Bariatric Cookbook

1000 Plus Easy to Cook and Friendly Recipes for Before and After the Gastric Sleeve Weight Loss Procedure

By

TRACY HUBBARD

© **Copyright 2021 by TRACY HUBBARD- All rights reserved.**

This document is geared towards providing exact and reliable information in regard to the topic and issue covered. The publication is sold with the idea that the publisher is not required to render accounting, officially permitted, or otherwise, qualified services. If advice is necessary, legal, or professional, a practiced individual in the profession should be ordered.

From a Declaration of Principles, which was accepted and approved equally by a Committee of the American Bar Association and a Committee of Publishers and Associations.

In no way is it legal to reproduce, duplicate, or transmit any part of this document in either electronic means or in printed format. Recording of this publication is strictly prohibited, and any storage of this document is not allowed unless with written permission from the publisher. All rights reserved.

The information provided herein is stated to be truthful and consistent, in that any liability, in terms of inattention or otherwise, by any usage or abuse of any policies, processes, or directions contained within is the solitary and utter responsibility of the recipient reader. Under no circumstances will any legal responsibility or blame be held against the publisher for any reparation, damages, or monetary loss due to the information herein, either directly or indirectly.

Respective authors own all copyrights not held by the publisher.

The information herein is offered for informational purposes solely and is universal as so. The presentation of the information is without contract or any type of guaranteed assurance.

The trademarks that are used are without any consent, and the publication of the trademark is without permission or backing by the trademark owner. All trademarks and brands within this book are for clarifying purposes only and are owned by the owners themselves, not affiliated with this document.

TABLE OF CONTENTS

4 INTRODUCTION

5 BASICS OF GASTRECTOMY

12 BREAKFAST

60 LUNCH

115 DINNER

166 SNACKS AND DESSERTS

219 CONCLUSION

220 INDEX

INTRODUCTION

Removal of a part or all the stomach by a surgery called gastrectomy. Lymphoma and Adenocarcinoma of your stomach may be removed with this technique, as well as other malignant or benign stomach neoplasms. Partial gastrectomy may also be used to treat less frequent benign tumors of your stomach wall or stomach. Because the surgery removes gastric-acid-secreting parietal cells & stops the synthesis of a gastrin hormone, it is frequently used to cure ulcers since it destroys these cells and removes the underlying cell components that create an ulcer. Gastrointestinal surgery is currently utilized as the last option for patients with ulcers that have been perforated or are bleeding, rather than as the first choice of therapy.

Several procedures may remove part of the stomach, but the most frequent is an antrectomy. The first piece of the gastrointestinal tract is subsequently re-joined to the leftover stomach (duodenum). Subtotal gastrectomy, a more invasive treatment, involves removing the whole stomach, including the antrum, in addition to three-quarters of the stomach. Reattaching the stomach directly to either the duodenum or the jejunum, an even more distal digestive tract section may be possible after that.

While the protracted survival percentages of people who have stomach cancer who have had a gastrectomy vary greatly (usually about 90% for those with initial stage cancer and fewer than 10% for those with metastatic cancer), there are some commonalities: Gastrectomy is often followed with gastric lymphadenectomy (lymph nodes removal linked with the stomach), which has been shown to enhance survival rates in certain patients with stomach cancer. When the antrum is entirely excised, the risk of ulcer recurrence the following gastrectomy is extremely low (less than 2%). The most serious side effect of gastrectomy is malnutrition, which results from the patient's reduced capacity to eat and their stomach's reduced ability to process food.

CHAPTER ONE

BASICS OF GASTRECTOMY

Surgery to remove all or part of your stomach is known as a gastrectomy. Three basic gastrectomy types are available:
- A partial gastrectomy is a procedure in which a portion of the stomach is surgically removed. Remove the bottom portion of the body, if possible.
- As the name suggests, a complete gastrectomy removes the whole stomach.
- The sleeve gastrectomy is a procedure that removes the left portion of the stomach. Weight-loss surgery often includes this procedure as part of the treatment.

When your stomach is removed, you will still eat and drink. The surgery may need certain lifestyle adjustments on your part.

1.1 Why you may need a gastrectomy?

In cases when previous therapies have failed to alleviate the symptoms, a gastric procedure may be necessary. Your doctor may recommend the gastrectomy to treat:
- noncancerous tumors or benign cancers
- inflammation
- stomach wall perforations
- bleeding
- your stomach growths or polyps
- stomach cancer
- duodenal ulcers or severe peptic

Obesity may be treated with certain forms of gastrectomy. Having a smaller stomach causes it to load faster. To help you lose weight, do this. If all other treatments have been unsuccessful, gastrectomy may be an alternative. Treatments that are less intrusive include:
- Diet
- Medication
- Exercise
- Counseling

1.2 Types of gastrectomy
A gastrectomy may be divided into three main categories:

Partial gastrectomy
Throughout the partial gastrectomy, the surgeon removes the bottom portion of the stomach. If you've cancer cells in your lymph nodes, these may be removed as well.
The surgeon will perform this procedure to seal off the duodenum. A portion of the small intestine called the duodenum gets food that has been partly digested from the stomach. You'll then link the rest of the stomach to the intestines.

Complete gastrectomy
This treatment, also known as a full gastrectomy, removes the whole stomach. Your esophagus will be surgically connected to the small intestine by your surgeon. Normally, the esophagus joins the neck and stomach through the esophagus.

Sleeve gastrectomy
Up to 75 percent of your stomach during the sleeve gastrectomy might well be surgically removed. The surgeon will reshape your stomach into tube form by removing tissue from the side. Smaller, longer stomachs result from this method.

1.3 How to prepare for a gastrectomy?
Before the procedure, the doctor will conduct blood or imaging tests. These measures will guarantee that you are in good health before the operation. Besides a physical exam, you'll also be given an evaluation of the medical records.
Speak to your doctor if you've been taking the medication during your visit. Consider bringing over-the-counter medications and vitamins with you. Before surgery, you may be required to cease using certain medications.
Pregnant women should also notify their doctor about any medical issues, including diabetes.
You should quit smoking if you're a cigarette smoker. Smoking delays the healing process. As a result, it may lead to further consequences, such as infection & lung disease.

1.4 How gastrectomy is performed?

It is possible to do a gastrectomy in two distinct techniques. General anesthesia is used for all procedures. This implies that you would not experience any discomfort since you'll be asleep throughout the procedure.

Open surgery

During open surgery, a single big incision is made. A surgeon will perform a muscle, skin, or tissue excision to get access to the stomach.

Laparoscopic surgery

Laparoscopic surgery seems to be a minimally invasive procedure. Small incisions & specialized instruments are needed for this procedure. As a result, the recovery period is shorter with this kind of treatment. Laparoscopically guided gastrectomy or "Keyhole surgery" is another name for this procedure (LAG).

In most cases, open surgery is preferable over LAG. With fewer problems, it's a more sophisticated procedure.

Certain illnesses, including stomach cancer, might need open surgery rather than laparoscopic surgery.

1.5 The risks of gastrectomy

The risks of a gastrectomy include:
- Reflux acid
- Diarrhea
- Maldigestion or gastric syndrome dumping
- Incision wound the infection
- An infection within the chest
- Bleeding inside
- Gastrointestinal leakage at the surgical site
- Vomiting
- Nausea
- Narrowing, esophageal scarring, or constriction as a result of stomach acid seeping into the esophagus (stricture)
- Small bowel blockage
- Deficiency vitamin
- Loss weight
- Bleeding
- Breathing difficulty
- Pneumonia
- Adjacent structures damage

Speak to your doctor about all of your current and past medical conditions, as well as any drugs you're taking. Make preparations for the treatment by following all of the instructions you've been given. As a result, you'll be taking fewer chances.

After gastrectomy
Following a gastrectomy, the doctor will stitch up the wound & wrap it up. Recovering in the hospital room is what you'll do. A nurse will keep an eye on the vital signs during your rehabilitation.
You should anticipate being in a hospital for 1-2 weeks following the procedure. Your nasal to stomach tube will likely be in place at this time. Your doctor will be able to drain any liquid from your stomach using this method. As a result, you won't feel nauseous.
A tube in the vein will be feeding you until you become able to eat or drink normally.
All new symptoms or discomfort that medication manages should be reported promptly to the doctor.

1.6 Lifestyle changes
You might even have to change your dietary habits when you return home. Changes that may be made include:
- limiting the amount of fiber in your diet by eating fewer meals often
- Consume foods that are iron, calcium, vitamin C & D-rich meals
- Supplementation with vitamins

The gastrectomy's recovery period might be rather lengthy. Your stomach & small intestines will eventually grow. You will be likely to feed more fiber and bigger meals due to this. Routine blood tests will be necessary to ensure that you receive adequate minerals and vitamins after the surgery.

1.7 Gastric Sleeve Diet
Gastric sleeve surgery may be a life-changing experience, and you're possibly looking further to your newer physique & learning to eat differently. After gastric sleeve surgery, you'll have to adjust to a new way of living.
Your pre-and post-surgery diets are special and designed to help you heal and prevent issues. At some point, in the long run, your diet will turn toward assisting you to develop healthy lifestyles so that you may lose weight & keep it off for good.

Pre-gastric sleeve diet
Pre-surgery nutrition goals include reducing the size of your liver. As a result of being overweight, your liver is likely to be full of fat cells. This causes it to be bigger than necessary. In the vicinity of your stomach, you'll find your liver. A gastric sleeve operation is more difficult for the doctor to perform and more harmful for you if you have a big liver.
You will be given a pre-surgery diet to practice, starting two weeks before your planned treatment. Calorie or carbohydrate intake is restricted, focusing on avoiding sugary and starchy foods like potatoes, pasta, & bread. You'll consume a diet of lean protein, veggies, and water for the most part. Your doctor may give you a daily calorie target.
You'll be on a simple liquid diet for two days before surgery. If you're looking to lose weight and stay healthy, you may want to include a no protein shake each day, as well as water and decaffeinated tea or coffee, Jell-O or sugar-free popsicles. It is best to stay away from caffeinated or carbonated drinks.

Week 1 diet

In the 1st week following the operation, you'll be on the same simple liquid diet as before. As a result, the risk of postoperative problems such as intestinal blockage and stomach leakage will be minimized. This routine will assist you in allowing your body to recuperate. Following are the tips to remember:

- Keep hydrated by drinking lots of water. See whether electrolyte beverages like low-calorie Gatorade can help you stay properly hydrated.
- Don't ingest sugary beverages. When so much sugar rushes into the intestines, a condition known as dumping syndrome may occur. This causes severe nausea, exhaustion, diarrhea, and, in extreme cases, even vomiting. Sugar, on the other hand, is a calorie-dense food. It's better to prevent it now than let it get out of hand.
- In addition, caffeine might cause acid reflux & dehydration.
- Gas & bloating may be exacerbated by many kinds of carbonated drinks, including sugary and low-calorie varieties as well as seltzer. Post-operatively, & maybe even long-term, they must all be eliminated.

Week 2 diet

A liquid-only diet will be introduced during the 2nd postoperative week. Among the choices are:

- shakes no-sugar nutrition, including Ensure Light
- breakfast instant drinks
- protein powder made shakes
- thin broth & cream-based soups
- milk unsweetened
- nonfit pudding sugar-free
- ice cream, & sorbet, frozen yogurt nonfat, sugar-free
- nonfit Greek yogurt plain
- no pulp fruit juices
- hot cereal thinned

During this time, you may experience a rise in your hunger. That's normal, but it's not a cause to stop eating solids. Solids are still too much for the system to manage. As a consequence, vomiting or other issues may arise. Making sure your body is getting enough water and nutrients can help you prepare for the next phase in the diet. Still, carbonated drinks & caffeine are not recommended.

Week 3 diet

You may begin including soft, pureed meals into your diet around week three. Chew your meal fully almost 25 times when eating, if feasible. Non-fibrous vegetables, lean protein sources, & other low-fat, sugar-free foods may be used. Increasing daily protein intake is essential. Drink protein no-sugar smoothies or take eggs every day if you do not like the flavor of lean pureed protein sources. Included in the list of foods to consume are:

- baby food jarred
- tofu silken
- cooked, white fish pureed
- soft-boiled or soft-scrambled eggs
- soup
- cheese cottage
- juice canned fruit
- ripe mango or mashed bananas
- hummus
- mashed or pureed avocado
- Greek yogurt plain

During this period, avoid solid & chunky meals and also caffeine. Additionally, basic foods with little or no flavor must be your mainstay. Some spices might well aggravate heartburn.

Week 4 diet

Now that you've been out of the hospital for a month, you can eat solid meals again. Your new healthy-eating abilities should be put to the test right now. Sugar or fat & hard-to-digest meals like fibrous vegetables, steak, & nuts should be avoided. White potatoes, Pasta, & other high-carb meals should also be avoided. At this point, it is normally possible to resume moderate amounts of caffeinated drinks. Included in the list of foods that may be added are:

- well-cooked fish & chicken
- vegetable well-cooked
- potatoes sweet
- cheese low-fat
- fruit
- cereal low-sugar

Week 5 diet and beyond

It seems to be the time to start putting your different dietary habits into long-term action now, where you can consume solid meals. Incorporate one new meal at a time into your diet so that you can observe your body's response. Sugary sweets & soda are among the foods you must avoid completely or only consume occasionally from now on. All other foods may be reintroduced if they don't cause any negative reactions.

Make smart meal choices, such as those high in nutrients, and stay away from those high with empty calories. It's possible to stay on track by eating three modest meals per day and limiting yourself to a few snacks. Make careful to stay hydrated at all times.

1.8 Guidelines and tips

Post-surgical recuperation advice includes the following:
- Food may be pureed in a food processor or blender.
- Learn to distinguish between bodily hunger & emotional hunger.
- Remember that your stomach may expand and settle in size over time if you do not overeat.
- Slow down and enjoy your food.
- Stay away from non-nutrient calories.
- Avoid foods that are high in sugar concentrations.
- Avoid trans fats or meals that are fried, processed, or fast-food-like in any way possible.
- Drinking low-calorie or water Gatorade may help prevent dehydration.
- At the same time, don't drink and eat
- It's best to consult your doctor before taking any bariatric vitamins or supplements.
- Incorporate physical activity into your daily routines and routines. Walking is a good place to start, but don't be afraid to try other activities that you love, such as swimming or dancing.
- You should avoid drinking alcohol. Weight-loss surgery like gastric sleeve operations or other bariatric procedures may intensify and speed up the effects of alcohol.
- NSAIDs, including aspirin, ibuprofen, or naproxen, should be avoided. If you use these under pain relievers, your stomach's natural defenses may be weakened.

Chapter 2: Breakfast Recipes

1. High Protein Jell-O Mousse Full Liquids Stage
Prep Time: 10 Mins, Cook Time: 25 Mins, Servings: 2
Ingredients
- 1 small box Black Cherry Jell-O (sugar-free)
- 2 containers of Dannon light and fit Cherry Greek yogurt
- ½ cup of water
- 2 scoops of NOW unflavored whey (or other unflavored protein powder)

Instructions
- Simmer the water but avoid boiling.
- Transfer the sugar-free jello mixture into a bowl, add water, and set aside while arranging the rest of the ingredients.
- Now, put it all into the mixing bowl. Blend it to smooth mixture.
- Pour the mixture into four ramekins and leave them aside to cool.

Nutrition Information
Calories: 102.5 kcal, Carbohydrates: 5 g, Protein: 19.5 g, Fats: 0.2 g

2. Instant Pot Asparagus Soup
Prep Time: 10 Mins, Cook Time: 10 Mins, Servings: 4
Ingredients
- 2 lb. asparagus, cut into 2 inches pieces (remove tough ends)
- 1 tbsp butter
- 2 cups of chicken broth (fat-free)
- 1 clove garlic (minced)
- 1 small onion (chopped)
- Salt and pepper (to taste)

Instructions
- Melt all butter in the Instant Pot by setting it to sauté. Cook, stir to combine, for 3 mins after adding the onion. Cook for another min after adding the minced garlic.
- After turning off the Instant Pot, add the chicken broth and asparagus. Close the Instant Pot's lid and seal it. Set the lever is in the locked position. Set the timer for 10 mins using the manual button.
- When the timer goes off, let off the pressure. Remove the cover lid when the pin comes out.
- Blending the soup by hand blender is a better option. Combine the half and half, pepper, and salt in a mixing bowl (to taste). Serve it.

Nutrition Information
Calories: 102.5 kcal, Carbohydrates: 5 g, Protein: 19.5 g, Fats: 0.2 g

3. Crock-Pot Chicken Kale Soup
Prep Time: 15 Mins, Cook Time: 6 hr 15 Mins, Servings: 6
Ingredients
- 1 tbsp olive oil
- 14 oz chicken bone broth
- 2 lb chicken breast or thigh (boneless and skinless)
- ½ cup olive oil
- ⅓ cup onion
- 5 oz baby kale leaves
- 32 oz chicken stock
- Salt to taste
- ¼ cup lemon juice

Instructions
- Take a large skillet, heat 1 tbsp of oil on medium heat.
- Season the chicken with pepper and salt before placing it on the hot skillet.
- Reduce the heat and cover the pan. Cook the chicken for approximately 15 mins, or till the core temperature rises to 165 degrees Fahrenheit.
- Place the shredded chicken in the crockpot.
- Take a blender, mix the chicken broth, olive oil, and diced onion until smooth. Fill the crockpot halfway with a mixture of chicken broth.
- Cover and stir the remaining Ingredients in the crock cooker.
- Cook for 6 hours on low, stirring one or two times throughout that cooking period.

Nutrition Information
Calories: 261 kcal, Carbohydrates: 21 g, Protein: 14.1 g, Fats: 21 g

4. Protein Packed Black Bean and Lentil Soup
Prep Time: 10 Mins, Cook Time: 35 Mins, Servings: 1
Ingredients
- 2 garlic cloves (minced)
- 1 tbsp olive oil
- 2 carrots, peeled and diced small
- 1 yellow onion
- 1 cup dried lentils
- 15 oz of diced tomatoes can
- 1 tsp chili powder
- 15 oz black beans can (drained)
- ½ tsp black pepper
- ½ tsp cumin
- ½ tsp kosher salt
- 4 cups vegetable broth
- ½ tsp red pepper, crushed

Instructions
- Add olive oil to a big saucepan and fry the garlic for 1 min. Continue to sauté the carrots and onions until the onion is soft, about 5 mins.
- Cover and mix all remaining Ingredients.
- Boil at medium heat, then lower to low heat and cook for 25-30 mins, or until carrots and lentils are cooked.

Nutrition Information
Calories: 171 kcal, Carbohydrates: 29 g, Protein: 10 g, Fats: 2 g

5. Instant Pot Split Pea Soup w/ Ham
Prep Time: 5 Mins, Cook Time: 35 Mins, Servings: 6
Ingredients
- ½ medium white onion (diced)
- 2 tbsp vegetable oil
- 1 ½ cups diced ham
- 3 medium carrots (sliced)
- 2 cups of water
- 4 cups chicken broth, low sodium
- 1 bay leaf
- 1 lb. of dried split peas
- Salt and black pepper

Instructions
- Set the instant pot at a sauté setting. Add the onion and vegetable oil to a warm pan. Please make sure the onions are transparent before adding them to the pan. It will take 3–5 mins.
- Ham, carrots, broth, split peas, bay leaf, and water should all be added to the instant pot.
- After 20 mins, let it release naturally for 10 mins.
- For releasing all pressure, conduct a manual discharge by moving the valve toward you.
- Sprinkle with salt to taste. Serve immediately in a soup dish.

Nutrition Information
Calories: 214 kcal, Carbohydrates: 21 g, Protein: 17 g, Fats: 6 g

6. Mexican Egg Casserole
Prep Time: 10 Mins, Cook Time: 30 Mins, Servings: 2
Ingredients
- 1 small green pepper (finely diced)
- 1 small onion (diced)
- 1 log of chorizo sausage (get mild to avoid spicy food)
- 1 can tomatoes & chiles (get mild to avoid spicy food)
- 1 cup + ¼ cup shredded Mexican blend cheese
- 1 can of beans (kidneys and black beans are suggested)
- 6 eggs (or equivalent liquid egg substitute)
- ½ cup milk
- Salt, Cajun, pepper, seasoning blend

Instructions:
- Toss the green peppers, serranos, and onion into a nonstick pan. Simmer them till tender.
- Remove the chorizo from the cover and place it into the pan. Warm the tomatoes and chilies thoroughly.
- Take a large mixing bowl, whisk together milk and six eggs, then season to taste. Beat it by adding 1 cup cheese.
- Take a casserole dish, spread out the meat and vegetable mix.
- Pour the egg mixture and fold it gently.
- Preheat oven up to 350°F and bake for 30 mins, or till fully set. As the dish cools, sprinkle more cheese at the top, and allow it to melt.

Nutrition Information
Calories: 152 kcal, Carbohydrates: 5 g, Protein: 16 g, Fats: 7 g

7. Healthy Smoked Salmon Sushi Bowl
Prep Time: 20 Mins, Cook Time: 20 Mins, Servings: 4
Ingredients
Ginger sesame dressing
- 2 cups of cooked rice
- 1 clove Garlic (pressed)
- 2 inches Ginger (grated)
- 1 tbsp Soy sauce (gluten-free soy sauce or use tamari)
- 1 to 2 tbsp honey
- 1 tbsp and 1 tsp Sesame oil
- 3 tbsp rice vinegar

Spicy mayo
- 2 tbsp of mayonnaise
- ½ tsp soy sauce (gluten-free or use tamari)
- 3 to 4 tbsp of sriracha

Bowls
- 1 to 2 ripe avocados
- 12 oz smoked salmon
- 1 to 2 carrots, shaved
- 1 cucumber (AKA English cucumber), shaved into strips
- nori seaweed, cut into strips

Instructions
- Cook the rice and cool them. Brown rice is recommended for nutrition, and it takes 10 mins, and regular cooking rice takes 30-45 mins.
- Take a small bowl, whisk together all Ingredients until thoroughly blended. As required, check, and adjust the flavors. Set aside the sauce.
- Whisk together the mayonnaise, soy sauce, and sriracha in the bowl until the thoroughly blended season to taste as required. Add more mayo for milder spice and extra sriracha for hotter heat. Set aside the spicy mayo.
- Ready all vegetables as directed above and peel the salmon layers. A veggie platter or sharp knife can be used.
- If you're serving sushi bowls, it'd be great to put smoked salmon, all vegetables, and extra toppings on a plate.
- Combine the rice, smoked salmon, carrots, sliced avocado, cucumber, green onions, and nori strips in a bowl.
- Take a bowl to combine the rice, smoked salmon, carrots, sliced avocado, cucumber, green onions, and nori strips. Pour spicy mayo and some of the ginger sesame sauce on top. Enjoy right now.
- Any leftovers should be kept in different airtight containers. The sauces and rice can keep in the refrigerator for up to a week.

Nutrition Information
Calories: 252 kcal, Carbohydrates: 56 g, Protein: 16 g, Fats: 8 g

8. Hasselback Baked Caprese Chicken
Prep Time: 5 Mins, Cook Time: 25 Mins, Servings: 2
Ingredients
- 4 medium-sized chicken breasts (boneless skinless)
- 1 tbsp olive oil
- 1 log buffalo mozzarella (thinly sliced)
- 3 plum tomatoes, thinly sliced
- Salt and pepper to taste
- ½ cup fresh basil leaves

Balsamic glaze
- ½ cup of balsamic vinegar
- 3 tbsp of brown sugar

Instructions
- Preheat your oven to around 400 degrees Fahrenheit. Make significant, broad horizontal incisions in chicken breast. Season the prepared chicken with pepper and salt after rubbing it with olive oil.
- Tomatoes and mozzarella are thinly sliced and stuffed into cuts of chicken breast, followed by basil in each incision. Bake for 25 mins, or till chicken is thoroughly cooked.
- Meanwhile, put a small saucepan on the stove, boil brown sugar and balsamic. Cook over medium heat for about 10-12 mins or until the mixture thickens achieved.
- Remove the chicken from the oven and coat it with balsamic dressing. If preferred, top with more fresh basil. Serve the dish with a salad or other side dish.

Nutrition Information
Calories: 401 kcal, Carbohydrates: 14g, Protein: 34 g, Fats: 23 g

9. Chicken with Spinach and Tomato
Prep Time: 5 Mins, Cook Time: 20 Mins, Servings: 6
Ingredients
- 2½ lb. chicken breast (skinless boneless) cut into 1" pieces
- 2 tbsp olive oil
- Salt
- 2 cloves garlic minced
- Ground black pepper
- 7 oz. baby spinach
- 15 oz. canned diced tomatoes
- Grated parmesan cheese optional
- 15 oz. canned diced tomatoes

Instructions
- Place a big saucepan over medium heat and coat it with olive oil.
- Add the garlic and chicken to the heated oil. Salt & pepper to taste.
- Add the spinach, tomatoes, and mushrooms when the pinkish shade of chicken and the fluids run clear. Cook till the liquid has been reduced to roughly half its original volume. If necessary, season the dish.
- If preferred, top with cheese right before serving.

Nutrition Information
Calories: 173 kcal, Carbohydrates: 11 g, Protein: 40g, Fats: 6 g

10. Crock Pot Stuffed Peppers with Ground Turkey
Prep Time: 30 Mins, Cook Time: 4 hr, Servings: 6
Ingredients
- 6 bell peppers (tops, seeds, and membranes removed)
- ½ cup sweet onion, finely diced
- 1 lb. ground turkey 93/7
- ½ tsp of garlic powder divided
- 1 ½ cups cooked rice
- ¼ tsp pepper
- 1 tsp of dried herbs divided thyme or rosemary

- 1 tsp salt
- 1 ½ tsp of Worcestershire sauce divided
- 12 oz. can tomato sauce
- 1 tsp salt

Instructions
- Remove the peels and seeds from 6 bell peppers (red, green, orange, or yellow) by cutting off the tops.
- Mix uncooked ground turkey, chopped onion, cooked rice, 14 tsp garlic powder, salt, pepper, 12 tsp of dried herbs, and 1 tsp of Worcestershire sauce in a large mixing dish. Mix until everything is well blended.
- Fill bell peppers with the rice-turkey mixture in equal proportions. Place bell peppers in a slow cooker (6-quart) with their tops on.
- Cook for about 4 hours at the high flame or cook for 8 hours on low with ¼ cup of water.
- Take a medium-sized bowl, stir ¼ tsp garlic powder, tomato sauce, ½ tsp Worcestershire sauce, and ½ tsp dried herbs during the final 30 mins of cooking. Remove the tops off all bell peppers and cover them with tomato sauce. Finish the cooking for the last 30 mins. Add Mozzarella cheese if preferred.
- Cut a tiny incision in the bottom of peppers just before serving to drain any extra liquid.
- Enjoy! Garnish bell pepper beside fresh parsley.

Nutrition Information
Calories: 342 kcal, Carbohydrates: 49 g, Protein: 25 g, Fats: 4 g

11. Dill and Caper Egg Salad
Prep Time: 20 Mins, Cook Time: 20 Mins, Servings: 6
Ingredients
- 8 large, hard-boiled eggs (whites separated from yolks) and chopped fine
- 3 tbsp capers (drained)
- ¾ to 1 cup finely chopped celery
- 3 tbsp olive oil
- 2 tsp fresh lemon juice
- 2 tbsp whole grain mustard
- ¼ tsp acceptable sea salt
- ¼ tsp black pepper
- ¼ tsp granulated garlic
- 1 tbsp (packed) chopped fresh dill

Instructions
- Toss the shredded egg white, capers, and celery in a small bowl.
- Use a spoon to mash egg yolks in a small bowl until smooth. Combine the lemon juice and mustard oil in a mixing bowl. If the combination isn't soft enough, then add extra oil. Whisk in the salt, dill, garlic, and pepper after you've reached the appropriate consistency. Season with salt and pepper to taste.
- Fold the egg, celery, and caper combination in the yolk mix until completely incorporated.
- Serve right away with more fresh dill on top or keep in an airtight jar in the fridge. It can be stored for 3 days.

Nutrition Information
Calories: 201 kcal, Carbohydrates: 7 g, Protein: 10 g, Fats: 0 g

12. Instant Pot Southern Deviled Eggs
Prep Time: 5 Mins, Cook Time: 10 Mins, Servings: 12
Ingredients
- 12 eggs
- 1 tbsp Dijon mustard
- Dash paprika (for each deviled egg)
- ½ cup mayonnaise
- Salt and pepper (to taste)

Instructions
- The hard-boiled egg can be made in an Instant Pot or boiled in water on the stovetop for 10 mins.
- To boil these eggs on the stovetop, set them in a pan, then cover them with 1 inch over the eggs. Boil water, reduce to low heat, and cook for 10 mins.
- Allow the boiled eggs to cool in ice water for 5 mins after cooking.
- Boiled eggs should be peeled.
- Boiled eggs should be cut in half.
- Remove the yolk and set it in a basin.
- Combine mayonnaise, relish, mustard, and salt/pepper with the egg yolks. Stir until everything is well blended.
- Fill each boiled egg white shell with the egg yolk fill.
- Sprinkle paprika over every deviled egg and garnish with chopped parsley, cilantro, or green onions.

Nutrition Information
Calories: 85 kcal, Carbohydrates: 1 g, Protein: 5 g, Fats: 6 g

13. Bacon Ranch Chicken Crust Pizza
Prep Time: 10 Mins, Cook Time: 35 Mins, Servings: 8
Ingredients
Crust:
- ⅓ Cup mozzarella, shredded (40 grams)
- 1 lb ground chicken
- ⅓ cup parmesan cheese, shredded (30 grams)
- 1 large egg
- 1 tsp Italian seasonings basil, rosemary, oregano, and thyme
- Salt and ground black pepper to taste

Sauce:
- ⅓ cup sour cream
- ¼ tsp dried chives
- ⅓ cup avocado mayonnaise
- ¼ tsp dried parsley
- ¼ tsp garlic powder
- ¼ tsp dried dill
- ⅛ tsp onion powder
- dash pepper
- ⅛ tsp salt

Instructions
- Preheat the oven up to 400 degrees Fahrenheit. Use parchment paper to line a pizza pan.
- Use a large mixing basin and combine all crust Ingredients. After that, roll into a ball.
- Set the meatball in a pizza pan coated with parchment paper. Roll out in a vast circle and top with a layer of parchment sheet. Remove the parchment sheet from the top. Is there part of the crust attached to the paper? Then use a rubber spatula to scrape it off. Return it to the core crust.
- Preheat oven at 400°F and bake meat crust for about 20-25 mins, or till the top is browned.
- Take a mixing bowl and combine the sauce Ingredients meanwhile the crust is baking.
- Remove the crust from the oven. Flip it over on the pan and peel away the parchment paper.
- Put ½ cup sauce over prepared pizza crust. Spread ½ cup of cheese. 12 Bacon and chopped tomatoes must be sprinkled on top.
- Return the pizza to the oven. Bake for 10 mins at 400°F. Serve with the leftover ranch sauce in 8 slices.

Nutrition Information
Calories: 284 kcal, Carbohydrates: 2g, Protein: 18 g, Fats: 23g

14. Roasted Acorn Squash with Cranberries, Goat Cheese, And Balsamic Glaze
Prep Time: 10 Mins, Cook Time: 25 Mins, Servings: 2
Ingredients
- 1 acorn squash (~3 lb)
- ½ tsp dried rosemary
- ⅓ cup dried cranberries
- 1½ to 2 oz goat cheese, crumbled
- ½ cup balsamic vinegar
- ¼ tsp black pepper

- 1½ tbsp olive oil
- ⅛ tsp salt

Instructions
- Preheat your oven to around 375 °F. Meanwhile, microwave for 4 mins to make the acorn squash easier to chop. Remove the bottom and top. After cutting in half (lengthwise), chop into 12-3/4-inch pieces. Use a parchment sheet or foil and line the baking sheet.
- Place the squash slices on a plate. Season with rosemary, salt, and pepper. Drizzle the olive oil. Bake for 20-25 mins, or until vegetables are soft.
- Allow the squash to cool after it has been removed from the oven. Drizzle with balsamic glaze, dried cranberries, and crumbled goat cheese.

Nutrition Information
Calories: 252 kcal, Carbohydrates: 56 g, Protein: 16 g, Fats: 8 g

15. The Best Cauliflower Mash Recipe
Prep Time: 5 Mins, Cook Time: 15 Mins, Servings: 4
Ingredients
- 1 tsp salt plus more to season
- 1 head cauliflower, quartered
- 1 tbsp butter/olive oil
- 1 garlic clove
- Pepper to taste

Instructions
- Add cauliflower (along with garlic clove), butter or oil, and water. Purée water 1 tbsp at instance until smooth. Serve with salt and pepper.

Nutrition Information
Calories: 43 kcal, Carbohydrates: 3.8g, Protein: 1.4 g, Fats: 3 g

16. Vegan Lentil Loaf Recipes
Prep Time: 30 Mins, Cook Time: 35 Mins, Servings: 10
Ingredients
- 3 cups cooked green lentils (about 1 cup, dried)
- 2 tbsp olive oil
- 4 garlic cloves (chopped)
- 1 large carrot (chopped)
- 1 large onion (chopped)
- 1 celery stalk, portobello mushrooms, and red bell pepper (chopped)
- ½ tbsp of vegan Worcestershire sauce
- ½ cup of quinoa (already cooked)
- 1 tbsp tamari
- ½ cup oats
- 2 tbsp ground flax seeds with 6 tbsp water

Glaze
- 2 tbsp balsamic vinegar
- 1 tbsp maple syrup
- ¼ cup ketchup

Instructions
- Allow 5 mins for the powdered flax seeds to form a gel after mixing with water.
- Take a pan and heat the olive oil over medium to high heat. Allow the garlic, onions, carrots, red pepper, celery, and mushrooms to brown in the pan. Fry for 10 to 15 mins, often stirring to prevent the vegetables from burning. Pepper, salt, paprika, and herbs can season the dish.
- Turn down the heat at a medium level. Add the red wine for deglazing the pan. Combine the tomato paste, ketchup, and vegan Worcestershire sauce in a bowl.
- Combine the vegetable combination, quinoa oats, lentils, and flax eggs in a food processor. Pulse just until mixed, but not so much that the texture is lost.
- Pour this lentil paste into the pan and evenly distribute it.
- To prepare the glaze, whisk together the ketchup, maple syrup, and balsamic vinegar, then spread it evenly over the loaf.
- Preheat oven up to 350°F and bake for 35-45 mins.
- Allow for 30 mins of cooking time before taking from the pan.

Nutrition Information
Calories: 177 kcal, Carbohydrates: 27 g, Protein: 8 g, Fats: 4g

17. Pumpkin, Goat's Cheese, And Sage Tart in A Broccoli Crust
Prep Time: 30 Mins, Cook Time: 35 Mins, Servings: 6
Ingredients
Broccoli & Cheese Crust:
- 100 g/1 cup ground almonds
- 400 g/14 oz broccoli florets, roughly chopped
- 2 tbsp grated Parmesan cheese
- salt and freshly ground black pepper
- 2 eggs, beaten

Filling:
- low-fat cooking spray or mist
- 4 eggs
- 400 g/14 oz pumpkin (peeled and chopped)
- 100 g/4 oz goat's cheese (sliced)
- 1175 g/6 oz ricotta (or burrata)
- 15 fresh sage leaves

Instructions
- Prepare the oven at 200 degrees Celsius/400 degrees Fahrenheit/gas mark 6.
- Prepare your crust by pulsing the broccoli into tiny grain-like bits in a food processor.
- Mix thoroughly with the parmesan, almonds, eggs, salt, and pepper to taste in a mixing bowl.
- The non-stick baking paper should be used to line (22-cm/8-inch) non-stick pie tin/pan. Use the backside of a wooden spoon to press the crust mixture equally over the edges and base of the tin/pan. Cook for about 20 mins or till getting golden brown in the oven.
- Meanwhile, sprinkle the pumpkin with low-fat cooking spray and lay it in a roasting dish. Season and bake for 20 mins, or until soft but still firm, alongside the tart crust.
- Combine the ricotta (or burrata), eggs, and salt and pepper to taste in a mixing bowl. Fill the pre-baked tart crust with cooked pumpkin. Top with goat cheese, egg mixture, and some fresh sage leaves. Spritz with a low-fat cooking spray or spritz once more.
- Transfer to the oven for another 25-30 mins, or till the egg mixture has set, risen, and become golden.
- Cut into wedges and serve warm/cold.

Nutrition Information
Calories: 300 kcal, Carbohydrates: 7.4 g, Protein: 19.4 g, Fats: 21.3 g

18. Turkey Vegetable Tray
Prep Time: 20 Mins, Cook Time: 35 Mins, Servings: 16
Ingredients
- 2 cups baby carrots
- 2 red bell pepper
- 1 yellow bell pepper
- 1 crown broccoli
- candy eyeballs
- 2 cups baby carrots
- 1 cup snap peas
- 2 cucumbers

Instructions
- Cut the bottom of red pepper to create the face. Use a small carrot for the beak, a slice of yellow pepper to make snoods, and a few candy eye balls
- Gather and prepare your vegetables for the body. Wash them and chop them into manageable portions.
- Arrange the cucumber slices in a half-circle on the plate. Then, stack the red and yellow peppers, carrots, and

broccoli pieces in smaller half circles. At the bottom, add the snap peas.
- Then add your favorite dip to the mix. In the dip dish, put this turkey face created out of peppers.

Nutrition Information
Calories: 25 kcal, Carbohydrates: 5 g, Protein: 1 g, Fats: 9 g

19. Cilantro Lime Sauce + Instant Pot Drumsticks for WW
Prep Time: 5 Mins, Cook Time: 20 Mins, Servings: 3
Ingredients
- 1 tbsp olive oil
- 4 cloves garlic, minced
- 6 drumsticks
- 1 tsp crushed red peppers
- 1 lime Juice
- 1 tsp cayenne pepper
- ½ cup chicken broth, low sodium
- 2 tbsp cilantro, chopped

Instructions
- Adjust the Instant Pot to sauté and add some olive oil. Put the drumsticks to the hot oil. Sprinkle the drumsticks with the seasoning. Turn the drumsticks with tongs and brown for 2 mins on each side.
- Use the Instant Pot to combine the lime juice, chicken broth, and cilantro. Set its pressure valve to lock and secure the lid. Cook for 9 mins on high pressure. Allow the pressure to dissipate when you've finished naturally.
- Place the drumstick on a baking sheet. Let it boil for about 3-5 mins, or until golden brown. Serve while still heated, garnished with extra cilantro.

Nutrition Information
Calories: 311 kcal, Carbohydrates: 7 g, Protein: 28 g, Fats: 5 g

20. Creamy Shrimp Scampi Puree
Prep Time: 8 Mins, Cook Time: 0 Mins, Servings: 8
Ingredients
- 1 lb Shrimp
- 4 Cloves garlic, minced
- 2 tbsp Olive oil
- 2 tbsp Low fat plain Greek yogurt
- ¼ cup Parsley, chopped

Instructions
- Heat little olive oil in a large pan over medium-high heat.
- Dry the shrimp and place them in the heated pan. Cook, tossing halfway through, for 2-3 mins, or until barely pink. Cook for another min, or until garlic is aromatic.
- Transfer to a heat-resistant bowl. Toss in the Greek yogurt and parsley to coat.
- Fill a food processor halfway with the contents and pulse until smooth.

Nutrition Information
Calories: 91.8 kcal, Carbohydrates: 0.9 g, Protein: 14.1 g, Fats: 3.7 g

21. Turkey Tacos with Refried Beans Puree
Prep Time: 21 Mins, Cook Time: 21 Mins, Servings: 8
Ingredients
For beans
- 1 cup No salt added pinto beans (rinsed and drained)
- 1 Clove garlic, minced
- 2 tbsp Cilantro, chopped
- 1 Clove garlic, minced

For turkey
- ¼ tsp Garlic powder
- ¼ tsp Mild chili powder
- ¼ tsp Cumin
- ½ lb Lean ground turkey
- ¼ tsp Paprika

Instructions
- Heat about 2 tbsp of water in a sauté pan at medium heat to prepare the beans. Put garlic in it and Sauté for 1 min, or until garlic is aromatic. Bring the chicken broth and pinto beans to a boil. Reduce the flame to medium-low and continue to cook for another 5 mins.
- Mash the beans using a potato masher or a fork can also be used. Cook for the next 3-4 mins or until the liquid has evaporated. Remove the pan and add 2 tbsp of chopped cilantro.
- Heat the chili powder, paprika, garlic powder, and cumin in a sauté pan to create the turkey. allow 1 min of toasting
- Add 2 tbsp turkey and 2 tbsp water. Cook for about 6-8 mins. Continue stirring to break any clumps or until well cooked. To avoid drying the pan, add another 1 tbsp of water as the water evaporates.
- Blend the beans and turkey in any good food processor until pureed.

Nutrition Information
Calories: 68.1 kcal, Carbohydrates: 5.4 g, Protein: 10 g, Fats: 0.9 g

22. Chimichurri Chicken Puree
Prep Time: 13 Mins, Cook Time: 13 Mins, Servings: 5
Ingredients
- ½ lb Lean ground chicken
- ½ tsp Paprika
- ¼ tsp Dried oregano
- ¼ cup Parsley
- 2 tbsp Cilantro
- 2 Cloves garlic, peeled
- 2 tsp Apple cider vinegar

Instructions
- Add 2 tbsp water, heated in a sauté pan over medium-high heat. Combine the paprika, chicken, and oregano in a bowl. Cook for about 6-8 mins, turning to break any clumps, or till well cooked.
- Combine cilantro, parsley, garlic, 3 tbsp of water, and apple cider vinegar in a food processor or blender. Pulse until the Ingredients are coarsely minced.
- Toss in the chimichurri and toss to combine.
- Return to the food processor. Blend until completely smooth.

Nutrition Information
Calories: 47.6 kcal, Carbohydrates: 5 g, Protein: 5.6 g, Fats: 4g

23. Salmon Salad
Prep Time: 20 Mins, Cook Time: 16 Mins, Servings: 4
Ingredients
Salmon
- 1½ tbsp olive oil
- 4 salmon fillets (about 1 lb)

Honey Mustard Dressing
- 2 tbsp honey
- 3 tbsp olive oil
- 1 tbsp apple cider vinegar
- 1 ½ tbsp Dijon mustard
- pepper (to taste)
- Kosher salt

Instructions
- Preheat your oven to 400 degrees Fahrenheit. To make cleanup easier, line a baking dish with parchment paper. Place the salmon in the pan (skin side down). Rub olive oil over the fish and season with pepper and salt. Bake the salmon for about 12-18 mins, or until the thickest portion reaches 145°F temperature. Allow salmon to cool slightly before serving.
- Blend the olive oil, Dijon mustard, honey, and cider vinegar until smooth. Season with salt and pepper.
- In all four large salad dishes, add two cups of spinach. Walnut, Red onion, avocado, goat cheese, and blueberries are good additions. Serve with cooked salmon on top. Serve salads with other dressing.

Nutrition Information
Calories: 767 kcal, Carbohydrates: 26 g, Protein: 44 g, Fats: 57 g

24. Vegetarian Chili Mac
Prep Time: 10 Mins, Cook Time: 20 Mins, Servings: 1
Ingredients
- 1 cup chopped onion
- 1 tbsp olive oil
- 2 medium carrots (chopped)
- 15 oz can dice tomatoes
- 1 bell pepper (chopped small)
- 8 oz elbow macaroni pasta
- 15 oz can black beans
- 15 oz can red kidney beans
- 2 cups shredded cheese
- 2 cups water

Instructions
- Take a pot or skillet and heat some olive oil over medium heat. Cook, occasionally turning, till the onion, carrots, and bell pepper are cooked for approximately 6 mins.
- Cook, constantly stirring, for 30 seconds after adding the garlic, chili powder, salt, and cumin into the pan.
- Add diced tomatoes, green chilies, black beans, pasta, kidney beans, and water, and stir to combine.
- Raise and simmer the mixture to a low simmer. Cover it and cook for 12-15 mins. Stir occasionally until the pasta is cooked and a significant quantity of liquid has been absorbed.
- Remove from the stove and mix with the cheese, keeping a slight topping. The remaining cheese should be sprinkled on top. Serve.

Nutrition Information
Calories: 447 kcal, Carbohydrates: 63 g, Protein: 23 g, Fats: 12 g

25. Poached Chicken
Prep Time: 5 Mins, Cook Time: 20 Mins, Servings: 4
Ingredients
- 2 chicken breasts, boneless, skinless
- 1 tsp salt
- Coldwater

Instructions
- Place the chicken in the pan with a lid. In the pan, arrange these chicken breasts to form one layer. Fill the pot with cold water till the water level is approximately 1 inch above these pieces.
- Season with salt and any other aromatics you choose.
- Place the saucepan, uncovered, on the stovetop at medium heat. Low boil it and then reduce to low heat.
- Reduce the heat, cover the lid, and continue cooking for 6 to 11 minutes. Keep cooking until the internal temperature of chicken pieces reach 165°F.
- Before slicing the chicken, remove it from the water and leave it for 5-10 mins.

Nutrition Information
Calories: 73 kcal, Carbohydrates: 2 g, Protein: 12 g, Fats: 2 g

26. Hard-Boiled Eggs
Prep Time: 5 Mins, Cook Time: 12 Mins, Servings: 1
Ingredients
- 6 large eggs

Instructions
- A lidded pot will be required. Add 1 or 2 inches of cold water to the pot. In the same saucepan, crack the eggs. Then fill the saucepan with cold water till it reaches a height of 3/4 to 1 inch over the eggs.
- Bring the saucepan to boil on the stovetop on high heat.
- Allow the eggs to remain in the boiling water for 8–12 mins.
- Transfer these eggs to a pot of ice water. Allow 5 mins for the eggs to cool before peeling.
- Serve right away. It can be stored for 1 week.

Nutrition Information
Calories: 63 kcal, Carbohydrates: 1 g, Protein: 6 g, Fats: 4

27. Chicken Florentine Pasta Bake
Prep Time: 35 Mins, Cook Time: 3 Mins, Servings: 1
Ingredients
- 1 tbsp olive oil
- 12 oz farfalle pasta
- 2 eggs
- 1 yellow onion (chopped)
- 1 ¼ cups milk
- 2 cups shredded cooked chicken
- 1½ tsp dried Italian seasoning
- ¼ cup grated Parmesan cheese
- 2 cups shredded Monterey jack cheese (8 oz)

Instructions
- Preheat the oven up to 350 degrees Fahrenheit. Set aside a baking dish (13x9-inch) sprayed with cooking oil.
- Follow the Instructions for cooking the pasta. Pour the water and put it aside.
- Heat some olive oil over medium heat. Remove the pan from the heat and put it aside.
- Take a large bowl to mix the milk, eggs, Italian seasoning, red pepper flakes, salt and pepper, onion, spinach, sun-dried tomatoes, artichokes, cooked chicken, parmesan cheese, and Monterey jack cheese.
- Gently stir the pasta so that everything is equally distributed.
- Place the spaghetti baking dish that has been prepared. Bake for 25 mins, covered with foil.
- Prepare the topping: Combine the paprika, breadcrumbs, Parmesan, and melted butter in a small bowl. To blend, stir everything together.
- Sprinkle this topping over the dish and bake for another 10 mins.

Nutrition Information
Calories: 523 kcal, Carbohydrates: 48 g, Protein: 31 g, Fats: 9 g

28. Instant Pot Lentil Soup
Prep Time: 20 Mins, Cook Time: 8 Mins, Servings: 2
Ingredients
- 1 medium yellow onion (chopped)
- 2 medium carrots (chopped)
- 2 tbsp olive oil
- 4 cloves garlic (minced)
- 2 ribs celery (chopped)
- 1 ½ tsp dried thyme
- 6 cups (low sodium) vegetable broth
- 1 tsp ground cumin
- 15 oz can fire-roasted crushed tomatoes
- 1 ½ cups dry green or brown lentils

Instructions
- Apply Sauté feature of your Instant Pot and heat some olive oil. Cook, often turning, until the carrots, onion, and celery are cooked (approximately 5 mins are required).
- Season with salt, pepper and add the thyme, garlic, cumin, smoky paprika, and garlic powder. Cook for 30 seconds while stirring.
- Pour the broth in it. Stir in the mashed lentils and tomatoes
- Adjust the steam nozzle to the closing position and close the Pot lid. Set the pressure cooker on high for 8 mins.
- Allow the air pressure to naturally release for 10 mins after the cooking time has ended.
- Allow all the steam to leave and the pin to fall to the bottom before gently opening the Pot lid. Use a large bowl and combine the chopped spinach and the soup. If preferred, top with grated Parmesan cheese.

Nutrition Information
Calories: 130 kcal, Carbohydrates: 23 g, Protein: 6 g, Fats: 1 g

29. Instant Pot Quinoa
Prep Time: 5 Mins, Cook Time: 1 Mins, Servings: 1
Ingredients
- 1 cup dry quinoa
- 1 cup water (vegetable broth or chicken broth)

Instructions
- Rinse the quinoa for 1 min under cold water. Drain it.
- In an Instant Pot, combine the water, quinoa, and salt (if using). Turn the steam nozzle to the locking position and close the lid.
- Set your pressure cooker setting to high pressure for 1 min.
- Allow the pot to release when the cooking time is finished naturally. Carefully remove the cover from the Instant Pot.
- To smooth and separate the quinoa, use a fork.

Nutrition Information
Calories: 104 kcal, Carbohydrates: 18 g, Protein: 4 g, Fats: 2 g

30. Instant Pot Butter Chicken
Prep Time: 15 Mins, Cook Time: 10 Mins, Servings: 4
Ingredients
- 1 small onion (chopped)
- 3 tbsp unsalted butter
- 1 tbsp minced fresh ginger
- 3 tbsp unsalted butter
- 1 tbsp garam masala
- 2 tsp smoked paprika
- 1 red bell pepper (chopped)
- 2 lb chicken thighs or breast
- 1 red bell pepper (chopped)
- 1 cup whole fat coconut milk

Instructions
- Set the Instant Pot at sauté mode and pour in the butter. Add the onions after butter has melted. Cook for 2 to 3 mins.
- Cook and constantly stir for 30 seconds after adding the garlic, bell pepper, and ginger to the saucepan.
- Combine the garam masala, cumin, smoked paprika, turmeric, and salt in a large mixing bowl.
- Stir in ¼ cup of water.
- Toss in the chicken and tomato sauce.
- Push the steam valve to lock and close the Pot lid.
- Release the pressure when the cooking time has passed.
- Allow the chicken to rest on a clean chopping board. Meanwhile, whisk together the coconut milk and the sauce in the Instant Pot.
- Move the chicken pieces to the Instant Pot, cut them into bite-size pieces.
- If wanted, serve the sauce and chicken over rice with naan and chopped cilantro.

Nutrition Information
Calories: 355 kcal, Carbohydrates: 13 g, Protein: 36 g, Fats: 18 g

31. Honey Garlic Instant Pot Pork Tenderloin
Prep Time: 10 Mins, Cook Time: 4 Mins, Servings: 1
Ingredients
- 1 lb pork tenderloin
- ½ cup water
- 2 tsp olive oil
- 3 cloves garlic (minced)
- 2 tsp olive oil
- 2 tsp cornstarch

Instructions
- Cut these tenderloins in halves to get two smaller pieces. They can fit in the Pot easily.
- Season the pork tenderloin on both sides with salt & pepper.
- In the Instant Pot, heat some olive oil in sauté mode. Brown the pork t for 2-3 mins on each side.
- Add ½ cup water and cook.
- Combine the Instant Pot's garlic, soy sauce, honey, and ginger. Return the meat to the Instant Pot.
- Set the steam valve to the closing position and shut the lid.
- Cook for 4 mins on high pressure using the Manual or Pressure Cook option.
- Allow the pork to rest for a while on a cutting board.
- Combine the 2 tbsp cornstarch and 1 tbsp water in a small dish. Turn the Instant Pot off.
- Pork should be sliced and served with the sauce.

Nutrition Information
Calories: 297kcal, Carbohydrates: 21 g, Protein: 34 g, Fats: 9 g

32. Instant Pot Stuffed Peppers
Prep Time: 15 Mins, Cook Time: 16 Mins, Servings: 1
Ingredients
- ½ lb lean ground beef
- 1 cup cooked brown rice
- 4 or 5 medium-large bell peppers
- 15 oz can diced tomatoes
- 8 oz can tomato sauce
- 4 or 5 medium-large bell peppers
- 2 tsp dried Italian seasoning
- 1 cup shredded cheese
- 1 tsp garlic powder

Instructions
- Remove the tops of all bell peppers and set them aside. If these bell peppers aren't standing up, cut a little piece off the bottom to help them stand up.
- Combine the ground beef, onion, cooked rice, diced tomatoes, ¼ cup tomato sauce, garlic powder, Italian seasoning, salt, pepper, and half cheese in a large mixing bowl. Stir till everything is well combined.
- Fill the bowl of your Instant Pot with 1 cup of water (for an 8-quart pot, use ½ cups water). In the saucepan, put the metal trivet.
- Fill the bell peppers to the brim with the filling. In the Instant Pot, place the peppers over the trivet. 1 tbsp tomato sauce, spooned on top.
- Turn the steam valve to the closing position and shut the Instant Pot cover.
- When the cooking time is up, quickly relieving the pressure by gently turning the steam release valve towards the venting position using the handle of a long spoon.
- The remaining cheese can be sprinkled over the peppers. To melt the cheese, replace the Instant Pot cover for a few minutes. Serve.

Nutrition Information
Calories: 298 kcal, Carbohydrates: 30 g, Protein: 23 g, Fats: 10 g

33. Instant Pot Pulled Pork
Prep Time: 20 Mins, Cook Time: 1 hour, Servings: 1
Ingredients
- 1 tbsp chili powder
- 1 tbsp brown sugar
- 1 tsp garlic powder
- 1 tsp onion powder
- 1 tbsp brown sugar
- 1 tsp ground cumin
- 1 cup barbecue sauce
- 2 tbsp apple cider vinegar
- 3-4 lb boneless pork shoulder/pork butt

Instructions
- Stir all spice rub Ingredients in a bowl until thoroughly blended.
- Trim the extra fat from the pork and cut it into four pieces. The spice rub should be applied on all sides of the pork.
- Turn the Instant Pot insert to sauté mode and pour in the olive oil. Put the pork in the pot when heated and brown on both sides.
- Shut off the Instant Pot. Add half chicken broth should be added to the saucepan. Combine the remaining broth,

apple cider vinegar, barbecue sauce, and honey in a large mixing bowl (or brown sugar). To blend, stir everything together.
- Place the meat into the Instant Pot. Put the cover back on. Place the steam nozzle in the closed position. Put Instant Pot to high-pressure cooking for 60 mins.
- It will take around 15 mins to pressure formation in the Instant Pot. Release the pressure after the cooking time has passed.
- Place the meat in a large mixing bowl.
- Cook the sauce, stirring regularly until slightly thickened, about 4-5 mins in the Instant Pot. Turn the Instant Pot off.
- Meanwhile, shred the meat with two forks. Return it to the strained sauce and stir it in again. If preferred, serve the pork with burger buns and more barbecue sauce.

Nutrition Information
Calories: 356 kcal, Carbohydrates: 23 g, Protein: 33 g, Fats: 14 g

34. Mango Smoothie
Prep Time: 5 Mins, Cook Time: 5 Mins, Servings: 10 oz.
Ingredients
- ¼ cup plain Greek yogurt
- ½ medium banana (frozen)
- ¾ cup milk (dairy or dairy-free)
- ¼ tsp vanilla extract
- 1 ½ cups frozen mango pieces

Instructions
- Take a blender, combine all of the ingredients. Blend until smooth. Add extra milk as needed to thin down the smoothie. Serve right away.

Nutrition Information
Calories: 173 kcal, Carbohydrates: 31 g, Protein: 7 g, Fats: 4 g

35. Greek Pasta Salad
Prep Time: 20 Mins, Cook Time: 10 Mins, Servings: 1
Ingredients
- ⅓ cup red wine vinegar
- ⅔ cup olive oil
- 2 tsp dried oregano
- 1 tsp garlic powder
- 1 lb short pasta shapes
- 1 tsp dried basil
- 2 bell peppers
- 1 cucumber
- ½ cup finely chopped red onion
- 1-pint cherry tomatoes
- ¾ cup kalamata olives
- ¼ cup chopped fresh parsley
- ½ cup crumbled feta cheese

Instructions
- Take a small bowl, whisk the dressing Ingredients in it. Remove from the equation.
- A big saucepan of salted water should be brought to a boil. Cook the pasta according to the Instructions on the box. Using a colander, drain the pasta. Drain carefully after rinsing with cold water. Use a large mixing bowl to combine the pasta and the sauce.
- While you cut the veggies and prepare the additional pasta salad Ingredients, allow the pasta to cool down. To prevent the spaghetti from sticking together, stir it periodically.
- In the same bowl as the spaghetti, combine the cucumber, bell peppers, red onion, tomatoes, feta, kalamata olives, and parsley. Mix in the dressing until everything is nicely mixed.
- Before serving, chill the salad for 2 hours.

Nutrition Information
Calories: 285 kcal, Carbohydrates: 33 g, Protein: 7 g, Fats: 14 g

36. Baked Chicken Breast
Prep Time: 5 Mins, Cook Time: 18 Mins, Servings: 1
Ingredients
- 4 boneless, skinless chicken breasts
- 1 tsp dried oregano
- 1 tsp paprika
- 1 tbsp olive oil
- ½ tsp garlic powder
- Salt and pepper

Instructions
- Preheat the oven up to 450 °F. Use the foil to line a baking pan.
- If the chicken breasts are more rigid in some areas than others, use a meat mallet to press them equal thickness.
- Drizzle oil over all sides of the chicken breasts and place them on the baking pan.
- In a small dish, mix the spice rub Ingredients.
- The spice rub should be applied to all parts of the chicken.
- Chicken breasts should be baked as per their size: 5-6 oz breasts should be baked for 13-16 mins, 8 oz breasts should be baked for 16-19 mins, and 11-12 oz breasts should be baked for 22-26 mins. Check that the chicken has achieved a warmth of 165 °F on the inside.
- Remove the instant pan from the oven, cover loosely with foil, and set aside for 5-10 mins before serving and slicing the chicken.

Nutrition Information
Calories: 146 kcal, Carbohydrates: 26 g, Protein: 24 g, Fats: 4 g

37. Instant Pot Chicken and Mushrooms
Prep Time: 15 Mins, Cook Time: 4 Mins, Servings: 4
Ingredients
- 1 tbsp olive oil
- 1 cup chopped yellow onion
- 1 ½ lb boneless (skinless chicken thighs)
- salt and pepper
- ½ tsp dried oregano
- 2 cloves garlic (minced)
- ½ tsp paprika
- 2 cups chicken broth
- 1 cup dried orzo pasta

Instructions
- In the Instant Pot, heat the olive oil on sauté setting till it is hot. Season the chicken thighs generously with pepper and salt.
- Put the chicken in a single layer in the Instant Pot. Remove the chicken to a clean platter after browning it for 3-4 mins on each side.
- In the Instant Pot, combine the onion and mushrooms. Cook for about 2-3 mins, or until they begin to soften. Cook and constantly stir for 30 seconds after adding the garlic to the saucepan.
- Combine the garlic powder, dried oregano, paprika, 14 tsp salt, and chicken broth in a large saucepan. Scrape off any parts adhered to the base of the saucepan.
- Add the orzo and mix well. Cover the Instant Pot and put the chicken thighs over everything else. Adjust the seal position as necessary.
- Set the pressure cooker on high for 4 mins. It will take around 10 mins for the Instant Pot to achieve pressure, after which the cooking time will begin to clock down. Quickly release the pressure after the cooking time is over.
- Open the Pot cover after removing steam. Use an instant-read thermometer to make sure the chicken is cooked through to 165° F. If preferred, garnish with Parmesan cheese and parsley.

Nutrition Information
Calories: 422 kcal, Carbohydrates: 36 g, Protein: 42 g, Fats: 12 g

38. Chicken Stir Fry
Prep Time: 23 Mins, Cook Time: 12 Mins, Servings: 1
Ingredients
- ⅓ cup soy sauce
- 2 tbsp honey
- ½ cup chicken broth
- 2 tbsp minced fresh ginger

- 3 cloves garlic (minced)
- 2 tsp sesame oil
- 1 tbsp cornstarch

For Serving
- 4 cups rice, cooked

Instructions
- Take a dish or jar and add all the stir fry sauce Ingredients. Set aside after whisking everything together.
- Take a large pan or wok, heat 1 tbsp oil at medium heat.
- When the saucepan is heated, add cubed chicken. Cook and toss periodically until browned or nearly cooked through approximately 4 to 5 mins. Place the chicken on a platter that has been cleaned.
- In the same pan, add olive oil (remaining). Cook for about 2 mins after adding the carrots and broccoli. Put the bell peppers and stir fry for another 2 to 3 mins or crisp-tender.
- To recombine the sauce, whisk it together. Return the chicken to the pan, along with the sauce. Cook for another 2 - 3 mins, or until the chicken is fully cooked and the sauce has become thickened.
- Add the green onions and stir to combine. Overcooked rice, serve with stir fry.

Nutrition Information
Calories: 366 kcal, Carbohydrates: 28 g, Protein: 30 g, Fats: 13 g

39. Perfect Instant Pot Hard Boiled Eggs
Prep Time: 1 Min, Cook Time: 5 Mins, Servings: 1

Ingredients
- Eggs (up to 12)
- 1 cup water
- Ice + water

Instructions
- Take an Instant Pot and pour 1 cup of water. In the pot, place a trivet or a steamer rack
- On the upper edge of the rack, arrange the eggs in a layer.
- Move the valve towards the sealing setting and close the Instant Pot lid.
- Set to the pressure/manual cook, high pressure. Adjust the cooking time for 5 mins using the +/- button.
- After the cooking time, arrange a 5-min natural release in case of 6-quart Instant Pot. If Instant Pot is 8 quarts, rapidly release the air pressure when the cooking time is up.
- After the float valve lowers, open it. Carefully remove the cover and move the eggs to a dish right away.
- Allow 5-10 mins for the eggs to chill in the cold water before peeling.

Nutrition Information
Calories: 70 kcal, Carbohydrates: 26 g, Protein: 6 g, Fats: 5 g

40. Graham Cracker Recipe
Prep Time: 20 Mins, Cook Time: 14 Mins, Servings: 1

Ingredients
- ¼ cup packed light brown sugar
- 1 tsp baking powder
- 2 ¼ cups white whole wheat flour
- ½ tsp salt
- ¼ tsp cloves
- 6 tbsp cold unsalted butter *(cubes)*
- 1 tsp cinnamon
- ¼ cup honey
- ¼ cup plus 1 tbsp cold milk

Instructions
- Preheat your oven to around 350 degrees Fahrenheit.
- Take the food processor bowl, combine the brown sugar, white whole wheat flour, salt, baking powder, cinnamon, and cloves.
- Pulse the butter cubes 10 times in the food processor to incorporate the butter.
- In a food processor, combine the milk and honey. Pulse the dough until it comes together.
- Take the dough from the processor and divide it in half.
- All portions of dough should be rolled into a ball, then flattened and shaped into a square. You may trim the rough edges of the dough and re-roll it if desired.
- Cut the dough into graham shapes using a pastry, pizza cutter, or knife. Separate the crackers only after they've been baked.
- Carefully move the crackers to a baking sheet.
- Bake the crackers for about 12 to 15 mins
- Allow the crackers to cool over the baking sheet before separating them.

Nutrition Information
Calories: 56 kcal, Carbohydrates: 9 g, Protein: 1 g, Fats: 2 g

41. Instant Pot Black Beans
Prep Time: 10 Mins, Cook Time: 1 hour, Servings: 1

Ingredients
- 3 ½ cups water
- 1-lb dry black beans
- 3 cloves garlic (minced)
- ½ tsp ground cumin
- ½ onion (chopped)
- ¼ tsp pepper
- ½ tsp chili powder
- 1 tsp salt

Instructions
- Dry beans should be rinsed and picked over to remove tiny stones or other dirt.
- In an Instant Pot, combine black beans (soaked or not), onion, water, garlic, pepper, cumin, and chili powder. Stir.
- Set the steam pressure valve to the locking position and close the Pot lid.
- At high pressure, use the Manual button or pressure cook to set the cooking time:
- Beans that have not been soaked should be cooked for 25 mins for harder beans, and 30 mins will be required for softer beans.
- Soaked Beans: For stronger beans, soak for 8 minutes; for softer beans, 10 minutes.
- It will take 10-15 mins for the Instant Pot to achieve pressure, after which the cooking time starts.
- Allow 15 mins for the pressure to release once the cooking time has ended naturally.
- Use a long spoon, gently move, the quickly remove any leftover pressure. Carefully open the Instant Pot cover after all the steam releases and the pin has dropped.
- Add the salt and mix well. Serve it immediately.

Nutrition Information
Calories: 145 kcal, Carbohydrates: 27 g, Protein: 9 g, Fats: 1 g

42. Instant Pot Pinto Beans
Prep Time: 10 Mins, Cook Time: 25 Mins, Servings: 1

Ingredients
- ½ small white onion (chopped)
- 4 cloves garlic (minced)
- 1 lb dry pinto beans
- 1 tsp chili powder
- 1 jalapeño (chopped)
- ¼ tsp black pepper
- 1 tsp cumin
- 4 cups water
- ½ tsp salt

Instructions
- Rinse and sieve through the beans to remove min stones or other dirt.
- Take an Instant Pot, add the beans (unsoaked or soaked). Stir together the water and the other Ingredients, except the salt.

- Set the steam pressure valve to the locking position and seal the Pot lid. Use the manual button or pressure cook on high pressure, adjust the cooking time as follows:
- 30 mins for unsoaked beans and 15 mins for soaked beans.
- It will take roughly 10-15 mins for the Instant Pot to achieve pressure, after which the cooking time starts. Allow the air to release naturally
- Gently remove the Instant Pot cover after the pin has fallen. Stir in the beans and season with salt to taste.
- Cooled beans may be kept in a sealed jar for up to 4 days in the refrigerator or 3 months in the freezer.

Nutrition Information
Calories: 136 kcal, Carbohydrates: 25 g, Protein: 8 g, Fats: 1 g

43. Sautéed Green Beans with Parmesan
Prep Time: 10 Mins, Cook Time: 5 Mins, Servings: 1
Ingredients
- ¾ lb fresh green beans (stem ends trimmed)
- 2 tsp olive oil
- 1 oz. grated Parmesan cheese (¼ cup)

Instructions
- Take a large pan, heat the olive oil overheat. Cook, occasionally turning until the green beans are crisp-tender. Cooking time may vary based on the skillet's temperature, and 4-6 mins are suggested.
- Season with salt.
- Remove the pan from the heat and toss in the Parmesan cheese. Serve accordingly.

Nutrition Information
Calories: 49 kcal, Carbohydrates: 4 g, Protein: 2 g, Fats: 2g

44. Tuna Salad
Prep Time: 10 Mins, Cook Time: 10 Mins, Servings: 1
Ingredients:
- 2 cans (5 oz. each) tuna in water, drained
- ¼ cup plain Greek yogurt (or mayonnaise)
- 2 tbsp relish
- 2 tbsp red onion, finely chopped
- 2 tbsp celery, chopped
- salt and pepper (to taste)

Instructions:
- Take a medium dish, place the drained tuna.
- Combine the Greek yogurt, relish, celery, red onion, and a pinch of salt and pepper in a mixing bowl.
- Stir everything together using a fork till completely blended. Taste and season with extra pepper and salt, if necessary.
- Tuna salad may be served with rolls, bread, crackers, or croissants. Serve the tuna salad over a bed of lettuce in avocado halves or hallow tomatoes for a low-carb option.

Nutrition Information
Calories: 78 kcal, Carbohydrates: 3 g, Protein: 15 g, Fats: 2 g

45. Banana Smoothie
Prep Time: 5 Mins, Cook Time: 5 Mins, Servings: 1
Ingredients
- ¼ cup Greek yogurt (vanilla or plain)
- 1 cup banana, sliced (frozen is best)
- ¼ tsp vanilla extract
- ¼ cup milk (almond, dairy, etc.)

Instructions
- In a blender, combine all the ingredients. Blend till completely smooth. Add extra milk if necessary to get the desired consistency.
- Serve right away.

Nutrition Information
Calories: 8 kcal, Carbohydrates: 39 g, Protein: 9 g, Fats: 3 g

46. How to Cook Brown Rice
Prep Time: 5 Mins, Cook Time: 30 Mins, Servings: 1
Ingredients
- ½ tsp salt (optional)
- 8 cups water
- 1 cup long-grain brown rice

Instructions
- Take a big saucepan with a tight-fitting cover, boil water in it.
- Rinse the rice using a fine-mesh sieve under cool running water.
- Mix the rice and lower the heat after the water has reached a boil. Cook the rice for 30 mins, uncovered.
- Turn the heat off. Pour boiled rice in a strainer. Set aside for 10 seconds to drain. Return the cooked rice to the heated pot. Cover these right away. Allow 10 mins for the rice to rest before serving. It will steam, become fully and light throughout this time.
- Toss the rice with a fork and serve.

Nutrition Information
Calories: 136 kcal, Carbohydrates: 28 g, Protein: 2 g, Fats: 1 g

47. Healthy Carrot Cake Muffins
Prep Time: 15 Mins, Cook Time: 15 Mins, Servings: 4

Ingredients
- 2 eggs
- 1 cup unsweetened applesauce
- ¼ cup melted unsalted butter
- ½ cup pure maple syrup
- ½ tsp salt
- 1 tsp baking soda
- 1 tsp cinnamon
- ¼ tsp ground nutmeg
- 2 tsp vanilla extract
- ¼ tsp ground ginger
- 1 ½ cups of white whole wheat flour
- 1 ½ cups peeled grated carrot
- ¼ tsp ground cloves

Instructions
- Preheat the oven up to 350 °F. Line the muffin pans using paper liners or cooking spray (nonstick spray).
- Beat the eggs, maple syrup, and applesauce in a large mixing dish. Take a separate bowl to whisk the melted butter and egg yolks together.
- Whisk together the cinnamon, baking soda, cloves, salt, nutmeg, ginger, and vanilla till a smooth mixture form.
- Gently mix the oats, wheat flour, and grated carrot using a spatula. Make sure the batter isn't over-mixed. It will become a thick batter.
- Fill all muffin cups nearly to the top with the batter, dividing the 12 muffin cups equally. Bake for 18 to 20 mins, till a toothpick inserted in the middle of a muffin, turns clean.
- Allow 5 mins for the muffins to cool before transferring to a wire rack.

Nutrition Information
Calories: 174 kcal, Carbohydrates: 28 g, Protein: 4 g, Fats: 6 g

48. Paleo Apple Cinnamon Bread
Prep Time: 15 Mins, Cook Time: 60 Mins, Servings: 4
Ingredients:
- 1½ cups unsweetened applesauce
- ½ cup creamy almond butter
- 4 eggs (room temperature)
- ¼ cup coconut oil (melted)
- 1 tsp of vanilla extract
- ¼ cup coconut sugar
- 2 tsp cinnamon
- ¼ tsp sea salt
- 1 tsp baking powder
- 1 medium apple, diced
- 1 tsp baking powder
- ½ cup pecans (chopped and toasted)

Instructions:
- Heat oven up to 350 degrees Fahrenheit and grease a 9″x5″ loaf pan.
- Mix the eggs, applesauce, coconut oil, vanilla extract, coconut sugar, and nut butter in a large mixing bowl until well blended.
- Take a large mixing bowl, combine cinnamon, coconut flour, baking soda, sea salt, baking powder. Combine the pecans and apple chunks in a mixing bowl.
- Pour the mixture into the pan and smooth it out evenly.
- Preheat your oven to 350°F and bake for about 50-60 mins. The tip should Boz back slightly when squeezed, and a tester inserted in the middle must look clean.
- Remove from the oven and cool for 12 hours. Keeping leftovers in an airtight container is a good idea.

Nutrition Information
Calories: 223 kcal, Carbohydrates: 15 g, Protein: 7 g, Fats: 15 g

49. Healthy Blueberry Lemon Muffins
Prep Time: 15 Mins, Cook Time: 35 Mins, Servings: 6
Ingredients
Wet
- ¼ cup unsweetened applesauce
- 2 tbsp coconut oil melted
- 2 large eggs
- ½ cup low-fat buttermilk
- ⅓ cup honey or agave nectar
- ½ cup low-fat yogurt

Dry
- 1 cup all-purpose flour
- 1 ¼ cups whole wheat flour
- 1 tsp baking powder
- 1 ¼ cups whole wheat flour
- 2 lemons finely grated zest
- 1 ¼ cups whole wheat flour
- 1 cup frozen blueberries

Instructions
- Preheat oven up to 425 degrees Fahrenheit (220 degrees Celsius). Grease the 6-cup giant muffin tray lightly.
- Take a medium mixing bowl, combine the applesauce, coconut oil, and honey or agave nectar. Whisk in the eggs until they are thoroughly mixed. Set aside after whisking in the yogurt and buttermilk.
- Except for blueberries, combine remaining dry Ingredients in a large mixing bowl. Combine all Ingredients (wet and dry) in a mixing bowl and whisk until mixed. Don't overmix it, as a few clumps are acceptable.
- Use a spatula to mix the blueberries into the batter gently.
- Distribute the batter evenly among the six large muffin cups.
- Reduce the oven temperature to 400 degrees Fahrenheit (205 degrees Celsius) and bake for about 20 mins. Lower the heat up to 350°F and bake for another 15 mins.
- Allow the muffins to cool after removing them from the oven.

Nutrition Information
Calories: 109.5 kcal, Carbohydrates: 9.5 g, Protein: 9.5 g, Fats: 3.9 g

50. Pancake Muffins
Prep Time: 15 Mins, Cook Time: 15 Mins, Servings: 1
Ingredients
- ¾ cup white whole-wheat flour
- 4 tbsp. unsalted butter
- 1 ½ tsp. baking powder
- ½ tsp. baking soda
- 4 tbsp. unsalted butter
- ½ tsp. salt
- ¾ cup mashed ripe banana
- 2 large eggs
- 4 tbsp. unsalted butter
- 1 tsp. pure vanilla extract

Instructions
- Preheat the oven up to 375 °F. Paper liners should be used to line the muffin tin.
- Melt butter in a microwave-safe bowl in your microwave. Allow cooling slightly before serving.
- Whisk the baking powder, white whole-wheat flour, salt, all-purpose flour, baking soda in a large mixing basin until thoroughly blended.
- Add the maple syrup, mashed banana, vanilla, and eggs to the bowl containing the melted butter. Take a separate bowl, whisk together the buttermilk and the egg yolks.
- Stir together the wet and dry Ingredients until just incorporated. Avoid overmixing.
- Scoop the mixture into the muffin cups. Fill each approximately 3/4 full and equally distribute the batter among the 12 wells. 15 mins in the oven
- Allow pancake muffins to cool for five min before transferring to a wire rack. Just before serving, sprinkle maple syrup on each maple syrup.

Nutrition Information
Calories: 142 kcal, Carbohydrates: 20 g, Protein: 3 g, Fats: 5 g

51. Fruit on The Bottom Yogurt
Prep Time: 5 Mins, Cook Time: 5 Mins, Servings: 4
Ingredients
- 4 cups (245 grams) plain Greek
- 3 cups blueberries
- 4 tbsp. unsalted butter
- ¼ cup sliced almonds, toasted
- 1 tbsp cornstarch
- 4 fresh raspberries

Instructions
- Take a mixing bowl to combine the yogurt and 1 ½ tsp of honey. Blend well until everything is well combined. Refrigerate it.
- Heat the blueberries, 3 tbsp of honey, and 2 tsp water in a small skillet over medium-low heat.
- Combine the 1 tsp cold water and cornstarch in a small mixing dish and stir until completely dissolved.
- When the blueberries simmer, they'll eventually break down.
- Cook until the corn starch mixture thickens, then remove from the heat.
- Refrigerate until cold and solidify, then transfer to containers.
- Pour the yogurt over the fruit that has been allowed to cool.
- Serve with almonds and raspberries.

Nutrition Information
Calories: 170 kcal, Carbohydrates: 30 g, Protein: 6 g, Fats: 2 g

52. Easy breakfast roll-ups
Prep Time: 15 Mins, Cook Time: 35 Mins, Servings: 6
Ingredients
- 1 egg
- Salt and pepper
- 1 tsp water or milk
- 1 soft taco size flour tortilla
- Fillings: baby spinach, avocado, bacon, tomatoes, cheese, crumbled sausage

Instructions
- Whisk the milk/water and egg until smooth in a small mixing basin. If desired, place the tortilla on a platter and add cheese topping.
- Spray a pan equal to the size of a tortilla with cooking spray. Preheat a pan at the medium-low flame and pour the egg mixture into it. To guarantee that the egg touches the pan's bottom, gently tilt the pan. Cook till the egg is fully cooked and the liquid has evaporated. Add pepper and salt to taste.
- Slide the fried egg immediately on top of the tortilla/cheese.
- Optional fillings may be placed on top of the egg.

- Roll up the tortilla tightly without ripping it or displacing the fillings. Serve by cutting the slice in half.

Nutrition Information
Calories: 150 kcal, Carbohydrates: 13 g, Protein:8.6 g, Fats: 7.3 g

53. Freezer Breakfast Sandwiches
Prep Time: 15 Mins, Cook Time: 20 Mins, Servings: 6
Ingredients
- Salt & pepper, to taste
- 6 large eggs
- 6 slices sharp cheddar cheese
- 6 English muffins
- Plastic wrap
- 18 small slices of deli ham

Instructions
- Preheat the oven up to 350 °F. Use a nonstick spray and coat a large muffin tray or tiny ramekins. In each ramekin, crack 1 egg. Gently puncture each yolk with a sharp knife.
- Bake for 10-15 mins, or until eggs are set. Remove the eggs from the ramekins and set them aside to cool somewhat. If desired, season with salt and pepper.
- Meanwhile, cut the English muffins into slices. On top of every English muffin, place one piece of cheese and three sham slices.
- Finally, add the egg layer.
- Cover in the plastic wrap and place in the freezer.
- Take the sandwiches and wrap them in a paper towel to reheat. Microwave them on high for 1 min at 50% power. Turn the sandwich over. Microwave them for 1 min over regular power.

Nutrition Information
Calories: 210 kcal, Carbohydrates: 26 g, Protein: 12 g, Fats: 7 g

54. Spinach + Feta Breakfast Quesadillas
Prep Time: 10 Mins, Cook Time: 15 Mins, Servings: 6
Ingredients
- ½ red onion (diced)
- 2 tsp olive oil
- 4 eggs
- ⅛ tsp salt
- ½ cup feta (crumbled)
- 4 handfuls of spinach leaves
- ⅛ tsp pepper
- 1 cup mozzarella cheese
- 2 tsp olive oil
- 4 tortillas

Instructions
- Heat tbsp of olive oil in a nonstick skillet over medium heat.
- Sauté the bell pepper and red onion for 5-7 mins, or until tender. The eggs should be whisked together before being added to the pan with feta cheese and spinach. Scramble for 2-3 mins, until the eggs are fully cooked, and feta and spinach have been well combined.
- Turn off the heat in the pan.
- Add 2 tortillas to a clean pan.
- Spread a quarter of the filling mixture over half of a tortilla. Top with a quarter of a cup of mozzarella cheese.
- Cook for 2-3 mins on each side, till golden and the cheese has melted. Press the other half of this tortilla over the topping.
- Allow it to cool fully before placing it in the meal prep box (for about 1-2 days).
- Refrigerate for up to four days or freeze for three months.

Nutrition Information
Calories: 442 kcal, Carbohydrates: 41 g, Protein: 21 g, Fats: 22 g

55. Butternut Squash Breakfast Wraps
Prep Time: 20 Mins, Cook Time: 25 Mins, Servings: 6
Ingredients
- ½ cup wilted Spinach
- 16 Turkey Sausage Links, cooked
- 1 cup Cheddar Cheese, Shredded
- 16 Turkey Sausage Links, cooked
- 6 Eggs
- 6 Whole Wheat High Fiber Tortillas
- Salt and Pepper
- 3 Tbsp Butter
- ¼ cup Milk

Instructions
- Melt half butter portion in a pan over medium flame.
- Sprinkle pepper and salt over cubed butternut squash.
- Add half squash to the boiling butter. Cook until it gets brown. Toss in the pan and cook until golden brown on both sides and squash becomes tender.
- Set aside on a dish and continue to sauté the remaining squash.
- Cook the turkey sausages till they are thoroughly done. Cut into tiny pieces and set aside over a platter.
- Wilt the spinach in a pan until it is completely wilted.
- Cheese should be shredded.
- Whisk the milk, eggs, salt, and pepper in the mixing bowl.
- In the same pan, melt the remaining butter and bring to a simmer. Cook the eggs until they are scrambled.
- To assemble, cheddar cheese, eggs, spinach, squash, and sausage on each tortilla wrap. Let's wrap things up.

Nutrition Information
Calories: 109.5 kcal, Carbohydrates: 9.5 g, Protein: 9.5 g, Fats: 3.9 g

56. Gingerbread Baked Oatmeal Cups (Muffins)
Prep Time: 20 Mins, Cook Time: 25 Mins, Servings: 2
Ingredients
- 2 cups milk
- 2 ¼ cups old-fashioned oats
- 2 large eggs
- 2 tbsp molasses
- ¼ cup pure maple syrup
- ½ tsp baking powder
- ¼ cup pure maple syrup
- ¼ tsp nutmeg
- ¼ cup pure maple syrup

Instructions
- Preheat the oven up to 350 °F. Employ silicone liners or coat the wells of the muffin tray by using cooking spray. Pour 3 tbsp oats into all wells.
- Combine eggs, milk, maple syrup, vanilla, and molasses in the 4-cup liquid measuring bowl. Whisk everything together until it's smooth.
- Mix salt, baking powder, ginger, cloves, cinnamon, and nutmeg in a small basin. Pour the dry items into the wet ones and whisk to mix. Fill the muffin tray wells nearly to the top with the wet Ingredients. In the measuring cup, re-mix the wet Ingredients as required to keep them well blended.
- Bake for 24-26 mins or until the oatmeal cups are firm. Allow cooling in the pan for 5 mins. Warm the dish before serving.

Nutrition Information
Calories: 245 kcal, Carbohydrates: 39 g, Protein: 8 g, Fats: 6 g

57. Easy Overnight Oats Recipe
Prep Time: 5 Mins, Cook Time: 5 Mins, Servings: 1
Ingredients
- ½ cup milk
- ½ cup old-fashioned oats
- ¼ tsp pure vanilla extract
- ½ tsp pure maple syrup
- For serving; fresh fruit, slivered almonds, other nut butter, etc.

Instructions
- take a glass jar or dish and combine the milk, oats, vanilla, and maple syrup. cover and shake or stir in case of the bowl. (If you're preparing a larger quantity, combine the ingredients in a mixing bowl.)

- Refrigerate for about 6 hours and 4 days in the refrigerator. Just before serving, stir in the toppings.
- Before serving, stir in any desired toppings, such as chia seeds, peanut butter, blueberries, yogurt, dried fruit, almonds, honey, banana, nuts, and so on.

Nutrition Information
Calories: 226 kcal, Carbohydrates: 36 g, Protein: 9 g, Fats: 5 g

58. Chia Overnight Spiced Oats
Prep Time: 5 Mins, Cook Time: 45 Mins, Servings: 4
Ingredients
- 3 cups rolled oats old fashioned
- 3 tbsp brown sugar
- 2 tbsp chia seeds
- 2 ½ cups almond milk, unsweetened
- 2-3 tsp chai spice homemade mix
- Toppings: dried fruit sliced almonds

Instructions
- Take a medium mixing bowl to combine the chia seeds, oats, spices, and brown sugar. Stir in the almond milk until it is well incorporated. Refrigerate overnight, covered with plastic wrap.
- Enjoy the breakfast.

Nutrition Information
Calories: 157 kcal, Carbohydrates: 26 g, Protein: 5 g, Fats: 4 g

59. Blueberry Baked Oatmeal Cups
Prep Time: 10 Mins, Cook Time: 25 Mins, Servings: 12
Ingredients
- 3 cups (300 grams) old-fashioned rolled oats
- 1 tsp of ground cinnamon
- 1 cup (240 ml) milk
- 1 tsp of baking powder
- ¼ tsp salt
- ¼ cup honey
- 2 tbsp (light or dark) brown sugar
- 1 tsp extract vanilla
- 2 eggs large
- 1 cup blueberries fresh

Instructions
- Preheat your oven to 350 degrees Fahrenheit. Set aside a (12-count) muffin tray that has been sprayed with cooking spray (nonstick).
- Take a large mixing basin, whisk together the baking powder, oats, salt, and cinnamon.
- Whisk together the eggs, milk, honey, vanilla extract, and brown sugar in a separate dish until well blended. Combine the wet and dry ingredients in a mixing bowl and stir until thoroughly combined.
- Use a big spoon, evenly spread the mixture among the muffin pan's 12 holes. Make sure all cups have an equal quantity of oats and liquid. Using your fingers, carefully press the blueberries into all oatmeal cups.
- Bake for 25-27 mins at 350°F, or until the oatmeal cups' tops is hard. Remove from oven and let it cool for about 5-10 mins in the pan.
- Remove all oatmeal cups and cool completely on a wire rack.

Nutrition Information
Calories: 126 kcal, Carbohydrates: 23 g, Protein: 3.7 g, Fats: 2.6 g

60. Perfect Steel Cut Oats
Prep Time: 5 Mins, Cook Time: 25 Mins, Servings: 3
Ingredients
- 1 cup steel-cut oats
- 1 cup almond milk
- 3 cups water
- 1/8 tsp salt
- ¼ tsp cinnamon
- ½ tsp vanilla extract
- 1 tsp pure maple syrup

Instructions
- Combine the milk and water (if used). Over medium-high heat, bring to a boil.
- Reduce the heat and add salt and oats to the pan.
- Cook, often stirring, for 20-30 mins or till the oats reach your preferred texture. Cook for about 20-25 mins if you want chewier oats; cook longer if you wish to soften oats, adding extra liquid as required.
- Remove the pan and mix in the cinnamon, maple syrup, and vanilla extract.
- As desired, add toppings.

Nutrition Information
Calories: 169 kcal, Carbohydrates: 27 g, Protein: 6 g, Fats: 3 g

61. Strawberry Chia Overnight Oats
Prep Time: 5 Mins, Cook Time: 5 Mins, Servings: 4
Ingredients
- ½ cup milk
- ¼ cup Greek yogurt
- ½ cup old fashioned oats
- ¼ tsp vanilla extract
- ½ cup old fashioned oats
- ¼ cup sliced strawberries
- 1 ½ tsp chia seeds

Instructions
- In a glass jar or dish, combine all items except the strawberries. To mix, cover securely with a lid, then shake vigorously (or stir).
- Refrigerate for at least one night.
- Before serving, mix in the strawberries and serve. Overnight oats are usually eaten cold, although they may be warmed in your microwave if needed.

Nutrition Information
Calories: 286 kcal, Carbohydrates: 45 g, Protein: 16 g, Fats: 5 g

62. Egg Muffins with Kale, Roasted Red Peppers, and Feta Cheese
Prep Time: 10 Mins, Cook Time: 20 Mins, Servings: 2
Ingredients
- 2 large eggs
- 5 egg whites
- ¼ cup skim milk/almond milk
- 1 tbsp green onion, chopped
- Salt and pepper to taste
- ¼ cup chopped roasted red peppers
- ¼ cup fresh chopped kale
- ¼ cup crumbled feta cheese

Instructions
- Preheat oven up to 350 degrees ° F. Using cooking spray, spray 8 muffin pan cups. Make sure the cups are adequately sprayed.
- Whisk the eggs and their whites in a mixing bowl. Sprinkle with salt to taste after whisking in the skim milk. Combine the kale, green onion, and red peppers in a mixing bowl.
- Fill the muffin cups equally with the egg mixture. Divide the cheese among the muffin cups.
- Bake for about 20 mins, or till the middle of the egg muffins is hard. Remove the eggs from the oven and use a butter knife lightly to go around each one. Warm the dish before serving.

Nutrition Information
Calories: 319 kcal, Carbohydrates: 20 g, Protein: 21 g, Fats: 16 g

63. Mini Wonton Quiche
Prep Time: 15 Mins, Cook Time: 20 Mins, Servings: 2
Ingredients
- 12 wonton wrappers
- 4 turkey breakfast sausage links
- ¼ cup frozen spinach (thawed and drained)
- 1/3 cup finely chopped red pepper
- 2 tbsp finely chopped green onion
- ¼ cup milk

- 5 large eggs
- ¼ tsp salt
- 1 cup shredded cheese

Instructions
- Preheat the oven up to 350 °F.
- Using a nonstick spray, coat a 12-cup muffin tray. 1 wonton wrapper should be used to line each cup.
- Scramble breakfast sausage in a medium pan. Transfer the pan from the stove and add spinach, green onion, and red pepper.
- Whisk the salt, eggs, and milk in a medium mixing basin.
- Fill the wonton wrappers with the cheese and sausage mixture.
- Fill wonton cups with egg mixture. Cook for 20 mins or until the eggs are completely set.

Nutrition Information
Calories: 91 Kcal, Carbohydrates: 1.6 g, Protein: 7.1 g, Fat: 4.1 g

64. Ham, Cheese, and Veggie Frittatas
Prep Time: 20 Mins, Cook Time: 20 Mins, Servings: 4
Ingredients
- ½ cup minced onion
- 2 tsp olive oil
- 1 ½ cups baby spinach
- ½ cup chopped bell pepper
- ¾ cup chopped cooked ham
- 1 cup cooked quinoa
- ¾ cup grated cheddar
- 7 eggs
- ½ cup unsweetened milk
- 1/8 tsp pepper
- ½ tsp salt

Instructions:
- Preheat your oven up to 350 degrees. Grease e a muffin tray with silicone liners or spray with cooking spray (can be lined with paper liners).
- Take a medium pan and heat the olive oil over medium heat. Cook, stirring periodically, for 3-5 mins, or until the bell pepper and onion are softened. Cook them for about 30 sec or until the spinach is slightly wilted. Place the veggies in a large mixing bowl.
- Add the cheddar cheese, ham, and cooked quinoa to the bowl containing veggies.
- Mix the milk and eggs in a measuring cup. Combine the pepper and salt in a mixing bowl.
- In the prepared muffin tray, divide the mixture equally among the 12 wells.
- Preheat oven to 180°F. Bake for about 18 to 22 mins, or until set. Allow cooling for 3 mins in the pan. Remove each frittata from the pan by running a tiny rubber spatula. Serve.

Nutrition Information
Calories: 214kcal, Carbohydrates: 9 g, Protein: 15 g, Fats: 13g

65. Strawberry Banana Baked Oatmeal
Prep Time: 20 Mins, Cook Time: 40 Mins, Servings: 1
Ingredients
- 1 cup ripe banana, mashed
- 3 cups milk
- 2 eggs
- 2 tsp vanilla extract
- ¼ cup pure maple syrup
- 1 tsp baking powder
- ½ tsp salt
- 1 tsp cinnamon
- 4 cups old-fashioned oats

Instructions
- Preheat the oven up to 350 °F. Grease a (size: 9x13-inch) baking dish lightly.
- Whisk together the eggs, mashed banana, milk, maple syrup, vanilla, salt, cinnamon, and baking powder in a mixing dish. Stir in the oats, then the strawberries, until everything is well mixed.
- Carefully transfer the mixture to the baking dish that has been prepared. Preheat oven to 350°F and bake for about 35-40 mins.
- Allow for a 5-min rest before serving. Serve the oats with more strawberries on top.

Nutrition Information
Calories: 291 kcal, Carbohydrates: 48 g, Protein: 10 g, Fats: 7 g

66. Easy Granola Recipe - 4 Ingredients
Prep Time: 8 Mins, Cook Time: 35 Mins, Servings: 4
Ingredients:
- 5 cups old-fashioned oats
- 3 tbsp coconut oil
- ½ cup pure maple syrup
- ¾ tsp cinnamon

Instructions:
- Preheat the oven up to 300 °F. Using parchment paper, prepare the rimmed baking sheet.
- In a large mixing basin, combine the oats.
- Microwave coconut oil, maple syrup, and coconut oil in 30-second intervals in a measuring cup until melted. Add the cinnamon and mix well. Pour over oats and whisk to incorporate.
- Spread the granola over the baking sheet in an equal layer. Bake for about 20 mins, stirring halfway through. Bake for another 15 mins, or until gently brown, pressing down into an equivalent layer.
- Remove from the oven and cool thoroughly before storing in an airtight container. Granolas can be kept in an airtight jar for two weeks and stored in the freezer for optimal results.

Nutrition Information
Calories: 234 kcal, Carbohydrates: 38 g, Protein: 5 g, Fats: 7 g

67. Healthy Pancakes
Prep Time: 10 Mins, Cook Time: 5 Mins, Servings: 1
Ingredients:
- 2 cups white whole wheat flour
- 2 tbsp butter
- 2 tsp powder baking
- ½ tsp baking soda
- 2 large eggs
- ½ cup applesauce, unsweetened
- 2 tbsp honey
- ½ tsp ground salt
- 1 tsp extract vanilla
- 1 & ¼ cups milk

Instructions:
- Remove the butter from the heat and put it aside to cool.
- Mix wheat flour, baking powder, baking soda, & salt in a large mixing basin.
- Combine the applesauce, eggs, milk, honey, and vanilla extract in a medium mixing bowl. Use a separate bowl to whisk the melted butter and the egg yolks.
- Pour dry Ingredients plus wet Ingredients & mix just until combined. The mixture will become thick. Since your pancakes will be flat instead of light and fluffy, don't add more milk.
- Over medium heat, heat a pan, and cooking spray should be used sparingly. Scoop a scant ¼ cup of batter over a hot grill. Cook the first side of the steak.
- Cook till the other side of the pancakes is browned, approximately 2 mins longer. Serve right away.

Nutrition Information
Calories: 108 kcal, Carbohydrates: 17 g, Protein: 4 g, Fats: 3 g

68. Chocolate Black Bean Blender Muffins {High Protein}
Prep Time: 8 Mins, Cook Time: 18 Mins, Servings: 1
Ingredients
- 3 eggs

- ½ cup unsweetened cocoa powder
- 15 oz can of black beans
- ½ cup plain Greek yogurt
- ½ cup old-fashioned rolled oats
- 1 tsp powder baking
- ½ cup pure maple syrup or honey
- ½ cup bittersweet chocolate chips
- 2 tsp vanilla extract

Instructions
- Preheat the oven up to a temperature around 350 degrees Fahrenheit. Use silicone or paper liners to line a muffin tray.
- Take an electric blender and mix all the ingredients except the chocolate chips. Blend until completely smooth.
- Fill every muffin cup nearly to the top with the batter in the preheated muffin tray. 4 to 5 chocolate chips should be placed on top of every muffin.
- Bake until a toothpick placed in the middle of a cupcake comes out clean, about 18-20 minutes. Cool in the pan for 5 mins before transferring to a wire rack.

Nutrition Information
Calories: 143 kcal, Carbohydrates: 24 g, Protein: 7 g, Fats: 4 g

69. Air Fryer Steak
Prep Time: 5 Mins, Cook Time: 12 Mins, Servings: 1
Ingredients:
- 2 tsp olive oil
- ⅛ tsp garlic powder
- 2 Ribeye, Sirloin (1-inch thick)
- salt and pepper

Instructions:
- Allow 20-30 mins for the steaks to reach room temperature.
- Preheat the air fryer to 400 °F for about 5 mins.
- Olive oil should be rubbed all over the steaks. Garlic powder, salt, and pepper should be sprinkled on both sides of the steaks.
- Place the steaks to form a single layer in your air fryer without overlapping (Cook in two batches). Air fried the steaks for around 5 mins at 400°F. Cook for another 3-9 mins.
- Allow 5 mins for the steaks to rest before serving. If desired, top with garlic butter.

Nutrition Information
Calories: 506 kcal, Carbohydrates: 1 g, Protein: 46 g, Fats: 36 g

70. Beef Enchiladas
Prep Time: 30 Mins, Cook Time: 1 hour, Servings: 1
Ingredients
- 1 cup finely chopped yellow onion
- 2 tsp olive oil
- 1 lb ground beef
- 1 ½ tsp chili powder
- 3 cloves garlic (minced)
- 1 ½ tsp ground cumin
- ½ tsp ground salt
- ½ tsp dried oregano
- ¼ tsp black pepper
- 19 oz red enchilada sauce
- 12 oz shredded cheddar

Instructions
- Preheat your oven to 350 degrees Fahrenheit.
- Use a large pan to heat little olive oil on medium-high heat. Cook, occasionally stirring, until the onion is softened, about 2-4 mins. Cook the ground beef it is browned.
- Cook, constantly stirring, for 30 seconds after adding the garlic, chili powder, dried oregano, cumin, salt, and pepper. Turn off the heat in the pan.
- ½ cup enchilada sauce should be spread in the bottom of the prepared baking dish.
- Take one tortilla and place ½ cup of prepared meat filling in the center of the tortilla to make each enchilada. ¼ cup grated cheese sprinkled on the meat filling. Roll this tortilla properly and set it in prepared baking pans.
- Pour the remaining sauce on the enchiladas' tops. Sprinkle the remaining cheese on the top.
- Adjust the oven temperature to 350°F and bake for about 25-30 mins. As desired, garnish with toppings.

Nutrition Information
Calories: 312 kcal, Carbohydrates: 18 g, Protein: 22 g, Fats: 17 g

71. Instant Pot Chicken and Rice
Prep Time: 20 Mins, Cook Time: 20 Mins, Servings: 1
Ingredients
- 1 cup chopped onion (1 small onion)
- 1 tbsp olive oil
- 4 medium carrots
- 1 ½ cups long-grain brown rice
- 3 cloves garlic (minced)
- 1 ½ cups chicken broth
- 1 lb chicken breasts
- 1 cup frozen peas

Instructions
- In a 6 quart or bigger Instant Pot, heat olive oil on the sauté setting. Combine the carrots and onion in a large mixing bowl. Cook, occasionally stirring, for approximately 3 mins. Turn the Instant Pot off.
- Add the garlic and mix well. Dijon mustard, brown rice, Italian seasoning, salt, pepper, garlic powder, and chicken stock are added to the pan. Over the rice mixture, arrange the chicken breasts.
- Turn the pressure release valve to lock and close the Pot lid. Cook for about 20 mins at high pressure in a pressure cooker.
- Allow 10 mins to release its pressure naturally
- After that, gently relieve the pressure by turning the release valve toward the venting position.
- Place the chicken on the chopping board. Stir them into Instant Pot, cover, and set aside for 5 mins to cook the peas through.
- Chicken should be cut into bite-size pieces. Move the chicken to the pot with the rice mixture.
- If preferred, garnish with parsley and Parmesan.

Nutrition Information
Calories: 378 kcal, Carbohydrates: 47 g, Protein: 30 g, Fats: 8 g

72. Spaghetti Squash
Prep Time: 25 Mins, Cook Time: 55 Mins, Servings: 1
Ingredients
- 1 tbsp olive oil
- 1 medium spaghetti squash
- 1 lb ground beef
- salt and pepper
- 1 bell pepper (chopped)
- 1 cup finely chopped yellow onion
- 3 cloves garlic (minced)
- 1 cup shredded mozzarella cheese
- ⅓ cup grated Parmesan cheese

Instructions:
- Heat your oven to 400 degrees Fahrenheit temperature. Using parchment paper, line a baking sheet.
- Remove a tiny portion of the spaghetti squash's base and stem tips. Then, gently cut the squash into half (lengthwise) with a sharp knife, standing the squash on flat sides.
- Drizzle some olive oil into the squash and massage it to distribute it evenly. Season to taste with pepper and salt. Arrange the squash on the baking sheet that has been prepared.
- Roast the squash for about 30 to 40 mins in a preheated oven. Avoid overcooking the squash.

- Allow the squash to cool till it is safe to handle. Then divide the squash into filaments with a fork. Preheat your oven to 375 degrees Fahrenheit.

Nutrition Information
Calories: 271 kcal, Carbohydrates: 17 g, Protein: 18 g, Fats: 16 g

73. Instant Pot Mac and Cheese
Prep Time: 10 Mins, Cook Time: 3 Mins, Servings: 1
Ingredients
- 4 cups water
- 16 oz uncooked white
- 2 tbsp unsalted butter
- salt and pepper
- 4 oz sharp cheddar cheese
- salt and pepper
- ½ cup milk *(warmed)*

Instructions
- Combine the water, pasta, salt, pepper, garlic powder, and paprika in an Instant Pot. Stir everything together well.
- Place the pressure release valve in the locking position and close the Pot lid. Cook the elbow pasta for around 3 mins or white elbow pasta for 4 mins at high pressure.
- Shred the cheese and reheat the milk while the pasta cooks.
- Move the releasing pressure valve towards the venting position to relieve the pressure quickly.
- Open the Instant Pot cover and put the butter to the pot after all steam has been released. It resulted in a pin drop. Slowly whisk in the cheese, then milk. Season with salt and pepper if necessary.

Nutrition Information
Calories: 409 kcal, Carbohydrates: 44 g, Protein: 20 g, Fats: 19 g

74. How to Cook Spaghetti Squash
Prep Time: 5 Mins, Cook Time: 35 Mins, Servings: 1
Ingredients
- 1 tbsp olive oil
- salt and pepper
- Squash spaghetti

Instructions
- Preheat your oven to 400 degrees Fahrenheit. Using parchment paper, line a baking sheet.
- Cut your spaghetti squash into half lengthwise or crosswise, depending on whether you want longer or shorter strands.
- Remove the seeds using a spoon
- Drizzle the olive oil on the sliced side of these squash and massage it in evenly. Season with pepper and salt. Arrange these squash halves on the baking sheet that has been prepared.
- Roast the squash for about 30-40 mins in a preheated oven, or till just get tender when pricked with a fork. Make sure the squash doesn't overcook.
- Allow the squash to cool before separating the threads with a fork. As preferred, serve with marinara sauce.

Nutrition Information
Calories: 106 kcal, Carbohydrates: 17 g, Protein: 2 g, Fats: 5 g

75. Greek Salad
Prep Time: 20 Mins, Cook Time: 20 Mins, Servings: 1
Ingredients
- 1 green bell pepper
- 1 large cucumber
- 1 cup cherry or grape tomatoes (halved)
- ½ small red onion (thinly sliced)
- 4 oz block feta cheese
- ⅔ cup pitted kalamata olives
- salt and pepper *(to taste)*

Instructions
- Bring a small bowl, whisk together all the dressing Ingredients in it. Whisk everything together until it's smooth. Remove from the equation.
- Use a large bowl to combine the cucumber, red onion, bell pepper, tomatoes, and feta cheese. Toss and adjust the amount of dressing as required. To increase taste, add more salt and pepper to the salad. Serve.

Nutrition Information
Calories: 258 kcal, Carbohydrates: 8 g, Protein: 6 g, Fats: 23 g

76. Black Bean Burger Recipe
Prep Time: 15 Mins, Cook Time: 12 Mins, Servings: 1
Ingredients
- 15 oz can of black beans
- ⅓ cup chopped red bell pepper
- 2 green onions
- ⅔ cup pitted kalamata olives
- 1 large egg
- ⅔ cup pitted kalamata olives
- 1 tsp smoked paprika
- ½ tsp cumin
- 1 tbsp ketchup

Instructions
- Place the black beans in a large mixing basin after patting them dry. Mash the beans with a fork or a potato masher until they are entirely mashed along with bigger chunks of beans in the mixture. Combine the panko breadcrumbs, onion, red bell pepper, and garlic in the same bowl as the beans.
- Combine the ketchup, eggs, cumin, smoked paprika, chili powder, salt, and black pepper in a medium mixing bowl. Mix everything till adequately blended.
- Transfer this mixture into the dish along with black beans, scraping all of the spices and eggs into the bean mixture with a bit of spatula. Stir everything together until it's thoroughly blended.
- Divide this mixture into four equal sections, then form every portion into a 12-inch-thick burger.
- Assemble and serve.

Nutrition Information
Calories: 160 kcal, Carbohydrates: 26 g, Protein: 10 g, Fats: 2 g

77. Air Fryer Chicken Breast
Prep Time: 10 Mins, Cook Time: 7 Mins, Servings: 1

Ingredients
- 1 tsp paprika
- 1 tbsp ketchup
- ½ tsp garlic powder
- 1 tbsp ketchup
- 2 boneless, skinless chicken breasts
- 1 tbsp ketchup

Instructions
- Combine the paprika, brown sugar, dried oregano, onion powder, garlic powder, salt, and pepper in a small bowl. Stir until everything is well blended.
- Using paper towels, pat the chicken dry. Lb chicken breasts uniformly in a zip bag using a rolling pin.
- All edges of this chicken should be rubbed with olive oil and spice.
- In the air fryer, arrange the chicken to form a layer. Cook for 8 mins at 400°F, then set aside to rest for about 5 mins before serving.

Nutrition Information
Calories: 85 kcal, Carbohydrates: 3 g, Protein: 12 g, Fats: 3 g

78. Chicken & Black Bean Mole Puree
Prep Time: 12 mins, Cook Time: 12 Mins, Servings: 8
Ingredients:
- ½ lb ground chicken lean
- 1 Minced Clove of Garlic
- 3 tbsp raw almonds

- 1 cup black beans
- ½ tbsp raw cacao powder
- ¼ cup chicken broth
- 1/2 tsp paprika
- ¼ tsp coriander
- ¼ tsp oregano dried
- ⅛ tsp cinnamon
- ¼ tsp garlic powder
- 2 tbsp chopped cilantro

Instructions
- Add 2 tbsp water and heat in a sauté skillet over medium heat Cook for 1 min. Stir often till garlic is aromatic.
- Cook for 6 to 8 mins, tossing to break the chicken, till it is cooked through. To avoid pan drying, pour 1 tbsp of water as the water evaporates.
- Add 2 tbsp of water, paprika, soaked almonds, chicken broth, cacao, oregano, cumin, cinnamon, coriander, and garlic powder in a blender. Blend until completely smooth.
- Bring the chicken, sauce, and black beans to a boil. Pulse the mixture in a food processor with the cilantro till smooth.
- Almonds may be soaked quickly by placing them in a small saucepan and covering them with water. Boil and then lower to low heat. Continue to cook for a further 15 to 20 mins.
- Serve warm.

Nutrition Information
Calories: 109.5 kcal, Carbohydrates: 9.5 g, Protein: 9.5 g, Fats: 3.9 g

79. Easy Banana Spinach Smoothie
Prep Time: 5 mins, Cook Time: 5 Mins, Servings: 1
Ingredients
- ⅔ cup Greek yogurt
- 1tbsp of the almond butter
- ½ banana
- 1 scoop vanilla protein powder
- ¾ cup water
- Handful spinach

Instructions
- Blend all Ingredients in a blender till desired consistency is formed.

Nutrition Information
Calories: 365 kcal, Carbohydrates: 26 g, Protein: 46 g, Fats: 8 g

80. Berry Avocado Smoothie
Prep Time: 5 mins, Cook Time: 5 Mins, Servings: 1
Ingredients
- ¼ cup blueberries
- 1 cup strawberries (5 oz)
- ½ of an avocado
- ½ cup low-fat milk
- ½ cup 2% Greek yogurt
- 1 tsp raw honey, optional

Instructions
- Use a blender to combine the blueberries, avocado, yogurt, strawberries, and milk.
- Blend till completely smooth.
- Taste and, if desired, add some honey.
- Serve immediately or keep refrigerated for 2 days.

Nutrition Information
Calories: 352 kcal, Carbohydrates: 39 g, Protein: 22 g, Fats: 16 g

81. Cocoa Almond Protein Smoothie
Prep Time: 5 mins, Cook Time: 5 Mins, Servings: 1
Ingredients
- ¼ cup plus 2 tbsp of milk *(almond, dairy, etc.)*
- ¾ cup Greek yogurt
- 1 medium banana *(sliced and frozen)*
- 2 tbsp almond butter
- ½ tbsp unsweetened cocoa powder
- ¾ cup ice cubes
- 2 tsp ground flaxseed *(optional)*

Instructions
- In a blender and blend all recipe Ingredients. Mix till smooth.
- Enjoy!

Nutrition Information
Calories: 471 kcal, Carbohydrates: 45 g, Protein: 27 g, Fats: 23 g

82. Nutty Waffles
Prep Time: 5 mins, Cook Time: 5 Mins, Servings: 1
Ingredients
- 1 tbsp Smucker's Natural Peanut Butter
- 1 KNOW Better waffle (toasted)
- ½ small banana, sliced

Instructions
- Take a toasted KNOW Better waffle and spread one dollop of Smucker's Natural Peanut Butter.
- Add ½ of a (sliced) banana on top.

Nutrition Information
Calories: 433 kcal, Carbohydrates: 25 g, Protein: 20 g, Fats: 35 g

83. Pumped Up Avocado Toast
Prep Time: 5 mins, Cook Time: 5 Mins, Servings: 1
Ingredients:
- 3 Sausage Turkey Breakfast links
- 1 slice of Ezekiel Sprouted Whole Grain Bread
- ¼ avocado (mashed)

Instructions
- Piece three links and serve over a piece of Ezekiel Sprouted Whole Grain Bread, smothered with one-quarter avocado.

Nutrition Information
Calories: 260 kcal, Carbohydrates: 21 g, Protein: 16 g, Fats: 3 g

84. Cinna-Berry Parfait
Prep Time: 5 mins, Cook Time: 5 Mins, Servings: 1
Ingredients:
- ½ cup blueberries
- 6 oz Fage 2% Plain Greek Yogurt
- ½ cup of KIND Cinnamon Oat Clusters with Flax Seeds

Instructions:
- Add half a cup of blueberries to a bowl
- Add half cup oat with flax seeds. For a perfect balance, add yogurt.

Nutrition Information
Calories: 340 kcal, Carbohydrates: 50 g, Protein: 24 g, Fats: 9 g

85. Banana Nut Oatmeal
Prep Time: 5 mins, Cook Time: 5 Mins, Servings: 1
Ingredients:
- ½ cup skim milk
- 1 Thin Banana Bread Bowl
- 1 oz. crushed walnut

Instructions:
- For an added boost of omega-3s, make the oatmeal using skim milk.
- Add one oz of crumbled walnuts.

Nutrition Information
Calories: 430 kcal, Carbohydrates: 41 g, Protein: 14 g, Fats: 23 g

86. Protein Pancakes
Prep Time: 5 mins, Cook Time: 5 Mins, Servings: 1
Ingredients
- 1 tbsp maple syrup
- ½ cup Birch Bender Protein Pancake Mix
- ¼ cup sliced almonds

Instructions
- Prepare pancakes and drizzle with 1 tbsp of maple syrup.
- Sprinkle sliced almonds over them.

Nutrition Information
Calories: 360 kcal, Carbohydrates: 42 g, Protein: 21 g, Fats: 12.5 g

87. Tofu Scramble and Toast
Prep Time: 5 mins, Cook Time: 5 Mins, Servings: 1
Ingredients:
- 1 cup spinach
- ½ cup firm tofu
- 1 slice from Ezekiel Sprouted Whole Grain Bread
- ¼ cup Bob's Red Mill Large Flake Nutritional Yeast
- Turmeric (to taste)

Instructions:
- Lightly fry ½ cup of firm tofu. Add turmeric, ¼ cup Bob's Red Mill Large Flake Nutritional Yeast, and spinach in a skillet. Put in a toasted piece of Ezekiel Sprouted Whole Grain.

Nutrition Information
Calories: 290 kcal, Carbohydrates: 25 g, Protein: 27 g, Fats: 6 g

88. Protein Cereal and Berries
Prep Time: 5 mins, Cook Time: 5 Mins, Servings: 1
Ingredients:
- 1 cup Silk Protein Nutmilk
- 1 ¼ cup of Kashi GO LEAN
- 1 cup sliced strawberries

Instructions:
- Prepare cereal (Kashi GO LEAN) in nut milk.
- Pour in a bowl and add a cup of strawberries.

Nutrition Information
Calories: 360 kcal, Carbohydrates: 55 g, Protein: 23 g, Fats: 10 g

89. Ricotta Toast
Prep Time: 5 mins, Cook Time: 5 Mins, Servings: 1
Ingredients:
- 2 slices Ezekiel Sprouted Whole Grain Bread
- ½ cup Polly-O part-skim ricotta cheese
- ½ cup blackberries
- 1 tsp honey

Instructions:
- Add ½ up of cheese and Drizzle 1 tsp of honey on top of two pieces of toasted Bread for a bit of sweetness.
- Add ½ cup blackberries.

Nutrition Information
Calories: 390 kcal, Carbohydrates: 46 g, Protein: 25 g, Fats: 10 g

90. Veggie Bagel
Prep Time: 5 mins, Cook Time: 5 Mins, Servings: 1
Ingredients:
- 1 Dave's Killer Bread Epic Everything Bagel (sliced and toasted)
- ½ sliced tomato
- 1-oz goat cheese
- ¼ cup shredded carrots
- ½ cup raw spinach
- ¼ cup cucumber slices

Instructions:
- Take a toasted bagel. Spread 1 oz. Goat's cheese over it.
- Put ½ cup raw spinach, ½ of sliced tomato, ¼ cup cucumber slices, and ¼ cup shredded carrots on top.

Nutrition Information
Calories: 390 kcal, Carbohydrates: 58 g, Protein: 20 g, Fats: 6 g

91. Overnight Oats
Prep Time: 5 mins, Cook Time: 5 Mins, Servings: 1
Ingredients:
- ½ cup almond milk, unsweetened
- ½ cup Fage 0% Fat-Free Yogurt
- 1-oz pecans, chopped
- 1 tbsp honey
- ½ cup rolled oats
- Cinnamon (to taste)

Instructions:
- Mix rolled oats, ½ cup of Fage fat-free yogurt, and almond milk.
- Stir till smooth. Refrigerate for the night.
- Before serving, add chopped pecans, cinnamon, and honey.

Nutrition Information
Calories: 485 kcal, Carbohydrates: 49 g, Protein: 21 g, Fats: 24 g

92. Apple and Peanut Butter Smoothie
Prep Time: 5 mins, Cook Time: 5 Mins, Servings: 1
Ingredients:
- 1 scoop of Sun Warrior Blend Raw Plant-Based Complete Protein Powder Vanilla
- 1 cup of unsweetened almond milk
- 1 sliced apple
- Sprinkle of nutmeg
- 1 tbsp Smucker's Natural Peanut Butter
- Cinnamon to taste

Instructions:
- Add one sliced apple, 1 cup almond milk, 1 scoop of Sun Warrior Blend Raw Plant-Based Complete Protein Powder Vanilla, 1 tbsp of Smucker's Natural Peanut Butter in a blender.
- Sprinkle cinnamon and nutmeg in a blender.
- Blend till a smooth mixture is formed.
- Pour in glass and serve.

Nutrition Information

Calories: 284 kcal, Carbohydrates: 22 g, Protein: 20 g, Fats: 12.5 g

93. Peanut Butter and Chocolate Smoothie
Prep Time: 5 mins, Cook Time: 5 Mins, Servings: 1
Ingredients:
- 1 cup almond milk, unsweetened
- 1 tbsp Smucker's Natural Peanut Butter
- 1 medium banana
- ¼ cup soft tofu
- 1 tsp cocoa powder
- 1 cup steamed and cooled cauliflower

Instructions:
- Blend almond milk, banana, peanut butter, and all other Ingredients in a blender.
- Blend all items thoroughly.
- Enjoy!

Nutrition Information
Calories: 340 kcal, Carbohydrates: 33 g, Protein: 18 g, Fats: 17 g

94. Toast and Lox
Prep Time: 5 mins, Cook Time: 5 Mins, Servings: 1
Ingredients:
- 2 slices of Grain Bread Whole
- 2 oz of Sliced Salmon Smoked
- 2 tbsp of Organic Valley Cream Cheese

Instructions:
- Toast the slices of whole-grain bread.
- Layer 2 tbsp of Organic Valley Cream Cheese.
- Top with sliced salmon.

Nutrition Information
Calories: 360 kcal, Carbohydrates: 30 g, Protein: 21 g, Fats: 17 g

95. Elvis's Toast
Prep Time: 5 mins, Cook Time: 5 Mins, Servings: 1
Ingredients:
- 2 tbsp of Smucker's Natural Peanut Butter
- 2 slices of Bread Sliced Thin
- 1 small banana, sliced

Instructions:
- Toast slices of Bread Sliced Thin.
- Top the toast with banana slices and 2 tbsp of Smucker's Natural Peanut Butter

Nutrition Information
Calories: 440 kcal, Carbohydrates: 50 g, Protein: 15 g, Fats: 19 g

96. Pumpkin Pie Oatmeal
Prep Time: 5 mins, Cook Time: 5 Mins, Servings: 1

Ingredients:
- 1 scoop of Sun Warrior Blend Raw Plant-Based Protein Powder Vanilla
- ½ cup rolled oats
- 2 tbsp brown sugar
- ½ cup pureed pumpkin
- Sprinkle of nutmeg and cinnamon
- ½ cup pureed pumpkin

Instructions:
- Make oatmeal with water. Add 1 scoop of Sun Warrior Blend Raw Plant-Based Complete Protein Powder in it.
- Add the other Ingredients and mix well. Sprinkle with cinnamon and nutmeg.

Nutrition Information
Calories: 520 kcal, Carbohydrates: 57 g, Protein: 27 g, Fats: 22 g

97. Peanut Butter Granola Breakfast Cookies
Prep Time: 10 Mins, Cook Time: 10 Mins, Servings: 15

Ingredients
- 1 tsp baking powder
- 1 medium ripe banana, mashed
- 1 tsp baking soda
- ½ cup coconut sugar
- ¼ cup plain yogurt
- 1 tsp of baking soda
- 1 large egg
- ½ cup of dried cranberries
- 1 tsp baking soda
- ½ cup semisweet chocolate chips
- 2 cups of white whole wheat flour

Instructions
- Preheat your oven to 350 °F. Using parchment paper, prepare a baking sheet.
- Combine baking soda, flour, baking powder, granola, and salt in a large mixing basin.
- Beat sugar, banana, peanut butter, egg, yogurt, and vanilla in a large mixing bowl using an electric mixer until smooth.
- Slowly stir the flour mix into the liquid mix until the dough comes together. Combine the chocolate chips and cranberries in a mixing bowl.
- Use the prepared baking sheet and roll the dough into 1-inch balls. Bake at 350°F for 9 mins. Cool for around 5 mins on the baking sheet before transferring to a cooling rack.

Nutrition Information
Calories: 102.5 kcal, Carbohydrates: 5 g, Protein: 19.5 g, Fats: 0.2 g

98. Carrot Cake Breakfast Cookies
Prep Time: 20 Mins, Cook Time: 15 Mins, Servings: 5

Ingredients
- 1 cup oat flour
- 2 & ¼ cups old-fashioned oats
- 2 tsp cinnamon
- ½ cup flaxseed ground
- ½ tsp soda baking
- ½ tsp fresh ground salt
- ½ tsp nutmeg
- 1 cup grated carrot
- 1 cup unsweetened applesauce
- 1 cup finely chopped or grated apple

Instructions
- Preheat your oven to around 350°F. Line baking pans by using parchment paper.
- Combine flour, oats, flaxseed, cinnamon, salt, nutmeg, and baking soda in a mixing dish.
- Whisk all the honey or maple syrup, applesauce, egg, and vanilla in a medium mixing bowl or measuring cup. Melt the butter and pour it into the mixture.
- Mix the wet Ingredients with dry Ingredients and whisk until everything is well incorporated. Fold in the shredded carrot and apple gently.
- Drop ¼-cup dough on baking sheets using a measuring cup or large scoop. Gently shape the cookies with your fingers and flatten them somewhat.
- Bake for 14-15 mins, or until gently brown and firm.
- Allow cookies to rest for a few moments over the baking sheet before transferring for cooling.

Nutrition Information
Calories: 146 kcal, Carbohydrates: 23 g, Protein: 3 g, Fats: 5 g

99. Chia Seed Peanut Butter Banana Breakfast Cookies
Prep Time: 10 Mins, Cook Time: 15 Mins, Servings: 12

Ingredients
- 2 cups old fashioned oats
- 3 small ripe bananas, mashed
- 3 tbsp ground flax seed
- 1 ½ tsp cinnamon
- ¼ tsp sea salt
- 1 ½ tsp vanilla extract
- 1 tbsp chia seeds

Peanut Butter Drizzle
- ½ cup of Peanut flour
- ¼ - ½ cup of almond milk, unsweetened

Instructions
- Preheat your oven to around 350 °F. Use parchment paper to prepare a baking sheet.
- Mash the banana in a big mixing bowl. Combine other Ingredients in a mixing bowl.
- Divide the dough into 12 mounds using a tiny cookie scoop. Spread each cookie to approximately ¼ inch using a glass bottom (coated with nonstick spray) or moisten your palm slightly.
- Bake for 13-15 mins, or till the cookies are slightly hard to the touch but still soft.
- Allow the cookies to cool on the cookie sheet before transferring to the wire rack to cool completely.
- Whisk the ¼ cup milk and peanut flour in a small bowl until smooth. If this one is too thick, add more. Drizzle a little bit of chocolate on each biscuit.
- Use the refrigerator to store them.

Nutrition Information
Calories: 110 kcal, Carbohydrates: 29 g, Protein: 0 g, Fats: 0.2 g

100. Blueberry Carrot Cake Bars (Gluten-Free)
Prep Time: 15 Mins, Cook Time: 15 Mins, Servings: 1

Ingredients
- ½ cup Almond Flour
- 1 ½ cups Oat flour
- 1 tsp baking powder
- ¼ cup tapioca flour or arrowroot
- ½ tsp salt kosher
- 1 egg
- 1 cup non-dairy milk
- ½ cup raw sugar
- 2/3 cup to 1 cup shredded carrot
- 2 tbsp melted coconut oil or butter
- 2/3 cup to 1 cup blueberries (extra for topping)
- Optional toppings: ½ cup of vegan cashew frosting, vegan coconut frosting, and 1/3 cup gluten-free granola

Instructions
- Adjust oven temperature to 350 degrees Fahrenheit. Use parchment paper to line a simple brownie pan or an 8x8 pan.
- Whisk the flours, baking powder, and salt in a mixing dish. Add the sugar and mix well.
- Combine vanilla extract, yogurt, milk, and egg separately. Mix the dry Ingredients first. Slowly add the coconut oil & cinnamon.
- Combine the blueberries and carrots in a mixing bowl. Pour into a brownie pan that has been lined.
- Bake for about 30-35 mins.
- Allow it cool for about 10 mins on a baking sheet.

- Before slicing, apply your optional topping. Extra granola and berries may be placed on top.
- Cut into slices and serve.

Nutrition Information
Calories: 225 kcal, Carbohydrates: 26 g, Protein: 7 g, Fats: 6 g

101. Lemon Almond Flour Shortbread Cookies
Prep Time: 12 mins, Cook Time: 8 mins, Servings: 20
Ingredients
- 6 tbsp slightly softened unsalted butter
- ½ cup granulated sugar
- 2 tbsp lemon zest
- ½ tsp salt
- ½ tsp almond extract
- 2 ½ cups Finely Powdered Almond Meal or Flour (Bob's Red Mill)

Instructions
- Beat the sugar and butter with an electric mixer until smooth and creamy. Wipe the bowl's sides thoroughly.
- Mix the lemon zest at a slower speed until thoroughly mixed. Then add the almond extract and salt to it.
- Stir the almond flour at low speed in three batches and mix until everything is mixed. At first, the batter will be crumbly, but keep mixing at a slower speed until it blends. Stop mixing until the dough starts to cling together.
- Separate the dough into two halves. Wrap each half in plastic wrap into a ball shape. Spread it out a little further to level it out. Let it rest in the freezer for two mins or 1 day.
- Heat the oven before baking the cookies at 350 °F. Line two baking pans with parchment paper.
- Divide the dough into 14-inch-thick pieces using a sharp knife. Layer the cookies (1 inch apart) on the lined baking pans. Bake for 7 to 10 mins, or until the top and bottom side of the cookies are just brown. Make sure the cookies aren't over-baked.
- Cool the cookies for 10 mins on the baking pan. Serve immediately or store them in an airtight container for 5-6 days or the freezer for 3 months.

Nutrition Information
Calories: 71 kcal, Carbohydrates: 4 g, Protein: 1 g, Fat: 5g

102. Instant Pot Steel Cut Oats
Prep Time: 3 mins, Cook Time: 4 mins, Servings: 3
Ingredients
- 1 cup oats (steel cut)
- 3 cups water
- 1/2 tsp vanilla extract
- Toppings: milk, maple syrup, fruits, cinnamon, nuts, etc.

Instructions
- In an Instant Pot, combine the oats, water, and vanilla extract and stir.
- Set the steam valve to the proper position and latch the Instant Pot cover.
- Set the Cooking time to 4 mins at high pressure.
- After a few minutes, pressure will achieve, and the time will clock down. Leave the Pot until it automatically vents after the cooking time has ended.
- Adjust the steam valve carefully to a vent position to ensure that pressure and steam have escaped. Remove the lid from the Instant Pot.
- Toss the oats with the toppings of your choice and serve.

Nutrition Information
Calories: 155 kcal, Carbohydrates: 26 g, Protein: 6 g, Fat: 2g

103. Easy Overnight Oats
Prep Time: 5-8 mins, Cook Time: 0 mins, Servings: 1
Ingredients
- 1/2 cup simple oats
- 1/2 cup milk
- 1/2 tsp pure maple syrup
- 1/4 tsp pure vanilla extract
- Optional servings: fresh fruit, nuts, sliced/slivered almond, nut butter, etc.

Instructions
- Combine the oats, milk, vanilla extract, and maple syrup in a glass jar or dish. Cover the lid & shake or mix in a bowl.
- Refrigerate for at least six hr or up to 3 days in the refrigerator. Just before serving, mix the oats.
- Stir in any desired toppings and serve.

Nutrition Information
Calories: 226 kcal, Carbohydrates: 36 g, Protein: 9 g, Fat: 5g

104. Black Bean and Sweet potato with Quinoa
Prep Time: 15-20 mins, Cook Time: 25-30 mins, Servings: 2
Ingredients
- 1 & ½ tbsp olive oil
- 1 medium-sized chopped red onion
- 4 cloves minced garlic
- 4 cups peeled and chopped (½-inch pieces) sweet potatoes
- 2 tbsp chili powder
- 1 tbsp cumin
- 1 tsp dried oregano
- 1/2 tsp smoked paprika
- ½ tsp salt
- 1/4 tsp black pepper
- 6 oz. can tomato paste
- 28 oz. can dice tomatoes
- 2 and 1/2 cups or more vegetable broth
- ¾ cup drained quinoa
- 2 cans drained black beans

Instructions
- In a large saucepan/Dutch oven, heat 1 tbsp of oil over medium heat. Cook for 2 to 3 mins, occasionally turning until the onion is softened. Add the garlic and cook for 30 secs.
- Turn the heat to a high flame, pour the remaining oil, and stir the sweet potatoes. Cook for 5 mins with periodically stirring.
- Add the salt, chili powder, oregano, cumin, smoked paprika, and tomato paste. Cook for 2 to 3 mins, occasionally stirring, to bring out the seasonings and tomato paste flavors.
- Add the chopped tomatoes, quinoa, broth, and black beans.
- Reduce the heat and cook for 25 mins, or until the potatoes and quinoa are cooked.
- Garnish with Greek yogurt/sour cream, shredded cheese, avocado, cilantro, chopped red and green onion, and a squeeze of lemon juice.

Nutrition Information
Calories: 280 kcal, Carbohydrates: 52 g, Protein: 7 g, Fat: 5g

105. Instant Pot Baked Potatoes
Prep Time: 5 mins, Cook time 20 mins, Servings: 1
Ingredients
- 4 medium scrubbed Russet potatoes

Instructions
- In an Instant Pot, pour 1 cup of cold water and put the metal trivet.
- Use a fork to stab the sides of the potato in a few places.
- Arrange the pricked potatoes on the trivet.
- Set the steam valve to the latching position and close the lid.
- Set the Manual/Pressure Press Cook to 16 mins for medium potatoes and 20 mins for large potatoes. The pressure will be achieved after 8 to 12 mins for the Instant Pot.
- When the Cooking time is over, turn off the Instant Pot and allow the pressure to relax naturally for 10 mins. Then, gently move the steam valve to the vented position with

the handle of a long spoon to quickly release any leftover pressure.
- Remove the Instant Pot cover after the float valve has dropped.

Nutrition Information
Calories: 168 kcal, Carbohydrates: 38 g, Protein: 4 g, Fat: 0g

106. Perfect Steel Cut Oats
Prep Time: 5-7 mins, Cook Time: 20-25 mins, Servings: 1
Ingredients
- 3 cups water
- 1 tbsp butter
- 1 cup almond milk
- 1 cup steel-cut oats
- 1/8 tsp salt
- 1/2 tsp vanilla extract
- 1 tsp pure maple syrup
- 1/4 tsp cinnamon

Instructions
- In a medium saucepan, sauté the oats in butter for a few mins. Pour the milk or water and simmer on medium-high heat.
- Add the salt, then turn the heat down to a gentle simmer.
- Cook the oats for 20 to 30 mins, or until the preferred texture is obtained. Add extra liquid as required.
- Turn off the flame and mix in the cinnamon, vanilla extract, and maple syrup.
- Garnish with favorite toppings and serve.

Nutrition Information
Calories: 169 kcal, Carbohydrates: 27 g, Protein: 6 g, Fat: 3g

107. Kale Smoothie
Prep Time: 6-7 mins, Cook Time: 0 mins, Servings: 1
Ingredients
- 3 cups kale leaves without tough stalks
- ½ banana
- 1 cored and sliced pear
- ¾ cup water/coconut water
- 1 & ½ cup frozen peaches
- 1 cup frozen mango
- 1 cup plain Greek yogurt
- 1 & ½ tsp honey

Instructions
- Add the kale, banana, chopped pear, and water in a blender and mix until smooth.
- Mix the frozen peaches, mango, and Greek yogurt. Blend until completely smooth. Blend with a bit more water if the smoothie is too thick. If you want the smoothie to be sweeter, add a little honey. Serve right away.

Nutrition Information
Calories: 197 kcal, Carbohydrates: 40 g, Protein: 11 g, Fat: 1g

108. Spinach Salad with Bacon and Eggs
Prep Time: 5-10 mins, Cook Time: 0 mins, Servings: 1
Ingredients
For Vinaigrette:
- 3 tbsp extra virgin olive oil
- 2 tbsp apple cider vinegar
- 1 tsp Dijon mustard
- 1/8 tsp black pepper
- 1/8 tsp Kosher salt
- 1 tbsp honey

For Spinach Salad
- 8 cups baby spinach
- 1 medium sliced cucumber
- 8 cremini mushrooms sliced
- 4 slices cooked and crumbled bacon
- 4 hard-boiled eggs

Instructions
- In a dish or jar, place the vinaigrette ingredients. Cover the lid and whisk or shake until the ingredients blend well together.
- Add the spinach, sliced cucumbers, and mushrooms to a mixing bowl. Toss the salad with the dressing. Place the cooked and crumbled bacon and eggs on top. Serve it right away.

Nutrition Information
Calories: 241 kcal, Carbohydrates: 10 g, Protein: 11 g, Fat: 18g

109. Frozen Chicken Breasts in the Instant Pot
Prep Time: 08 mins, Cook Time: 12-15 mins, Servings: 2
Ingredients
- 1.5 lb frozen and boneless skinless chicken breasts
- 1 cup water or low-sodium chicken broth
- salt and pepper
- Optional seasonings: dried oregano, garlic powder, or paprika

Instructions
- In the Instant Pot, put the frozen chicken breasts. Pour the broth in. Pat the chicken with salt, pepper, and other seasonings to taste.
- Cover the top and adjust the steam valve to sealing mode.
- Select "Manual/Pressure Cook" and set the cook duration (at high pressure) for 16 mins.
- The pressure will be achieved after 10 secs and the cooking time will start to count down.
- Let the pot alone for 10 mins to naturally release the pressure. Set the steam valve to the vented position. Allow the rest of the steam to escape before proceeding. Make sure the float pin is down before removing the lid.
- Measure the chicken temperature with an instantaneous read thermometer to ensure the temperature is at least 165 °F.
- Set aside for 5 mins to cool before chopping or shredding the chicken.

Nutrition Information
Calories: 196 kcal, Carbohydrate: 20 g, Protein: 35 g, Fat: 5g

110. Easy Crockpot Shredded Chicken
Prep Time: 15 mins, Cook Time: 2 hr 50 mins, Servings: 2
Ingredients
- 3 lb boneless and skinless chicken breasts
- 3/4 cup low-sodium chicken broth
- 1 tsp dried oregano
- 1/2 tsp garlic powder
- 1/2 tsp salt
- 1/4 tsp black pepper

Instructions
- Add all of the listed Ingredients and mix well in a crockpot.
- Cover and simmer for 2 to 3 mins on high or until cooked and readily shreds with a fork.
- Take out the chicken from the crockpot and save the liquid. Allow the chicken to cool and shred it. Stir in broth from the saucepan to add flavor and moisture and serve it hot.

Nutrition Information
Calories: 169 kcal, Carbohydrate: 10 g, Protein: 30 g, Fat: 4g

111. Instant Pot Shredded Chicken
Prep Time: 10 mins, Cook Time: 16 mins, Servings: 2 cups
Ingredients
- 3 lb boneless and skinless chicken thighs/breasts
- 1 cup low-sodium chicken broth
- 1 tsp dried oregano
- 1/2 tsp garlic powder
- 1/2 tsp salt
- 1/4 tsp black pepper

Instructions
- Place the chicken in an Instant Pot and pour the chicken broth into the pot. Season the chicken with salt, dried oregano, pepper, and garlic powder.
- Adjust the steam release valve to the sealed mode and close the lid.

- Cook for 11 mins on high pressure for smaller chicken breasts or 16 mins for larger chicken breasts.
- Once the Pot beeps to indicate that the cooking time is up, quickly reduce the pressure (turn the steam release valve to venting mode).
- Let the steam dissipate entirely, and the needle fall. Then gently open the Instant Pot's cover and, with an instant thermometer, check the chicken's internal temperature to at least 165 °F.
- Remove the chicken meat and save the broth. Allow the chicken to cool before shredding it. Stir in approximately half the chicken broth and serve it hot to add flavor and moisture.

Nutrition Information
Calories: 169 kcal, Carbohydrates: 15 g, Protein: 30 g, Fat: 4g

112. Healthy Strawberry Muffins
Prep Time: 10-12 mins, Cook Time: 15-20 mins, Servings: 2 muffins
Ingredients
- 1 ½ cups freshly chopped strawberries
- ¼ cup all-purpose flour
- 4 tbsp unsalted butter/coconut oil
- 1 cup unsweetened applesauce/Greek yogurt or mashed ripe banana
- ½ cup pure maple syrup/honey
- ¼ cup milk
- 1 tsp vanilla extract
- 2 eggs
- 1 tsp baking powder
- ½ tsp baking soda
- ½ tsp salt
- 1 cup white wheat flour
- ½ cup all-purpose flour

Instructions
- Heat the oven to 375 °F before baking.
- Grease a muffin tray with oil or line it with parchment liners.
- Gradually mix the chopped strawberries with 1/4 cup of all-purpose flour in a basin.
- Soften the butter in the microwave in a bowl until butter is completely melted.
- Add the applesauce/mashed ripe banana or Greek yogurt in the same dish as the butter. Combine the milk, honey or maple syrup, vanilla, and eggs in a mixing bowl. Whisk everything together until it's smooth.
- Combine the salt, baking powder, and baking soda in a mixing bowl. Whisk everything together until it's smooth.
- Combine the whole white wheat flour and half a cup of all-purpose flour in a mixing bowl. Mix with a spoon/rubber spatula until thoroughly mixed. Toss in the strawberries mixture until they are well distributed. Spoon the mixture into the muffin tins.
- Bake them for 16 to 18 mins, or until a toothpick inserted in the middle comes out clean. Set the muffins aside for 5 mins to cool before transferring them to a cooling rack.
- Serve the muffins right away or store them in an airtight container with a paper towel on top for up to 3 days at room temperature.

Nutrition Information
Calories: 163 kcal, Carbohydrates: 26 g, Protein: 4 g, Fat: 5g

113. Healthy Apple Muffins (One Bowl Recipe)
Prep Time: 12 mins, Cook Time: 15-20 mins, Servings: 2
Ingredients
- 4 tbsp unsalted butter
- 1/2 cup honey/pure maple syrup
- 1/2 cup unsweetened applesauce
- 1/2 cup plain Greek yogurt
- 1/4 cup milk
- 2 large eggs
- 1 tsp vanilla extract
- 1 tsp baking soda
- 1/2 tsp baking powder
- 1/2 tsp salt
- 1 1/2 tsp cinnamon
- 1 ½ cups white whole wheat flour
- 1 ½ cup large, chopped baking apple

Instructions
- Heat the oven to 350 °F. Coat standard or small muffin tins with cooking spray.
- Melt the butter in the microwave at a high temperature in a bowl.
- In the same dish as the butter, combine the milk, applesauce, eggs, honey/maple syrup, plain Greek yogurt, and vanilla extract. Whisk everything together until it's smooth.
- Toss in the salt, cinnamon, baking soda, and baking powder with the prepared wet Ingredients in the mixing bowl. Whisk everything together until it's smooth.
- Finally, stir in the whole white wheat flour until it's nearly thoroughly mixed.
- Stir in the diced apple, keeping a few bits for the muffin tops if preferred. Mix in the apple with the rubber spatula until everything is well mixed.
- Spoon the mixture into the oiled muffin tins and place the apple bits on top.
- Bake for 16 to 18 mins, or until a toothpick inserted in the middle comes out clean.
- Cool for 10 mins in the pan before transferring to a cooling rack.
- Serve them right away or store them for up to 3 days in the freezer.

Nutrition Information
Calories: 134 kcal, Carbohydrates: 22 g, Protein: 4 g, Fat: 4g

114. Easy Grilled Chicken Recipe
Prep Time: 12 mins, Cook Time: 20 mins, Servings: 2
Ingredients
- ¼ cup olive oil
- ¼ cup lemon juice
- 3 cloves minced garlic
- 1 tsp dried oregano
- ¼ tsp chili powder
- ½ tsp salt
- ½ tsp pepper
- 4 boneless and skinless chicken breasts

Instructions
- Mix the olive oil, salt, pepper, garlic, lemon juice, oregano, and chili powder in a small bowl. Whisk everything together until it's smooth.
- Smack the chicken breasts with a mallet/rolling pin in a zip-lock plastic bag until they are an equal thickness (approximately half inches thick).
- Put the prepared marinade into the bag, close it and toss the chicken to cover both sides. Refrigerate the chicken for 30 mins to 2 hr before serving.
- Clean the grill grates. Heat the grills to medium-high and grease them with oil.
- Grill each side of the marinated chicken for 5 to 8 mins until done. Grill the chicken on a hotter portion for a few mins, then transfer it to a lower temp for the most excellent grill and juicy chicken.
- Set aside to cool for 5 mins before serving the chicken.

Nutrition Information
Calories: 160 kcal, Carbohydrates: 12 g, Protein: 28 g, Fat: 4g

115. Strawberry Banana Smoothie
Prep Time: 08 mins, Cook Time: 0 mins, Servings: 1
Ingredients
- 2 cups frozen strawberries
- 1 fresh/frozen medium banana
- 1 cup almond milk

- ½ cup plain Greek yogurt

Instructions
- Blend all Ingredients and mix until smooth and serve it in a mason jar.

Nutrition information
Calories: 117 kcal, Carbohydrates: 25 g, Protein: 2.3 g, Fat: 2.0g

116. Blueberry Spinach Breakfast Smoothie
Prep Time: 08 mins, Cook Time: 0 mins, Servings: 1

Ingredients
- 3 tbsp simple oats
- 1 cup fresh spinach
- 1 cup blueberries (frozen)
- 1/3 cup plain Greek yogurt
- ¾ cup milk
- 1/8 tsp cinnamon

Instructions
- Blend all the above Ingredients, mix until smooth, and serve it in a mason jar.

Nutrition Information
Calories: 168 kcal, Carbohydrates: 26 g, Protein: 9 g, Fat: 4g

117. Teriyaki Chicken and Veggie Noodle
Prep Time: 20 mins, Cook Time: 15-20 mins, Servings: 1 bowl

Ingredients
- ¼ cup low-sodium soy sauce
- 2 tbsp honey
- 2 tbsp water
- 1 tbsp rice vinegar
- 1 tbsp cornstarch
- 12 oz. Asian noodles (refrigerated)
- 1 tbsp olive oil
- 1 lb. chicken breasts, boneless
- salt, and black pepper
- 2 thinly sliced carrots
- 1 thinly sliced bell pepper
- 2 cups chopped broccoli
- 1 cup snow peas
- 2 cloves minced garlic
- 1 tsp finely chopped fresh ginger

Instructions
- Combine the rice vinegar, soy sauce, water, honey, and cornstarch in a mixing bowl and put it aside.
- Boil the noodles as directed on the box. Drain the water and put it aside.
- Add the olive oil and place the chicken with salt and pepper seasoning in a heated pan. Cook for 5 to 7 mins, often tossing, until well cooked.
- Stir in the veggies. Cook for a few mins until the vegetables are crisp-tender.
- Mix the sliced ginger and garlic. Cook, constantly stirring, for 30 secs. Pour the sauce and cook for approximately 1 min until the sauce has thickened. Stir in the boiled noodles and mix thoroughly. Serve it hot.

Nutrition Information
Calories: 442 kcal, Carbohydrates: 56 g, Protein: 34 g, Fat: 9g

118. Slow Cooker Broccoli, Cheddar, and White Bean Soup
Prep Time: 15-20 mins, Cook Time: 2-3 hr, Servings: 1.5 cup

Ingredients
- 1 small yellow chopped onion
- 1 lb. broccoli crowns (chopped)
- 15 oz. can drain cannellini beans
- 2 cloves minced garlic
- ½ tsp salt
- ¼ tsp crushed black pepper
- 3 ½ cups low-sodium vegetable broth
- 1 ½ cups fresh spinach
- 6 oz. shredded cheddar cheese

Instructions
- Add the onion, garlic, broccoli, beans, salt, pepper, and broth to a cooker.
- Cook on low flame for 5 to 6 hr or on high flame for 3 hr, until broccoli flower is tender.
- Add the spinach and simmer for another 5 mins.
- Puree the soup in portions with a tabletop blender until smooth. Pour the soup into the cooker. Combine 4 oz. Shredded cheddar and mixed it well. Serve the soup in bowls with the leftover shredded cheddar on top.

Nutrition Information
Calories: 332 kcal, Carbohydrates: 31 g, Protein: 20 g, Fat: 16g

119. Oatmeal Breakfast Smoothie
Prep Time: 08 mins, Cook Time: 0 mins, Servings: 1

Ingredients
- ¼ cup uncooked simple oats
- ½ medium banana
- ½ cup plain Greek yogurt
- ¾ cup frozen mango
- ¾ cup strawberries or ½ cup blueberries (frozen)
- ¾ cup milk of choice

Instructions
- Blender all the ingredients together, mix until smooth and serve it in a mason jar.

Nutrition Information
Calories: 200 kcal, Carbohydrates: 38 g, Protein: 9.8 g, Fat: 3.0g

120. Vegetarian Portobello Mushroom Fajitas
Prep Time: 20 mins, Cook Time: 08 mins, Servings: 2

Ingredients
- 2 tbsp olive oil
- 2 tbsp lime juice
- 2 cloves minced garlic
- ½ finely chopped jalapeno
- ¼ cup finely chopped cilantro
- ¼ tsp salt
- 1/8 tsp pepper
- 2 portobello mushrooms
- 2 thinly sliced bell peppers
- 1 sliced onion
- 1 avocado
- 8 whole-grain tortillas
- Serving: 15 oz. can drain black beans

Instructions
- In a large mixing bowl, mix the olive oil, garlic, salt, pepper, lime juice, jalapeño, and cilantro to make the marinade.
- Use a moist cloth to wipe the mushrooms. Remove the stem and take out the gills with a knife or spoon. Cut the mushrooms into half-inch thick pieces and stir them into the marinade basin.
- Mix the sliced onions and bell peppers in the bowl to mix.
- Toss the veggies and marinated mushrooms in hot oil in a big saucepan. Cook for approximately 8 mins or until veggies are soft.
- Peel and pit the avocado until then. In a mixing bowl, mash the avocados and add a squeeze of lemon juice and a sprinkle of salt, if preferred.
- Serve the veggies with mashed avocados and black beans in warmed tortillas.

Nutrition Information
Calories: 398 kcal, Carbohydrates: 60 g, Protein: 10 g, Fat: 16g

121. Almond Butter Chia Overnight Oats
Prep Time: 08 mins, Cook Time: 0 mins, Servings: 1

Ingredients
- 1 cup of simple oats
- 1 tsp pure syrup maple
- ¼ tsp extract vanilla
- ¼ cup of Greek yogurt plain
- 1 ½ tsp chia seeds
- 2 tsp almond butter
- ½ cup milk

- Optional toppings: fresh berries, sliced banana, chopped almonds, or more chia seeds

Instructions
- Combine the oats, milk, almond butter, yogurt, vanilla extract, maple syrup, and chia seeds in a glass jar or dish. Stir until everything is thoroughly blended. Store in refrigerator for up to 2-3 days.
- Before serving, mix and garnish with chosen toppings. Enjoy!

Nutrition Information
Calories: 369 kcal, Carbohydrates: 44 g, Protein: 17 g, Fat: 14g

122. One-Pot Spanish Chickpea Chicken
Prep Time: 15-20 mins, Cook Time: 30-40 mins, Servings: 1

Ingredients
- 1 tbsp olive oil
- 1.25 lb. boneless and skinless chicken thighs
- salt and pepper
- 1 small, chopped onion
- 1 chopped red bell pepper
- 4 cloves minced garlic
- 1 tsp smoked paprika
- ½ tsp cumin
- 15 oz. can chop tomatoes
- 1 ¾ cups low-sodium chicken broth
- 1 cup rinsed and drained brown rice (long grain)
- 15 oz. can drain chickpeas
- Freshly chopped parsley

Instructions
- Stir the salt and pepper seasoned chicken in heated oil in a large pan. Cook for 3 mins until both sides are browned and dish out in a clean platter.
- Add the chopped onions and red bell peppers. Cook on a medium flame for 2 to 3 mins until veggies are softened. Mix in the garlic and stir for 30 secs.
- Stir in the cumin, chopped tomatoes, salt, pepper, smoked paprika, and broth. To combine, stir everything together. Combine the brown rice and drained chickpeas. Place the cooked chicken again into the skillet's mixture.
- Reduce the heat, cover the lid, and simmer for 35 to 40 mins with no remaining liquid. To ensure that the rice cooks evenly, carefully stir it after every 10 mins.
- Garnish with some parsley and serve.

Nutrition information
Calories: 526 kcal, Carbohydrates: 61 g, Protein: 40 g, Fat: 14g

123. Slow Cooker Chicken, Broccoli, and Rice Casserole
Prep Time: 15 mins, Cook Time: 2-3 hr, Servings: 5

Ingredients
- 1 small, chopped onion
- 1 cup drained brown rice (long grain)
- 1 tbsp Dijon mustard
- 1 tsp garlic powder
- 1 tsp dried thyme
- 1/2 tsp salt
- 1/4 tsp black pepper
- 2 cups low-sodium chicken broth
- 1 lb. boneless and skinless chicken breasts
- 1 lb. chopped broccoli
- 1/2 cup plain Greek yogurt
- 1/2 cup Parmesan cheese (grated)
- 1 cup cheddar cheese (shredded)

Instructions
- Add the brown rice, onion, garlic powder, salt, pepper, Dijon mustard, and dried thyme in the slow cooker.
- Add the broth and mix until everything is thoroughly mixed.
- Place the chicken and stir to combine. Season the chicken with black pepper.
- Cook for 2 1/2- 3 1/2 hr on high flame, or until chicken meat is cooked and all liquid has absorbed.
- Cook, steam, or roast the broccoli when cooking time is nearly up.
- Cut the chicken into small pieces on a chopping board once the rice and chicken are done.
- Toss the rice with plain Greek yogurt (optional), Parmesan cheese, and cheddar cheese. Stir everything together.
- Chop the chicken into small pieces and mix the prepared broccoli in the slow cooker. Serve after a quick stir.

Nutrition Information
Calories: 375 kcal, Carbohydrates: 33 g, Protein: 30.5 g, Fat: 12.4g

124. Creamy Avocado Vegetarian Burritos
Prep Time: 8 mins, Cook Time: 10-15 mins, Servings: 4

Ingredients
- 1 tbsp olive oil
- 2 thinly sliced bell peppers
- 1 thinly sliced onion
- salt and pepper
- ½ cup plain Greek yogurt
- ½ tbsp lime juice
- ¼ tsp chili powder
- 2 tbsp freshly chopped cilantro
- 15 oz. can drain pinto beans
- 4 large whole wheat tortillas
- 1 cup shredded Monterey jack cheese
- 2 small, chopped avocados

Instructions
- In a large pan, add the sliced onions and bell peppers in heated oil and cook for a few mins until softened. To taste, sprinkle some salt and pepper.
- Combine the yogurt with lemon juice, chili powder, and chopped cilantro in a bowl.
- In a saucepan, add the beans and warm them for a few mins. To warm the tortillas, place them in the microwave between paper towels.
- Spread a quarter of the yogurt mixture along the middle of each tortilla. Add the onions, peppers, beans, cheese, and avocado to the top. Wrap the tortillas and serve.

Nutrition Information
Calories: 563 kcal, Carbohydrates: 55 g, Protein: 21 g, Fat: 31g

125. Kale Quinoa Salad with Blueberries
Prep Time: 25 mins, Cook Time: 0 mins, Servings: 1

Ingredients
For Salad:
- 1 cup quinoa
- 6 cups chopped kale
- 15 oz. can drained chickpeas
- 1 cup blueberries
- 4 oz. crumbled goat cheese
- ½ cup sliced almonds
- 1 peeled and chopped avocado

For Dressing
- ¼ cup extra virgin olive oil
- ¼ cup lime juice
- 2 tbsp honey
- 1 ½ tsp Dijon mustard
- ¼ tsp Kosher salt
- black pepper to taste

Instructions
- Rinse the quinoa and drain it. Pour water (2 cups) in a pan with quinoa and boil. Cover the top, and boil on low flame for approximately 15 mins, or until all of the water has been absorbed. Set aside to cool.
- Prepare the dressing until then. Mix all of the dressing Ingredients. Toss the kale with the prepared dressing with your hands.
- Once the quinoa has cooled, combine it with the kale, add the chickpeas (optional), almonds, blueberries, goat cheese, and avocado in a mixing bowl. To mix, gently toss everything together. Serve.

Nutrition Information

Calories: 734kcal, Carbohydrates: 74g, Protein: 26g, Fat: 42g

126. Grilled Zucchini Boats
Prep Time: 25 mins, Cook Time: 15 mins, Servings: 2
Ingredients
- ½ cup quinoa
- 1 cup water
- 4 large zucchinis
- 1 tbsp olive oil
- 1 tbsp fresh lime juice
- ½ tsp dried oregano
- 1/8 tsp kosher salt
- 1 cup cherry tomatoes
- ½ cup pitted kalamata quartered olives
- ¼ cup red onion (finely chopped)
- 1 tbsp freshly chopped parsley
- ¼ cup crumbled feta cheese

Instructions
- In a small pan, add the drained quinoa and 1 cup of water. Cover the lid and boil it on a low heat setting. Cook for 10 min, or until all of the liquid has been absorbed. Allow it to cool in a large mixing basin.
- Preheat a grill pan or grill on medium heat until then. Cut the zucchini in two (lengthwise) and scrape the insides with a tiny metal spoon. Apply olive oil to the cut sides of the zucchini. Grill them for 4-6 mins, until crisp-tender. Place in a baking tray to cool.
- Combine the salt, lemon juice, and oregano in a mixing bowl. Pour it on quinoa.
- Add the Chopped red onion and parsley, tomato halves, and olives. Combine them with the quinoa in a mixing bowl. Add the feta cheese and stir everything together.
- Spoon the filling into the grilled zucchini boats. Serve them hot or refrigerate them until ready to use.

Nutrition Information
Calories: 204kcal, Carbohydrates: 24g, Protein: 7g, Fat: 10g

127. Tuscan White Bean Soup
Prep Time: 10-15 mins, Cook Time: 20 mins, Servings: 1
Ingredients
- 2 tbsp olive oil
- 2 medium and chopped sweet potatoes
- 1 medium onion
- 4 celery ribs
- 3 cloves garlic
- ½ tsp dried rosemary
- ½ tsp dried thyme
- ½ tsp salt
- 1/8 tsp black pepper
- 2 cans drained cannellini beans
- 4 cups low-sodium vegetable broth
- 1 medium chopped bunch kale without tough stems

Instructions
- In a large saucepan/Dutch oven, add the onion, celery, and sweet potatoes in heated olive oil and cook for 5 mins over medium heat. Stir in the garlic, salt, pepper, rosemary, and thyme cook for 30 secs. Add the beans and stock in a saucepan.
- Turn the flame to high and bring the mixture to a boil. Cook for another 10 min with a closed lid, or until potatoes are cooked. Toss the chopped kale and cook for 2 mins until the kale has wilted. Serve.

Nutrition Information
Calories: 221kcal, Carbohydrates: 39g, Protein: 11g, Fat: 5g

128. Gingerbread Coffee Cake
Prep Time: 15 mins, Cook Time: 45 mins, Servings: 10 pieces
Ingredients
- 1 & ½ cups all-purpose flour
- 1 & ½ cups whole wheat flour
- ¼ cup+2 tbsp packed brown sugar
- ½ tsp salt
- 1 & ½ tsp ginger
- 1 tsp cinnamon
- ½ tsp cloves
- ½ tsp nutmeg
- ½ cup cold unsalted butter
- 2 tbsp melted unsalted butter
- 1 tsp baking soda
- ½ tsp baking powder
- 1 large egg
- ¾ cup unsweetened applesauce
- ½ cup molasses
- 1/3 cup buttermilk or simple milk
- ¼ cup pure maple syrup

Instructions
- Heat the oven before baking to 350 °F. Grease the springform pan (8-inch) with some cooking oil and put it aside.
- Mix all the dry Ingredients (salt, cinnamon, 1/4 cup brown sugar, all-purpose flour, nutmeg, whole wheat flour, ginger, and cloves) in the electric mixer. Mix until everything is mixed correctly.
- Mix in the chilled butter squares at low rpm until the biggest pieces are equivalent to tiny peas.
- In the meantime, make the crumble topping, mix 1 cup of the dry Ingredients, 2 tbsp of brown sugar, and 2 tbsp of melted butter.
- In the mixer bowl, add the baking powder and baking soda with the dry Ingredients until well combined.
- Mix the buttermilk, egg, applesauce, maple syrup, and molasses in a mixing basin.
- Transfer the egg mixture into the dry Ingredients while running at low speed. Turn the mixer speed to moderate and beat for 2 min, or until the batter is smooth.
- Transfer the prepared batter into greased pan and top with crumble topping. Put it in a preheated oven for 40 to 45 mins, or until the cake is done. Before serving, let the coffee cake cool on a wire rack.

Nutrition Information
Calories: 342kcal, Carbohydrates: 53g, Protein: 5g, Fat: 12g

129. Spinach Pesto Pasta
Prep Time: 25 mins, Cook Time: 5 mins, Servings: 1
Ingredients
For Spinach Pesto:
- 3 cups fresh spinach
- 1 clove garlic
- ½ cup toasted walnuts
- ½ cup shredded Parmesan cheese
- ¼ tsp Kosher salt
- 1/8 tsp black pepper
- ¼ cup extra virgin olive oil

For Pasta:
- ¾ lb. trimmed green beans
- 8 oz. whole wheat rotini pasta
- 2 cups cooked and cubed chicken breast
- 8 oz. cherry/grape tomatoes cut in halves

Instructions
- In a food processor, combine all pesto components except olive oil. Process until the mixture is chopped finely. Add oil in a steady flow via the feed tube while the processor is running, and process until thoroughly blended,
- Boil water with salt in a big pot. Add the beans in the boiling water and cook for 2-5 min, or until crisp-tender. Scooped out into a dish of cold water using a slotted spoon. After a few mins, remove the green beans from the cold water and dry them on a clean towel.
- Add the pasta to the already boiling salt water and cook as directed on the box. Strain the pasta (keep 1/2 cup of the cooking pasta water for later use). Put the pasta in a pan.
- Place a handful of green beans on a cutting board and chop in half. Toss in the beans and chicken with the noodles in the pan. Mix the pesto mixture and a splash of the pasta

boiling water to loosen the sauce. Toss in the tomatoes carefully.
- Serve the spaghetti hot or chilled and enjoy.

Nutrition Information
Calories: 633kcal, Carbohydrates: 54g, Protein: 39g, Fat: 30g

130. Apple Cinnamon Cookie Energy Bites
Prep Time: 20 mins, Cook Time: 0 mins, Servings: 2 dozen
Ingredients
- 2 cups simple oats
- ¼ cup crushed flaxseed
- ¾ tsp cinnamon
- ½ cup almond butter
- ¼ cup+1 tbsp honey
- 1 tsp vanilla extract
- pinch of salt
- 1 cup grated apple

Instructions
- Combine the flaxseeds, oats, and cinnamon in a large mixing basin. Add the honey, vanilla, almond butter, and sprinkle of salt in a separate dish or liquid measuring cup and mix until well blended. Pour the oat mixture over it and stir until it is uniformly covered. Add the grated apple and mix well.
- With the help of a cookie scoop, divide the mixture into tbsp-sized parts and roll it into a ball with your palms (damp your hands to avid stickiness).
- Serve them right away or keep the energy bites refrigerated inside an airtight container for 3-4 days. Enjoy!

Nutrition Information
Calories: 161kcal, Carbohydrates: 19g, Protein: 5g, Fat: 8g

131. Peanut Butter Granola Bars {No Bake}
Prep Time: 10 mins, Cook Time: 10 mins, Servings: 1
Ingredients
- 1 ½ cups quick oats
- 1 cup puffed brown rice cereal
- ½ cup dry roasted chopped peanuts
- 1 cup peanut butter
- ½ cup honey
- 1 tsp vanilla extract
- ¼ tsp salt

Instructions
- Line a baking tray (8x8 inch) with parchment paper and put it aside.2. Combine the instant oats, peanuts, and brown rice cereal in a large mixing dish.
- In a microwave-safe dish, add peanut butter and honey. Microwave for 45 secs, then stir in the vanilla and salt and mix until smooth. If necessary, microwave for another 15 secs to re-melt.
- Stir in the peanut butter mixture into dry Ingredients until equally distributed throughout the oat mixture.
- Fill the baking pan with prepared batter and flatten it evenly into the pan. Before cutting into bars, chill for at least one min.
- Keep refrigerated for up to a week in an airtight container.

Nutrition Information
Calories: 214kcal, Carbohydrates: 22g, Protein: 7g, Fat: 13g

132. Homemade Greek Yogurt
Prep Time: 45 mins, Cook Time: 0 mins, Servings: 4 cups
Ingredients
- 8 cups milk or fat-free milk
- 1 tbsp plain yogurt or homemade yogurt

Instructions
- Boil the milk in a medium saucepan, stirring periodically until it reaches 180°f. The milk will be heating and frothing but not boiling at this temperature.
- Add the hot milk into a container and chill to 110-115 °F (suitable for yogurt culture). Add the yogurt and mix. Cover the container top with a lid or plastic wrap and cover it in a thick dishcloth.
- Preheat the oven for one min at any temperature. Turn off the oven, then place the wrapped container inside. Shut the microwave door and leave the yogurt inside for 8-12 mins. During incubation, keep the oven warm (about 110 °) and resume the 1 min warming cycle as required.
- When it appears like yogurt with liquid on top, it's done. This liquid (whey) must be drained to make thick Greek yogurt. Put a fine-mesh cloth or sieve over a big basin. Top with cheesecloth or two layers of paper towels. Pour the yogurt on top of it and wrap it with plastic wrap. Refrigerate it for 8 hr to drain the whey (discard the liquid or save it for baking).
- Spoon the yogurt into sealed containers and refrigerate it. Homemade yogurt lasts a week.

Nutrition Information
Calories: 319kcal, Carbohydrates: 31g, Protein: 21g, Fat: 13g

133. Loaded Coffee Smoothie
Prep time: 5 mins, Cook Time: 0 mins, Servings: 1
Ingredients
- 1 medium frozen and sliced banana
- 1/2 cup strong and chilled brewed coffee
- 1/2 cup milk
- 1/4 cup rolled oats
- a spoonful of nut butter (optional)

Instructions
- Blend all the listed Ingredients in a blender until smooth, add additional milk as
needed to attain desired consistency. Serve immediately with a chocolate sprinkling.

Nutrition Information
Calories: 257kcal, Carbohydrates: 46g, Protein: 7g, Fat: 5g

134. Cocoa Almond Protein Smoothie
Prep Time: 5 mins, Cook Time: 0 mins, Servings: 1
Ingredients
- ¾ cup Greek yogurt
- ¼ cup+2 tbsp milk
- 1 medium sliced and frozen banana
- ½ tbsp unsweetened cocoa powder
- 2 tbsp almond butter
- Optional: 2 tsp ground flaxseed
- ¾ cup ice cubes

Instructions
- Blend all the listed Ingredients in a blender until smooth, add additional milk as needed to attain desired consistency. Pour it in a glass, dust some cocoa powder and place some banana slices on top and serve.

Nutrition Information
Calories: 470kcal, Carbohydrates: 43g, Protein: 26g, Fat: 22g

135. The Busy Mom's Oatmeal Bowl
Prep Time: 5 mins, Cook Time: 5 mins, Servings: 2
Ingredients
- 1 1/2 frozen and sliced bananas
- 2 tbsp peanut butter
- 1 tbsp chia seeds
- 1 1/2 tbsp honey
- 1/2 cup oats
- 10 oz. almond milk

Instructions
- Layer items in the blender as directed.
- Choose smoothie mode or blend on low-high speed until all components are well blended and served.

Nutrition Information
Calories: 470kcal, Carbohydrates: 43g, Protein: 26g, Fat: 22g

136. Banana Raspberry Smoothie
Prep Time: 5 mins, Cook Time: 0 mins, Servings: 1
Ingredients
- 1 medium sliced and frozen banana
- 1/2 cup fresh or frozen raspberries
- 1 cup unsweetened Almond milk

- 1/4 cup vanilla Greek yogurt
- 1/4 cup simple rolled oats/quick oats
- 1/2 tbsp honey or more to taste

Instructions
- Blend all the listed Ingredients in a blender until smooth. Add additional honey as needed. Pour it in a glass and serve.

Nutrition Information
Calories: 360 kcal, Carbohydrates: 40 g, Protein: 16 g, Fat: 10 g

137. Peanut Butter Banana Smoothie
Prep Time: 5 mins, Cook Time: 0 mins, Servings: 1
Ingredients
- ¾ cup ice cubes
- 1 medium frozen and sliced banana
- ¾ cup Greek yogurt
- ½ cup milk
- 2 tbsp peanut butter

Instructions
- Blend all the listed Ingredients in a blender until smooth. Pour it in a glass and serve.

Nutrition Information
Calories: 456kcal, Carbohydrates: 44g, Protein: 28g, Fat: 21g

138. Tropical Pineapple Carrot Smoothie
Prep time: 10 mins, Cook Time: 0 mins, Servings: 2
Ingredients
- 1 cup unsweetened almond coconut milk
- 1 orange juice
- 1 cup frozen pineapple
- 1/2 cup frozen mango
- 1/2 a fresh banana
- 2-3 peeled and chopped carrots
- sweeten as desired

Instructions
- In a blender, add liquid Ingredients first.
- Add carrots and fruits, and blend for a few mins until a smooth and creamy texture is attained.
- According to the blender's performance, add more liquid to the smoothie as needed and adjust to the desired thickness.

Nutrition Information
Calories: 135kcal, Carbohydrates: 30g, Proteins: 2g, Fats: 2g

139. Beet Berry Apple Chia Smoothie
Prep time: 05 mins, Cook Time: 0 mins, Servings: 1
Ingredients
- 3 small, cooked beets
- 2 cups blueberries (frozen)
- 1 cup unsweetened apple juice
- 1 cup light canned coconut milk
- 1 tbsp chia seeds
- 1/8 tsp crushed cinnamon

Instructions
- Blend all the listed Ingredients in a blender until smooth. Pour it in a glass and serve.

Nutrition Information
Calories: 495kcal, Carbohydrates: 80g, Proteins: 9g, Fats: 17g

140. Raspberry Peanut Butter Smoothie
Prep time: 08 mins, Cook Time: 0 mins, Servings: 1
Ingredients
- 1 1/2 cups raspberries (frozen)
- 1 medium frozen banana
- 2 tbsp peanut butter
- 1/4 cup plain Greek yogurt
- 6 tbsp ice cubes
- Optional garnishing: fresh raspberries

Instructions
- Blend all the listed Ingredients well until smooth. Add more water if needed. Pour it in a glass and garnish with some fresh berries on top. Serve.

Nutrition Information
Calories: 375kcal, Carbohydrates: 43g, Protein: 16g, Fat: 19g

141. Mango Avocado Smoothie
Prep time: 08 mins, Cook Time: 0 mins, Servings: 2
Ingredients
- 1 cup Frozen Mango Chunks
- ½ banana
- ½ cup ice
- ½-1 cup Pineapple Juice
- ½ almond milk/water
- ¼ avocado

Instructions
- Blend all the listed Ingredients well until smooth. Adjust the consistency by adding more pineapple juice. Pour it in a glass and serve.

Nutrition Information
Calories: 155kcal, Carbohydrates: 29g, Protein: 2g, Fat: 4g

142. Blueberry Coconut Water Smoothie (With Hemp Hearts)
Prep Time: 15 mins, Cook Time: 0 mins, Servings: 1 person
Ingredients
- 1 ½ cups blueberries (frozen)
- 1 cup coconut water
- ½ cup Greek or full-fat plain yogurt
- ¼ tsp coconut extract
- 1 tbsp hemp hearts

Instructions
- Blend all Ingredients well until smooth puree forms. Pour it in a glass and serve.

Nutrition Information
Calories: 301kcal, Carbohydrates: 49g, Protein: 17g, Fat: 5g

143. Raspberry Peach Smoothie Shake
Prep Time: 5 mins, Cook Time: 0 mins, Servings: 1
Ingredients
- 1 cup unsweetened frozen raspberries
- ¾ cup freshly chopped peach
- ¼ cup plain Greek yogurt
- 1/3 cup milk
- 1 tsp honey

Instructions
- Blend all Ingredients well until smooth. Add extra milk as required. Serve with raspberries on top.

Nutrition Information
Calories: 216kcal, Carbohydrates: 38g, Protein: 7g, Fat: 6g

144. Immunity Boosting Orange Smoothie
Prep Time: 5 mins, Cook Time: 0 mins, Servings: 1
Ingredients
- 1 large, peeled orange
- ½ medium banana
- 1 cup frozen mango chunks
- ½ cup almond milk
- ¼ tsp vanilla extract

Instructions
- Blend all listed Ingredients well until smooth, add extra milk as required. Serve with mango chunks on top.

Nutrition Information
Calories: 232kcal, Carbohydrates: 52g, Protein: 3.2g, Fat: 2.0g

145. Spinach & Apple Detox Smoothie
Prep time: 5 mins, Cook Time: 0 mins, Servings: 2
Ingredients
- 2–3 cups packed spinach
- 1/2 cup unsweetened almond milk
- 1 banana

- 1 Granny Smith apple (chopped)
- 1 cup cubed cucumber
- 4 dates
- 1 tbsp flax seeds
- A squeeze of lime juice
- 6 ice cubes
- For garnishing: chia or hemp seeds, unsweetened shaved coconut

Instructions
- Blend the almond milk, spinach, and banana first. Add the dates, flaxseeds, cucumber, apple, and lemon juice and blend for 3-4 mins until smooth. Add ice cubes and pulse for a few secs. Serve into two glass jars and garnish as desired. Serve this away, or keep it refrigerated for later!

Nutrition Information
Calories: 495kcal, Carbohydrates: 80g, Proteins: 9g, Fats: 15g

146. Tropical Green Chia Seed Smoothie
Prep Time: 05 mins, Cook Time: 0 mins, Servings: 1
Ingredients
- 1 cup chopped kale (loosely packed)
- 1/3 small frozen banana
- 3/4 cup pineapple (frozen and chunks)
- 1/2 cup frozen mango
- 1 small, peeled orange
- 2 tsp chia seeds
- 1/3 cup Unsweetened Silk Almond Milk

Instructions
- Blend all the above Ingredients well until smooth, add extra milk as required. Serve with pineapple chunks on top.

Nutrition Information
Calories: 291kcal, Carbohydrates: 62g, Protein: 7g, Fat: 4g

147. Green Monster Smoothie
Prep Time: 5 mins, Cook Time: 0 mins, Servings: 1
Ingredients
- 1 frozen banana
- 1 cup pineapple (frozen chunks)
- 1 sliced pear
- 1 peeled and chopped orange
- 3 cups baby spinach leaves loosely packed
- 2 tbsp crushed flaxseed (optional)
- 1 cup cold water

Instructions
- Blend all the above Ingredients well until smooth. Add extra water as required. Serve with some crushed flaxseeds on top.

Nutrition Information
Calories: 149kcal, Carbohydrates: 33g, Protein: 3g, Fat: 2g

148. Metabolism Boosting Smoothie
Prep time: 05 mins, Cook Time: 0 mins, Servings: 1
Ingredients
- 1/2 cup brewed and potent green tea
- 1/4 cup low-fat Greek yogurt
- 1/4 cup quick oats
- 1/2 banana
- 1/2 cup mixed berries

Instructions
- Blend all smoothie Ingredients in the above order until smooth. Serve.

Nutrition Information
Calories: 210kcal, Carbohydrates: 39g, Protein: 9g, Fat: 3g

149. Pumpkin Smoothie
Prep Time: 5 mins, Cook Time: 0 mins, Servings: 1
Ingredients
- 1/4 cup+2 tbsp simple oats
- 1/4 cup canned pumpkin puree
- 3/4 cup plain Greek yogurt
- 1 medium chopped apple
- 1/2 small frozen sliced banana
- 1/2 cup desired milk
- 1/8 tsp pumpkin pie spice
- 1/2 cup ice cubes

Instructions
- Pulse the oats in a high-speed blender for approximately 30 secs, or until finely chopped. Mix in the remaining Ingredients until smooth. Serve right away.

Nutrition Information
Calories: 187kcal, Carbohydrates: 32g, Protein: 11g, Fat: 2g

150. Blueberry Spinach Breakfast Smoothie
Prep Time: 5 mins, Cook Time: 0 mins, Servings: 1
Ingredients
- 3 tbsp simple oats
- 1 cup spinach (fresh)
- 1 cup blueberries (frozen)
- 1/3 cup plain Greek yogurt
- 3/4 cup desired milk
- 1/8 tsp cinnamon (optional)

Instructions
- Pulse the oats in a high-speed blender for approximately 30 secs, or until finely chopped. Mix in the remaining Ingredients until smooth. Serve right away.

Nutrition Information
Calories: 168kcal, Carbohydrates: 26g, Protein: 9g, Fat: 4g

151. Apple-Pear Oatmeal Smoothie (aka Apple Pie Smoothie)
Prep time: 5 mins, Cook Time: 0 mins, Servings: 1
Ingredients
- 1/2 cup simple oats
- 1 cup plain Greek yogurt
- 1 medium chopped apple
- 1 medium chopped pear
- 1/4 cup preferred milk
- 1/4 tsp ground cinnamon
- pinch of crushed nutmeg
- 1/4 tsp pure vanilla extract
- 1 cup ice cubes

Instructions
- Pulse the oats in a high-speed blender for approximately 30 secs, or until finely chopped. Blend the remaining components and mix until smooth. On top, dust some cinnamon and serve it right away.

Nutrition Information
Calories: 261kcal, Carbohydrates: 45g, Protein: 14g, Fat: 3g

152. Strawberry & Honey Banana Soft Serve
Prep Time: 5 mins, Cook Time: 0 mins, Servings: 3 cups
Ingredients
- 2 1/2 cups frozen sliced banana
- 1 1/2 cups frozen sliced strawberry
- 1 cup Honey Almond Milk

Instructions
- Chop the frozen fruits several times in a blender until it is coarsely chopped.
- Reduce the speed and gradually pour the almond milk until it is well absorbed and creamy.
- Serve right away or store in tiny portions in the freezer to take out and enjoy later.

Nutrition Information
Calories: 427kcal, Carbohydrates: 85g, Protein: 9g, Fat: 10 g

153. Chocolate-Dipped Almond Butter Banana Bites
Prep time: 10 mins, Cook Time: 0 mins, Servings: 12 bites
Ingredients
- 3 large bananas
- 1/3 cup preferred nut butter
- 1/2 cup melted chocolate

Instructions

- Cut bananas into thick (1/4-1/2 inch) slices.
- Sprinkle nut butter on top of each slice and make a sandwich of two.
- Arrange them on a sheet pan lined with wax paper and freeze for at least a min, or until solid.
- Melt the chocolate and dip it in the frozen banana pieces.
- Place each chocolate-dipped banana bite on a sheet pan and put it in the freezer for another min.
- Transfer them to an airtight container and store them in the refrigerator for up to two weeks.

Nutrition Information
Calories: 46kcal, Carbohydrates: 5g, Protein: 1g, Fat: 3g

154. Millet Porridge Recipe
Prep time: 5 mins, Cook Time: 20 mins, Servings: 1
Ingredients
- 1 tbsp butter
- 1 cup uncooked millet
- 2 cup unsweetened coconut milk
- 1 cup water
- 1/8 tsp salt
- Toppings: raspberries, maple syrup, and toasted pecans

Instructions
- Pulse the millet in a coffee/spice grinder until it reaches a crumbly or flour texture.
- Add the butter and melt it on a low flame in a pan.
- Toast the millet in melted butter, often stirring, for 2-3 mins.
- Stir in the water, coconut milk, and salt in it.
- Bring to a simmer, then lower to low heat and cook, stirring periodically, for 15 to 20 mins until a porridge-like consistency is achieved. Add more milk as required.
- Garnish with toasted nuts, blueberries, and maple syrup on top.

Nutrition Information
Calories: 190kcal, Carbohydrates: 36 g, Protein: 6 g, Fat: 2 g

155. Make-Ahead Vegetarian Holiday Frittata Recipe
Prep Time: 15 mins, Cook Time: 35 mins, Servings: 8
Ingredients
- 2 tbsp olive oil
- 2 cups onion (thinly sliced)
- 1 clove minced garlic
- 1 small, shredded zucchini
- 2 cups cooked spaghetti (squash)
- 1/2 cup halved tomatoes (sundried)
- 8 large eggs
- 1/4 cup milk
- 1 cup grated mozzarella cheese
- 1 tsp salt
- 1/2 tsp pepper
- 1/2 tsp dried oregano

Instructions
- Heat the oven before baking to 400 °F.
- In an iron skillet (8-inch), Sauté the onions in heated oil for 15 mins over medium heat, or until beautifully caramelized. Cook for another min after adding the garlic.
- Stir in the spaghetti squash, zucchini, and sundried tomatoes until well mixed.
- Mix the eggs, cheese, milk, oregano, salt, and pepper in a bowl. Pour the mixture over the veggies in the skillet, ensure everything is uniformly distributed, and cover the egg mixture.
- Cook the eggs on low heat until the sides of the eggs have set. Put it in a preheated oven and bake for 10 mins at 400°F or until cooked. Grill for 1-2 mins, or until the top is lightly browned.

Nutrition Information
Calories: 102kcal, Carbohydrates: 3g, Protein: 10g, Fat: 5g

156. Banana Nut Toaster Pop-Ups for Busy Weekday Mornings
Prep Time: 30 mins, Cook Time: 10 mins, Servings: 15 pop-ups
Ingredients
- 3 cups rolled simple oats
- 2 tsp baking soda
- 2 tsp baking powder
- 1 tsp cinnamon
- 1/2 tsp salt
- 1 cup soy milk
- 2 beaten eggs
- 1 ripe banana
- 1/4 cup maple syrup
- 1 cup roasted and chopped walnuts

Instructions
- Pulse the oats in a processor until fine like flour.
- Add the prepared oat flour to a clean bowl. Mix the salt, cinnamon, baking powder, and baking soda in flour.
- Mash the banana in a clean mixing bowl until it has a homogeneous mashed texture. Add the beaten eggs, milk, and maple syrup and blend them well.
- Blend the wet and dry ingredients in a mixing basin and whisk to combine. Mix the walnuts.
- Heat a grill over medium-high heat. Co at the surface with butter and pour the batter with a measuring cup (1/4 cup). Flatten it out into a circular form with the measuring cup if the batter is thick.
- Cook each side for 2 to 3 mins until done, then transfer to a cooling rack and serve.
- Or arrange them in a layer on a baking tray and freeze for 1 to 2 mins. Take out the pop-ups and vacuum seal them in a Food Saver sealed bag. Freeze for those hectic weekday mornings!

Nutrition Information
Calories: 230kcal, Carbohydrates: 38g, Protein: 8g, Fat: 6g

157. Apple Cinnamon Oat Muffins
Prep Time: 20 mins, Cook Time: 20 mins, Servings: 12 muffins
Ingredients
- 1 & 2/3 cup quick oats
- 1 cup all-purpose flour
- 3/4 cup coconut sugar/brown sugar
- 2 tsp cinnamon
- 1 tsp baking powder
- 1 tsp baking soda
- 1 tsp salt
- 2 eggs
- 1 tsp vanilla
- 1 & ½ cup low-fat buttermilk
- 1 & ½ cup peeled and grated apples

Instructions
- Heat the oven before baking to 400 °F.
- In a food processor, combine the oats and the other Ingredients and pulse them 5-6 times, or until the oats resemble coarse flour.
- In a large mixing basin, combine the oat flour, all-purpose flour, salt, cinnamon, baking soda, and baking powder. Mix vigorously until adequately blended.
- Beat eggs in a separate dish, add sugar, buttermilk, and vanilla. Toss in the shredded apple after whisking everything together.
- Combine the egg mixture with dry Ingredients in a large mixing bowl and combine well.
- Pour 3 tbsp batter into each cupcake liner and dust sugar on top.
- Bake for 18 to 20 mins or until a toothpick inserted in the middle comes out clean.
- Take it out from the oven and set it on a wire rack.
- Serve it right away or stored in an airtight container for 2 days or in the freezer (reheat anytime a quick and substantial breakfast is needed).

Nutrition Information
Calories: 200kcal, Carbohydrates: 29.6g, Protein 4g, Fat: 7.1g

158. The Busy Mom's Oatmeal Bowl
Prep Time: 5 mins, Cook Time: 0 mins, Servings: 2
Ingredients
- 1 ½ frozen and chopped bananas
- 2 tbsp peanut butter
- 1 tbsp chia seeds
- 1 ½ tbsp honey
- 1/2 cup oats
- 10 oz. almond milk

Instructions
- In a blender, layer the ingredients as per the manufacturer's directions.
- Turn on the smoothie mode or mix at low-high speeds until all Ingredients are thoroughly combined.
- Serve right away.

Nutrition Information
Calories: 150kcal, Carbohydrates: 28g, Protein: 5g, Fat: 2.5g

159. Lemon Zest Springtime Spinach Muffins
Prep Time: 10 mins, Cook Time: 20 mins, Servings: 12 muffins
Ingredients
For muffins
- 2 eggs
- 3/4 cup applesauce
- 1/3 cup lemon juice
- 1 tbsp lemon zest
- 1 tsp vanilla extract
- 1/4 cup avocado oil
- ¼ cup unsweetened almond milk
- 3–4 oz. roughly chopped baby spinach
- 2/3 cup light brown sugar
- ½ tsp salt
- 1 ½ tsp baking soda
- 1 cup whole wheat flour
- 1 cup all-purpose flour

For Glaze
- 2 cups powdered sugar
- 2 tsp lime juice fresh
- 2-3 tsp of milk almond

Instructions
- Heat the oven before baking to 375°F and line a muffin tray with liner or spray with nonstick cooking spray.
- Add milk, eggs, oil, vanilla extract, lemon juice, applesauce, lemon zest, and spinach in a blender; mix well until all spinach is mixed.
- Combine salt, sugar, and baking soda in a large dish. Once everything is mixed correctly, whisk in the flours until they are entirely integrated.
- Slowly pour in the spinach mixture and stir until a thick batter forms.
- Divide the batter equally between the muffin pans.
- Bake for 18 to 20 mins in a preheated oven. Leave it to cool about 5 min before transferring to a cooling rack.
- To prepare a glaze, Whisk lemon juice with powdered sugar. Add ½ tsp of almond milk and mix until the desired consistency is reached.
- Drizzle the glaze over the cooling muffins and serve right away.
- Stored the un-glazed muffins in an airtight container for up to 3 days. Before serving, drizzle with glaze.

Nutrition Information
Calories: 329kcal, Carbohydrates: 10 g, Protein: 9g, Fat: 18g

160. Healthy Freezer Breakfast Burritos
Prep Time: 20 mins, Cook Time: 2 mins, Servings: 8 burritos
Ingredients
- 1 lb sausage (breakfast)
- 1/2 finely diced yellow onion
- 1/2 cored and diced red pepper
- 12 eggs
- A few dashes of hot sauce
- 8 burrito-sized tortillas
- 2 cup shredded cheddar cheese
- 1 cup chopped spinach

Instructions
- Cook the sausage in a heated pan for 2 mins until it is browned and crumbled. Take it out in a dish.
- Add the chopped onions and bell pepper to the skillet and stir for 3 to 5 mins until softened. Meanwhile, gently whisk the eggs in a large mixing dish.
- Turn the heat down to medium and scramble the eggs until fully cooked.
- Stir in the spicy sauce if used.
- Turn the heat and let the egg scramble mixture cool fully.
- Fill a tortilla with the prepared filling. Drizzle 1/4 cup of cheese on top, then firmly roll. Place the baking sheet repeats the process until all of the burritos are done.
- Freeze the baking sheet for about 1 min, or until solidly frozen, then move the burritos to the sealed bag or wrap each burrito separately in plastic wrap.
- To reheat the tortilla, remove it from the plastic wrap and cover it loosely in a paper towel. Microwave each side for 45 secs on high.

Nutrition Information
Calories: 365kcal, Carbohydrates: 40g, Protein: 21g, Fat: 12g

161. Pumpkin Spice Cinnamon Rolls
Prep Time: 25 mins, Cook Time: 25 mins, Servings: 12 rolls
Ingredients
For dough
- 1 cup pumpkin puree
- 2 eggs
- ¼ cup butter, softened
- 4 ¼ cup all-purpose flour
- ¼ cup warmed milk
- 1 tsp cinnamon
- 3 tbsp brown sugar
- 1 ½ tsp salt
- 2 tsp yeast

For filling
- ¾ cup sugar
- 1 tbsp cinnamon
- Raisins
- For the glaze:
- 1 cup confectioners' sugar
- 1 tbsp butter
- 1 ½ tbsp milk

Instructions
- Whisk the heated milk with yeast, then put aside for 5 min.
- Whisk the eggs, butter, brown sugar, pumpkin, cinnamon, and salt separately. Pour the yeast mixture in. With an attached beater, mix everything at low speed until well blended.
- Attach the dough hook, add half a cup of flour, and mix on medium-low until thoroughly combined.
- Cover and set aside for 1 and a half mins to expand in a warm environment.
- Heat the oven before baking to 375 °F.
- When the dough has doubled in size, spread out on to a rectangle board (12x15 inch) until it is approximately 1/4 inch thick.
- Sprinkle the filling equally over the rolled dough and spread it out.
- Cut the dough into 12 even pieces by rolling it into a spiral loaf.
- In an oiled pan (9x13), place uncooked rolls.
- Bake for about 20-25 mins or until golden brown.
- Leave the rolls for 5 mins to cool, and prepare the glaze by mixing melted butter, milk, and sugar.
- Drizzle the glaze over the cinnamon buns and serve warm.

Nutrition Information
Calories: 290kcal, Carbohydrates: 47g, Protein: 4g, Fat: 9.8g

162. Carrot Cake Lactation Breakfast Cookies for New Moms
Prep Time: 10 mins, Cook Time: 10 mins, Servings: 12
Ingredients
- ½ cup all-purpose flour
- ½ cup whole wheat flour
- ½ cup rolled oats
- ½ tsp baking powder
- 1/4 tsp salt
- ½ tsp cinnamon
- 3 tbsp granulated sugar
- 1/3 cup brown sugar
- 2 tbsp yeast
- 1/4 cup warmed coconut oil
- 1 egg
- 1 tsp vanilla extract
- ½ cup grated carrots
- ½ cup raisins
- 1 tsp unsalted butter
- 1/3 cup pecans

Instructions
- Heat the oven before cooking to 350 °F.
- In a saucepan, roast the pecans in melted butter on medium heat for 2-5 mins. Take them out in a dish and put them aside.
- Combine the dry Ingredients (oats, flours, salt, baking powder, cinnamon, and Brewer's yeast) in a large mixing dish.
- Whisk the egg with sugar, oil, and vanilla separately. Slowly whisk in the dry Ingredients until they are well incorporated.
- Add the roasted pecans, carrots, and raisins, and mix well.
- Scoop tbsp-sized scoops of dough onto a cookie sheet and flatten them into round cookie-shaped discs.
- Bake for 10 mins and then set aside to cool.

Nutrition Information
Calories: 146kcal, Carbohydrates: 23g, Protein: 3g, Fat: 5g

163. Sweet Potato Breakfast Hash
Prep Time: 15 mins, Cook Time: 5 mins, Servings: 4
Ingredients
- 2 sweet potatoes
- 4 large green onions
- 1 kale bunch
- 5 large eggs
- salt and black pepper to taste

Instructions
- Peel sweet potatoes and slice them into tiny pieces. Wash the kale and green onions and slice them into small pieces.
- In a large pan, sauté sweet potatoes with heated olive oil over medium heat until tender. Season with salt and pepper. Stir in the chopped onions and sauté for a few mins until tender.
- Fry the desired number of eggs in a separate pan.
- Toss in chopped kale with the sweet potato combination and cook until wilted, seasoning with salt and pepper as required.
- Place the fried egg on top and serve.

Nutrition Information
Calories: 102kcal, Carbohydrates: 9.6g, Protein: 6g, Fat: 7g

164. Healthy Freezer Breakfast Sandwiches
Prep Time: 15 Mins, Cook Time: 10 Mins, Servings: 6
Ingredients
- 6 English muffins
- 6 cheese slices
- 6 cooked sausage patties
- 6 eggs

Instructions
- Cook the eggs until the yolks are no longer runny.
- If desired, lightly brown each muffin.
- Layer the muffin base with sausage, egg, and cheese.
- Let the cheese melt.
- Put the muffin top on top of the cheese.
- Use plastic wrap to wrap each sandwich and place them in a freezer.
- To reheat, take from plastic and cover in a paper towel loosely. Microwave for 1-2 min, or until well heated.

Nutrition Information
Calories: 328, Carbohydrates: 30g, Protein: 21g, Fats: 15g

165. Toddler-Approved Banana Mini Muffins
Prep Time: 10 mins, Cook Time: 15 mins, Servings: 30 mini muffins
Ingredients
- 2 cups all-purpose flour
- ½ cup packed brown sugar
- 1 tsp crushed cinnamon
- 1 tsp baking soda
- 1/4 tsp salt
- 1 cup water
- 1/4 cup butter
- 2 cups pulped bananas
- Mini cupcake liners (30) or cooking spray

Instructions
- Heat the oven before cooking to 350 degrees Fahrenheit. Spray tiny muffin tins with cooking spray or line with small cupcake liners.
- Mix water with butter in a wide mixing dish. Combine the flour, cinnamon, salt, brown sugar, and baking soda. Add the banana and mix well.
- Fill each tiny muffin cup halfway with batter.
- Bake in a preheated oven for 18 mins, or until a toothpick inserted in the center comes out clean. Put it aside for 5 min to cool.
- Keep refrigerated or frozen for more than three months.

Nutrition Information
Calories: 68kcal, Carbohydrates: 12g, Protein: 3g, Fats: 5g

166. Fajita Breakfast Casserole
Prep Time: 10 mins, Cook Time: 2 mins, Servings: 2
Ingredients
- 1 tbsp olive oil
- 1/2 cup sliced onion
- 1 1/2 cup sliced bell peppers
- 4 eggs
- 1/2 tsp minced garlic
- 1/2 tsp vegetable seasoning
- Salt and pepper to taste
- For garnishing: limes, cilantro, and avocado

Instructions
- Add the oil, onions, garlic, sliced bell peppers, and seasoning and cook on high heat for 1 to 2 mins.
- Put the eggs on the veggies. Reduce the heat to a medium setting.
- Cover the lid and cook for approximately 1 to 2 mins, or until the eggs are cooked.
- Turn the flame off and top with limes, avocado, and cilantro. Serve with a toast.

Nutrition Information
Calories: 241kcal, Carbohydrates: 11g, Protein: 12g, Fat: 16g

167. DIY Just Crack an Egg Recipe
Prep Time: 1 min, Cook Time: 3 mins, Servings: 1
Ingredients
- 1/4 cup cooked and diced sweet potato
- 1/4 cup low-sodium diced bacon
- 1 tbsp cheddar cheese
- 1/8 cup diced onions
- 1/8 cup diced bell peppers
- 1/8 cup low-sodium diced ham
- 1/8 cup cooked and diced sweet potato
- 1 tbsp cheddar cheese
- Meat Lovers/High Protein Egg Scramble:

- ¼ cup homemade turkey sausage
- ⅛ cup low-sodium diced bacon
- ⅛ cup low-sodium diced ham
- Veggie Lovers Egg Scramble:
- ⅛ cup diced mushrooms
- ⅛ cup chopped broccoli
- ⅛ cup chopped cauliflower
- 1 tbsp diced onion
- ⅛ cup diced bell peppers
- Anti-inflammatory Egg Scramble:
- ⅛ cup cooked and diced sweet potato
- ⅛ cup homemade turkey sausage
- ⅛ cup chopped broccoli
- 1 tbsp diced onions
- Southwest Egg Scramble:
- ¼ cup diced poblano peppers/Anaheim
- ⅛ cup canned black beans
- ⅛ cup chopped bell peppers
- ⅛ cup chopped kale
- ⅛ cup homemade turkey sausage

Instructions
- To make your desired egg, spray a zip-lock bag with oil and add the desired ingredients.
- Add one egg (or two) to it and give it a good stir.
- Pour the egg mixture into a microwave-safe bowl, cup, or Mason jar.
- Microwave for 1 and a half minutes, then whisk and cook for another minute.

Nutrition Information
Calories: 86kcal, Carbohydrates: 7g, Protein: 3g, Fat: 5g

168. Mocha Coffee Creamer with Almond Milk
Prep Time: 10 mins, Cook Time: 2 mins, Servings: 17
Ingredients
- 1 can unsweetened full-fat coconut milk
- 3 tbsp unsweetened almond milk unsweetened
- 2 tbsp coconut crystals
- 2 tsp cocoa powder
- 1 tsp vanilla extract

Instructions
- Combine vanilla, coconut milk and almond milk, coconut crystals, and cocoa powder in a small saucepan.
- Stir constantly on low flame until the coconut crystals and cocoa powder are fully dissolved.
- Turn off the flame. Allow resting for 20 mins for a cooling period before transferring to an airtight glass container/bottle.
- Refrigerate for up to 3 months or freeze for 5-7 days.

Nutrition Information
Calories: 60kcal, Carbohydrates: 3g, Protein: 1g, Fat: 6g

169. Dairy-Free Egg Bites
Prep Time: 10 mins, Cook Time: 20 mins, Servings: 7
Ingredients
- 8 eggs
- 3/4 cup crumbled tofu
- 1/4 cup unsweetened almond milk
- 1/2 tsp onion powder
- 1/2 tsp pepper
- 1 tsp parsley
- 1 tsp dried dill
- 14 slices turkey bacon
- Salt to taste

Instructions
- Heat the oven before baking to 375 °F.
- Place turkey bacon (2 1/2 slices) in each cupcake tin.
- Blender all remaining Ingredients for 30-60 secs or until smooth.
- Fill each cup with egg mixture and seal the top with Aluminum foil.
- Place the tray on the oven's top rack. Put a cake pan filled with water on the lower rack of the oven under the egg bits.
- Cook the egg bits for 20 mins and allow them to cool for about 5 mins.

Nutrition Information
Calories: 204kcal, Carbohydrates: 2g, Protein: 17g, Fat: 14g

170. Turkey Chorizo Breakfast Casserole with Eggs
Prep Time: 10 mins, Cook Time: 20 mins, Servings: 4
Ingredients
- Turkey Chorizo
- 1 lb. minced turkey
- 1 tsp onion powder
- 1 tsp garlic salt
- 4 tbsp chili powder
- 1 tbsp cumin
- 1 tbsp crushed coriander
- 1 tbsp oregano
- 1 tsp pepper
- 2 tsp paprika
- ¼ tsp cinnamon
- 1 tsp crushed red pepper flakes
- 1 tbsp fennel seed
- ¼ cup apple cider vinegar
- Chorizo and Eggs Casserole
- ½ lb. homemade turkey chorizo
- 8 eggs
- ¼ cup unsweetened almond milk
- ½ tsp pepper
- 1 chopped red bell pepper
- 1 chopped zucchini

Instructions
- Mix the onion and garlic powder, cumin, turkey, chili powder, red pepper flakes, oregano, paprika, powdered coriander, pepper, cinnamon, fennel spice, and apple cider vinegar. Toss the ingredients together with your hands and leave it for a few mins to marinate.
- Whisk the eggs with almonds and leave them aside.
- Coat a pan with nonstick cooking spray and place it over medium heat. Add the marinated turkey, zucchini, and bell peppers once the pan is heated. Break up any big bits using a spatula. Cook for 10 mins, or until the veggies are tender and the chorizo is fully cooked.
- Lower the flame and crack the eggs on top of the chorizo and veggies. Stir constantly until the eggs are scrambled.
- Serve with corn or whole wheat flour tortillas.

Nutrition Information
Calories: 325 kcal, Carbohydrates: 13 g, Protein: 41 g, Fat: 13g

171. Starbucks Egg White Bites with Red Pepper and Turkey Bacon
Prep Time: 10 mins, Cook Time: 8 mins, Servings: 7
Ingredients
- 14 slices uncooked turkey bacon
- 1 cup chopped spinach
- 1 large, diced tomato
- 1 cup diced bell peppers
- 12 egg whites
- ¾ cup plain Greek yogurt
- ¾ cup cottage cheese
- 1 tsp dried basil
- 1 cup shredded mozzarella cheese

Instructions
- Heat oven before baking to 375 °F.
- Coat a muffin tray with nonstick spray. Fold a turkey bacon piece inside of each cupcake pan cup.
- Combine the bell peppers, spinach, and tomatoes in a mixing dish. Then, evenly spread the veggies into each cupcake pan's cups.
- Whisk the egg whites and add the cottage and mozzarella cheese, Greek yogurt, and basil. Mix everything well.

- Divide the egg mixture equally among the cups. Wrap foil around the pan.
- Place a baking pan filled with water on the oven's lowest shelf. Then, lay the egg bits on the top shelf of the oven.
- Cook the egg bits for 20 minutes and cool for 5 minutes before serving.

Nutrition Information
Calories: 224kcal, Carbohydrates: 4g, Protein: 22g, Fat: 12g

172. Flour Free Pancakes
Prep Time: 5 mins, Cook Time: 10 mins, Servings: 4
Ingredients
- 6 eggs
- 1 tsp vanilla extract
- 1 tbsp cinnamon
- 1 tbsp olive oil
- ¾ cup cottage cheese
- ¾ cup uncooked rolled oats

Instructions
- Heat a pan (lightly coated with nonstick cooking spray) over medium heat.
- Combine the olive oil, eggs, vanilla, cinnamon, oats, and cottage cheese in a blender. Blend on high speed until completely smooth.
- Pour a batter (1/4 cup) onto the heated pan. Cook for a few mins until bubbles appear on top and the edges begin to dry. Make the pancakes with the same process.
- Serve with fruits, butter, or maple syrup on top.

Nutrition Information
Calories: 221kcal, Carbohydrates: 14g, Protein: 16g, Fat: 11g

173. Low Carb Cloud Bread with Greek Yogurt
Prep Time: 10 mins, Cook Time: 25 mins, Servings: 1
Ingredients
- 3 eggs
- 3 tbsp plain Greek Yogurt
- ¼ tsp baking powder

Instructions
- Heat the oven to 300 °F before baking. Line a baking tray with parchment paper.
- Whisk the egg yolks and Greek yogurt together until smooth.
- Whip egg whites with 1/4 tsp baking powder until frothy.
- Mix the egg whites with the beaten egg yolk mixture.
- Drop the scoopful of batter with a cookie spoon and gently tap it on the counter to release any large air bubbles before baking.
- Bake at 300°F for 25 mins or until lightly browned. Sprinkle some sea salt on top and place it on a cooling rack.

Nutrition Information
Calories: 224kcal, Carbohydrates: 3g, Protein: 21g, Fat: 13g

174. Healthy Copycat Starbucks Egg Bites
Prep Time: 10 mins, Cook Time: 8 mins, Servings: 7
Ingredients
- 6 eggs
- 1 cup grated cheddar cheese
- 3/4 cup cottage cheese
- 3/4 cup Greek yogurt plain
- 1/2 cup sun-dried tomatoes
- 1/4 cup basil, chopped
- 1 tsp salt

Instructions
- Mix the eggs, salt, cheddar and cottage cheese, and yogurt in a blender. Mix all items in a blender for 30 secs.
- Grease 2 silicone food molds with coconut or olive oil. Inside of each cup, put the sun-dried tomatoes and basil. Fill each cup with batter (approximately 3/4 capacity).
- Wrap the silicone molds with foil securely. Fill the Instant Pot with water (2 cups) and set the rack on the pan's bottom. Stack the molds (slightly off-set) on top of the rack.
- Cook for 8 mins on high pressure. Allow the pressure to subside naturally. Remove the silicone molds and set them aside to cool. Remove the foil from the mold and pop the eggs out. Refrigerate for 1 week in an airtight container. When ready to eat, microwave for 30 secs.

Nutrition Information
Calories: 170kcal, Carbohydrates: 6g, Protein: 15g, Fat: 10g

175. Zucchini and Sausage Breakfast Casserole Skillet
Prep Time: 10 mins, Cook Time: 40 mins, Servings: 4
Ingredients
- 1 tbsp butter
- 3 eggs beaten
- 3 cups grated zucchini grated
- 1/3 cup grated Pepper Jack cheese
- 1/2 cup diced red bell pepper
- 1/4 cup chopped onion finely
- ½ lb. turkey sausage

Instructions
- Heat the oven before cooking to 350 degrees Fahrenheit.
- Cook the onions and zucchini in melted butter until the onions are transparent and the zucchini is tender.
- Stir in the sausage and cook until it is thoroughly done.
- In an oiled pan (8x8), toss the onions, zucchini, and sausage mixture.
- In a separate pan, make the scrambled eggs and sprinkle them on the sausage.
- Spread cheese on top and bake for 35 to 40 mins.

Nutrition Information
Calories: 221kcal, Carbohydrates: 6g, Protein: 19g, Fat: 14g

176. Sweet Homemade Sausage Recipe
Prep Time: 8 mins, Cook Time: 6 mins, Servings: 4
Ingredients:
- 1 lb. minced turkey/chicken
- 1 tsp cinnamon
- 1 tsp nutmeg
- ½ chopped green apple
- 1/4 cup low-sodium bone broth
- 2 tbsp coconut oil
- Salt to taste

Instructions
- Combine all the listed Ingredients with hands and make 12 tiny patties.
- Heat the oil in a big skillet and cook patties in heated oil. Cook each side for 5 mins or bake in a preheated oven (375 degrees F) for 25 mins, or until its internal temperature reaches 165°F.

Nutrition Information
Calories: 206 kcal, Carbohydrates: 4 g, Protein: 28 g, Fat: 9 g

177. Muffin Egg Cups
Prep Time: 9 min, Cook Time: 26 mins, Servings: 6
Ingredients
- 12 large eggs
- 2 cups chopped broccoli
- Cooking spray
- Salt and pepper to taste

Instructions
- Heat the oven before cooking to 350°F and coat the muffin tins with a cooking spray.
- In a large mixing bowl, beat a dozen eggs with some salt and pepper3. Prepare the vegetables as per the pack Instructions and set them aside to cool.
- Chop the veggies and fill all muffin cups with good vegetables.
- Add cheese on top and pour the whisked eggs.
- Bake for 20 to 25 mins, or unless a toothpick in the middle comes out clear.

Nutrition Information
Calories: 136kcal, Carbohydrates: 3g, Protein: 12g, Fat: 8g

178. Chewy Granola Bars with Almond & Cranberry - No Bake
Prep Time: 20 Mins, Cook Time: 5 Mins, Servings: 1
Ingredients
- ¼ cup coconut oil
- ½ cup peanut butter, preferably creamy and unsalted
- 2 cups rolled oats
- 1 tsp pure vanilla extract
- ½ cup shredded unsweetened coconut
- 1 tsp ground flaxseeds
- ½ cup oat flour
- ½ tsp ground cinnamon
- 1/8 tsp salt leave out the salt if your nut butter is salted
- 1 tbsp dried cranberries divided (use organic if needed)
- 1 tbsp sunflower seeds
- 2 tbsp raw almonds divided

Instructions
- Take a (9x9) square pan (for thicker bars) or a 9x13 rectangle pan (for thinner bars). Line with foil or parchment, gently coated with cooking spray.

Make Date Paste:
- In a medium saucepan at medium-low heat, combine the dates and water. While the mixture is heated up, mash it down using a fork. Continue swirling and mashing. After around 3-5 mins, the dates will get softened. It's OK if some pieces remain; as long as the paste is smooth, it's ready to use.

Make Granola Bars:
- Add some peanut butter and coconut oil to the saucepan after smoothing and melting the date mixture. Remove from heat after the mixture gets soft and the coconut oil becomes melted, stirring regularly (about 1 min). Remove the pan and add the vanilla essence.
- Gently fold in the shredded coconut, oat flour, ground cinnamon, and salt (if using).
- Take a spatula or big spoon, carefully fold in the flaxseeds, and roll oats. Combine the half almonds, sunflower seeds, and cranberries in a mixing bowl.
- Pour the granola mix into the pan that has been prepared.
- Use a flat spatula, spread the mixture evenly, and push down firmly. Evenly distribute the dried cranberries and remaining almonds. To flatten, press down hard with a spatula once more. To set, chill for 1 hour in the freezer, 3 hours in the refrigerator, or overnight.
- Remove the frozen or chilled bars from the refrigerator and place them on a cutting board with the foil overhang. Cut into rectangles using a sharp knife.
- Keep the bars in an airtight container.

Nutrition Information
Calories: 215 kcal, Carbohydrates: 26 g, Protein: 4 g, Fats: 11 g

179. One Bowl Blueberry Oatmeal Breakfast Cookies
Prep Time: 10 Mins, Cook Time: 20 Mins, Servings: 12
Ingredients
- ½ cup of oat flour or tapioca
- ½ cup flax + chia meal
- ½ tsp soda baking
- ¼ tsp freshly ground salt
- 1½ cup old fashioned oatmeal
- 3 tsp cinnamon
- ½ cup applesauce
- 1 cup mashed banana
- 2 Tbsp chia seeds
- 4 Tbsp coconut oil
- ½ tsp vanilla
- ¾ cup blueberries
- ¼ cup sorghum (molasses, honey, maple syrup)

Instructions
- Preheat your oven to 350°F and line a baking sheet with parchment paper.
- In a large mixing dish, combine chia meal, flax, tapioca, salt, oatmeal, cinnamon, baking soda, and chia seeds. Mix thoroughly.
- Combine applesauce, coconut oil, mashed banana, sweetener, and vanilla extract in a mixing bowl.
- Mix until everything is well combined.
- Lastly, fold in the blueberries.
- Place a spoonful of the mixture over the cookie sheet, press down gently. Continue until the cookie sheet is completely loaded.
- Cook for 20-25 mins, or until well done.
- Place over a cooling rack. Keep refrigerated in an airtight container.

Nutrition Information
Calories: 110 kcal, Carbohydrates: 29 g, Protein: 0 g, Fats: 0.2 g

180. Low Carb Pizza Casserole
Prep Time: 20 Mins, Cook Time: 55 Mins, Servings: 4
Ingredients
- 14 oz cauliflower florets
- 2.5 oz Pepperoni
- 2 lb of Italian Sausage
- 1 tbsp of Olive Oil
- 8 oz sliced Mushrooms
- 1 Pepper, green
- 12 oz of Mozzarella cheese
- 1.5 cups Pasta Sauce
- ¼ cup powdered Parmesan cheese
- 1 tsp of Italian Seasoning

Instructions
- Cauliflower must be steamed. 1 cup of water inside a microwave dish with sliced cauliflower & Microwave on high for 3 mins, or till the cauliflower is soft, covered with a moist paper towel. Don't overcook your food!
- Using a paper towel, gently dry the cauliflower. Remove from the equation.
- Preheat your oven to around 400 degrees Fahrenheit.
- Cook your Italian Sausage for about 15 mins in a big pan over medium-high heat. Remove the extra fat from the sausage when cooking and keep it aside.
- To drain extra water, sauté mushroom in the same pan with olive oil approximately 10 mins over medium to high heat. When you're finished, set it away.
- Spray a 13-by-9-inch casserole dish with non - stick cooking spray, then put 12 cups spaghetti sauce over the bottom.
- In a large mixing bowl, combine the cauliflower, Italian sausage, mushroom, & peppers. Toss everything together until it's evenly distributed.
- Half of the mixture should be spread in the dish.12 cup spaghetti sauce, 12 pepperonis, and 6 oz mozzarella cheese
- Distribute the remaining topping mix over the cheese, then top with the pepperonis, ½ cup of pasta sauce, then 6 oz mozzarella cheese.
- Combine grated Parmesan cheese & Italian Seasoning in a small bowl.
- Top the dish with the Grated parmesan mixture plus 10 pieces of pepperoni.
- Bake for 30 minutes, until the cheese, is completely melted and the dish is warmed through.

Nutrition Information
Calories: 519 kcal, Carbohydrates: 7 g, Protein: 27 g, Fat: 43 g

181. The Best Keto Meatloaf Muffins
Prep Time: 5 Min, Cook Time: 15 Mins, Servings: 11
Ingredients:
- 1 lb of Ground Beef
- Chopped Onion one cup
- One Egg

- 1 cup breadcrumbs
- ¼ tsp Onion Powder
- ¼ tsp Garlic Powder
- ¼ Tsp Italian Seasoning
- ¼ tsp Salt
- ¼ tsp Black pepper

Instruction:
- Preheat your oven to around 350-degree Fahrenheit and butter a muffin tray.
- Add ground beef, egg, chopped onion, pork panko, onion powder, Italian Seasoning, salt, and pepper in a mixing bowl, then mix until thoroughly mixed.
- A quarter cup of the ingredients should be formed into a puck and placed inside a muffin tray.
- Top each small meatloaf with half tbsp Kitchen Ketchup.
- Bake for approximately 15 mins.

Nutrition Information
Calories 171 kcal, Fat 10.8g, Carbs 2.5 g, proteins 15.7g

182. Bacon Cheeseburger Casserole
Prep Time:30 Mins Cook Time:35 Mins Servings: 10
- 1 tbsp of avocado oil
- 1.5 lb of ground beef
- 1 tsp of onion powder
- 1 tsp parsley
- 1 tsp garlic powder
- 1 tsp salt
- ½ tsp pepper
- 20 oz cauliflower rice frozen
- ⅓ cup coconut floor
- ¼ tsp salt

Sauce
- 1 tbsp butter
- 1 tbsp coconut flour
- 1 ½ cups cream
- 2 tbsp mustard
- 8 oz cheddar cheese

Instructions
- Preheat your oven to around 400 degrees Fahrenheit. Place your bacon on a baking dish in an equal layer, then bake for twenty Mins or till crisp.
- In a big pan, heat the oil and put the ground beef. Sauté till golden brown. Combine the onion powder, salt, parsley, garlic powder & pepper in a mixing bowl. Drain with a spoon & place it in a bowl to keep it warm.
- Cook for 5 min in a microwaveable dish with iced cauliflower rice. Mix in the coconut flour & salt well. Place aside.
- When the bacon is golden, transfer it to a paper towel-lined pan. When completely cool, cut into pieces.

Prepare the Sauce
- Mix the coconut flour after adding the butter to the skillet. Lower the heat, then continue to whisk until the flour is incorporated with the butter. Continue to whisk in the cream & mustard till it thickens.

Assembly
- Half cup sauce should be spread on the bottom of a 9 X 13 baking dish.
- Distribute the cauliflower combination equally over the sauce.
- Spread 4 oz of cheddar cheese over the rice.
- Distribute the ground meat equally over the cheese.
- Pour ½ of the leftover sauce well over beef.
- Spread the leftover cheddar on the sauce.
- Add the leftover sauce over the top.
- Wrap & bake for 30 mins.
- Uncover, then bake for a further 5 mins.
- Let it cool for 15-20 mins before serving.

Nutrition information
Calories: 504kcal, Carbohydrates: 7g, Protein: 21g, Fat: 42g

183. Protein brownie
Prep Time: 15 Min, Cook Time: 25 Min Servings: 5
Ingredients:
- Choco protein powder 32-34 grams
- 1 tbsp of coconut flour
- 2 tbsp of sweetener
- ½ tsp baking powder
- 1-2 tbsp of cocoa powder
- 1 egg
- A quarter cup of milk
- 1 tbsp of Choco chips

Instructions
- Set aside a cereal dish or a shallow mug that has been greased.
- Put the protein powder, baking powder, coconut flour, Sugar, & cocoa powder inside a bowl and stir well.
- Mix the egg & milk in a bowl, then put into the dry Ingredients and stir until well combined. If preferred, sprinkle with chocolate chips.
- Transfer from the microwave after 1 min and eat right away.

Nutrition information
Calories: 125kcal, Carbohydrates: 6g, Protein: 14g, Fat: 5g

184. BLT Chicken Salad
Prep Time: 5 min, Cook Time: 20 min, Servings: 4
Ingredients
- 2 boneless chickens
- 5 pieces of bacon
- ¼ cup of green onion chopped
- ½ cup cherry tomatoes
- ½ cup of mayonnaise
- ½ tsp of grounded black pepper

Instructions
- Cover chicken breasts with cold water in a medium saucepan until both breasts are filled with at least 1 inch of water.
- Bring to a simmer in an open saucepan on the fire.
- Low the heat and cover the pot with a cover.
- Remove the chicken from the stove after 15 min of simmering.
- Cook the bacon just on the stove as the chicken cooks — fry till crispy over moderate flame.
- Place fried bacon on a paper towel to absorb excess oil before chopping into chew pieces.
- Mix mayonnaise, chopped onion, & black pepper in a mixing bowl.
- Remove the chicken breast piece from the water after it's done cooking & shred it on a cutting board.
- Mix the shredded chicken, green onion, mayo and pepper combination, cherry tomatoes, & bacon in a mixing bowl.
- Combine all the Ingredients inside a large mixing bowl and stir until well blended.
- Enjoy right now or save it for later.

Nutrition information
Calories: 172.3kcal, Carbohydrates: 21.3g, Protein: 2.2g, Fat: 9.8

185. Golden red & orange Bell pepper soup recipe
Prep Time: 15 min, Cook Time: 35 min, Servings: 6
Ingredients:
- A quarter cup of extra virgin oil
- ½ diced small onion
- 2 carrots diced and peeled
- 1 celery stalk
- Sea salt & black pepper
- 8 bell peppers finely chopped
- 1 sweet potato chopped
- 4 cups vegetable broth
- 3 tsp of chopped marjoram

- sliced avocado
- fresh cilantro, finely chopped

Instructions
- Heat the olive oil inside a big pot over low heat. Combine the onions, celery, carrot, and a sprinkle of salt & black pepper in a large mixing bowl. Cook for 4 mins.
- Cook, occasionally stirring, till the bell peppers are tender, about 6 mins.
- Combine the potatoes & broth in a large mixing bowl. Add salt & pepper, then cover it with a lid.
- Bring the water to a simmer. Reduce the heat and stir in the marjoram. Cook for about 20 mins.
- Allow the broth to cool before transferring it to a mixer in batches, then pureeing until it gets smooth. Dilute the soup using water if necessary. If required, adjust the taste by adding salt and black pepper. Let the broth be heated in the pan till ready to serve.

Nutrition information
Calories, 137 Kcal, Carbohydrates 11 g, Proteins: 6 g, Fat: 9 g

186. Instant Pot Chicken Chile Verde
Prep Time: 25 Mins Cook Time: 20 Mins Servings: 5

Ingredients
- Anaheim peppers, remove seeds and ribs
- 1 tbsp of garlic minced
- 2 serrano peppers
- Chicken broth 1-32 oz
- 1 Sliced onion
- 2 chicken breasts
- 2 chicken thighs
- Cilantro one bundle
- 6 tomatillos
- 1 tbsp cumin
- ½ tsp salt
- ½ tsp pepper
- 1 cup water
- Half red onion

Instructions
- In a pressure cooker, combine the chicken, diced peppers, white onion, diced peppers, tomatillos & garlic.
- Add chicken broth & water to cover the items.
- Cumin, salt, pepper, and Maggi to taste.
- Set the Pressure and the time to 20 mins. Allow for the discharge of natural Pressure.
- When the Pressure subsides, remove the chicken, and puree the soup in a blender. Return the shredded chicken to the soup.
- In a bowl, combine 1/3 cup of water & ¾ of the cilantro. B lending with immersion. This should be added to the soup.
- To serve, top with additional cilantro & red onion.

Nutrition information
Calories, 112 Kcal, Carbohydrates 10 g, Proteins: 7 g, Fat: 2 g

187. Keto Spaghetti Squash Au Gratin
Prep Time: 20 Min, Cook Time: 20 Min Servings: 4-5

Ingredients
- 1 spaghetti squash
- 2 tbsp of butter
- 1 onion minced
- 2 minced garlic cloves
- 1 tsp of fresh thyme minced
- 1 cup of shredded parmesan
- ¼ cup cream
- Salt & pepper

Instructions
- Preheat the broiler to high.
- Extract the noodle-like filaments from the spaghetti squash utilizing your preferred method, drain the excess water in a strainer, and leave it aside.
- In a skillet, melt butter on moderate heat. In the same skillet, sauté the onion, thyme, and garlic for about 1 min or until fragrant.
- Toss in the strained spaghetti squash until everything is well combined. Combine the cream & half of the cheese in a mixing bowl. Boil for 5 mins, then sprinkle with the remaining cheese and grill for 3-5 mins. Serve with more thyme over the top.

Nutrition information:
Calories, 115 Kcal, Carbohydrates 6 g, Proteins: 8 g, Fat: 7 g

188. The Best No-Carb Cloud Bread with Only 4 Ingredients
Prep Time: 10 Mins, COOK TIME: 20 Mins, Servings: 6

Ingredients
- 3 eggs
- 3 Tbsp cream cheese
- ¼ tsp baking powder

Instructions
- Preheat your oven to around 150 Celsius.
- Separate your eggs; the whites must be free of yolk.
- Combine the egg yolks, sweetener, and cream cheese in a mixing dish and whisk till smooth; leave aside.
- In another bowl, whisk the egg whites with ¼ tsp of baking powder until they are frothy. It takes around 5-6 Mins to beat your eggs to the appropriate consistency with an electric blender.
- Slowly mix the yolk into the egg white, mixing carefully & slowly so as not to break the fluffiness.
- Take the following steps as soon as possible. Otherwise, the mixture will begin to melt: Place the mixture over a greased sheet in 10 to 12 even circles, sprinkle with rosemary & your chosen spices, then bake.
- Bake for 17 to 20 mins.
- Then broil for 1 min, occasionally stirring, till golden brown. Remember to keep an eye on them at this point to prevent them from burning.
- When you take it out of the oven, it's ready to eat right away!

Nutrition information
Calories, 143 Kcal, Carbohydrates 10 g, Proteins: 9 g, Fat: 3 g

189. Cajun Sausage Cauliflower Rice (Keto & Low Carb)
Prep Time: 25 Min, Cook Time: 35 Min Servings: 5

Ingredients
- cauliflower rice froze 6 cups
- 1 pack of sliced andouille sausage
- 1 bell pepper one
- 1 yellow onion
- 1 tbsp of olive oil
- 1 tbsp of Cajun Seasoning
- Pepper and salt

Instructions
- In a skillet over moderate heat, heat 2 tbsp olive oil; cook the chopped bell pepper & onions with the olive oil for a few mins.
- Cook for 3-4 mins or till the sausages begins to brown.
- In the same pan, put cauliflower rice frozen and the Cajun spice; mix and simmer for another 5 mins, or till the cauliflower rice gets warmed.
- Taste to determine if you need to add extra Cajun Seasoning. Add a pinch of salt, garlic powder, pepper for taste.

Nutrition Information
Calories, 121 Kcal, Carbohydrates 7 g, Proteins: 12 g, Fat: 4 g

190. Vegan Lentil, Haricot Bean & Chickpea Soup
Prep Time: 25 Min, Cook Time: 35 Min Servings: 5

Ingredients
- 2 tbsp of olive oil
- 1 finely chopped red onion
- 3 chopped garlic cloves
- 400g chopped tomatoes
- 850ml of vegetable stock
- 140g red lentils

- 200g of chickpeas
- 100g of haricot beans
- Lemon juice 2tbsp
- ½ finely chopped red and green pepper
- Extra virgin olive oil
- freshly ground pepper and sea salt
- Basil leaves for garnishing

Instructions
- Sauté the onions and cloves in a small pan until brown. Combine the onion, oil, & garlic. Bring the remaining Ingredients to a simmer, then reduce to low heat and cook for 20 mins. If necessary, add extra boiling water. Make it chunky in a mixer if you prefer it that way. Season. Test your taste buds. Garnish with basil leaves & a spray of extra virgin olive oil. Serve with crusty bread.

Nutrition Information
Calories: 175 Kcal, Carbohydrates: 12 g, Proteins: 16 g, Fat: 9 g

191. Healthy Strawberry and Lemon Sugar-Free Popsicles
Prep Time: 10 Mins, Cook Time: 4 Hr 10 Mins, Servings: 10
Ingredients
- ½ cup of fresh lemon juice
- 1 and ½ of cup water
- ½ cup of sweetener
- 1 lb frozen strawberries

Instructions
- In a mixing blender, assemble all the ingredients.
- Stir for 45-60 sec, or until the mixture is smooth.
- Fill the popsicle mold halfway with the combined mixture.
- Put the popsicle sticks in the mold and cover it with the lid.
- keep for 4 Hr in the freezer
- To soften the popsicles, take the popsicle mold from the freezer and wash the bottom and sides of the mold underwater.
- Dish the popsicles straight from the mold.

Nutrition information
Calories: 17 Kcal, Carbohydrates: 3 g, Protein: 7 g, Fats: 9 g

192. Lemon Garlic Butter Salmon Baked in Foil
Prep Time:10 Mins Cook Time:10 Mins, Servings: 4-6
Ingredients
- 1.5 lb of salmon fillet
- 1 tbsp of olive oil
- 3 cloves of garlic
- 2 tbsp of lemon juice
- 1 tsp of Italian Seasoning
- ¼ tsp of salt
- black pepper
- 2 tbsp of butter

Instructions
- Preheat your oven to around 400 degrees Fahrenheit. Put a big slice of aluminum foil in a baking dish large enough to contain all the salmon.
- Using olive oil, lightly coat the foil. On top, arrange the fish fillets.
- 1 tbsp olive oil drizzled on the top and garlic equally distributed. Top with Seasoning, salt, & pepper, then drizzle with fresh lemon juice. Make a butter smear. Seal the foil around the fish.
- Bake it for 10-15 mins or till salmon readily flakes. Serve right away.

Nutrition information
Calories: 328kcal, Fat: 20g, Carbs: 1g, Protein: 34g

193. Keto Chicken Enchiladas
Prep Time: 10 Min, Cook Time: 25 MIN, Servings: 4
Ingredients
- 2 lb of chicken
- 1-2 tbsp olive oil
- 1 cup diced onion
- 1-4 green chilis
- 1 tsp of cumin
- ½ tsp of chili powder
- 1 jar of enchilada sauce
- 2 cups of shredded cheese
- non-stick cooking spray

Instructions
- Preheat your oven to 350 degrees Fahrenheit. Preheat the olive oil in a frying pan at medium heat. Cook for 3-4 Mins, or until the onions soften.
- Cook till the mouth chicken is golden exterior, then add the cinnamon and chili powder. The poultry will not be thoroughly done at this time and will continue to cook inside the oven. Mix in the green chilis that have been drained.
- You can use fried chicken. Reduced carbs enchiladas are a great way to use up remaining shredded chicken.
- Place a generous dollop of enchilada sauce solely on a single side of every tortilla, then spread it out evenly.
- Place roughly half a cup of chicken in the center of the tortilla.
- Add a good amount of cheese on the top.
- Put the tortillas inside the baking tray, either side down or up, in the baking tray.
- Overtop the keto chicken enchiladas, add the leftover enchilada sauce.
- So spread the remaining cheese over the surface of the low sugar enchiladas recipe.
- Baking and Serving
- Bake for approximately 15-20 mins, or till the cheese has melted & the meat is cooked through.
- Serve with avocado, salsa, sour cream, or chives just on the side and garnish with cilantro if preferred.

Nutrition Information
Calories: 500 kcal, Carbohydrates: 8 g, Protein: 42 g, Fat: 29 g

194. Sour Cream Chicken Enchiladas
Prep Time: 5 Min, Cook Time: 30 Min, Servings: 6
Ingredients:
- 3 tbsp of butter
- 6 tsp of water
- 2 cups of chicken broth
- ½ tsp of salt
- ⅛ tsp of chili powder
- ¼ tsp dried oregano
- 4 oz of green chiles
- 3 whole chicken breasts
- 1 cup of sour cream
- 3 cups of riced cauliflower
- 2 cups of grated cheese

Thickening (pick one)
- 3 Tbsp of Flour
- 1.5 Tbsp of Corn Starch
- 3 Tbsp of arrowroot powder

Instructions
- Melt the butter in a wide pan at medium heat.
- Put the thickening agent plus cold water into the skillet and whisk till smooth.
- Add the chicken broth. Stir for 2 to 3 mins till smooth & thickened.
- Stir in the salt, oregano, chili powder, green chilies, and chicken pieces. Simmer for fifteen min, covered, till fully cooked through.
- Remove the chicken from the skillet, turn heat to medium, and cut it into mouth-sized pieces.
- Return chicken & cauliflower rice to pan using the sour cream sauce.
- Mix well. 5 mins covered in the pan
- Cover with cheese, then melt.

- Serve.

Nutrition information
Calories: 456 kcal, Carbohydrates: 8 g, Protein: 36 g, Fat: 30 g

195. Healthy Breakfast Burritos
Prep Time: 20 mins Cook Time:18 mins Servings: 7
Ingredients
- 8 eggs
- ½ cup whipping cream
- 2 tbsp butter
- 1 lb of bacon
- 7 tortillas
- 1 ½ cups of cheddar cheese
- ¼ cup of white cheddar cheese
- ½ tsp of salt
- ½ tsp of pepper

Instructions
- Heat the butter over moderate flame.
- Whisk in the thickening agent and water until smooth.
- Pour the broth. Mix for 2–3 mins to smooth and thicken.
- Add the salt, chili powder, oregano, green chilies, then chicken. Cook covered for 15 Mins.
- Take chicken from pan, reduce heat to low, and slice.
- Add sour cream sauce over chicken and cauliflower rice.
- Blend well. 5 mins covered.
- Melt cheese on top.
- Serve.

Nutrition information
Calories: 405 kcal, Carbohydrates: 17g, Protein: 22g, Fat: 34g

196. Skinny Meatloaf Muffins with Barbecue Sauce
Prep Time: 15 Mins, Cook Time: 40 Mins, Servings: 12
Ingredients:
- 1 package of turkey breast
- 1 sliced whole-wheat bread
- 1 cup onions
- 1 egg
- 2 tbsp Worcestershire sauce
- ½ cup barbecue sauce
- ¼ tsp salt
- Fresh pepper

Instructions
- Preheat your oven to 350°F. Grease a standard muffin tray. Set aside.
- For crumbs: 1 whole-wheat toast Put in the food processor, then mix it until formed into crumbs.
- Stir in the sauce and 12 cup BBQ sauce. Mix well using hands or a big spoon.
- Fill the Nine muffin cups with the meatloaf mixture. ¾ tbsp barbecue sauce on each meatloaf muffin, distribute evenly.
- . Bake for 40 min. Loosen each muffin off the pan using a knife. Remove to a platter.

Nutrition Information
Calories: 203 kcal, Carbohydrates: 14 g, Protein: 22 g, Fat: 14g

197. Chipotle Chicken Fajita Bowls
Prep Time: 10 Mins, Cook Time: 20 Mins, Servings: 4
Ingredients
For Chicken
- 1–1.5 lb of chicken breast
- ½ to 1 tsp of chipotle powder
- 2 tbs of avocado oil
- 2 tbs of tomato paste
- 1 tsp of garlic salt
- Salt and pepper
- Juice of lime

For Cauliflower Rice
- 4 cups of riced cauliflower
- ¼ cup of chopped cilantro
- Juice of lime
- 1 tsp of garlic salt
- Salt & Pepper

For Fajita Veggies
- 4 sliced bell pepper
- 1 onion, sliced
- 1 tbs olive oil
- 1 tsp of garlic salt
- 1 tsp of cumin

Instructions
- Combine the oil, chipotle powder, lime juice, garlic salt, and tomato paste in a mixing bowl.
- Dry the chicken breasts, then put them inside a freezer bag along with the marinade.
- Spray a hot pan using cooking spray.
- Sauté riced cauliflower, salt garlic salt & pepper till soft.
- Set up a dish of cauliflower and lime juice plus cilantro.
- 1 tbsp oil and chopped onions 1 to 2 Mins sauté.
- Sauté bell peppers, salt, & cumin till soft yet crunchy. Set aside.
- Cook the chicken for 4 to 5 mins each side or until no pinker.
- Serve with cauliflower rice & fajita veggies.
- If preferred, add lime, cilantro, and avocado.

Nutrition information
Calories: 356, Carbohydrates: 12, Protein 42g, fat 34g

198. Keto French Toast
Prep Time: 5 Mins, Cook Time:10 Mins, Servings: 1
Ingredients
- 1 tbsp of coconut flour
- 1¼ tbsp butter melted
- 1 egg
- 1 tsp cream cheese
- ¼ tsp baking powder
- ¼ tsp cinnamon
- pinch nutmeg

For the French Toast
- 1 egg
- ¼ cup whipping cream
- ¼ tsp powdered Sugar

Instructions
- Melt the butter in a basin. Mix the remaining Ingredients, then whisk until mixed.
- Microwaves for 90 sec.
- Take from microwave then cool for a few Mins.
- Half the bread.
- 1 egg & ¼ cup of whipping cream whisked in a flat dish
- Dip bread in egg, then thick whipping cream.
- 1 tbsp of butter in a pan, crisp each side.
- Add ¼ tsp of sugar or sweetener
- Berries go well with Keto French Toast.

Nutrition information
Calories: 352kcal, Carbohydrates: 6g, Protein: 12g, Fat: 30g

199. Keto Pumpkin Bread
Prep Time:15 Mins, Cook Time:55 Mins, Servings: 10
Ingredients
For Bread:
- 5 eggs
- ½ cup of coconut oil
- 2 tbsp butter
- 1 cup of pumpkin puree
- 4 tsp pie spice
- 1 ½ cup powdered Sugar
- 10 tbsp of coconut flour
- ½ tsp salt
- 1 ½ tsp baking powder
- 1 tsp vanilla extract

For Icing:
- 4 tbsp powdered monk fruit

- 1 tsp butter
- 2 tsp whipping cream

Instructions

For Bread:
- Melt the coconut oil & butter together.
- Combine the eggs, Monk fruit Powdered, vanilla, pumpkin puree, pumpkin pie spices in a mixing bowl.
- Slowly drizzle in the melted coconut oil. Slowly drizzle in the heated coconut oil.
- Whisk together the salt, coconut flour, & baking powder.
- Combine the flour mixture with the other Ingredients and stir thoroughly.
- Put into a greased pan or line with parchment paper.
- Bake for 1 Hr & 15 mins in a 350-degree oven.

To make the icing:
- Melt the butter, carefully stir in the Lakanto Monk fruit Powdered.
- Pour in whipping cream till the mixture is thinned out. If necessary, add more or less.
- Drizzle on top of warm bread.

Nutrition Information
Calories: 253 kcal, Carbohydrates: 6 g, Protein: 12 g, Fat: 17 g

200. Keto Waffles
Prep Time: 20 Mins, Cook Time: 5 Mins, Servings: 4

Ingredients
- 9 tbsp coconut oil
- 6 tbsp butter
- 15 eggs
- 1 cup coconut flour
- 3 oz of cream cheese
- 3 tbsp whipping cream
- 5 tbsp of Swerve Confectioners
- 1 tbsp of cinnamon
- 1 ½ tsp of salt
- 1 ½ tsp baking powder

Instructions
- In a high-powered blender, mix all Ingredients. Remove the cover, scrape the sides using a spatula, and re-blend high.
- The waffle maker should be preheated, then put 1/3 cup batter over the waffle grid. Spread the batter with a spatula or, indeed, the measuring cup.
- Lakanto Maple Syrup is suitable for Ketogenic diets.

Nutrition information
Calories: 221 kcal, Carbohydrates: 4.2 g, Protein: 13.9 g, Fat: 4.3 g

201. Keto Chocolate Mint Buttons
Prep Time: 1 Hr, Cook Time: 2 Hr, Servings: 4

Ingredients
- 2 oz of softened cream cheese
- 2 ¼ cups erythritol
- ¼ tsp of mint extract
- 2 drops green food color
- ½ cup of whipping cream
- 5 oz of chocolate chips

Instructions
- Set aside one baking sheet lined with parchment paper.
- Add the softened cream cheese plus ½ cup of powdered sweetener in a small mixing bowl.
- Combine the mint essence and the green food coloring in a mixing bowl.
- Slowly add the remaining powdered sugar, about ½ cup at once, until everything is mixed. Clean down the bowl's edges as needed. Use a blender or your hands to blend the ingredients. Use it if you've got a stand mixer but be cautious not to overbeat the sugar mixture.
- Take the dough, then roll it into a ball on your palms. Each ball should be placed on a cooking pan.
- For around 1 Hr, freeze the mints till they are hard.
- In a medium microwave-safe bowl, mix the cream with chocolate and heat for 1-2 mins.
- Move the chocolate mixture to a sealed bag. Allow the chocolate to sit for a while when it has the consistency of yogurt.
- Using a Ziploc bag, cut the edge off and pour the chocolate into the center of every mint.
- Refrigerate for at least an Hr, so chocolate has hardened. Refrigerate for up to 2 weeks.

Nutrition information
Calories: 121kcal, Carbohydrates: 3g, Protein: 3g, Fat: 10g

202. Instant Pot Italian Sausage
Prep Time: 5 Mins, Cook Time: 6 Mins, Servings: 5

Ingredients
- 1-2 Tbsp of olive oil
- Italian sausages 5
- 1 cup of chicken broth

Instructions
- Put the Instant Pot at High sauté.
- In a small amount of olive oil, lightly brown Italian Sausage on both sides, approximately 2-3 mins each.
- Place the Italian Sausage on a platter, then transfer them from the Pressure Cooker.
- Place a shelf on the base of the saucepan and put the chicken broth into it, and the sausages links should be placed at the top of the rack.
- Cook approximately 6 mins on Pressure. Enjoy!

Nutrition information
Calories 230kcal, carbs 1g, Protein 25g, fat 23g

203. Chicken Sausage in Oven
Prep Time: 30 Min, Cook Time: 20, Min Servings: 4

Ingredients
- 1 lb of chicken sausage
- 1 sliced bell pepper
- ½ sliced yellow onion
- 8 oz of broccoli florets
- 1 lb of potatoes
- 2 tbsp of olive oil
- ½ tsp of sea salt
- 1/tsp black pepper

Instructions
- Preheat oven to 375°F with oven rack in the middle.
- Grease a baking sheet using cooking spray and otherwise olive oil, then arrange the chicken sausages on it.
- Cooking time for the chickens in the oven is 20 mins. After 10 mins, turn the chicken sausages using tongs. Cook the sausages for approximately 10-15 mins more, just until the temperature of your chicken reaches 165°F.

Nutrition Information
Calories: 173 kcal, Carbohydrates: 7 g, Protein: 14.2 g, Fat: 9.6 g

204. Stuffed Italian Sausage
Prep Time: 5 Mins, Cook Time: 30 Mins, Servings: 5

Ingredients
- 1 lb of Italian sausage links
- 1 cup of marinara sauce
- 5 strings of cheeses
- Italian Seasoning including fresh basil or parmesan cheese

Instructions
- Preheat your oven to 400°F with a rack in the middle.
- Slice your Italian sausage links vertically, barely cutting midway into the meat.
- Insert a string cheese within each sausage link, then crimp the top closed over the cheese. Fill a 9 by 9 baking tray with filled sausages.
- Pour the marinara sauce well over sausages.
- Bake the filled sausages for approximately 30 mins or till they achieve a temp of 160°F.

Nutrition Information
Calories: 133 kcal, Carbohydrates: 5.4 g, Protein: 9.2 g, Fat: 3.1 g

205. Keto Cranberry Sauce Recipe

Prep Time: 5 Mins, Cook Time: 20 Mins, Servings: 5
Ingredients
- 12 oz of cranberries
- ¾ cup of powdered sweetener
- 1 cinnamon
- 1 tsp of orange zest grated
- ¾ cup of water

Instructions
- combine your fresh cranberries, Sugar, orange zest, & water in a pan.
- Put the cranberry sauce to a simmer, stir, then cover.
- Boil approximately 15 mins till the cranberries explode and the sauce thickens. While cooking, stir the mixture often.
- Refrigerate the sauce for several Hr to solidify.
- It's served hot or cold.
- Refrigerate cranberry sauce for 2 weeks.

Nutrition Information
Calories: 108 kcal, Carbohydrates: 4 g, Protein: 7.4 g, Fat: 2.3 g

206. Cajun Slow Cooked Kielbasa
Prep Time: 10 Mins, Cook Time: 4 Hr, Servings: 8
Ingredients
- 2 packs of kielbasa
- 2 sliced bell peppers
- 1 large, sliced onion
- 1 Tbsp of Cajun seasoning
- 3 garlic cloves
- 15 oz of diced tomatoes
- 15 oz of tomato sauce
- ½ tsp sea salt
- 1 tsp of dried basil

Instructions
- Slice the kielbasa in half vertically.
- Pour a very little oil into a medium saucepan on moderate flame. Brown the kielbasa on both sides.
- Add kielbasa, onion, bell peppers, Cajun spice, garlic, diced tomatoes, refined salt, tomato sauce, plus dried basil herbs to the crockpot. Combine them all.
- Combine them all 3 hr on High flame until the crockpot kielbasa dish is cooked through and begins to bubble.
- Serve with rice, grits, cauliflower rice, spaghetti, or cornbread.

Nutrition Information
Calories: 143 kcal, Carbohydrates: 3 g, Protein: 10.4 g, Fat: 7.3 g

207. Cajun Dry Rub Wings
Prep Time: 8 Mins, Cook Time: 35 Mins, Servings: 3
Ingredients
- chicken wings cut into vignettes
- 1 tbsp of olive oil
- 2 tbsp of Cajun Seasoning
- 1 tbsp of hot wing sauce

Instructions
- Preheat your oven to 425 F with a shelf in the middle.
- Dehydrate the wings using a paper towel
- Mix the wings, Cajun spice, and olive oil. Combine them.
- Place the wings on a baking tray, with skin side up.
- After 15 mins, flip the sides of the wings. Bake the Cajun drying rub wings for more than 10 Mins more until they get crispy & brown to your choice.
- Spread hot wing sauce on wings after baking to get extra spicy wings.

Nutrition information
Calories 350kcal, carbohydrates 9g, Protein 13g, fats 28g

208. Alcohol Infused Strawberries
Prep Time: 1 Hr 15 Mins, Cook Time: 1 Hr 15 Mins, Servings: 5
Ingredients
- 1 lb of Strawberries
- 1 Bottle of Prosecco
- 1 Cup of Sugar

Instructions
- Wash your strawberries and put them in the dish.
- Pour a fresh bottle of prosecco well over strawberries.
- Refrigerate the strawberries for a minimum of one Hr, but preferably overnight. Stir to ensure complete saturation.
- Strain them and dry strawberries entirely by putting them on a paper towel.
- Before serving, dip the strawberries in the Sugar. Rotate to coat your strawberries thoroughly.

Nutrition Information
Calories: 102 kcal, Carbohydrates: 3.2 g, Protein:7.5 g, Fat: 1.7 g

209. Healthy Baked Chicken Tenders
Prep Time: 10 Mins, Cook Time: 10 Min, Servings: 3
Ingredients
- 2 lb of chicken tenders
- ¼ cup of melted Butter
- 2 Tbsp of Chicken rub

Instructions
- Preheat your oven to 400F & place a rack in the center of the oven.
- A baking sheet with uncooked chicken.
- Brush the tenders using olive oil or melted butter on a single side.
- Apply chicken rub on the oiled or melted butter-brushed side.
- Brush the second side of the chicken tenders using oil or butter, then sprinkle with the chicken rub.
- If preferred, rotate the chicken about after 5 Mins and then continue to cook on either side until the internal temperature reaches 160F.
- Wait 5 Mins before serving the chicken.

Nutrition Information
Calories: 139 kcal, Carbohydrates: 8.9 g, Protein: 11.8 g, Fat: 8.1 g

210. How to Cook Bratwurst on the Stove
Prep Time: 10 Mins, Cook Time: 20 Mins, Servings: 5
Ingredients
- 1 lb bratwurst
- 2 bottles beer
- ¼ cup of butter
- 1 large, sliced onion

Instructions
- Put the brats, one sliced onion, beer, plus ½ stick butter pieces to a large pan or Dutch oven. Pour the beer to cover the meat.
- Bring the beer mixture to a low simmer, then boil the bratwurst for 10 Mins.
- For serving, scoop out the delicious onions along with the bratwurst. 3 min each side in the little oil till they get brown. To properly cook, the temp should be 160F.

Nutrition Information
Calories: 156 kcal, Carbohydrates: 4 g, Protein: 9.9 g, Fat: 3 g

211. Air Fryer Boiled Eggs
Prep Time: 5 Mins, Cook Time: 14 Mins, Servings: 5
Ingredients
- 6-12 raw eggs

Instructions
- 3-Min preheating of the air fryer.
- 6-12 eggs per basket in air frying. They may roll and not be uniformly spaced, but it's OK.
- For full-boiled eggs, cook in the air fryer for approximately 14-15 mins, without flipping. When making boiled eggs inside an air fryer for the first time, check each egg after 13 Mins to see if it's done.
- Prepare a water bath in a medium dish with cold water plus ice cubes. Immerse your air fryer eggs in water for 5 mins to finish frying.

Nutrition Information
Calories: 187 kcal, Carbohydrates: 11.5 g, Protein: 17.3 g, Fat: 6.4 g

212. Egg and Avocado Salad
Prep Time: 10 Min, Cook Time: 15 Min, Servings: 2

Ingredients
- 4 chopped boiled eggs
- 1 chopped avocado
- 1 tbsp of mayo
- 1 tsp of Dijon mustard
- 1 Tbsp of fresh dill
- 1 Tbsp of diced chives
- ½ tsp sea salt
- ¼ tsp of black pepper

Instructions
- Prepare the Ingredients by slicing the fresh herbs and hard-cooked eggs.
- Add mayonnaise, fresh chives, sea salt, Dijon mustard, dill, and powdered black pepper in a bowl.
- Combine the Ingredients. For a chunkier texture, crush the avocados and eggs alternatively, leave in tiny cubes and fold gently.
- Serve with greens, a sandwich, or crackers.

Nutrition Information
Calories: 174 kcal, Carbohydrates: 7 g, Protein: 12.5 g, Fat: 9.9 g

213. Boiled Chicken Tenders
Prep Time: 2 Mins, Cook Time: 12 Mins, Servings: 4

Ingredients
- 1 lb of chicken tenders uncooked

Instructions
- put 1 lb of raw chicken tenderloins and cover it using cold water.
- Put the pot's lid on. Let the water to a boil.
- Reduce the heat to medium as soon as the water begins to bubble. Sauté your chicken tenders for approximately 2-3 mins more with the lid on, or until they reach an internal temperature of 160 F.
- Use the chicken in the pre-cooked chicken recipes, such as salads, soups, and casseroles.

Nutrition Information
Calories: 163 kcal, Carbohydrates: 7.2 g, Protein: 9.1 g, Fat: 4.9 g

214. Air Fryer Chicken Tenders
Prep Time: 5 Mins, Cook Time: 8 Mins, Servings: 4

Ingredients
- 1 lb of raw chicken tenders
- 2 tsp of olive oil
- 1 tsp of chicken rub

Instructions
- Preheat your air fryer approximately 400 degrees Fahrenheit.
- Spray the chicken tenders using oil before sprinkling or brushing on the chicken rub.
- Incorporate the rub in the crucial chicken flesh.
- Cook for 8-9 mins in the air fryer, flipping after five min. Because the tenders are so thin, it's technically OK to omit the flip, but you like it.

Nutrition information
Calories: 204kcal, Carbohydrates: 6g, Proteins: 24g, Fat: 7g

215. Frozen Asparagus in Air Fryer
Prep Time: 5 Mins, Cook Time: 10 Mins, Servings: 4

Ingredients
- ½ lb of asparagus frozen
- 2 tsp of olive oil
- ¼ tsp of sea salt
- ¼ tsp of black pepper
- 2 tbsp of shredded parmesan

Instructions
- Preheat your air fryer for about 5 mins at 400 degrees Fahrenheit.
- Combine the asparagus, olive oil, sea salt, and black pepper in a medium-sized mixing bowl. To mix, toss everything together.
- Inside the air fryer basket, arrange the asparagus in a uniform layer.
- Air fry the asparagus for a maximum of 8-9 mins, turning halfway through after 4-5 mins.
- If using parmesan cheese, put it in the last Min of frying or until it is completely melted.
- Enjoy! With asparagus, serving lemon slices is a great touch.

Nutrition information
Calories 526kcal, Carbohydrates 5g, Protein 28g, Fat 33g

216. Greek Tomato Cucumber Salad
Prep Time: 15 Mins, Cook Time: 15 Mins, Servings: 4

Ingredients
- 1 cup sliced cucumbers
- 2 cups sliced tomatoes
- ½ thinly sliced red onion
- 1 cup olives
- Feta cheese
- 1 sliced green pepper
- ½ cup of red vinegar
- ½ tsp of dried oregano
- ¼ tsp of sea salt

Instructions
- Slice the onions, green pepper, and cucumber for the tomato-cucumber salad components. You may either skip the grape-sliced tomatoes or cut them into wedges when you're using regular tomatoes.
- Combine the cucumbers, kalamata olives, and tomatoes in a mixing dish. Mix the Ingredients with a splash of red vinegar, oregano, & sea salt. Before serving, top with feta cheese cubes. Enjoy!

Nutrition Information
Calories: 143 kcal, Carbohydrates: 6.8 g, Protein: 14.2 g, Fat: 9.7 g

217. Air Fryer Chicken Fajitas
Prep Time: 10 Mins, Cook Time: 15 Mins, Servings: 6

Ingredients
- 1 lb of chicken breast, finely sliced
- 3 colored bell peppers
- 1 sliced red onion
- 2 tbsp of olive oil
- 3 tbsp of fajita seasoning

Instructions
- Preheat your air fryer to 370 degrees Fahrenheit for five min.
- Cut the chicken breast flesh into mouthpieces by thinly slicing it. Cut the peppers & onion into slices.
- Combine the chicken strips, olive oil, onion, bell peppers, & fajita spice in a mixing bowl. Mix the two.
- Cook the fajitas for 14 to 16 mins, turning every 5 mins, till they fully cooked through, and the peppers and onions get softened, evenly spreading the vegetables and chicken in the base of your air fryer basket.
- Toss with salsa, sour cream, and tortillas before serving. Enjoy!

Nutrition Information
Calories: 185 kcal, Carbohydrates: 4.3 g, Protein: 9.6 g, Fat: 7.7 g

218. Tuna Stuffed Peppers
Prep Time: 20 Min, Cook Time: 25 Min, Servings: 4

Ingredients
- 2 colored bell peppers
- ½ cup of mayo
- 2 tbsp of lemon juice
- 1 minced celery stalk
- 2 chopped pickles
- 2 tbsp minced red onion
- 2 cans of albacore tuna

- ½ tsp of sea salt
- ¼ tsp of black pepper
- fresh herbs for garnishing
- 2 oz of cheddar cheese shredded

Instructions
- Preheat your oven to 400 degrees Fahrenheit.
- Prepare all the items as directed in the ingredient list, including slicing, chopping, draining, and so on.
- Discard the inner layer & seeds from the bell peppers by slicing them in half.
- To soften the pepper halves, roast them for 15 mins on a baking pan.
- In a separate bowl, add the other Ingredients.
- Distribute the tuna mixture equally among the four bell pepper halves, pressing the mixture down until the peppers are filled.
- Over the surface of each pepper, place ½ of cheese.
- Bake for about 5-10 mins, or till the tuna is well cooked and the cheese has melted.
- Serve with chopped parsley as a garnish.

Nutrition Information
Calories: 153 kcal, Carbohydrates: 5.6 g, Protein: 10.8 g, Fat: 3.5 g

219. Greek Salad Bowl with Chicken
Prep Time: 30 Min, Cook Time: 25 Min, Servings: 4
Ingredients
- ½ thinly sliced red onion
- ½ cup of kalamata olives
- 1 cup sliced cucumbers
- Tomatoes
- Feta cheese
- ½ sliced green pepper
- 4 chicken breasts thinly sliced
- 1 lb of cauliflower rice
- 4 cups of lettuce
- tzatziki sauce
- fresh dill
- ¼ cup vinegar

Instructions
- Cut two chicken breasts piece in half, removing the fat. Blot dry the chicken breasts to help them crisp up.
- Place the chicken cutlets on a baking tray.
- Olive oil & melted butter in a small basin. Drizzle the chicken with the oil & butter mixture. Add salt and pepper to the chicken.
- Bake your thin chicken breasts for approximately 12 to 13 mins, or till they reach 160 F. Cooking time includes flipping the chicken. Wait for 5 mins before serving the chicken.

Greek Salad
- The Greek salad is sliced onions, cucumber, green pepper, and tomato.
- Combine the veggies, red vinegar, dill, & feta cheese crumbles. Set aside.

Cauliflower Rice
- Melt butter in a medium skillet. Drizzle the pan with olive oil.
- Put the 1 lb of cauliflower rice in the pan, then simmer until tender. Season to taste.

Assemble:
- Stack the veggies in a dish. Place the lettuce in the bowl.
- place Greek salad on lettuce
- Top with cauliflower rice and sliced chicken breast. Enjoy!

Nutrition Information
Calories: 149 kcal, Carbohydrates: 3.6 g, Protein: 7.6 g, Fat: 2.8 g

220. Healthy Tzatziki Sauce
Prep Time: 10 Mins, Cook Time: 10 Mins, Servings: 8

Ingredients
- 1 cup Greek yogurt
- 1 cup chopped cucumber
- 1 tbsp olive oil
- ½ tsp of sea salt
- ¼ tsp of black pepper
- 2 minced garlic cloves
- 1 ½ Tbsp of fresh dill
- 1 tsp lemon juice

Instructions
- Peel and finely slice the cucumber.
- Set aside a small dish filled with dill and lemon-flavored Greek yogurt.
- Mix the sauce Ingredients thoroughly.
- Serve on the spot or refrigerate for 1-2 hr.
- You may eat it with Greek salad or flatbread.

Nutrition Information
Calories 35kcal, carbohydrate 2g, Protein 3g, fats 2g

221. Healthy Baked Thin Chicken Breast
Prep Time: 7 Mins, Cook Time: 12 Mins, Servings: 8
Ingredients
- 1.5 lb of chicken
- 1 Tbsp of olive oil
- 1 Tbsp melted butter
- ½ tsp of sea salt
- ¼ tsp black pepper ground

Instructions
- Preheat your oven to 400°F.
- Cut two big breasts of chicken in half, removing the fat. Blot dry chicken breasts to help them crisp up.
- Put the baking sheet with chicken cutlets.
- Add olive oil & butter in a small basin. Drizzle the chicken with olive oil butter.
- Add salt and pepper to the chicken.
- Bake the sliced chicken breasts for approximately 12 to 13 mins, or till they reach 160 F. Cooking time includes flipping the chicken.
- Wait for 5 mins before serving the chicken. With pan juices. Enjoy!

Nutrition Information
Calories: 147 kcal, Carbohydrates: 4.8 g, Protein: 13.2 g, Fat: 5 g

222. Air Fried Radishes
Prep Time: 6 Mins, Cook Time: 14 Mins, Servings: 3
Ingredients
- Radishes one bunch
- 1/3 tbsp of Olive Oil
- ½ tsp of black pepper
- ¾ tsp of Sea Salt
- ¼ cup of parmesan, shredded

Instructions
- Preheat the air fryer at 400F.
- Trim radishes and slice them in half lengthwise in a dish.
- Pour in the sea salt, pepper, then olive oil.
- Toss to cover radishes in the mixture.
- Preheat the air fryer for about 10 to 12 mins, flipping halfway. The final two mins of cooking time may be added with grated parmesan cheese.

Nutrition Information:
Calories 49kcal, Carbs 1g, Proteins 2g, Fats 4g

223. Air Fryer Whole Chicken Wings
Prep Time: 5 Mins, Cook Time: 20 Mins, Servings: 6-7
Ingredients
- 1.25 lb of chicken wings
- 1 Tbsp of olive oil
- ½ tsp of sea salt

- ¼ tsp of black pepper
- ¼ cup of red-hot Sauce
- ½ cup of melted butter

Instructions
- Preheat your air fryer for five min at 400°F.
- Dry the chicken wings using paper towels. Add the entire wings, salt, pepper, and olive oil to a medium bowl. Mix them well.
- Spread the chicken wings in an equal layer inside the air fryer basket. Fry for 9 mins topside down, then flip.
- Air fried the wings for 8 to10 mins more till done and crispy. Melt butter in the microwave or a small saucepan. Add the wings to the butter & Frank's red hot sauce mixture and coat them well.
- Refry the wings for about 1 to 2 mins.
- Immediately serve with cheese & celery.

Nutrition Information
Calories: 99 kcal, Carbohydrates: 1.3 g, Protein: 5.1 g, Fat: 1.9 g

224. Air Fryer Country Style Ribs
Prep Time: 5 Mins, Cook Time: 45 Mins, Servings: 4
Ingredients
- 2 lb of ribs
- 2 Tbsp of pork rub (dry)
- BBQ sauce

Instructions
- preheat at 360 F the air fryer for approximately 5 min.
- Dry the ribs using paper towels. Spread the dry rub across each side of the ribs with sanitized hands.
- Cover the ribs with foil to keep them moist.
- Cook for twenty Mins, turn them, then cook for 20 Mins until done.
- Brush with BBQ sauce, then air fried for 1 to 2 extra Mins for a grilled look.
- Serve with baked beans, coleslaw, & cornbread.

Nutrition Information
Calories: 127 kcal, Carbohydrates: 2 g, Protein: 6.4 g, Fat: 1.3 g

225. BBQ Air Fryer Ribs
Prep Time: 7 Mins, Cook Time: 45 Mins, Servings: 3
Ingredients
- 1 rack of back ribs
- 2 tbsp of dry pork rub
- ¼ cup of BBQ sauce

Instructions
- Preheat your air fryer for about 5 mins at 360°F.
- Blot the ribs rather than rinse them off.
- Cut the rib rack in two using a sharp knife.
- 2 tbsp of spice on the fleshy side of each rib, 1 tbsp on each half. Press the seasonings gently into the flesh to help the rib mix attach to the ribs.
- Wrap them securely in foil and air-fried them flesh side down.
- After 20 Mins, turn the pork ribs inside the air fryer. Cook for 20 mins more, keeping the meaty side up.
- Open all foil packaging carefully and baste the ribs as desired. 5 mins longer, air-fried the ribs until the sauce brown and looks "grilled."

Nutrition Information
Calories: 106 kcal, Carbohydrates: 4.3 g, Protein: 6.8 g, Fat: 2.8 g

226. Frozen Salmon in Air Fryer
Prep Time: 5 Min, Cook Time: 10 Mins, Servings: 4
Ingredients
- 3-4 fillets of salmon
- 1 tbsp of olive oil
- 2 tsp seasoning of garlic herb

Instructions
- Preheat your air fryer for about 5 Mins at 390°.
- Brush with oil or butter, i.e., melted. Season the fillets well with garlic herb seasoning. You may use salt and black pepper rather than roasted garlic & herb.
- Put the fish inside the air fryer, keeping the skin-side down. After 10-12 mins, the salmon fillets should be flaky and have reached an internal temp of 120 to 125 degrees. Cook medium fish at 130 to140 degrees. Wait for 5 mins before serving the salmon.

Nutrition Information
Calories: 219 kcal, Carbohydrates: 13.2 g, Protein: 15 g, Fat: 10.1 g

227. Iced Matcha Latte Starbucks Copycat
Prep Time: 5 Mins, Cook Time: 5 Mins, Servings: 1
Ingredients
- 1 tsp of matcha tea powder
- 1 tbsp of honey
- 12 oz of milk

Instructions
- Fill your cup with 12 oz raw almond or ordinary milk, one matcha tea packet, and a sweetener.
- Blend until the Ingredients are fully incorporated.
- You may use this recipe for hot matcha latte instead of iced.

Nutrition Information
Calories: 77 kcal, Carbohydrates: 3 g, Protein: 5.2 g, Fat: 1.6 g

228. Chicken Wing Brine Recipe
Prep Time: 15 Mins, Cook Time: 10 Mins, Servings: 8
Ingredients
- 8 cups of water
- ½ cup of kosher salt
- 1 tbsp of black peppercorns
- fresh parsley or thyme
- 6 small cloves of garlic

Instructions
- A large saucepan with water, black peppercorns, kosher salt, garlic cloves, & herbs. Keep the heat to medium, cover the saucepan, and simmer the mixture.
- Cook approximately 5 mins once hot. Take the mixture from the stove.
- Let the brine cool fully.
- After the brine has cooled, add chicken wings. The water should fully cover the chicken wings.
- Refrigerate the wings brine for 1 to 2 Hr.
- Wash the chicken using cold water after removing the wings. Dry them using a cloth.
- They're now prepared to use with your favorite wings' recipe.

Nutrition Information
Calories 8kcal, Carbs 1g, Proteins 1 g, Fats 0 g

229. Air Fryer Bone-in Chicken Thighs
Prep Time: 5 Mins, Cook Time: 16 Mins, Servings: 4
Ingredients
- 2 lb of chicken thighs
- 1 Tbsp of olive oil
- 2 Tbsp of dry chicken rub

Instructions
- For 5 min preheating your air fryer.
- Remove the skin from chicken thighs. Towel dry the chicken.
- Pour the oil across each side of the chicken, then sprinkle using a dry chicken rub.
- After 8 Mins, turn the skin downside bone-in chicken thighs. Cook for approximately 7 to 8 mins more till the chicken reaches 165F.
- Based on the type of air fryer, it may take more than 20 mins to cook our chicken.

Nutrition Information

Calories: 123 kcal, Carbohydrates: 6.9 g, Protein: 14.4 g, Fat: 7.1 g

230. Stove Top Chicken Thighs
Prep Time: 8 Mins, Cook Time: 22 Mins, Servings: 4
Ingredients
- 4 thighs of chicken
- ¾ tsp of sea salt
- ½ tsp of garlic powder
- ½ tsp of smoked paprika
- ½ tsp of black pepper
- ½ cup of chicken broth
- 2 tbsp of olive oil

Instructions
- Preheat a big skillet with olive oil. You can use a cast-iron pan to brown the chicken and strongly suggest it for optimal results.
- Trim the chicken thighs of any significant fat or skin bits and dry them using paper towels.
- Set aside a small dish of each of the following Ingredients. Season each side of the chicken.
- With tongs, lay the top portion down inside the skillet for 4 to 5 mins until lightly browned. Brown the chicken on either side for 4 to 5 mins.
- Cook for a further 12 to 15 mins till the temp of the chicken reaches 165F.
- If desired, garnish with parsley and chives.

Nutrition Information
Calories: 107 kcal, Carbohydrates: 3.9 g, Protein: 7.2 g, Fat: 6.1 g

231. Baked Dry Rub Chicken Wings
Prep Time: 10 Mins, Cook Time: 40 Mins, Servings: 12
Ingredients
- 1 ½ lb of chicken
- 2 Tbsp of olive oil
- 2 Tbsp of chicken rub
- 1 Tbsp of baking powder

Instructions
- Preheat your oven to 425F with a central rack.
- Set the chicken wings aside after drying them by using paper towels. Blotting them thoroughly removes unnecessary moisture and helps them crisp up while frying!
- Take 1 tbsp of olive oil, 2 tbsp of chicken rub, plus 1 tbsp of baking powder Mix well till all chicken is coated with rub spice.
- Cooked wings on something like a baking sheet, skin side up. After 20 Mins, flip the wings. Bake for 15 to 25 mins more till crispy & brown of your preference.
- Serve with BBQ, Ranch, or other sauces.

Nutrition Information
Calories: 89 kcal, Carbohydrates: 1 g, Protein: 2.4 g, Fat: 0.8 g

232. Keto Air Fryer Chicken Tenders
Prep Time: 10 Mins, Cook Time: 8 Mins, Servings: 3-4
Ingredients
- 1 lb of chicken tenders
- 1 egg
- ½ cup of almond flour
- ½ cup of Parmesan cheese, grated
- ½ tsp of garlic salt
- ¼ tsp of black pepper
- ½ tsp of paprika
- olive oil

Instructions
- Preheat for five mins at 400F to the air fryer.
- Two small low bowls for breading the chicken First, beat the egg, then mix the almond flour, garlic salt, grated parmesan, black pepper, & paprika in the second dish.
- Put a chicken tender in the egg first, letting the excess egg drop back inside the bowl.
- Then coat the chicken tender with the almond flour and parmesan mixture on both sides. Repeat with the egg wash plus coating mix for the remainder of the tenders.
- Put the chicken into the air fryer, then spray with olive oil.
- After 4 mins, turn the chicken over and spray the other side with olive oil. Roast a chicken till it reaches 160F.
- Wait 5 mins before you serve the chicken. You may eat them plain or dipped in the sauce!

Nutrition Information
Calories: 95 kcal, Carbohydrates: 3 g, Protein: 8 g, Fat: 2.1 g

233. Stuffed Pepper Soup
Prep Time: 10 Mins, Cook Time: 20 Mins, Servings: 6
Ingredients
- 1 lb of ground beef
- 2 bell peppers
- 3 cups of beef broth
- 1 onion, diced
- 2 tsp of minced garlic
- 2 cans tomatoes, diced
- tomato sauce
- 2 tsp of Worcestershire
- 1 tsp of garlic salt
- ½ tsp black pepper
- 2 tsp of Italian Seasoning
- ½ cup of uncooked white rice
- 1 cup of cheddar cheese

Instructions
- Put Instant Pot to High sauté and brown the ground meat. Cook for 3 mins longer to soften the onion.
- Mix in the beef broth, scrape the browned meat from the base.
- Discard any uncooked rice that hasn't been mixed in with the other Ingredients.
- Cook for 10 mins at high pressure.
- Let the soup settle for 5 mins before making a rapid release.
- If cold pre-cooked rice, put it in the instant pot after the soup has finished cooking and heat it on Sauté till the rice gets heated through.
- Garnish each bowl with cheddar cheese as well as other toppings.

Nutrition information
Calories 372kcal, carbs 19g, proteins 29g, fats 30g

234. Baked Sausage Patties
Prep Time: 5 Mins, Cook Time: 18 Mins, Servings: 6
Ingredients
- 1 lb of sausage patties

Instructions
- Preheat your oven at 400 degrees and place the center oven rack.
- Wrap a baking tray with parchment or foil for easier cleaning.
- Arrange the sausage patties on a baking sheet in one layer, spacing them apart.
- Bake the patties for about18 mins, turning them halfway through (after 8 to 9 mins).
- You may test the interior temperature of the Sausage using a digital thermometer (minimum 160F+). Enjoy!

Nutrition Information
Calories: 133 kcal, Carbohydrates: 4.6 g, Protein: 6.1 g, Fat: 1.7 g

235. Keto Chocolate Covered Strawberries
Prep Time: 5 Mins, Cook Time: 2 Mins, Servings: 4
Ingredients
- 8 oz of chocolate chips Sugar-free
- 16 oz of whole strawberries

- 1 Tbsp of coconut oil

Instructions
- Rinse and dry the strawberries. Dry each fruit well before coating it with melted chocolate.
- Put parchment paper over a baking sheet.
- Fill a standard size bowl with chocolate chips and coconut oil. Microwave chocolate chips for 2-2 ½ Mins, stirring after every 30 seconds, till thoroughly melted.
- Pour the melted chocolate over the strawberries, allowing the excess to shift back into the bowl.
- Well, before the chocolate solidifies, you may coat the strawberries with sprinkles, cocoa powder, and crushed coconut.
- Place keto chocolate-coated strawberries on parchment paper. After immersing all strawberries, refrigerate the baking sheet for ½ Hr to firm the chocolate.
- Chill them beforehand until the chocolate solidifies to sprinkle chocolate and white chocolate over berries. Refrigerate the adorned strawberries until serving.
- The strawberries can be stored in the fridge for 2 to 3 days, but they are best eaten that day or the following day to avoid softening and discoloring.

Nutrition information
Calories: 55g. carbs 1g, proteins 1g, fats 4g

236. Healthy Baked Chicken Tenders
Prep Time: 10 Mins, Cook Time: 10 Mins, Servings: 7

Ingredients
- 2 lb of chicken tenders
- ¼ cup of Butter
- 2 Tbsp of Chicken rub

Instructions
- Preheat your oven at 400F and put center oven rack.
- A baking sheet with uncooked chicken.
- Brush the tenders using olive oil and melted butter on one side.
- Apply chicken rub on the oiled or melted butter-brushed side.
- Brush the second side of the chicken tenders using butter or olive oil and sprinkle with the chicken rub.
- If preferred, rotate the chicken every 5 mins, and continue cooking on either side until the internal temperature reaches 160F.
- Wait 5 mins before serving the chicken.

Nutrition Information
Calories: 168 kcal, Carbohydrates: 6.8 g, Protein: 17.3 g, Fat: 10.1 g

237. Air Fryer Bell Peppers and Onions
Prep Time: 7 Mins, Cook Time: 8 Mins, Servings: 4

Ingredients
- 2 colored bell peppers
- 1 onion
- 1 Tbsp of olive oil
- 1 tsp of sea salt
- ½ tsp of black pepper
- ½ tsp of Italian Seasoning
- 1 tsp of balsamic vinegar

Instructions
- preheat for 5 mins at 370 degrees for the air fryer.
- Prep the peppers & onions as the air fryer heats. Combine the peppers, Italian spice, olive oil, onions, and balsamic vinegar in a large bowl.
- The spiced bell peppers & onions will be overlapping and not in one layer in the air fryer.
- Cook for 8 to 10 mins, turning or rotating the basket halfway. After 8 mins, the peppers become soft and cooked thoroughly, but simmer for 10 to 12 mins more if you want them somewhat browned.
- To serve, combine the bell peppers & onions with balsamic vinegar.
- Enjoy!

Nutrition information
Calories: 62kcal, carbs 8g, proteins 1g, fats 4g

238. Hearty Instant Pot Hot and Sour Soup
Prep Time: 10 Mins, Cook Time: 20 Mins, Servings: 7

Ingredients
- 8 cups of chicken broth
- 12 oz of mushrooms
- 8 oz of bamboo shoots
- ¼ cup of soy sauce
- ¼ cup wine vinegar
- 2 Tbsp of minced ginger
- 1 tsp of garlic salt
- 1 tsp of chili garlic sauce
- 2 tsp of sesame oil
- 2 tbsp of cornstarch
- 3 eggs, finely whisked
- 10 oz of firm tofu
- 3-4 green sliced onions

Instructions
- Stock tofu cubes, green onions, bamboo shoots, vinegar, fresh ginger, soy sauce, garlic salt, oil, chili-garlic sauce in a pressure cooker.
- 1 min on Manually High temperature. It will take 10 to 12 mins to reach Pressure.
- When the soup is under Pressure, beat the eggs.
- After cooking, conduct a 5 min natural release. Remove Pressure from the pot. Open the lid.
- ¼ cup heated broth in a mixing bowl. Mix in the cornstarch well. Stir for 1 min or until the soup thickens.
- Add the beaten eggs in a narrow stream while swirling the soup to produce egg ribbons.
- To get the soup hotter, add additional chili garlic sauce and extra vinegar for the sourer. You may also season to taste.
- Add green onions on top. Enjoy!

Nutrition information
Calories 115kcal, carbs 6g, proteins 10g, fats 6g

239. Keto Sausage & Egg Casserole Omelet
Prep Time:15 Mins, Cook Time:22 Mins, Servings: 2

Ingredients
- 1 lb sausage
- ½ chopped bell pepper
- ¼ chopped onion
- 7 eggs
- ¾ cup whipping cream
- 2 cups of cheese
- 1 tsp of regular mustard
- dash nutmeg
- ½ tsp of salt
- ¼ tsp of pepper

Instructions
- Oil a 9 by 13 casserole dish.
- Brown sausage inside a pan until half-done, then add sliced bell pepper & onion. Then remove the grease.
- In a mixer, mix all ingredients, saving ¼ cup of cheese for topping.
- Put the egg mixture over the sausage & vegetables in the casserole dish and toss with a spoon to incorporate everything.
- Bake for 20-23 Mins with the saved cheese on top. Enjoy!

Nutrition information
Calories: 312kcal, Carbohydrates: 2g, Protein: 12g, Fat: 28g

240. Keto Quiche Recipe with Bacon & Cheese
Prep Time:10 MINS, Cook Time: 22 MINS Servings: 8

Ingredients
- 6 eggs

- ⅔ cup of whipping cream
- 6 pieces of cooked bacon
- 1 ½ cup grated Cheese
- ½ tsp of salt
- ½ tsp of pepper
- 1 tbsp of bacon grease

Instructions
- Preheat your oven and oil the 10.25 In an iron pan with 6 bacon bits and 1 tbsp bacon grease.
- Six eggs, four bacon crumbles, 2/3 cup of whipping Cream, one cup of cheese, salt & pepper
- Whisk vigorously to get air to the egg mixture. A blender is also possible.
- Grease the cast-iron skillet. 1 tbsp grease in a cast iron skillet, beat eggs.
- After 19 mins, transfer to a plate & top with ½ cup cheese and two crumbled bacons.
- Place onto a top rack for about 1-2 mins until cheese melts.
- Enjoy

Nutrition information
Calories: 169 kcal, Carbohydrates: 2.7 g, Protein: 7.7 g, Fat: 2.4 g

241. Keto Muffins with Lemon & Blueberries
Prep Time:12 Mins, Cook Time:26 Mins, Servings: 12
Ingredients
- 4 eggs
- 2 egg whites
- 5½ tbsp of butter
- ¼ cup of sour cream
- 3 oz of cream cheese
- 1 cup sweetener
- 4 tbsp of lemon juice
- 1½ tsp of baking powder
- ½ tsp of salt
- ½ cup of coconut flour
- ¾ cup blueberries

Instructions
- Preheat your oven to around 350F.
- Mix in melted butter, sour Cream, eggs, cream cheese, plus Monk Fruit Sweetener.
- 2 and½ tbsp of lemon zest and 4 tbsp of lemon juice should be mixed.
- Mix in the coconut flour, salt, baking powder, and blueberries.
- Twelve muffin pans filled with batter oil your muffin tray thoroughly.
- Add blueberries to the mixture in each pan till all berries are utilized. Mix the batter to include the blueberries. They should still be there!
- Bake for 20 min. Remove, cover with aluminum foil, and re-bake for 3-5 Mins. Using a knife or toothpick, test one or two muffins for doneness. If it's clean, they're nearly there!

Nutrition information
Calories: 193 kcal, Carbohydrates: 7.6 g, Protein: 13.5 g, Fat: 9.7 g

242. Low Carb Mixed Berry Muffins
Prep Time:10 Mins, Cook Time:28 Mins, Servings: 16
Ingredients
- 6 eggs
- 9 tbsp melted butter
- ¼ cup sliced strawberries
- ¼ cup of fresh blueberries
- ½ tsp cinnamon
- 2 tbsp sour cream
- 1 ½ tsp vanilla
- 2 tbsp of whipping Cream
- ½ cup and 2 tbsp of coconut flour
- ½ tsp salt
- 1 ½ tsp baking powder
- 1 cup powdered Sweetener

Instructions
- Preheat your oven to 350.
- Melt the butter.
- Then mix in the eggs, powdered sugar, sour cream, whipping Cream & vanilla.
- Beat in the butter plus coconut flour till incorporated.
- Mix in the strawberries & blueberries at moderate speed till well blended.
- Fill muffin tins with batter. Keto baking uses standard muffin liners and pans. They are great.
- For a golden-brown top or getting a clean toothpick in the middle, bake for 25 to 30 Mins.

Nutrition information
Calories: 112kcal, Carbohydrates: 3g, Protein: 2g, Fat: 9g

243. French Toast
Prep Time:45 Mins, Cook Time:15 Mins, Servings: 14
Ingredients
- ½ cup of coconut flour
- 10 tbsp of butter
- 8 eggs
- 1 ¼ oz of cream cheese
- 1 ½ tsp baking powder
- 2 tsp cinnamon
- ¼ tsp nutmeg

For French Toast:
- 5 eggs
- 1 cup of HWC
- 2 tbsp butter
- 2 tsp sweetener

Instructions
- Preheat your oven to 350°F.
- Melt butter & cream cheese.
- Stir in the remaining ingredients.
- Grease a pan using oil or butter.
- Bake for 40 to 50 mins, till a knife put into the middle comes out clean.
- After a few mins, take bread from the skillet and slice.

For French toast
- Pour egg and cream into a casserole dish.
- Whisk until well blended.
- Cover both sides of bread with egg mixture.
- Melt the butter on a griddle.
- Brown the toast coated with the egg mix in the butter.
- Transfer to a plate and sprinkle with Sweetener.

Nutrition information
Calories: 231kcal, Carbohydrates: 4g, Protein: 6g, Fat: 21g

244. Christmas Morning Breakfast Casserole
Prep Time: 10 Min, Cook Time: 40 Min, Servings: 5
Ingredients
- 6 slices of bread
- 1 lb of hot sausage
- 2 cups of shredded cheese
- 3 eggs
- ¾ cup of evaporated milk
- 1 ¼ cup milk
- 1 tsp mustard
- 1 tsp Worcestershire sauce
- ½ tsp salt
- dash pepper
- dash nutmeg

Instructions
- Trim bread crusts & cut into squares. Brown sausage & drain. Make a nutmeg-mustard sauce by mixing all ingredients. Well, mix.

- Mix in meat and bread. Refrigerate in a 13 by 9 casserole dish. Thaw before baking for 30 to 45 mins at 350°F until golden. Chill for 10 mins before serving!

Nutrition information
Calories 366kcal, Carbs 18.5g, Fat 30.3g, Protein 18.5g

245. Jamie's Breakfast Casserole
Prep Time: 10 Min, Cook Time: 20 Min Servings: 6
Ingredients
- 1 can of crescent rolls
- 12 eggs
- 2 cups shredded cheese
- 1 lb. of cooked breakfast
- Salt & pepper
- Salsa, chiles, onions, mushroom

Directions
- Oil a 9 by 13-inch casserole tray. Spread unbaked crescent rolls for the "crust."
- Spread cooked meat over "crust." pour whisked eggs over the meat. Spread cheese on top of eggs. Thirty-five to forty-five mins at 350°F or till set. Cool for 10 mins before serving!

Nutrition information
Calories: 262kcal, Carbohydrates: 2g, Protein: 12g, Fat: 22g

246. Bacon, Egg, & Cheese Biscuit Casserole
Prep Time: 35 Min, Cook Time: 55 Min, Servings: 9
Ingredients
For Biscuit Layer
- 4½ tbsp of butter
- ⅓ cup of coconut flour
- 2 tbsp of full fat cream
- 4 eggs
- ¼ tsp salt
- ¼ tsp baking powder
- 1⅓ cup of shredded cheddar cheese,

For Bacon, Egg, & Cheese Layer
- 4 large eggs
- 2 Tbsp of Whipping Cream
- Salt & Pepper
- 7 slices of cooked bacon
- 2 cups of grated cheddar cheese

Instructions
- The oven is preheated to 400°F.
- Oil a casserole dish.
- For the Biscuit Layer, stir in coconut flour & baking powder.
- Add cheese.
- Put baked batter in a casserole
- With 2 tbsp of Whipping Cream plus salt/pepper, beat 4 eggs.
- Spread over the biscuit layer.
- Bake for fifteen mins or till eggs are nearly done.
- Transfer to a plate and cover with shredded cheese & bacon.
- Stir frequently till cheese melts.

Nutrition information
Calories 104kcal, carbs 1g, proteins 8g, fats 7g

247. Sausage Breakfast Casserole
Prep Time:10 Mins, Cook Time:20 Mins, Servings: 12
Ingredients
- 1 lb of breakfast sausage
- 4 ½ tbsp melted butter
- 1/3 cup of coconut flour
- 2 tbsp of sour cream
- 4 eggs
- ¼ tsp salt
- ¼ tsp baking powder
- 2 cups of shredded cheese

Instructions
- Grease by using oil or butter a 9 by 13 casserole dish.
- Mix melted butter, eggs, salt, & sour cream.
- Stir in coconut flour plus baking powder.
- Put browned sausage with cheese.
- Pour batter into a casserole dish.
- Bake approximately 20 to 25 mins till the edges start to brown.
- Enjoy!

Nutrition information
Calories: 231kcal, Carbohydrates: 4g, Protein: 6g, Fat: 21g

248. Cooking Turkey Bacon in the Oven
Prep Time: 5 Mins, Cook Time: 20 Mins, Servings: 8
Ingredients
- 1 pack of turkey bacon

Instructions
- Preheat the oven at 400°F with a rack there in the middle. Put Parchment paper on a baking sheet.
- Put the bacon on parchment paper over the oven rack.
- Set a timer for 20 mins and turn the bacon after 10 mins. Monitor the bacon after Eighteen mins. However, 20 mins are the recommended cooking time for crispy turkey bacon.

Nutrition information
Calories: 262kcal, Carbohydrates: 2g, Protein: 12g, Fat: 22g

249. Kielbasa and Sauerkraut on the Stovetop
Prep Time: 7 Mins, Cook Time: 25 Mins, Servings: 4
Ingredients
- 1 package Polish kielbasa (13.5 oz), sliced into ½" pieces
- 1 Tbsp butter
- 1 Tbsp olive oil
- 1 medium onion, sliced
- 3 garlic cloves, minced
- 2 cups sauerkraut, undrained
- ½ tsp fine sea salt
- ¼ tsp ground black pepper

Instructions
- Melt butter & olive oil in a medium pan. Cook for 7 to 9 mins till golden and done through. Set aside.
- Fry the chopped onion over medium-low heat for approximately 10 mins till softened & browned. Don't burn the onion. Add the crushed garlic and simmer for 1 min.
- Put the salt & pepper, sauerkraut on the skillet. Put the sausages into the pan and simmer for 6 to 8 Mins until the sauerkraut is heated and your sausage is cooked through.
- Enjoy!

Nutrition Information
Calories: 293 kcal, Carbohydrates: 7 g, Protein: 13 g, Fat: 14 g

250. Air Fryer Boneless Turkey Breast
Prep Time: 5 Mins, Cook Time: 1 Hr 45 Mins, Servings: 5
Ingredients
- 2.5-3 lb of turkey, boneless & frozen

Instructions
- 5 mins at 350 F for Air Fryer
- Extract frozen turkey out of the plastic bag and cover in foil.
- Skin-down inside the air fryer. Cook for 60 Mins at 350°F
- Cook in foil for about 30 mins on the other side.
- Discard the foil and continue cooking for 15 to 20 minutes until the turkey achieves 150 F. Cook until the internal temperature reaches 150 F.
- Serve after 15 to 20 Mins of rest.

Nutrition information
Calories 120kcal, carbs 1g, Protein 20g, fats 1g

251. Instant Pot Bacon
Prep Time: 10 Mins, Cook Time: 10 Mins, Servings: 3
Ingredients
- 5-6 slices of raw bacon
- 1 tbsp of olive oil

Instructions
- Set the Pressure Cooker to Sauté High & cook till the Pot displays Hot.
- One tbsp of oil in the base of the saucepan will assist the bacon does not stick.
- Five entire bacon strips should fit in the Pot, giving space on all sides.
- To get wonderfully crisp bacon, fry it for approximately seven mins, turning it halfway through.
- Take the bacon & drain the fat. Put water into the saucepan to puree the stuck-on particles.

Nutrition Information
Calories: 159 kcal, Carbohydrates: 7 g, Protein: 11.2 g, Fat: 14 g

252. How to Cook Chicken Tenderloin
Prep Time: 10 Mins, Cook Time: 10 Mins, Servings: 16
Ingredients
- 2 lb chicken tenderloin (or called chicken tenders)
- ¼ cup butter, melted or olive oil
- 2+ Tbsp Chicken rub, store-bought

Instructions
- Preheat an oven at 400°F and place a rack in the middle.
- A baking tray with uncooked chicken tenders. Coat the tenderloin using olive oil and otherwise melted butter on one side.
- In a small bowl, assemble all ingredients and mix well.
- Coat the chicken tenderloins with more oil or butter, then season with more chicken rub on the second side.
- Grill the chicken for 10 mins, turning after 5 mins if desired, and then cook for a few min on the other side till the internal temp reaches 160°F. It's best to use a digital thermometer to check the chicken's temp because ovens cook differently sometimes.
- Serve the chicken after a few mins rest.

Nutrition Information
Calories: 123 kcal, Carbohydrates: 4.3 g, Protein: 10.2 g, Fat: 2.7 g

253. Air Fryer Boneless Turkey Breast
Prep Time: 5 Mins, Cook Time: 1 Hr 45 Mins, Servings: 12
Ingredients
- 2.5-3 lb of frozen turkey

Instructions
- For five mins at 350 F for Air Fryer
- Take out frozen turkey from a plastic bag & cover in foil.
- Skin-down inside the air fryer. For 60 Mins at 350°F
- Cook in foil for about 30 mins on the other side.
- Discard the foil and continue cooking for 15 to 20 mins longer until the turkey achieves 150 F. Cook till the internal temperature reaches 150 F if the turkey browns too soon.
- Serve after 15 to 20 mins of rest.

Nutrition information
Calories 120kcal, carbs 1g, Protein 20g, fats 1g

254. Keto Blueberry Coconut Flour Pancakes
Prep Time:10 Mins, Cook Time:10 Mins, Servings: 4
Ingredients
- 4 eggs
- 1 egg white
- 2 tbsp of coconut oil
- 2 tbsp of powdered Sweetener
- 2 oz of cream cheese
- 1 tsp vanilla
- 1 tsp cinnamon
- 6 tbsp of coconut flour
- ½ tsp baking powder
- pinch of salt
- 1/3 cup of fresh blueberries

Instructions
- Beat chilled coconut oil & Cream cheese till smooth. Finally, lastly, vanilla and Powdered Sweetener. Mix at high speed till batter is mixed.
- Mix the remaining ingredients except for the blueberries on medium speed until incorporated. Don't use heaping tbsp of coconut flour. Mix gently.
- Oil Butter griddle and place ¼ cup batter over hot grill, next 4 to 5 blueberries.
- When the pancake's surface starts to bubble, gently turn it over.
- Serve with maple syrup.

Nutrition information
Calories: 139 kcal, Carbohydrates: 3.2 g, Protein: 7.8 g, Fat: 1.9 g

Chapter 3: Lunch Recipes

1. Quick & Easy Herb-Crusted Cauliflower Steaks
Prep Time: 10 mins, Cook Time: 35 mins, Servings: 1
Ingredients
- 1 cauliflower head
- 1 tbsp olive oil
- ½ tsp black pepper ground
- 1 tsp salt kosher
- 3 minced garlic cloves
- 1 tsp basil dried
- ½ tsp oregano dried
- ½ tsp thyme dried
- 2 tbsp plain Greek yogurt
- 1 tbsp mustard Dijon
- ½ cup panko breadcrumbs whole-grain
- 2 tbsp fresh chopped parsley

Instructions
- Preheat the oven to 400°F. Place your cauliflower steaks over a parchment-lined baking pan. Season with pepper and salt before applying the olive oil. Take the bread out of the oven after approximately 20 mins, when it's golden and tender.
- A tiny cup of yogurt & mustard is all that is needed to make the garlic & herb seasoning. Mix thoroughly. Remove your cauliflower from the oven, then pour the herb mix on the roasted cauli. Gently press your panko into cauliflower after sprinkling it on the yogurt mixture. The cauliflower should be returned to your oven & baked for another 15 mins, or until it is browned and crispy.
- Fresh parsley is a nice touch.

Nutrition Information
Calories: 125 kcal, Carbohydrates: 18 g, Protein: 6 g, Fat: 5 g

2. Oven-Fried Pickles
Prep Time: 5 mins, Cook Time: 20 mins, Servings: 12
Ingredients
- 16 oz hamburger sliced pickles jar
- 3 egg whites
- ¼ cup flour whole-wheat
- ½ cup breadcrumbs panko
- ½ tsp powder garlic
- 1 tsp paprika smoked
- ¼ tsp kosher salt

Instructions
- Bake at 450°f for about 30 mins. Set aside one baking sheet that has been sprayed using a nonstick spray.
- Pat your pickles dry after draining them. Gently whisk your egg whites inside a mixing bowl. You'll need a medium-sized bowl to incorporate all of the ingredients.
- Using egg white, dip the pickles into it, & then coat them with a combination of Panko and breadcrumbs. Set a baking sheet by placing the pickles together in a thin layer on it.
- After 10 mins within an oven, take the pickles from the oven & flip them over. Ten more mins within the oven will make it crispy. Serve immediately with a choice of dipping sauces.

Nutrition Information
Calories: 79kcal, Carbohydrates: 14g, Protein: 4g, Fat: 1g

3. Easy Garlic Lemon Green Beans
Prep Time: 2 mins, Cook Time: 10 mins, Servings: 4
Ingredients
- 1 lb fresh green beans
- 1 tbsp olive oil
- 4 finely minced garlic cloves
- 1 tsp juice lemon
- 2 tsp zest lemon

Instructions
- Bring a big saucepan of water onto a rolling boil over high heat. Your green beans should be added to the pot and cooked for 3 mins at a rolling boil when the water has reached a rolling boil.
- Pat your beans dry with a paper towel once they have been drained.
- In a medium skillet, heat some olive oil over medium heat. Add both green beans & garlic when the oil is heated. Cook your beans until they start to blister, stirring often. To this, add lemon juice & the zest. Cook your beans until they are soft but still have a crunch.
- Serve with the rest of the zest on top.

Nutrition Information
Calories: 69 kcal, Carbohydrates: 9 g, Protein: 2 g, Fat: 4 g

4. Slow Cooker Spinach and Mozzarella Frittata
Prep Time: 15 mins, Cook Time: 1 hr, Servings: 4
Ingredients
- 1 tbsp olive oil extra virgin
- ½ cup diced onion
- 1 cup divided shredded mozzarella cheese
- 4 eggs
- 2 tbsp milk 1%
- 4 egg whites
- ¼ tsp pepper black
- ¼ tsp pepper white
- 1 cup chopped baby spinach
- 1 diced Roma tomato
- salt

Instructions
- Add the oil to a small pan and sauté the onion for approximately 5 mins on moderate flame.
- Apply a little coat of cooking spray to the interior of the slow cooker.
- A large bowl should be used to mix the onion, mozzarella cheese, & the rest of the ingredients; whisk them together, and then pour them into the slow cooker. On top of the egg mixture, sprinkle the leftover cheese.
- Cook on Medium for 2 hrs, or unless the eggs are fully set & a knife pierced in the middle comes out clear. Cover the pan halfway during the cooking time.

Nutrition Information
Calories: 127 kcal, Carbohydrates: 3 g, Protein: 9 g, Fat: 9 g

5. Crustless Vegetable Quiche
Prep Time: 15 mins, Cook Time: 30 mins, Servings: 2
Ingredients
- 1 tbsp olive oil
- 2 small diced yellow onion
- 2 minced garlic cloves
- ½ cup pepper diced red bell
- ½ cup bell pepper diced
- ½ cup sliced zucchini
- 6 florets broccoli
- ¼ cup tomatoes diced sun-dried
- 3 large eggs
- 4 large egg whites
- 2 tbsp low-fat milk
- 1 tsp oregano dried
- ½ tsp pepper black
- sea salt

Instructions
- The oven should be preheated at 425°F.

- Sauté onion & garlic in oil within a large pan over moderate heat for 4 mins or until soft. Toss in the vegetables & continue to cook for another 2 mins before adding the sun-dried tomatoes.
- Mix the eggs, milk, egg whites, seasonings, & parmesan cheese in a small mixing bowl. Toss the sautéed veggies into a 9" pie plate sprayed with cooking spray. Cover all of the vegetables with the egg mixture.
- For the first 10 mins, preheat the oven to 425°F; then, drop the temperature to 350°F & bake for another 20-25 mins. To finish the dish, remove foil, then sprinkle the leftover parmesan cheese over the top of the dish. Once the quiche puffs & a knife put in the middle come out clear, it's done baking.

Nutrition Information
Calories: 141 kcal, Carbohydrates: 15 g, Protein: 11 g, Fat: 5 g

6. Stuffed Bell Pepper Pizzas
Prep Time: 15 mins, Cook Time: 35 mins, Servings: 8
Ingredients
- 5 bell peppers removed stems & seeds
- 1 lb turkey lean ground
- ½ cup diced yellow onion
- ¾ cup sauce pizza
- ½ cup of mozzarella cheese shredded part-skim
- ¼ cup chopped basil fresh

Instructions
- Preheat your oven to 375°F.
- Break up the ground turkey while it cooks on moderate flame. Cook your turkey till it has lost its pink hue and is well done. Remove any excess fat by squeezing it out.
- Sliced onion & pizza sauce should be added to the turkey mixture.
- Bake the peppers for 25 mins, then remove them from the oven.
- Take out of the oven, cover with cheese, & bake for another 10 mins, unless the cheese has melted & is slightly browned if desired. Before serving, add a few sprigs of fresh basil.

Nutrition Information
Calories: 179 kcal, Carbohydrates: 7 g, Protein: 13 g, Fat: 11 g

7. Crunchy Kale and Brussels Sprout Salad with Creamy Dijon Dressing
Prep Time: 15 mins, Cook Time: 15 mins, Servings: 2
Ingredients
For Dressing
- 1 tbsp juice lemon
- 2 tbsp mustard Dijon
- ¼ cup plain Greek yogurt
- 1 tsp of honey
- 2 minced garlic cloves
- ¼ tsp salt kosher

For Salad
- 3 cups of kale lightly chopped & stem removed
- 2 cups shaved thin Brussels sprouts
- ¼ cup thinly sliced red onion
- ¼ cup sesame seeds toasted
- 1 chopped gala apple
- ¼ cup roughly chopped pecans

Instructions
For Dressing
- In a large bowl, mix all of the ingredients unless well combined. Before using, let it sit for 10 mins.

For Salad
- Divide the kale & Brussels sprouts into the serving dishes & toss to coat with the

dressing. The dressing should be drizzled over the salad before adding additional ingredients. It's time to eat!

Nutrition Information
Calories: 109 kcal, Carbohydrates: 10 g, Protein: 3 g, Fat: 7 g

8. Greek Stuffed Peppers with Tzatziki Sauce
Prep Time: 15 mins, Cook Time: 25 mins, Servings: 4
Ingredients
For Tzatziki Sauce
- ½ cup plain Greek yogurt
- ¼ cup shredded cucumber
- ½ tsp salt kosher
- 2 tsp olive oil extra-virgin
- 2 tsp juice lemon
- 2 tsp dill dry
- 2 minced garlic cloves

For Peppers
- 6 seeds removed bell peppers
- 1 lb turkey ground
- 3 minced garlic cloves
- ¼ cup minced red onion
- 2 tbsp roughly chopped oregano fresh
- 1 chopped Roma tomato
- ½ cup chopped zucchini
- 1 cup cooked quinoa
- 1 tsp salt kosher
- ¼ cup crumbled fat-free feta cheese

Instructions
For Tzatziki Sauce
- Mix all of the ingredients well. Allow almost 10 mins for the flavors to come together before serving.

For Peppers
- Preheat your oven to 375°F. Use nonstick spray to coat a casserole dish & then add the peppers to the pan.
- Place the pan over medium heat. Remove from heat and break up the turkey into tiny pieces while it cooks in a separate pan. Add both onion and garlic after approximately three mins of cooking. Continue cooking until your turkey is roasted & the onions become tender.
- Toss in the oregano, tomatoes, zucchini & quinoa, then season with salt. Toss in the other ingredients, except the feta, until well-combined. Bake sliced peppers for 25 mins after filling them with the mixture. Bake for a further 10 mins with the feta added in.
- Serve with some tzatziki sauce drizzled over the top.

Nutrition Information
Calories: 254 kcal, Carbohydrates: 19 g, Protein: 21 g, Fat: 11 g

9. Slow Cooker Balsamic Chicken
Prep Time: 10 mins, Cook Time: 4 hrs, Servings: 3
Ingredients
- 4-6 chicken breasts boneless & skinless
- 29 oz tomatoes cans diced
- 1 thinly sliced medium onion
- 4 cloves garlic
- ½ cup vinegar balsamic
- 1 tbsp olive oil extra virgin
- 1 tsp oregano dried
- 1 tsp basil dried
- 1 tsp rosemary dried
- ½ tsp thyme
- black pepper ground

Instructions
- In your slow cooker, add salt, chicken breasts, olive oil, & pepper to every breast, onion slices on top, & dried herbs & garlic cloves. Cook over low for 6-8 hrs. Tomatoes & vinegar are poured on top.
- Serve on hair pasta after cooking on high for four hrs.

Nutrition Information
Calories: 96 kcal, Carbohydrates: 7 g, Protein: 11 g, Fat: 3 g

10. Skinny Spinach and Feta Baked Egg
Prep Time: 5 mins, Cook Time: 15 mins, Servings: 4
Ingredients
- 1 cup squeezed spinach cooked
- 4 eggs large
- ½ cup fat-free feta cheese

Instructions
- The oven should be preheated at 375 degrees & a muffin tin should be sprayed with nonstick spray.
- In four muffin tins, divide your spinach & set it in the base of each. Each spinach should be topped with an egg & feta cheese.
- For a firmer yolk, bake for five minutes within the oven. Carefully take the muffins from muffin tins once they've been baked, and it's time to eat.

Nutrition Information
Calories: 114 kcal, Carbohydrates: 1 g, Protein: 8 g, Fat: 8 g

11. Dairy-Free Sour Cream
Prep Time: 10 Mins, Cook Time: 25 Mins, Servings: 4
Ingredients
- 1 & ½ cups raw cashews
- 2/3 cup of water
- 2 tbsp vinegar apple cider
- 2 tbsp freshly squeezed lemon juice
- ½ tsp salt to taste
- 2 tbsp chopped chives

Instructions
- In a glass bowl, add cashews. Add water until cashews are thoroughly submerged.
- Allow the mixture to sit in the covered basin for at least 6-8 hrs.
- A blender may be used to process the cashews after they have been soaked
- Add the rest of the ingredients & water to the pot and stir to combine. Blend until the mixture resembles thick, creamy yogurt. Chill for almost a week after storing in your glass jar with a lid. If preferred, top with chives before serving.

Nutrition Information
Calories: 106 kcal, Carbohydrates: 6 g, Protein: 3 g, Fat: 8 g

12. Parmesan Roasted Zucchini
Prep Time: 10 mins, Cook Time: 30 mins, Servings: 0.5 cup
Ingredients
- 4 large zucchinis
- 2 tsp powder garlic
- ½ tsp black pepper ground
- ¼ cup reduced-fat grated parmesan cheese
- 2 tbsp olive oil extra-virgin

Instructions
- The oven should be preheated to 350°F. Set aside one baking sheet sprayed using non-stick spray.
- Using a vegetable peeler, cut the zucchini into quarter-inch circles & arrange them on the baking pan.
- Add the pepper, garlic powder, & parmesan cheese to a medium bowl, then mix well. Make a slight coating of oil & sprinkle your parmesan mix over the zucchini.
- Bake for around 30 mins, or unless the top is just beginning to brown. It's time to eat!

Nutrition Information
Calories: 100 kcal, Carbohydrates: 8 g, Protein: 4 g, Fat: 6 g

13. Cucumber Quinoa Salad with Ground Turkey, Olives, & Feta
Prep Time: 10 Mins, Cook Time: 25 Mins, Servings: 5
Ingredients
- ½ lb turkey sausage ground
- 3 large cucumbers
- 1 sliced thin small red onion
- 1 cup sliced grape tomatoes
- ½ cup olives kalamata
- ½ cup crumbles fat-free feta cheese
- 1 & ½ cup cooked quinoa
- 2 tbsp chopped mint fresh
- 2 minced garlic cloves
- 1 tbsp chopped oregano fresh
- 1 tbsp juice lemon

Instructions
- Cook your turkey sausage in a wide pan over medium heat. As your sausage cooks, cut it into tiny pieces. Drain any remaining liquid and let it cool thoroughly.
- Combine your turkey sausage with other ingredients after it has cooled. Serve after chilling thoroughly.

Nutrition Information
Calories: 97 kcal, Carbohydrates: 10 g, Protein: 6 g, Fat: 4 g

14. Plant-Based Borscht | Oil-Free Recipes
Prep Time: 10 mins, Cook Time: 30 mins, Servings: 6
Ingredients
Borscht
- 1 large carrot
- ½ lb root celery
- 1 medium red onion
- 1 medium zucchini
- 1 medium tomato
- ½ large bell pepper
- 6 oz small red cabbage
- ½ lb medium beets
- 3 cups broth vegetable
- 2 lemons
- salt & pepper
- ¼ cup chopped parsley fresh

Instructions
- Wash the veggies by first peeling and rinsing them.
- A medium grater may be used to process the celery, zucchini, carrots, & red cabbage. The beets can also be grated.
- The tomato, onion, & bell pepper should be cut into cubes no more than half an inch in size.
- Cook the veggies for 3-5 minus in a pan of water before sprinkling with salt and pepper: Sauté vegetables and liquid till al dente in the same way you would do with oil in a hot pan using a spatula & more broth if this evaporates. Continue to deglaze with broth if necessary.
- To simmer, bring 3 cups of vegetable broth to your boil in a big saucepan, then decrease heat.
- Add salt & pepper, then simmer for about 20-25 mins, until the vegetables are soft.
- Squeeze in 1 lemon juice for a classic tart flavor.

Nutrition Information
Calories: 78 kcal, Carbohydrates: 17 g, Protein: 3 g, Fat: 1g

15. Lemon Ginger Detox Drink
Prep Time: 2 mins, Cook Time: 2 mins, Servings: 8
Ingredients
- 12 oz water
- ½ juiced lemon
- ½ knob of grated ginger root

Instructions
- Add lemon juice into a water glass. Using a zester, grate fresh ginger finely and add it to water. It's a great way to begin the day, and you won't regret it!

Nutrition Information
Calories: 11 kcal, Carbohydrates: 2 g, Protein: 1 g, Fat: 0 g

16. One-Skillet Chicken and Broccoli Dinner
Prep Time: 10 mins, Cook Time: 30 mins, Servings: 5
Ingredients
Chicken & Broccoli Dinner
- 1 tbsp olive oil extra virgin
- 12-18 oz chicken breasts boneless & skinless
- 2 cups florets broccoli
- 2 minced garlic cloves
- ½ cup chopped yellow onion
- ½ cup sliced celery
- ¼ cup broth chicken
- ¼ tsp sea salt or kosher
- ¼ tsp pepper black

Sauce
- ¼ cup aminos coconut
- 2 tbsp Sriracha vegetable

Instructions
- Cook the chicken for 8 mins in a pan with olive oil on medium heat. Remove and reserve the chicken. Toss in the broccoli florets and sauté for a few mins. Set aside the broccoli.
- It is important to cook for around 5-8 mins till the celery gets softened & the onion is transparent. Toss in the garlic & heat for another 30 secs or till it's aromatic. Toss with the pepper and salt before adding the broth. The chicken should be heated through in approximately 5 mins.
- To make the sauce, combine all ingredients in a bowl and simmer for one more min. Serve and revel in the delicacies!

Nutrition Information
Calories: 130 kcal, Carbohydrates: 5 g, Protein: 21 g, Fat: 3 g

17. Skinny Cheeseburger Boats
Prep Time: 15 mins, Cook Time: 25 mins, Servings: 12

Ingredients
- 1 lb lean beef ground
- 1 diced onion small
- ½ tsp salt sea
- ½ tsp pepper black
- 3 medium bell peppers
- 2/3 cup divided ketchup
- 1 tbsp mustard
- 5 bars of reduced-fat cheddar cheese

Instructions
- Preheat the oven to 375°F.
- Slice every bell pepper vertically six times, starting at the indentation and working your way out. Set aside the peppers.
- A large bowl should incorporate all of the ingredients for the meatloaf.
- Add the meat mixture to the boats. The meat should be done in approximately 20 mins on a parchment-covered baking pan.
- Top every boat with a quarter of a cheese slice, then return the boats to your oven & bake for another 5 mins, till the cheese has melted.

Nutrition Information
Calories: 237 kcal, Carbohydrates: 9 g, Protein: 18 g, Fat: 15 g

18. Chocolate Peanut Butter Oatmeal Bars
Prep Time: 10 mins, Cook Time: 30 mins, Servings: 10

Ingredients
- 2 cups oats rolled
- 2 cups milk coconut
- ½ cup mashed banana
- ¼ cup no sugar peanut butter
- ¼ cup almond meal or almond flour
- ¼ cup unsweetened cocoa powder
- 2 tbsp flaxseed ground
- ¼ cup chopped peanuts
- 1 tbsp powder vanilla clean protein

Instructions
- Set the oven temperature to 35°F. Apply nonstick spray to a casserole dish.
- Mix all the ingredients in a mixing bowl unless they are well incorporated. Evenly distribute and softly press the mix into the casserole dish.
- Allow cooling before slicing into squares. Serving suggestion: Slice & serve hot, then chill before serving.

Nutrition Information
Calories: 217 kcal, Carbohydrates: 17 g, Protein: 7 g, Fat: 15 g

19. Oven Baked Zucchini Chips
Prep Time: 10 mins, Cook Time: 30 mins, Servings: 5

Ingredients
- 1 large zucchini
- 1/3 cup breadcrumbs whole-grain
- ¼ cup reduced-fat Parmesan cheese finely grated
- ¼ tsp pepper black
- sea salt or Kosher
- 1/8 tsp powder garlic
- 1/8 tsp pepper cayenne
- 3 tbsp low-fat milk

Instructions
- The oven should be preheated at 425°F.
- Toss the Parmesan cheese, breadcrumbs, & other seasonings into a large mixing dish. Cover both sides of the zucchini slices, soak them in milk, then dredge them in breadcrumbs. The crumbs may need to be pressed into zucchini slices to adhere.
- Spray a cookie sheet using cooking spray & arrange zucchini in a crisscross pattern.
- Place the rack over the cookie sheet if you are using the rack. Bake for 15 minutes, then flip and bake for another 10-15 minutes, till golden brown. Before keeping it in a sealed jar, let it stand at room temperature.

Nutrition Information
Calories: 99 kcal, Carbohydrates: 12 g, Protein: 6 g, Fat: 3 g

20. Sweet Potato Black Bean Quinoa Bites
Prep Time: 5 mins, Cook Time: 20 mins, Servings: 10

Ingredients
- 2 cups cooked quinoa
- 2 beaten eggs
- 1 cup mashed sweet potatoes
- 2 tbsp chopped cilantro fresh
- 2 tsp powder garlic
- 1 tsp cumin ground
- 1 tsp paprika
- 2 tsp powder chili
- 1 tsp turmeric
- ½ tsp salt kosher
- 15 oz black beans

Instructions
- Set the oven temperature to 350°F. Use parchment paper to cover a baking pan.
- Toss together the other ingredients in a mixing bowl, excluding black beans, then stir to blend well. Using a spoon, gently stir in the beans till they are evenly distributed.
- Using approximately 2-3 tsp of mixture per burger, gently shape into patties & put on the baking pan. It's done when the top is just starting to brown, which takes around 15–20 mins at 350°F. A firmer patty may be served either cold or hot according to personal preference.

Nutrition Information
Calories: 94 kcal, Carbohydrates: 16 g, Protein: 5 g, Fat: 2 g

21. Toasted Coconut Coffee Sweetener
Prep Time: 10 Mins, Cook Time: 25 Mins, Servings: 6

Ingredients
- ¾ cup unsweetened shredded coconut
- ¼ cup sugar coconut
- 2 tbsp honey
- ½ cup of water

Instructions
- Set the oven temperature to 350°F. Ten mins in the oven should be enough time for the coconut to get a golden-brown color. To avoid burning, stir your coconut every two mins while baking.
- Add all the other ingredients, including the roasted coconut, to a pot and bring to a boil. Don't stir! Simmer for roughly 5 mins at a boil on moderate flame. Cool & steep for two hrs after removing from the heat.

- Strain your syrup thru a cheesecloth or coarse sieve after it's cooled down. Store in the refrigerator for almost a week in a sealed container.

Nutrition Information
Calories: 15 kcal, Carbohydrates: 2 g, Protein: 2 g, Fat: 1 g

22. Baked Lemon Salmon and Asparagus Foil Pack
Prep Time: 10 mins, Cook Time: 15 mins, Servings: 4
Ingredients
- 16-24 oz salmon
- 1 lb fresh asparagus
- 1 tsp kosher salt
- ½ tsp black pepper ground
- 2 tbsp olive oil
- ¼ cup fresh lemon juice
- 1 tbsp chopped thyme fresh
- 2 tbsp chopped parsley fresh
- 2 tbsp lemon zest

Instructions
- Preheat your oven to 400°F
- Spray four big sheets of Al foil using a nonstick spray. Stack each package of asparagus on top of the other to form a thin layer next to each other. Salt & pepper to taste using half the amount.
- Toss a piece of salmon over asparagus before serving. Pour olive oil, thyme, lemon juice, & the rest of the pepper and salt over the chicken breasts and toss. A thin Al foil packet should be placed on a baking pan, with the salmon surrounded by the packets. Bake for about 15 mins.
- Each package should be cautiously opened but be aware of the steam produced! Top with lemon zest & parsley. Serve & revel in the delicacies!

Nutrition Information
Calories: 386 kcal, Carbohydrates: 7 g, Protein: 32 g, Fat: 26 g

23. Tuna Zucchini Noodle Bake
Prep Time: 10 mins, Cook Time: 20 mins, Servings: 6
Ingredients
- 4 medium zucchinis
- 2 tsp olive oil
- ½ cup diced yellow onions
- 12 oz drained tuna cans
- 1 tbsp paste tomato
- 15 oz drained diced tomatoes
- ½ cup milk skim
- 1 tsp dried thyme
- ½ tsp kosher salt
- ¼ tsp black pepper ground
- ¼ cup grated parmesan cheese
- ½ cup of cheddar cheese shredded fat-free

Instructions
- Spray a pan using nonstick spray and heat the oven to 400°F. In a casserole dish, evenly distribute the zucchini. Set away for later.
- Oil should be heated in a big pan, then add chopped onion & cook for 2 mins. Cook for another min or so after adding the tuna & tomato paste. Salt & pepper to taste are added to a tomato mixture after the chopped tomatoes have been added. Toss within parmesan & heat till melted.
- Toss your zucchini noodles with the tuna mixture and serve Cheddar cheese should be sprinkled on top. The cheese should be melted and bubbling after 15 mins of baking with the lid off.

Nutrition Information
Calories: 164 kcal, Carbohydrates: 10 g, Protein: 18 g, Fat: 7 g

24. Moroccan Chicken Salad with Chimichurri Dressing
Prep Time: 15 mins, Cook Time: 15 mins, Servings: 3
Ingredients
For Chimichurri Dressing
- 1 clove garlic
- 1 cup fresh cilantro
- ¼ cup of parsley
- 1 tbsp lemon juice
- 4 tbsp olive oil
- ¼ tsp kosher salt
- red pepper crushed

For Salad
- 1 & ½ cups chicken breasts boneless & skinless
- 6 cups of arugula baby
- 1 cup shredded carrot
- 1 cup chopped cucumber
- ¼ cup seeds pomegranate
- ¼ cup fat-free crumbles feta cheese
- ¼ cup chopped almonds

Instructions
For Chimichurri Dressing
- Process till finely chopped & well combined in your food processor. Set a portion of your time aside.

For Salad
- Toss the ingredients together in a medium bowl. Chimichurri Dressing should be drizzled over the top of each dish. It's time to eat!

Nutrition Information
Calories: 300 kcal, Carbohydrates: 10 g, Protein: 23 g, Fat: 19 g

25. Squash and Kale Gratin Casserole
Prep Time: 15 Mins, Cook Time: 25 Mins, Servings: 6
Ingredients
- 1 squash kabocha
- 3 minced garlic cloves
- ½ tsp rosemary dried
- ½ tsp thyme dried
- 1/3 cup of coconut milk
- ½ tsp kosher salt
- ¼ tsp black pepper ground
- 2 cups roughly chopped kale
- 1 cup roughly chopped spinach
- ¼ cup roughly chopped yellow onion
- 3 tbsp water
- ½ cup panko breadcrumbs whole-wheat
- 2 tbsp honey

Instructions
- Bake at 450°F for about 30 mins. Apply nonstick spray to a casserole dish.
- Add the rosemary, thyme, squash, garlic, & coconut milk to a medium saucepan. When squash is fork-tender & mash-able, could you bring it to your boil? Remove the squash from the heat & mash it until there are no more lumps. Use pepper and salt.
- Add the spinach, onion, kale, & water to a small saucepan. Make sure that the onions are tender & the kale is wilting. To keep the veggies from adhering to a pan, you may have to add extra water. Squash should be incorporated into the mixture with ease.
- Dump the ingredients into a well-greased casserole dish. Sprinkle the panko breadcrumbs & honey over the top. Bake for about 15-20 minutes unless the top is browned and crispy.

Nutrition Information
Calories: 104 kcal, Carbohydrates: 19 g, Protein: 3 g, Fat: 3 g

26. The Best Savory Southwest Tofu Egg Scramble
Prep Time: 5 mins, Cook Time: 10 mins, Servings: 4
Ingredients
- 1 tbsp olive oil
- ¼ cup chopped small bell pepper
- 4 oz cubed small tofu extra-firm
- ¼ cup chopped small red onion
- 1 cup roughly chopped kale
- ½ tsp cumin ground
- 1 tsp powder chili
- 6 lightly beaten egg whites

- 2 tbsp chopped cilantro fresh

Instructions
- The oil should be heated in a big skillet. Add the pepper, onion, tofu, & greens after it's heated through. While turning often, cook your onion till it is translucent and kale is cooked. Add the cumin and the chili powder and mix well. Add some egg whites one at a time, constantly stirring to scramble them. Remove from heat & egg whites become firm but just not browned. Serve with some cilantro & take pleasure in.

Nutrition Information
Calories: 107 kcal, Carbohydrates: 5 g, Protein: 10 g, Fat: 6 g

27. Baked-to-Perfection Salmon Foil Packet with Mushroom & Garlic Recipe
Prep Time: 10 mins, Cook Time: 20 mins, Servings: 8

Ingredients
- 1 tbsp olive oil
- 4 minced garlic cloves
- 1 cup sliced red onion
- 2 cups sliced mushrooms
- ¼ tsp salt kosher
- 1 tsp thyme dried
- 2 tbsp chopped parsley
- ¼ cup broth vegetable
- 24 oz salmon fillets boneless

Instructions
- The oven should be preheated to 450°F
- In a medium skillet, heat your olive oil over medium heat. Add the garlic, onion, & mushrooms once the oil is heated. To release the moisture, cook your mushrooms & onions together for a few mins. Pour in the thyme, salt, & parsley, then add broth & water. Stir till the mixture reaches a simmer, then turn off the heat.
- Spray nonstick spray on four big sheets of foil before laying them out. Each plate should include a salmon fillet in the middle. Top each package with some mushroom mix, distributing the mixture equally. Place the package on the baking sheet, then seal the edges with a little water.
- Remove from oven once 15 mins of baking time have passed. Before opening the packages, allow them to cool for five mins. The steam may be dangerous!

Nutrition Information
Calories: 406 kcal, Carbohydrates: 5 g, Protein: 36 g, Fat: 26 g

28. 4-Ingredient Protein Pancakes
Prep Time: 5 mins, Cook Time: 10 mins, Servings: 4

Ingredients
- ½ cup mashed banana
- 3 large egg whites
- ¼ tsp powder baking
- 1 tbsp powder vanilla protein

Instructions
- In a mixing bowl, combine all ingredients and stir until smooth.
- Add some non-stick spray to a pan and heat it over medium-high heat. A quarter of the batter should be put in. To get the best results, cook pancakes for 3-4 minutes or until they bubble within the middle. Flip & cook for the next 2-3 mins, or until the meat is done. Remove the cooked pancake from the pan & continue making them with the remaining batter. Between batches of pancakes, use a spray to keep the pan from sticking.
- Your preferred nut butter or fresh fruit may be added to the top!

Nutrition Information
Calories: 57 kcal, Carbohydrates: 6 g, Protein: 7 g, Fat: 1 g

29. White Bean Avocado Toast
Prep Time: 10 mins, Cook Time: 10 mins, Servings: 4

Ingredients
- ½ cup drained & rinsed canned white beans
- 2 tsp paste tahini
- 2 tsp juice lemon
- ½ tsp salt kosher
- ½ avocado pit removed & peel
- 4 sliced bread whole-grain
- ½ cup tomatoes grape

Instructions
- Combine the tahini, beans, lemon juice, & salt in a medium bowl and mix well. It's time to get down to business.
- Combine diced avocado with the leftover lemon juice & salt in a separate bowl. Gently mash with a potato masher.
- Toast the bread and top it with mashed beans. Add the avocado & tomatoes to the beans for a delicious finishing touch.

Nutrition Information
Calories: 140 kcal, Carbohydrates: 19 g, Protein: 6 g, Fat: 5 g

30. Warm Chicken Salad Over Arugula with Creamy Dill Dressing
Prep Time: 10 mins, Cook Time: 15 mins, Servings: 6

Ingredients
- 1 tbsp olive oil
- 8-12 oz chicken breasts boneless & skinless
- 1 cup fresh asparagus
- ½ cup tomatoes grape
- ¼ tsp salt kosher
- ¼ tsp black pepper ground
- ½ cup yogurt Greek
- 1 tsp dill dry
- 2 tbsp juice lemon
- 1 tbsp vinegar red wine
- 1 tbsp mustard Dijon
- 1 tbsp mustard whole-grain
- 4 cups of baby arugula

Instructions
- Olive oil should be heated in a big pan over medium heat. Chicken should be cooked after 5 mins or so, depending on how well you want your meat to be. Add tomatoes & asparagus. Increase the heat to medium, then add pepper and salt. Cook for another 5 mins or so unless the meat is cooked thru & the tomatoes fully blistered.
- In the meantime, add the yogurt, dill, vinegar, lemon juice, & mustards to a bowl and mix well. Set the mixture aside for later use.
- Serve arugula in a variety of ways. You may use around 3 tbsp of yogurt dressing to coat roughly 3 cups of chicken. Spoon some arugula on top of it. If desired, top with more dressing.

Nutrition Information
Calories: 167 kcal, Carbohydrates: 5 g, Protein: 20 g, Fat: 8 g

31. Oil-Free Pesto
Prep Time: 5 mins, Cook Time: 5 mins, Servings: 4

Ingredients
- 2 cups spinach
- ¼ cup of parmesan cheese
- 3 diced garlic cloves
- ¼ cup freshly squeezed lemon juice
- salt

Instructions
- In a food processor, mix all the ingredients & pulse till a pesto-like consistency is achieved.
- Keep chilled until you're ready to serve.

Nutrition Information
Calories: 23 kcal, Carbohydrates: 2 g, Protein: 2 g, Fat: 1 g

32. Mediterranean Chopped Salad with Salmon, Cucumber, and Mint
Prep Time: 10 mins, Cook Time: 10 mins, Servings: 3

Ingredients
- 2 cups roughly chopped romaine lettuce
- 2 chopped small tomatoes

- 1 chopped small cucumber
- 1 chopped small bell pepper
- ¼ cup chopped small parsley fresh
- 2 tbsp chopped small mint fresh
- 1 tbsp juice lemon
- 2 tsp zest lemon
- 24 oz filets salmon
- ½ tsp salt kosher
- ¼ tsp black pepper ground

Instructions
- If you don't have a broiler, preheat your oven to 500°F.
- Toss the romaine lettuce with the radishes and the rest of the ingredients in a large salad bowl. Toss well & put away.
- Salmon fillets should be placed on a baking pan that has been sprayed with nonstick spray. Salt & pepper to taste. Cook for approximately 10 mins over the oven broiler, till the top, is gently browned & the meat is cooked through. Halfway through the cooking time, check your salmon & move the pan if necessary to get an equal browning.
- To serve, divide the salad among serving dishes and top with the salmon. Top the salmon with the lemon zest.

Nutrition Information
Calories: 390 kcal, Carbohydrates: 8 g, Protein: 36 g, Fat: 23 g

33. Curried Coconut Mussels
Prep Time: 10 mins, Cook Time: 20 mins, Servings: 6
Ingredients
- 2 tbsp water
- ½ cup diced yellow onion
- ½ cup diced bell pepper
- 3 minced garlic cloves
- ½ tsp black pepper ground
- 2 tbsp powder curry
- 1 cup milk coconut
- ½ cup broth vegetable
- 2 lb washed & cleaned mussels
- ¼ cup chopped cilantro fresh

Instructions
- Salt & pepper to taste, and then add the bell pepper, onion, & garlic to the water in a big pan over moderate heat. It's time to let the onions soften! It is possible to add water & the veggies cling to the pan.
- Toss in the curry powders, hot peppers, coconut milk, & veggie broth. To avoid curry powder lumps in the soup, whisk everything together well. Add your muscles to the simmering mixture. When all the mussels have opened, cover & simmer for 5-6 mins, or till they're done cooking. Unopened mussels should be thrown away.
- Serve in individual serving dishes with some chopped cilantro on top. Serve with brown rice & quinoa if preferred.

Nutrition Information
Calories: 331 kcal, Carbohydrates: 15 g, Protein: 29 g, Fat: 18 g

34. Southwestern Brussels Sprout Coleslaw
Prep Time: 15 mins, Cook Time: 45 mins, Servings: 4
Ingredients
- 4 cups shaved Brussels sprouts
- 1 cup roughly chopped kale
- ½ cup charred corn kernels
- 3 tbsp finely minced red onion
- 1 tbsp minced jalapeno
- ¼ cup diced tomatoes
- ¼ cup juice lime
- 1 cup mashed avocado
- 2 tsp honey
- ½ tsp salt kosher
- 1 tsp cumin ground
- 1 tbsp powder chili

Instructions
- Toss your Brussels sprouts, greens & corn with the onion, jalapeño, & tomatoes in a big bowl before serving. Toss gently.
- Combine the additional ingredients in a medium bowl to create a sauce. Add the avocado sauce to Brussels sprouts & stir till everything is covered. Before serving, put the dish in the fridge for almost 30 mins.

Nutrition Information
Calories: 123 kcal, Carbohydrates: 19 g, Protein: 4 g, Fat: 5 g

35. Healthier Olive Garden Garlic Rosemary Chicken
Prep Time: 10 mins, Cook Time: 25 mins, Servings: 6
Ingredients
- 2 tbsp olive oil
- 2 minced garlic cloves
- 2 cups sliced mushrooms fresh
- 24-32 oz chicken breasts boneless & skinless
- ½ tsp salt kosher
- ¼ tsp black pepper ground
- 3 tbsp minced rosemary fresh
- ¼ cup wine Chardonnay dry white
- 1 cup low sodium chicken broth
- 3 cups spinach baby

Instructions
- In a big pan, heat some olive oil over moderate flame. Once the oil is heated, add mushrooms & garlic, then cook for a further min or two. Take the mushrooms from the pan after they have been gently browned.
- Add the leftover olive oil to the pan where the mushrooms had cooked. Then, add your chicken breast, season with pepper, salt, & rosemary. On every side, cook for approximately 6-8 mins, and the chicken must be cooked thoroughly on both sides. Remove your chicken & place it in a warm place to protect it from drying out.
- Add the mushrooms back into the pan. Add both wine & chicken stock to the pan and bring to a boil. After 5 mins, remove from heat; broth should be reduced to a thickening consistency. Add chopped spinach & simmer for a few mins till wilted, then remove from the heat.
- Serve the chicken with the spinach & mushroom sauce over top of it.

Nutrition Information
Calories: 336 kcal, Carbohydrates: 4 g, Protein: 48 g, Fat: 13 g

36. Vegetarian Pizza Casserole
Prep Time: 25 mins, Cook Time: 30 mins, Servings: 6
Ingredients
- 4 cups shredded zucchini
- ½ tsp salt
- 2 large eggs
- ½ cup grated low-fat parmesan cheese
- 1 cup cheese skim mozzarella
- 1 tbsp olive oil
- ½ cup chopped yellow onion
- ½ cup chopped green pepper
- 1 cup shredded carrot
- 2 cups chopped button mushrooms
- 2 tsp seasoning Italian
- 15 oz no sugar sauce jar marinara
- ½ cup fat-free ricotta cheese

Instructions
- Preheat the oven to 400°F. Use nonstick spray to coat a baking dish.
- Sprinkle salt over the zucchini & place it in a strainer to drain. Allow the zucchini to rest for 10 mins before pressing it to extract all of the water. Once pressed, the parmesan, eggs, & mozzarella go into a big bowl with the zucchini. Pour the mixture into the baking dish and push down firmly. To get a beautiful golden-brown color, bake for around 15-20 mins. Remove from the oven and let cool.
- Meanwhile, warm the olive oil in a big pan over medium-high heat. Add the pepper, carrot, onion, & mushroom

after they've warmed through. When the onion & pepper are tender, remove from the heat. Cooked pasta and tomato sauce should be added last. Take off the heat after it reaches a simmer. Put ricotta cheese over zucchini crust using a spoonful and sprinkle it about.
- Bake for another 10-15 mins within the oven. Before serving, cool for around 5 mins.

Nutrition Information
Calories: 237 kcal, Carbohydrates: 14 g, Protein: 15 g, Fat: 15 g

37. "Flush the Fat Away" Lentil and Vegetable Soup
Prep Time: 10 mins, Cook Time: 35 mins, Servings: 4
Ingredients
- 2 cups rinsed dry lentils
- 1 cup rinsed dry quinoa
- 2 shredded carrots
- 1 potato sweet
- 1 diced yellow onion
- 2 minced garlic cloves
- 5 cups low-sodium vegetable broth
- 4 oz green chilis diced
- 2 tsp powder chili
- 1 tsp cumin
- ¼ tsp crushed flakes red pepper
- 1 tsp pepper black
- ½ tsp sea salt
- 2 cups of chard torn & packed
- 1 chopped avocado
- ½ cup chopped cilantro fresh

Instructions
- A big saucepan should be used for this recipe, except for chard, avocado & cilantro. A low boil is achieved by bringing the mixture to your boil & then reducing the heat to maintain a simmer.
- Cook for approximately 30 mins, or until the lentils & quinoa are cooked.
- Add shredded Swiss card & simmer for approximately 5 mins, or till wilted.
- Garnish with sliced avocado & fresh cilantro before serving.

Nutrition Information
Calories: 272 kcal, Carbohydrates: 45 g, Protein: 14 g, Fat: 5 g

38. Low-Carb Philly Cheesesteaks
Prep Time: 10 mins, Cook Time: 10 mins, Servings: 3
Ingredients
- ½ tbsp olive oil
- 2 lb lean sliced sirloin steak
- ½ tsp salt kosher
- ¼ tsp black pepper ground
- 2 tsp oregano leaves dry
- 1 sliced yellow onion
- 1 sliced bell pepper green
- 1 sliced bell pepper red
- 8 large lettuce leaves
- ½ cup shredded provolone cheese
- 2 tbsp roughly chopped cilantro fresh

Instructions
- Add some olive oil to a medium-sized pan and bring it to a boil. The steak should be
seasoned with pepper and salt once the pan is heated. Onions, red and green bell peppers should be added. Depending on the thickness of the beef, heat for 5-10 mins, or unless the meat is cooked thru, and the vegetables are softened.
- Your lettuce cups should be filled with the mixture, & the cheese should be sprinkled on top. Cilantro is a great addition! Serve it hot!

Nutrition Information
Calories: 319 kcal, Carbohydrates: 7 g, Protein: 29 g, Fat: 19 g

39. 15-Min Zucchini Noodle Tomato Salad with Balsamic Dressing
Prep Time: 15 mins, Cook Time: 15 mins, Servings: 2
Ingredients
- 2 medium zucchinis
- 1 cup shredded carrots
- 2 cups tomatoes grape
- 2 tbsp fresh basil
- 1 tbsp minced red onion
- 3 tbsp vinegar dark balsamic
- 1 tbsp paste tomato
- 1 clove garlic
- 2 tsp honey

Instructions
- Make long noodles out of the zucchini by using a spiralizer & putting them in a big basin.
- Zucchini is ready to be served with the addition of carrots, basil, tomatoes, & red onion.
- Blend the garlic, tomato paste, vinegar, & honey in your blender until smooth. Pour this smooth mix over zucchini. Mix the veggies with the dressing until evenly coated using a fork.
- Please wait until you're prepared to serve before putting it in the fridge.

Nutrition Information
Calories: 47 kcal, Carbohydrates: 10 g, Protein: 2 g, Fat: 1 g

40. Easy Roasted Beet and Pecan Salad
Prep Time: 5 mins, Cook Time: 40 mins, Servings: 6
Ingredients
- 1 lb peeled red beets
- 2 tbsp olive oil
- ½ tsp salt kosher
- 2 tbsp honey
- 5 cups spinach baby
- ¼ cup chopped pecans
- ¼ cup fat-free crumbles blue cheese
- 1 tbsp vinegar dark balsamic

Instructions
- Preheat the oven to 400°F.
- Mix the beets, salt, olive oil, & honey in a large bowl until well-combined. Add the beets and toss them to cover the spices. Place on a baking pan and smooth out the top. Beets should be roasted for 30-40 mins, or till they are soft. Let cool fully after removing from oven
- Place fresh spinach over a serving platter. The cooled beets should be topped with them. On the beets, scatter the pecans & blue cheese. To finish, add the honey, balsamic vinegar, & olive oil. It's time to eat!

Nutrition Information
Calories: 114 kcal, Carbohydrates: 11 g, Protein: 3 g, Fat: 7 g

41. Plant-Based Ground Beef Recipe
Prep Time: 10 mins, Cook Time: 45 mins, Servings: 3
Ingredients
Meat Base
- 1 cup rinsed quinoa
- 2 cups low-sodium vegetable broth
- ½ tsp pepper black
- ½ tsp salt
- 1 cup finely diced walnuts raw
- 3 tbsp paste tomato
- 1 tbsp yeast nutritional
- ½ cup no sugar salsa
- ¼ tsp powder garlic
- 2 tsp powder chili
- 2 tsp cumin

Italian
- ½ cup sauce marinara
- ¼ tsp powder garlic
- 2 tsp Italian seasoning or dried oregano

Instructions
- In a small saucepan, combine broth, salt, quinoa, & pepper; bring to your boil; decrease heat, and simmer for 12-15 minutes, unless the stock is absorbed. Allow the pot to sit for five mins after turning off the flame and covering it.
- Preheat the oven to 400°F.
- Toss the quinoa with the rest of the ingredients and mix well. Spread out on a baking sheet in an even layer. Bake for 15 mins, mix, & spread out evenly over the sheet.
- Serve with your favorite Italian or Mexican recipes after removing the sheet. To extend the shelf-life of your vegan meat, store it in the freezer.

Nutrition Information
Calories: 91 kcal, Carbohydrates: 13 g, Protein: 4 g, Fat: 3 g

42. Sesame Kale Salad with Ginger Soy Dressing
Prep Time: 20 mins, Cook Time: 20 mins, Servings: 4
Ingredients
For Salad
- 4 cups roughly chopped kale
- 1 cup finely chopped Brussels sprouts
- ½ cup shredded red cabbage
- ½ cup shredded carrots
- ½ cup thinly sliced cucumber

For Dressing
- 2 tbsp vinegar rice
- 1 tbsp sauce soy
- 1 tsp honey
- 1 tsp grated ginger fresh
- 1 tsp seeds sesame
- 1 tsp zest orange

Instructions
For Salad
- Toss all of the ingredients together in a medium bowl until well-coordinated. Serve in various bowls and serve with roughly 2 tbsp dressing drizzled over the top.

For Dressing
- Whisk the ingredients together in a mixing bowl. Allow sitting for a minimum of five mins. Before spreading the dressing on the salad, please give it a brief swirl.

Nutrition Information
Calories: 89 kcal, Carbohydrates: 17 g, Protein: 6 g, Fat: 2 g

43. Roasted Beet and Hazelnut Vegetable Dip
Prep Time: 5 mins, Cook Time: 1 hr 10 mins, Servings: 8
Ingredients
- 1 & ½ lb unpeeled beets washed
- 2 minced garlic cloves
- 2 tbsp fresh thyme leaves
- ½ tsp salt kosher
- ½ tsp black pepper ground
- 2 tbsp vinegar apple cider
- ¾ cup of hazelnuts
- 2 tsp syrup maple

Instructions
- Preheat the oven to 400°F.
- Place your beet on a big sheet of Al foil over a level surface. Salt & pepper to taste; garlic & thyme to taste; vinegar to taste; salt to taste; pepper to taste; garlic to taste. Place your beets over a baking pan and cover them with Al foil. Bake for an hr, or unless the beets are tender and can be pierced with a knife. Remove from heat and allow to cool to the touch.
- Bring water in a big pot to your boil while you're at it. Boil your hazelnuts for around 4 mins once they've reached a rolling boil. Rinse & pat dry your hazelnuts once they have been drained from the water. Toasted for three mins over a baking pan after being completely dry. Take out the nuts and toast for a further three mins. Remove & let to cool before putting it back in.
- Peel the beets' skins after they are cold enough to handle by gently rubbing them off. Toss the roasted hazelnuts, salt, pepper, vinegar & maple syrup with the beets in your food processor, then pulse until smooth. Blend until completely smooth.
- You may also serve it with some of your preferred raw vegetables.

Nutrition Information
Calories: 110 kcal, Carbohydrates: 9 g, Protein: 3 g, Fat: 8 g

44. Baked Tofu Chunks with Star Anise Marinade
Prep Time: 5 Mins, Cook Time: 40 Mins, Servings: 4
Ingredients
- 1 lb tofu firm
- 2 tbsp wine rice
- 2 tbsp tamari
- 2 tsp palm sugar coconut
- ¼ tsp freshly ground powder star anise
- ½ tsp freshly ground Sichuan peppercorns

Instructions
- Slice a tofu block into 4-5 rectangular planks by slicing it in half lengthwise & sideways. If necessary, add more vegetable broth to the pan to replace what has evaporated & to deglaze the pan.
- Bake your tofu planks for around 20 mins at 400°F over a baking sheet. Allow the planks to cool.
- Slice your planks into half-inch squares & marinate them in the fridge for almost an hr before cooking them.
- Seasoned tofu cubes may be added to any salad or rice dressing for a blast of flavor.

Nutrition Information
Calories: 188 kcal, Carbohydrates: 8 g, Protein: 19 g, Fat: 10 g

45. Turkey Sausage Egg Roll Bowl
Prep time: 15 Mins, Cook Time: 35 Mins, Servings: 4
Ingredients
- 1 lb turkey sausage ground
- 1 tbsp sesame oil
- 1 cup shredded carrot
- 4 cups shredded green cabbage
- 1 cup shredded red cabbage
- ½ cup sliced thin yellow onion
- 4 minced garlic cloves
- 1 tbsp minced ginger fresh
- 1 tbsp sauce soy
- ½ tsp salt kosher
- ½ tsp black pepper ground
- ¼ cup chopped green onions
- ¼ cup chopped cilantro fresh

Instructions
- A big skillet should be heated over medium-high heat. Then add your turkey sausage & heat, often turning, until it is well cooked. Drain sausage of any extra fat.
- Using a medium-sized saucepan, heat sesame oil over medium-high heat. Then add cabbage (including red cabbage), carrots, onions, soy sauce, garlic, ginger, & salt/pepper to the sausage. It should take 3-4 mins of cooking for the cabbage to wilt but not completely lose its crisp.
- Toss in green onions & cilantro before serving.

Nutrition Information
Calories: 255 kcal, Carbohydrates: 12 g, Protein: 24 g, Fat: 13 g

46. 3-Ingredient Vanilla Frosting
Prep Time: 5 mins, Cook Time: 5 mins, Servings: 16
Ingredients
- 8 oz reduced-fat cream cheese
- ¼ cup of honey
- 1 tsp vanilla pure

Instructions
- In a large bowl, combine all of the ingredients & beat for 3-5 mins.

- Please keep it in the fridge until you're ready to use it over the cupcake.

Nutrition Information
Calories: 53 kcal, Carbohydrates: 4 g, Protein: 1 g, Fat: 4 g

47. Broccoli and Mushroom Stir-Fry
Prep Time: 10 mins, Cook Time: 20 mins, Servings: 6
Ingredients
- 2 cups of broccoli
- ¼ cup chopped small red onion
- 3 minced cloves garlic
- 2 cups sliced mushrooms
- ¼ tsp red pepper crushed
- 2 tsp grated ginger fresh
- ¼ cup of vegetable broth
- ½ cup of carrot shredded
- ¼ cup of cashews
- 2 tbsp vinegar rice wine
- 2 tbsp low-sodium soy sauce
- 1 tbsp sugar coconut
- 1 tbsp seeds sesame

Instructions
- Combine all of these ingredients in a big pan over high heat & cook until the vegetables are tender but not mushy. Broccoli & onions should be cooked until they have softened and become transparent. Vegetables will not stick if you add enough broth and additional as required.
- Make a paste by combining all of the ingredients in a food processor. Cook for around 2 mins, stirring often. Sesame seeds may be used as a garnish. Serve with brown rice as a side dish.

Nutrition Information
Calories: 114 kcal, Carbohydrates: 15 g, Protein: 5 g, Fat: 5 g

48. Homemade Roasted Tomato Soup
Prep Time: 5 mins, Cook Time: 45 mins, Servings: 6
Ingredients
- 10 sliced Roma tomatoes
- 1 tbsp olive oil
- ½ tsp salt kosher
- ¼ tsp black pepper ground
- ¼ cup vinegar dark balsamic
- 2 cups broth vegetable
- ½ cup milk skim
- 2 tbsp honey
- ¼ cup fresh basil
- cheese parmesan

Instructions
- Preheat the oven to 400°F. Spread chopped tomatoes out on the baking sheet that has been lined with Al foil. Add salt, vinegar, & pepper to taste. Drizzle with olive oil. Approximately 30-35 mins, or unless your tomatoes start burning, depending on the size of the tomatoes.
- In tiny batches, mix the roasted tomatoes in a blender unless smooth. Add water to thin it up if the tomato mix is thick to combine. Add the pulverized tomatoes to a large saucepan and bring to a boil.
- Add the milk, vegetable broth, & honey to the pureed tomatoes in a soup pot while the soup is simmering on moderate flame. Bring the mix to the simmer, stirring often. Ten mins of simmering are required. The basil should be sprinkled on the serving dishes.
- Parmesan cheese, if preferred, may be sprinkled on top of the pasta.

Nutrition Information
Calories: 117 kcal, Carbohydrates: 19 g, Protein: 3 g, Fat: 4 g

49. Baked Tofu Chunks with Cajun Spice Dry Rub
Prep Time: 30 Mins, Cook Time: 20, Servings: 4
Ingredients
- 5 tsp salt
- 2 tbsp paprika
- 2 tbsp powder garlic
- 1 tbsp oregano dried
- 1 tbsp thyme dried
- 1 tsp cayenne pepper
- 1 tbsp pepper black
- 1 tbsp powder onion
- 1 tsp palm sugar coconut
- 1 lb tofu extra-firm

Instructions
- Set aside the spices for later use.
- Slice any tofu block into 4-5 rectangular planks by slicing it in half lengthwise & sideways. If necessary, add more vegetable broth to the pan to replace what has evaporated & to deglaze the pan as you do so.
- Apply spice mix to the planks one at a time, ensuring they are well covered.
- Bake the covered tofu slabs for around 20 mins at 400°F on a baking sheet. Wait until the slabs have cooled before handling them.

Nutrition Information
Calories: 212 kcal, Carbohydrates: 15 g, Protein: 20 g, Fat: 11 g

50. Dairy-Free Parmesan Cheese in Under 5 Mins
Prep Time: 5 mins, Cook Time: 5 mins, Servings: 4
Ingredients
- 1 cup raw cashews
- ¼ cup yeast nutritional
- 1/8 tsp powder garlic
- ½ tsp salt (sea)

Instructions
- To make the sauce, put all ingredients within blender & pulse until smooth and resembles parmesan cheese, about 30 pulses. Over-processing might cause the mixture to clump.
- Refrigerate in a sealed jar.

Nutrition Information
Calories: 89 kcal, Carbohydrates: 6 g, Protein: 5 g, Fat: 6 g

51. A Healthy Coffee Creamer
Prep Time: 20 Mins, Cook Time: 35 Mins, Servings: 3
Ingredients
- 1 cup raw almonds
- 10 dates pitted
- 2 cups water purified
- ½ tsp vanilla pure

Instructions
- Set nuts in a mixing bowl, cover using a kitchen towel, & let soak for a few hrs or overnight.
- Add dates & filtered water to a dish, then cover within the refrigerator for at least one to two hrs before creating the creamer.
- If you have time, soak the almonds for 8-10 hrs. Toss out the soaking solution.
- Almonds should be washed in the colander after being soaked in hot water. Blend dates and almonds in a blender if you have one.
- Dates & almonds should be crushed to a fine powder in a food processor or blender.
- Then, gently pour the blended ingredients through the nut bag & into a big basin. Gently squeeze your bag with both hands till all liquid has been released. Stir in the optional vanilla extract until well-combined.
- Store your creamer inside the refrigerator in a jar with a lid.
- In the refrigerator, nut creamer may be stored for almost a week.

Nutrition Information
Calories: 110 kcal, Carbohydrates: 10 g, Protein: 3 g, Fat: 7 g

52. 30-Min Lemon Basil Shrimp and Asparagus Recipe
Prep Time: 15 Mins, Cook Time: 35, Servings: 5

Ingredients
- 2 tbsp water
- 2 minced garlic cloves
- 2 tbsp finely minced yellow onion
- 1 lb medium size shrimp fresh
- ½ tsp grated ginger fresh
- ½ tsp salt kosher
- ¼ tsp black pepper ground
- ¼ tsp red pepper crushed
- 1 tbsp juice lemon
- 1 lb ends trimmed asparagus
- 1 tsp zest lemon
- 3 tbsp roughly chopped basil fresh

Instructions
- The garlic & onion are added to a large pan over moderate heat with the water. The garlic & onion should be aromatic after approximately a min of cooking.
- Serve immediately with a side of asparagus & a side of shrimp and ginger sauce. If onions & garlic have absorbed all water, add more water to the mixture. Cover and let sit for around 2 mins before sprinkling with salt and pepper. Stir, then put the lid back on. Continue to boil the shrimp until they are pink, firm, and fully done. Ideally, the asparagus must be lime green & just starting to soften but still have a little crunch when done.
- Lemon zest & fresh basil may be added at this point. It's time to eat!

Nutrition Information
Calories: 110 kcal, Carbohydrates: 7 g, Protein: 18 g, Fat: 1 g

53. Rainbow Salsa Recipe
Prep Time: 10 mins, Cook Time: 10 mins, Servings: 5
Ingredients
- 2 diced small tomatoes
- 1 habanero minced pepper small
- 1 diced small bell pepper yellow
- ¼ cup chopped cilantro fresh
- 1 diced small red onion
- 1 tbsp juice lime
- 1 tsp kosher salt
- 14 oz drained & rinsed black beans

Instructions
- Mix all of the ingredients well together before serving. Wait a few mins until serving to allow the flavors to meld.

Nutrition Information
Calories: 79 kcal, Carbohydrates: 15 g, Protein: 5 g, Fat: 0 g

54. Yam Balls with Coconut & Pecans Recipe
Prep Time: 1 hr, Cook Time: 15 mins, Servings: 2 balls
Ingredients
- 4 medium sweet potatoes
- ¼ cup syrup maple
- 2 tsp zest orange
- 1 tsp ginger ground
- 1 tsp cinnamon
- 1 large egg white
- ¼ tsp salt kosher
- 2 & ½ cups unsweetened shredded coconut
- ¾ cup chopped pecans

Instructions
- The oven should be preheated at 425 °F. Set aside the baking sheet that has been lined using parchment paper.
- The yams should be well cleaned and dried. Prick the surface using a fork on all four sides after patting it dry. Bake for around 40-50 mins, or until tender, on a baking sheet that has been lined with parchment paper. Yams should be cold enough to handle after being taken out of the oven.
- Line a separate baking sheet using parchment paper & lower the oven temp to 350°F.
- After they've cooled down, split the yams in half & scoop out the flesh into a medium-sized mixing bowl. Make a smooth paste by pulverizing the ingredients in a food processor in a medium saucepan; combine maple syrup with orange zest, cinnamon, ginger root, & egg white.
- Combine the pecans, coconut, & the rest of the maple syrup in a separate mixing bowl & stir until well combined. Gently roll these yam balls within coconut pecan mix before forming them into two-inch balls. To make the ball, gently push the coconut into it. On the 2nd baking sheet, place 1" apart.
- Bake for approximately 15 mins at 350 degrees. Before serving, let it sit for a few mins to cool somewhat.

Nutrition Information
Calories: 222 kcal, Carbohydrates: 19 g, Protein: 3 g, Fat: 16 g

55. Creamy Broccoli Soup Recipe
Prep Time: 10 Mins, Cook Time: 25 Mins, Servings: 10
Ingredients
- 4 cups of broccoli florets
- 3 cups no sugar vegetable broth
- ¼ tsp salt
- ½ tsp pepper black
- 1 cup canned coconut milk

Instructions
- Set aside half a cup of steamed florets for later use.
- In a blender, combine the first four ingredients, except for the diced florets, in that sequence. A creamy texture may be achieved by blending the ingredients for an extended period.
- Stir in the remaining chopped broccoli & coconut milk, then bring the soup to a boil over moderate flame.
- Whole-grain croutons may be added if desired.

Nutrition Information
Calories: 53 kcal, Carbohydrates: 2 g, Protein: 1 g, Fat: 5 g

56. No-Bake Almond Energy Balls
Prep Time: 35 mins, Cook Time: 35 mins, Servings: 20
Ingredients
- 1 cup dry oats old-fashioned
- ¼ cup natural almond butter
- ¼ cup honey agave syrup
- ¼ cup finely diced almonds
- ½ tsp vanilla extract pure
- ¼ cup chocolate chips mini

Instructions
- In a medium bowl, add all of the ingredients & stir well.
- Refrigerate the mixture for approximately 30 mins, or until it is somewhat firm and manageable to work with. A baking sheet should be used to roll out the dough into 1-inch balls.
- Serve right away or keep in a sealed jar in the refrigerator.

Nutrition Information
Calories: 139 kcal, Carbohydrates: 18 g, Protein: 4 g, Fat: 6 g

57. Chocolate Chip Coconut Cookies
Prep Time: 25 Mins, Cook Time: 30 Mins, Servings: 18
Ingredients
- 2 tsp extract vanilla
- 1 large egg
- 1/3 cup sugar coconut
- ½ cup melted & cooled coconut oil
- 1 cup white flour whole-wheat
- ½ tsp soda baking
- ½ cup chocolate chips semisweet
- ½ cup unsweetened shredded coconut

Instructions
- Set the oven temperature to 350 degrees.
- The oil and sugar should be combined in a bowl with the vanilla & the egg. Mix till a homogeneous mixture is achieved. Add flour & baking soda, then stir until they're

evenly distributed. Incorporate chocolate chips & coconut by folding them in.
- Drop your batter onto the baking sheet that has not been coated with cooking spray. Bake your cookies for 7-8 mins, or unless the edges start to brown. Before serving, allow the food to come to room temperature.

Nutrition Information
Calories: 198 kcal, Carbohydrates: 18 g, Protein: 2 g, Fat: 14 g

58. Curry Chicken Casserole Recipe
Prep Time: 15 mins, Cook Time: 20 mins, Servings: 4
Ingredients
- 1 cup cooked brown rice
- 3 cups of broccoli
- 14 oz drained & rinsed chickpeas
- 2 cups cooked & shredded chicken
- 3 tbsp melted coconut oil
- ½ cup diced small onion
- 3 minced garlic cloves
- 2 tbsp paste tomato
- 1 cup milk coconut
- ½ cup plain Greek yogurt
- 1 cup shredded low-fat cheddar cheese
- 4 tsp powder curry

Instructions
- Preheat your oven to 400°F Set aside a casserole dish that has been sprayed with cooking spray.
- Mix the broccoli, chickpeas, cooked rice, & chicken. Toss everything together and put it away.
- In a small skillet, melt some coconut oil. When the oil is heated, green onions & sauté often turn until they soften. Add the garlic & tomato paste, then mix well. One minute of cooking time is needed for the garlic to become aromatic.
- Reduce the heat to low, whisk in some milk, and simmer until thickened. Add the cheese, yogurt, & curry powder to the mixture and mix well. The mixture should begin to thicken after being simmered for 2-3 mins, stirring regularly.
- The sauce should be poured on top of the chicken & broccoli. Mix everything well, then add the chicken & lay it out within the casserole dish you've prepared.
- It should take between 15 and 20 mins to cook through.

Nutrition Information
Calories: 304 kcal, Carbohydrates: 13 g, Protein: 14 g, Fat: 23 g

59. Citrus Brussels Sprout and Pecan Salad
Prep Time: 25 mins, Cook Time: 25 mins, Servings: 0.5 cup
Ingredients
- 1 lb Brussels sprouts
- ¼ cup no sugar dried cranberries
- 1 cup peeled & chopped apple
- ½ cup roughly chopped pecans
- ¼ cup fat-free blue cheese
- ¼ cup cooked & crumbled turkey bacon
- 2 tbsp olive oil
- 2 tbsp balsamic vinegar white
- 1 tbsp maple syrup pure
- 1 tsp mustard Dijon

Instructions
- Mix the Brussels sprouts, blue cheese, pecans, cranberries, apple, & bacon in a mixing bowl. Toss everything together and put it in the fridge for later.
- Blend the maple syrup, vinegar, olive oil, and mustard inside a blender until smooth. To make a dressing, mix well. Combine the Brussels sprout combination with the completed dressing in a large bowl and stir to coat all ingredients. Before serving, allow the mixture to settle for around 10 mins & then refrigerate.

Nutrition Information
Calories: 209 kcal, Carbohydrates: 17 g, Protein: 5 g, Fat: 15 g

60. One-Pot Sesame Chicken Recipe
Prep Time: 10 Mins, Cook Time: 20 Mins, Servings: 5
Ingredients
- 2 tbsp oil sesame
- 1 lb chicken breasts boneless & skinless
- 1 peeled carrot
- 3 tbsp low-sodium soy sauce
- 2 tbsp honey
- ¼ tsp red pepper crushed
- 1 tsp grated ginger fresh
- 1 minced garlic clove
- 1 tbsp cornstarch
- 2 tbsp sesame seeds
- ¼ cup sliced green onion

Instructions
- Moderate heat for sesame oil. Heat the oil over medium heat in a skillet, then add both chicken & carrots. Cook chicken till it is firm & fully done. Any remaining liquid should be drained.
- All ingredients, excluding sesame seeds & green onion, should be combined in a small dish. Pour the sauce over the chicken after it's done cooking. Bring to your boil & cook for one min, or unless the sauce thickens, and the chicken is well-coated. Add sesame seeds and mix well. Green onions may be added at this point if desired. If preferred, serve over brown rice.

Nutrition Information
Calories: 278 kcal, Carbohydrates: 14 g, Protein: 28 g, Fat: 12 g

61. Egg Stuffed Baked Portobello Mushroom
Prep Time: 10 mins, Cook Time: 20 mins, Servings: 4
Ingredients
- 4 stems removed portobello mushrooms
- 2 tbsp olive oil
- ½ tsp kosher salt
- ¼ tsp black pepper ground
- ¼ tsp powder garlic
- 4 large eggs
- 2 tbsp grated parmesan cheese
- ¼ cup chopped parsley fresh

Instructions
- Set the oven's broiler to the highest setting and prepare the food. Al foil may be used to cover a baking pan.
- Both sides of the mushroom caps should be slathered using olive oil before cooking. Toss with a halved quantity of salt, pepper, & garlic powder. Broil for 5 mins on every side, or unless the meat is just done.
- Remove the mushrooms from the oven & drain off all the liquid. Adjust the oven temp to 400°F.
- Top every mushroom with some parmesan cheese & an egg. Bake for 15 mins, or until the egg whites have set.
- Salt, pepper, & garlic powder are all that are needed to complete the seasoning. Toss the parsley on top of the dish and serve.

Nutrition Information
Calories: 188 kcal, Carbohydrates: 6 g, Protein: 12 g, Fat: 14 g

62. Spicy Asian Brussels Sprouts
Prep Time: 10 mins, Cook Time: 30 mins, Servings: 6
Ingredients
- 1 lb fresh Brussels sprouts
- 3 tbsp low-sodium soy sauce
- 2 tbsp olive oil
- 1 tbsp honey
- 1 tbsp juice lemon
- 2 minced garlic cloves
- ¼ tsp red pepper crushed

Instructions
- Preheat the oven to 400°F. Set aside the baking sheet that has been lined using parchment paper.
- Add sliced Brussels sprouts to a medium bowl, along with the other ingredients, and mix well unless the sprouts are

completely covered in oil. Place the baking sheet with the mixture in a uniform layer.
- Sprouts should be golden & crispy after 30 mins of baking; flip them halfway through the time.

Nutrition Information
Calories: 134 kcal, Carbohydrates: 16 g, Protein: 5 g, Fat: 7 g

63. Roasted Sweet Potatoes with Turmeric and Cardamom Recipe
Prep Time: 10 mins, Cook Time: 40 mins, Servings: 8
Ingredients
- 2 peeled & diced sweet potatoes
- 2 minced garlic cloves
- 2 tsp turmeric ground
- 2 tbsp olive oil
- 1 tsp cardamom ground
- 1 tbsp fresh thyme leaves

Instructions
- Preheat the oven to 400°F.
- Toss the other ingredients together in a big dish, excluding the fresh thyme. Pour the ingredients and oil into a large bowl and mix well. After placing the potatoes over the baking sheet, bake for around 30-40 mins, rotating the potatoes halfway through until they're tender.
- Remove your potatoes from the oven when they're fork-tender & sprinkle them with thyme. Serve & revel in the delicacies!

Nutrition Information
Calories: 141 kcal, Carbohydrates: 19 g, Protein: 2 g, Fat: 7 g

64. Healthier "Energy-Boosting" Granola Recipe
Prep Time: 5 mins, Cook Time: 15 mins, Servings: 5
Ingredients
- 1 & ½ cups of rolled gluten-free oats
- ½ cup seeds pumpkin
- ½ cup sesame seeds
- 2 tbsp honey
- 2 tbsp melted coconut oil

Instructions
- Set the oven temperature to 350°F.
- Combine all of the ingredients. A baking sheet should be used to distribute the granola evenly. During the 15 mins of baking, mix the granola every 8 mins. Before storing in an airtight container, let it chill to room temperature.
- The granola is great on top of oatmeal or mixed with Greek yogurt for a hearty breakfast.

Nutrition Information
Calories: 93 kcal, Carbohydrates: 9 g, Protein: 3 g, Fat: 6 g

65. Slow Cooker Carrot Turmeric Soup
Prep Time: 10 mins, Cook Time: 4 hrs 10 mins, Servings: 7
Ingredients
- 6-8 peeled & chopped carrots
- 1 chopped onion
- 4 cups broth vegetable
- ½ cup milk coconut
- 1 tsp powder curry
- ½ tsp ginger ground
- 2 tsp turmeric ground
- ¼ cup plain Greek yogurt

Instructions
- In your slow cooker, combine all ingredients, excluding the yogurt, then cook for around 4 hrs on high.
- Blend your soup in the blender till it's creamy and frothy. Batches of work may be required for this.
- Stir in the yogurt till the soup is creamy & smooth, then return to your slow cooker. Serve at once.

Nutrition Information
Calories: 92 kcal, Carbohydrates: 11 g, Protein: 2 g, Fat: 5 g

66. Quick and Easy Marinara
Prep Time: 5 mins, Cook Time: 35 mins, Servings: 8
Ingredients
- 28 oz plum tomatoes whole peeled
- 1 tbsp olive oil extra virgin
- 1 small, diced yellow onion
- 2 minced garlic cloves
- 1 tbsp vinegar balsamic
- salt & black pepper freshly cracked
- 1 tbsp freshly chopped basil

Instructions
- Pulse chopped tomatoes in your food processor till they are completely smooth. Set away for later.
- Over moderate flame, sauté the onion and garlic in the oil in a skillet.
- For approximately 5 mins, add onion & continue to cook until translucent. Add garlic, then simmer for a min or so until it's fragrant.
- Add the balsamic vinegar, tomato puree, salt & pepper to the mixture. Upon reaching a simmer, turn the heat down to low. At this point, the sauce should be thick and well-combined, perhaps 20-25 mins in total, with constant stirring.
- Add chopped basil & adjust the seasoning to your liking with a pinch of salt and pepper.

Nutrition Information
Calories: 53 kcal, Carbohydrates: 7 g, Protein: 1 g, Fat: 3g

67. Clean Eating Oven Roasted Mushrooms
Prep Time: 5 mins, Cook Time: 30 mins, Servings: 4
Ingredients
- 4 cups mushrooms the whole button
- 2 tbsp olive oil
- 2 minced garlic cloves
- 2 tbsp vinegar dark balsamic
- ½ tsp salt kosher
- 2 tbsp chopped parsley fresh

Instructions
- Preheat the oven to 400°F. Set aside the baking sheet that has been lined using parchment paper.
- Add the mushrooms to a large bowl and toss to mix. A mixture of garlic, vinegar, olive oil, & salt Toss your mushrooms well to cover them within the oil. Place the baking sheet with the mixture in a uniform layer. About 30 mins in the oven, with a half-turn halfway through cooking time.
- Top with fresh parsley after removing it from your oven. It's time to eat!

Nutrition Information
Calories: 91 kcal, Carbohydrates: 5 g, Protein: 3 g, Fat: 7 g

68. This Sun-Dried Tomato Chicken Makes Clean Eating Simple
Prep Time: 15 Mins, Cook Time: 25 Mins, Servings: 6
Ingredients
- 2 tbsp olive oil
- 1 sliced yellow onion
- ¾ cup roughly chopped sundried tomatoes
- 4 chicken breasts boneless & skinless
- 2 minced garlic cloves
- 1 tsp seasoning Italian
- 1 & ½ cups light coconut milk
- 1 cup broth chicken
- ¼ cup roughly chopped basil fresh

Instructions
- Preheat the oven to 400°F.
- Olive oil should be heated in a wide oven-safe pan. Make sure to sear each chicken breast side inside the heated oil unless it's slightly browned. There is no need to worry about overcooking the chicken; it'll be returned to your pan for further cooking later.
- Make sure you use the same pan you used to cook the chicken. When the onion is tender and transparent, add the garlic and cook for another min. Add the coconut

milk, Italian spice, & broth to the mixture. Return your chicken to sauce mix & bring it to a boil.
- Place the dish within the oven & seal the edges with Al foil. Chicken should be cooked thoroughly in around 15-20 mins. To serve, remove from the oven and garnish with basil.

Nutrition Information
Calories: 372 kcal, Carbohydrates: 13 g, Protein: 19 g, Fat: 27 g

69. Savory Carrot Bacon
Prep Time: 5 mins, Cook Time: 20 mins, Servings: 9
Ingredients
- 1 tbsp tahini
- 1 tbsp sesame oil
- 2 tsp sauce soy
- 1 tbsp honey
- 1 tsp mustard Dijon
- ½ tsp smoke liquid
- 2 sliced carrots large

Instructions
- Preheat the oven to 400°F. Using parchment paper, prepare the baking sheet.
- Carrots may be sliced into tiny strips using a sharp knife. To avoid breaking the carrot strips, don't press too hard.
- All ingredients for this dish may be mixed in a separate bowl and whisked together

until smooth. Apply the mixture on all sides of strips of carrot.
- Place a single layer of seasoned carrot strips over a baking sheet. Remove from your oven after ten mins of cooking time. Turn each piece of carrot over & bake again. Lightly browned & crisp, continue cooking for another 5-10 mins. Remove from the pan when it has cooled down a little.
- Allow to cool entirely in the original container, uncovered. Keep at room temp with a loose covering.

Nutrition Information
Calories: 85 kcal, Carbohydrates: 9 g, Protein: 1 g, Fat: 6 g

70. Tuscan Salad Recipe with Mixed Greens and Lemon Caper Vinaigrette
Prep Time: 15 mins, Cook Time: 15 mins, Servings: 2
Ingredients
For Salad
- 1 cup chopped romaine lettuce
- 1 cup arugula baby
- 1 cup of radicchio
- 2 cup spinach baby
- ½ cup fat-free provolone cheese
- ¼ cup of capers
- 4 peeled & sliced eggs boiled
- ½ cup roughly chopped salmon cooked

For Dressing
- 1 & ½ tbsp juice lemon
- 1 tsp honey
- 1 tsp mustard Dijon
- 2 tbsp olive oil
- ½ tbsp capers

Instructions
For Salad
- In a medium bowl, add all of the ingredients & gently mix.

For Dressing
- A blender with all the ingredients should mix them unless smooth. A dressing may be drizzled over the top and enjoyed!

Nutrition Information
Calories: 377 kcal, Carbohydrates: 6 g, Protein: 25 g, Fat: 28 g

71. Rise and Shine with These Greek Egg Muffins!
Prep Time: 5 mins, Cook Time: 20 mins, Servings: 5
Ingredients
- 2 large eggs
- 4 large egg whites
- ½ cup milk skim
- ½ tsp salt kosher
- ¼ tsp white pepper ground
- ¼ cup diced small tomatoes
- ¼ cup diced small red onion
- ¼ cup diced small black olives
- 1 tbsp roughly chopped parsley fresh
- ¼ cup crumbles fat-free feta cheese

Instructions
- Spray a six-cup muffin tray using nonstick spray & heat the oven to around 350 degrees Fahrenheit.
- Salt & pepper to taste are added to the milk and eggs in a large bowl. Whisk vigorously until the mixture is somewhat foamy, then remove from the heat. Add the rest of the ingredients and mix.
- Fill every muffin cup approximately three-quarters of the way with the egg mix. Bake for around 15-20 mins unless the muffins are cooked through & slightly browned over the top. Cook and enjoy right away, and then refrigerate & reheat for healthy breakfast on the road.

Nutrition Information
Calories: 45 kcal, Carbohydrates: 2 g, Protein: 5 g, Fat: 2 g

72. Slow Cooker Roasted Sugared Pecans
Prep Time: 5 mins, Cook Time: 3 hrs, Servings: 12
Ingredients
- 1 lb halved pecan
- ½ cup melted butter
- ¼ cup sugar coconut
- 2 tbsp honey
- 1 & ½ tsp cinnamon ground
- ¼ tsp clove ground
- ¼ tsp nutmeg ground

Instructions
- Make your slow cooker and add the pecans to it. Toss the pecans in the melted butter and mix until evenly coated. Toss in the rest of the ingredients & pecans until well-coated.
- Stirring periodically, cook for around 3 hrs over high with the cover OFF.
- The finished product should be spread out on a baking sheet. Completely cool down. Store tightly wrapped within the pantry rather than the refrigerator to preserve freshness.

Nutrition Information
Calories: 267 kcal, Carbohydrates: 9 g, Protein: 3 g, Fat: 26 g

73. Loaded Southwest Corn and Zucchini Skillet
Prep Time: 5 mins, Cook Time: 10 mins, Servings: 4
Ingredients
- 1 tbsp oil olive
- 2 minced garlic cloves
- ¼ diced small red onion
- 3 diced medium zucchinis
- 1 cup frozen corn kernels
- ¼ tsp oregano leaves dried
- ½ tsp cumin ground
- ½ tsp salt kosher
- ¼ tsp black pepper ground
- 2 tsp juice lime
- 2 tbsp chopped cilantro fresh
- 3 tbsp finely grated fat-free cheddar cheese

Instructions
- Olive oil should be heated in a big skillet. Add the onion, zucchini, garlic, & corn to the pan once it's heated. The zucchini should be tender, and the onion should be transparent when the dish is done cooking.
- Add the salt, pepper, oregano, cumin, & lime juice to the mixture and mix it well. Stir and heat for a min. Remove from the heat and mix within cilantro & feta cheese.

Nutrition Information
Calories: 146 kcal, Carbohydrates: 14 g, Protein: 5 g, Fat: 8 g

74. Baked Kale and Eggs with Ricotta
Prep Time: 15 Mins, Cook Time: 30 Mins, Servings: 6
Ingredients
- 1 tbsp olive oil
- 6 cups roughly chopped stems removed kale
- 2 minced garlic cloves
- ¼ cup fat-free ricotta cheese
- ¼ cup fat-free feta crumbles
- 4 large eggs
- 1/3 cup tomatoes grape
- ¼ tsp black pepper ground
- ½ tsp kosher salt

Instructions
- The oven should be preheated at 350°F. Set aside a casserole dish sprayed using non-stick spray.
- Olive oil should be heated over medium-high heat in a big pan. Add the greens & garlic to the pan after it's at a safe temperature. Cook your kale unless it is wilted & tender, then serve. Remove from the stove and let it cool.
- In a mixing bowl, combine the ricotta & feta cheeses and stir well.
- To bake the kale, place your cooked kale within the baking dish that was previously prepared. Put a beaten egg into those four wells you've made within kale. Dotting the cheese mix around the eggs over the kale using a spoon, roughly every mouthful. Top with sliced cherry tomatoes & season with salt & pepper to your liking. The whites should be done and brown in about 20-25 minutes.

Nutrition Information
Calories: 170 kcal, Carbohydrates: 4 g, Protein: 11 g, Fat: 12 g

75. Blueberry French Toast Casserole
Prep Time: 15 mins, Cook Time: 30 mins, Servings: 3
Ingredients
- 2 cups bread whole-grain
- 4 large egg whites
- 1 cup of milk coconut
- 2 tbsp maple syrup pure
- 1 tsp extract vanilla
- ½ tsp extract almond
- 1 tsp cinnamon ground
- 1 cup fresh blueberries

Instructions
- The oven should be preheated at 350°F & a casserole dish should be sprayed using non-stick spray. Set aside your sliced bread within the dish that has been made.
- The other ingredients, excluding the blueberries, should be mixed well in the mixing dish. After you've moistened bread cubes completely, pour the remaining liquid over them. Toss your bread with blueberries before serving.
- Bake for around 30-40 mins, or unless the casserole is gently browned & bread cubes have absorbed all of the liquid from the casserole.

Nutrition Information
Calories: 123 kcal, Carbohydrates: 13 g, Protein: 4 g, Fat: 7 g

76. Sweet Potato and Zucchini Casserole
Prep Time: 20 mins, Cook Time: 25 mins, Servings: 8
Ingredients
- 1 tbsp olive oil
- ½ cup diced small yellow onions
- 2 diced medium zucchini
- 2 minced garlic cloves
- 1 lb sausage ground turkey
- 15 oz no sugar diced tomatoes
- 2 tbsp no sugar tomato paste
- 1 tbsp seasoning Italian
- 2 sweet peeled & sliced potatoes medium
- ½ cup shredded fat-free mozzarella cheese
- 2 tbsp grated parmesan cheese
- 2 tbsp chopped parsley fresh

Instructions
- Set the oven temperature to 350°F. Set aside casserole dish sprayed using non-stick spray.
- Olive oil should be heated in a big skillet. Add the onions, zucchini, & garlic to the pan once heated. When the onions start to soften, remove them from the heat. Toss within turkey sausage, slice it into tiny pieces, & cook unless it's no longer pink. Stir in tomato paste, chopped tomatoes, & Italian seasonings. Just before the mixture reaches a simmer, stir continuously. Removing the food from the heat is necessary.
- Your sweet potato rounds should be placed in the casserole dish that has been preheated. Mix within sausage, then sprinkle with some mozzarella & parmesan. The potatoes should be done in around 25-30 mins. The cheese may be covered with foil if something starts to burn too much during the cooking process.
- Preparation: Sprinkle with some parsley on the plate.

Nutrition Information
Calories: 193 kcal, Carbohydrates: 12 g, Protein: 15 g, Fat: 9 g

77. Ham and Egg Cups
Prep Time: 10 mins, Cook Time: 20 mins, Servings: 2
Ingredients
- 12 slices of ham all-natural low sodium
- 3 large eggs
- 3 large egg whites
- ½ cup milk skim
- 2 chopped green onions

Instructions
- Preheat the oven to 350 degrees Fahrenheit.
- Spray the muffin tray using non-stick spray and set it aside for later. Create a cup form by pressing every ham piece into a muffin tray.
- Pour the milk and egg whites into a mixing dish and stir well. Pour the mixture into ham cups unless they are approximately three-quarters full.
- 20 mins in the oven should be enough time for the egg yolks to firm up entirely. After removing from heat, allow it to cool.

Nutrition Information
Calories: 92 kcal, Carbohydrates: 3 g, Protein: 10 g, Fat: 5 g

78. Butternut Squash and Turkey Bacon Salad
Prep Time: 10 mins, Cook Time: 20 mins, Servings: 4
Ingredients
For Salad
- 1 peeled & cubed butternut squash
- 2 tbsp olive oil
- ½ tsp kosher salt
- ½ tsp cinnamon ground
- 6 cups arugula baby
- ¼ cup sliced red onion
- ¼ cup chopped walnuts
- ¼ cup low-fat feta cheese
- ¼ cup no sugar dried cranberries
- 4 strips cooked & chopped turkey bacon

For Dressing
- ¼ cup of olive oil
- 1 tbsp mustard Dijon
- 2 tbsp vinegar apple cider
- 2 tsp honey
- ½ tsp rosemary ground

Instructions
For Salad
- 400° Fahrenheit is the ideal temperature for baking. A large bowl of olive oil, squash, and salt/cinnamon. Combine all ingredients and toss to cover the squash in a large bowl. Roast for around 20-30 mins unless the vegetables are fork tender. Cool fully after removing from the oven.

- Once your squash has cooled, add it with the rest of the salad ingredients & toss gently to blend. Put the mixture in serving dishes to serve.

For Dressing
- Blend the ingredients in your blender. Blend for around 1 min on high speed. Mix with salad dressing and serve. Refrigerate any dressing that you don't use right away.

Nutrition Information
Calories: 296 kcal, Carbohydrates: 13 g, Protein: 5 g, Fat: 26 g

79. Hashbrown, Spinach, Tomato, and Feta Pie
Prep Time: 20 mins, Cook Time: 40 mins, Servings: 4
Ingredients
- 2 cups shredded potatoes
- ¾ cup low-fat crumbled feta cheese
- 1 cup grape tomatoes cut in half
- 3 cups of baby spinach
- 1 tbsp olive oil
- 2 large eggs
- 2 large egg whites
- ¼ cup milk skim
- ½ tsp salt kosher
- ¼ tsp black pepper ground

Instructions
- Set the oven temperature to 375°F.
- Nonstick spray may be used to line a pie plate to prevent sticking. Shredded hashbrown potatoes should be added to a pan, then patted into an even layer to provide a crisp crust. Bake in the oven for a total of ten mins. Sprinkle some feta cheese on top of the crust after taking it out of the oven. Set aside for now.
- Olive oil may be heated in a shallow pan over medium-low heat. Add tomatoes & spinach once the oil is heated. Place the feta cheese on top of the wilted spinach within hashbrown crust.
- Combine the milk, salt, eggs, & pepper in a large mixing bowl. Top with the rest of the feta, spinach & tomatoes. A medium brown crust should form after approximately 30 mins of baking time, at which point the dish is done baking. Slice and serve the meat once it has rested for 10 mins.

Nutrition Information
Calories: 145 kcal, Carbohydrates: 12 g, Protein: 7 g, Fat: 8 g

80. Roasted Green Beans and Mushrooms
Prep Time: 10 mins, Cook Time: 20 mins, Servings: 2
Ingredients
- 2 minced garlic cloves
- 2 tbsp oil olive
- 2 cups end trimmed green beans
- 2 cups fresh mushrooms
- ½ tsp black pepper ground
- 2 tsp low-sodium soy sauce

Instructions
- 400° Fahrenheit is the ideal temperature for baking.
- Combine all the ingredients in a mixing bowl. Add the mushrooms, oil, & beans; toss to cover gently.
- A uniform layer should be spread on the baking sheet. Bake for about 20-15 mins, or until the bread is golden brown and crispy. Enjoy your meal while it's still piping hot.

Nutrition Information
Calories: 87 kcal, Carbohydrates: 5 g, Protein: 2 g, Fat: 7 g

81. Chocolate Peanut Butter Popcorn
Prep Time: 15 mins, Cook Time: 15 mins, Servings: 6
Ingredients
For Popcorn
- 8 cups unseasoned popped popcorn
- 1 tbsp oil coconut
- ¼ cup butter peanut
- 2 tbsp syrup maple

For Chocolate Drizzle
- 1 & ½ tbsp coconut oil
- ¼ cup chocolate chips semisweet

Instructions
For Popcorn
- On a baking sheet, evenly distribute your popped popcorn.
- Melt the peanut butter, coconut oil, & maple syrup in a big saucepan. Pour the peanut butter on the popped kernels & gently toss till every kernel is covered. Take a break and let it cool off.

For Chocolate Drizzle
- Melt coconut oil & chocolate chips in a medium saucepan unless smooth. Let the peanut popcorn cool before drizzling it with the caramel sauce.
- It's time to eat!

Nutrition Information
Calories: 164 kcal, Carbohydrates: 13 g, Protein: 3 g, Fat: 12 g

82. Tomato, Ham, and Poached Egg English Muffin
Prep Time: 15 mins, Cook Time: 15 mins, Servings: 5
Ingredients
- 3 tsp olive oil
- 4 slices low-sodium ham
- 1 tomato
- 2 English muffins whole-wheat
- 4 poached eggs
- ¼ tsp coarsely ground black pepper

Instructions
- In a medium-sized pan, warm some olive oil. Cook till your tomatoes are somewhat mushy & the ham becomes golden brown, then remove the ham from the pan and set it aside.
- Top your English muffin along with ham & tomato. On top of it, place the fried egg. Sprinkle with coarse powdered black pepper & drizzle with leftover olive oil.

Nutrition Information
Calories: 209 kcal, Carbohydrates: 16 g, Protein: 13 g, Fat: 11 g

83. Snowball Cookies
Prep Time: 10 mins, Cook Time: 10 mins, Servings: 12
Ingredients
- 1 cup organic unsalted butter
- ½ cup sugar organic confectioners
- 1 tsp extract almond
- 2 & ¼ cups flour whole-wheat
- ½ cup ground fine walnuts

Instructions
- Set the oven to 400°F.
- Gather your ingredients in a small bowl and whip them together with a mixer. Before serving, stir in both flour & walnuts at a moderate speed.
- Place the 1" balls on a baking sheet about 1" apart and flatten slightly. Take them out of the oven when they are just beginning to brown, and cool completely after removing them from the oven. Add more confectioners' sugar to the dough before rolling it out.

Nutrition Information
Calories: 118 kcal, Carbohydrates: 10 g, Protein: 2 g, Fat: 8 g

84. Flourless Blueberry Oatmeal Muffins
Prep Time: 15 Mins, Cook Time: 25 Mins, Servings: 10
Ingredients
- 2 & ½ cups rolled oats old-fashioned
- 1 & ½ cups of milk almond
- 1 lightly beaten egg large
- 1/3 cup maple syrup pure
- 2 tbsp melted coconut oil
- 1 tsp extract vanilla
- 1 tsp cinnamon ground
- 1 tsp powder baking
- ¼ tsp salt

- 1 tsp grated lemon zest
- 1 cup fresh blueberries

Instructions
- In a medium bowl, mix both oats & almond milk. Overnight, cover & refrigerate.
- Set the oven temperature to 375°F. Nonstick spray is used to line the muffin pan.
- Stir your soaked oats to mix gently with the other ingredients. Fill your muffin tin approximately ¾ of the way with the batter.
- About 20 mins in the oven, or until the tops are browned. Serve it hot.

Nutrition Information
Calories: 122 kcal, Carbohydrates: 19 g, Protein: 3 g, Fat: 4 g

85. Sweet Potato Cookies
Prep Time: 10 mins, Cook Time: 15 mins, Servings: 12

Ingredients
- 1 cup mashed sweet potato
- ½ cup butter almond
- 2 tbsp honey
- ¼ cup of flour
- 1 tsp baking soda
- ½ tsp vanilla extract

Instructions
- The oven should be preheated at 350°F.
- Mix all the ingredients in a medium-sized bowl. Drop using tsp onto a baking sheet.
- Allow the bread to bake for 15 mins or till it's golden brown and crispy. Enjoy your meal when it has cooled down for 10 mins!

Nutrition Information
Calories: 188 kcal, Carbohydrates: 18 g, Protein: 5 g, Fat: 12 g

86. Juicy Slow Cooker Turkey Breast
Prep Time: 15 mins, Cook Time: 3 hrs, Servings: 6

Ingredients
- 1 cup low-sodium chicken broth
- 1 garlic head
- 1 peeled yellow onion
- 1 & ½ tsp powder garlic
- 1 & ½ tsp powder onion
- 1 tsp paprika
- 2 tbsp olive oil
- 1 tsp thyme leaves dried
- ½ tsp salt kosher
- 1 tsp black pepper ground
- 4 lb turkey breast boneless & skinless

Instructions
- Slow cooker: Add some chicken broth. Make a "shelf" for your turkey breast by placing the garlic & onion halves within the slow cooker.
- Salt, pepper & olive oil are all that's needed to bring the spices together in a shallow dish. Prepare a mixture of the ingredients and massage your turkey breast on both sides. Put the turkey within a slow cooker over onion & garlic halves.
- To cook the turkey breast, cover & cook for 7-8 hrs on low heat or until it is done. Before serving, drizzle the drippings over the turkey breast.

Nutrition Information
Calories: 47 kcal, Carbohydrates: 3 g, Protein: 1 g, Fat: 4 g

87. Spiced Molasses Sweet Potatoes
Prep Time: 10 Mins, Cook Time: 35 Mins, Servings: 8

Ingredients
- 3 peeled potatoes medium
- 3 tbsp molasses
- 1 tbsp honey
- 1 tsp cinnamon
- 1 tsp orange zest
- ½ tsp nutmeg
- ¼ tsp ground ginger
- ¼ tsp kosher salt
- ¼ tsp cayenne pepper
- 3 tbsp plain Greek yogurt

Instructions
- Make 1-inch pieces out of your sweet potatoes. Fill a big soup pot halfway with water, then add the mixture. Prepare over high heat till potatoes are fork tender.
- Bring out a big mixing dish. Whip in the rest of the ingredients unless well-combined.
- It's time to eat!

Nutrition Information
Calories: 80 kcal, Carbohydrates: 18 g, Protein: 1 g, Fat: 0 g

88. Turkey Sweet Potato Stew
Prep Time: 10 mins, Cook Time: 1 hr 15 mins, Servings: 6

Ingredients
- 2 tbsp olive oil extra virgin
- 1 diced small yellow onion
- 1 diced small green pepper
- 3 minced garlic cloves
- 1 peeled & diced carrot large
- 2 peeled & diced sweet potatoes
- 3 cups of boneless & skinless cooked & shredded turkey breast
- 28 oz tomatoes diced
- 1 tbsp paprika smoked
- 1 tsp oregano dried
- 1 tsp coriander ground
- ¼ tsp crushed pepper flakes red
- 6 cups low-sodium chicken broth
- ¼ cup plain Greek yogurt
- 2 tbsp chopped cilantro fresh

Instructions
- The oil should be heated to medium-high heat in a wide soup pot. Mix in the carrots and onions. Cook unless the onions become translucent, but the carrots remain firm. All other ingredients, excluding yogurt & cilantro, should be mixed in. Stir often while the mixture comes to your boil. Simmer for approximately an hr after bringing to a boil.
- Top with both yogurt & cilantro before serving.

Nutrition Information
Calories: 311 kcal, Carbohydrates: 18 g, Protein: 30 g, Fat: 14 g

89. Baked Vegetable Omelet
Prep Time: 15 mins, Cook Time: 40 mins, Servings: 7

Ingredients
- ½ cup diced small red onion
- ½ cup diced small bell pepper green
- 1 cup roughly chopped baby spinach
- 5 large egg whites
- 3 eggs
- ¼ cup of skim milk
- ½ tsp kosher salt
- ¼ tsp black pepper ground
- ½ cup low-fat cheddar cheese

Instructions
- Set the oven temperature to 375°F. Apply nonstick spray to a casserole pan.
- Eggs should be foamy, and the veggies should be evenly distributed throughout the mixture. Pour the mixture into a pan, then top with the shredded cheese to assemble. When the egg is done and faintly browned, bake for another 40 minutes. Remove the foil once the top begins to brown. Continue baking till the cake is made.
- After 10 mins of resting, slice and serve.

Nutrition Information
Calories: 121 kcal, Carbohydrates: 4 g, Protein: 11 g, Fat: 7 g

90. Red Lobster's Cheddar Biscuits
Prep Time: 20 mins, Cook Time: 10 mins, Servings: 6

Ingredients
- ½ tsp powder garlic
- ¼ tsp salt
- ¼ tsp cayenne pepper
- ½ tsp onion powder
- ½ cup flour whole-wheat
- ¼ cup flour almond
- 2 tbsp flour coconut
- 2 tsp powder baking
- ¼ cup low-fat parmesan cheese
- 2 tbsp plain Greek yogurt
- 3 tbsp skim milk
- ½ cup sharp low-fat cheddar cheese
- 3 tbsp olive oil

Instructions
- The oven should be preheated at 350°F.
- Garlic, cayenne pepper, salt, & onion powder should be mixed in a medium bowl.
- Separately, in a large mixing bowl, mix all flours, baking powder & the remaining three-quarters of a spice mix. Indent the center of the flour mixture after it's all mixed. Mix your dry ingredients with the yogurt & milk. One tbsp of milk at the moment may be added to make the dough more stickable. Incorporate the shredded cheese into dough unless it's equally dispersed.
- Make a mixture of olive oil and the rest of the spices. You may use a tbsp to portion approximately ¼ cup of dough onto a baking sheet. Half of your oil & spice mixture should be brushed onto biscuits' tops. Baking time should be between 10 and 15 minutes, or until the biscuits brown. Immediately after removing from oven, spray leftover oil & spice mix on the surface. Serve it hot.

Nutrition Information
Calories: 212 kcal, Carbohydrates: 14 g, Protein: 8 g, Fat: 15 g

91. Truffle Whipped Potatoes
Prep Time: 15 Mins, Cook Time: 30 Mins, Servings: 6

Ingredients
- 1 lb gold potatoes Yukon
- 2 tbsp truffle oil black
- 3 tbsp plain Greek yogurt
- ¼ cup milk skim
- ½ tsp salt
- ¼ tsp chopped thyme fresh

Instructions
- Place the potatoes in a big soup pot with the skins on and fill them with water. Boil until the potatoes are tender, then remove from heat and cool. Transfer to the mixing dish after draining.
- In a medium bowl, combine potatoes with the rest of the ingredients and mix well. Whip till fluffy using a mixer set to moderate speed. Add a spoonful of skim milk if the potatoes have become too dry.
- It's time to eat!

Nutrition Information
Calories: 83 kcal, Carbohydrates: 11 g, Protein: 2 g, Fat: 4 g

92. Cajun Roast Turkey
Prep Time: 20 Mins, Cook Time: Servings: 6

Ingredients
- 10 lb thawed the whole turkey

For Rub
- 2 tsp salt kosher
- 2 tbsp pepper cayenne
- 2 tbsp powder garlic
- 2 tbsp paprika smoked
- 1 tbsp oregano dried
- 1 tbsp thyme dried
- 3 tsp black pepper ground
- 1 tbsp powder onion
- 3 tbsp olive oil extra virgin

Roasting
- 5 smashed garlic cloves
- 1 quartered yellow onion
- 4 chopped celery stalks
- 3 peeled & chopped carrots
- 2 chopped green peppers
- 5 fresh oregano stems
- 10 fresh thyme stems
- 1 water quart

Instructions
- Place your roasting rack upon the top of a sheet of foil-lined Al foil in the roasting pan. Apply a little coat of nonstick spray before cooking. Place the cleaned and dried turkey within a preheated roasting pan.

For Rub
- Prepare a mixture by combining all of the rub ingredients. Use a pastry brush or your hands to apply the paste to the turkey. Spray nonstick spray on a sheet of Al foil. Overnight refrigeration is recommended.

Roasting
- The oven should be preheated at 350°F.
- Toss the ingredients together in a big bowl, except for the water. Stuff your turkey with the mix & spread the rest of the mix around it within the pan. Just add enough water to cover the base of your turkey within a pan. A new piece of foil, gently coated with nonstick spray, should be placed on top of the previous one.
- Bake for around 3 hrs or unless the core temperature reaches 165 degrees, depending on the size of your pan. Keep an eye on the water level & add extra if necessary. For 15-20 mins of roasting, remove the turkey's skin.

Nutrition Information
Calories: 329 kcal, Carbohydrates: 11 g, Protein: 49 g, Fat: 14 g

93. Baked Zucchini, Spinach, and Feta Casserole
Prep Time: 10 mins, Cook Time: 45 mins, Servings: 4

Ingredients
- 2 tbsp olive oil
- 2 diced small zucchini
- 3 cups spinach baby
- 2 diced small yellow squash
- ¼ cup fat-free crumbled feta cheese
- ¼ cup grated low-fat parmesan cheese
- ¼ cup panko breadcrumbs whole-wheat
- 2 large egg whites
- ½ tsp salt kosher
- 2 tsp powder garlic
- ½ tsp black pepper ground
- 1 tsp basil leaves dried

Instructions
- The oven should be preheated at 400°F. Set aside a casserole dish sprayed using non-stick spray & ready to use.
- Olive oil should be heated in a big skillet. Once heated, add the zucchini, spinach, & yellow squash to the pan. The spinach should be wilted & the squash should be tender after approximately 5 mins of cooking. Mix well in a mixing bowl after draining off any remaining fluid.
- Add the rest of the ingredients to the spinach mix within a bowl. Spread the ingredients evenly in the preheated casserole dish after mixing thoroughly. A light golden top should be achieved in 30-40 mins. Before serving, allow the food to cool somewhat.

Nutrition Information
Calories: 162 kcal, Carbohydrates: 20 g, Protein: 6 g, Fat: 8 g

94. Orange Glazed Roasted Carrots
Prep Time: 10 mins, Cook Time: 30 mins, Servings: 6

Ingredients
- 3 tbsp olive oil
- 2 tsp grated ginger fresh
- 1 zested & juiced orange
- 6 peeled & sliced carrots large

Instructions
- Set the oven temperature to 350°F.
- Mix everything in a big dish, including the oiled carrots, & toss to cover them within the oil. Spread out on the baking sheet in an equal layer. If you want your carrots softer & browned, roast them for 30-45 mins. Serve right away and have a great time!

Nutrition Information
Calories: 150 kcal, Carbohydrates: 14 g, Protein: 1 g, Fat: 10 g

95. 1-2-3 Pumpkin Butter
Prep Time: 5 mins, Cook Time: 20 mins, Servings: 26
Ingredients
- 29 oz purée pumpkin
- 1 cup sugar coconut
- 1 cup no sugar apple juice
- 2 tsp cinnamon ground
- 1 tsp ginger ground
- ½ tsp nutmeg ground
- ½ tsp clove ground
- 2 tsp juice lemon

Instructions
- Mix all the ingredients except the lemon juice in the medium saucepan and bring to a boil over moderate flame. Stir often while bringing the mixture to a boil, then reduce the heat to a simmer.
- A fragrant, rich stew should be ready in about 15-20 mins. Stirring often once again.
- Stir within lemon juice when the dish has cooled. Before putting it in a sealed jar, make sure it is thoroughly cooled.

Nutrition Information
Calories: 29 kcal, Carbohydrates: 7 g, Protein: 8 g, Fat: 2 g

96. Brussels Sprouts Gratin
Prep Time: 10 mins, Cook Time: 40 mins, Servings: 6
Ingredients
- 1 lb trimmed & sliced Brussels sprouts
- 1 tsp kosher salt
- 1 tbsp olive oil
- ½ tsp pepper black
- 2 tbsp whole-wheat flour white
- 1 cup milk skim
- 2 tbsp butter
- ¾ cup cheese skim white cheddar
- ¼ cup shredded parmesan cheese

Instructions
- 400° Fahrenheit is the ideal temperature for baking.
- Add salt, olive oil, & pepper to Brussels sprouts, then toss. Bake for around 30 mins, pulling the dish out of your oven once to rotate the sprouts.
- Melt butter in a small saucepan over low heat. Pour in some flour and stir until the mix forms one ball & starts to brown, then remove from heat. Whisk your milk into the mixture as you add it. For thickening, add cheddar cheese & stir until incorporated. Sprinkle parmesan cheese on top of Brussels sprouts before serving. The cheese should be bubbling & beginning to brown after another 10-15 mins of baking.

Nutrition Information
Calories: 171 kcal, Carbohydrates: 9 g, Protein: 8 g, Fat: 12 g

97. Orange Glazed Chicken and Sweet Potato Kebabs
Prep Time: 15 Mins, Cook Time: 45 Mins, Servings: 9
Ingredients
- 2 peeled sweet potatoes
- 16-24 oz chicken breasts boneless & skinless
- 1 large fennel bulb
- ¼ cup juice orange
- ½ tsp red pepper crushed
- 2 tbsp honey
- 2 tbsp oil olive
- 1 tbsp minced ginger fresh
- 1 tbsp chopped thyme fresh
- 3 tbsp chopped parsley fresh

Instructions
- A grill or oven should be preheated to 450°F.
- Cover your sweet potatoes using water in a big saucepan and bring to a boil. Bring to your boil, then simmer for five mins to complete the cooking process. Rinse with cold water after draining.
- Skewers with fennel, boiling sweet potato, & chicken cubes should be placed on each other. Re-fill the skewer till it's full.
- Gather all of the ingredients for the dressing in a shallow dish and whisk well. Apply the mixture on the skewers one at a time. Cook for around 6-8 mins on a baking pan or straight on your grill. Apply more orange juice mix to your brush as you turn. A few more mins in the oven will help to ensure that your chicken is well-done, as well as the potatoes.
- Sprinkle using fresh thyme & parsley after removing from grill. Serve right away and have a great time!

Nutrition Information
Calories: 281 kcal, Carbohydrates: 16 g, Protein: 17 g, Fat: 16 g

98. Slow Cooker Meatball and Potato Soup | Easy Meal Prep Ideas
Prep Time: 20 Mins, Cook Time: 35 Mins, Servings: 4
Ingredients
Meatballs
- 1 lb ground turkey lean
- ½ tsp pepper black
- ½ tsp salt sea
- ½ tsp powder chili
- ¼ tsp crushed flakes red pepper
- 1 cup gluten-free panko breadcrumbs
- ½ diced yellow onion
- 1 tbsp oil olive

Soup
- 3 large russet potatoes
- 1 sliced carrot thinly
- ½ tsp pepper black
- ½ tsp salt sea
- turmeric pinch
- ½ tsp crushed flakes red pepper
- ½ diced yellow onion
- 3 minced garlic cloves
- 5 cups broth chicken
- 13 & ½ oz can coconut milk
- 3 cups loosely packed baby spinach
- 2 slices nitrate-free bacon

Instructions
- Mix the meatball ingredients in your bowl and form 1" meatballs.
- Add oil into a large pan over medium heat, then add meatballs & brown from all sides until just cooked through. It's important to remember that the meatballs must only be gently browned on the exterior before serving.
- Then, add all of the soup ingredients, excluding baby spinach & bacon, to your slow cooker and mix to blend. Incorporate the meatballs & simmer for a further 6-8 hrs on low. Crumble the bacon into tiny pieces & reserve.
- Add spinach at ending of cooking time & simmer for about 10 mins, or till wilted. When presenting the soup, sprinkle the top with crumbled bacon chunks.

Nutrition Information
Calories: 258 kcal, Carbohydrates: 20 g, Protein: 13 g, Fat: 15 g

99. Sweet and Sour Green Beans
Prep Time: 30 Mins, Cook Time: 40 Mins, Servings: 6
Ingredients
- 1 lb fresh ends trimmed green beans
- 3 slices of turkey bacon chopped nitrate-free

- ½ cup diced yellow onion
- 2 tbsp vinegar apple cider
- 2 tbsp honey
- ½ tsp kosher salt

Instructions
- Bring the water pot to your boil in a big saucepan. After 2-3 mins, add the green beans & simmer for another 2-3 mins. To prevent your beans from overcooking, quickly rinse and immerse them into cold water. Drain all the residual water when the food has cooled.
- Cook diced bacon in a pan over medium heat. The onion should be added when the bacon is just beginning to brown, & the bacon should be crispy. Mix in some green beans that have been drained. As they start to blister from the exterior, continue cooking for a few more mins. Mix honey, vinegar, & salt into the mixture. Then toss everything together until it's evenly coated. Remove from the stove & serve.

Nutrition Information
Calories: 104 kcal, Carbohydrates: 19 g, Protein: 4 g, Fat: 2 g

100. 3-Ingredient Crispy Garlic Broccoli
Prep Time: 5 mins, Cook Time: 15 mins, Servings: 4

Ingredients
- 2 lb florets broccoli
- 5 minced garlic cloves
- 2 tbsp olive oil

Instructions
- Prepare your baking sheet by lining it using parchment paper & preheating the oven to 425°F.
- Toss all ingredients together & spread them out evenly over a baking sheet. Bake the broccoli for around 15 mins, till it is crisp-tender. It's time to eat!

Nutrition Information
Calories: 129 kcal, Carbohydrates: 13 g, Protein: 7 g, Fat: 8 g

101. Egg and Bacon Stuffed Acorn Squash
Prep Time: 15 mins, Cook Time: 30 mins, Servings: 20

Ingredients
- 1 large acorn squash
- 1 tbsp oil olive
- ¼ tsp salt kosher
- ¼ tsp black pepper ground
- 4 large eggs
- ¼ tsp thyme leaves dried
- 2 slices cooked & crumbled turkey bacon

Instructions
- Preheat the oven to 425°F. Set aside a wide baking sheet by lining it using parchment paper.
- Remove the squash's ends & toss them. Cut the squash into half lengthwise and then into four rounds, one on top of the other. Remove seeds from the middle of each one.
- Use olive oil & salt & pepper to season your squash rings from all sides. Bake for around 15 mins, or unless the vegetables are fork-tender, on the lined baking sheet.
- After taking it out of the oven, lower the temperature to 350°F. Using an eggbeater, break one egg into every acorn slice & bake for around 12 mins, or unless the yolk is set. Add herbs & bacon to the dish. It's time to eat!

Nutrition Information
Calories: 163 kcal, Carbohydrates: 12 g, Protein: 8 g, Fat: 10 g

102. Pumpkin Pie Pancakes
Prep Time: 10 mins, Cook Time: 20 mins, Servings: 6

Ingredients
- 3 large eggs
- ½ cup milk coconut
- ½ tsp extract vanilla
- 1 tbsp honey
- ½ cup puree pumpkin
- 1 cup flour coconut
- ½ tsp cinnamon
- ¼ tsp ground clove
- ¼ tsp ground nutmeg
- ½ tsp baking soda
- ½ tsp powder baking
- 2 tsp coconut oil

Instructions
- Eggs, vanilla, honey, milk, & pumpkin are mixed in a big bowl. To get the best results, mix well. Flour, cloves, nutmeg, cinnamon, & baking soda are sifted into a second bowl. The moist pumpkin mix should be added to your dry ingredients & gently stirred until everything is incorporated. Make sure you don't overdo it when it comes to combining ingredients!
- Medium heat should be used for a skillet, and some coconut oil should be drizzled over a medium-hot pan. Pour roughly some batter into the pan after it has melted. Cook for around 3-4 mins of cooking time unless the middle of the pancakes is just starting to boil. Cook for the next 2-3 mins after carefully flipping the pan. You may continue this method as many times as necessary to use up all of your pancake batters in this manner. In between batches of pancakes, use the leftover coconut oil to coat the pan.
- As an optional garnish, you may drizzle honey over the top of the heated dish!

Nutrition Information
Calories: 182 kcal, Carbohydrates: 16 g, Protein: 6 g, Fat: 10 g

103. Slow Cooker Thai Chicken Satay
Prep Time: 20 mins, Cook Time: 2 hrs, Servings: 8

Ingredients
- 1 tbsp oil olive
- 6 chicken tenders boneless & skinless
- 1 stalk chopped lemongrass
- 1/3 cup coconut milk lite
- 2 tbsp sauce fish
- 1 tbsp juice lime
- 1 tbsp soy sauce lite
- 1 tsp sauce chili garlic
- 1 tbsp nectar agave
- 1 tsp ginger ground
- 1 tsp turmeric
- 2 minced garlic cloves

Instructions
- Heat some olive oil to moderate flame in your frying pan on a stove. You must cook the outsides of the chicken; the inside should remain raw. Then transfer to your slow cooker.
- Pour the other ingredients on the chicken & combine well. Cook for around 3-4 hrs on low heat. Serve over brown rice & Asian veggies.

Nutrition Information
Calories: 375 kcal, Carbohydrates: 8 g, Protein: 25 g, Fat: 25 g

104. Carrot Soup with Pumpkin Seeds
Prep Time: 5 mins, Cook Time: 25 mins, Servings: 3

Ingredients
- 5 cups broth vegetable
- 2 cups cooked & mashed carrots
- ½ cup puree pumpkin
- 1 tsp cumin ground
- ½ tsp coriander ground
- ¼ tsp pepper cayenne
- ½ tsp salt kosher
- ½ tsp cinnamon ground
- ½ tsp turmeric ground
- ½ cup plain Greek yogurt
- ¼ cup toasted & shells removed pumpkin seeds
- 2 tbsp olive oil extra virgin

Instructions
- In a big soup pot, combine the broth, carrots, pumpkin puree, salt, cinnamon, cayenne, cumin, coriander,

& turmeric using a hand blender or food processor. Stirring regularly, bringing the soup to your boil, then lowering the heat to a simmer is the way to go. Simmer for another 20 mins or more, stirring often. Overly thick soup may be thinned by adding half a cup of warmed broth at a time.
- Top the soup with pumpkin seeds, yogurt, & olive oil before serving. Serve at room temperature.

Nutrition Information
Calories: 119 kcal, Carbohydrates: 8 g, Protein: 4 g, Fat: 2 g

105. Cheesy Chicken Chili Dip
Prep Time: 25 Mins, Cook Time: 30 Mins, Servings: 6
Ingredients
- 1 tbsp olive oil
- 2 minced garlic cloves
- 1 diced sweet onion
- 2 seeded & diced jalapeno peppers
- 1 seeded & diced poblano pepper
- 1 cup yogurt Greek
- 8 oz cheese Neufchatel
- ½ cup grated cheddar cheese
- 4 oz green chiles diced
- 1 tsp sea salt or kosher
- 2 boneless & skinless cooked chicken breasts
- 1 tbsp powder chili
- 2 tsp cumin
- ½ tsp pepper black
- 1 tsp oregano dried
- ¼ cup chopped cilantro

Instructions
- The oven should be preheated to 400°F.
- Olive oil should be heated in a large sauté pan. Add garlic, jalapeño, onion, & poblano peppers after the oil has heated up. It's done when it's soft. Remove from the heat source and let it cool to room temperature.
- Mix Greek yogurt & Neufchatel cheese in a large dish. On low, add the onion & pepper combination and the rest of the ingredients, omitting fresh cilantro, & mix until well-combined.
- Use cooking spray to coat the casserole dish. Spread the ingredients out evenly on the platter. Bake for 15-20 mins, or until the mixture is hot and bubbling. Top with chopped cilantro.
- Use your favorite cracker and tortilla chip as a dip!

Nutrition Information
Calories: 166 kcal, Carbohydrates: 9 g, Protein: 15 g, Fat: 8 g

106. Slow Cooker Eggplant Lasagna
Prep Time: 25 mins, Cook Time: 2 hrs, Servings: 4
Ingredients
- 2 peeled & sliced eggplants
- 1 cup low-fat cottage cheese
- 1 & ½ cups low-fat mozzarella cheese
- 1 egg large
- 24 oz spaghetti sugar-free sauce jar
- 1 tsp salt kosher
- ½ tsp pepper
- 1 diced bell pepper
- 1 diced onion

Instructions
- The excess liquid within eggplants should be easily leached for about 15 mins

over paper towels. Mix up the mozzarella, cottage cheese, & egg in a separate bowl while you're waiting.
- The base of your slow cooker should be covered with about a quarter of tomato sauce, and ¼ of your eggplant slices are placed on top of the other ingredients, including onions, peppers, & cheese. Repeat the layering process three times.
- Cook for around 5-6 hrs on low heat.

Nutrition Information
Calories: 221 kcal, Carbohydrates: 19 g, Protein: 14 g, Fat: 10 g

107. Italian Spaghetti Squash Casserole
Prep Time: 25 Mins, Cook Time: 15 Mins, Servings: 4
Ingredients
- 1 medium spaghetti squash
- ½ cup of water
- 2 tsp oil olive
- 1 lb turkey sausage ground
- 1 diced small yellow onion
- 1 diced small green pepper
- 15 oz drained diced tomatoes
- 24 oz marinara no sugar sauce jar
- ¾ cup low-fat ricotta cheese
- ¾ cup of mozzarella cheese shredded low-fat
- ¼ cup chopped basil fresh

Instructions
- Make sure your oven is preheated at 375°F. Set aside casserole dish sprayed using non-stick spray & ready to use. A separate baking dish should be reserved.
- Slice your squash in half and remove the seeds. Squash should be placed in a separate baking dish & some water should be sprinkled around it. Bake for about 40 to 45 minutes unless the meat is fork-tender and juicy. Fork out the squash's inside when it has cooled down a little. Spaghetti noodles should be the result of the squash. Set away in a big basin for later use.
- Olive oil should be heated in a big skillet. Toss in your turkey sausage, onions, & peppers as soon as the sausage is heated. Break your turkey into tiny pieces & heat until the veggies are tender, and your turkey is heated through. Add tomatoes & marinara after draining the extra liquid. Remove from the heat & stir to mix. Take care not to overwork the mixture. Pour the mix into a medium bowl that contains spaghetti squash & stir well to coat it. Sprinkle fresh mozzarella cheese before placing it in a casserole dish.
- Bake for 30 mins, or unless the cheese gets melted & bubbling. Add fresh basil after taking it out of the oven. Allow 10 mins of rest time before serving.

Nutrition Information
Calories: 210 kcal, Carbohydrates: 10 g, Protein: 16 g, Fat: 12 g

108. Easy 6-Ingredient Sesame Chicken
Prep Time: 5 mins, Cook Time: 20 mins, Servings: 4
Ingredients
- 12-16 oz chicken breasts boneless & skinless
- 3 minced garlic cloves
- 1 tbsp finely grated ginger fresh
- ¼ cup low-sodium soy sauce
- 3 tbsp honey
- 2 tbsp sesame seeds

Instructions
- High-heat skillet: Cook your chicken till it's firm & golden brown.
- Add the ginger and garlic, then simmer for a further one-min period. Slowly turn down the heat to medium, then add soy sauce & honey to the mixture, stirring constantly. Heat through until a thick sauce develops and coats the chicken. Sesame seeds may be added at this point if you'd like.
- Enjoy with a side of quinoa.

Nutrition Information
Calories: 331 kcal, Carbohydrates: 16 g, Protein: 24 g, Fat: 19 g

109. Ground Turkey and Sweet Potato Skillet
Prep Time: 10 mins, Cook Time: 25 mins, Servings: 4
Ingredients
- 1 lb turkey ground
- 1 tbsp oil olive
- 2 minced garlic cloves

- 1 diced bell pepper yellow
- 1 cup small onion diced
- 1 tbsp cumin ground
- 1 tbsp powder chili
- ½ tsp salt kosher
- 2 peeled & diced medium sweet potatoes
- ½ cup of water
- ½ cup of mozzarella cheese low-fat part-skim
- ¼ cup roughly chopped cilantro

Instructions
- Cook your ground turkey in a big pan, breaking it up as it cooks. Add some olive oil, bell pepper, garlic, & onion after the meat has finished cooking. The onion & pepper should start to wilt at this point. Add the chili powder, cumin, and salt, then combine well.
- Add water & sweet potatoes. Bring to your boil, then remove the lid and simmer for 15 mins. Potatoes should be boiled for 8-10 mins, or till they are tender, and the water has gone. Additional water may be added, if possible, to protect your potatoes from being dried out during cooking.
- Remove the pan from heat when the mozzarella is on top. Allow the cheese to soften under the cover. Well before serving, garnish with fresh cilantro.

Nutrition Information
Calories: 229 kcal, Carbohydrates: 16 g, Protein: 19 g, Fat: 11 g

110. One Pan Apple Cinnamon Pork Chops
Prep Time: 15 Mins, Cook Time: 25 Mins, Servings: 6
Ingredients
- 12 oz pork chops boneless lean
- ½ tsp salt kosher
- ¼ tsp clove ground
- 2 tbsp olive oil extra virgin
- 2 sliced green apples
- 1 sliced yellow onion
- ¼ cup vegetable broth or chicken broth
- 1 tsp cinnamon ground
- 1 tbsp honey

Instructions
- Pat pork chops dry using a paper towel after rinsing them in cold water. Use salt & ground cloves to season all sides.
- On moderate flame, add some olive oil to a medium-sized skillet. Add the pork chops when the pan is heated. Pork chops should be cooked thoroughly and lightly browned on all sides. Place on a cooling rack.
- Using a similar pan, sauté the apples & onion inside the leftover oil until soft. Add broth & cinnamon, then cook for some more mins. Bring the mixture to a rolling boil. Maintain a high flame and cook till the liquid is gone. Combine the honey, pork chops, & mustard.
- It's time to eat!

Nutrition Information
Calories: 279 kcal, Carbohydrates: 18 g, Protein: 18 g, Fat: 15 g

111. Slow Cooker Thai Curry Soup
Prep Time: 15 mins, Cook Time: 3 hrs, Servings: 4
Ingredients
- 2 tbsp paste red curry
- 24 oz milk coconut
- 2 cups low-sodium chicken stock
- 2 tbsp sauce fish
- 1 tbsp honey
- 2 tbsp creamy peanut butter
- 4 chicken breasts boneless & skinless
- 1 thinly sliced bell pepper red
- 1 seeded & minced jalapeno pepper
- 1 thinly sliced onion
- 1 cup sprouts bean
- 1 tbsp minced ginger fresh
- 1 cup frozen peas
- 1 cup frozen corn
- 1 tbsp juice lime
- As garnish cilantro

Instructions
- Cook over low for 8 to 10 hrs, occasionally stirring, until the sauce thickens and becomes creamy. Add the rest of your ingredients to your slow cooker, excluding lime juice, then mix.
- This recipe may be made on a low setting of 5-6 hrs or a high setting of 3-4 hrs. Serve with fresh cilantro & lime juice.

Nutrition Information
Calories: 365 kcal, Carbohydrates: 21 g, Protein: 19 g, Fat: 23 g

112. Easy Skillet Potatoes with Eggs and Turkey Sausage
Prep Time: 20 Mins, Cook Time: 35 Mins, Servings: 8
Ingredients
- 1 tbsp olive oil
- ½ cup diced small yellow onion
- 4 cups peeled & diced small Idaho potatoes
- ½ cup diced small green pepper
- 1 lb ground sausage turkey
- 2 lightly beaten whole eggs
- 6 lightly beaten egg whites
- ¼ cup milk skim
- ½ tsp salt kosher
- ¼ tsp white pepper ground
- ½ cup shredded cheddar cheese

Instructions
- Medium-high heat some olive oil inside a big skillet. Once the onion, potatoes, & green pepper are warmed, add them to the stew and cook until soft. Cook your potatoes until they start to color and are fork tender.
- Using roughly meat in each piece, add chopped turkey sausage onto the pan. Sausage is cooked by stirring it and breaking it into tiny chunks.
- Whip up egg whites & milk in a separate dish while your turkey sausage cooks. Season with salt & pepper.
- Add eggs mixture to the pan after the sausage has finished cooking. Move the eggs about the pan with a wooden spoon while they cook & scramble.
- Remove the pan from heat after the eggs have set. Cover the dish with the shredded cheese & bake for a few mins so that the cheese melts. It's time to eat!

Nutrition Information
Calories: 376 kcal, Carbohydrates: 16 g, Protein: 21 g, Fat: 26 g

113. One-Pot Chicken and Veggie Ramen Stir-Fry
Prep Time: 5 mins, Cook Time: 15 mins, Servings: 6
Ingredients
- 2 packet noodles
- 2 tbsp oil sesame
- 1 cup peas snow
- 1 cup sliced red pepper
- 1 cup florets broccoli
- 1 cup sliced yellow onion
- 2 minced garlic cloves
- 1 tbsp grated ginger fresh
- 2 chicken breasts boneless & skinless
- 3 tbsp honey
- ½ cup low-sodium soy sauce
- 3 tbsp vinegar rice
- ¼ tsp crushed pepper flakes red

Instructions
- Bring a big saucepan of water to your boil. When the water is boiling, add some Ramen noodles. Cook for 5-8 mins, or until the vegetables are fork tender. Prepare a bowl for the drained and collected water.
- Some sesame oil should be heated in a wide pan over medium heat. Snow peas, broccoli, red peppers, and onion should be added to the pot once it's heated. Cook both onions & peppers until they start to soften, stirring often, & then remove from pan. Add the leftover sesame oil to

your skillet and continue to cook on medium heat. Add ginger, chicken, & garlic to the pan after it's heated through. Cook your chicken until it has completely lost its pink color. Drain the remaining fluids from your body.
- When you're done cooking the chicken & veggies for dinner, add the soy vinegar, honey, & pepper flakes. Simmer for a few mins until it thickens. Cooked noodles may be added to coat them with the sauce.
- Place over a serving plate and pass the food once it's hot.

Nutrition Information
Calories: 234 kcal, Carbohydrates: 17 g, Protein: 24 g, Fat: 8 g

114. 5-Ingredient Pesto Pasta Salad
Prep Time: 10 Mins, Cook Time: 25 Mins, Servings: 6
Ingredients
- 1 lb whole-wheat cooked & cooled rotini pasta
- 1/3 cup of pesto
- 12 oz roasted drained & chopped small peppers jarred
- 1 & ½ cups low-fat provolone cheese
- 2 cups of baby spinach

Instructions
- In a large bowl, combine the pasta with the pesto & stir to coat. Add the rest of the ingredients and mix well.
- Serve after 30 mins of sitting in the refrigerator.

Nutrition Information
Calories: 215 kcal, Carbohydrates: 13 g, Protein: 12 g, Fat: 13 g

115. Instant Pot Shrimp and Grits
Prep Time: 20 Mins, Cook Time: 30 Mins, Servings: 4
Ingredients
- 1 tbsp olive oil
- 1 lb medium-sized, thawed shrimp
- ½ tsp salt kosher
- ¼ tsp crushed pepper flakes red
- 1 & ½ cups chicken broth or vegetable broth
- 1 tbsp unsalted butter
- ½ cup grits quick
- ½ cup of sharp shredded cheddar cheese
- 2 tbsp chopped cilantro fresh
- 1 tsp paprika smoked

Instructions
- On your Instant Pot, hit the "Sauté" key. To change the temperature, use the "Adjust" button. Olive oil should be heated to a medium-high temperature before the shrimp may be added. Stirring often, cook your shrimp till they are pink & firm to the touch. Remove from pot & place on a cooling rack to retain the heat.
- Scrape your Instant Pot with a spatula after adding the broth & butter. Add the grits and mix well. To increase the pressure, push the "Manual" key followed by the "Adjust" key. Set a timer for around 7 mins, then put the lid over the pot and ensure any vent is closed. Before beginning the cooking process, your Instant Pot would preheat and wait for 5 mins before lifting the cover & venting the pot.
- Add some cheddar cheese and mix well. Serve in dishes topped with shrimp that have been cooked. Add paprika & cilantro to the top. It's time to eat!

Nutrition Information
Calories: 299 kcal, Carbohydrates: 20 g, Protein: 23 g, Fat: 14 g

116. Poblano and Turkey Sausage Casserole
Prep Time: 25 Mins, Cook Time: 35 Mins, Servings: 6
Ingredients
For Casserole
- 2 peppers poblano
- 1 tbsp oil olive
- 1 lb turkey sausage lean ground
- ¼ cup diced yellow onion
- 5 large egg whites
- 5 eggs
- ½ cup of skim milk
- ¼ cup of plain Greek yogurt
- 1 tsp salt kosher
- ½ tsp pepper black
- 1 cup shredded cheddar cheese
- 4 cups shredded hash browns

For Avocado Tomato Topping
- 1 pitted & diced avocado peeled
- 1 cup diced tomatoes
- ¼ cup diced green onions
- ¼ tsp salt kosher

Instructions
For Casserole
- The oven should be preheated to a high broil setting.
- Apply olive oil to the skin side of every pepper half & lay it on a baking sheet. Bake for 10-15 mins, or till blackened and soft. Use tongs to extract from the oven. Cover and put away charred peppers inside a small dish using plastic wrap as soon as possible.
- Set a casserole dish & lower the temperature of the prepared oven to around 350 degrees.
- Cook the turkey sausage inside a large pan, breaking it up into bits as it heats until it's done. Add onion & sauté till translucent 7 the sausage isn't any longer pink, approximately halfway through the cooking process. Remove from the heat, discard the fat, and let cool completely before serving.
- Remove any charred peel from peppers while your sausage is chilling. Toss the diced peppers with the sausage & onion mixture.
- Combine egg whites, milk, yogurt, yolks, & seasonings in a medium bowl. Whisk unless there are no clumps of yogurt left. Serve with a side of cheese & hash potatoes. Hash brown is well covered in the egg mixture after thorough mixing.
- For approximately 1 hr & 30 mins, cover the casserole dish using Al foil & bake it. Bake for extra 10-15 mins, or unless the top starts to brown, after removing the lid. After 10 mins, slice and serve the dish. Spritz with the tomato and avocado sauce.

For Avocado Tomato Topping
- Mash your avocado with a fork. Add the rest of the ingredients & stir them in well. Roasted Poblano & Sausage Casserole is a great accompaniment.

Nutrition Information
Calories: 306 kcal, Carbohydrates: 19 g, Protein: 22 g, Fat: 16 g

117. Easy Turkey Sausage with Peppers & Onions
Prep Time: 10 mins, Cook Time: 15 mins, Servings: 8
Ingredients
- 1 lb rope sausage turkey
- ½ tbsp oil olive
- 1 cup sliced green pepper
- 1 cup sliced yellow pepper
- 1 cup sliced red onion

Instructions
- Add all ingredients to a big pan and cook over medium-high heat. Stir often as you cook until the peppers & onions are just beginning to soften.
- Serve with brown rice like a side dish.

Nutrition Information
Calories: 363 kcal, Carbohydrates: 6 g, Protein: 18 g, Fat: 30 g

118. Southwestern Stuffed Pepper Soup
Prep Time: 15 mins, Cook Time: 6 hrs 35 mins, Servings: 4
Ingredients
- 1 lb ground turkey lean
- 1 onion diced medium
- 2 minced garlic cloves
- 2 seeded & chopped bell peppers
- 29 oz fire-roasted tomatoes diced
- 4 cups fat-free chicken broth
- 6 oz paste tomato
- 1 tsp oregano dried

- 1 tsp salt sea
- ½ tsp pepper black
- ¼ cup of cilantro divided freshly chopped
- 2 cups cooked brown rice
- ½ cup Greek yogurt or sour cream

Instructions
- Ground turkey & chopped onion are cooked in a big saucepan on medium heat, breaking up the turkey since it cooks. Drain the fat from the turkey once it's cooked until it's no longer pink.
- Except for rice, cilantro, & sour cream, combine all other ingredients into a large saucepan and heat through. Using medium heat, bring to your boil, then decrease your simmer's heat. After 30 mins, the meat should be done & the peppers should be softer. Keep warm for around 6-8 hrs, covered.
- Cook rice according to package directions, then add the rest of the sour cream, cilantro, & salt to taste. 5 more mins of cooking time
- Serve along with the rest of the diced cilantro on top.

Nutrition Information
Calories: 209 kcal, Carbohydrates: 22 g, Protein: 14 g, Fat: 8 g

119. Caprese and Smashed Avocado Toast
Prep Time: 20 Mins, Cook Time: 25 Mins, Servings: 5
Ingredients
- ¼ cup balsamic vinegar dark
- 1 pit removed & peeled avocado
- 2 tsp juice lemon
- 4 slices of toasted rye bread
- 1 diced Roma tomato
- 4 oz low-fat mozzarella cheese
- ¼ cup chopped basil fresh

Instructions
- Bring your vinegar to a moderate boil in a medium saucepan. Cook until the sauce has decreased & thickened to your simmer. Allow cooling before storing.
- The avocado & lemon juice should be combined. A few bits of avocado seem ok, as long as your avocado is pureed. Toast four pieces of rye bread and equally spread your avocado on each one. The tomato & mozzarella should be topped.
- Fresh basil & chilled balsamic sauce should be drizzled over the dish. It's time to eat!

Nutrition Information
Calories: 201 kcal, Carbohydrates: 12 g, Protein: 8 g, Fat: 14 g

120. Grilled Shrimp and Radish Chopped Salad
Prep Time: 15 mins, Cook Time: 5 mins, Servings: 5
Ingredients
- 2 lb peeled & deveined shrimp raw
- 1 tbsp oil olive
- ½ tsp salt kosher
- 1 tsp coarsely ground black pepper
- 2 tbsp mayonnaise clean
- ¼ tbsp juice orange
- 2 tsp honey pure
- 2 cups roughly chopped kale
- 3 sliced radishes
- ½ cup sliced fennel
- ¼ cup chopped parsley

Instructions
- Grill over high heat for a few mins. Shrimp is ready to be tossed in olive oil with pepper and salt. Turn halfway during the grilling process to ensure even charring. As little as a min and a half per half, Shrimp would be bright pink & firm. Grilled food should be cooled before serving.
- Orange juice, Mayonnaise, and honey are all you need for this recipe. Set aside for now.
- Combine the chilled shrimp with the radish, fennel, greens, & parsley in a mixing basin. Make sure to mix the ingredients with mayonnaise sauce thoroughly. It's time to eat!

Nutrition Information
Calories: 411 kcal, Carbohydrates: 10 g, Protein: 63 g, Fat: 14 g

121. Instant Pot Corn on the Cob with Chipotle Sauce
Prep Time: 5 mins, Cook Time: 15 mins, Servings: 3
Ingredients
For Corn
- 4 ears corn husked sweet
- 1 & ½ cups warm water
- 1 tsp salt kosher

For Sauce
- 1 cup plain Greek yogurt
- ¼ cup pureed chipotle peppers
- 2 tsp juice lime
- 2 tbsp chopped cilantro fresh

Instructions
For Corn
- Corn should be placed on an Instant Pot steam rack, and salt and water should be added to the mixture. Close its lid and assure that vent is shut off. Press your "Manual" key, then use the "Adjust" button to adjust the pressure to a high level, and then release. For around 5 mins, set a timer. This should take a few minutes for your Instant Pot to warm up before starting the timer. Wait 10 mins before gently lowering the steam & removing the cover after the 5 mins are up. Serve your corn with the chipotle dipping sauce.

For Sauce
- Juice from one lime & peppers should be added to the yogurt mixture. Drizzle over some cooked corn over the cob once removed from the heat. Serve with a sprinkling of fresh cilantro.

Nutrition Information
Calories: 153 kcal, Carbohydrates: 22 g, Protein: 9 g, Fat: 5 g

122. Chimichurri Sauce
Prep Time: 5 mins, Cook Time: 5 mins, Servings: 4
Ingredients
- ½ cup finely chopped Italian parsley
- ¼ cup finely chopped cilantro
- 1 finely diced onion small
- 1 finely minced garlic clove
- 1 finely chopped chili pepper red
- 2 tbsp vinegar red wine
- 1 tbsp fresh lemon juice
- ½ cup olive oil extra virgin

Instructions
- Mix all the ingredients in a bowl & serve over your preferred meat or pasta dish.

Nutrition Information
Calories: 64 kcal, Carbohydrates: 1 g, Protein: 2 g, Fat: 7 g

123. Slow Cooker Salisbury Steaks
Prep Time: 25 mins, Cook Time: 2 hrs 30 mins, Servings: 8
Ingredients
Steaks
- 1 tsp olive oil
- ½ cup diced white onion
- 1 & ½ lb ground beef lean
- ½ cup breadcrumbs panko
- 1 egg large
- ¼ cup low-sodium beef broth
- 1 tsp garlic dried
- 1 tsp salt kosher
- ½ tsp pepper black
- 8 oz sliced mushrooms

Gravy
- 2 cups low-sodium beef stock
- 2 tbsp ketchup
- 1 tbsp mustard yellow

- 1 tbsp vinegar red wine
- 1 tsp sauce Worcestershire
- 2 tbsp butter
- 2 tbsp flour

Instructions
- On the burner, heat olive oil to medium-high. Onions should be tender and transparent when they're cooked.
- Beef, salt, breadcrumbs, beef broth, egg, dried garlic, & pepper should all be combined in a mixing bowl. Using the similar pan in which the onions had browned, form patties & cook for approximately two mins from each side. Cover the bottom of the slow cooker along with mushrooms & simmer on low for 8 to 10 hrs.
- Pour the rest of the ingredients, excluding the butter & flour, on the patties & mix well.
- 5 hrs on low is the recommended cooking time. Butter & flour should be whipped together. Removing the meat patties from your slow cooker, mix with the flour. Return your patties to a sauce after whisking them to you thicken them.

Nutrition Information
Calories: 313 kcal, Carbohydrates: 11 g, Protein: 28 g, Fat: 17 g

124. Melon Berry Salad with Feta
Prep Time: 15 mins, Cook Time: 15 mins, Servings: 4
Ingredients
- 2 cups melon cantaloupe
- 1 cup of feta cheese low-fat crumbles
- 2 cups melon honeydew
- 2 cups of watermelon
- 1 cup of blueberries
- 2 tbsp olive oil
- 2 tbsp juice lime
- ½ tsp salt kosher
- 1 cup of blackberries

Instructions
- Combine the honeydew, cantaloupe, & watermelon with the lime juice, olive oil, & salt in a big mixing bowl. To ensure that all ingredients are well-coated in oil, combine everything and stir thoroughly. Add blueberries, blackberries, & feta cheese. To evenly distribute all berries, give the salad a little spin.
- It's time to eat!

Nutrition Information
Calories: 114 kcal, Carbohydrates: 13 g, Protein: 3 g, Fat: 6 g

125. Jalapeno Popper Casserole
Prep Time: 20 mins, Cook Time: 45 mins, Servings: 3
Ingredients
- 1 lb cauliflower
- 8 oz low-fat cream cheese
- ½ cup low-fat Greek yogurt
- ½ cup low-fat sour cream
- ½ cup shredded low-fat cheddar cheese
- ½ lb cooked & crumbled turkey bacon
- ½ cup seeded & diced jalapeno peppers
- 1 tsp powder garlic
- ½ tsp salt
- 1 lb chicken breasts boneless & skinless

For Topping
- ¼ cup low-fat cheddar cheese
- ½ lb cooked & crumbled turkey bacon
- 1 thinly sliced jalapeno

Instructions
- Cauliflower may be baked in a 400-deg oven over the baking sheet. Roast the cauliflower florets for approximately 20 mins, or till they are soft and pliable. Drain all liquid by transferring it to the colander.
- In a medium bowl, combine the following 8 ingredients & whisk with a hand mixer till smooth.
- With the spoon, combine the cauliflower & chicken into the mixture.
- Transfer this mixture to a casserole dish lightly coated using cooking spray & taste for seasoning.
- Bake for around 25-30 mins, unless the cheese is bubbling & the bacon is crispy.

Nutrition Information
Calories: 376 kcal, Carbohydrates: 9 g, Protein: 29 g, Fat: 25 g

126. Lemon and Garlic Sweet Potato Salad
Prep Time: 30 mins, Cook Time: 1 hr, Servings: 12
Ingredients
- 2 lb peeled sweet potatoes
- 2 tsp zest lemon
- ¼ cup fresh lemon juice
- 1 tbsp vinegar apple cider
- 4 minced garlic cloves
- 2 tsp mustard Dijon
- 2 tsp mustard whole-grain
- 1 tbsp honey pure
- 1 tsp salt kosher
- 2/3 cups oil olive
- ¼ cup chopped tarragon

Instructions
- A big saucepan should be filled with enough water to cover the potatoes, so bring it to a boil. Cover and simmer for approximately 20 minutes unless the potatoes are fork tender. After draining and cooling, proceed.
- Meanwhile, put all of your ingredients into a blender & mix until smooth. Add some olive oil slowly while mixing till the mixture is creamy. Set aside for now.
- Once your potatoes have cooled, dice them, and add them to a big bowl. Sprinkle some tarragon over top of the dressing. Gradually stir in a little amount.
- Almost 30 mins before serving, freeze the dessert.

Nutrition Information
Calories: 216 kcal, Carbohydrates: 21 g, Protein: 2 g, Fat: 15 g

127. Arugula, Mushroom, and Tomato Poached Egg Toast
Prep Time: 15 Mins, Cook Time: 25 Mins, Servings: 2
Ingredients
- 1 tbsp oil olive
- ¼ cup sliced mushrooms
- ¼ tsp salt kosher
- 2 slices sourdough bread whole-wheat
- 1/3 cup arugula baby
- 1 sliced tomato
- 2 poached eggs large
- ¼ tsp coarsely ground black pepper

Instructions
- Heat your olive oil inside a small pan over medium-low heat. Once the oil is heated, add both mushrooms & salt. The mushrooms should be mushy & the liquid from them released, so cook them till they are.
- Toasted your bread to an appropriate level of doneness, whereas the mushrooms cooked.
- Arugula & tomato go on top of every piece of bread. Place the cooked mushrooms over the tomato and cover with a lid to keep them warm. Sprinkle coarse pepper over the poached egg before gently placing it over mushrooms.
- It's time to eat!

Nutrition Information
Calories: 220 kcal, Carbohydrates: 17 g, Protein: 10 g, Fat: 13 g

128. Spicy Sesame Cucumber Salad
Prep Time: 15 mins, Cook Time: 15 mins, Servings: 3
Ingredients
- 1 tbsp low-sodium soy sauce
- 1 tbsp vinegar rice
- 2 tsp oil sesame
- 1 tsp honey
- 2 tsp seeds sesame
- ¼ tsp red pepper crushed
- 3 cups sliced cucumber

- 1 sliced red onion
- 1 diced small jalapeno
- ¼ cup chopped cilantro fresh

Instructions
- Pour everything into a medium bowl & stir until well-combined. Taste and adjust seasoning if necessary. Stir in jalapeño, red onion, & cucumber. Stir gently till the sauce is well distributed among the food.
- Serve with a garnish of cilantro.

Nutrition Information
Calories: 38 kcal, Carbohydrates: 4 g, Protein: 1 g, Fat: 3 g

129. Grilled Avocado & Peach Salad
Prep Time: 20 Mins, Cook Time: 35 Mins, Servings: 4
Ingredients
- 3 pit removed peaches
- 2 pit removed, & sliced avocados peeled
- 1/3 cup oil olive
- 2 tbsp vinegar white balsamic
- 1 tsp honey
- ½ tsp salt kosher
- 2 cups arugula baby
- 2 cups spinach baby
- 2 cups chopped romaine lettuce
- ¼ cup toasted pine nuts

Instructions
- Grill over high heat for a few mins. Some olive oil should be applied to the peach & avocado slices, and it's time to save some of that olive oil for later.
- Griddle the peaches & avocados until they are slightly browned on both sides. Approximately 3-5 mins on each side. Remove it off the grill. Make wedges out of the roasted peaches by cutting them in half.
- Make a well-blended mixture of vinegar, honey, & sea salt in a food processor or blender. Blend the remaining olive oil into a slow, steady stream unless well-combined.
- Combine all three salad ingredients with your hands in an enormous bowl. Toss your greens with roughly some dressing. Serve in separate bowls. Put peaches & pine nuts on top of the avocado. If necessary, add extra dressing.
- It's time to eat!

Nutrition Information
Calories: 197 kcal, Carbohydrates: 13 g, Protein: 2 g, Fat: 17 g

130. Red Pepper Sun-Dried Tomato Sauce
Prep Time: 10 mins, Cook Time: 10 mins, Servings: 5
Ingredients
- 16 oz roasted drained red peppers
- 4 oz sun-dried drained tomatoes
- 2 tbsp olive oil extra virgin
- 2 halved garlic cloves
- ½ tsp salt sea
- ½ tsp pepper black
- ½ cup diced red onion
- ¼ cup packed basil leaves
- 1 tbsp vinegar balsamic

Instructions
- Pulse the food processor till the mixture is smooth. Till you're prepared to use the sauce, keep it in a closed container.

Nutrition Information
Calories: 178 kcal, Carbohydrates: 5 g, Protein: 1 g, Fat: 18 g

131. Tex-Mex Quinoa Bowl
Prep Time: 30 Mins, Cook Time: 45 Mins, Servings: 3
Ingredients
- 2 tbsp oil coconut
- 1 cup diced onion
- 2 chicken breasts boneless & skinless
- 3 tsp seasoning taco
- 2 tbsp water
- ¾ cup frozen corn kernels
- 2 cups cooked quinoa
- 1 tbsp fresh lime juice
- ½ cup reduced-fat cheddar cheese
- 2 tbsp chopped cilantro
- 2 cups diced tomatoes
- ½ diced avocado
- 2 tbsp fat-free sour cream

Instructions
- Coconut oil may be heated in a pan over medium-high heat. Chopped chicken breast & onion should be cooked together, and the chicken must be cooked to the point when it isn't any longer pink. Taco spice, water, & corn are all good additions. Simmer over low heat until all of the water is gone.
- Place the quinoa inside a medium-sized sauté pan and cook, often stirring, until the quinoa is tender. To toast & warm the quinoa, give it a quick toss in the pan. Add both lime juice & the leftover taco spice. Remove from the heat.
- Serve quinoa into bowls by sprinkling it on top. Sprinkle with a mixture of chicken & corn. Add sour cream & cheese to the top of the dish.

Nutrition Information
Calories: 200 kcal, Carbohydrates: 20 g, Protein: 10 g, Fat: 10 g

132. Cajun Shrimp & Sausage "Pasta" with Butternut Squash
Prep Time: 30 Mins, Cook Time: 25 Mins, Servings: 4-6
Ingredients
- 8 oz of Andouille style sausage sliced
- ½ lb of Shrimp peeled & deveined
- 1 large, diced tomato
- 1 tbsp of tomato paste
- 1-2 tsp of Cajun seasoning
- 12 oz of Butternut Squash noodles
- 1 sliced jalapeno pepper
- shredded Parmesan cheese
- salt & pepper, to taste

Instructions
- Coat a skillet with cooking spray & brown the sausage. Stir in the shrimp until they are gently browned. Remove the pan from the heat.
- Spray the pan once more & add the onions. Before adding the tomatoes, cook for 1 min. Cook for another 2 mins (tomatoes may release water).
- If the mixture is too thick, add tomato water & paste (up to one-fourth cup). Season with salt and pepper. Simmer for 2-3 mins.
- Cook for 10 mins or until the noodles are tender. In the final 5 mins, add the cooked sausage & shrimp to just warm through. Serve with cheese & jalapenos on top.

Nutrition Information
Calories: 136, Carbohydrates: 8 g, Protein: 20 g, Fats: 5 g

133. No-Flour, Low-Sugar Pumpkin Chocolate Chip Cookies
Prep time: 5 mins, Cook time: 17 mins, Servings: 12-15
Ingredients
- sweetener (no-calorie) equivalent to ¼ cup of sugar
- brown sugar (no-calorie) sub equivalent to ¼ cup of brown sugar
- 2 tbsp of butter or light butter stick
- ¼ cup of pumpkin puree, pure
- ½ tsp of vanilla extract, pure
- 1 egg, large
- ¾ cup of almond flour, finely ground
- ½ cup or 30g protein powder, vanilla or unflavored
- ½ tsp of baking soda
- ¼ tsp of salt
- ½ cup chocolate chips, sugar-free

Instructions
- Preheat the oven to 350 Fahrenheit.

- Combine butter, sweeteners, pumpkin, & vanilla in a dish with a stand mixer or hand mixer & "cream." (NOTE: Sugar substitutes do not cream the same way as ordinary sugar.) The butter may clump together. That's OK as far all Ingredients are combined.) Mix in the egg completely.
- Combine coconut & almond flour, salt (plus protein powder, if using), baking soda in a separate bowl & stir well. Mix with the wet Ingredients till the dough forms. Put chocolate chips (sugar-free).
- Using a spoon or cookie scoop, drop piles of dough onto parchment-lined baking sheets. Bake for 15 mins, or till the interior of the cookie is done. Allow cooling on a cooling rack.

Nutrition Information
Calories: 131, Carbohydrates: 10 g, Protein: 12 g, Fats: 6 g

134. Take on Shakshuka
Prep time: 5 mins Cook time:15 mins, Servings: 4
Ingredients
- 1large sliced onion
- 1 tbsp of olive oil
- 20 oz of canned tomatoes (fire-roasted)
- 2-3 tomatoes (Roma, on the vine, etc.) chopped (optional)
- 2cloves minced garlic
- Salt & pepper, to taste
- 2 tsp of paprika (you may use smoked paprika)
- 1/2 tsp of cumin
- 1/4 tsp of chili powder
- 4 eggs, large
- 1bunch parsley/cilantro

Instructions
- Preheat a pan on medium flame & add the oil, followed by the onions. Cook for approximately 2 mins or until softened.
- Put the garlic in the pan & continue to sauté for another min before tossing in the bottled & fresh tomatoes.
- Stir in the spices, including the pepper & salt.
- In tomato mixture, make 4 "holes." Each hole should be filled with a whole egg. Cover the skillet and reduce the flame to medium-low.
- Cook for 6-8 mins, or till eggs are perfectly poached. Remove the pan from the heat & set it aside to cool. The tomato sauce will thicken as it sits.

Nutrition Information
Calories: 90, Carbohydrates: 14 g, Protein: 19 g, Fats: 5.1 g

135. Easy Weeknight Steak Fajita Skillet
Prep time: 15 mins, Cook time: 30 mins, Servings: 4
Ingredients
- 1 tbsp of olive oil, extra-virgin
- 1medium sliced yellow onion
- 1 red sliced bell pepper
- 1 sliced yellow bell pepper
- 2 tsp of minced garlic
- 1/2 lb of thin-cut steak, slice into strips
- Salt & pepper, to taste
- 1 tsp of cumin, divided
- 1 tsp of Coriander, divided
- 1 tsp of chili pepper, divided
- One pinch of cayenne pepper
- 4cups of frozen cauliflower rice
- 2 tbsp of tomato paste
- 1/3 cup of water

Instructions
- Preheat a pan on medium flame until it is hot. Pour in the oil.
- Cook the onion, garlic & peppers in a skillet until they are cooked, approximately 5-7 mins.
- While the veggies are cooking, throw the steak strips in the dish with 1/2 of each spice, pepper & salt.
- Add the meat to the pan & cook until it is browned.
- Stir in the cauliflower rice & heat until it has thawed, then add the tomato paste, other spices, & water, if necessary. (Add water if the sauce is thick to incorporate the tomato paste.)
- Reduce the flame to medium-low & cover the pan. Allow 10-15 mins to cook, stirring often.
- Adjust spices to taste. Add jalapeno peppers, grated cheese, cubed avocado, or other toppings to taste.

Nutrition Information
Calories: 110, Carbohydrates: 12.3 g, Protein: 14 g, Fats: 3 g

136. Sugar-Free Egg Nog with Added Protein
Prep time:30 mins, Cook time: 10 mins, Servings: 8
Ingredients
- 4 egg yolks
- 1/3cip of Sola granular sweetener + 1 additional tbsp)
- 1pint Fair life 2% milk or 2% milk of you like
- 1c up of half & half
- 2 tsp of rum extract
- 1 tsp of nutmeg
- 4 egg whites
- 1scoop or 30 g protein powder, unflavored

Instructions
- Beat the eggs with a stand mixer on low speed in the mixing bowl, gradually adding the sweetener until mixed well. The color of the egg yolks should soften & thicken.
- In a large skillet, combine the milk & half-and-half & heat on low-medium flame. Bring to a boil, then remove from the heat.
- Whisk or beat the yolks for a couple of seconds before gently ladling in a 3/4 cup of the heated mixture while continually mixing. To gradually increase the temp of the eggs, slowly drizzle in the liquid. Repeat three times more, finishing with a 20-second milk/egg combination mix.
- Immediately whisk the milk/yolk mixture & add it to the remaining boiling liquid in the skillet. Reduce the heat to medium & continue to cook till the internal temp reaches 160 degrees.
- Stir in the nutmeg & rum essence. Place in a bowl, cover, & chill for 2 hrs.
- Whip egg whites in a stand mixer or bowl, gradually adding protein powder & more sugar. To stiff peaks, beat.
- Take the cooled milk/yolk combination out of the fridge & whisk in the egg white combo. Incorporate the egg whites softly into the milk/yolk mixture until completely mixed. The mixture will seem to bubble & thick.
- Refrigerate the dish till ready to be served. The eggnog will keep up to a week in the fridge.

Nutrition Information
Calories: 112, Carbohydrates: 7 g, Protein: 15 g, Fats: 5.3 g

137. No-Flour, Low-Sugar Snickerdoodles
Prep time: 5 mins, Cook time: 12 mins, Servings: 10-12
Ingredients
- 1cup of almond flour +1 additional tbsp
- 1/4 tsp of baking powder
- 1/4 tsp of salt
- 1/2 tsp of cream of tartar
- 1/2stick butter melted, unsalted
- 2-4 tbsp of Sola granular
- 1/2 egg or 2 tbsp of Egg Beaters
- 1/2 tsp of pure vanilla extract

Instructions
- Preheat the oven to 350°F & prepare a baking tray with baking parchment.
- Combine almond flour, salt, baking powder, & cream of tartar in a mixing dish. Put it aside.
- In a separate dish, cream the butter & sweetener until smooth, then add the vanilla

& egg. Mix the wet Ingredients & dry Ingredients completely, smooth out any clumps of almond flour.

- The consistency must be similar to a light cookie batter. If it is more like cake mix, stir in another tbsp of almond flour & chill for 30 mins,
- In a dish or bowl, combine the remaining sweetener and cinnamon. Drop heaping spoonsful of batter into the mix & gently coat.
- Place dough in 2 rows on a baking tray & flatten it into a disc shape with a spoon.
- Bake for 15 mins, then take out from oven & cool for 5 mins on a cookie sheet before moving to a wire rack.

Nutrition Information
Calories: 100, Carbohydrates: 15 g, Protein: 14 g, Fats: 5 g

138. No-Flour, Low-Sugar Ginger Cookies
Prep time: 5 mins, Cook time: 11 mins, Servings: 10
Ingredients
- 1 cup of almond flour + 1 additional tbsp.
- ¼ tsp of baking powder
- ¼ tsp of salt
- ½ tsp of ground ginger
- ½ tsp of ground cinnamon
- ¼ tsp of nutmeg
- ¼ tsp of allspice
- ½ stick butter melted, unsalted
- 3 tbsp of Sola granular (or your favorite one)
- ½ egg or 2 tbsp of Egg Beaters
- ½ tsp of pure vanilla extract

Instructions
- Preheat the oven to 350 Fahrenheit.
- Combine almond flour, salt, baking powder, ginger, nutmeg, cinnamon, & allspice in a large mixing bowl. Set aside after fully mixing.
- In a separate dish, thoroughly mix the sweetener & butter before adding the vanilla & egg & combining again.
- Stir together the wet Ingredients & dry Ingredients well, being careful to break up any clumps of almond flour.
- The consistency must be similar to light cookie dough. If the mixture resembles cake batter, add another tbsp of almond flour & stir completely before wrapping it in clingfilm. Freeze for approximately 30 mins after wrapping it in a wrapping sheet.
- Separate two big pieces of baking paper & place one on the work area. Put the dough ball on the baking parchment & wrap it with another piece. Roll the dough out flat with a rolling pin.
- Working rapidly, make as many patterns as you can with the cookie cutters to eliminate the leftover dough. Place the parchment paper on a cookie sheet and set it aside. Return any leftover dough to the freezer & continue the procedure till the cookie tray is filled or you run out of dough. (For round cookies, you might have to use the final piece of dough to form flattened discs.)
- Bake for 12 mins while remaining close to the oven. The bottoms of them may soon catch fire.
- Immediately transfer the biscuits to a wire rack using a cookie spatula.

Nutrition Information
Calories: 127, Carbohydrates: 10 g, Protein: 11 g, Fats: 6 g

139. No-Flour Low Sugar Cookie Base Recipe
Prep time: 5 mins, Cook time: 12 mins, Servings: 10-12
Ingredients
- 1cup of almond flour +an additional tbsp
- 1/4 tsp of baking powder
- 1/4 tsp of salt
- 1/2stick butter softened, unsalted
- 2 tbsp of Sola granular (or your favorite one)
- ½ egg or 2 tbsp Egg Beaters
- 1/4 tsp of pure vanilla extract

Instructions
- Preheat the oven to 350 Fahrenheit.
- Combine the almond flour, salt & baking powder in a mixing dish. Put it aside.
- In a separate dish, cream together the sweetener & butter until smooth, then add the vanilla & egg. Mix the dry & wet Ingredients completely, smooth out any clumps in almond flour.
- The dough must have the consistency of light cookie dough. If the mixture resembles cake batter, use another spoonful of almond flour. Put in the refrigerator for 30 mins before serving.
- Drop spoonsful of cookie dough in 2 rows, approximately 2 inches apart, on a baking sheet coated with baking parchment. Flatten them with a spoon into a disc.
- Bake for 14 mins at 350°F. Remove from the oven & cool for 5 mins on the baking tray before moving to a wire rack.

Nutrition Information
Calories: 119, Carbohydrates: 20 g, Protein: 16 g, Fats: 5.9 g

140. You-Sized Four Cheese Mashed Cauliflower
Prep time: 15 mins, Cook time: 30 mins, Servings: 3-4
Ingredients
- 1 tbsp of butter
- 1 tsp of xanthan gum
- 1cup of milk
- 1/3cup grated cheddar cheese
- 1/4cup of grated mild cheddar cheese
- 1/3cup grated asiago cheese (or whatever you like!)
- 1/3cup shredded Parmesan
- (optional) smoked paprika
- 12 oz. of frozen cauliflower rice
- salt & pepper, to taste

Instructions
- Preheat the oven to 350 Fahrenheit.
- Preheat a pan on medium flame until it is hot, then add the butter & cook till it is barely melted. Whisk in the xanthan gum till it forms a paste.
- Pour the milk & whisk again to remove any lumps. Cook for 1-2 mins, or until it thickens.
- To begin the melting procedure, whisk in the mild cheddar cheese, sharp cheddar, & third cheese. Allow for 5-7 mins of cooking time. The cheese mix will become rough at first, then smoother.
- Combine the package of cauliflower rice (still frozen) with the heated cheese mixture in a mixing dish. Bake, uncovered, for approximately 30 mins or till cheese is melted to your preference, in ramekins or a casserole dish.

Nutrition Information
Calories: 140, Carbohydrates: 12 g, Protein: 19.9 g, Fats: 4.3g

141. Apple-Pecan Chicken Salad
Prep time: 5 mins, Cook time: 0 mins, Servings: 1-2
Ingredients
- 4 oz chicken breast (cooked & diced)
- 2 tbsp minced yellow onion
- 1/2 diced sweet apple
- 2 tbsp pecan pieces, crushed
- 1/4 tsp of Garlic Powder
- 2 tsp of Dijon mustard
- 1 tbsp of mayo (low or full fat, your choice!)
- Salt & pepper, to taste

Instructions
- In a mixing bowl, mix all ingredients & combine well! Refrigerate until ready to serve.

Nutrition Information
Calories: 120kcal, Carbohydrates: 10 g, Protein: 12 g, Fats: 5 g

142. Yummy Fall Pork & Apple Stew
Prep time: 15 mins, Cook time: 5 hrs., Servings: 8
Ingredients
- 3 diced slices of bacon
- 2 lb of pork country, ribs cubed
- 1medium sliced yellow onion

- 1 tsp of salt
- 1/2 tsp of ground black pepper
- 1 tsp of dried sage
- 1 tsp of minced garlic
- 1 tsp of ground ginger
- 1 tsp of Dijon mustard
- 1 tsp of chopped basil leaves
- 1inch chopped rosemary sprig needles
- 1/2 tsp of nutmeg
- 4 cups of broth (like you can use chicken or pork)
- 1cup hard cider
- ¼ cup of cooking wine or apple cider vinegar
- 3cup butternut squash or sweet potato, diced
- 3medium sliced Honeycrisp apples

Instructions
- Set the crockpot to medium & add the bacon bits if it has a stovetop option. Fry until the fat is rendered, then remove & set aside.
- Increase the heat to high & add the country ribs, scorching both sides. Remove.
- Toss all of the herbs & spices together in a dish. Stir in the onions, spices, & mustard in the crockpot once all of the bacon fat is mixed. Return the meat to the pot.
- Pour in the broth, sweet potatoes, cider (or squash) & simmer on low for 4 hrs.
- Add the apple slices & simmer for one additional hr.
- If desired, garnish with fresh sage (chopped) or whole grain mustard.

Nutrition Information
Calories: 123, Carbohydrates: 11 g, Protein: 15 g, Fats: 4 g

143. Bacon Cheeseburger Meatballs
Prep time: 20 mins, Cook time: 30 mins, Servings: 16
Ingredients
- 1 lb of ground turkey, 90% lean
- 1 egg, large
- 1 small, grated zucchini
- 1 small finely minced or diced yellow onion
- (optional) 1cup of textured vegetable protein
- 1/4 tsp of salt
- 1/4 tsp of ground black pepper
- 1/2 tsp of Garlic Powder
- 1 tsp of smoked paprika
- 1/3cup of real bacon bits
- 1/2cup of reduced-fat grated cheddar cheese

Sauce
- 1/2cup ketchup, low sugar
- 1/4cup of yellow mustard
- 1/4cup of reduced-fat mayo
- 2 tbsp of no-sugar-added relish

Instructions
Meatballs
- Preheat the oven to 350 Fahrenheit. Combine the turkey, zucchini, egg, onion, & textured vegetable protein in a mixing dish. Mix thoroughly.
- Combine the seasonings, bacon pieces, & half of the cheddar cheese in a mixing bowl. Recombine the Ingredients.
- Preheat oven to 350°F. Line a baking tray. Scoop out a big spoonful using a tbsp measure, roll into balls with hands (mixture may be quite soft), & set on a prepared baking tray.
- Bake for 28 mins, or till well cooked. Top with the remaining cheese. Use Everything Sauce as a dipping or a topping.

Everything Sauce
- In a mixing dish, combine all of the ingredients & stir thoroughly. Refrigerate until ready to use.

Nutrition Information
Calories: 138, Carbohydrates: 7.8 g, Protein: 18 g, Fats: 5.3 g

144. Crockpot Curry Chicken
Prep time:10 mins, Cook time:4 hrs., Servings: 6
Ingredients
- 1 lb chicken thighs (boneless +skinless)
- 1/4 tsp of each salt & pepper
- 1 medium chop of yellow onion
- 1 sliced red bell pepper
- 1 carrot diced, large
- 1cup of forum green peas
- 3 tbsp of curry powder
- 1 tsp of minced garlic
- 2cup of light coconut milk
- 1cup of chicken broth, low sodium
- 1 tbsp of corn starch
- 1 tbsp of water
- 3cup of cauliflower rice

Instructions
- Rinse the chicken & pat it dry. Season to taste with pepper & salt.
- Combine the chicken, carrots, onion, peas, curry powder, bell pepper, & garlic. Cook on low flame for 4 hrs, with coconut milk & chicken broth.
- Take the chicken out of the crockpot & shred it on a platter.
- In a mixing dish, combine equal parts of cornstarch & water & whisk till the paste forms. Pour the cornstarch mixture in the crockpot to the liquid & whisk, whereas the chicken is not in the crockpot. Allow 10 minutes to simmer before placing the chicken in the crockpot.
- Cook for another hr. before serving on top of cauliflower rice.

Nutrition Information
Calories: 139, Carbohydrates: 7 g, Protein: 19 g, Fats: 10.2 g

145. Smoky Cabbage Rolls
Prep time: 25 mins, Cook time: 30 mins, Servings: 12
Ingredients
- 12 cabbage leaves
- 1 medium diced yellow onion
- 1 lb of lean ground turkey
- 1cup of cauliflower rice
- 1/4 tsp of salt
- 1/4 tsp of pepper
- 2 tbsp of smoked paprika
- 1/2 tsp of Italian seasoning
- 2 tbsp of Worcestershire sauce
- 10 oz of can whole tomatoes (without salt added)
- 1/2 tsp of Garlic Powder
- 1/2 tsp of onion powder
- 1 tsp of no-calorie sweetener

Instructions
- Preheat the oven to 350 Fahrenheit.
- Bring a saucepan of water to a boil & put the metal strain over this boiling water. Place the cabbage leaves in a sieve & steam until they are wilted but not fully soft (about 5 mins). Put everything in a dish & put it aside.
- Coat a pan with cooking spray & place it on medium flame to heat it. Cook the onions for 1-2 mins, or till onions are softened. Put the turkey in the pan & cook the turkey until it is thoroughly cooked.
- Combine the salt, smoked paprika, pepper, Italian seasoning, & one tbsp of Worcestershire sauce in a large mixing bowl. Add the cauliflower rice last. Allow this mixture to simmer for another 2 mins.
- Pulse full tomatoes with can liquid in a food processor or blender until pureed. Pulse in the garlic & onion powder & the leftover Worcestershire sauce.
- Assemble the rolls as follows. Spoon roughly two oz of the beef mixture onto a clean surface or cabbage leaf. Then fold in the long ends & roll long ways as roll a burrito. Serve in a casserole dish.
- Spread tomato sauce on the top of the packed & rolled leaves.

- Bake uncovered for 15-20 mins for a little less juicy cabbage roll.
- Bake covered (with foil) for 20 mins for more juicy cabbage rolls.

Nutrition Information
Calories: 126, Carbohydrates: 8.9 g, Protein: 16 g, Fats: 7 g

146. Citrusy Crockpot Pork Tacos with Spicy Green Sauce
Prep time: 15 mins, Cook time: 6 hrs., Servings: 6-8
Ingredients
Pork filling
- 1 lb. of pork country ribs
- 1/2 tsp of salt
- 1/2 tsp of ground black pepper
- 1 tsp of minced garlic
- 1/2 tsp of smoked paprika
- (optional)1/2 tsp of ground chipotle pepper
- 2 cups of Tropicana 50 no-sugar-added orange juice
- 1 tsp of orange zest

Green Sauce
- 1bunch cilantro, fresh
- 2 peeled cloves garlic
- 1 jalapeno pepper
- 1 lime juice
- 2-3 tbsp of water
- 1 tsp of olive oil, extra-virgin
- 1/4cup of Greek yogurt, unflavored

Tacos/Toppings
- 1head of curly leaf lettuce
- 1 sliced red bell pepper
- 1 sliced orange bell pepper

Instructions
- In a crockpot, combine the ribs, pepper, salt, garlic, chipotle pepper & paprika (if using). Cook on low flame for 6 hrs, covered with orange zest plus juice & water. Allow the meat to continue to warm by shredding it with forks.
- To prepare the sauce, pulse cilantro, jalapeno, garlic, lime juice, Greek yogurt & olive oil till smooth in a food processor or blender. It should be possible to sprinkle the sauce. If it's too thick, thin it out with water & re-mix.
- To prepare taco shells, remove the leaves from the curly leaf lettuce bunch & remove the steam with a knife. Fill all of the tacos with roughly 1-2 oz of pork, peppers, one tbsp of yogurt & one tsp of green sauce.

Nutrition Information
Calories: 134, Carbohydrates: 8.1 g, Protein: 20.5 g, Fats: 5 g

147. Lower Carb Orange Bars
Prep time: 20 mins, Cook time: 30 mins, Servings: 9-12
Ingredients
Crust
- 2 cups crushed high fiber cereal
- 4 oz of cream cheese softened low fat
- ¼ cup no-calorie sweetener
- 1/2 tsp. of ground cinnamon

Filling
- ¾ cup no-calorie sweetener
- 2 tbsp of corn starch
- 4large eggs
- 4 navel oranges juice, large
- 1 orange zest
- 1 lemon juice, large

Instructions
Make crust
- Preheat the oven to 350 Fahrenheit.
- Pulse cereal crumbs, sweetener, softened cream cheese, & cinnamon in the food processor until the blend resembles wet sand.
- Use parchment paper to line an 8x8 baking sheet. Bake for 12-15 mins after pressing crumbs in the baking dish.

Make filling
- Mix the cornstarch & sweetener in a mixing dish & stir thoroughly with a fork. Put the eggs & continue to beat till the batter is entirely mixed.
- Whisk together the orange juice & lemon juice, as well as the orange zest. The combination will be runny.
- Slowly pour the mix over the crust & bake for 26-30 mins, or till fully set.
- Cool completely (approximately one hr) on a wire rack to cool before putting it in the fridge for 3 hrs. Lift the whole sheet out when ready to serve & slice into desired size pieces.

Nutrition Information
Calories: 106, Carbohydrates: 13.3 g, Protein: 12.7 g, Fats: 8 g

148. Smoky, Spicy (and vegan!) Roasted Brussels Sprouts
Prep time: 10 mins, Cook time: 20 mins, Servings: 5
Ingredients
- 1bag (25-30 in a bag) whole Brussels sprouts, fresh
- 1 minced clove of garlic
- 1/2 tsp of salt
- 1/2 tsp of pepper
- 1 tsp of smoked paprika
- 1 tsp of ground cumin
- (optional), 1/2 tsp of ground chipotle powder
- ¼ cup of olive oil, extra-virgin

Instructions
- Preheat the oven to 425 Fahrenheit.
- Remove the stems from Brussels sprouts & slice them in half, putting them in a mixing dish.
- Add the spices & garlic, followed by the oil. Toss till all the sprouts are well covered.
- Place sprouts in an equal layer on a baking tray lined with parchment paper. Bake for 15-20 mins, or till the desired doneness.
- Set aside to cool somewhat before serving.

Nutrition Information
Calories: 116, Carbohydrates: 10.9 g, Protein: 17 g, Fats: 10.1 g

149. Crispy Cauliflower Tots
Prep time: 15 mins, cook time: 20 mins, servings: 18
Ingredients
- 3 cups (drained & cooked), cauliflower florets
- 1 tbsp of onion flakes,
- 1 tsp of Garlic Powder
- 1/2 tsp of smoked paprika
- 1/4 tsp of salt
- 1/4 tsp of white pepper
- 1 egg beaten, large
- 1/2cup of shredded cheddar cheese

Instructions
- Preheat the oven to 425 Fahrenheit.
- Puree cauliflower florets in the food processor once they've been cooked & drained. Use a sieve or cotton cloth to drain away from the extra water. Empty the cauliflower onto a dish after it has been squeezed of water.
- Stir in the spices completely.
- Mix in the egg & cheese till everything is well blended.
- Preheat oven to 350°F. Line a baking tray with baking paper. Portion the batter into the palms of the hand & form into a cylinder utilizing a tiny scope or melon baller. Place all of the tots on a baking tray with care.
- Bake for 18-20 mins, turning halfway during the cooking time.

Nutrition Information
Calories: 129, Carbohydrates: 7.9 g, Protein: 11 g, Fats: 4 g

150. Protein Pumpkin Cheesecake Cups
Prep time: 10 mins, Cook time: 10 mins, Servings: 4
Ingredients
Pumpkin Cheesecake Fluff
- 1/2cup of canned pumpkin (not pumpkin pie filling!)
- 1serving of Bariatric Pal Protein 1Cinnamon Swirl flavor

- 8 oz cream cheese softened, low fat
- 2 tbsp of Greek yogurt vanilla, low fat
- 1/2 tsp of pumpkin pie spice
- No-calorie sweetener, to taste

Topping
- ½ cup of crushed cereal
- 2 tbsp of walnut pieces
- (optional), whipped topping, low-calorie

Instructions
- Mix pumpkin & protein powder in a dish. With the help of a hand mixer, beat on medium speed until completely incorporated.
- Beat cream cheese, pie spice & Greek yogurt for 1-2 mins on medium speed, then for 1-2 mins on high speed, or till smooth.
- Place a half-cup portion in each of 4 cups. (NOTE: You will need more cups if you're using a lower quantity of each cup.)
- Combine nuts & cereal in a blender & pour equal quantities of topping into each cup. To serve, garnish with heavy cream & a pinch of cinnamon (if preferred).

Nutrition Information
Calories: 130, Carbohydrates: 17 g, Protein: 14 g, Fats: 6.6 g

151. Olive Garden Knock-Off: Tilapia Piccatta
Prep time: 10 mins, Cook time: 15 mins, Servings: 2

Ingredients
For Tilapia
- 1 tbsp of olive oil, extra-virgin
- 2 tilapia filets (defrost if frozen)
- Salt & pepper
- 1 tbsp of all-purpose flour or cornstarch
- 1/2 tbsp of butter
- ¼ cup of Champagne vinegar or white wine cooking vinegar
- 1 lemon juice, large
- 1 tsp minced garlic
- 1 tbsp of capers

For Parmesan-crusted zucchini
- 1 zucchini sliced into round shape 1/4 inch thick, medium
- ½ cup of shredded Parmesan cheese
- 1/3 cup of Egg Beaters or 2 eggs
- cooking spray, non-stick

Instructions
Make Tilapia
- Preheat a skillet on medium flame until hot, then coat liberally with cooking spray.
- Sprinkle the fish with pepper & salt on each side & set it in the heated pan. Cook for 2 mins on both sides, or until the salmon is well cooked. Remove the pan from the heat.
- Reduce the flame to low & whisk in the butter & flour until the sauce simmers & thickens. Continue whisking for another 2-3 mins after adding the garlic, wine, or Champagne vinegar & lemon juice.
- Finally, put the capers & simmer for about a min. Taste your mix. It must be bright, but not to the point of making you pucker! If something does, add a smidgeon of milk (approximately a tsp.) to the mix to settle it down. Alternatively, if you like, you may add additional butter!
- Put the fish on plates & top with an appropriate quantity of sauce.

Make zucchini
- Put the cheese in one dish & the eggs in the other.
- Dip zucchini rounds in cheese & then in egg, & finally back in cheese.
- Heat a pan on medium flame until it's hot, then thoroughly coat it with cooking spray. Place the coated zucchini in the pan and cook for 2-3 mins on both sides. If you turn the zucchini too soon, the crust may not have formed & will cling to the skillet instead of sticking to the zucchini!
- Place the zucchini on the paper towel to absorb the excess liquid till ready to be served.

Nutrition Information
Calories: 107, Carbohydrates: 16 g, Protein: 12 g, Fats: 6 g

152. Low-Carb Lemon Bars: Recipe Fail (and recovery!)
Prep time: 25 mins, Cook time: 30 mins, Servings: 12

Ingredients
Filling
- 8 lemons juiced
- 1 cup of liquid egg substitute (like Egg Beaters)
- 3 egg yolks only
- ¾ cup of Splenda (or your preferred sweetener, equivalent to ¾ cup of sugar)
- 1 tbsp of corn starch

Crust
- 1 cup of high fiber cereal
- 1 cup of coconut flour
- 2 tbsp of Splenda
- 5 oz of cream cheese (low fat) softened
- pinch salt

Instructions
- Preheat the oven to 350 Fahrenheit.
- Prepare the filling by combining cereal, sweetener, coconut flour, & salt in a dish. Mix in melted cream cheese till a crumbly sand-like paste develops, which may be formed into loose balls in your palm.
- Place the crumb mix into an eight-by-eight baking sheet lined with baking paper. Allow the crust to cool after baking for 15 mins.
- Mix lemon juice, egg yolks, liquid egg replacement, & sweetener in a dish. Using a mixer at moderate speed, thoroughly whisk the ingredients. Mix in the cornstarch well one more.
- Scoop the lemon mix over the crust & place the whole baking tray on the oven's bottom rack. Bake for 20-30 mins, or till the lemon custard is slightly firm to the touch.
- Allow cooling before using the paper to remove the whole dish from the baking tray. Slice into cubes & store in a sealed jar in the refrigerator till ready to serve.
- Powdered sugar (sugar-free) is sprinkled over the shown bars, which is created by combining one-fourth cup of Splenda with two heaping tsp of cornstarch.

Nutrition Information
Calories: 114, Carbohydrates: 9.5 g, Protein: 11.5 g, Fats: 2.9 g

153. Easy Crockpot Chicken Tortilla Soup
Prep time: 20 mins, Cook time: 6 hrs., Servings: 8-10

Ingredients
- 1 lb of chicken breast tenderloins
- 1 tsp of black pepper
- 1 tsp of salt
- 2 cups of jarred black bean salsa, your favorite one
- 1 tsp of ground chipotle powder (you can omit if you do not like spicy)
- 2 tsp of McCormick Mexican Spice blend (your favorite one Mexican spice blend)
- 1 tsp of ground cumin
- 8 oz of queso Blanco sliced (or you may use cojita)
- 4 cups of water
- 2 cups of frozen corn
- 10 oz of black beans(optional)
- 10 oz of diced tomatoes
- 4.5 oz of mild green chiles
- 2 tbsp of fresh chopped cilantro
- (optional), lime & additional cilantro & cotija cheese for garnish

Instructions
- Rinse & pat dry the chicken tenderloins before putting in the crockpot, season both halves with pepper & salt.
- Pour the salsa container over the chicken, season with spices, & simmer on low flame for 4 hrs.

- Shred the cooked chicken (it should be completely done). Add the tomatoes, water, extra beans, corn, chilies, & cilantro to the crockpot. Allow another 2 hrs for the mixture to simmer.
- Garnish with more cheese & cilantro if preferred, as well as a squeeze of lime juice (fresh).

Nutrition Information
Calories: 120, Carbohydrates: 15 g, Protein: 12.2 g, Fats: 6.6 g

154. Thai Shrimp Skillet
Prep time: 60 mins, Cook time: 30 mins, Servings: 4
Ingredients
Shrimp
- 1 lb of shrimp 25 ct. or larger, steamed
- 1 lime Juice
- 1 lime zest
- 2 tbsp of fish sauce
- 2 tbsp of peanut oil
- 2 tsp of freshly grated ginger
- 2-3 crushed garlic cloves garlic

Peanut Sauce
- 6 oz of coconut milk
- 5 tbsp of Chika PB powder
- 1 tbsp of lime Ponzu sauce
- 1 tbsp of fish sauce
- 2 tbsp of Thai chili garlic sauce
- 2 tsp freshly grated ginger
- 2-3 crushed garlic cloves garlic

The Veggies
- 1/2 sweet sliced into strips of red bell pepper
- ½ sliced into strips sweet orange pepper
- 1 medium sliced onion
- ½ diced sweet potato
- 1/3 diced of an eggplant

Garnish
- cilantro
- chopped peanuts

Instructions
- In a zip-lock storage bag, mix the marination Ingredients & your protein also. Allow a minimum of 30 mins to marinate.
- Preheat a pan on medium flame, then add the sweet potato & peanut oil (add the sweet potato at once as peanut oil starts to smoke quickly). Stir for 3-4 mins, till it begins to get soft, then put the other veggies & stir, sautéing till they're as tender as you like.
- In a mixing dish, whisk together all of the ingredients for the peanut sauce while the vegetables are cooking. Ensure that all of the peanut powder is blended & there is no dry powder visible!
- Drain the marinating liquid from the protein & return it to the skillet, including the sauce, to warm it up.
- Garnish with cilantro & peanuts while still heated.

Nutrition Information
Calories: 136, Carbohydrates: 6 g, Protein: 5 g, Fats: 1 g

155. Spaghetti Squash Ramen with Shrimp
Prep time: 15 mins, Cook time: 15 mins, Servings: 2-4
Ingredients
- 1 cup of cooked spaghetti squash (or uncooked small spaghetti squash)
- 1 tsp of sesame oil, divided
- 1 tbsp of soy sauce (low sodium), divided
- 2 cups of chicken broth, low sodium
- 1 Peeled garlic clove
- 1/2 tsp of grated ginger
- 8 sliced mushrooms
- 8 cooked medium shrimp, peeled & deveined
- 1 hard boil egg
- 2 tbsp of chopped green onion
- 1 small sliced red hot chili pepper (optional)

Instructions
- Preheat the oven to 400 Fahrenheit. Discard the seeds & pulp from the spaghetti squash, then score the interior with the help of a fork before spreading a half tsp of sesame oil & a half tbsp of soy sauce within Roast for 15-20 mins, or till fork tender, on a baking tray put both of the halves. Remove the squash from the skin & place it in a dish when it's done. Put it aside.
- Combine the leftover sesame oil, chicken broth, soy sauce, ginger & garlic in a small saucepan. Bring to the boil, then lower to the low flame setting. If using frozen shrimp, put them in the batter & simmer until done. Reduce the flame to a low simmer & put the mushrooms just before the end of the cooking time.
- Meanwhile, make a boiled egg (hard-boiled) by placing one egg in steaming for 7-8 mins. Bring to tepid water right away & soak for 2-3 mins before peeling & slicing in half.
- To make the ramen bowl, start with the required quantity of spaghetti squash, shrimp, broth, mushrooms, & half of the boiled egg in the bowl. Decorate with red hot chilies peppers (sliced) & green onions, if preferred.

Nutrition Information
Calories: 115, Carbohydrates: 7 g, Protein: 14 g, Fats: 9 g

156. Fake Grits
Prep time: 10 mins, Cook time: 10 mins, Servings: 6
Ingredients
- 2/3 cup of water
- 3 cups of cauliflower florets
- 1/3 cup of cream soup, low fat (any flavor you like)
- 1/4 cup of grated Parmesan cheese
- 2 tbsp of milk
- Salt & pepper, to taste

Instructions
- Bring water in a saucepan & bring to a boil & then add cauliflower florets. Cook until the vegetables are quite tender (about 10-13 mins).
- Drain & then mash. It should be mashed to the point where the cauliflower no longer resembles florets. Continue mashing if you notice florets.
- Combine the cream soup, milk & cheese in a mixing bowl. Use additional milk & soup to make thinner "grits." Use less milk/ cream soup for thicker "grits." Make a thorough mix.

Nutrition Information
Calories: 139, Carbohydrates: 5 g, Protein: 9 g, Fats: 4 g

157. Summer Shrimp Salad with Watermelon Champagne Vinaigrette
Prep Time: 15 Mins, Cook Time: 25 Mins, Servings: 3
Ingredient
- 10-12 Shrimp shelled, cooked & deveined
- 1/4 tsp of Garlic Powder
- Salt & Pepper, to taste
- 4 cups of Spring Salad Mix
- 10 Watermelon balls, seedless
- 2 tbsp of Crumbled Goat Cheese
- 2 tbsp of Pepitas

Champagne Vinaigrette dressing
- 3 tbsp of champagne vinegar
- 2 tbsp of olive oil, extra-virgin
- 1 tsp of Honey Dijon mustard
- 3 tbsp of watermelon juice
- ½ tsp of minced garlic
- ¼ tsp of black pepper

Instructions
Salad
- Coat a skillet liberally with cooking spray & place it on medium flame to warm up.
- If the shrimp are frozen, place them in a strainer & rinse them under cold water. If not, add pepper, garlic powder & salt to taste. Cook for approximately 2-3 mins, rotating once in the heated pan. Remove them from the oven & set them aside to cool.

- Toss salad greens with goat cheese, watermelon, & pepitas in a dish. Toss the salad with tongs after adding half of the dressing.
- Divide the mixture equally between the 2 plates. Serve with shrimp on top.

Dressing
- Combine vinegar, garlic, oil, watermelon juice, & pepper in a mixing bowl. Refrigerate for a minimum of 1 hr before filtering into a dish or dressing container via a sieve.

Nutrition Information
Calories: 146, Carbohydrates: 10.6 g, Protein: 13 g, Fats: 7 g

158. Citrusy Crockpot Pork Tacos with Spicy Green Sauce
Prep time: 15 mins, Cook time: 6 hrs., Servings: 6-8

Ingredients

Pork filling
- 1 lb of pork country ribs
- ½ tsp of salt
- ½ tsp of ground black pepper
- 1 tsp of minced garlic
- ½ tsp of smoked paprika
- ½ tsp of ground chipotle pepper(optional)
- 2 cups of Tropicana
- 1 tsp of orange zest

Green Sauce
- 1bunch of fresh cilantro
- 2 peeled cloves garlic
- 1 jalapeno pepper stems removed, (& discard seeds if you do not want too spicy)
- 1 lime juice
- 2-3 tbsp of water
- 1 tsp of olive oil, extra-virgin
- ¼ cup of Greek yogurt, unflavored

Tacos/Toppings
- 1head of curly leaf lettuce
- 1sliced red bell pepper
- 1sliced orange bell pepper

Instructions
- In a crockpot, combine the ribs, pepper, salt, garlic, chipotle pepper (if you like) & paprika. Cook on low flame for 6 hrs, covered with orange zest plus juice & water. Allow the beef to continue to warm by shredding it with forks.
- To prepare the sauce, pulse jalapeno, Greek yogurt, cilantro, lime juice, garlic & olive oil until smooth in a food processor or blender. It should be possible to sprinkle the sauce. If it's too thick, thin it out with water & re-mix.
- To prepare taco shells, remove the leaves from the curly leaf's bunch of lettuce & remove the steam with a big knife. Stuff every taco with one-two oz pork, one tbsp of yogurt, peppers, & one tsp of green sauce.

Nutrition Information
Calories: 116, Carbohydrates: 10 g, Protein: 9 g, Fats: 2 g

159. Spicy Beans & Sausage
Prep time: 10 mins, Cook time: 8 hrs, Servings: 6

Ingredients
- 8 oz of diced Andouille sausage
- 1 chopped yellow onion
- 2 seeded & chopped tomatoes
- 3 minced cloves garlic
- 1 lb of Great Northern beans dry
- 2 tsp of Cajun spice blend (like McCormick)
- ½ tsp kosher salt
- 1 tsp of smoked paprika
- 1diced jalapeno pepper
- 4 cups of broth, low sodium
- 2 cups of water

Instructions
- Coat a pan with cooking spray & place it on medium flame to heat up. Cook till one side of the sausage is browned. Cook for another 2 mins with the tomato & onions before putting garlic & cooking for another min.
- Transfer the Ingredients of the pan to a crockpot & add the beans, peppers, water, spices & broth. Stir everything together well.
- Cover the crockpot & simmer on low flame for 8 hrs, or till the beans are tender & the liquid has thickened.

Nutrition Information
Calories: 106, Carbohydrates: 8.0 g, Protein: 15.9 g, Fats: 6 g

160. Tilapia with Fire Roasted Tomato Sauce
Prep time: 10 mins, Cook time: 30 mins, Servings: 4

Ingredients
- 1 small sliced yellow onion
- 12-15 trimmed & chopped stalks of skinny asparagus woody stem
- 1 tbsp of olive oil
- 1 tsp of minced garlic
- 16 oz of canned tomatoes, fire-roasted
- 4 tilapia filets, frozen
- 1-2 tbsp of Cajun seasoning (to taste)

Instructions
- Preheat a pan on medium flame until it is hot. Add the oil to the pan & stir it around.
- Toss the onions in oil & cook for 2 mins before tossing in the garlic & asparagus. Cook for another 2 mins.
- Stir in the tomatoes (fire-roasted) & heat to a gentle boil before adding 4 frozen tilapia fillets.
- Sprinkle the Cajun seasoning on top & cover the pan. Reduce the flame to low & cook for 20-25 mins, or till the fish slice easily with a fork.

Nutrition Information
Calories: 145, Carbohydrates: 9.2 g, Protein: 8.7 g, Fats: 5 g

161. Low-Carb Flatbread
Prep time: 15 mins, Cook time: 15 mins, Servings: 1

Ingredients
- 1 flatbread, low carb (like flat out & Aldi Fit or Active)
- an assortment veggie sliced or diced (flavor you like)
- 1 diced Fit & Active Chicken Sausage (like Chipotle flavored)
- ¼ cup of grated cheese (like Cheddar Jack)
- one pinch of salt
- one pinch of pepper
- cooking spray, non-stick

Instructions
- Preheat the oven to 350 Fahrenheit. Spray the flatbread with cooking spray on both ends & place it on a baking tray. If preferred, season with a pinch of salt. Bake for 8-10 mins, or until sides are lightly browned & flatbread is crispy. Allow cooling after removing from the oven.
- In a medium-film skillet, sauté the vegetables until they're slightly wilted but not entirely limp. Put it aside.
- Using a nonstick spray, re-sauté the chopped chicken sausage till it's warmed through. Put it aside.
- Spread half of the cheese on the flatbread first. Then add the veggies & meat over the top. Add the leftover cheese last. Re-spray everything with cooking spray.
- Bake for 5 mins at 350°F, or till cheese melts. Enjoy a piece of pizza!

Nutrition Information
Calories: 129, Carbohydrates: 12.0 g, Protein: 15 g, Fats: 8 g

162. Pioneer Woman Inspired Chicken Zoodle Casserole
Prep time: 3 hrs., Cook time: 45 mins, Servings: 4

Ingredients
- 6medium sized zucchini cut into spaghetti shapes
- ½ tsp of salt
- 1small diced onion

- 1 diced green pepper
- 1/3 cup of sliced pimentos jarred
- 1 lb of diced cooked chicken meat
- ½ tsp of smoked paprika
- ¼ tsp of ground cayenne pepper or chipotle powder
- 8 oz of reduced-fat cream of mushroom soup
- 2 cups of grated cheddar cheese

Instructions
- Spiralize the zucchini into zoodles a few hrs before preparing the dinner, season liberally, & store in a sealed container in the fridge. When preparing to cook, spin them 4-5 times in a salad spinner to remove extra salt & water.
- Preheat the oven to 350 Fahrenheit.
- Cook the chicken completely if you have not previously done so, using any manner

you like. 1 l b of cooked chicken chunks should result (or shredded chicken, if utilizing a rotisserie chicken).
- Combine zoodles, diced veggies, chicken, & seasonings in a mixing basin. Toss with chopsticks until everything is well combined.
- Stir in the cream of mushroom soup with tongs throughout the whole zoodles, cheese & meat.
- Pour into a nine-by-thirteen casserole dish & sprinkle with shredded cheese. Bake for 45 mins, or until the cheese is melted.

Nutrition Information
Calories: 110, Carbohydrates: 9.3 g, Protein: 11.1 g, Fats: 6.1 g

163. Protein Mini-Cheesecakes
Prep time: 20 mins, Cook time: 30 mins, Servings: 4
Ingredients
Cheesecake Filling
- 8 oz of Greek yogurt (low fat) cream cheese softened
- 1 large egg
- 4 oz of Salted Caramel flavored Greek yogurt(fat-free) like Oikos Triple Zero
- 1/3 cup of whey isolate protein powder (unflavored or vanilla)
- ½ cup of Sola granular

Optional Crust
- 2 tbsp of Greek yogurt (low fat) cream cheese softened
- 2/3 cup of high-fiber cereal, lightly sweetened, (Fiber One)

Instructions
Make Crust
- Preheat the oven to 325 Fahrenheit.
- Use parchment paper to line the bottoms of mini-spring shape pans.
- In the food processor, combine cereal & cream cheese till clumps resemble tiny springform. Bake for 8-10 mins after pressing into springform pans.

Make Cheesecake
- Mix cream cheese, yogurt, egg, yogurt, vanilla, sweetener & protein in a mixing bowl. For 1min, beat on medium speed with the hand mixer, then increase to high for 2 mins. Make sure you get rid of all the bumps!
- Pour the mixture over the crumb crust. In a baking dish, place the pans. Boil water

in another dish & put it on the bottom rack of the oven. Place the cheesecakes in the center of the oven. Preheat oven to 350°F & bake for 25-30 mins.
- Turn off the oven & open the oven door slightly. Allow cheesecakes to cool in the oven till completely cold.
- To serve, carefully lift the cheesecake out of the springform pan using the baking paper.

Nutrition Information
Calories: 89, Carbohydrates: 10.6 g, Protein: 12 g, Fats: 4.4 g

164. No-Flour, Low-Sugar Thumbprint Cookies
Prep time: 5 mins, Cook time: 25 mins, Servings: 10
Ingredients
- 1/2cup of cream cheese (can utilize reduced fat but not fat-free!)
- ¼ cup of brown sugar substitute (like Splenda Brown Sugar blend)
- 1 egg, white part
- ½ tsp of vanilla extract
- 2 cups of almond flour
- ¼ tsp of salt
- ¼ cup walnuts, finely chopped (optional)
- 2/3 cup of sugar-free or low-sugar jelly

Instructions
- Preheat the oven to 325°F & line baking pans with parchment paper.
- Separate the egg & combine the cream cheese, egg white & sugar substitute in a blender.
- Mix in the vanilla, salt & almond flour until well combined.
- Allow dough to chill for 15 mins before rolling into balls.
- Form dough into balls & dip them in egg white before rolling them in walnuts, if using.
- Place cookies approximately 2 inches apart on the baking pan. Preheat oven to 350°F & bake for 8-10 mins.
- Remove the cookies and press a huge fingerprint into each one, filling it with jam.
- Cook for a further 12-15 mins or so. Remove from the oven & cool on a baking sheet.

Nutrition Information
Calories: 121, Carbohydrates: 12.6 g, Protein: 10 g, Fats: 5.1 g

165. No-Flour, Low-Sugar Peanut Butter Cookies
Prep time: 5 mins, Cook time: 15 mins, Servings: 10-12
Ingredients
- 1cup of creamy peanut butter
- 1 large egg, white part
- 1 tsp of pure vanilla extract
- ½ tsp of Cinnamon(optional)
- ½ cup of brown sugar blend substitute (like Splenda Brown Sugar Blend)
- 1/3 cup of almond flour

Instructions
- Preheat the oven to 350°F & prepare a sheet for cookies using parchment paper.
- Combine peanut butter, vanilla extract, egg white, cinnamon (optional), & brown sugar mixture in a mixing dish. Make a thorough mix.
- Stir in the almond flour until it is completely mixed.
- Form balls of dough and lay them on a baking sheet approximately two inches away from each other. Press the dough ball into a disc shape using a fork, creating a crisscross pattern on cookies.
- Bake for 12-15 mins, then set aside to cool.

Nutrition Information
Calories: 101, Carbohydrates: 10.1 g, Protein: 13 g, Fats: 7.5 g

166. No-Flour, Lower-Sugar Chewy Pecan Cookies
Prep time: 5 mins, Cook time: 20 mins, Servings: 10
Ingredients
- 1/2cup of pecan butter
- 1.5 cup of almond flour
- 6 tbsp of no-calorie sweetener
- ¼ cup of milk (like vanilla almond milk, unsweetened)
- 1 tsp of vanilla extract
- 1/2 tsp of salt
- 10 halves of pecan

Instructions
- Preheat the oven to 350 Fahrenheit. Using parchment paper, prepare a cookie sheet.
- In a mixing bowl, combine all ingredients except the pecan halves & stir thoroughly. If the mix seems too moist, add another two tbsp of almond flour. Add two tbsp of additional milk if it is too dry.
- Place the dough on a baking sheet & place a pecan in the center.

- Bake for 15-20 mins, then take out from the oven & cool on a wire rack.

Nutrition Information
Calories: 108, Carbohydrates: 12 g, Protein: 14.4 g, Fats: 4 g

167. Protein Infused Cranberry Sauce
Prep time: 0 mins, Cook time: 35 mins, Servings: 16
Ingredients
- 10 oz of BiPro Protein Watereither flavor will do
- no-calorie sweetener (equivalent to 1 cup sugar)
- 12 oz of whole cranberries
- 1 tsp of lemon zest or orange zest

Instructions
For Cranberry Sauce
- In a saucepan, combine the sweetener & protein water. Bring it to a boil, then reduce to low flame & continue to cook till the sweetener is completely dissolved (there may be bubbles with no-calorie sweeteners, which is OK).
- Stir in the cranberries, cover, & return to a boil. Reduce the heat to a low simmer right away to prevent the liquid from boiling over the stove.
- Cook over low heat till the liquid has thickened significantly (usually 18-20 mins). Remove from the heat & set aside to cool fully in a jar. (This takes around 1-2 hrs.) Refrigerate for at least 2 hrs before serving.

For Cranberry Jellied Sauce
- Cook the cranberries for a further 5 mins after lowering the heat, as directed in steps 1 & 2.
- Pour the cranberries & juice onto a sieve set in a bowl. Mash the fluid out of the skins with a wooden spoon, scraping the bottom of the sieve often.3. Return the fluid to the saucepan & simmer on low flame until it has thickened significantly (about 18-25 mins).
- Take the pan from the heat & place it in a container. Allow the fluid to cool completely (usually takes 1-2 hrs.). Before serving, chill for a minimum of 2 hrs.

Nutrition Information
Calories: 112, Carbohydrates: 7.7 g, Protein: 10.2 g, Fats: 3 g

168. Thanksgiving Super Food Stuffing
Prep time: 15 mins, Cook time: 30 mins, Servings: 4-5
Ingredients
- 2 cup chicken broth, low sodium
- 1/3 cup red quinoa
- 1/3 cup of amaranth
- 1 small diced onion
- 1 small diced red pepper
- 1 small diced green pepper
- 1 lb turkey breakfast sausage (Jennie-O)
- 1 diced honey crisp apple (peeled, if desired)
- Salt & pepper to taste
- 1/4 tsp ground sage

Instructions
- Take the chicken stock to boil in a saucepan. Reduce the flame to low & simmer the quinoa & amaranth for approximately 30 mins, swirling often. When small white coils erupt from the quinoa, it is time to mix. (Please note that some fluid may remain.)
- Meanwhile, coat a pan with cooking spray & heat it on medium flame. Sauté for 1-2 mins, or till peppers & onion are softened.
- Put the sausage & heat until it is browned, tearing it up into little pieces.
- Stir in the amaranth/quinoa mixture & chopped apple before adding the seasonings.
- Put into a baking tray & bake for 25-30 mins at 350°F, or till the filling is crispy on top.

Nutrition Information
Calories: 130, Carbohydrates: 9 g, Protein: 11.1 g, Fats: 3.1 g

169. Cauliflower Crust Turkey Pot Pie
Prep time: 30 mins, Cook time: 30 mins, Servings: 6-9

Ingredients
- 1 cup diced carrots
- 1 cup frozen peas
- 1/2 cup diced onions
- 1 tsp minced garlic
- 16 oz of diced or shredded cooked turkey meat
- 1 cup of cooked quinoa
- 10.5 oz cream of chicken soup, low-fat
- 1/2 cup of skim milk
- 3 cup cauliflower rice or florets
- Salt & pepper, to taste
- 1 egg, large
- ½ cup reduced-fat grated cheddar cheese
- 1/4 cup grated Parmesan cheese
- 1 tsp chopped parsley

Instructions
- Preheat the oven to 350 Fahrenheit.
- Coat a big pan with cooking spray & place it on medium flame to heat up.
- Add the carrots, peas & onions to the pot. Cook for around 2 mins (2-4 mins if carrots & peas were frozen). Cook for another min after adding the garlic.
- Stir in the chopped turkey breast flesh & quinoa until everything is well combined. Stir in the milk & cream of chicken soup. Allow the batter to bubble for a few mins. Remove the pan from the heat.
- Steam cauliflower florets until soft (about 6-7 mins). Drain the water & squeeze the excess out using a cheesecloth. Place in a mixing dish.
- Season the cauliflower with pepper & salt before adding the cheddar cheese & egg. Make a thorough mix.
- Spread the veggie/meat mixture equally in a smaller casserole dish (eight-by-eight) & bake. Spread the cauliflower mixture evenly over the top. Finish with parsley & parmesan cheese.
- Bake for 28-30 mins or till the "crust" is fully done & browned as you like.

Nutrition Information
Calories: 125, Carbohydrates: 10 g, Protein: 10.9 g, Fats: 2.2 g

170. Zoodle Ravioli
Prep time: 15 mins, Cook time: 30 mins, Servings: 4
Ingredients:
- 1 small, sliced onion,
- 1 clove minced of garlic (or 1 tsp of jarred minced garlic)
- 1 lb of lean ground turkey, Salt & pepper, to taste
- 15 oz of can pumpkin puree, not pumpkin pie filling
- ½ tsp of cinnamon ½ tsp nutmeg
- 1 tbsp tomato paste
- 2 cups of part-skim ricotta cheese
- ½ cup shredded parmesan cheese
- 1 tsp Italian seasoning
- 2 medium zucchinis, cut lengthwise thick strips
- Optional: More Italian blend grated cheese

Instructions
- Preheat the oven to 350 Fahrenhei2. Preheat a big pan on medium flame & coat it with cooking spray once it's heated. Add the onion & cook for 1-2 mins, or until it is soft. Cook until the beef is browned, then add the garlic, salt, ground turkey, pepper, & Italian seasoning.
- Stir in the canned pumpkin, nutmeg & cinnamon before adding the tomato paste. Return on low flame, cover, & let it simmer.
- Combine the ricotta & Parmesan cheese, salt, Italian seasoning & pepper in a mixing bowl. Make a thorough mix.
- Cut 2 zucchini slices into a plus sign form to make the ravioli. Place a good amount of ricotta in the middle, then fold the lower piece of zucchini first, then the top one. In an eight-by-eight inches casserole dish, place it upside down.

- Bake for 28-30 mins after finishing each ravioli with the meat/pumpkin sauce. If desired, top with more cheese.

Nutrition Information
Calories: 342, Carbohydrates: 22 g, Protein: 29 g, Fats: 15 g

171. Sweet Potato Toast with Egg
Prep time: 10 mins, Cook time: 10 mins, Servings: 4
Ingredients:
- 1 medium sliced sweet potato
- 1 tbsp olive oil (extra-virgin)
- 1 large sliced yellow onion
- 4 cups baby spinach
- 2 whole cloves of garlic
- 10 halved cherry tomatoes
- 4 large poached eggs
- Salt & pepper, to taste
- Optional: Fresh grated Parmesan cheese

Instructions
- To make sweet potato toast, toast sweet potatoes in a standard toaster oven or toaster (toaster oven suggested) until fork tender. Put it aside.
- Preheat a pan on medium flame until it is hot. Swirl the oil around in the pan.
- Add the onion & cook for 1-2 mins, or until it softens. After that, toss in the spinach, cherry garlic, garlic. Cook until the spinach has softened but is still firm. Remove the pan from the heat.
- Half-fill a second pan with water and one tbsp of white vinegar. Bring the mixture to a moderate simmer.
- Separate 4 eggs into 4 bowls or ramekins. To remove the eggs, gently dip ramekins in hot water. Cover the pan & heat for 1-2 mins, or till all 4 eggs are done & the yolk is completely coated with white.
- Remove the eggs with a slotted spoon & place them on a clean cloth.
- To serve the meal, start with a slice of sweet potato toast, then add the spinach combination, followed by a poached egg.
- If preferred, top with freshly grated Parmesan cheese.

Nutrition Information
Calories: 164, Carbohydrates: 15 g, Protein: 10 g, Fats: 7 g

172. Turkey Burritos
Prep time: 15 mins, Cook time: 30 mins, Servings: 8
Ingredients:
- cooking spray, nonstick
- 1 large, diced onion
- 1 large diced green pepper
- 1- lb lean ground turkey
- ½ tbsp of cumin
- ½ tbsp of coriander
- 1 tsp minced garlic
- ½ tbsp smoked paprika
- 10 oz of can petite diced tomatoes, low sodium
- 10 oz of can black beans, drained & rinsed
- (Optional) 2 oz of green chiles
- 8 taco-sized high-fiber, low-carb tortillas
- ½ cup of 2% grated cheddar cheese

Topping (all optional):
- Salsa
- Unflavored Greek yogurt, for topping
- Sliced jalapenos
- Diced avocados

Instructions
- Preheat the oven to 350 Fahrenheit.
- Preheat a large pan on medium heat & coat with cooking spray before using.
- Cook for 1-2 mins, till onion, garlic & green pepper are softened. Cook until the ground turkey is browned, break up the meat & mix in the veggies.
- Reduce the flame to low & add the spices, black beans, tomatoes, & chilies. Cook for roughly 10 mins.
- Layout the tortilla on a level surface. Fill the tortilla with a heaping half cup of meat/vegetable mixture. Fold the bottom & top of the tortilla on the mixture of meat & wrap it into a burrito shape.
- Arrange each burrito in a thirteen-by-nine inches casserole dish side by side. Before wrapping the burritos with aluminum foil, spray the tops with cooking spray. 25 mins in the Sprinkle with shredded cheese and bake for an additional 5 mins, or till cheese gets melted to your liking.
- Toppings: Greek yogurt, salsa, or anything else you want!

Nutrition Information
Calories: 240, Carbohydrates: 19 g, Protein: 9 g, Fats: 10 g

173. Spicy Vegetarian Chili
Prep time: 20 mins, Cook time: 30 mins, Servings: 10
Ingredients:
- 1 tbsp of olive oil (extra-virgin
- 1 large diced yellow onion
- 1 green diced bell pepper
- 1 red diced bell pepper
- 2 minced garlic cloves
- 1 large, diced butternut squash
- 1 lb of textured vegetable protein or medium-firm tofu
- 3 cups of water
- 20 oz of diced petite tomatoes (low sodium)
- 10 oz of black beans, drained & rinsed
- 10 oz of red kidney beans (light), drained & rinsed
- 10 oz of red kidney beans (dark), drained and rinsed
- 1 diced jalapeno pepper, with seeds (you can omit seeds to reduce spiciness)
- 2 tbsp of chili powder
- ½ tbsp ground chipotle powder
- 2 tsp lime juice
- Salt and pepper, to taste

Instruction
- Preheat a big saucepan on medium flame until it is hot. Swirl the olive oil all around the base of the saucepan.
- Combine the onions, garlic, peppers & squash in a large mixing bowl. Reduce the flame to medium-low. Cover & simmer for approximately 10 mins, or till squash is cooked, stirring often.
- Combine the water, textured vegetable protein, tomatoes, jalapeno peppers, lime juice, beans & spices in a large mixing bowl. Make a thorough mix. Reduce flame to low & cover once more. Continue to cook for another 20 mins.
- The combination should have transformed from a brilliant to a deeper crimson when finished. There should be some liquid in it, but not much. If you want additional liquid, go ahead & add it, but make sure to fix the spices.

Nutrition Information
Calories: 270, Carbohydrates: 45 g, Protein: 31 g, Fats: 2 g

174. Meatball Ramekins
Prep time:15 mins, Cook time:45 mins, Servings: 4
Ingredients:
- ½ medium sliced white onion
- 1 cup cream of mushroom soup (low-fat)
- ½ cup milk, low-fat (suggested: Fair life 0% milk)
- 1 tbsp of Worcestershire sauce
- 1 tbsp of flat-leaf parsley, fresh chopped
- ¼ tsp of salt
- ¼ tsp of pepper
- 1/8 tsp nutmeg
- 12 Aldi Fit & Active® Turkey Meatballs
- 3 whole crushed wheat Wasa crackers
- 1 tbsp of melted unsalted butter
- ¼ tsp of garlic powder
- 4 tbsp of grated Parmesan cheese

Instructions
- Preheat the oven to 350 Fahrenheit.

- Preheat a pan on medium flame until it is hot. Swirl the oil around the pan.
- Cook for 1-2 mins or until softened onions. Stir in the cream soup, parsley, milk, salt, Worcestershire sauce, nutmeg & pepper, then bring to a boil.
- Fill a 5 oz. Ramekin with three meatballs each. Pour a large amount of sauce over the meatballs. Bake for approximately 30 mins, covered with aluminum foil.
- Combine garlic powder, crackers, butter, & Parmesan cheese in a mixing bowl. Sprinkle the mixt on top of ramekins & bake for more than 10 mins uncovered.
- Serve with zucchini noodles (ribbon-cut zoodles) that have flash boiled in boiling water for 1-2 mins, then spiced to taste. Do you have no idea how to create zoodles? Bariatric Foodie has a tutorial on how to do it.

Nutrition Information
Calories: 234, Carbohydrates: 27 g, Protein: 13 g, Fats: 9 g

175. Roasted Veggies and Couscous
Prep time:5 mins, Cook time: 20 mins, Servings: 8
Ingredients
- 10 oz of couscous, box bought from the store (flavor you like)
- oil or butter (if you want to add)
- 2-3 cups of roasted vegetables
- Salt and Pepper, to taste
- fresh grated Parmesan cheese (optional)
- 1 lb cooked chicken breast (diced) or other protein

Instructions
- Prepare the couscous according to the package instructions.
- While the couscous remains hot, add the roasted vegetables to the saucepan (especially if you're using pre-cooked). At this stage, you may also put your protein. Besides the chicken, chopped cooked pork, fish, or shrimp are more options.
- Toss with your favorite spices &, if wanted, Parmesan cheese.

Nutrition Information
Calories: 135, Carbohydrates: 8.8 g, Protein: 12.3 g, Fats: 5.5 g

176. Power Chicken Salad
Prep time:10 mins, Cook time:15 mins, Servings: 4
Ingredients:
- ¼ cup of Greek yogurt
- 1 tbsp of light mayo
- 1 tbsp of Dijon mustard
- ¼ tsp of garlic powder
- ¼ tsp of Herbs de Provence
- ½ a medium diced red onion
- ½ cup of shelled edamame, cooked & cooled
- 6 oz of chicken breast meat, canned
- Salt & pepper, to taste
- Toasted pepitas, shelled pumpkin seeds
- Optional: 1 medium sliced jicama

Instructions
- Combine Greek yogurt, mayonnaise, mustard, herbs & garlic powder in a mixing dish. Make a thorough mix.
- Toss in the red onion, chicken meat & edamame until fully combined and evenly covered. To taste, season with salt & pepper.
- Refrigerate for at least 1 hr. before serving. Heat a small pan on the stovetop when fully cooked, but do not add any oil. Toss in the pepitas & toast till fragrant (about 1-2 mins).
- Toss the final salad with pepitas & serve with high fiber crackers or jicama slices.

Nutrition Information
Calories: 150, Carbohydrates: 5 g, Protein: 18 g, Fats: 6 g

177. Spicy Beans & Sausage
Prep time: 10 mins, Cook time: 8 hrs., Servings: 6
Ingredients
- 8 oz of diced Andouille sausage
- 1 roughly chopped yellow onion
- 2 diced tomatoes
- 3cloves minced garlic
- 1 lb of dry Great Northern beans
- 2 tsp of Cajun spice blend
- 1/2 tsp of kosher salt (finely ground)
- 1 tsp of smoked paprika
- 1 diced jalapeno pepper
- 4 cups of broth (low sodium)
- 2 cups of water

Instructions
- Coat a pan with cooking spray & place it on medium flame to heat up. Put the sausage in the pan & cook till one side of the sausage is browned. Cook for another 2 mins with the tomato & onions before putting the garlic & cooking for another min.
- Transfer the mixture of the pan to the crockpot & add the beans, peppers, water, spices & broth on the top. Stir everything together well.
- Cover the crockpot & simmer on low for 8 hrs, or till the beans are tender & the liquid has thickened.

Nutrition Information
Calories: 135, Carbohydrates: 11.2 g, Protein: 8 g, Fats: 2 g

178. Easy Refrigerator Pickles
Prep time: 20mins, Cook time:0 mins, Servings: 1
Ingredients
- 5 lb of pickling cucumbers (sliced)
- 4 cups of white vinegar
- 2 cups of water
- 2 tbsp of kosher salt (finely ground)
- 6cloves garlic (whole)
- 2 tbsp of pre-made pickling spice
- 2 tsp of red pepper flakes (optional)
- 5-6 fresh sprigs of dill

Instructions
- In a sieve, thoroughly rinse the cucumbers. Put it aside.
- Bring the water & vinegar to a low boil in a saucepan. Reduce the flame to low. Bring the brine back to the boil with the salt, pickling spice, garlic, & red pepper flakes (if using) before switching off the flame & leaving the brine to rest.
- Fill the gallon canning jar halfway with dill, then cucumbers. When the brining liquid has cooled, ladle it over the cucumbers & carefully close the container.
- Leave it out for a few hrs to start the pickle party, then put it in the fridge for 3 days before eating.

Nutrition Information
Calories: 109, Carbohydrates: 4.9 g, Protein: 10.2 g, Fats: 3 g

179. PB&J Protein Shake
Prep time: 3 mins, Cook time: 0 mins, Servings: 1
Ingredients
- 1cup of milk (of your choice)
- 1scoop of BiPro USA Strawberry whey protein
- 3 strawberries hulled (large)
- 1 tsp of sweetener of your choice (no-calorie)
- 1 tbsp of powdered peanuts
- 1-3 ice cubes
- whipped cream, optional
- chopped peanuts, optional for garnish

Instructions
- In the blender, combine the milk, sugar, protein, strawberries, & powdered peanuts for approximately a min.
- Add two-three ice cubes if preferred, & mix till ice is pulverized.
- Garnish with peanuts & whipped cream, if preferred.

Nutrition Information
Calories: 120, Carbohydrates: 11 g, Protein: 10 g, Fats: 3 g

180. Strawberry Shortcake Protein Shake
Prep time: 5 mins, Cook time: 0 mins, Servings: 1
Ingredients
- 1 cup of milk (of your choice)
- 1/8 tsp of pure vanilla extract
- 3 hulled & diced strawberries
- sweetener(no-calorie) of your choice (optional & to taste)
- 2-5 ice cubes
- 1 shortbread cookie crumbled (sugar-free)

Instructions
- In the blender, combine the vanilla, milk, sweetener (if you want), protein & strawberries. For a full min, blend everything.
- Blend in the ice cubes for another min, or till smooth.
- Fill a cup halfway with the mixture & sprinkle with cookie crumbs. If desired, a dollop of whipped cream may be added to the top.

Nutrition Information
Calories: 110, Carbohydrates: 5.5 g, Protein: 7.8 g, Fats: 5 g

181. Jicama Fish Tacos
Prep time:10 mins, Cook time: 10 mins, Servings: 2
Ingredients
- 2cups of water
- 2 slices of jicama
- 4 oz of tilapia filet (thawed)
- 1 tsp of McCormick Cajun Seasoning (salt-free)
- 1/8 tsp of salt
- 1/3 cup of slaw mix (your choice)
- 1small sliced red hot chili pepper
- 1 tbsp of fresh cilantro
- 1-2 tbsp of Ranch dressing

Instructions
- Fill a pan halfway with water & place it on medium flame. Bring the water to a boil.
- Place the jicama "taco shells" in the boiling water & cook for 2 mins. They must be flexible but not softened, and water should be discarded.
- Sprinkle both sides of a defrost tilapia fillet with Cajun spice & salt on a clean cloth. Using nonstick frying spray, coat the pan.
- Spray the pan with cooking spray & place it on medium flame to heat up again. Cook for 3 mins on both sides, or till fish is cooked through.
- To make the tacos, start by putting half of the fish into each shell. Slaw mixture, peppers (if used), cilantro, plus ranch dressing are served on the side.

Nutrition Information
Calories: 105 Kcal, Carbohydrates: 7.5 g, Protein: 8 g, Fats: 4 g

182. Dee Dee's Cheesy Squash and TVP Casserole
Prep Time: 30 Mins, Cook Time: 1 Hour, Servings: 4
Ingredients
- 3 thinly sliced zucchini squash
- 2 thinly sliced yellow squash
- 1 medium thinly sliced onion
- 1 cup TVP (Textured Vegetable Protein)
- 1 cup + ½ cup desired cheese
- 1 tsp Italian Seasoning
- Garlic salt and black pepper, to taste

Instructions
- Combine onion, squash, zucchini, cheese, TVP, and Italian spices in a mixing bowl. Refrigerate for about 30 mins (this enables the water in the vegetables to escape), re-hydrate the TVP, and enable it to absorb the taste.
- Transfer the mixture to an 8-inch casserole dish sprayed with non-stick cooking spray. Bake for 1 hour in the oven. Turn the oven off and top with a generous amount of cheese and leave it in the oven to cool.

Nutrition Information
Calories: 95 kcal, Carbohydrates: 9 g, Protein: 15 g, Fat: 0 g

183. Secret Sauce
Prep time: 5 mins, Cook time: 10 mins, Servings: 4
Ingredients
- 1 small, chopped onion
- 1 small chopped green pepper
- 1 clove minced garlic
- Finely chopped zucchini and red peppers
- 1 lb. lean minced turkey
- 2 Turkey Italian sausages without casings
- 2 oz. tomato paste
- 1 jar spaghetti sauce
- A pinch of salt and pepper
- ½ tsp. Italian spice

Instructions
- Set a greased pan on medium heat. Add the chopped onions and bell peppers. Sauté until veggies are tender. Stir in the minced garlic and sauté for another 3 mins until aromatic.
- Add the turkey and sausages and brown them until thoroughly. Add the tomato paste and mix. Stir in the tomato sauce and cook on reduced heat; add more water if needed.
- Boil for another 5 mins on low heat.

Nutrition Information
Calories: 230 kcal, Carbohydrates: 19.68 g, Protein: 20.70g, Fat: 8g

184. Nik-a-doodles
Prep time: 5 mins, Cook time: 15 mins, Servings: 12
Ingredients
- 1 small piece of butter
- ½ cup of sugar
- 1 large egg
- 1 tsp. vanilla extract
- ¼ cup Brown Sugar Cinnamon syrup, sugar-free
- 1 cup baking mix (low-Carb)
- ½ tsp. Salt
- ½ tsp. baking soda
- 1 tsp. tartar cream
- 1 tsp. cinnamon, additional

Instructions
- Heat the oven before cooking to 400 °F.
- Combine the butter and sugar substitution in a mixing basin. Whisk in the egg and the vanilla extract.
- Mix the dry components in another bowl. Mix the ingredients (dry and wet) and blend well to make a smooth batter. Spoon out a batter on a greased baking sheet and bake for 15 mins.

Nutrition Information
Calories: 96 kcal, Carbohydrates: 5.87 g, Protein: 5.53 g, Fats: 5.8g

185. Nutty Apple Protein Baked Oatmeal (or Bars)
Prep time: 10 mins, Cook time: 20 mins, Servings: 12 bars
Ingredients
- 1 cup quick oats
- 3 scoops vanilla/unflavored protein powder
- A pinch of salt
- ½ tsp. cinnamon
- 1.5 cup milk
- ¼ cup sugar-free pancake syrup
- 2 beaten eggs
- ¼ cup powdered peanut
- ¼ cup natural peanut butter
- 1 small, chopped apple
- ¼ cup chopped walnuts

Instructions
- Heat the oven before cooking to 350 °F.
- Blend all dry components in a bowl and put them aside.
- In a separate dish, combine all of the wet ingredients. Combine the wet and dry components well.
- Add the chunky Ingredients, stir well, and then transfer into a greased casserole dish.

- Bake for 15 mins, or until crust is golden brown and the edges are firm. Or cook the oat bars for 30 mins, or until the edges are golden.
- Cool them completely before slicing them into bars.

Nutrition Information
Calories: 100 kcal, Carbohydrates: 20g, Proteins: 6.3 g, Fats: 1.7g

186. Protein Pumpkin Custard
Prep time: 10 mins, Cook time: 30 mins, Servings: 6
Ingredients
- 2 egg white
- 3/4 cup sweetener without calories
- 2 scoops of vanilla whey protein
- 1 3/4 cup pumpkin puree
- 2/3 cup non-fat evaporated milk
- ½ tsp. pumpkin pie spice

Instructions
- Heat the oven before cooking to 350 °F.
- Whisk egg whites in a mixing basin until foamy.
- Whisk in the sweetener until it is completely mixed. Mix in the protein and repeat the process.
- Toss in the pumpkin puree with pumpkin pie seasoning. Blend until well combined.
- Whisk in the evaporated milk until the batter is lump-free.
- Fill 6 ramekins with the mixture and place them on a baking dish in a water bath.
- Put it in a 350-degree oven for approximately 30 minutes or check it after about 25 minutes since oven temperatures vary.

Nutrition Information
Calories: 96 kcal, Carbohydrates: 13.1g, Proteins: 15.5g, Fat: 1g

187. Ramekin Peach Pies
Prep time: 10 mins, Cook time: 12 mins, Servings: 4
Ingredients
Crust
- 1/3 cup low-carb baking mix
- 1 tbsp. diced butter
- 1 sachet sweetener with no calorie
- 1 pinch salt
- 1 tbsp. ice water

Filling
- 4 cups diced peach without sugar
- 4 sachets sweetener with no calorie
- ¼ tsp lemon juice
- ½ tsp low-carb baking mix
- 1 pinch Cinnamon

Instructions
- To make the crust, combine the salt and Splenda in a mixing bowl, then chop in the butter and mix it with a fork. Add half teaspoons and more cold water until a dough forms. Refrigerate the dough.
- Combine the peaches, sweetener, and lemon juice in a mixing dish. Add the thickening agent and whisk one more. Fill the ramekins halfway with peaches and put them aside.
- Cut the small dough ball into two halves, place it on the peaches, and make a hole in the middle. Brush some more butter on top.
- Bake for approximately 10-12 mins in a preheated oven at 350 degrees or until the top is beautiful and brown. Let it cool before serving.

Nutrition Information
Calories: 97g, Carbohydrates: 8.5 g, Protein: 10g, Fat: 1.3g

188. No-flour Oatmeal Raisin Cookies
Prep time: 10 mins, Cook time: 20 mins, Servings: 6
Ingredients
Dry
- 1 cup quick oats
- 1/8 tsp. salt
- ½ tsp. baking soda
- ¼ tsp. pumpkin pie spice

Wet
- ½ stick baking butter substitute, low calorie
- 1 egg
- 1 cup no-calorie sweetener
- ½ tsp vanilla

Additions
- ¼ cup raisins
- ¼ cup chopped roasted walnuts

Instructions
- Heat the oven before cooking to 350 °F.
- Blend the oats (½ cup) in a food processor or blender. Take out in a bowl with the remaining oats.
- Mix the baking soda, salt, and spices and set it aside.
- Combine butter and sugar substitute in a mixing bowl. Mix in the egg until thoroughly combined. Finally, stir in the vanilla extract.
- Mix the wet and dry components until a dough forms. Add the nuts and raisins and stir to combine.
- Roll the batter into small balls with the help of a spoon. Place them on a greased cookie sheet, then press them down with the back of the spoon to make a disc.
- Bake them for 8-10 mins until done.

Nutrition Information
Calories: 80 kcal, Carbohydrates: 8 g, Protein: 6 g, Fat: 2g

189. No-Flour Almond Butter Cookies
Prep time: 10 mins, Cook time: 20 mins, Servings: 6 cookies
Ingredients
- 1 cup almond butter
- 1 cup Splenda
- 1 egg
- ½ tsp. pure vanilla extract
- ½ tsp. butter extract
- Raw almonds (optional)

Instructions
- Heat the oven before cooking to 350 °F.
- Combine all the components with a hand blender in a mixing bowl, ensuring the egg is well mixed to make the dough a little sloppy.
- Shape the dough into a ball with a big spoon. Transfer the balls to a greased baking tray and mash them down with the back of the spoon to make a disc.
- Bake in an oven for 10 mins. Top each cookie with almond and press it into the cookie while it's still soft.
- Let it cool completely before serving.

Nutrition Information
Calories: 100 kcal, Carbohydrates: 12 g, Protein: 5 g, Fat: 3g

190. Quickie Salisbury Steak and Rice
Prep time: 10 mins, Cook time: 15 mins, Servings: 2
Ingredients
- Cooking spray, non-stick
- 1 large, sliced onion ring
- 2 tsp garlic, minced
- 2 turkey burgers
- 1.5 - 2 cup beef broth
- ¼ cup Atkins Baking Mix
- ¼ cup cold water
- 1 cup frozen cauliflower florets
- 2 cup water
- Salt and black pepper, to taste

Instructions
- Set a greased pan on medium heat until it becomes ready. Add the onions and sauté for a few mins until lightly browned. Stir the minced garlic and fry for a few mins.
- Add the patties and beef broth, cover the top and cook the burgers on medium to low heat.
- Meanwhile, boil the cauliflower florets in a small saucepan until fully cooked on medium heat.

- Remove the burgers from the gravy once they're done. Mix the baking mix with cold water.
- Set the heat to a high flame and allow the stock to boil. Whisk in the baking mix/water combination with one hand and continue whisking with the other until it is completely combined and thickens.
- Return the burgers to the sauce, cover, and cook for approximately 10 mins.

Nutrition Information
Calories: 230 kcal, Carbohydrates: 15 g, Protein: 25 g, Fat: 8 g

191. Banana Peanut Butter Protein "Minute Pudding"
Prep time: 5 mins, Cook time: 0 mins, Servings: 2-4
Ingredients
- ½ cup cottage cheese
- 1 scoop Chike Banana Magic protein powder
- 2 tbsp. PB2 powdered peanuts
- Sweetener without calorie, to taste

Instructions
- Add the Banana and peanut powder, sweetener, and cheese to a blender and process for 5 mins.
- Pour into the glasses and enjoy your pudding.

Nutrition Information
Calories: 98 kcal, Carbohydrates: 5 g, Protein: 10 g, Fat: 3 g

192. Fall Harvest Protein Baked Oatmeal
Prep time: 10 mins, Cook time: 20 mins, Servings: 4-6
Ingredients
Dry
- 1 cup quick oats
- 2 scoops vanilla/unflavored protein powder
- 1/8 tsp. salt
- 1 tsp. pumpkin pie spice
- ½ cup chopped nuts

Wet
- 1 + ¼ cup milk
- ½ cup canned pumpkin
- ¼ cup maple syrup, sugar-free
- ¼ cup sweetener with no calorie
- 1 tsp. vanilla extract
- 1 egg beaten

Instructions
- Heat the oven before cooking to 350 °F.
- In a mixing basin, add the dry ingredients and mix well until well combined.
- Mix the pumpkin, milk, syrup, and Splenda separately. Mix everything well and add the beaten eggs and whisk again.
- Mix the wet and dry components in a mixing bowl and whisk until well combined.
- Grease a baking tray with cooking spray (non-stick) and pour the ingredients into it. Bake for 15-20 mins, or until the top is golden brown and the sides are slightly toasted.

Nutrition Information
Calories: 100 kcal, Carbohydrates: 15 g, Protein: 17.3g, Fat: 5g

193. Chocolate Chip Cookie Protein Shake
Prep time: 5 mins, Cook time: 0 mins, Servings: 1
Ingredients
- 8 oz. milk
- 1 scoop chocolate protein powder
- 1 tbsp. unsweetened cocoa powder
- 1 tbsp. Davinci cookie dough syrup without sugar
- 1/8 tsp. imitation butter extract
- Ice

Instructions
- Add the cocoa powder, protein powder, syrup, and butter extract in a blender and mix by the Triple X Method and enjoy.

Nutrition Information
Calories: 150 kcal, Carbohydrates: 8 g, Protein: 35g, Fat: 2.5g

194. Peanut Butter Cup Protein Shake
Prep time: 5 mins, Cook time: 0 mins, Servings: 1
Ingredients
- 1 cup milk
- 1 scoop Chike Chocolate Bliss protein powder
- 1 tbsp PB2
- ½ tbsp. cocoa powder, unsweetened
- Sweetener with no calorie, to taste
- Ice

Instructions
- Blend everything by using Triple X Method. Skip the ice to make it a warm drink.

Nutrition Information
Calories: 160 kcal, Carbohydrates: 6 g, Protein: 30g, Fat: 3g

195. Sausage Quinoa & Roasted Veggie Soup
Prep time: 10 mins, Cook time: 25 mins, Servings: 1
Ingredients
- 1 medium chopped onion
- 1 large clove minced garlic
- 1 pkg. low-fat diced turkey smoked sausage
- 4 cups washed and chopped Swiss Chard
- 1 + 3 cup water
- 2 cored tomatoes
- 4 cups roasted veggies
- 1 cup uncooked quinoa
- Salt and pepper
- 1 tsp Herbs de Provence

Instructions
- Coat a big saucepan with non-stick cooking spray and set it on medium heat. Mix in the onions and sauté until browned, then add the garlic and cook for a few mins until fragrant.
- Toss in the sausage and cook until the sausage is browned. Add 1 cup of water and the Swiss chard. Allow the liquid to boil, stirring to dislodge any particles at the base of the kettle.
- Add the tomatoes and cover for 5 mins. Remove the cover and the peel from the tomatoes. Mash them with a potato masher.
- Add 3 more cups of water, roasted vegetables, and quinoa. Stir everything together well.
- Cook for approximately 25 mins, or until the chard has wilted and the quinoa has thoroughly cooked. Take it off from the heat and leave it covered for another 10 mins before eating.

Nutrition Information
Calories: 250 kcal, Carbohydrates: 18 g, Protein: 22 g, Fat: 3g

196. Farmer's Market Scramble
Prep time: 10 mins, Cook time: 20 mins, Servings: 2
- ½ large thinly sliced onion
- ½ diced green pepper
- ½ diced red pepper
- ¼ diced small zucchini
- ¼ diced yellow squash
- 1 clove minced garlic
- ¼ tsp. Italian seasoning
- 2 large beaten eggs
- 2 large beaten egg whites
- 2 oz. preferred cheese
- 1 large, halved tomato (optional)
- Salt and black pepper, to taste

Instructions
- Heat the greased pan on medium heat. Toss in the garlic, all vegetables, and Italian seasoning, cook for a few mins until gently colored and tender.
- Place eggs in the cracks of the vegetables and gently stir them with the vegetables.
- Take it off the heat, spread cheese on the top, or mix it with vegetables.
- Lastly, add the fresh tomatoes on top or skip this step.

- Add some salt and black pepper on top and enjoy.

Nutrition Information
Calories: 250 kcal, Carbohydrates: 12 g, Protein: 19g, Fat: 8g

197. Pumpkin Chili
Prep time: 20 mins, Cook time: 30 mins, Servings: 4
Ingredients
- 1 medium yellow diced onion
- 1clove minced garlic
- 1lb. lean minced meat
- 15 oz. canned drain black beans
- 15 oz. canned drain white beans
- 15 oz. canned drain kidney beans
- 12 oz. no-sugar tomato soup
- 15oz. canned pumpkin filling
- 1tbsp. chili powder
- 1tsp. crushed cumin
- 1tsp. crushed coriander
- 1tsp. Cinnamon
- Salt & pepper
- ½ tsp. crushed chipotle powder

Instructions
- Spray a saucepan liberally with non-stick cooking spray, place it over medium heat, and let it heat up before adding the chopped onions. Sauté the chopped onions for 2 mins or until tender.
- Mix the garlic and cook for another minute or two.
- Add the minced beef and simmer until it is fully cooked. Stir in all of the beans and mix everything well.
- Stir in the pumpkin, soup, and spices. Let the soup simmer.
- Cover the top and cook for approximately 30 mins on low heat. Place in the refrigerator and enjoy it the next day.

Nutrition Information
Calories: 206 kcal, Carbohydrates: 14 g, Protein: 18g, Fat: 5g

198. Pumpkin Chai Protein Shake
Prep time: 5 mins, Cook time: 0 mins, Servings: 1
Ingredients
- 1 cup milk
- 1 scoop vanilla protein powder
- 2 pumpkin pie protein shake starter cubes
- 1 tbsp. sugar-free Davinci Chai Concentrate
- Sweetener, to taste
- Optional: Whippage and an additional dusting of cinnamon

Instructions
- Add the protein powder, milk, shake starters and concentrate and mix everything using the Triple X Technique in a blender.

Nutrition Information
Calories: 206 kcal, Carbohydrates: 8 g, Protein: 24 g, Fat: 3g

199. Protein Pumpkin Bread
Prep time: 10 mins, Cook time: 1 hour, Servings: 6 pieces
Ingredients
- 1 1/3 cup whole wheat flour
- 1 cup sweetener with no calorie
- 1 ¼ tsp baking powder
- ½ tsp baking soda
- 2 tsp pumpkin pie spice
- 12 oz. canned pumpkin
- 3 scoops vanilla protein powder
- ¼ cup no-sugar applesauce

Instructions
- Combine all of the ingredients first, except the applesauce, then add the applesauce and mix it one more time.
- Transfer the prepared mixture into a greased loaf pan (8x4 inch). Bake for 50-55 mins, or until a toothpick inserted into the center comes out clean.

Nutrition Information
Calories: 150 kcal, Carbohydrates: 8.7 g, Protein: 10g, Fat: 5g

200. Spicy Bean Dip
Prep time: 10 mins, Cook time: 0 mins, Servings: 1
Ingredients
- 1 can of black beans
- 1 can corn
- 1 can of black-eyed peas
- 1 can green chilis
- 1 can chopped tomatoes
- 1 diced red onion
- 1 diced green bell pepper
- 8 oz. of Italian dressing
- Pickled Jalapenos, optional

Instructions
- Add the drain and rinse beans and corn in a large bowl.
- Add the drained tomatoes and can chilies to the mixing bowl.
- Chop the onion and bell peppers and toss them in with the beans in the mixing basin. Add Italian seasoning and chopped jalapenos.
- Mix them well and put them in the fridge overnight before eating.

Nutrition Information
Calories: 200 kcal, Carbohydrates: 20 g, Protein: 6 g, Fat: 3g

201. Meatball Bake Faux-Lasagna
Prep time: 10 mins, Cook time: 45 mins, Servings: 2
Ingredients
- ½ lb beef ground
- ¼ cup TVP
- ¼ cup water
- ½ jar sauce spaghetti
- 3 sliced grilled zucchinis
- 3 sliced and grilled yellow squash
- 1 pkg Turkey Meatballs Trader Joe
- 8 oz. soft goat cheese
- 2 tsp of pesto
- ½ cup grated mozzarella
- ½ cup grated Romano cheese

Instructions
- Heat the oven before cooking to 350 °F.
- Combine the TVP with water in a small dish and put it aside.
- Cook minced beef with spaghetti sauce and soak TVP in a skillet. Season with salt and garlic.
- Combine the pesto with goat cheese in a separate bowl.
- With olive oil spray, coat a baking tray (9x13). Spread the meat and TVP sauce mixture on the baking sheet. Layer the top with goat cheese and pesto mixture, grilled zucchini, and squash. Place the meatballs evenly over the top and drizzle with the remaining 3/4 cup spaghetti sauce.
- Top with Romano and mozzarella cheeses and bake for 30-45 mins, or until bubbling and heated.

Nutrition Information
Calories: 305 kcal, Carbohydrates: 18 g, Protein: 24g, Fat: 8g

202. Noodle-less Lasagna
Prep time: 15 mins, Cook time: 45 mins, Servings: 2
Ingredients
Meat Sauce
- 1tbsp olive oil extra-virgin
- 1 diced onion small finely
- 1 finely diced green pepper
- 1tsp minced garlic
- 1lb. minced lean turkey
- 8oz. Italian Sausage
- 1 jar spaghetti sauce

Ricotta Layer
- 16 oz. ricotta cheese part-skim
- ½ cup shredded Parmesan cheese
- ½ tsp crushed pepper
- 1 egg large

Noodles
- 3-4 zucchini, 7-8 inches long

Topping
- 2 cups shredded Italian-blend cheese
- 1tsp Italian seasoning, optional

Instructions
- Heat the oven before baking to 350 °F.
- Cut zucchini into long, flat slices lengthwise. Lay them on a kitchen towel, season with salt, and then let them aside for 10-15 minutes to absorb any extra moisture. Cook/roast or grill the raw zucchini to eliminate even more water.
- Preheat a big saucepan over medium heat until it's hot. Pour in the oil and stir it around the pan.
- Add the diced green bell pepper and onions and cook for 3 mins until veggies are softened.
- Toss in the meat, brown meat, and garlic in the veggies. Cook until the meat is completely cooked.
- Stir in the spaghetti sauce and cover with a lid. Cook it on low heat for 15 to 20 minutes until the sauce boils and becomes a deeper crimson color.
- Thoroughly combine egg, ricotta, cheese, and pepper in a large bowl.
- Pour 1/3 of the beef sauce mixture into a casserole dish (9x13 inches). Layer the top with zucchini noodles and ricotta mixture.
- Pour the final 1/3 of the prepared sauce and repeat the layering process.
- If preferred, top with cheese and Italian spice for garnish.
- Bake for 40 mins at 350 degrees or until the cheese is crusted on top.

Nutrition Information
Calories: 209 kcal, Carbohydrates: 14 g, Protein: 18 g, Fat: 12g

203. Meat Crust Pizza
Prep time: 20 mins, Cook time: 25 Mins Servings: 6-8

Ingredients
Crust
- 1 lb. lean minced meat
- ½ packet dry onion soup mix
- ¼ tsp. freshly crushed black pepper
- 1medium egg

Toppings
- Ham
- Pepperoni
- Thinly sliced green peppers
- 1 cup jarred spaghetti sauce
- 1.5 cup part-skim mozzarella cheese
- ¼ cup shredded Parmesan cheese

Instructions
- Heat the oven before cooking to 350 °F.
- Combine the meat, egg, soup, and spices in a large mixing basin. Add a few spoons of breadcrumbs if the mixture is moist.
- Layout plastic sheet on a clean surface. Wrap the meatball tightly in plastic wrap. Roll the meat into the thick disc (½-inch) with a rolling pin. Line a baking tray with cooking spray (non-stick).
- Place the rolled disc (without plastic wrap) on it. Bake for 30 min until meat is cooked.
- Cover the top with spaghetti sauce, cheese, and toppings. Bake for another 10-15 mins, until the topped cheese has melted or browned on top.
- Add the grated Parmesan cheese, chili flakes, or anything else you'd want.

Nutrition Information
Calories: 250 kcal, Carbohydrates: 20 g, Protein: 18 g, Fat: 8g

204. Taco Soup
Prep time: 10 mins, Cook time: 15 Mins Servings: 15

Ingredients
- 1 lb. boneless chicken or beef
- ½ cup diced onion
- 28 oz. diced tomatoes
- 1-2 package taco seasoning
- 3-4 oz. can chop green chili
- 4 cup chicken/beef broth
- 4 cup water
- 14 oz. can drain black beans
- 17 oz. can drain corn
- Shredded Cheese
- Tortilla/corn chips

Instructions
- Mix the onion, meat, tomatoes, green chili, taco spice, broth, and water in a crockpot. Allow cooking on low all night.
- Shred the cooked meat and cook on low heat, stirring periodically.
- Before serving, add the black beans and corns, and if necessary, add more liquid.
- Serve with smashed chips and grated cheese on top.

Nutrition Information
Calories: 118 kcal, Carbohydrates: 9.2 g, Protein: 8 g, Fat: 5.5g

205. TVP Tuna
Prep time: 15 mins, Cook time: 0 mins, Servings: 1

Ingredients
- 4 oz. can tuna
- ¼ cup vegetable protein, textured
- 1 tbsp. mayo
- 2 tbsp. Greek yogurt
- 1 tsp. Dijon mustard
- 1 tbsp. finely chopped onions
- Pinch of salt and pepper
- a dash of garlic powder

Instructions
- Combine the tuna, spices, liquid, and TVP in a mixing dish. Let it rest until TVP soaks the liquids.
- Combine mayonnaise, yogurt, and mustard in a separate bowl. Mix thoroughly.
- Combine the tuna and mayonnaise mixture, then toss the onions and stir again.
- Serve with apple slices because this combination is a winning combination.

Nutrition Information
Calories: 250 kcal, Carbohydrates: 20 g, Protein: 25 g, Fat: 9g

206. Red Hot Faux-Tato Salad
Prep time: 15 mins, Cook time: 0 mins, Servings: 1

Ingredients
- 1 large fresh cauliflower head
- 4 large hard-boiled diced eggs
- 1 medium finely chopped sweet onion
- 1 cup Greek Yogurt
- ½ cup Kraft Low-Fat Horseradish-Dijon
- Low-fat Mayo
- ¼ cup Horseradish
- Aldi Mustard
- ¼ cup dill pickles, chopped
- ½ bunch freshly minced Italian Parsley
- ½ bunch freshly minced dill
- Salt, Pepper to taste
- ½ tsp. Garlic powder
- ¼ cup Frank's Red-Hot sauce
- 2 tsp Paprika

Instructions
- Fill a pan with water and a little bit of salt.
- Separate the cauliflower (florets) from the stem and place them in a saucepan of boiling water. Boil them and cook for another 5 mins on low heat, or until it is fork soft. Mash it with a masher or pulse it in a processor until it resembles lumpy mashed potatoes.

- Mix the Greek yogurt, mustard, and mayonnaise, together in a separate dish until fully blended. Add a bit of salt, pepper, and a pinch of garlic powder. Add the chopped onions, dill, parsley, and pickle relish until everything combines.
- Mix the cauliflower, chopped eggs, and yogurt mixture with a rubber spatula until it's well combined. Add additional salt and pepper as required.

Nutrition Information
Calories: 100 kcal, Carbohydrates: 10 g, Protein: 7 g, Fat: 4g

207. Gypsy's Cilantro Lime Chicken
Prep time: 20 mins, Cook time: 15 mins, Servings: 2
Ingredients
- 4 boneless chicken breast halves
- ¼ cup lemon juice
- ½ cup freshly chopped cilantro
- 6 cloves chopped garlic
- 1 tbsp. honey
- 1 tbsp. olive oil
- ½ tsp. salt
- ¼ tsp. pepper

Instructions
- Flatten the chicken pieces to an equal thickness (approximately ½ inch) and transfer them to the side dish.
- Combine olive oil, garlic, lime juice, cilantro, honey, salt, and pepper in a small bowl. Pour the mixture over the chicken and flip it to coat evenly. Marinate for at least 30 mins or up to 24 hours in the refrigerator.
- Grill each side of the marinated chicken on medium heat for 4-6 mins or until cooked well.

Nutrition Information
Calories: 280 kcal, Carbohydrates: 18 g, Protein: 28g, Fat: 5g

208. "Kick Arse" Veggie Chili
Prep time: 15 mins, Cook time: 25 mins, Servings: 4
Ingredients
- 2 cup TVP
- 4 cup water
- ¼ tsp. Onion powder
- ¼ tsp. garlic powder each
- salt and pepper to taste
- 1 medium diced onion
- ½ skinned and diced eggplant
- 1 diced zucchini
- 1 diced yellow squash
- 1 clove minced garlic
- 1 can drain and dice tomatoes
- 1 can drain black beans
- 1 can drain light red kidneys
- 1 can drain dark red kidneys
- 3 tbsp. chili powder
- 1 tbsp. unsweetened cocoa powder
- ¼ tsp. cayenne pepper

Instructions
- Combine water (2 cups), garlic powder, onion powder, salt, and pepper in a large mixing bowl. Add the TVP and then rest for around 20 minutes to re-hydrate thoroughly.
- In the meanwhile, chop the vegetables.
- Coat a saucepan with cooking spray and set it aside to heat up. Toss in the onions, squash, and eggplant. Sauté until softened, then stir in the garlic and cook until fragrant.
- Stir in the re-hydrated TVP, beans, and tomatoes until everything is thoroughly combined.
- Add the remaining water and spices as needed to get a little soupy texture.
- Bring everything to a boil, then reduce to low heat and cook for approximately 20 or a few more mins.

Nutrition Information
Calories: 227 kcal, Carbohydrates: 35 g, Protein: 22.5 g, Fat: 1.5g

209. Cheesy Chicken, Broccoli & "Rice" Casserole
Prep time: 10 mins, Cook time: 30 mins, Servings: 4
Ingredients
- 2 large grilled and chopped chicken breasts
- 1 small finely diced onion
- 3 cups cauliflower rice
- 1 package frozen broccoli pieces
- 1 can low-fat cheddar cheese soup
- ½ cup milk
- 1 cup shredded sharp/mild cheddar cheeses
- Salt and pepper to taste
- Onion powder and garlic powder to taste

Instructions
- Heat the oven before cooking to 350 °F.
- Boil/steam the broccoli until it reaches the appropriate texture and drains.
- In a non-stick pan, sauté the onions and add the spices.
- Combine the chicken, sautéed onion, cooked broccoli, and cauliflower rice in a large mixing basin.
- Mix the cheese soup, milk, and ½ cheese in a mixing bowl and thoroughly combine
- Place in a baking tray and sprinkle the remaining cheese.
- Bake for 30 min, or until the cheese is completely melted.

Nutrition Information
Calories: 218 kcal, Carbohydrates: 22 g, Protein: 18g, Fat: 6g

210. Cauliflower Pizza Crust
Prep time: 10 mins, Cook time: 10 mins, Servings: 4
Ingredients
- ¼ cup raw grated cauliflower
- 2 oz. 75% fat-free cheese
- 1 egg white
- 4 turkey pepperoni slices
- 1 tbsp. pizza sauce
- Italian spices

Instructions
- Combine the cheese, cauliflower, egg white, and Italian spice in a mixing bowl.
- Spread the ingredients evenly in a medium frying pan coated with non-stick cooking spray. Cook each side for a few mins, or until golden brown.
- Top with a dollop of pizza sauce, pepperoni slices, and the remaining cheese.
- Cover with a lid to allow the cheese to melt or bake it for a few more minutes.

Nutrition Information
Calories: 272 kcal, Carbohydrates: 14 g, Protein: 24g, Fat: 8g

211. Protein Cookies
Prep time: 20 mins, Cook time: 15 mins, Servings: 48 cookies
Ingredients
- 3/4 cup calorie-free sweetener
- 1 cup rolled oats
- 1 cup vanilla whey protein powder
- ½ cup soy flour
- 1 3/4 tsp baking soda
- ½ tsp baking powder
- ½ tsp salt
- 2 tsp crushed cinnamon
- 1 tsp crushed nutmeg
- 1 tsp crushed ginger
- 1 tsp vanilla extract
- 1 can pumpkin puree
- 3 tbsp. plain Greek yogurt
- 2 eggs
- 3 tbsp. crushed flax seeds
- 1 cup diced fresh cranberries
- ½ cup chopped roasted walnuts (optional)

Instructions
- Heat the oven before cooking to 175 °C.

- Combine the Splenda, protein powder, oats, soy flour, salt, cinnamon, ginger, nutmeg, baking powder, and baking soda in a large mixing dish.
- Combine the eggs, pumpkin, and yogurt in another mixing bowl. Mix dry ingredients and fold in the walnuts, flax seeds, and cranberries.
- Create 48 big balls, flatten them on a baking tray, or make little muffins using a mini muffin pan.
- Bake in an oven for 9 to 12 mins (avoid over baking).

Nutrition Information
Calories: 190 kcal, Carbohydrates: 20g, Protein; 10g, Fat: 8g

212. Cinnamon Muffins
Prep time: 10 mins, Cook time: 15 mins, Servings: 6 muffins
Ingredients
- 3/4 cup whole wheat pancake mix
- ½ tsp cinnamon
- ½ tsp baking soda
- 2 tbsp. Splenda brown sugar
- 2 scoops of vanilla protein powder
- ½ cup milk
- ¼ cup sugar-free pancake syrup

Instructions
- Heat the oven before cooking to 350 °F.
- Combine the pancake mix, protein powder, baking soda, brown sugar, cinnamon, and milk in a bowl. Stir until the mixture is completely smooth.
- Fold in the maple syrup and mix.
- Butter the muffin pans and spoon the batter into muffin cups until they are 3/4 full.
- Bake for 16 mins.

Nutrition Information
Calories: 130 kcal, Carbohydrates: 18 g, Protein: 14g, Fat: 3g

213. Curried Chickpeas
Prep time: 10 mins, Cook time: 5 hours, Servings: 1
Ingredients
- 1 lb. chickpeas
- 1 small, chopped onion
- 1 clove minced garlic
- Finely diced raw carrots
- 10 oz. vegetable stock
- 10 oz. light coconut milk
- 4 cup water
- ½ tbsp. cumin and coriander each
- 2-3 heaping tbsp. curry powder
- ¼ tsp red pepper flakes (optional)

Instructions
- Add onions, garlic, and carrots to the crockpot, then layer the beans on top.
- Cook for 5-6 hours on reduced heat, or until the chickpeas are cooked.

Nutrition Information
Calories: 220 kcal, Carbohydrates: 23 g, Protein: 18g, Fat: 4g

214. Low-Carb pancakes
Prep time: 10 mins, Cook time: 15 mins, Servings: 4
Ingredients
- 1 pkg+ extra tsp. Protein Baking Mix
- 1 tbsp. banana pudding mix, sugar-free
- 2 tbsp. unflavored Greek yogurt
- 3 tbsp. milk
- 1 beaten egg
- ¼ tsp. pure vanilla extract

For topping:
- low-calorie butter spray
- ¼ banana, sliced
- ¼ cup sugar-free pancake syrup
- 1/8 tsp. rum extract
- 1/8 tsp. cinnamon

Instructions
- Coat a grill pan with non-stick butter spray and place it on medium heat to heat up.
- Meanwhile, in a mixing bowl, thoroughly combine all ingredients. If the batter is too thick, add a tablespoon of milk at a time until it approaches the consistency of a pudding.
- Drop piles of the mixture on a pan with a spoon and spread them out into circles. Cook each side for 1-2 mins on one side. When done, transfer to a plate.
- To create the topping, place a small pan (7 1/8 inch) on medium heat and coat it with non-stick cooking spray. Spray the bananas with butter spray and cook for a few mins. Add the pancake syrup and allow to boil before lowering the heat. Stir in the rum essence and cinnamon, then serve on top of the pancakes.

Nutrition Information
Calories: 480 kcal, Carbohydrates: 24g, Proteins: 23 g, Fat: 0g

215. Spaghetti Squash Ramen with Shrimp
Prep Time: 15 Mins, Cook Time: 15 Mins, Servings: 2-4
Ingredients
- 1 spaghetti squash, cooked
- 1 tsp of sesame oil, divided
- 1 tbsp of low-sodium soy sauce, low-sodium, divided
- 2cup of chicken broth, low sodium
- 1 peeled clove garlic
- ½ tsp of grated ginger
- 8 mushrooms, sliced
- 8 cooked medium shrimp, peeled & deveined
- 1hardboiled egg
- 2tbsp of chopped green onion
- 1 sliced small red hot chili pepper

Instructions
- Preheat the oven to 400 Fahrenheit.
- Discard the seeds & pulp from the spaghetti squash, then score the interior with the help of the fork before spreading half tsp of sesame oil & half tbsp of soy sauce within.
- Roast for 18-20 mins, or till fork tender, on the baking tray with both halves. Remove the squash from the skin & place it in a dish when it's done. Put anything away.
- Combine the leftover sesame oil, garlic, chicken broth, soy sauce & ginger in a saucepan. Bring to the boil, then lower to a low flame. Add the shrimp to the mix if they are frozen, then cover & simmer till done. Reduce the flame to a low simmer & add mushrooms just before the cooking time.
- Meanwhile, make a boiled egg (hard boil) by submerging one egg in boiling water for 7-8 mins. Bring to cold water right away & soak for 2-3 mins before peeling & slicing in half.
- To make the ramen bowl, start with the required quantity of broth, spaghetti squash, shrimp, mushrooms, & ½ boil egg (hard boil) in the bowl. Top with chopped red-hot chilies & green onions, if preferred.

Nutrition Information
Calories: 122 kcal, Carbohydrates: 3.1 g, Protein: 21 g, Fats: 8.1 g

216. Spicy Chipotle Pork Stew
Prep time: 30 mins, Cook time 8 hrs., Servings: 4-6
Ingredients
- 1 pound of country ribs
- 1 tsp of salt
- 1 tsp of pepper
- 1 tsp of ground cumin
- 1 tsp of ground coriander
- 2 bay leaves
- 1cup of water
- 1 can of chipotle peppers in adobo sauce
- 10 ounces tomatoes, diced (drained of excess liquid)
- 2 cups of vegetables (your choice)
- ¼ cup of part-skim ricotta cheese (serve with each serving)

Instructions
- Combine the ribs, cumin, salt, water, pepper, coriander & bay leaves. Cook for around 6 hrs. on low heat.
- Discard the bones from meat & bay leaves. Using 2 forks, shred the meat.
- Puree 1-2 of chipotle peppers (if you want it somewhat hot) or 2-4 peppers (if you want to like it extremely spicy) in the blender with the chopped tomatoes. Combine it with the chopped tomatoes & your mixed veggies in a crockpot.
- Cook for another 2 hrs. Serve with a dollop of ricotta cheese & a sprig of cilantro on top.

Nutrition Information
Calories: 221 kcal, Carbohydrates: 9 g, Protein: 20.2 g, Fats: 6 g

217. Chicken Lasagna Roll-Ups with Zoodles
Prep time: 10 mins, Cook time: 1 hr., Servings: 3-4

Ingredients
- 2-3 zucchini
- ½ tbsp olive oil, extra-virgin
- 1 small, diced yellow onion
- 2 cups of baby spinach
- 1 cup ricotta cheese, part-skim
- 1 egg beaten, large
- ¼ tsp of ground black pepper
- ¼ tsp of Italian spice
- ½ cup of shredded Parmesan cheese
- 1 pound thin-sliced chicken breasts, boneless, skinless
- 1 jar spaghetti sauce, your favorite
- 2 cup of shredded mozzarella cheese

Instructions
- Preheat the oven to 350 Fahrenheit.
- Slice the zucchini in spaghetti-shaped zoodles with a vegetable spiralizer. Set aside the zoodles with a pinch of salt.
- Preheat a skillet on medium flame until it is hot. Swirl the oil around in the pan. Cook for 1-2 mins, or till onions are softened. The spinach should then be added & cooked until barely wilted. Allow 5-6 mins for cooling.
- In a dish, thoroughly combine egg, ricotta, pepper, parmesan cheese & spice. Mix in the onions & spinach once more.5. Make every roll-up by placing one chicken breast flat down the side on a chopping board or work surface. Put a ricotta/vegetable mixture on top & fold it up carefully.
- Pour into an 8-by-8-inch casserole dish.
- Cover with canned sauce, cover, & bake for 40-45 mins in the oven.
- Sprinkle the cheese on top & simmer for another 15 mins, uncovered.
- Fill a small saucepan halfway with water and bring to a boil. Before returning to the dish, drop zoodles into hot water & cook for just 1-2 mins.
- Put zoodles in the small dish & serve with a chicken roll-up to complete the meal. Pour the sauce on the top &, if preferred, sprinkle with more parmesan cheese.

Nutrition Information
Calories: 131 kcal, Carbohydrates: 11.5 g, Protein: 13 g, Fats: 9.0 g

218. Baked Eggplant Parmesan with Zoodles
Prep time: 20 mins, Cook time: 1 hr., Servings: 4-5

Ingredients
- 1 medium sliced eggplant
- 2 egg whites
- 1 cup of whole-wheat breadcrumbs
- ½ cup of shredded Parmesan cheese
- 1 tsp of Italian seasoning
- ½ tsp of salt
- ¼ tsp of black pepper
- 1 jar marinara sauce, low sugar
- 1 zucchini sliced into thick spaghetti shaped zoodles, large
- 1 sliced yellow onion, small
- 1 sliced green pepper, small
- ½ cup of grated mozzarella cheese

Instructions
- Preheat the oven to 400 Fahrenheit.
- Prepare the dredging station by whisking the egg whites in a small bowl, & on a plate, mix the parmesan cheese, pepper & salt.
- Dip eggplant pieces in egg whites first & then into the bread crumb combination. When done, put on the rack inside a baking tray to cool.
- Bake for 25 -30 mins, or till the eggplant is soft & the coating is crunchy.
- To make the sauce, first, soften the peppers & onions in the pan coated with cooking spray for 2-3 mins. Cover & cook for approximately 20 mins with the marinara sauce.
- After salting & discarding the extra water from the zoodles, cook them in water for 2-3 mins. [NOTE: If preparing lunches ahead of time, don't cook the zoodles. The zoodles will be properly cooked once you reheat the meal.
- Arrange the zoodles on the dish to plate the meal. Top with a slice of cooked eggplant, approximately one-third cup of or more the sauce mix,

Nutrition Information
Calories: 114 kcal, Carbohydrates: 14.6 g, Protein: 23 g, Fats: 5 g

219. Zoodle Lo Mein
Prep Time: 10 Mins, Cook Time: 15 Mins, Servings: 2

Ingredients
- Whole clove of garlic
- 1 zucchini sliced into thick spaghetti shaped zoodles, large
- 3 ounces of matchstick carrots
- ½ cup of shelled edamame
- 2 tsp of sesame oil
- 2 tbsp of soy sauce, low sodium
- (optional), ½ tbsp of sriracha sauce
- 6-8 shrimp shelled, large & deveined
- 2 tbsp scallions, chopped
- (optional) 1 tsp of whole sesame seeds

Instructions
- Generously coat a wok or pan with cooking spray, place it on medium flame, & allow it to become extremely hot. Cook, constantly stirring, till the garlic is golden brown. Put it aside.
- Combine zoodles, shrimp, soy sauce, carrots, & edamame with oil (sesame oil), sriracha sauce (if using) in a large mixing bowl.
- Toss for 2-3 mins with tongs till cooked thoroughly. Serve with sesame seeds or scallions as a garnish.

Nutrition Information
Calories: 145 kcal, Carbohydrates: 11 g, Protein: 23 g, Fats: 7 g

220. Protein Strawberry Cheesecake Cheeseball
Prep time: 15 mins, Cook time: 3 hr., Servings: 1

Ingredients
- 16 ounces of Greek yogurt cream cheese, low-fat
- ¾ cup of no-calorie sweetener
- (optional) 1 tsp of cream of tartar
- ½ tbsp of vanilla extract
- 3 servings of protein powder, unflavored
- ½ cup of strawberry jelly, sugar-free (like Fit & Active from Aldi)
- 2 cup of strawberries, diced
- 2 cups of crushed high fiber cereal OR 4 whole graham crackers

Instructions
- Cream together the cream cheese, vanilla, sweetener, cream of tartar, & protein powder in a hand mixer/ mixing bowl or the stand mixer till thoroughly combined. Scrape down the edges of the dish a couple of times to ensure that everything is incorporated.
- Drain any leftover liquid from the jelly inside the jar before adding it to the cream cheese mixture. If you're using

chopped strawberries, toss them in as well. Gently incorporate it into the mix using a flat spatula. (Folding Means repeatedly flipping the batter to spread things throughout without necessarily blending it.) There should still be strawberry jelly swirls in there.)
- Place on a big sheet of clingfilm, wrap it up, & roll it into a ball. Refrigerate for at least 3 hrs.
- Place smashed graham cracker or fiber cereal crumbs on a platter & distribute them out when ready to serve. Put the cheese mix in the middle of the crumbs & cover the ball with your hands. Refrigerate till ready to serve.

Nutrition Information
Calories: 145 kcal, Carbohydrates: 14.4 g, Protein: 11 g, Fats: 8 g

221. Raspberry Walnut Goat Cheese Cheeseball
Prep time: 15 mins, Cook time: 2hr 45 mins, Servings: 1
Ingredients
- 16 ounces of Greek yogurt cream cheese, Low-fat
- 4 ounces of plain goat cheese
- 2servings protein powder, unflavored
- ¾ cup of sweetener (your choice)
- ½ cup of raspberry preserves, sugar-free (like Fit & Active from Aldi)
- 2 cups of chopped walnuts

Instructions
- Cream together the protein powder cream cheese, sweetener & goat cheese in a bowl or stand mixer on medium speed until fully incorporated.
- Add the preserves & incorporate them into cream cheese mix with a flat spatula. (Folding means gently flipping over but not mixing in.) Swirls of raspberry should still be visible.
- Wrap the mixture in a wide piece of wrapping sheet & roll it into the ball. Refrigerate for a minimum of 3 hrs before serving.
- Set a dry pan on medium flame on the stove for 35-40 mins before you're ready to be served. Cook until the walnuts are aromatic, approximately a min (about 3- mins). Allow it cool completely on a big platter, distributing the nuts evenly over the surface.
- To make the cheeseball, lay the balls in the middle of the walnut plate & cover it with your hands. Keep refrigerated until ready to serve. This meal lasts around 2-hrs at the party table. (However, it would not last long.) (Believe me.)

Nutrition Information
Calories: 139 kcal, Carbohydrates: 11 g, Protein: 21 g, Fats: 6 g

222. Mint Mocha Protein Pudding
Prep time: 10 mins, Cook time: 50 mins, Servings: 4
Ingredients
- 1box or 0.5 ounces instant chocolate pudding mix, sugar-free
- 2servingsof BiPro USA Chocolate protein powder
- 1 tsp of Cafe Bustillo instant decaffeinated espresso
- 1 tbsp cocoa powder, unsweetened
- 2 cups of cow's milk (Fair life increased protein milk)
- 1/8 tsp of peppermint extract
- 4 tbsp whipped cream
- (optional)2-3 peppermints, sugar-free

Instructions
- Combine the pudding mix, cocoa powder, protein & instant espresso in a mixing dish. To incorporate everything, whisk it together completely.
- Mix in the milk & extract with the hand mixer on medium speed for a few secs before switching to high. If you've one, you may also use the stand mixer. Start slowly and gradually increase your tempo to smooth out any lumps. Scrape the bowl halfway through to ensure you've included all dry items.
- The mix should begin to be set up immediately. Split it up into 4 cups & set aside. Before serving, chill the glasses for 1 hr. NOTE: The pudding might be a little harder than regular pudding since you have added protein (mousse-like).
- If preferred, sprinkle with sugar-free peppermint (crushed) & whipped cream bits before serving.

Nutrition Information
Calories: 125 kcal, Carbohydrates: 10.9 g, Protein: 13 g, Fats: 7.5 g

223. Mint Chocolate Protein Pots de creme
Prep time: 5 mins, Cook time: 20 mins, Servings: 4
Ingredients
- 1 cup of milk (your choice)
- 2servings of chocolate protein powder (your favorite one)
- 1/8 tsp of mint extract
- 2 tbsp cocoa powder, unsweetened
- 2tbsp of sweetener, no-calorie
- ½ tsp of vanilla extract
- 2 eggs, large

Instructions
- Preheat the oven to 325 Fahrenheit. Set a kettle or saucepan of water to boil as well.
- In the blender, mix the milk, cocoa powder, protein, vanilla extract & sweetener until smooth (about 16-20 secs). Blend in the eggs one more.
- In the baking dish, place 4 ramekins. Using 4 ramekins, divide the mixture equally. Put the baking tray on the center rack in the oven that has been preheated.
- Fill the baking tray halfway with hot water and pour it over the ramekins.
- Bake for 18-20 mins but check on it after 10 mins. The top may immediately produce a brownie-like crust. They might still be a bit dangly when you jiggle the ramekins, but the interior must not be watery. It's not a huge deal if you cook them far beyond the exact point when they're jiggly. The finished texture is more fudge-like than custard-like.

Nutrition Information
Calories: 90 kcal, Carbohydrates: 10 g, Protein: 10.1 g, Fats: 4 g

224. Sweet (and Salty) Potato Casserole
Prep time: 15 mins, Cook time: 30 mins, Servings: 2
Ingredients
- 1 sweet potato, large +skinned
- 1serving protein, unflavored (BiPro USA)
- ¼ tsp of pumpkin pie spice
- 1-2 tbsp of sweetener, no-calorie
- 2tbsp of butter, unsalted
- ½ cup of chopped pecans
- 1/8 tsp of salt

Instructions
- Preheat the oven to 350 Fahrenheit.
- Fill a small saucepan halfway with water & bring to a boil. Boil the sweet potato till it is extremely soft (about 8-10 mins).
- Mash the sweet potato well in a dish, then put protein powder, sugar, & pie spice & mix them again. You may use an immersion blender if you want a completely smooth texture.
- Divide the sweet potato combination into many ramekins or a tiny casserole dish.
- Melt the butter in a saucepan. Toss in the pecans & salt till they are evenly covered.
- Toss the nut mixture on top of the tiny casseroles or ramekins & bake for 13-15 mins, or till the nuts are roasted.

Nutrition Information
Calories: 131 kcal, Carbohydrates: 8.8 g, Protein: 9.8 g, Fats: 5 g

225. Thanksgiving Meatballs w/Mashed Cauliflower and Craisin Sauce
Prep time: 30 mins, Cook time: 1 hr., Servings: 20
Ingredients
Meatballs
- 1 pound of lean ground turkey

- ½ small, grated zucchini
- ¼ tsp of salt
- ½ tsp of ground sage
- ½ tsp of celery flakes
- ¼ tsp of black pepper

Whipped Cauliflower
- 1 small head of cauliflower slice into florets
- 2 tbsp of cream cheese, reduced fat
- 2 tbsp of Parmesan cheese shredded
- 2 tbsp of milk
- ¼ tsp of parsley

Craisin Sauce
- 2 cups of water
- 1 cup of craisins, low sugar
- ¼ tsp of lemon juice or zest
- ¼ cup of sweetener, no-calorie

Instructions
Make meatballs
- Combine spices, ground beef & zucchini in a dish & stir by hand till fully incorporated. Scoop up gobs of meat mixture with a tbsp measure & shape it into balls with the hands. Before wrapping with aluminum foil, put in the baking tray & add approximately 2 tsp of water. Cook for 40 mins, or till meatballs are well cooked.

Make whipped cauliflower
- Fill a small saucepan halfway with water and bring to a boil & put the cauliflower florets in this boiling water cook till cauliflower florets are very soft, approximately 7-8 mins. Put them back in the pot after draining the water. Mash the cream plus Parmesan cheese & milk together with a masher or an immersion blender till smooth. To produce a whipped consistency, combine the items in the food processor.

Make craisin sauce
- In a saucepan, bring two cups to a boil. Cook for 5-7 mins after adding the lemon zest & craisins. The raisins will plump up a lot. Remove the craisins from the water & throw them in the blender. Blend in the sweetener until it is completely smooth. If desired, chill the dish before serving.

Assemble
- Place the required quantity of whipped cauliflower (each mound comprises one-fourth cup of mashed cauliflower). Finish with a dab of craisin sauce & meatballs on top.

Nutrition Information
Calories: 100 kcal, Carbohydrates: 8 g, Protein: 11 g, Fats: 10 g

226. Apple Crumble Ramekins
Prep time: 10 mins, Cook time: 35 mins, Servings: 2
Ingredients
Apple filling
- 2 Granny Smith or Pink Lady apples (small) peeled, cored & sliced
- 3 tbsp of sweetener, no-calorie
- ¼ tsp of apple pie spice

Topping
- 1 tbsp of butter
- ½ cup of high fiber cereal
- 1 tbsp almonds, sliced
- 1 tbsp of sweetener, no-calorie

Instructions
- Preheat the oven to 350 Fahrenheit.
- Coat a skillet with cooking spray & place it on medium flame to heat up. Put the apples in a heated pan & cook till apples are cooked, approximately 3 mins, by adding apples, sugar, & pie spice. Fill ramekins halfway with the mixture.
- Pulse the butter, cereal, sweetener & almonds in a bullet-shaped blender or the mini-food processor till it's well combined (will start to clump a little). Pour the mixture into each ramekin.
- Bake for 32-35 mins, or till the topping is crisp & the filling starts bubbling over the top.

Nutrition Information
Calories: 89 kcal, Carbohydrates: 5 g, Protein: 7 g, Fats: 6.1 g

227. No-Sugar-Added Ramekin Blueberry Cobblers
Prep time: 5 mins, Cook time: 30 mins, Servings: 2
Ingredients
Filling
- 16 ounces of mixed berries
- ¼ tsp of lemon juice
- 1/3 cup of sweetener, no-calorie
- 1 tbsp of corn starch

Topping
- ½ cup of oats quick
- ¼ tsp of pie spice (any kind)
- 1 tbsp of butter
- 1/8 tsp of salt

Instructions
- Preheat the oven to 340 Fahrenheit.
- Combine the berries and lemon juice in the dish
- Mix in the sweetener & corn starch completely. It's OK if it looks clumpy (as cornstarch does).
- Pulse the spices, oats, & butter in the mini food processor or a bowl until a rough meal texture (clumpy texture).
- Scoop out the berry mixture into each ramekin. Serve with a dollop of oat topping on top.
- Bake for 32-35 mins, then turn off the oven and leave the ramekins in there to cool. Warm with whipped cream on top!

Nutrition Information
Calories: 97 kcal, Carbohydrates: 7.7 g, Protein: 9.2 g, Fats: 7 g

228. Summer Shrimp Salad with Watermelon Champagne Vinaigrette
Prep Time: 15 Mins, Cook Time: 1 hr 15 Mins, Servings: 2-3
Ingredients
- 10-12 Shrimp shelled & deveined, cooked
- ¼ tsp of Garlic Powder
- Salt & Pepper, to taste
- 4 cups of Spring Salad Mix
- 10 Seedless Watermelon balls
- 2 tbsp of Crumbled Goat Cheese
- 2 tbsp of Pepitas

Champagne Vinaigrette dressing
- 3 tbsp of champagne vinegar
- 2 tbsp extra-virgin olive oil
- 1 tsp of Honey Dijon mustard
- 3 tbsp of watermelon juice
- ½ tsp minced garlic
- ¼ tsp of black pepper

Instructions
Salad
- Coat a skillet liberally with cooking spray & place it on medium flame to heat up.
- You should rinse shrimp through a filter with cold water. If not, add salt, garlic powder & pepper to taste. Put the shrimps in the heated pan & cook for 2-3 mins, turning them once. Remove them from the heat & set them aside to rest.
- Toss salad greens with goat cheese, watermelon & pepitas in a dish. Toss the salad with chopsticks after adding half of the dressing.
- Divide the mixture equally between the 2 plates. Serve with shrimp on top.

Dressing
- Combine vinegar, garlic, oil, watermelon juice & pepper in a mixing bowl. Refrigerate for a minimum of 1 hr before filtering into a dish or dressing bottle via a sieve

Nutrition Information

Calories: 140 kcal, Carbohydrates: 12.3 g, Protein: 5 g, Fats: 9 g.

229. No-Sugar-Added Chocolate Hazelnut Spread
Prep time:10 Mins, Cook time:15Mins, Servings: 2
Ingredients
- 1 cup of chopped hazelnuts
- 4 ounces of baking chocolate
- 1 tbsp extra-virgin olive oil
- ½ cup of milk
- ¾ cup of sweetener, no-calorie
- 1 tsp of pure vanilla extract
- 1/8 tsp of salt

Instructions
- Melt the chocolate in a microwave-proof dish for 10-secs until completely melted.
- Preheat a dry pan on the burner (don't use nonstick spray, simply let it alone). Toss the hazelnuts & toss them about for a min or 2 till you can scent them. Remove from the heat as soon as possible.
- In the food processor or the blender, combine nuts, oil, melted chocolate, milk, salt, vanilla & sweetener until smooth. If it is not smoothing out or mixing, add a spoonful of milk at a time until it does.
- Pour into a clean jar (you may use a glass jar). This isn't a recipe for preserving food. Refrigerate for up to a month before using.

Nutrition Information
Calories: 141 kcal, Carbohydrates: 11 g, Protein: 15 g, Fats: 6.5 g

230. Meatless Mexican Frittata (Featuring McCormick Perfect Pinch Mexican Spice)
Prep time: 15 mins, Cook time: 30 mins, Servings: 8
Ingredients
- 1 small diced green pepper
- 1 small diced yellow pepper
- 1 medium diced tomato
- 1 small diced yellow onion
- 1 cup black beans, cooked
- 1 tsp of McCormick Perfect Pinch Mexican Spice
- ½ tsp of baking powder
- 6 eggs, large
- 1 cup of grated Mexican blend cheese
- Greek yogurt (unflavored)& salsa for topping

Instructions
- Preheat the oven to 350 Fahrenheit.
- Coat an oven-proof skillet with cooking spray & place it on medium heat to heat up.
- Put the peppers, onions & tomatoes & cook them for 1-2 mins till they are softened. Toss in the black beans & seasonings.
- In a separate dish, whisk the baking powder & a little amount of egg. Add the remainder of the egg and whisk it in with the fork until it is well absorbed (if you just add baking powder to the egg, it will clump).
- Pour the eggs over the cooked bean mixture/veggies and spread them evenly until they resemble a large, flattened egg pancake.
- Use a wooden spoon to swirl the eggs within the circle gently, but don't touch the sides since you would like them to set. Place the whole pan in the oven for approximately 10 mins, or till the top of the frittata is done & the cheese is melted to your preference after the edges have set.
- Slice & serve while still hot!

Nutrition Information
Calories: 120 kcal, Carbohydrates: 10 g, Protein: 10.1 g, Fats: 7 g

231. Panera Knock-Off: "Something Chicken Stew"
Prep time: 10 mins, Cook time: 5 hr., Servings: 4
Ingredients
- 2 chicken breast tsp-marinated in Italian seasoning
- 6cups chopped assorted vegetables
- 1 tsp of garlic, minced
- 1 tsp of Mediterranean seasoning
- 1 tsp of lemon juice
- 4cups of water
- 1-2 tbsp of tomato paste
- 2 cups quinoa or couscous, cooked
- ¼cup almonds (sliced) for garnish
- Salt & pepper, to taste

Instructions
- Place everything in a crockpot except the tomato paste & cook on low flame for 4 hrs.
- The chicken must be cooked thoroughly meanwhile your return. Transfer it to a chopping board with chopsticks & chop it into the required pieces. Place the chicken in the crockpot once again.
- Check the spices in the broth & make any necessary adjustments. Mix the tomato paste until it is completely dissolved in the boiling liquid. Allow another 35-40 mins to pass.
- To serve, put a tiny quantity of couscous, rice, quinoa, or whatever you're using in the bowl. Serve with a stew side and enjoy with chopped almonds on top.

Nutrition Information
Calories: 137 kcal, Carbohydrates: 9.3 g, Protein: 13.1 g, Fats: 5.4 g

232. Apple-Cinnamon Protein Muffins
Prep time: 10 mins, Cook time: 25 mins, Servings: 16
Ingredients
Dry
- 1cup of oat flour
- 1 cup of soy flour
- ½ cup of vanilla protein powder (any flavor you like)
- 1 tsp of baking powder
- 1 tsp of baking soda
- ½ tsp of salt

Wet
- 1 sweet apple, large (Honeycrisp or Pink Lady, etc.) shredded
- 1 tsp of vanilla
- 1.25 cup of sweetener, no-calorie
- 1 tsp of Cinnamon
- ¼ tsp of nutmeg
- 2 beaten eggs, large
- ¼ cup of milk

Instructions
- Preheat the oven to 350 Fahrenheit.
- If you've oat flour, that's fantastic, and it's simple to create if you don't have one. In the blender, combine a cup of instant oats & whiz till flour forms. Place it in a mixing dish with the remainder of dry items & mix them.
- Add the shredded apple with other wet ingredients in a separate dish, stirring to incorporate.
- Combine the wet & dry ingredients in a mixing bowl. It'll seem that there isn't enough moist material but keep on mixing.
- When it's finished, it must be rather thick. After that, pour the milk & whisk it in. This softens it up (it should be the thickness of cooked oats).
- Fill the cupcake pans three-fourth the way with batter.
- Bake for 18-25 mins, or till a fork inserted in the center comes out dry. Allow time for cooling. You can put almost anything on top of them. On top, enjoy whipped Greek yogurt, cream cheese, or a dollop of peanut butter.

Nutrition Information
Calories: 133 kcal, Carbohydrates: 11.4 g, Protein: 20.1 g, Fats: 7.1 g

233. Crustless Pizza Casserole
Prep time: 15 Mins, Cook time: 35 Mins, Servings:2-3
Ingredients
- 2cups diced veggies (which you like)
- 1 minced clove of garlic
- 1 pound of Italian-style ground meat
- salt & pepper, to taste
- 1& ½ cup of spaghetti sauce or pizza sauce (which you like)

Instructions

- Preheat the oven to 350 Fahrenheit.
- Preheat a pan on a medium flame for 2-3 mins before spraying it with cooking spray or one tbsp of oil. Add the vegetables and cook for 2-3 mins, or till they are tender. Add the garlic cook for another min or two.
- Stir in the ground beef and veggies, splitting it up with the spatula as needed. Cook until the meat is fully cooked. Using a strainer, drain any extra liquid from the meat.
- Reduce the flame to medium-low & toss in the sauce until it is completely combined. Simmer for 5-7 mins, or until the sauce darkened in color. The consistency of the mixture must be saucy, not soupy. Because the vegetables will continue to release liquid as they simmer, you do not want the sauce to be overly liquid. Drain some of it.
- Pour the mixture into an eight-by-eight casserole dish & smooth it out evenly. Now begins the exciting part. Toppings! Like pepperoni & black olives on the pizza, so topped them, as well as grated cheese.
- Like pepperoni & black olives on the pizza, so topped them, well as grated cheese.
- Cooked for approximately 20 mins, long enough for the pepperonis to crisp up a little & the cheese to melt. It is technically done once the cheese has melted, so cook it for as long as you want till it is to your liking!

Nutrition Information
Calories: 125 kcal, Carbohydrates: 12 g, Protein: 20.2 g, Fats: 6.1 g

234. Low-Carb Ramekin Shepherd's Pie
Prep time: 20 mins, Cook time: 30 mins, Servings: 4
Ingredients
- ½ medium finely diced yellow onion
- ½ pound of lean ground meat
- 8 ounces of peas &carrots
- ½bag or 2 cups of frounces cauliflower florets
- 4 ounces of cream of mushroom soup, low-fat
- 2-3 Laughing Cow pieces
- 1/3cup of grated cheddar cheese
- Salt & Pepper, to taste

Instructions
- Preheat the oven to 350 Fahrenheit. Boil some water in a small saucepan.
- Heat a pan on a medium flame for a few mins. Add the onions after spraying them with frying spray. Cook for around 2 mins.
- Brown the ground beef & stir with onions till the meat is thoroughly cooked. If required, drain. Cauliflower florets must be dropped into a kettle of boiling water.
- Stir in the peas & carrots. Then pour the soup & whisk it in. If the soup isn't thick enough to coat the beef, add a quarter cup of milk. Leave the mixture to heat completely before setting it aside.
- Drain & puree the cauliflower florets when cooked (approximately 4-5 mins after coming to the boil). When the florets are still heated, add the Laughing Cow slices. Mix with a spoon till the mix becomes a puree (it may not look precisely like mashed potatoes, but it will bind together & will no longer resemble shredded cauliflower).
- Line a baking sheet with ramekins. One-fourth cup meat/veggie combination ladled in Top with a quarter cup of cauliflower mixture & a sprinkling of grated cheese.
- Bake for 12-15 mins, or till cheese melts &, if desired, browned in ramekins.

Nutrition Information
Calories: 105 kcal, Carbohydrates: 10.9 g, Protein: 12 g, Fats: 5.2 g

235. Peanut Stew
Prep time: 15 mins, Cook time: 40 mins, Servings: 4
Ingredients
- 1 tbsp of olive oil
- 1 small diced yellow onion
- 3 diced tomatoes
- 2 minced cloves of garlic
- 1can or 12-15 ounces of peas& carrots
- ½ tsp of ground cumin
- ½ tsp of turmeric
- ½ tsp of ground coriander
- 1 tsp of garam masala
- 2cups of water
- 1cup of creamy peanut butter
- 4 ounces of tomato paste
- ¼cup of sriracha sauce
- 3cans or 15 ounces of garbanzo beans
- 4cups of baby spinach
- Salt & pepper, to taste

Instructions
- Preheat the soup pot on medium flame until it is hot. Toss in the garlic, olive oil & tomatoes. Cook for 2- 3 mins.
- Stir in the carrots & peas and all the water & spices and reduce the flame to low. Allow the liquid to come to a boil while covered.
- In the mixing bowl, blend peanut butter and tomato paste till fully incorporated. Before putting everything again into the saucepan, spoon part of the vegetable mix into the dish & use it to thin it out.
- Add the spicy sauce and stir thoroughly.
- Stir in the baby spinach & garbanzo beans at the end. (At this stage, if you're using roasted chicken flesh, add it!) Cover the saucepan and cook for 26-30 mins on medium heat.

Nutrition Information
Calories: 107 kcal, Carbohydrates: 10.4 g, Protein: 14.4 g, Fats: 8 g

236. Eggplant Parmesan Casserole
Prep Time: 15 Mins, Cook Time: 45 Mins, Servings: 2-4
Ingredients
- 1medium diced eggplant
- 1small sliced yellow onion
- 1 green chopped pepper
- 2 cups of spaghetti squash
- ½ cup of diced tomatoes
- 1jar Alfredo sauce, light
- 1.5 cup of grated Italian-style cheese

Instructions
- Preheat the oven to 350 Fahrenheit.
- Coat the eggplant, green pepper & onions with nonstick cooking spray, sprinkle with salt, Italian seasoning & pepper, and place on the parchment-lined baking sheet. Roast it for around 25 mins.
- Toss the tomatoes, roasted vegetables & spaghetti squash in a mixing bowl. If desired, season with salt and pepper since this is the greatest method to get flavor into the dish.
- Toss in any sauce you're using until it's fully combined. Garnish with cheese & transfer to a casserole dish. Bake for 20 mins, or until cheese melts & desired brownness is achieved.

Nutrition Information
Calories: 115 kcal, Carbohydrates: 13 g, Protein: 13.6 g, Fats: 5.8 g

237. PB&B Greek Yogurt
Prep time: 20 mins, Cook time: 30 mins, Servings: 4
Ingredients:
- 6 ounces of container Greek yogurt, unflavored
- sweetener, No- calorie (to taste)
- 1 tbsp of peanut butter powder (like PB Fit)
- ½ serving of Blue Diamond Blueberry Almonds

Instructions:
- Combine yogurt, peanut butter powder & sweetener in a mixing dish.
- Almonds are sprinkled on top.
- Also, CRUNCH!

Nutrition Information
Calories: 85 kcal, Carbohydrates: 9 g, Protein: 11 g, Fats: 5 g

238. Cheesy Chicken & Broccoli Bake
Prep time: 15 mins, Cook time: 30 mins, Servings: 2
Ingredients
- 8 ounces of cubed chicken breast
- 2cups of frounceen cauliflower florets
- 1 cup of frounceen broccoli florets
- 8 ounces of reduced-fat cream of chicken soup
- 1 cup grated cheese (which you like)
- ½ cup shredded Parmesan cheese
- onion powder, salt, garlic powder, pepper (to taste)

Instructions
- Preheat the oven to 350 Fahrenheit.
- Preheat a skillet (coated with cooking spray) on medium heat. Put the chicken in the pan & cook until the chicken is done.
- Boil broccoli & cauliflower till tender (approximately 7-10 mins if cooked together), then mash both of them with a potato masher.
- Add the chicken to the mashed broccoli/cauliflower saucepan and stir in the stock. Stir everything together completely.
- Place in a mini-casserole dish & sprinkle with both kinds of cheese. Bake for about 30 mins at 350°F or until cheese is melted to your preference.

Nutrition Information
Calories: 101 kcal, Carbohydrates: 9.9 g, Protein: 12.9 g, Fats: 4.7 g

239. Tilapia Verde
Prep Time: 20 Mins, Cook Time: 30 Mins, Servings: 4
Ingredients
- ¼ cup of water
- ½ sliced onion, small
- 2 cups of baby spinach
- 2 tsp of minced garlic
- ½ yellow squash sliced into halved
- 2 tilapia filets about 4 ounces
- 1 cup of salsa Verde
- Salt & pepper, to taste

Instructions
- Pour water into a skillet on medium flame. Add all of the vegetables & garlic to this hot water.
- It must be quite watery at this time. Remove the lid & cook for another 5 mins on low flame.
- Serve right away or put in the lunch container if you bring it with you. It's that simple!

Nutrition Information
Calories: 145 kcal, Carbohydrates: 11 g, Protein: 23 g, Fats: 7 g

240. Chicken Chorizo Skillet
Prep time: 5 mins, Cook time: 15 mins, Servings: 4
Ingredients
- 3links chorizo sausage casings removed
- 4chicken breasts, boneless plus skinless, cubed
- 1 medium sliced into strips yellow onion
- 1 green sliced into strips bell pepper
- 1 sliced red or orange bell pepper
- 6 beaten eggs
- 2 tsp of garlic, minced
- ¼ tsp of ground cumin
- ¼ tsp of ground coriander
- ¼ tsp of chili powder
- 1 cup grated Mexican blend cheese
- Salt &pepper, to taste

Instructions
- Preheat the oven to broil mode.
- Coat a big, oven-proof skillet with cooking spray & place it on a medium temp to heat.
- Add the chorizo & simmer for approximately 2 mins, occasionally stirring, before adding the chicken (chorizo needs some time to omit some oil). Stir sausage & chicken until both are done thoroughly.
- Sauté the onions, bell peppers, garlic, & seasonings until they are softened. Add roasted potatoes in as well if you're using them.
- Make a hole (well) in the center of the pan, re-spray if necessary, and crack the eggs into it. Before putting them into the veggie/meat combination, fully scramble them with the wooden spoon.
- Sprinkle with cheese & set in the broiler for 1-2 mins, or until the cheese is melted & browned to your liking.

Nutrition Information
Calories: 145 kcal, Carbohydrates: 11 g, Protein: 23 g, Fats: 7 g

241. Thai Shrimp Skillet
Prep time: 60 mins, Cook time: 30 mins, Servings: 4
Ingredients
Shrimp
- 1-pound steamed shrimp
- 1 lime juice
- 1 lime zest
- 2 tbsp of fish sauce
- 2 tbsp of peanut oil
- 2 tsp freshly grated ginger
- 2-3 crushed cloves of garlic

Peanut Sauce
- 6 ounces of coconut milk
- 5 tbsp of Chika PB powder
- 1 tbsp of lime Ponzu sauce
- 1 tbsp of fish sauce
- 2 tbsp of Thai chili garlic sauce
- 2tsp of freshly grated ginger
- 2-3crushed cloves of garlic

The Veggies
- ½ sliced sweet red bell pepper
- ½ sliced sweet orange pepper
- 1medium sliced onion
- ½ diced sweet potato
- 1/3 diced eggplant

Garnish
- cilantro
- crushed peanuts

Instructions
- In a zip-lock storage bag, combine the marination ingredients & the protein. Allow a minimum of 30 mins to marinate.
- Preheat a pan on medium flame, then add the sweet potato & peanut oil (add sweet potato quickly as peanut oil starts to smoke quickly). Stir for 3-4 mins, till it begins to tender, then add the additional veggies & mix, sautéing till they are as tender as you like.
- In a mixing dish, whisk together all of the ingredients for the peanut sauce while the vegetables are cooking. Ensure all peanut powder is blended and there is no dry powder visible!
- Drain the protein from the marination liquid & return it to the skillet, along with peanut sauce, to warm it up.
- Garnish with peanuts & cilantro while still hot.

Nutrition Information
Calories: 115 kcal, Carbohydrates: 10.1 g, Protein: 21.3 g, Fats: 7.0 g

242. Taco Soup
Prep time: 20 mins, Cook time: 20 mins, Servings: 8
Ingredients
Soup
- 1small diced yellow onion
- 1small diced green pepper
- 1 minced clove of garlic
- 1 pound of lean ground meat
- 1pack of taco seasoning
- 1 tsp of cumin
- 1 tsp of coriander
- 1 tsp of onion powder

- A pinch of cayenne peppers
- Salt & pepper, to taste
- 4 ounces of tomatoes & chiles
- 1 cup of prepared salsa
- 10-ounce s black beans
- 2 cups of chicken broth or water

Garnishments (optional)
- sliced jalapenos
- Greek yogurt, unflavored
- grated Mexican blend cheese

Instructions
- Coat a saucepan liberally with cooking spray & place it on medium flame to heat up. Sautee the green pepper & onion until tender, approximately 3 mins. Sauté for another 1 or 2 after adding the garlic.
- Brown, the ground beef, stirring in the pepper, onions & garlic while it cooks. If necessary, drain the meat mixture. Stir in spices or taco seasoning (not both) well.
- Combine the tomatoes, salsa, chiles & black beans in a large mixing bowl. Add the water or broth until the desired liquid level is reached. You like soup, but you do not want your seasonings to be too watered down.
- Reduce the flame to medium cover& bring to a boil. Remove from the heat & set aside for some time, covered, before serving in dishes with preferred toppings!

Nutrition Information
Calories: 103 kcal, Carbohydrates: 8.9 g, Protein: 11 g, Fats: 10 g

243. Protein Pumpkin Bread
Prep time: 10 mins, Cook time: 25 mins, Servings: 8

Ingredients
- 1can or 15 ounces of pumpkin puree
- 1cup of Splenda (or no-calorie sweetener equivalent to 1 cup of sugar)
- ¼ cup of Touraine Brown Sugar Cinnamon syrup
- 1 tbsp unsalted butter
- 2 eggs
- 1 tsp of vanilla extract
- 1 tsp of pumpkin pie spice
- 1cup of Big Train baking mix, low carb
- 1 tsp of baking soda
- ½ tsp of salt

Instructions
- Preheat the oven to 350 Fahrenheit.
- Use a hand mixer on medium, thoroughly incorporate pumpkin, syrup, sweetener& butter in a mixing dish. One at one time, crack the eggs, ensuring that the first is well mixed in the mixture before adding the second one. Mix in the pumpkin pie spice & vanilla once more.
- Sieve the baking soda, pancake mix & waffle mix & salt into the pumpkin mix & beat on medium until everything is well blended.
- Prepare a mini-loaf pan or brush it with cooking spray (with a little flour in it). If you do not have a mini-loaf pan, you can use a regular cupcake pan or loaf pan. Spoon the batter evenly into each hole, then smack the pan on the counter to disperse the batter & eliminate any trapped air.
- Bake for about 20-25 mins at 350°F, till a wooden skewer in the center comes out moist. Place the pan on a cooling rack & allow it to cool completely before removing the little loaves. Cover each loaf in the plastic wrapping & store in the refrigerator till ready to serve. This freeze well, but. Wrap them separately and carefully before freezing.

Nutrition Information
Calories: 109 kcal, Carbohydrates: 12.6 g, Protein: 13 g, Fats: 6.4 g

244. Super Juicy Meatloaf
Prep Time: 20 Mins, Cook Time: 30 Mis, Servings: 4

Ingredients
- 1 pound of lean ground meat
- 1 cup of diced onions
- 1 cup of grated zucchini
- Any other sliced veggies you want
- ¼ tsp of salt
- ¼ tsp of pepper
- ½ tsp of garlic salt
- ¼ tsp of red pepper flakes

Sauce
- 1 tbsp of Worcestershire sauce
- 1 cup of ketchup, low sugar
- ¼ steak sauce

Instructions
- Preheat the oven to 350 Fahrenheit.
- In a mixing bowl, add the meat, zucchini, onions & any other vegetables you are using, and the spices. Mix in the egg & the spoonful of Worcestershire sauce (or steak).
- For an entire loaf, bake for around 40 mins, and it should only take roughly 30 mins to make little loaves.
- Check the doneness of beef by my general method: put your finger into the thickest section of the loaf. It is not done if it feels spongy under the skin, and when you push on it, it should feel firm. Whether you are unsure if it is done after the stipulated time, switch off the oven & leave the loaf to cool in the oven.
- Remove the loaf from the oven and set it aside to cool for approximately 10 mins before slicing. Meanwhile, stir steak & ketchup (or Worcestershire sauce) together in a bowl until fully incorporated.
- Drizzle the sauce over the loaf & cut! If you're using tiny loaves, you may either place it on each loaf or lay it out in a dish on the tabletop for guests to pick what they want.

Nutrition Information
Calories: 131 kcal, Carbohydrates: 10.6 g, Protein: 14.6 g, Fats: 8 g

245. Crustless Pumpkin Cheesecake (with Sugar-free Salted Caramel Pecan Topping)
Prep time: 20 mins, Cook time: 30 mins, Servings: 4

Ingredients
Cheesecake
- 16 ounces of cream cheese, low-fat
- 6 ounces of Greek yogurt, unflavored
- 15 ounces of pumpkin puree does not have pie filling
- 2 eggs, large
- 3/4 cup of sweetener, no-calorie
- 1 tsp of pumpkin pie spice
- 1 tsp of pure vanilla extract

Topping
- 2 tbsp of butter
- 2 cups of pecans, chopped
- ½ cup of caramel sauce, sugar-free
- ¼ tsp of course sea salt

Instructions
- Arrange the oven racks so that one is at the base & the other one is in the middle. Preheat the oven to 325mFahrenheit & bring a big pot of water to a boil.
- Combine Greek yogurt & cream cheese in a mixing dish. Using a hand mixer, beat on medium till well blended.
- Blend in the pumpkin, sugar, vanilla, protein (if using) & pie spice until well blended.
- In another dish, whisk the egg whites till soft peaks form (3-4 mins on medium).
- CAREFULLY pour the egg whites into the cream cheese mixture & lightly fold them in using a wooden spoon or scraper (folding is lightly turning the mixture over on itself over & over again). Don't use the hand mixer & don't hurry!
- Spray a baking tray with cooking spray. Cover the bottom of a springform pan with baking parchment if you use it. Remove the batter from the bowl & spread it out evenly.
- Place a big baking dish on the lowest shelf of the oven & fill it halfway with boiling water. Place the baking dish on the middle oven rack.
- Bake for about 35 mins, or till the cheesecake appears to be largely set (it'll start to pull away from the sides of the

baking dish and will appear firm). Switch off the oven, push the door open, and leave the cheesecake inside until the oven cools down, which should take around 20–25 mins. If you're a perfectionist, ensure the top is completely flat! There will be some cracking, and that occurs. Tiny cracks are usually a sign that the oven should be turned off.
- Take out the cheesecake from the oven & place it on the cooling rack to cool completely before covering & refrigerating; 2-3 hrs will be enough. If you're using a springform pan, slide a knife along the edge of the cheesecake before removing it.

Nutrition Information
Calories: 138 kcal, Carbohydrates: 15 g, Protein: 11.4 g, Fats: 7.7 g

246. Mocha Toffee Protein Pie
Prep Time: 20 Mins, Cook Time: 30 Mins, Servings: 4
Ingredients
Pie filling
- 2-3 tsp of espresso flavored protein
- 1.5 ounces of box chocolate pudding mix, sugar-free
- 1.5 cup of skim milk
- 3 tbsp of Torani English Toffee syrup, sugar-free

Pie crust
- 2 cups crushed Fiber One Original cereal
- 2 tbsp of butter
- 1 tbsp of sweetener, no-calorie
- 2 tbsp of English Toffee syrup, sugar-free

Instructions
Make pie filling
- In a bowl, add two-three scoops of the protein powder (it doesn't matter how large the scoop is, as long as the protein is a minimum of 20g per scoop) with a pudding mix (sugar-free) & protein & stir well. Please keep in mind that the more protein you use, the thicker the filling will become. Then pour in 1 & half cups milk (cow's milk is excellent for pudding). Use a hand mixer or whisk to mix it. Do what you need to do! Simply mix till it begins to set.

Make crust
- A crumb crust may be made from a variety of Ingredients. I used to make cookies out of smashed graham crackers. Fiber One Original cereal is now my go-to cereal since it's somewhat sweet, easy to flavor, and has enough fiber to help balance the entire carload. You may, however, use whatever cereal you choose. If you are okay with it, you can also use graham crackers (but keep in mind that you'll be consuming a lot of carbohydrates & sugar). To create a crumb crust, mix two cups of whatever crumb you are using with roughly 2 tbsp of low-calorie baking spread or butter. Using the hands, mash them until they resemble wet sand. Then put the batter into a pie crust & bake for about 10-15 mins at 350 degrees Fahrenheit, or until firm.

Make topping
- As the pie crust has cooled & the filling has chilled, spoon the filling over the crust & level it out completely, the toppings! Serve with whipped cream (fat-free) or with sugar & some kind of decoration (cocoa powder, shavings, chocolate, etc.). Pretty food appeals to me. Refrigerate till ready to be served!

Nutrition Information
Calories: 119 kcal, Carbohydrates: 10.1 g, Protein: 6.2 g, Fats: 8.1 g

247. Bacon-Ranch Chicken Salad
Prep time: 10 mins, Cook time: 0 mins, Servings: 2-3
Ingredients
- 1 tbsp of Greek yogurt, fat-free
- 2 tbsp of ranch dressing, low-fat
- 1 tsp of mayo
- 1/8 tsp of onion powder
- 1/8 tsp of garlic powder
- 1/8 tsp of black pepper
- ½ tsp of hot sauce
- 8 ounces of canned chicken
- 1 tbsp of bacon bits
- 1 tbsp of scallions, chopped

Instructions
- Combine the yogurt, dressing, mayonnaise, spices, & spicy sauce in the mixing bowl.
- Take a bite of it. Use the garlic, onion powder & salt because one spoonful of ranch dressing adds without overpowering. As a result, add these spices to it. You might also simply utilize some dry ranch mix & a little extra Greek yogurt.
- Taste and adjust seasonings as needed. Mix in the chicken flesh completely. Mix in the bacon chunks once more.
- Put in the refrigerator till ready to serve!

Nutrition Information
Calories: 145 kcal, Carbohydrates: 11 g, Protein: 23 g, Fats: 7 g

248. WLS-Friendly Shamrock Shake
Prep time: 5 mins, Cook time: 0 mins, Servings: 1
Ingredients
- 4 ounces of milk (which you use)
- 1 serving of vanilla protein
- 2 tbsp of Davinci Peppermint Paddy syrup, sugar-free
- 5-8 drops of green food coloring
- 3-5 ice cubes
- 2 tbsp of whipped topping, low-cal
- 4-5 chocolate chips, sugar-free

Instructions
- Combine the milk, syrup, protein, syrup & food coloring. Blend for approximately 45 secs, or till the mixture is foamy.
- Blend in the food coloring & ice cubes till the ice is pulverized. If desired, top with chocolate chips & whipped topping.

Nutrition Information
Calories: 102 kcal, Carbohydrates: 10 g, Protein: 12.3 g, Fats: 5.3 g

249. Taco Casserole
Prep time: 30 mins, Cook time: 30 mins, Servings: 9
Ingredients
- 1 pound ground turkey
- 1 small, diced zucchini
- 1 small diced yellow onion
- 1 minced clove of garlic
- 1 pck of taco seasoning
- 10 ounces of black beans, drained & rinsed
- 8 ounces of canned refried beans, fat-free
- 8 ounces of canned tomatoes & chiles
- 2 cups of Mexican blend cheese

Instructions
- Preheat the oven to 350 Fahrenheit.
- Coat a pan with cooking spray and place it on medium flame to heat it. Sauté the vegetables with garlic till tender. Any extra liquid should be drained & transferred to the bowl.
- Brown, the ground beef, drain, & combine with the canned beans, chilies & tomatoes in the same dish.
- Stir in the taco seasoning completely, then pour into a 13-by-9-inch casserole dish.
- Evenly distribute refried beans (fat-free) on top (it may be simpler if you warm them in the microwave-safe dish for a min or two).
- Sprinkle with cheese & bake for about 30 mins at 350 degrees, or till the cheese is melted & slightly browned.
- Set aside for about 10-15 mins to cool before cutting & serving.

Nutrition Information
Calories: 114 kcal, Carbohydrates: 12.2 g, Protein: 23 g, Fats: 8.1 g

250. Classic Click Frap
Prep time: 20 mins, Cook time: 30 mins, Servings: 4

Ingredients
- 8 ounces of skim milk
- 1 scoop of Click
- 1 scoop chocolate whey
- 2 tbsp of Torani chocolate syrup, sugar-free
- 6-8 ice cubes
- 2 tbsp of either fat-free or sugar-free whipped cream

Instructions
- In the blender, combine everything except the whip page & ice, & whiz until smooth. Add whiz & ice once more. Enjoy in a lovely glass or pickle jar or mason jar.

Nutrition Information
Calories: 136 kcal, Carbohydrates: 13 g, Protein: 21 g, Fats: 6.1 g

251. Four Cheese Mashed Cauliflower
Prep time: 20 mins, Cook time: 30 mins, Servings: 4

Ingredients
- 1 head of cauliflower, large slice into florets
- 2-4 ounces of 3 different kinds of cheese
- 1 beaten egg
- 6 ounces of Greek yogurt
- 2 tbsp of melted light butter spread (like Blue Bonnet Light)
- ¼ cup of whole wheat breadcrumbs
- ½ cup of shredded Parmesan cheese
- Dashes of paprika, onion powder, salt, garlic powder & pepper.

Instructions
- Cauliflower florets should be cooked until soft, then drained & mashed.
- Except for the paprika, mix in cheeses, yogurt, & any spices you desire (keep cauliflower in the pan when you do this). Stir well before adding the egg.
- Fill a thirteen-by-nine casserole dish halfway with the mixture.
- Combine the breadcrumbs, butter & Parmesan cheese in the mixing bowl.
- Top with a dab or two of spread & paprika evenly over the cauliflower mixture.
- Preheat oven to 350°F & bake for 20 mins, or till top is attractively browned.

Nutrition Information
Calories: 125 kcal, Carbohydrates: 17 g, Protein: 13 g, Fats: 8 g

252. Rendition of Taco Soup
Prep time: 20 mins, Cook time: 30 mins, Servings: 4

Ingredients:
- 1 large, diced onion
- 1 diced green pepper
- 1 minced clove of garlic
- 1 pound of ground meat of (your choice)
- 1 can each of:
- Dark red kidney beans
- Light red kidney beans
- Black beans
- 2 cans tomatoes & chiles
- 1 pack taco seasoning
- Optional: A dash of either ground chipotle powder or cayenne pepper if you want spicy food
- Possible toppings): grated taco-blend cheese, Greek yogurt (unflavored), red onions, black olives, crumbled whole wheat tortillas.

Instructions:
- This follows the same steps as preparing evening chili. Spray a saucepan with nonstick cooking spray & place it on medium flame to heat it. Sauté the onions & peppers till they are tender.
- Add the meat to the pan & brown it fully, adding in peppers & onions. You might have to remove the liquid of the meat mixture afterward, based on the fat content of the ground beef.
- Drain & rinse the beans in a strainer (this eliminates most of the salt), then add them to the saucepan. Put the tomatoes and chilies in there as well. Combine everything in a mixing bowl. You must have about a pretty much of liquid in there. If not, don't worry; the tomatoes will release more water while the dish simmers.
- Mix in the taco seasoning & any other Ingredients. (If it does not have a deep enough taco flavor for you, add more onion powder, cumin, chili powder, coriander, garlic powder to taste.) You may also use an additional package of taco seasoning, but keep in mind that this will increase the salt content, so if you are on a low sodium diet, you might like to hold off!).
- Reduce the flame to a low setting & cover the pan. Cook, mixing every 10 mins or so, for approximately 30 mins.
- Serve immediately with the toppings of your choice.

Nutrition Information
Calories: 107 kcal, Carbohydrates: 10 g, Protein: 7 g, Fats: 4.9 g

253. Green Apple Hot Drink
Prep time: 20 mins, Cook time: 30 mins, Servings: 4

Ingredients
- 10-12 ounces of boiling water (based on your cup size)
- 1 pack of green tea (which you like)
- 1 pack of apple cider mix, sugar-free
- Optional: sweetener, no-calorie

Instructions
- Remove tea bag from boiling water after a min or two.
- Pour in the cider mixture, stir well, & enjoy!

Nutrition Information
Calories: 111 kcal, Carbohydrates: 13.3 g, Protein: 15 g, Fats: 6.1 g

254. Shrimp Faux Fried Rice
Prep time: 20 mins, Cook time: 30 mins, Servings: 4

Ingredients:
- About 1.5 cups of veggies (whatever you like)
- 1 bag of frounceen cauliflower florets (don't thaw!)
- 1 can (small) of baby shrimp, drained.
- 2 beaten eggs OR ½ cup of Egg Beaters
- 1 packet of fried rice seasoning OR ½ tsp each: onion & garlic powder with ¼ tsp of black pepper (crushed)
- ¼ cup of reduced-sodium soy sauce

Instructions:
- Put the cauliflower after the wok is heated (the cooking spray will start to generate a little bit of smoke).
- When the cauliflower is soft (approximately 4 mins, but keep an eye on it), mash it with a masher directly inside the wok to achieve an even texture. As shortly as you're able, puree the cauliflower, and do not wait till it's "soft."
- Then add the remainder of the vegetables and the Little' baby shrimp, & start cooking about 3 mins or so. Make sure the minced cauliflower & vegetables are well combined.
- After that, set everything aside for a moment, sprinkle the empty area with extra non-stick spray, then crack the egg into it. Before adding it to the vegetable mixture, scramble it.
- Finally, add the seasonings and soy sauce to the mixture & stir well. Take out the wok from the flame & take the mixture into the dish right away.

Nutrition Information
Calories: 135 kcal, Carbohydrates: 14.7 g, Protein: 11 g, Fats: 5 g

255. Cajun Scramble
Prep time: 20 mins, Cook time: 30 mins, Servings: 4

Ingredients:
- 1 ounce of diced onions
- 1 ounce of diced green peppers
- 1 slice of chopped Cajun chicken breast lunch meat
- 1/8 tsp of cumin
- 1/8 tsp of coriander
- 1/8 tsp of garlic powder
- black pepper (crushed), to taste

- ¼ cup of egg substitute or 1 beaten egg
- For topping; 1 ounce of your favorite grated cheese (like taco blender salsa)

Instructions:
- Spray a pan with cooking spray & set it aside to heat it on low flame.
- Cook for approximately 2 mins after adding the peppers & onions. Add the chicken & seasonings & heat until the onions begin to caramelize & the chicken develops a crust.
- If the pan has become dry, spray it with cooking spray before adding the eggs. Gently incorporate the eggs into the vegetable mixture till it is fully cooked.
- Place on a dish & sprinkle with cheese.

Nutrition Information
Calories: 116 kcal, Carbohydrates: 14.1 g, Protein: 13.3 g, Fats: 6 g

256. Chunky Monkey Protein Baked Oatmeal
Prep time: 15 mins, Cook time: 30 mins, Servings: 4
Ingredients:
- 1.5 cups oatmeal
- 3 scoops of chocolate protein
- 2 pinches salt
- 4 tbsp of cocoa powder, unsweetened (Nik Note: four tbsp also equal to ¼ cup)
- 1/3 cup Splenda
- 2 eggs
- 1.5 cups milk
- ¼ cup PB2
- ¼ cup peanut butter
- ¼ cup of aloha chocolate syrup, sugar-free (Davin/Toranici-style syrup, not Hershey's)
- 2 ripe bananas, sliced

Instructions:
- Preheat the oven to 350 Fahrenheit.
- Combine oats, protein, cocoa powder, salt, & Splenda in a mixing bowl (if using PB2 instead of peanut butter & banana pudding instead of bananas, do so now).
- Combine milk, syrups, eggs & peanut butter, if used, in a separate dish.
- Combine the wet Ingredients & dry Ingredients in the mixing bowl and combine well. After the mixture has been mixed, add the banana slices.
- Spread to a casserole dish (you may use eight-by-eight inches or whatever you choose). Keep in mind that the thinner the oats pieces are, the bigger the dish).
- Bake the backed oatmeal for 25 mins and oatmeal bars for 30 mins. Allow it to cool fully before slicing or serving.

Nutrition Information
Calories: 120 kcal, Carbohydrates: 12 g, Protein: 15.1 g, Fats: 7.1 g

257. Peaches & Cream Protein Baked Oatmeal
Prep time: 10 mins, Cook time: 25 mins, Servings: 2
Ingredients:
- 1.5 cup of quick oats
- 1/8 tsp of salt
- 1/3 cup of sweetener, no-calorie
- 2 scoops of protein powder
- 1.5 cup of milk
- 2 beaten eggs, beaten
- ½ bag of frounceen peaches
- 1-ounce cubed cream cheese
- ¾ cup of Ideal Brown Sugar substitute
- 3/4 cup of flour
- 1 tbsp of water
- 1.5 tbsp of cinnamon
- 1.4 cup of softened butter

Instructions:
- Preheat the oven to 350 Fahrenheit.
- Combine the oats, sweetener, salt & protein powder in a mixing dish.
- Mix in the milk, peaches & cubed cream cheese until well combined.
- Bake for about 12-15 mins, or till set & sides are browned, in a casserole dish (eight-by-eight inches).
- Allow cooling fully before slicing. When refrigerated, these make excellent breakfast bars, or you may reheat them up in the microwave oven for 15 secs or so.

Nutrition Information
Calories: 112 kcal, Carbohydrates: 13.7 g, Protein: 14 g, Fats: 9 g

258. Shrimp & Quinoa
Prep time: 15 mins, Cook time: 40 mins, Servings: 3
Ingredients:
- ¼ cup Canadian bacon, diced
- 2 -3 cloves of garlic, minced
- 1 diced onion
- ½ chopped green bell pepper
- One ¼ ½-ounce of diced petite- tomatoes, no-salt
- ¼ cup of dry white wine
- 2 tbsp of plain Greek-style yogurt, nonfat
- 1tsp of hot sauce
- ¼ tsp of salt
- 1ounce of shrimp with tails, peeled & deveined, with tails on
- ¾ cup of uncooked quinoa
- 3 cups of hot water
- (Optional) for garnish 1 tbsp, fresh chives, chopped

Instructions:
- In a nonstick pan, cook the bacon till crisp on medium heat. Remove the bacon from the pan and place it on a platter. Combine the garlic, bell peppers & onions in a large mixing bowl. Cook, often stirring, for approximately 8 mins or until the veggies are soft.
- Bring the tomatoes, hot sauce, wine, yogurt & salt to the boil, scraping the browned pieces from the base of the pan as needed. Reduce the flame to low and cook, uncovered, for 6 -8 mins, or till the flavors have mixed & the sauce has thickened. Toss the bacon back into the skillet. Put the shrimp & heat for 1- 2 mins, or until they become brilliant pink & are done through.
- Meanwhile, toast the quinoa in the cast-iron pan for approximately a min. Slowly mix the water & quinoa after adding the boiling water. Reduce the flame to low and continue to cook for another 7-10 mins, or till the quinoa is completely cooked. Remove the pan from heat.
- So over quinoa, spoon the shrimp mix. If preferred, finish with a sprinkling of chives.

Nutrition Information
Calories: 121 kcal, Carbohydrates: 11.3 g, Protein: 14.1 g, Fats: 7 g

259. Baked Protein Oatmeal Cinnamon Raisin
Prep time: 15 mins, Cook time: 30 mins, Servings: 2
Ingredients:
- 1/2 cup of quick oats
- 1/3 cup of sweetener, no-calorie (Splenda)
- 1/8 tsp of salt
- ¼ cup of Torani Brown Sugar Cinnamon syrup
- Up to ½ tsp or more cinnamon if you like it
- 1.5 cup of milk
- 2 beaten eggs
- 2 scoops of protein powder (Any powder, like vanilla, any whey, etc.)
- 1/3 cup of natural raisins (like Sun-Maid)

Instructions:
- Preheat the oven to 350 Fahrenheit.
- Combine the oats, sweetener & salt in a mixing dish.
- In a separate dish, whisk together the syrup, milk, cinnamon, eggs, & protein powder till fully blended (there must be no lumps of protein powder).
- Stir the liquid ingredients into the oat mixture well.
- Finally, add the raisins & stir to combine.
- Spray a square casserole dish (eight-by-eight inches) with cooking spray & pour the batter into it. Bake for15-20

mins, or till the oatmeal is firm & the sides are golden brown.
- Allow cooling completely before cutting.

Nutrition Information
Calories: 113 kcal, Carbohydrates: 13 g, Protein: 10.2 g, Fats: 9.9 g

260. Flourless Coconut Macaroons
Prep time: 10 mins, Cook time: 25 mins, Servings: 2-3
Ingredients:
- 1 egg white, large
- 3/4 cup of sweetener, no-calorie (like Splenda)
- 3 cups of coconut, unsweetened
- 2 tsp of coconut extract
- ¼ cup of chocolate chips, sugar-free

Instructions
- Preheat the oven to 350 Fahrenheit.
- Whip the egg white for 3 mins in the bowl until it is nice and fluffy.
- Add a 3/4 cup of sugar at a time, whisking after each transfer into the egg whites. As you add additional sweetness, the egg white mix should stiffen. Whip in the extract once more.
- Using the baking spatula, gently fold in the coconuts. You're carefully folding the batter back into itself to avoid deflating the egg whites. GENTLY!
- Stir in the chocolate chips once the coconut has been thoroughly mixed into egg white batter.
- Drop heaping spoonful of the batter onto a baking paper-lined baking tray. It's not going to hold together, and that's all right. Simply place everything in a little mound & make sure it is all near each other.
- Bake for 10 mins, or until sides are browned & cookie is firm. Before eating, remove from the oven & cool.

Nutrition Information
Calories: 137 kcal, Carbohydrates: 9 g, Protein: 10 g, Fats: 5.6 g

261. Banana Bread Recipe
Prep time: 10 mins, Cook time: 25mins, Servings: 6
Ingredients:
- 3 bananas, over-ripe
- ½ – ¾ cup of sweetener (no-calorie)
- 2 eggs, large
- 2 tsp of pumpkin pie spice
- 2 tsp of vanilla extract
- ½ cup of Quest Banana Flavored Protein powder, vanilla, unflavored
- ½ cup of soy flour or almond meal
- 1 tsp of baking powder
- ½ tsp of salt
- 1 cup of chopped walnuts

Instructions:
- Preheat the oven to 350 Fahrenheit.
- In the meantime, peel the bananas & mash them in a large dish.
- Mix in the sweetener, pie spice & extract completely. Add the eggs one at a time, fully mixing the first one before pouring the second.
- Combine the baking powder, protein powder, salt & almond or soy flour in another bowl.
- Mix the dry components into the wet items well. It will be a THICK mixture.
- Finally, toss in walnuts & stir well.
- Spray a mini loaf pan or standard loaf pan with cooking spray. The surplus batter was then split among the slots.
- Bake for about 15-20 mins, or until the top is golden brown & the edges are crisp.

Nutrition Information
Calories: 348 kcal, Carbohydrates: 25 g, Protein: 27 g, Fats: 17.41 g

262. Christmas Cookie Protein Shake
Prep time: 10 mins, Cook time: 15 mins, Servings: 1
Ingredients
- 8ounces of milk
- 1serving of vanilla protein powder
- 2 tbsp of butterscotch instant pudding mix, sugar-free
- 2 tbsp of cinnamon brown sugar syrup, sugar-free (Torani)

Instructions
- In the blender, combine all ingredients & blend for approximately a min, or till smooth & creamy. Blend in the ice till it is completely smooth.
- Combine the dry ingredients in a cup with approximately an oz of room milk to make it hot. Stir well to ensure that no lumps remain. Once all of the lumps have been removed, whisk in the remaining milk & microwave for 30 secs at a time till it reaches the required temperature.
- Garnish with decorative elements & whipped cream, if desired. Then it's time to SLURP!

Nutrition Information
Calories: 79 kcal, Carbohydrates: 5 g, Protein: 9 g, Fats: 5.4 g

263. Chicken & Rice
Prep time: 20 mins, Cook time: 30 mins, Servings: 6
Ingredients:
- 4 cups of an assortment of diced veggies (which you like)
- Either the remnants of 1 chicken carcass or two large chicken breasts
- ½ salt, garlic powder, black pepper, onion powder plus 1 bay leaf
- 3 cups of water
- 1 can cream of mushroom soup, low-fat
- A batch of cauliflower rice

Instructions:
- Sauté vegetables till tender in a big saucepan coated with cooking spray.
- Reduce the heat to low (if you have got an electric oven, like two or three settings) & cook for 1 hr with the chicken, spices & water, or carcass & chicken.
- Take the bones from the chicken carcass (the flesh should have come off) & discard them. Pull the meat apart by 2 forks if using chicken breasts. Discard the bay leaf & taste & adjust spices as needed.
- Stir in the soup, then cook for another 16-20 mins on low flame.
- Over cauliflower rice, serve.

Nutrition Information
Calories: 103 kcal, Carbohydrates: 6.2 g, Protein: 12.5 g, Fats: 5.7 g

Chapter 4: Dinner Recipes

1. Meatballs with Walnut Pomegranate Sauce
Prep Time: 15 Mins, Cook Time: 15 Mins, Servings: 4
Ingredients
Meatballs
- 1 lb ground turkey
- ½ cup of onion grated
- ½ cup chopped parsley fresh finely
- ½ tsp coriander ground
- 1 lime juiced & zested
- 1 tsp salt
- 2 tbsp olive oil

Pomegranate Sauce
- 2 tbsp olive oil
- ½ tsp grated onion
- 2 minced garlic cloves
- ½ tsp ginger grated
- ¾ cup walnuts finely chopped
- ½ tsp cumin
- ¼ tsp salt
- ¼ tsp black pepper
- 2 cups of pomegranate juice
- ¼ cup of pomegranate molasses
- 1 lime juiced & zested

Instructions
Meatballs
- Salt & pepper the turkey mixture, add coriander, onion, parsley, lime zest, & juice. The mixture should be well-combined by kneading it together.
- Set aside golf-ball racquetballs of beef for later use.
- Place paper towels on a dish.
- Bring the skillet to high heat & coat it with oil. Cook the meatballs for three Mins on each side until they're well browned. Three Mins is the maximum cooking time. Using paper towels, pat the meatballs dry.

Sauce
- Warm the oil in a large saucepan over medium heat. Make a sauce using onion, garlic, & ginger. Three Mins of cooking time is sufficient to soften the onion.
- Sauté the walnuts for a further 3 Mins. Add salt & pepper to the mixture. Pomegranate juice & molasses, respectively, should be added to the mixture. Add one lime juice and zest. Increase the seasoning to your liking.
- Bring the sauce to a simmer. Cover the meatballs with sauce & re-add them to the pan. Cook for a further three Mins with the lid on the pan.
- Serve over a grain of your choice while it's still warm. Adding pomegranate seeds & cilantro to the dish elevates the visual appeal, but it isn't required.

Nutrition Information
Calories: 447 kcal, Carbohydrates: 16 g, Protein: 31 g, Fat: 31 g

2. Herb Roasted Zucchini and Carrots
Prep Time: 15 Mins, Cook Time: 20 Mins, Servings: 1
Ingredients
- 3 cups of zucchini sliced
- 1 cup sliced yellow squash
- 2 cups sliced carrots
- 1 tbsp fresh, chopped oregano
- 2 tbsp fresh thyme leaves
- ½ tsp sea or kosher salt
- ¼ tsp black pepper
- 1 & ½ tbsp olive oil extra virgin

Instructions
- Preheat the oven to 425°.
- Vegetables should be marinated in olive oil with salt, herbs, and pepper in a dish before being served.
- After 20-25 Mins, the veggies should be crisp-tender yet brown and caramelized in spots.
- Serve & enjoy your meal!

Nutrition Information
Calories: 94 kcal, Carbohydrates: 11 g, Protein: 2 g, Fat: 5 g

3. Cheesy Stuffed Mushrooms
Prep Time: 5 Mins, Cook Time: 10 Mins, Servings: 2
Ingredients
- 8 oz diced mozzarella cheese
- 12 stems removed brown mushrooms
- ½ tsp olive oil

Crispy Topping
- ¼ cup panko breadcrumbs whole wheat
- 3 tbsp grated parmesan cheese
- 1 tbsp rosemary dried
- 1 tbsp parsley dried
- 1 tbsp basil dried
- 1 tbsp dill dried
- 1 small chopped finely red pepper
- ½ tsp salt kosher
- 1 zested lemon

Instructions
- The oven should be preheated to 350°F.
- Make sure all of the mushrooms on a lined tray are facing up.
- Every mushroom cap should have a cheese cube inserted inside the middle.
- Top every mushroom with a generous portion of a crispy topping mixture, which is made by combining the ingredients in a bowl.
- Bake for around 8-10 Mins, or unless the crust becomes golden brown, some balsamic vinegar drizzled over the top.
- Before serving, take out of the oven & brush with some olive oil.

Nutrition Information
Calories: 158 kcal, Carbohydrates: 8 g, Protein: 11 g, Fat: 10 g

4. Lemon and Thyme Chicken Salad
Prep Time: 15 Mins, Cook Time: 30 Mins, Servings: 2
Ingredients
- 1 juiced lemon
- 1 tbsp garlic minced
- 1 tbsp olive oil
- 2 tbsp thyme chopped fresh
- to taste salt
- to taste black pepper
- 1 lb chicken breast skinless & boneless
- 4 cups of arugula
- 1 sliced red onion
- 1 cup diced cucumber
- ¼ cup cheese feta

Creamy Thyme Dressing
- ¼ cup Greek yogurt fat-free
- 1 tsp garlic minced
- ½ tsp black pepper ground
- 1 tbsp thyme fresh
- 2 tbsp juice lemon
- 1 tbsp honey

Instructions
- A bowl should be used to combine all of the ingredients.
- Pour your lemon juice mixture over the chicken within the baking dish & bake for 30 Mins. Allow it to marinate for around 20-30 Mins, making sure it's well covered.

- Make sure you've got your oven on.
- After 30 Mins of baking, remove the chicken and turn it over.
- In the meanwhile, mix the dressing ingredients within a bowl.
- Combine red onion, arugula, & cucumber with dressing.
- Slice your chicken after it has rested for approximately five Mins.
- Layer chicken & feta on top of the salad, then drizzle the dressing on top.

Nutrition Information
Calories: 367 kcal, Carbohydrates: 15 g, Protein: 23 g, Fat: 25 g

5. Baked Cranberry Glazed Chicken Wings
Prep Time: 10 Mins, Cook Time: 45 Mins, Servings: 2
Ingredients
Chicken
- 2 lb drumettes chicken
- 2 tbsp oil avocado
- ½ tsp salt kosher
- 1 tsp powder garlic
- 1 tsp powder onion
- 1 tsp paprika
- ½ tsp pepper

Cranberry Glaze
- 1 & ½ cups frozen cranberries
- ½ cup of water
- ¼ cup of maple syrup
- 3 tbsp low sodium soy sauce
- 1 tsp minced fresh ginger
- ¼ tsp flakes red pepper

Instructions
- The oven should be preheated to 425°F. Coat the wings with avocado oil before placing them in a big dish.
- Before serving, the last step is adding the paprika, kosher salt, onion powder, garlic powder, & pepper to the mix.
- The wire rack should be placed on your baking sheet. 20 minutes from one side is enough time to get the wings ready for the rest of the meal. Bake for another 15 min on the opposite side, or unless the bread is browned and crispy.
- Your cranberry glaze may be made ahead of time and heated in a saucepan while your wings cook. Add water to a pot and bring it to a boil, then lower the heat & simmer for a few Mins.
- Mix the ingredients with a blender after simmering for 20 mins.
- Toss the wings within cranberry glaze & bake them for another 5-7 Mins in your oven.

Nutrition Information
Calories: 280 kcal, Carbohydrates: 14 g, Protein: 16 g, Fat: 18 g

6. Instant Pot Green Detox Soup
Prep Time:10 Mins, Cook Time: 12 Mins, Servings: 1
Ingredients
- 2 roughly chopped onions
- 2 tbsp oil olive
- 3 cups of roughly chopped zucchini
- 1 lb roughly chopped broccoli
- 1 lb kale dried & rinsed
- 4 cups vegetable broth low sodium
- ½ cup no stems finely chopped parsley
- ½ cup no stems finely chopped cilantro
- ¼ tsp salt
- 1 juice lemon
- 10 finely minced garlic cloves

Instructions
- Add olive oil & chopped onions to the Instant Pot by pressing the Sauté button. The onions should be tender and transparent after 5 Mins of cooking.
- Another 5 Mins of sautéing are required to add zucchini, broccoli, & kale. The kale will darken and wilt somewhat.
- Seal your Instant Pot with the lid closed and add the veggie broth. Set the timer for around 12 Mins at high pressure & use a manual timer.
- Allow the pressure to dissipate for five minutes before gradually releasing the pressure. Make sure the broccoli & zucchini become fork-tender when you remove the cover. They should be able to mix readily.
- It is time to get creative in the kitchen.
- When required, mix in batches in the blender.

Nutrition Information
Calories: 75 kcal, Carbohydrates: 11 g, Protein: 4 g, Fat: 3 g

7. Walking Taco Casserole
Prep Time: 5 Mins, Cook Time: 30 Mins, Servings: 2
Ingredients
- 1 lb turkey ground
- 1 diced medium yellow onion
- 1 tbsp powder chili
- 1 tsp cumin ground
- ¼ tsp salt kosher
- ¼ tsp paprika ground
- ¼ tsp powder garlic
- ¼ tsp oregano dried
- ½ cup of water
- 15 oz canned drained & rinsed black beans
- 4 oz green chilies diced
- 2 oz cream cheese low-fat
- 2 cups pita chips whole-grain
- ½ cup shredded cheese
- 1 cup shredded lettuce
- ½ cup chopped tomatoes
- Salsa & sour cream

Instructions
- Make sure the oven temperature is at 375 deg.
- Using a large pan, brown your ground turkey & chopped onion for approximately 5 Mins, once they're no longer pink.
- Salt, oregano, paprika, & water are added to the chili powder, powdered cumin, salt, & garlic powder. Take a pot and bring it to a boil over medium heat.
- Add the black beans, cream cheese, & green chiles. Remove the skillet from the heat after cream cheese has completely melted.
- Stack the chips & cheese on top of the turkey. Bake for around 20 Mins, covered with foil, unless your cheese is melted and bubbly.
- Before serving, garnish with chopped tomatoes & shredded lettuce. If desired, top with salsa & sour cream.

Nutrition Information
Calories: 320 kcal, Carbohydrates: 20 g, Protein: 35 g, Fat: 12 g

8. Cranberry Seed Bars
Prep Time: 15 Mins, Cook Time: 45 Mins, Servings: 1
Ingredients
- ½ cup fresh cranberries
- 1 tbsp ginger grated
- 1 tbsp zest orange
- ½ cup pepitas
- ½ cup raw sunflower seeds
- ½ cup unsweetened coconut flakes
- ¼ cup seeds chia
- ¼ cup seeds flax
- ¼ cup sesame seeds or hemp hearts
- ½ cup syrup date

Instructions
- A pan should be lined using parchment paper before baking.
- In your food processor, combine ginger, cranberries, & orange zest. Pulse till a paste form. One min. Combine ginger & orange zest into seed mix if you utilize dried cranberries. Toss pepitas & sunflower seeds into a large

dish with the rest of the ingredients. When finished, stir in the cranberry mixture.
- Warm your date syrup within the microwave for around 30 seconds to 1 Min.
- By hand, combine both seed mix & cranberry combination.
- Then, add some date syrup to the mixture & mix well.
- 45 Mins in the oven at 320°. Golden brown is the ideal shade. Slice into 4 parts, then cut each portion into thirds.

Nutrition Information
Calories: 136 kcal, Carbohydrates: 6 g, Protein: 5 g, Fat: 11 g

9. Egg Roll Bowl
Prep Time: 5 Mins, Cook Time: 20 Mins, Servings: 1
Ingredients
- 16 oz fat removed pork loin
- 2 tbsp divided sesame oil
- 1 sliced red onion
- 1 coleslaw mix bag veggie
- 1 tbsp soy sauce
- 2 clove minced garlic
- 1 tbsp minced ginger
- 1 sliced thinly green onion

Sweet Chili Mayo
- ¼ cup mayonnaise low fat
- 2 tbsp sauce sweet chili

Egg Roll Sauce
- 3 tbsp soy sauce
- 2 tbsp hot sauce
- 2 tsp powder garlic
- 3 tsp minced garlic

Instructions
- Set aside a small dish of sweet chili mayo ingredients for later use.
- Brush pork chops with egg roll sauce made from the following ingredients:
- In a medium-sized pan or wok, heat sesame oil over medium-high heat.
- Sear the pork for a few Mins in the pan before removing it from the heat.
- Flip the pig over and cook for another 5 Mins on High heat.
- Cook for a further 5 Mins on the opposite side.
- Set aside for a few Mins before serving.
- Cut into 1" pieces after 2-3 Mins.
- The onion should be sautéed for 5 minutes or transparent within the same skillet.
- Sauté your slaw for the next 3-4 Mins before adding the vegetables.
- For a Min, add ginger, garlic, and soy sauce.
- Return the meat to the pan and allow it to heat up.
- Remove from the stove & top with some green onion & sweet chili mayonnaise, then serve.

Nutrition Information
Calories: 322 kcal, Carbohydrates: 18 g, Protein: 30 g, Fat: 15 g

10. Air-Fried Edamame with Sweet Thai Chili Dressing
Prep Time: 10 Mins, Cook Time: 15 Mins, Servings: 3
Ingredients
- 2 cups shelled edamame
- 1 tsp oil sesame
- 1 juiced Mandarin orange
- 1 tbsp tamari
- 1 tsp grated ginger
- ¼ tsp powder chili
- 1 tsp fruit sweetener monk
- ½ tsp salt

Instructions
- Drain and pat dry the edamame using a paper towel. Gather up the edamame.
- Toss together the tamari, sesame oil, ginger & chili powder inside a cup & stir to combine. Shake well to coat edamame with sauce. Remove any excess liquid from the edamame by scooping it out with a spoon or placing it in a filter.
- Using the "Air Fryer" temperature at 400°F, fry the edamame for 5 Mins, then shake them around. Cook for an additional 5 to 8 Mins based on how dark you would like them to be; at the 10 min mark, keep a close eye on everything to avoid overheating.
- Top with sugar and salt after taking them out of the air fryer.

Nutrition Information
Calories: 79 kcal, Carbohydrates: 8 g, Protein: 6 g, Fat: 3 g

11. Healthy Buffalo Chicken Dip
Prep Time: 5 Mins, Cook Time: 20 Mins, Servings: 1
Ingredients
- 2 cups shredded cooked chicken breast
- ½ cup Greek yogurt non-fat
- 8 oz cottage cheese low fat
- ½ cup crumbles blue cheese
- ½ cup of low-fat shredded cheddar cheese
- ½ cup buffalo sauce red hot

Instructions
- The oven should be preheated at 350 degrees Fahrenheit.
- Pour all of the ingredients into a casserole dish & mix thoroughly.
- It should be hot and bubbling after 20 mins in the oven.

Nutrition Information
Calories: 100 kcal, Carbohydrates: 1 g, Protein: 9 g, Fat: 7 g

12. Authentic Everything Beef Tacos
Prep Time: 10 Mins, Cook Time: 20 Mins, Servings: 1
Ingredients
- 24 small yellow tortillas corn
- 1 full Beef slow cooker
- 1 cup finely chopped red onions
- 1 cup finely chopped cilantro
- 2 limes
- 1 cup Verde salsa
- 1 stemmed, seeded, medium jalapeño

Instructions
- Arrange the tortillas in an even layer on the hot, dry pan or grill one or two at a time. Over one side, heat for 1-2 Mins, then turn and cook for another 30 - 60 seconds. To reheat, place on a platter, cover using a dishtowel.
- It's time to pile the tortillas over top of one another after they're all warmed up. Twelve two-stack stacks must be available, and each tortilla should have the same quantity of shredded meat. Add onions & cilantro to the top.
- As a garnish, sprinkle with some lime wedges & salsa.
- Just before devouring your tacos, squeeze some lime juice over them. The salsa is ready to go.
- Add sliced or chopped jalapenos to your tacos for an extra kick. Enjoy!

Nutrition Information
Calories: 376 kcal, Carbohydrates: 20 g, Protein: 27 g, Fat: 21 g

13. Creamy Tomato Soup
Prep Time: 5 Mins, Cook Time: 25 Mins, Servings: 1
Ingredients
- 1-lb tomatoes
- 2 garlic head
- 2 quartered yellow onions
- ¼ cup chopped basil
- 1 tbsp oil olive
- 1 tbsp vinegar balsamic
- ¼ cup cream light
- ¼ cup grated parmesan

Instructions
- The oven should be preheated at 350 degrees Fahrenheit.

- Toss a baking sheet lined with Al foil with tomatoes, onion, and garlic.
- Drizzle olive oil & balsamic vinegar on top of the salad.
- 20 Mins in the oven
- The food processor may be used to puree the roast after it is removed from the oven
- Process until it's silky-smooth.
- Pour the mixture into a saucepan and bring it to simmer over a moderate flame, stirring constantly.
- Five Mins later, remove from heat and serve.
- Top with some parmesan cheese and the rest of the basil.

Nutrition Information
Calories: 126 kcal, Carbohydrates: 11 g, Protein: 4 g, Fat: 8 g

14. Macadamia Date Butter
Prep Time: 3 Mins, Cook Time: 3 Mins, Servings: 3
Ingredients
- 1 & 1/3 cup of nuts macadamia
- 2/3 cups of pitted dates
- 1 cup of milk almond

Instructions
- In your food processor, combine the nuts & dates. Make hummus-like consistency by adding some almond milk & blending until it's smooth.

Nutrition Information
Calories: 100 kcal, Carbohydrates: 6 g, Protein: 1 g, Fat: 9 g

15. Spicy Fish in Cherry Tomato and Harissa Sauce
Prep Time: 20 Mins, Cook Time: 1 hr, Servings:1
Ingredients
Harissa Sauce
- 2 roasted, peeled, & seeded bell peppers
- 1 sliced & seeded jalapeno
- 1 tsp cumin
- 2 cloves garlic
- 1 tsp coriander
- 2 tbsp olive oil
- 1 tsp turmeric

Tomato Sauce
- 8 smashed garlic cloves
- ¼ cup paste tomato
- 1 thinly sliced jalapeno cored
- 1 tbsp harissa store
- 1 tbsp paprika
- 1 tsp cumin
- 5 cups of tomato cherries
- ½ cup of water
- 4 fish fillets white
- 1 cup of cilantro

Instructions
Harissa Sauce
- Blend or pulse everything except the olive oil till a paste is formed. Make sure the mix is emulsified and smooth by adding a small amount of oil at a time while the engine is running. If not, then add oil & mix well. Refrigerator-safe for 1 week.

Tomato Sauce
- Just three Mins into the process, add garlic, tomato paste, jalapeño, and harissa to the pan. Stir in the paprika & cumin for 1 Min before serving. Add a moderate heat setting.
- 4 cups of fresh cherry tomatoes should be added. Simmer the water for about half an hr, then turn the heat down to low. For around 30 Mins, keep the dish covered.
- Add the remainder of the cup of cilantro and mix, save some sprigs for garnishing. Adjust the spices to your liking after tasting the sauce. Jalapeno and some harissa should be added to the mix.
- Top with tomatoes & a few pieces of fish. Increase the heat for simmering and then turn it off. 7-8 Mins of cooking time. The thicker the fillet, the longer it will take. For one-inch-thick fillets, you may use a dish cover.
- Set aside some cilantro for garnishing.

Nutrition Information
Calories: 198 kcal, Carbohydrates: 7 g, Protein: 36 g, Fat: 3 g

16. Creamy Plant-Based Pasta Sauce
Prep Time: 5 Mins, Cook Time: 25 Mins, Servings: 1
Ingredients
- 1 ½ cups onion diced finely
- 1 ¼ cup white wine dry
- 1 tbsp minced fresh thyme
- 6 cloves garlic
- ½ cup broth vegetable
- 1 tbsp juice lemon
- ½ cup cashews soaked raw
- 1 block soft tofu
- ¼ cup yeast nutritional
- 1 salt pinch
- 1 pepper pinch

Instructions
- Over medium-high heat, add the onion & wine to a large pan. Add the thyme & garlic after eight Mins of cooking. Continue cooking for another 8 Mins unless the onion/garlic combination is well-soaked up by its liquid.
- Make the creamy cashew sauce by combining vegetable broth, cashews, and lemon juice. Using an immersion blender, puree the onion/garlic mixture until no visible bits remain. Toss in nutritional yeast, tofu, and salt & pepper and mix well.
- Add the mixture back to the saucepan, along with wine, and heat till alcohol has been absorbed. If required, adjust the seasonings to your liking.
- Pasta or another grain may be used as a base. Servings are around three-quarters of a cup.

Nutrition Information
Calories: 196 kcal, Carbohydrates: 16 g, Protein: 5 g, Fat: 7 g

17. Low Carb General Tso's Chicken
Prep Time: 10 Mins, Cook Time: 30 Mins, Servings: 1
Ingredients
- 2 tbsp oil sesame
- 1 lb chicken thigh skinless boneless
- ¼ tsp salt
- ¼ tsp black pepper ground
- 1 head broccoli
- ¼ cup chopped green onion

Low Carb General Tsos' Sauce
- 1/3 cup soy sauce low sodium
- 1 cup of water
- 2 tbsp vinegar rice
- 2 tbsp fruit extract sweetener low carb
- 1 tbsp sauce hoisin
- 2 tbsp ketchup sugar-free
- 2 tsp oil sesame
- 2 minced garlic cloves
- ½ tsp chili flakes red

Instructions
- On medium heat, combine all sauce ingredients.
- Stir for around 5-10 Mins after bringing to the simmer & lowering the heat.
- Remove from fire and let to cool once thickened.
- Meanwhile, in a medium-sized pan, heat your sesame oil until shimmering. Sauté the garlic for one Min once it has been added to the pan.
- Next, add the chicken and cook for 8 mins or till browned, seasoning with pepper and salt along the way.
- After 3 Mins, add the broccoli.
- Allow the Teriyaki sauce to boil for five Mins before serving.
- Green onions may be added at this point if desired.

Nutrition Information
Calories: 411 kcal, Carbohydrates: 15 g, Protein: 24 g, Fat: 29 g

18. Life-Changing Keto Bread
Prep Time: 10 Mins, Cook Time: 1 hr, Servings: 1
Ingredients
- 2 cups seeds pumpkin
- ½ cup meal flax
- ½ cup of hazelnuts
- 2 tbsp seeds chia
- 1 cup of seeds sunflower
- 1/3 cup powder psyllium husk
- ½ cup flour coconut
- 1 stevia pinch
- 1/3 cup oil olive
- 1 & ½ cups of water

Instructions
- Put the pumpkin seeds inside your food processor and pulse until they look like oats. It doesn't have to be extremely fine, but it shouldn't be too bulky.
- Combine the flour, baking powder, sugar, and salt in a medium-sized bowl. Pour the oil and water into the dry ingredients and stir well.
- Prepare a one-lb loaf pan by lining it with parchment. Pour the mixture into the pan and use a spoon to pat it into form.
- Rest the bread on the counter for 2 hrs. When you carefully take the paper away from one edge, it's prepared to bake.
- The oven should be preheated at 350 degrees Fahrenheit.
- Bake for around 40 Mins in the oven. Bake the second side of the bread for another 20 Mins after removing it from the oven & inverting it onto the baking pan. When tapped, the sound should be hollow.
- Before slicing, allow the cake to cool fully. Make 14 equal-sized pieces. It's best when toasted.

Nutrition Information
Calories: 258 kcal, Carbohydrates: 13 g, Protein: 7 g, Fat: 21 g

19. Instant Pot Perfect Pulled Pork Shoulder
Prep Time: 5 Mins, Cook Time: 1 hr, Servings: 1
Ingredients
- 3 lb shoulder pork
- ½ cup juice orange
- ½ cup broth chicken

Instructions
- Slab and chop the shoulder into two-inch chunks. Skip this seasoning if you purchased pre-seasoned pork. Use your preferred rub or pepper and salt combination if it's raw.
- The pieces should be seared in the Pot using the Sauté option for 2-3 mins on each side. Do it in batches as necessary. If you skip this step, the fluids will be lost, so don't do it. A wooden spoon may be used to scrape any chunks of pork that may have gotten caught in the pan. This is essential aside from ensuring that nothing burns just on the bottom. If you receive an error alert, you'll need to begin again from the start.
- A 60-Min timer has been set. Open your Instant Pot and wait another 20 seconds before releasing the pressure. As soon as you've removed the pork, save a quarter-to-half cup of these juices for later use. Shred the meat using two forks.

Nutrition Information
Calories: 93 kcal, Carbohydrates: 1 g, Protein: 12 g, Fat: 4 g

20. Homemade Date Syrup
Prep Time: 5 Mins, Cook Time: 1 hr, Servings: 2
Ingredients
- 20 pitted dates
- 3 cups of water

Instructions
- To clean dates, give them a short rinse in warm water.
- Using a small pot, bring water & dates to a boil. Simmer for around 15-20 Mins.
- Remove dates and mash them with your potato masher after draining water from the saucepan.
- Use cheesecloth or a clean tea towel to line a sieve. Ensure to utilize enough fabric so that you might cover the date mix, then twist a bit on top, as you would twist the bag full of something like you would twist a bag. Cover a dish with a cheesecloth. Squeeze out all of the date mush in the cheesecloth using the cheesecloth. Remove any residual syrup from the cheesecloth with a rubber spatula.
- Pour some water into the pulped dates before putting them back in the saucepan. If you want extra syrup, just repeat steps 2 through 4.
- Finally, add all of the pulp liquid back into the pot and boil, stirring regularly, for 40-45 Mins. From warm honey to the deeper brown, the hue should progress.

Nutrition Information
Calories: 20 kcal, Carbohydrates: 5 g, Protein: 1 g, | Fat: 1 g

21. Air Fryer Cod Fish Cakes
Prep Time: 20 Mins, Cook Time: 15 Mins, Servings: 1
Ingredients
- 1 lb fillets cod
- 1 & ½ cups florets cauliflower
- 1 cup cooked quinoa
- 3 cloves garlic
- 2 mixed eggs
- 2 tbsp yeast nutritional
- ¼ cup sliced green onions
- 1 tbsp juice lemon
- 1 tsp salt
- ½ tsp pepper

Breading
- 2 tbsp flour almond
- 2 large egg whites
- ¼ cup of breadcrumbs

Instructions
- A pan or wok should have approximately an inch of water in it, and it should be heated to a rolling boil on high heat. Use your steamer basket for cooking the cauliflower. For 4-8 Mins, place a steamer basket on a pot of boiling water. If you don't have the steamer basket, you may utilize a sieve.
- Chop the cauliflower finely after it has chilled to handle. It is finely chopped and smoother, yet larger pieces have more granularity. Both too small and too large won't work properly.
- Cook the fish for 20 mins at 400°F. With 2 forks, grate the cheese when it has cooled.
- By hand, combine the flakes, fish, cauliflower, and the other ingredients. Add a half egg if the mix is too crumbly. Add breadcrumbs or quinoa if the mixture is too sticky.
- Create patties via hand. Set up 3 separate bowls: one for flour, one for egg white, and one for breadcrumbs. Before baking, each cake should be rolled in flour, next egg whites, and breadcrumbs. Prepare the fish cakes and arrange them on a plate. After chilling in the refrigerator, they may be cooked or saved for future use.
- When possible, let patties sit in the fridge for up to 24 hrs, and this will aid in maintaining the form.
- Air-fry for 10 Mins at 400 degrees in an air-fryer. Cook for a further five Mins on the opposite side.

Nutrition Information
Calories: 183 kcal, Carbohydrates: 19 g, Protein: 18 g, Fat: 4 g

22. Instant Pot Honey Garlic Chicken Thighs
Prep Time: 5 Mins, Cook Time: 12 Mins, Servings: 1
Ingredients
Sauce
- ½ cup of tamari
- ½ cup of no sugar ketchup
- 5 mashed garlic cloves

- 1/3 cup of honey
- 1 tsp seasoning Italian
- 2 tbsp parsley fresh chopped

Chicken and garnish
- 6 skinless, boneless chicken thighs
- 1 tbsp seeds sesame
- 2 tbsp sliced green onions

Instructions
- In a measuring cup, mix all of the sauce components, including water (if you've one). Be careful, to begin with, tamari, then honey, ketchup, etc., before moving on to other condiments. You won't have to scrape out any honey this way.
- Pour some sauce on your chicken thighs and seal the cover of the Instant Pot. If utilizing frozen thighs, cook on Higher Pressure for around 12 Mins; if utilizing fresh, cook for around 8 Mins. Before opening the valve, wait 5-10 mins for the pressure to drop normally.
- Chicken may be served by placing one leg per person on top of starch of your choosing and sprinkling sesame seeds & green onions on top of it.

Nutrition Information
Calories: 338 kcal, Carbohydrates: 19 g, Protein: 21 g, Fat: 19 g

23. Plant-Based Portobello Fajita Skillet
Prep Time: 5 Mins, Cook Time: 15 Mins, Servings: 1

Ingredients
- 4 portobello sliced mushrooms
- 2 sliced yellow onions
- 2 sliced bell peppers
- 2 tbsp oil olive
- 1 tbsp juice lime
- ½ tsp cumin ground
- ¼ tsp paprika smoked
- 1 tsp oregano
- 1 cayenne pepper pinch ground
- ½ tsp salt
- 1 tsp pepper

Portobello Marinade
- 3 juiced limes
- 2 tbsp vinegar red wine
- 2 tsp tamari
- 2 tsp date syrup
- 2 tsp cilantro
- 1 clove garlic
- ¼ tsp cumin
- ¼ tsp pepper black

Instructions
Marinate Mushrooms
- In a fluid measuring cup, combine the marinade. Marinate mushrooms by placing them inside a zip-lock plastic container or bag and shaking until they're completely covered. Allow almost 30 Mins of marinating time.

Bell Peppers & Onions
- Spritz olive oil & lime juice over the vegetables before serving.
- At medium-high heat, sauté the vegetables until they are tender. A few Mins to a few hrs.

Cook Mushrooms
- A wide skillet should be used to cook mushrooms over moderate flame until they are tender. A few Mins.
- Taste for crispiness and add extra spice, if necessary, after mixing mushrooms with the other veggies.

Nutrition Information
Calories: 146 kcal, Carbohydrates: 19 g, Protein: 4 g, Fat: 8 g

24. Air Fryer Mozzarella Sticks
Prep Time: 1 hr 15 Mins, Cook Time: 8 Mins, Servings: 1

Ingredients
- 1 large egg
- 1 tsp seasoning Italian
- ½ tsp salt garlic
- 1 cup panko breadcrumbs whole-wheat
- 8 mozzarella sticks low-fat
- cooking spray avocado oil

Instructions
- Set aside the beaten egg and water in a small dish.
- The garlic salt, Italian seasoning, & panko breadcrumbs should be combined in a separate bowl.
- In batches of one, coat each mozzarella stick with breadcrumbs and then dip it into the beaten egg to finish. Make sure that breadcrumbs stick to the cheese by pressing it hard. Continue breading the cheese by transferring it to the wax-lined baking sheet.
- Your mozzarella sticks should be frozen for 30 to 60 Mins after they've been breaded.
- Every mozzarella stick should be dipped in egg and then pressed into the breadcrumbs one more time. Continue to refrigerate for a further 30 to 60 Mins.
- Your air fryer should be preheated to 390°F.
- Using the avocado oil frying spray, coat the frozen mozzarella sticks & cook for around 6-8 Mins, till they are golden brown & melted inside. When using an air fryer, you will have to bake 2 batches of your mozzarella sticks at once.

Nutrition Information
Calories: 83 kcal, Carbohydrates: 6 g, Protein: 8 g, Fat: 3 g

25. Slow Cooker Bourbon Chicken
Prep Time: 15 Mins, Cook Time 2 hrs 20 Mins, Servings: 1

Ingredients
- 5 chicken breasts boneless & skinless
- ½ tsp ginger ground
- 4 minced garlic cloves
- ¼ tsp crushed chili flakes red
- ¼ cup sugar-free apple juice
- 3 tbsp honey or date syrup
- ¼ cup organic ketchup
- 3 tbsp vinegar apple cider
- ¼ cup of water
- ¼ cup good quality Bourbon
- ¼ cup low-sodium soy sauce
- 1 tsp sea salt or kosher
- ½ tsp pepper black
- ¼ cup sliced green onions

Instructions
- Place the chicken breasts in the slow cooker and stir. Pour the rest of the ingredients into a dish and mix well before pouring over the chicken. Set the timer for 4-5 hrs on low-medium or 2-3 hrs on medium-high. Remove the chicken from the oven and shred it. Continue cooking the chicken on medium for 15 more Mins.
- Brown rice, red quinoa, or farro may be served as a side dish with green onions over the top.

Nutrition Information
Calories: 380 kcal, Carbohydrates: 17 g, Protein: 32 g, Fat: 6 g

26. Sweet and Spicy Toasted Almonds
Prep Time: 5 Mins, Cook Time: 2 hrs, Servings: 1

Ingredients
- 2 tbsp sriracha gochujang
- 3 tbsp syrup maple
- 1 tsp yeast nutritional
- 2 cups raw almonds

Instructions
- The oven should be preheated at 250°F.
- Combine syrup, hot sauce, & nutritional yeast.
- Use a parchment paper or silicone pastry sheet to line the baking sheet. Set out the almonds inside a wide mixing dish and set aside. Swirl the basin to distribute the liquid mixture on the nuts properly.
- On the cookie sheet with a liner, distribute the nuts uniformly. For a full hr, bring the pot to a gentle simmer.

Rotate the camera once it's halfway through the shot. Taste a nut after 45 Mins to determine whether it's done baking. It should be less chewy or waxy and simply tastier overall. If it doesn't work, try again after 15 Mins.

Nutrition Information
Calories: 115 kcal, Carbohydrates: 7 g, Protein: 4 g, Fat: 9 g

27. Healthy Fried Green Tomatoes
Prep Time: 10 Mins, Cook Time: 20 Mins, Servings: 2
Ingredients
- 3 large green tomatoes
- ¼ cup flour whole wheat
- 3 large egg white
- 1 cup of almond meal
- ½ tsp paprika
- ½ tsp cumin
- ½ tsp salt
- ½ tsp black pepper ground
- ¾ cup Skinny Dip

Instructions
- Spray the baking sheet using non-stick spray & heat the oven to 400°f.
- Set up three separate bowls: one for the wheat flour, one for egg whites, & the third for the paprika, cumin, almond meal, salt & pepper.
- Tomato slices should be lightly coated in wheat flour and dredged in the egg whites before being cooked.
- Cover this with some almond meal & transfer it to your last bowl.
- Repeat this process till all the slices have been coated.
- The tomatoes should be golden brown after 20 Mins in the oven, at which time they should be turned over once.
- While the bread is baking, make your Ranch Dip dish.

Nutrition Information
Calories: 171 kcal, Carbohydrates: 12 g, Protein: 10 g, Fat: 10 g

28. Slow Cooker Carnitas
Prep Time: 10 Mins, Cook Time: 8 hrs, Servings: 4
Ingredients
- 3 lb shoulder pork
- 2 yellow peeled & sliced onions medium
- 6 peeled & smashed garlic cloves
- ¼ cup freshly squeezed orange juice
- ¼ cup freshly squeezed lime juice
- 1 tbsp oregano dried
- 1 tbsp cumin ground
- 1 tbsp powder chili
- 1 tsp salt sea
- 1 tsp pepper black

Instructions
- In the slow cooker, place the pork shoulder. Nestle the garlic and onions in the vicinity of the pork. Pour the mixture of lime juice, orange juice, and spices over the meat, then stir to coat it well. Use roughly half as much water as needed to cover the meat. Cover & cook for around 8 hrs on low heat. Shred the pork with two forks after it's done cooking.
- Makes a great filling for burritos, tacos, or sandwiches.

Nutrition Information
Calories: 343 kcal, Carbohydrates: 5 g, Protein: 24 g, Fat: 25 g

29. Low-Carb Avocado Breakfast Cups
Prep Time: 5 Mins, Cook Time: 15 Mins, Servings: 1
Ingredients
- 2 pits removed avocados halved
- 4 large eggs
- ½ tsp salt sea
- ½ tsp black pepper ground
- ¼ cup Mexican cheese shredded low fat
- ¼ cup of salsa

Instructions
- Preheat the oven to 450 degrees Fahrenheit before beginning.
- Using a spoon, scoop out a tiny amount of avocado flesh from each half and place it in a baking tray lined using baking paper.
- Break an egg into the middle of each side of an avocado.
- Salt & pepper each egg before cooking.
- Bake for 15 Mins, or unless the whites are completely set, within the baking dish.
- When one Min remains, top with cheese.
- Salsa is a great addition to this dish.

Nutrition Information
Calories: 249 kcal, Carbohydrates: 10 g, Protein: 10 g, Fat: 20g

30. Air Fryer Egg Roll Recipe
Prep Time: 20 Mins, Cook Time: 12 Mins, Servings: 1
Ingredients
- 1 tbsp oil sesame
- 1 lb turkey sausage ground
- 3 cups shredded green cabbage
- 1 shredded carrot medium
- 3 chopped scallions
- 4 minced garlic cloves
- 1 tbsp minced ginger
- 1 tbsp sauce soy
- 1 tbsp vinegar rice wine
- 12 egg wrappers roll
- cooking spray avocado oil

Instructions
- In a big, medium-sized pan, warm the sesame oil. Stir in the turkey sausage & heat until it's browned and crumbly. The sausage should be drained of any extra fat.
- Then add the other ingredients to the pan, along with the soy sauce & rice vinegar. It should take 3-4 Mins of cooking for the cabbage to soften but not completely lose its crisp. Place on a cooling rack and let it sit for a few Mins.
- Egg roll wrappers should be placed on a chopping board with one corner facing you whenever the filling is cold (like a diamond). Add some filling to the middle of the wrapper and seal it up.
- You may use a finger dipped in water to help seal the egg roll wrapper. Stack the wrapper's sides together. Eggrolls may be made by folding the bottom edge inward toward the center and then firmly rolling away from you.
- Keep doing this until all of the egg roll wrappers are used.
- Set the air fryer temperature to 390°F.
- Spray the egg rolls in the basket with avocado oil spray. When golden brown & crispy on one side, air fried for 6-8 mins on the other side. Egg rolls should be cooked for a further 3-4 Mins, till both sides are golden brown and crunchy. Based on the scale of the air fryer, you may need to cook your egg rolls into 2 batches.
- Ensure that the food is served at the correct temperature.

Nutrition Information
Calories: 117 kcal, Carbohydrates: 10 g, Protein: 9 g, Fat: 4g

31. Slow Cooker Honey Mustard Chicken
Prep Time: 10 Mins, Cook Time: 4 hrs, Servings: 1
Ingredients
- 4 fresh rosemary sprigs
- 4 skinless chickens
- 4 tbsp honey
- 4 tbsp mustard Dijon
- 2 tbsp olive oil extra virgin
- ½ tsp sea salt kosher
- ¼ tsp pepper black
- 1 tsp finely chopped rosemary fresh

Instructions
- In the slow cooker, place a rosemary twig beneath each chicken.

- You may make this dressing in a small dish by combining 1 tbsp of coarsely diced rosemary with the honey & mustard in a saucepan. Take care to coat each piece of chicken thoroughly with the mixture.
- Ensure the slow cooker is covered and set to either high or low for around 8 hrs or 4 hrs.

Nutrition Information
Calories: 385 kcal, Carbohydrates: 19 g, Protein: 19 g, Fat: 26g

32. Maple Coffee Ice Pops
Prep Time: 5 Mins, Cook time: 8 hrs, Servings: 1
Ingredients
- 3 tbsp syrup maple
- 1 & ½ cup strong black coffee
- 1 tsp cinnamon ground
- 1 cup cream coconut

Instructions
- Mix all the ingredients.
- Popsicle molds or large cups may be used for this.
- To freeze, insert one popsicle stick.
- Put in the fridge overnight till it is completely firm.

Nutrition Information
Calories: 160 kcal, Carbohydrates: 10 g, Protein: 2 g, Fat: 14g

33. Egg White Mini Breakfast Bites
Prep Time: 10 Mins, Cook Time: 20 Mins, Servings: 3
Ingredients
- ½ cup finely chopped bell peppers
- ½ cup finely chopped mushrooms
- 2 & ½ cups large egg-whites
- 3 tbsp high protein Greek yogurt
- 1/3 cup crumbled goat cheese

Instructions
- Pre-heat the oven to around 350 degrees Fahrenheit.
- Spray/line a tiny muffin tray with cooking spray.
- Fill one-third of each pan with mixed vegetables.
- Add a sprinkling of cheese to the mix.
- Mix your egg whites & yogurt in a shallow dish. Each may be filled to the same level. The modest size of the tins means that you may fill them to the brim.
- Bake for around 15 to 20 Mins.

Nutrition Information
Calories: 72 kcal, Carbohydrates: 2 g, Protein: 11 g, Fat: 2g

34. The Best Chicken Bacon Ranch Casserole
Prep Time: 10 Mins, Cook Time: 35 Mins, Servings: 2
Ingredients
- 6 slices turkey bacon
- 1 & ½ lb chicken breasts boneless skinless
- 1 tsp powder garlic
- 1 tsp powder onion
- 1 tsp divided kosher salt
- 4 cups uncooked cauliflower rice
- 8 oz low-fat softened cream cheese
- ½ cup of Greek yogurt
- 1 tbsp powder buttermilk
- 1 large egg yolk
- 1 tsp dill weed dried
- ½ tsp chives dried
- ½ cup mozzarella shredded
- 1 lb thawed & squeezed frozen spinach
- ½ cup cheddar cheese shredded

Instructions
- The oven should be preheated at 375° F. Set aside a casserole dish that has been sprayed with cooking spray.
- Cook your bacon for approximately 5 mins in a big skillet. However, do not discard the rendered drippings.
- Sprinkle half kosher salt over the chicken before adding it to the pan. Cook for approximately 5 Mins, or until the chicken isn't any longer pink inside the middle. Toss your cauliflower rice into the pan when it has been taken off the heat.
- To make the cream cheese mixture, add the cream cheese, egg yolk, Greek yogurt, buttermilk powder & dried dill, as well as the chopped-up mozzarella cheese & the frozen spinach in a big bowl, then mix well.
- Spread your chicken mixture evenly within a baking dish, then top with the cheese mixture. Grated cheddar cheese should be sprinkled on top.
- Bake for about 15 Mins. Bake for a further 10 Mins, or unless the bacon is bubbling and heated through.
- Allow 10 Mins of rest time before serving.

Nutrition Information
Calories: 282 kcal, Carbohydrates: 11 g, Protein: 32 g, Fat: 12g

35. Easy Sautéed Greens
Prep Time: 10 Mins, Cook Time: 10 Mins, Servings: 1
Ingredients
- 2 lb cleaned & dry spinach
- 2 tsp oil olive
- 1 tbsp ginger fresh
- 1 tbsp garlic
- 1 salt pinch
- 1 pepper pinch

Instructions
- Mix in some oil & heat the pan to medium-high heat.
- For thirty seconds while adding spinach, add garlic and ginger. Do not leave them there for more than a minor they may be burned.
- Stir in some spinach, cook until wilted, and remove from the heat. Strong heat and constant stirring are necessary to get wilted, but not slimy greens.
- Before serving, if preferred, sprinkle with lemon juice or vinegar.

Nutrition Information
Calories: 149 kcal, Carbohydrates: 18 g, Protein: 13 g, Fat: 6g

36. Air Fryer Pork Chops
Prep Time: 5 Mins, Cook Time: 10 Mins, Servings: 1
Ingredients
- 4 pork chops boneless
- cooking spray avocado oil
- 1 tsp salt kosher
- 1 tsp paprika smoked
- 1 tsp powder garlic
- 1 tsp powder onion
- ½ tsp mustard ground
- ½ tsp black pepper ground

Instructions
- For 5 Mins, heat your air fryer approximately 375°F.
- Spray all sides of the pork chops with avocado oil. Dispose of.
- Salt, onion powder, garlic powder, powdered mustard, & black pepper are all mixed in a larger basin. Make sure everything is well-combined.
- Place your pork chops within the air fryer in a solo layer & coat them with spice mixture.
- A temp of 145°F should be reached after 9-10 Mins of cooking.

Nutrition Information
Calories: 215 kcal, Carbohydrates: 10 g, Protein: 29 g, Fat: 9g

37. Quick & Easy Egg Muffins
Prep Time: 5 Mins, Cook Time: 20 Min, Servings: 3
Ingredients
- 1 tbsp oil olive
- 1 thinly chopped yellow onion
- 1 thinly diced bell pepper
- 1 cup thinly chopped brown mushrooms
- 1 cup chopped spinach
- 8 large eggs
- ½ cup cheddar cheese shredded
- ¼ tsp salt sea
- ½ tsp black pepper ground

Instructions
- Pre-heat your oven to around 350 deg Fahrenheit
- Heat some olive oil over medium-high heat in a small saucepan until it smokes.
- 2 to 3 Mins of sautéing the onion
- Add the bell peppers & mushrooms, then continue to cook for another 4 to 5 Mins, unless the vegetables are slightly browned.
- Toss in the spinach and cook until wilted.
- While preparing the eggs, please take off the heat & let it cool.
- Whisk your eggs in a small bowl & add the cheese, salt, & pepper, as well as the sautéed vegetables.
- Bake for around 10-12 mins, or unless the tops of the muffins are crisp.

Nutrition Information
Calories: 208 kcal, Carbohydrates: 7 g, Protein: 16 g, Fat: 13g

38. Keto Protein Fat BombsPrep Time10 Mins
Prep Time: 30 Mins, Cook Time: 15 Mins, Servings: 4
Ingredients
- 1/8 cup of pecans
- 1/3 cup meal flax
- 1/3 cup unsweetened coconut flakes
- 1 & ½ tbsp melted coconut oil
- ½ cup powder pea protein
- 1 tsp sweetener monk fruit
- 3 tbsp chocolate chips dark
- ¼ cup milk almond

Instructions
- Pulverize the pecans in your food processor until they are a fine powdery consistency.
- Pour in the rest of the ingredients and mix well. Once the ingredients have been well combined, add your almond milk gradually while mixing till no powder remains. Almond milk may be added in small amounts until the mixture is homogeneous. Add some chocolate chips to the batter in a mixing bowl and stir with a spoon.
- Roll a little portion of the mixture into a ball using a big spoon. 10 balls should be easy to come by.
- Make sure it's chilled for almost 30 Mins before serving. These may be stored for up to 3 weeks within the refrigerator.

Nutrition Information
Calories: 119 kcal, Carbohydrates: 6 g, Protein: 6 g, Fat: 9g

39. Avocado Tuna Salad
Prep Time: 10 Mins, Cook Time: 10 Mins, Servings: 2
Ingredients
- 12 oz light tuna canned chunk
- 1 mashed avocado
- 1 chopped red onion
- 1 cup chopped celery
- 1 chopped tomato medium
- 1 juiced lemon
- 1 tbsp extra virgin olive oil
- ½ tsp chili flakes red
- ½ tsp salt
- ½ tsp black pepper ground

Instructions
- Mix all ingredients in a wide bowl unless they are completely incorporated.
- Serving suggestions include a sandwich with crackers or a salad with lettuce.

Nutrition Information
Calories: 240 kcal, Carbohydrates: 12 g, Protein: 24 g, Fat: 12g

40. Air Fryer Buffalo Cauliflower
Prep Time: 15 Mins, Cook Time: 15 Mins, Servings: 1
Ingredients
- 1 beaten egg
- 1 cup of whole-wheat, gluten-free panko breadcrumbs
- 1 tsp paprika smoked
- ½ tsp powder garlic
- ¼ tsp salt kosher
- 1 cauliflower head
- cooking spray avocado oil
- ½ cup sauce buffalo

Instructions
- 375 degrees Fahrenheit should be the temperature of the air fryer when it's ready to be used.
- Beat the egg with water in a small dish and put it aside.
- Combine the garlic powder, panko, paprika, & salt in a separate bowl.
- Before drizzling your cauliflower florets within the panko mixture, dip them into the egg. Put a dish of breaded cauliflower on the counter while you continue to bread the rest of the cauliflower.
- Place the breaded pieces within the air fryer in a layer, spraying the bites with avocado oil spray as you go. Continue frying the cauliflower in batches, keeping the previously cooked heads warm in a 200°F oven.
- The florets should be golden brown & crispy after 10-15 Mins of air-frying.
- Before serving, mix the cauliflower with some buffalo sauce.

Nutrition Information
Calories: 114 kcal, Carbohydrates: 19 g, Protein: 6 g, Fat: 2g

41. Jerk Spiced Cashews
Prep Time: 4 Mins, Cook Time: 4 Mins, Servings: 1
Ingredients
- 2 cups unsalted cashews raw
- 1 tbsp oil sunflower
- 2 fresh sprigs of thyme
- 1 zest of lime
- 2 tsp finely chopped ginger fresh

Jerk Spice
- 1 tbsp salt
- 2 tbsp pepper black
- 1 tbsp dried thyme
- ½ tsp ground cloves
- ¾ tsp nutmeg
- 1 & ½ tsp cayenne
- 1 & ½ tsp cumin
- 1 & ½ tsp powder curry
- ¾ tsp cinnamon

Instructions
- Preheat the oven to around 350 degrees Fahrenheit.
- Combine all of the jerk spice ingredients in a medium, airtight jar.
- Using a spoonful of jerk spice, mix the first 5 ingredients in an airtight container in a small bowl.
- Cashews should be gently browned after baking for 4 Mins. Before eating, allow the dish to cool fully. For up maybe a week, store in an airtight container.

Nutrition Information
Calories: 276 kcal, Carbohydrates: 17 g, Protein: 8 g, Fat: 22g

42. Fresh Lime and Basil Fruit Salad
Prep Time: 10 Mins, Cook Time: 1 hr, Servings: 1
Ingredients
- 2.5 cups melon honeydew
- 1 cup of blackberries
- 2 cups raspberries
- 5-6 fresh basil leaves
- 1 juiced & zested lime

Instructions
- Mix all ingredients in a dish, carefully coat the fruit completely with lime juice before serving.
- For at least an hr, let it cool.

Nutrition Information
Calories: 50 kcal, Carbohydrates: 12 g, Protein: 1 g, Fat: 1g

43. Creamy Vegan Coleslaw
Prep Time: 5 Mins, Cook Time: 10 Mins, Servings: 1
Ingredients
- 2 cups shredded green cabbage
- 2 cups shredded red cabbage
- 2 shredded carrots medium
- 1 thinly sliced red onion

Creamy Dressing
- 2 tbsp vinegar apple cider
- 1 tbsp syrup agave
- 1 avocado
- 1 tsp salt sea
- 1 tsp black pepper ground

Instructions
- In a separate bowl, whisk together the dressing ingredients. Processed or blended ingredients in your food processor and a thick mayonnaise-like consistency should be achieved. The following morning, the product is mushy and will not keep properly.
- Using a large mixing bowl, combine all vegetables with all the dressing.
- Allow it cool for almost ten Mins before serving.

Nutrition Information
Calories: 146 kcal, Carbohydrates: 19 g, Protein: 3 g, Fat: 8g

44. Zucchini Fritters with Vegan Sour Cream Sauce
Prep Time: 20 Mins, Cook Time: 30 Mins, Servings: 2
Ingredients
- Sauce Sour Cream
- ½ cup sour cream homemade vegan
- ¼ tsp zest lemon
- 1 tbsp chopped dill fresh
- 1 tbsp minced chives fresh
- kosher salt & pepper

Fritters
- 1 tbsp flax seed ground
- 3 tbsp of water
- 1 lb coarsely grated zucchini
- 1 coarsely grated yellow onion
- 1 tsp salt
- ½ cup flour whole wheat
- ¼ tsp powder garlic
- fresh chopped parsley, dill

Instructions
Sauce Sour Cream
- In a mixing bowl, mix the ingredients for the sour cream sauce. Refrigerate, covered, till ready to serve.

Fritters
- The oven should be preheated to 400°F for the fritters. Set aside two baking sheets that have been lined with parchment paper. It is possible to bake the fritters two at a time if you do not have enough baking sheets.
- Mix your crushed flax seed & water into a small dish. Dispose of.
- Line a big strainer using a clean cheesecloth or dishcloth and place it in the dishwasher. In a colander, put the zucchini & onion that have been grated and add salt to it. Toss the zucchini with the seasoning and let it rest for 10 min to extract the zucchini's water.
- Remove much water from the fabric by twisting and squeezing the ends together. If there is too much humidity within fritters, they will crumble as they bake.
- In a large bowl, combine the grated zucchini and the rest of the ingredients. Using a mixer, blend the ground flax seed mix, flour, & garlic powder unless well mixed.
- Six mounds of batter should be placed on each baking sheet, using the measuring cup to scoop the batter out. Flatten all mounds into the round forms using the spoon.
- Bake the fritters for 10-15 Mins, unless they're golden brown & crispy on the outside. Flip the fritter with a spatula & continue to cook 10-15 Mins, or until the fritter is golden brown.
- Serve your fritters with sour cream and some fresh chopped herbs.

Nutrition Information
Calories: 121 kcal, Carbohydrates: 18 g, Protein: 4 g, Fat: 4g

45. Vegan "Chicken" Salad
Prep Time: 15 Mins, Cook Time: 15 Mins, Servings: 1
Ingredients
- 15 oz drained & rinsed chickpeas canned
- 2 tbsp diced red onion
- 1 diced stalk celery
- 1 tbsp dill fresh
- ¼ cup diced red grapes
- 1/3 cup vegan mayonnaise cashew-based
- ¼ tsp salt
- ¼ tsp pepper black

Instructions
- A fork and food processor may be used to mash Chickpeas. It is important to crush the chickpeas into little pieces so that no whole ones remain.
- Stir in the rest of the ingredients & mix well until they're evenly distributed throughout the mixture.
- Refrigerate for at least one hr before serving.

Nutrition Information
Calories: 121 kcal, Carbohydrates: 1 g, Protein: 1 g, Fat: 12g

46. Citrus Spritz Mocktail
Prep Time: 5 Mins, Cook Time: 5 Mins, Servings: 1
Ingredients
- 3 oz water sparking
- 1 sliced orange
- Ice
- 1 squeezed lime
- 5 raspberries

Instructions
- Three-quarters of the ice cubes should be placed in the glass before serving.
- Orange juice, orange slices, lime juice, & raspberries may all be added.
- Sparkling water is a wonderful accompaniment.

Nutrition Information
Calories: 39 kcal, Carbohydrates: 10 g, Protein: 1 g, Fat: 1g

47. 6-Ingredient Mediterranean Salad
Prep Time: 15 Mins, Cook Time: 15 Mins, Servings: 1
Ingredients
- 2 peeled & sliced avocados
- 12 halved cherry tomatoes
- 2 diced cucumbers medium
- ½ thinly sliced red onion
- 1 sliced tomato
- ¼ cup olive oil extra virgin
- 2 tbsp freshly squeezed lemon juice

Instructions
- Combine the veggies inside a serving dish. Toss your salad ingredients with the olive oil & lemon juice that have been whisked together in a mixing bowl. Salt & pepper to your liking.
- Enjoy!

Nutrition Information
Calories: 257 kcal, Carbohydrates: 17 g, Protein: 4 g, Fat: 22g

48. Slow Cooker Vegetable Omelets
Prep Time: 15 Mins, Cook Time: 2 hrs: Servings: 8
Ingredients
- 8 large eggs
- ½ cup grated parmesan cheese
- ½ tsp salt
- ¼ tsp pepper
- 1 tbsp olive oil extra virgin
- 1 coarsely chopped onion
- ½ cup peeled & diced carrots

- ¼ cup coarsely chopped string beans
- ½ cup peeled & diced potatoes
- ½ cup diced zucchini
- ¼ cup diced bell peppers red

Instructions
- Mix the eggs, salt, Parmesan cheese, and pepper in a small bowl.
- Sauté chopped onions for two Mins in olive oil on moderate flame before adding the rest of the ingredients. It's nearly done when it's been simmering for 10 Mins.
- Pour your egg mixture over the veggies within the slow cooker, ensuring they are firmly coated.
- 2 hrs on high heat.

Nutrition Information
Calories: 168 kcal, Carbohydrates: 8 g, Protein: 11 g, Fat: 10g

49. Coconut Milk Tapioca Pudding
Prep Time: 2 Mins, Cook Time: 25 Mins, Servings: 3
Ingredients
- 1/3 cup tapioca pearls small
- 1 cup milk almond
- 13 oz unsweetened canned coconut milk
- ¼ cup syrup maple
- 1 tsp extract vanilla
- 1 salt pinch
- 1 cut & cubed mango
- ½ cup rinsed & dried raspberries

Instructions
- For at least one hr, soak the tapioca pearls into almond milk. Drain nothing.
- Add the almond milk-tapioca pearl combination and the coconut milk to a saucepan. Immediately after bringing the mixture to a boil, reduce the heat to a simmer and whisk regularly to avoid scorching the pearls.
- Simmer the stew for twenty Mins, stirring every few Mins. Ensure the pudding simmer at a moderate and steady temperature to avoid overcooking.
- Add the vanilla, maple syrup, & salt just before serving. Take the pan off the heat and continue to stir for an additional 1-2 Mins.
- Traditional tapioca pudding is served chilled. If you've tiny ramekins or plates, divide the mixture into them. The ideal cool time is 2 hrs. Before eating heated pudding, allow it to cool for almost ten mins in the serving dish.
- 3 mango cubes & 2-3 raspberries on each ramekin should be enough to fill a quarter cup.

Nutrition Information
Calories: 181 kcal, Carbohydrates: 15 g, Protein: 2 g, Fat: 14g

50. The Easiest Air Fryer Chicken Breasts Recipe
Prep Time: 5 Mins, Cook Time: 20 Mins, Servings: 5
Ingredients
- ½ tsp salt kosher
- ¼ tsp powder garlic
- ¼ tsp black pepper ground
- ¼ tsp paprika smoked
- ¼ tsp oregano dried
- spray avocado oil
- 2 chicken breasts boneless skinless

Instructions
- Make sure the air fryer is preheated to 360°F before using it.
- Salt, smoked paprika, garlic powder, powdered black pepper, & dried oregano should be mixed in a small bowl.
- Spray the chicken breasts on the smooth side with avocado oil & sprinkle on the spice.
- Place the seasoned side of the breast within the air fryer. Spray the second side with the leftover seasoning and do so quickly.
- Cook the breasts for 8-10 Mins on one side, then turn them over & cook for another 5-10 Mins.

Nutrition Information
Calories: 66 kcal, Carbohydrates: 1 g, Protein: 12 g, Fat: 1g

51. Best Chewy Chocolate Chip Cookies
Prep Time: 20 Mins, Cook Time: 9 Mins, Servings: 1
Ingredients
- ¾ cup unsalted butter
- 1 & ¼ cup sugar coconut
- 2 & ¼ cup flour almond
- ½ tsp salt
- 1 tsp soda baking
- 1 large egg
- 1 large egg yolk
- 2 tsp vinegar apple cider
- 2 tsp vanilla
- 2 cups chocolate chips dark

Instructions
- Sift the almond flour into a small bowl and add the salt & baking soda.
- Melt the butter in a skillet over medium heat until it browns. Ideally, the color will be dark golden, and the scent should be nutty. To expedite the process, just squeeze out any sediment that collects.
- Refrigerate for 30 Mins after placing the butter in a pie pan.
- Sugar should be mixed in after one Min of beating the butter in an electric mixer with a paddle attachment. Cream for two Mins.
- Scrape down both sides & bottom of your bowl as you add the yolk, vinegar, egg, & vanilla.
- Slowly incorporate all dry ingredients into the batter at a moderate speed.
- Incorporate the chocolate by mixing at low rpm for 5-10 seconds.
- Refrigerate for at least three hrs before serving. If baked right away, the cookies will spread, but chilling the dough beforehand enhances the taste.
- The oven temperature should be 350 degrees.
- After 9-11 Mins, remove from the oven and let cool. While they are resting, they would bake, so undercooking them is ideal, and that's why they're so gooey. When the cookies are still warm, sprinkle some chocolate chips on top.
- Transfer the cookies to the cooling rack once five Mins of chilling time has elapsed.

Nutrition Information
Calories: 224 kcal, Carbohydrates: 18 g, Protein: 4 g, Fat: 16g

52. Spring Asparagus and Turkey Bacon Pizza
Prep Time: 15 Mins, Cook Time: 20 Mins, Servings: 1
Ingredients
- 1 Pizza Dough Chickpea Thin
- 2 tbsp oil olive
- 3 minced cloves garlic
- 2 cups of fat-free shredded mozzarella cheese
- 1/3 cup cooked & crumbled turkey bacon
- ½ cup of asparagus
- ¼ cup of red onion

Instructions
- Set the oven temperature to 400°F. Apply some non-stick spray to the pizza pan.
- Spread your chickpea pizza dough in a wide uniform layer on a pizza pan.
- Using the olive oil, coat the crust using garlic.
- Sprinkle some cheese on top of garlic oil, then add the rest of the toppings.
- If you want the cheese to brown & bubble, bake it for around 15-20 Mins. Before serving, let the pizza cool down a little.

Nutrition Information
Calories: 179 kcal, Carbohydrates: 5 g, Protein: 21 g, Fat: 9g

53. Slow Cooker Breakfast Casserole
Prep Time: 15 Mins, Cook Time: 4 hrs, Servings: 1
Ingredients
- 1 tsp oil olive
- 1 & ½ cups thinly sliced potatoes
- ½ cup no sugar salsa
- ¼ cup diced onion
- 1 seeded & diced jalapeño
- 5 large eggs
- ½ cup of mozzarella grated part-skim
- ¼ tsp sea salt kosher
- 1/8 tsp pepper black

Instructions
- Apply a generous amount of olive oil to the slow cooker's outside. An oil spray is another option. Place the onions, potatoes, jalapenos, and salsa in your slow cooker.
- Beat the eggs in a different bowl. Add salt & pepper to the mozzarella, then mix well. Ensure the potatoes are well submerged in the sauce before adding them to the slow cooker.
- After 4 hrs on low, or after potatoes are soft & the eggs have set, turn off your slow cooker.

Nutrition Information
Calories: 198 kcal, Carbohydrates: 14 g, Protein: 13 g, Fat: 10g

54. Quick and Easy Southwest Cucumber Avocado Salad
Prep Time: 10 Mins, Cook Time: 10 Mins, Servings: 1
Ingredients
- 2 large cucumbers
- 1 peeled & pit removed avocado
- 2 tbsp minced red onion
- 1 tbsp oil olive
- 3 tsp juice lime
- 2 tsp seasoning taco
- 1 tbsp minced fresh cilantro

Instructions
- Gently combine all of the ingredients in a large mixing bowl. Serve after 15 Mins of resting.

Nutrition Information
Calories: 132 kcal, Carbohydrates: 8 g, Protein: 2 g, Fat: 11g

55. Keto-Friendly Flavor Packed Turkey Burger
Prep Time: 15 Mins, Cook Time: 15 Mins, Servings: 1
Ingredients
- 1 lb turkey ground
- 1 tsp salt kosher
- ½ tsp black pepper ground
- 1 tsp powder garlic
- ¼ cup minced yellow onion
- 2 tsp Italian seasoning
- 1 half minced jalapeno pepper
- 1 tsp oil sesame
- 2 tsp oil olive
- 8 large lettuce leaves
- 1 pit remove avocado peeled
- 1 tomato
- ½ onion purple

Instructions
- In a mixing bowl, combine your turkey & all of the other ingredients except the onion & jalapeño, including kosher pepper and salt. To get the best results, mix well. Make 4 equal patties out of the mixture.
- The sesame & olive oils should be heated in a big skillet. Add your patties once they're heated. When browned, continue cooking for another 5-7 Mins. Cook for a further 5-7 Mins on the other side, unless your patty is well cooked. Allow cooling for approximately five Mins after removing from pan.
- Four lettuce leaves should be placed on a level surface while taking a break. Avocado slices, red onion, tomato, and jalapeño strips should be placed on the salad. Finish with some lettuce leaf on top of your turkey burger.

Nutrition Information
Calories: 263 kcal, Carbohydrates: 11 g, Protein: 29 g, Fat: 13g

56. Chocolate Hummus Fruit Dip
Prep Time: 5 Mins, Cook Time: 5 Mins, Servings: 2
Ingredients
- 1 & ½ cups drained garbanzo beans
- 2 tbsp tahini
- 2 tbsp syrup maple
- 4 tbsp cocoa powder unsweetened
- 1 tsp extract vanilla

Instructions
- In your food processor, mix all ingredients. Blend until completely smooth. Add some warm water if the mixture becomes too thick.
- To serve, top with chosen crackers or fresh fruit such as pretzels or graham.

Nutrition Information
Calories: 70 kcal, Carbohydrates: 10 g, Protein: 3 g, Fat: 3g

57. Easy Sea Salt Skillet Popcorn
Prep Time: 2 Mins, Cook Time: 5 Mins, Servings: 2
Ingredients
- 1 tbsp oil olive
- ¼ cup kernels popcorn
- 1 tsp salt sea

Instructions
- Melt the butter in a big, heavy pan over medium heat. Add the kernels after they've cooled down a little.
- Shake the skillet regularly with the cover on. Once the kernels start to pop, don't remove the lid from the frying pan.
- Proceed to stir the popcorn periodically as it pops. Popped kernels are prone to burning. Keep cooking unless the popping stops. As soon as you hear the popping, turn off the heat.
- Add a pinch of salt to the dish after removing the cover. Enjoy it while it's still warm!

Nutrition Information
Calories: 69 kcal, Carbohydrates: 8 g, Protein: 1 g, Fat: 4g

58. Easy Oven-Baked Meatballs
Prep Time: 15 Mins, Cook Time: 30 Mins, Servings: 3
Ingredients
- 1 lb lean beef ground
- ½ cup breadcrumbs panko
- 1 large egg
- ½ tsp salt kosher
- ½ tsp black pepper ground
- 1 tsp powder garlic
- ¼ cup minced yellow onion
- ½ tsp oregano dried
- ½ tsp basil dried
- 1 tsp oil olive

Instructions
- Set the oven temperature to 400°F. Using Al foil, coat the baking sheet using a nonstick spray.
- In a large bowl, combine all of the ingredients & thoroughly mix them. To bake, form into 1" balls, then put on the baking sheet that has been lined with parchment paper.
- Baking time should be between 15 and 20 minutes, depending on how browned you like your food. Add it to your preferred pasta meal or meatball appetizers.

Nutrition Information
Calories: 145 kcal, Carbohydrates: 5 g, Protein: 18 g, Fat: 5g

59. Turkey Sausage Brunch Burger
Prep Time: 5 Mins, Cook Time: 15 Mins, Servings: 1

Ingredients
- 8 slices turkey bacon
- 1 lb turkey ground
- 2 tsp blend Italian Seasoning
- ½ tsp seed fennel
- ½ tsp salt
- ¼ tsp pepper
- 2 tbsp oil olive
- 4 slices of Swiss cheese
- 4 large eggs
- 1 cup spinach baby
- 1 sliced tomato large
- 2 tbsp pesto basil

Instructions
- Cook the turkey bacon as per the package instructions.
- Mix the ground turkey, fennel, salt, Italian seasoning, and pepper in a wide mixing bowl with clean hands. Mix thoroughly. Assemble into four burgers
- In a large pan, heat the olive oil until shimmering and hot. If required, the burger patties should be cooked to an internal temperature of 165°F and browned on the exterior. Allow draining on a paper towel-lined platter or baking sheet.
- While still hot, top every burger with 2 pieces of turkey bacon and 2 pieces of Swiss cheese.
- Over-medium heat, eggs may be fried while the pan is still hot. Top every burger with 1 fried egg.
- Apply pesto to every brioche bun and use it as desired to build your burgers. On the bottom bun, arrange spinach and tomatoes in an equal layer. A burger patty covered with bacon, cheese, and an egg is all that is needed to complete the dish. The brioche bun on top completes the dish. Serve immediately while still hot.

Nutrition Information
Calories: 463 kcal, Carbohydrates: 5 g, Protein: 46 g, Fat: 29g

60. Chicken and Broccoli Stir-Fry
Prep Time: 5 Mins, Cook Time: 25 Mins, Servings: 2
Ingredients
- 3 tbsp soy sauce lite
- 1 tbsp honey
- 2 tsp juice lemon
- 2 tbsp oil sesame
- 1 tbsp flour or cornstarch
- 2 tsp seeds sesame
- 1 tbsp olive oil extra virgin
- 1 & ¼ lb chicken breasts boneless & skinless
- 1 coarsely chopped onion medium
- 1 peeled & finely chopped ginger root
- 2 cups florets broccoli
- ¼ tsp pepper black

Instructions
- Cornstarch & soy sauce are whisked together with the other ingredients, including honey, sesame oil, lemon juice, & zest. Put the mixture in a safe place.
- Set a large pan or wok on low flame and roast sesame seeds unless fragrant, about 2 Mins. Set aside the toasted seeds into a small bowl after they've been combined with the oil.
- Chicken should be gently browned when cooked in olive oil in the same skillet. Add the broccoli, onions, ginger, and pepper. 4 Mins of cooking time. Toss in the soy sauce mix & reduce the heat to moderate. To get the appropriate consistency, cook the sauce for no longer than 5 mins. Serve with a sprinkle of toasted sesame seeds. Enjoy!
- Enjoy Stir-fry with Broccoli and Chicken- quinoa or Brown rice may be used in this dish.

Nutrition Information
Calories: 256 kcal, Carbohydrates: 15 g, Protein: 35 g, Fat: 18g

61. Slow Cooker Jalapeno Chicken Flautas
Prep Time: 5 Mins, Cook Time: 6 hrs 15 Mins, Servings: 1
Ingredients
- 13 oz chicken breasts boneless & skinless
- 1 cup divided salsa mild
- ¼ cup low-fat cream cheese
- 1 sliced jalapeno
- ¼ tsp salt
- 1/8 tsp pepper
- 4 tortillas whole-grain
- ½ cup of cheese grated low-fat

Instructions
- Toss the chicken breasts with cream cheese, salsa, and seasonings in your slow cooker.
- 6 hrs on high heat.
- Shred the chicken with two forks after it's done cooking.
- Salsa, Shredded chicken, & cheese are all mixed in the tortilla.
- Roll out the tortillas.
- Over moderate flame, fry the flautas from both sides in a big, dry, nonstick saucepan.

Nutrition Information
Calories: 383 kcal, Carbohydrates: 17 g, Protein: 30 g, Fat: 22g

62. Coconut Milk Smoothie
Prep Time: 5 Mins, Cook Time: 5 Mins, Servings: 1
Ingredients
- 1 & ½ cups carton milk coconut milk
- 1 frozen banana
- 2 cups spinach raw baby

Instructions
- Blend all the ingredients in your blender unless they are completely emulsified. For a thick smoothie, add ice.

Nutrition Information
Calories: 184 kcal, Carbohydrates: 20 g, Protein: 2 g, Fat: 10g

63. Roasted Lemon and Dill Cauliflower
Prep Time: 5 Mins, Cook Time: 15 Mins, Servings: 1
Ingredients
- 1 core discarded cauliflower head
- 1 tbsp oil olive
- 1 tbsp zest lemon
- 1 tbsp finely chopped fresh dill
- 1 tsp salt sea

Instructions
- Preheat the oven to around 400°F.
- Put the florets of the cauliflower on a baking sheet with a rim.
- Dill and salt go well with olive oil & lemon zest. Toss to distribute the dressing over the florets evenly. One layer over the sheet pan is ideal.
- For a golden-brown finish, roast for an additional 15 mins. Oven cooking durations might vary, so be sure to keep an eye on everything.
- Serve hot, straight out of the oven.

Nutrition Information
Calories: 50 kcal, Carbohydrates: 6 g, Protein: 2 g, Fat: 3g

64. Easy At-Home Cold Brew
Prep Time: 5 Mins, Cook Time: 12 hrs, Servings: 1
Ingredients
- 1 cup coffee beans whole
- 4 cups water cold

Instructions
- Pulse the coffee beans into a grinder to coarse ground.
- A 5-6 cup drinking container works well for this. Pour the iced water on top of the ice cubes. Gently mix the beans to ensure that the water is evenly distributed throughout the beans. To preserve freshness, cover & refrigerate for at least 12 hrs.
- Pour the cold mix into a cheesecloth-lined strainer & place it over the bowl. Cold brew may be kept within the

fridge for almost a week if transferred to a storage container.
- Pour your cold brew in a cup and top it up with milk, water, or sugar to taste.

Nutrition Information
Calories: 215 Kcal, Carbohydrates: 12 g, Protein: 15 g, Fat: 4 g

65. Crab and Corn Salad
Prep Time: 10 Mins, Cook Time: 5 Mins, Servings: 1
Ingredients
- 8 oz meat crab
- 8 oz kernels corn
- 1 sliced thin Fresno chili
- ¼ cup chopped fine bell pepper green
- ¼ cup chopped fine green onion
- ½ tsp powder chili
- ¼ tsp ground cumin
- 2 tbsp chopped cilantro fresh
- 1 juiced & zested navel orange
- 1 juiced & zested lime

Instructions
- Mix all of the ingredients well. Allow the flavors to meld for 5 mins before serving. Serve at room temperature.

Nutrition Information
Calories: 82 kcal, Carbohydrates: 12 g, Protein: 8 g, Fat: 1g

66. Plant-Based Bell Pepper Nacho Boats with Avocado Sauce and Cashew Queso
Prep Time: 15 Mins, Cook Time: 10 Mins, Servings: 2
Ingredients
- Sauce Avocado
- 1 medium avocado
- ¼ cup leaves cilantro
- 2/3 cup of water
- ½ tsp salt kosher
- 1 tsp cumin ground
- 2 tbsp juice lime

Cashew Queso
- 1 cup hot water
- 1 cup raw cashews
- 3 tbsp yeast nutritional
- 1 tsp chili powder chipotle
- ½ tsp paprika smoked
- ½ tsp salt kosher
- ½ tsp powder garlic
- ½ tsp cumin ground

Nacho Boats
- 3 peppers bell
- ¾ cup no-sugar salsa
- cilantro leaves, pickled jalapeno

Instructions
Sauce Avocado
- Blend the ingredients for the avocado sauce until smooth. Add more water if necessary to reach desired consistency. Refrigerate the sauce till you are ready to utilize it.

Cashew Queso
- Blend the ingredients in a food processor or blender to create your cashew queso. Pour the sauce on the nachos and stir to combine, adding more water if necessary to thin it down enough to pour on the nachos. Cashews may be used as a thickening agent if your sauce has been over-watered. Refrigerate the sauce till you are ready to utilize it.

Nacho Boats
- Preheat your oven to 375°F for nacho boats. Parchment lined baking sheet is ready to be used immediately.
- A "cup" is formed when the natural curvature of a bell pepper slice makes a "cup" after the core & seeds are removed.

- Combine the ground beef & salsa in a mixing bowl. Fill your bell pepper canoes with a thin layer of the mixture and set them aside.
- Bake for 10 min, till the peppers, remain hot and slightly softened on a baking sheet.
- To reheat your cashew queso, cook it briefly in a medium saucepan.
- Put your peppers over a platter and attractively arrange them. Add extra garnishes, such as cilantro leaves, pickled jalapeño slices, chopped green or red onions, & olives, to the heated cashew queso & avocado sauce.

Nutrition Information
Calories: 197 kcal, Carbohydrates: 19 g, Protein: 7 g, Fat: 12g

67. Salsa Verde Chicken Casserole
Prep Time: 5 Mins, Cook Time: 35 Mins, Servings: 1
Ingredients
- 16 oz salsa jarred tomatillo
- 4 chicken breasts boneless & skinless
- 1 tsp powder garlic
- ½ tsp salt kosher
- ¼ tsp cumin ground
- ¼ tsp black pepper ground
- 4 oz shredded mozzarella

Instructions
- The oven should be preheated to 375°F.
- Spread tomatillo salsa on the bottom of a casserole dish.
- Put in chicken breasts & season those with cumin, salt, & black pepper.
- Over the top of the chicken, sprinkle on the leftover tomatillo salsa, then serve.
- For a 165-degree internal temperature, bake for 30-35 Mins.

Nutrition Information
Calories: 180 kcal, Carbohydrates: 6 g, Protein: 20 g, Fat: 7g

68. Stir-Fried Green Beans with Radishes
Prep Time: 10 Mins, Cook Time: 10 Mins: Servings: 4
Ingredients
- 1 lb quartered red radishes
- ½ sliced thin onion small
- 2 tbsp low-sodium soy sauce
- 1 lb trimmed green beans
- 2 tsp toasted sesame oil
- 1 tbsp toasted sesame seeds
- 1 tsp chili flakes red

Instructions
- Set moderate heat on a non-stick skillet.
- Adding soy sauce, radishes, and onions
- When the radishes brown and soften, remove them from the pan and set them aside.
- For a further 3-4 Mins, sauté the green beans till they are soft and crisp.
- Allow it cool before adding sesame seeds & oil. Garnish with a dash of hot sauce (optional).

Nutrition Information
Calories: 92 kcal, Carbohydrates: 14 g, Protein: 4 g, Fat: 3g

69. Healthy Instant Pot Lime Chicken
Prep Time: 10 Mins, Cook Time: 40 Mins, Servings: 0.5 cup
Ingredients
- 3 lb chicken breast boneless & skinless
- 2 cups broth chicken
- 3 zested & juiced limes
- ½ tsp salt kosher
- ¼ tsp black pepper ground
- 2 tsp cumin ground

Instructions
- Combine the chicken, salt, pepper, lime juice, chicken broth, lime zest, and cumin in your Instant Pot. Seal the lid & set the timer for 25 mins on manual

higher pressure. Afterward, apply a fast release to remove the remaining pressure completely. A fork may be used to pulverize the meat.
- Whether you're making tacos, quesadillas, or burritos, you can use chicken as a filler!

Nutrition Information
Calories: 275 kcal, Carbohydrates: 4 g, Protein: 49 g, Fat: 6g

70. Fast and Flavorful Chimichurri Shrimp
Prep Time: 5 Mins, Cook Time: 5 Mins, Servings: 1
Ingredients
- 2 cups fresh parsley
- ¼ cup fresh oregano
- 3 cloves garlic
- ½ tsp chili flakes red
- 2 tsp vinegar red wine
- 1/3 cup oil olive
- 1 tsp salt kosher
- 2 lb peeled & deveined shrimp large

Instructions
- The oregano, garlic, chili flakes, and parsley should be processed in the food processor. Pulse until the mixture is finely minced. Pulse till the vinegar & salt are incorporated into the mixture. All except 1 tbsp of olive oil should be added gradually unless well-combined.
- Set the broiler to a low setting. The remaining salt & olive oil should be mixed with the shrimp.
- Then broil for approximately 5 Mins unless the meat is cooked through. Before serving, remove from the oven and mix with chimichurri sauce.

Nutrition Information
Calories: 268 kcal, Carbohydrates: 2 g, Protein: 32 g, Fat: 14g

71. Pesto Chicken with Roasted Tomatoes and Green Beans
Prep Time: 5 Mins, Cook Time: 30 Mins, Servings: 1
Ingredients
- 1 lb ends trimmed green beans
- 1 cup tomatoes grape
- 1 tbsp oil olive
- salt kosher
- black pepper ground
- 4 chicken breasts boneless & skinless
- 2 tbsp pesto
- 4 fat-free mozzarella cheese

Instructions
- Preheat the oven to 425 degrees Fahrenheit.
- Toss your green beans & tomatoes with the oil, salt, & pepper in a large bowl. A baking sheet should be used to distribute the mixture evenly over it. Depending on the size of the beans & tomatoes, the dish should be baked for between 20 and 25 Mins.
- Pat your chicken breasts dry, then season with some salt & pepper while waiting for the chicken to finish cooking. In a large skillet over medium heat, reheat the leftover oil. A hot pan should be ready before you begin cooking the chicken. Spread some pesto over the brown side of your chicken after flipping the chicken over. To ensure that the meat is cooked thoroughly, cook for 5 Mins.
- Place fresh mozzarella slices over top of this cooked chicken. The cheese may be melted by placing a cover on the pan. Roasted beans & tomatoes may be served with the chicken.

Nutrition Information
Calories: 234 kcal, Carbohydrates: 10 g, Protein: 27 g, Fat: 10g

72. Low-Carb Cheesy Meatball Casserole
Prep Time: 15 Mins, Cook Time: 30 Mins, Servings: 3
Ingredients
- 2 lb ground turkey lean
- 1 cup freshly grated Parmesan cheese
- 2 large eggs
- ¼ cup grated onion
- 3 minced garlic cloves
- 2 tbsp chopped parsley
- 2 tsp seasoning Italian
- 1 tsp black pepper ground
- ½ tsp pepper flakes crushed
- kosher salt
- 24 oz marinara sauce jarred low carb
- ½ cup cheese ricotta
- ½ cup shredded mozzarella
- 3 tbsp chopped basil fresh

Instructions
- The oven should be preheated at 400°F.
- Combine ground turkey, eggs, Parmesan cheese, onion, garlic, parsley & Italian spice needed to form the meatballs.
- Scoop or roll your meatballs in 18 equal-sized balls with your hands. Put them in the baking pan.
- When they're done baking, remove the meatballs from the oven.
- Combine the meatballs, ricotta cheese, & marinara sauce. Bake for approximately 10 Mins, till the cheese melts & the sauce, is bubbling, then remove from the oven.
- Garnish with some fresh basil after removing from the oven.

Nutrition Information
Calories: 355 kcal, Carbohydrates: 4 g, Protein: 50 g, Fat: 14g

73. Blackberry Ginger Pork Chops
Prep Time: 10 Mins, Cook Time: 40 Mins, Servings: 1
Ingredients
- 1 cup of blackberries
- 1 tbsp grated ginger fresh
- 2 tbsp honey
- ¼ cup water
- ½ tsp kosher salt
- ¼ tsp cinnamon
- 1 juiced & zested lemon
- 1 tbsp oil olive
- 4 center-cut pork chops
- 1 tsp garlic granulated
- ¼ tsp black pepper ground
- ½ cup broth chicken

Instructions
- On a moderate flame in a small saucepot, combine blackberries, salt, cinnamon, ginger, honey, lemon juice & zest. Cook for around 15-20 mins, often stirring, after bringing to a boil.
- Olive oil should be heated at medium heat while your sauce is simmering. Sear pork chops for five Mins from each side after seasoning with garlic & pepper granules.
- Reduce the heat, add broth, and then cover to complete cooking, approximately 10-15 Minutes. Make sure the chops are roasted completely but not overdone after 7-8 Mins. A minimum internal temp of 145 degrees Fahrenheit is required. Serve with a sauce of blackberry ginger for dipping.

Nutrition Information
Calories: 298 kcal, Carbohydrates: 16 g, Protein: 30 g, Fat: 13g

74. Chocolate Raspberry Truffles
Prep Time: 10 Mins, Cook time: 3 hrs, Servings: 1 Truffle
Ingredients
Truffles
- 1 cup frozen raspberries
- 1 cup unsalted walnuts raw
- ½ cup desiccated coconut
- 6 pitted Medjool dates
- 3 tbsp powder cocoa
- 1 tsp extract vanilla
- ¼ tsp salt

Outer Coating
- ½ cup desiccated coconut
- 3 tbsp raspberries freeze-dried

Instructions
- In your food processor, combine all truffle ingredients & pulse until they form a homogeneous paste.
- Place the 1" balls over a baking sheet that has been lined with parchment paper.
- Refrigerate for fifteen to thirty Mins before using.
- Meantime, in a food processor, mix the ingredients for the outer coating & pulse 2 to 3 times or unless the coconut becomes pink.
- Ensure the truffles are out of the fridge before rolling each one in the coating.
- Re-chill in the fridge for approximately three hrs, or unless the cheese has set.

Nutrition Information
Calories: 144 kcal, Carbohydrates: 17 g, Protein: 2 g, Fat: 9g

75. Seared Tuna with Wasabi Cream
Prep Time: 10 Mins, Cook Time: 30 Mins, Servings: 1 steak
Ingredients
- 1 tbsp oil olive
- 24 oz steaks tuna
- ¼ cup sauce ponzu
- 1 tbsp paste wasabi
- 1 tbsp water
- 2 tsp minced fresh ginger
- 1 tbsp cream coconut
- 2 tsp aminos coconut

Instructions
- Tuna should marinate for around 10 mins in ponzu. In a pan, heat olive oil to medium-high heat. Sear the tuna for 3 mins on all sides in your skillet. Even after cooking, the core of the tuna would remain pink.
- In a mixing bowl, mix the rest of the ingredients until they form a smooth mixture. Tuna should be drizzled with the sauce.

Nutrition Information
Calories: 298 kcal, Carbohydrates: 2 g, Protein: 40 g, Fat: 13g

76. Broccoli Cashew Crunch Salad
Prep Time: 10 Mins, Cook time: 20 Mins, Servings: 1
Ingredients
- ¼ cup of mayonnaise
- 2 tsp vinegar apple cider
- 1 tsp honey
- ¼ tsp chili flakes red
- 1 lb broccoli
- 1 peeled & sliced thin carrot
- 1 chopped bell pepper red
- 1 sliced thin shallot
- ¼ cup cranberries dried
- ¼ cup chopped roasted cashews

Instructions
- Mix all ingredients well. Allow it to settle for 20 mins or a whole night. Serve ice-cold.

Nutrition Information
Calories: 114 kcal, Carbohydrates: 16 g, Protein: 3 g, Fat: 5g

77. Slow Cooker Everything Beef
Prep Time: 5 Mins, Cook Time: 6 hrs, Servings: 3
Ingredients
- 3 lb ground beef roast
- ¼ cup olive oil extra virgin
- ¼ cup chopped garlic
- 1 & ½ tsp salt sea
- 1 tsp pepper
- ½ cup broth vegetable

Instructions
- In a slow cooker, place the meat roast. Drizzle olive oil, sea salt, garlic, and pepper over the chicken. Pour vegetable broth on the beef's exterior.
- Assemble your meal by covering and cooking for 8 to 10 hrs, or 6 to 8 hrs, on low heat.
- Remove the meat from your crockpot once it is so soft that you can shred it using a fork.
- Make tacos with it, cover it with some teriyaki sauce, then serve it on brown rice for just an Asian touch. Enjoy!

Nutrition Information
Calories: 332 kcal, Carbohydrates: 2 g, Protein: 29 g, Fat: 23g

78. Blackened Sockeye Salmon
Prep Time: 5 Mins, Cook Time: 15 Mins, Servings: 1
Ingredients
- 12 oz salmon fillets sockeye
- 2 tbsp divided canola oil
- Spices Blackened
- 1 tbsp thyme dried
- 2 tsp powder garlic
- 1 tsp oregano dried
- 1 tbsp paprika
- 1 tbsp pepper black
- 1 tsp pepper cayenne
- sea salt kosher

Instructions
- Add the spices to a medium bowl and mix well.
- All sides of salmon should be coated with olive oil. Season all sides of the fish evenly. Toss the salmon with the leftover oil in a pan and cook over medium-high heat. On medium-low, cook salmon for 5-6 mins on all sides. The salmon must flake readily using a fork & the skin must be crispy.

Nutrition Information
Calories: 260 kcal, Carbohydrates: 4 g, Protein: 19 g, Fat: 19g

79. Orange Miso Wild Cod Recipe
Prep Time: 5 Mins, Cook Time: 18 Mins, Servings: 1
Ingredients
- 24 oz wild skinless cod fillet
- 2 tbsp miso paste mellow white
- ¼ cup soy sauce low sodium
- 1 tbsp honey
- 1 zested & juiced navel orange
- 1 tbsp ginger paste minced ginger

Instructions
- Set the oven temperature to 375°F.
- Combine navel orange zest and juice, soy sauce, miso paste, honey, coconut aminos, and chopped ginger in a large mixing bowl & stir until well combined. Stir till all ingredients are combined.
- Add some cooking spray to a baking sheet. Put in some parts of fish.
- Apply the miso glaze to the fish.
- For 10-15 mins in a 375-deg oven should do the trick.
- Increase oven temp to a high broil. Keep an eye on everything, checking every 2 to 3 mins to make sure you don't overheat.
- When the glaze has browned, and the fish isn't any longer transparent and flaky, it's done.

Nutrition Information
Calories: 200 kcal, Carbohydrates: 12 g, Protein: 32 g, Fat: 2g

80. Sriracha Salmon Power Bowl
Prep Time: 10 Mins, Cook Time: 40 Mins, Servings: 1
Ingredients
- ½ tbsp oil olive
- 6 oz skinless salmon
- 2 tsp Seasoning Old Bay
- ½ cup cubed sweet potatoes
- ½ tsp salt Kosher
- ¼ cup broth chicken

- ¼ cup shredded carrots
- ¼ cup of broccoli
- ¼ cup of arugula
- ½ cup of spinach
- 1 tbsp sriracha
- 1 wedges lime
- 1 tbsp chopped cilantro fresh

Instructions
- Set the oven temperature to 375 degrees. Rub olive oil & Bay Seasoning on the fish before cooking. Roast for around 18 to 22 mins, or unless crisp & flaky, in a medium baking dish.
- Sprinkle the sweet potato cubes with leftover olive oil & salt in a baking dish during the salmon's roasting. Bake at 375°F for 20 to 25 mins, unless the sweet potatoes become soft but not mush. Remove from the oven and let cool before serving.
- The nonstick skillet should be preheated to medium heat. Toss in some broccoli, matchstick carrots, & a quarter cup of chicken or veggie stock. Vegetables should be cooked for around 5 mins or until they're tender.
- Divide your baby arugula & baby spinach into 2 serving dishes and toss them together with the lemon juice. Sauteed veggies and sweet potatoes should be layered on top. Top each dish with skinless salmon. Serve with lime wedges, cilantro, & sriracha chili sauce drizzled over the top.

Nutrition Information
Calories: 216 kcal, Carbohydrates: 15 g, Protein: 19 g, Fat: 9g

81. Baked Apple Chips
Prep Time: 10 Mins, Cook Time: 2 hrs, Servings: 3
Ingredients
- 2 thinly sliced apples cored
- cinnamon

Instructions
- Make sure the oven is preheated at 275°F.
- Sliced apples should be placed on a parchment-lined cookie sheet.
- Add a dash of cinnamon on top (to taste).
- To bake for 2 hrs, set the timer to 2 hrs. After the first 60 Mins, rotate every slice to ensure equal cooking. To avoid overcooking them, you must check after 60 mins & every 30 mins after that.
- Remove these from your oven after they've browned and crisped up to your liking.

Nutrition Information
Calories: 32 kcal, Carbohydrates: 8.5 g, Protein: 12 g, Fat: 7 g

82. Paleo Friendly Meaty Veggie Roll-Ups
Prep Time: 10 Mins, Cook Time: 10 Mins, Servings: 3
Ingredients
- 12 thick deli meat slices unprocessed
- 1 cup sliced vegetables
- 12 optional chives

Instructions
- Take one or two slices from the meat case and pile as many veggies as you'd like over it. Utilize a chive to bind your roll together if desired.
- Rolls should be stored in a container to prevent odors from leaking out.
- Favorite Combinations of Flavors:
- Beef roast, carrot sticks, red pepper strips, & cucumber slices using mustard for the dipping.
- Chicken with red cabbage, apples, & pickle strips dipped in Dijon mustard.
- Turkey, avocado, bacon, & salsa for the dipping in a taco shell.

Nutrition Information
Calories: 71 kcal, Carbohydrates: 1.2 g, Protein: 11.3 g, Fat: 2g

83. Cabbage Garlic Veggie Soup
Prep Time: 10 Mins, Cook Time: 30 Mins, Servings: 2
Ingredients
- 2 tsp oil olive
- 1 chopped yellow onion
- 3 chopped celery stalks
- 3 chopped carrots
- 4 minced garlic cloves
- 8 oz beans green
- 6 cups low sodium vegetable broth
- 28 oz canned diced tomatoes
- 2 tbsp Seasoning Italian
- 2 tsp turmeric ground
- ½ tsp salt kosher
- ¼ tsp black pepper ground
- 1 green cabbage head
- 1 zucchini
- 1 squash yellow

Instructions
- In a small skillet, heat the olive oil to medium heat. Add the onions, celery, & carrots. Stirring constantly, cook for 5 mins until golden brown on both sides. Gather your ingredients and begin tossing them into a large pot.
- Then decrease the heat & simmer for another 15 Mins. A further 10 Mins of simmering are required for the vegetables to soften.

Nutrition Information
Calories: 74 kcal, Carbohydrates: 15 g, Protein: 3 g, Fat: 1g

84. Slow Cooker Chunky Beef and Potato Stew
Prep Time: 20 Mins, Cook Time: 4 hrs, Servings: 1
Ingredients
- 2 lb lean stew meat chuck
- ¼ cup of flour
- 2 tbsp extra-virgin divided olive oil
- 3 peeled & chopped potatoes large
- 14 & ½ oz fire-roasted tomatoes can be diced
- 1 minced garlic clove
- ½ cup chopped onion
- 1 tsp vinegar balsamic
- 1 leaf bay
- ½ tsp sea salt kosher
- ½ tsp pepper black
- 3-4 cups low-sodium beef broth
- 2 tsp sauce Worcestershire
- 1 tsp chopped dried oregano
- 1 tsp paprika

Instructions
- Pour the ingredients into a bowl & mix well. Toss the meat cubes with the flour mixture and then dredge them.
- On medium heat, add half of the oil to a medium skillet. A 30-sec sear on each side is sufficient to get medium-rare results when cooking beef cubes in the pan. Just tan the outside of the meat, not the inside, and toss it out of the way. Repeat with the leftover oil and meat cubes.
- Add the meat and the drippings to your slow cooker. The diced tomatoes, along with the liquid added to the onions, potatoes, & Worcestershire sauce.
- Add the balsamic vinegar, oregano, paprika, garlic, & bay leaf to the broth. Cook for around 4-6 hrs or 8-10 hrs, depending on how long you'd want it to cook. Stir thoroughly.

Nutrition Information
Calories: 233 kcal, Carbohydrates: 17 g, Protein: 23 g, Fat: 8g

85. Parchment Baked Fish and Vegetables
Prep Time: 15 Mins, Cook Time: 30 Mins, Servings: 1
Ingredients
- 2 gutted & halved whole fish
- 4 oz clams
- 8 spears asparagus
- 12 shrimp
- 2 diced zucchinis

- 8 halved cherry tomatoes
- 2 halved cloves garlic
- 1 halved lemon
- 4 fresh thyme sprigs
- 4 leaves basil
- 1 tsp oregano dried
- ½ cup white wine dry
- 2 tsp oil olive
- 1 tsp salt kosher
- ¼ tsp black pepper ground

Instructions
- Set the oven temperature to 375 degrees. Four 20-inch-long parchment paper should be cut from a sheet of paper. Layout each piece of parchment paper & divide the ingredients evenly among the pouches. Using butchers' twine, secure each packet. 30 Mins in the oven should do it. Serve it hot.

Nutrition Information
Calories: 106 kcal, Carbohydrates: 10 g, Protein: 7 g, Fat: 3g

86. Vegan Nut-Free Garlic Basil Pesto
Prep Time: 5 Mins, Cook Time: 10 Mins, Servings: 1
Ingredients
- 2 cups fresh basil leaves
- 3 garlic cloves
- ½ tsp salt Kosher
- 2 tbsp juice lemon
- 1/3 cup seeds sunflower
- 2 tbsp oil olive
- needed water

Instructions
- In your food processor, combine all ingredients except for olive oil and mix till the appropriate consistency is achieved. Pesto may be overly thick when all the olive oil is used. To thin it up, gradually add some water.

Nutrition Information
Calories: 44 kcal, Carbohydrates: 1 g, Protein: 1 g, Fat: 4g

87. Slow Cooker Pomegranate Chicken Breasts
Prep Time: 15 Mins, Cook Time: 6 hrs, Servings: 1
Ingredients
- 1 & ½ -2 lb chicken breasts boneless & skinless
- ½ tsp pepper black
- sea salt kosher
- 1 tsp coriander
- 1 tsp powder chili
- ¼ tsp pepper cayenne
- 2 tsp oregano dried
- 2 tbsp olive oil extra virgin
- 1 tbsp mustard Dijon
- 2 tbsp honey
- 2 minced garlic cloves
- 1 & ½ cups no sugar pomegranate juice
- 1 tbsp vinegar white balsamic

Instructions
- Add the herbs & spices to a medium bowl and stir well.
- Add the spices, herbs, & olive oil to a large bowl and combine well. Pat chicken dry using the paper towel after rinsing it. Place the chicken within a slow cooker, then coat with herb & oil mixture.
- Mix in a medium-sized bowl. Toss chicken breasts with a mixture of Dijon mustard & minced garlic, honey, pomegranate juice & balsamic vinegar.
- Cook for 4 to 6 hrs on low in your slow cooker. To serve the chicken, take it from your slow cooker & pour some of the liquid over it. A modest serving of spaghetti goes well with this juicy chicken. 165°F is the recommended setting for the Slow Cooker.

Nutrition Information
Calories: 279 kcal, Carbohydrates: 19 g, Protein: 26 g, Fat: 10g

88. Skinny Mini Desserts - Banana Pudding
Prep Time: 10 Mins, Cook time: 20 Mins, Servings: 4
Ingredients
- 10 whole almonds
- 2 tbsp cornstarch
- sea salt or kosher
- 3 tbsp palm sugar coconut
- 1 egg slightly beaten yolk
- ¾ cup of milk
- ½ tsp vanilla
- 2 thinly sliced bananas

Instructions
- Preheat the oven to around 325°F. While the pudding is being prepared, roast the almonds for around 12 mins at 350 degrees Fahrenheit. Almonds may be minced using your food processor after they have cooled.
- Salt & sugar should be added to the cornstarch mixture in your saucepan. Combine the dry ingredients with the egg yolk. Add the milk gradually & keep stirring until the mixture is well incorporated. Cook over medium-low heat, often stirring, until the sauce thickens and coats the back of a spoon. Continue to heat until it reaches a pudding-like texture.
- Remove from the heat and whisk in vanilla. Replace bananas into dessert dishes with pudding while it's still warm. Top your pudding with a layer of finely chopped almonds. If preferred, garnish with a dollop of whipped cream.

Nutrition Information
Calories: 102 kcal, Carbohydrates: 19 g, Protein: 2 g, Fat: 2g

89. Rustic-Style Italian Chicken
Prep Time: 5 Mins, Cook Time: 30 Mins, Servings: 1
Ingredients
- 24 oz chicken breast boneless & skinless
- ½ tsp salt kosher
- ¼ tsp black pepper ground
- 3 tbsp oil olive
- 1 pepper bell red
- 1 onion yellow
- 2 minced cloves garlic
- 15 oz no sugar diced tomatoes
- 1 tbsp seasoning Italian
- ½ cup chicken broth low sodium
- ¼ cup chopped parsley fresh

Instructions
- Apply Salt & pepper to your chicken before cooking it. On medium-low heat, add olive oil, and the chicken should be browned on all sides before being removed from the pan.
- Add the leftover olive oil, onion, red & yellow peppers, & garlic to the pan where the chicken was cooked. The veggies should only be cooked until they start to soften. Chicken stock, chopped tomatoes, & Italian spice are all added together in this step. The chicken should be returned to your pan and brought to a gentle simmer. Cover the pan and simmer it on low heat for approximately 20 Mins, unless the chicken has cooked through & very tender. Serve with a generous sprinkling of fresh parsley.

Nutrition Information
Calories: 337 kcal, Carbohydrates: 11 g, Protein: 38 g, Fat: 15g

90. Italian Sausage Kale Soup
Prep Time: 10 Mins, Cook Time: 45 Mins, Servings: 3
Ingredients
- 1 tbsp oil olive
- 1 diced yellow onion
- 2 diced carrots
- 2 diced celery stalks
- 3 minced garlic cloves
- 1 lb turkey sausage Italian

- 28 oz diced, canned tomatoes
- 1 tbsp seasoning Italian
- 6 cups broth chicken
- 2 tsp chili flakes red
- 15 oz drained & rinsed cannellini beans
- 1 lb kale roughly chopped stem removed

Instructions
- Over moderate flame, add olive oil to a big soup pot. In a large saucepan, cook sausage crumbles until crisp-tender. Then take it out of the pot.
- For 5 mins, cook the onions, carrots, & celery in a pan. Sauté the garlic for a further Min before removing it from the heat. Tomatoes with their juices and Italian spice are added to the pan, and the broth and chili flakes.
- For 20 Mins, bring to a boil and then decrease the heat to simmer. Cook the cannellini

beans & kale for a further 5-10 mins after adding them to the pot. Serve warm.

Nutrition Information
Calories: 168 kcal, Carbohydrates: 16 g, Protein: 12 g, Fat: 8g

91. Classic Italian Meatballs
Prep Time: 10 Mins, Cook Time: 10 Mins, Servings: 2
Ingredients
- 2 lb ground turkey lean
- 2 tsp oregano dried
- 2 tbsp freshly chopped Italian parsley
- 1 tsp pepper black
- sea salt or kosher
- ½ tsp crushed pepper flakes red
- 4 finely minced cloves of garlic
- 2 cups panko whole wheat
- 1 cup freshly grated parmesan cheese
- 2 large eggs

Instructions
- In a wide mixing bowl, combine all of the ingredients. Make (24) 1-inch meatballs out of the mixture.
- To prepare meatballs, heat a large pan with olive oil over medium heat & fry until browned & cooked over both sides. It's important to note that meatballs should not be cooked all the way through when added to a slow-cooker dish since they would continue to cook while within a slow-cooker.

Nutrition Information
Calories: 136 kcal, Carbohydrates: 13 g, Protein: 11 g, Fat: 5g

92. The Best and Easiest Glazed Ham Recipe for the Holidays
Prep Time: 5 Mins, Cook Time: 2 hrs 30 Mins, Servings: 4
Ingredients
- 1 bone-in unsliced & fully cooked ham
- cloves whole
- ½ cup of honey
- 2 tbsp packed brown sugar
- 2 tsp mustard Dijon
- 1 tsp vinegar apple cider

Instructions
- The oven should be preheated at 325 degrees Fahrenheit.
- Place your ham in a big casserole dish with a rack within the middle of the dish.
- Make deep incisions in the diamond pattern on the ham's surface. Use a full clove for every diamond point.
- Bake the ham for 2 hrs, till it hits a temperature of 130°F, and then remove it from the oven and let it rest.
- Add brown sugar, honey, & mustard to a saucepan and bring to a boil. Remove from the heat and set aside to cool somewhat.
- Remove your ham from the oven and toss the foil in the garbage. The ham should be coated with the glaze in a uniform layer all over.
- Additional 15-30 Mins of baking time is needed to attain a final temperature of 140 degrees Fahrenheit.
- Slicing and serving the ham should wait almost 15 mins as it rests. Make multiple vertical slices toward the bone for uncut meat and stop when the knife touches it. To release the slices, run your knife vertically along the bone. Repeat the same on the other side of the ham. You'll just need to create the vertical slice for a spiral sliced ham.

Nutrition Information
Calories: 333 kcal, Carbohydrates: 12 g, Protein: 28 g, Fat: 16g

93. Slow Cooker Pork Carnitas
Prep Time: 5 Mins, Cook Time: 8 hrs, Servings: 4
Ingredients
- 1 tbsp powder chili
- 1 tbsp paprika smoked
- 2 tsp cumin ground
- 2 tsp oregano dried
- 1 tsp salt kosher
- 1 tsp black pepper ground
- ½ tsp pepper flakes red
- 4 lb loin pork
- 1 quartered yellow onion
- 3 crushed cloves garlic
- 2 sliced limes

Instructions
- Combine the black pepper, oregano, salt, paprika, cumin, & red pepper flakes in a mixing bowl. Mix thoroughly. Rub both sides of the pork loin with the spice mixture. For optimal taste, cover & refrigerate for at least an hr & up to overnight.
- Slow cook your pork once it has rested for a few hrs. Toss some onion and garlic on top of the meat before cooking. Slice the limes and use the juice to season the meat before cooking it. The lime halves should also be added to the slow cookers. Cook your pork until it's cooked, about 4 hrs on high or 8 hrs on low.
- It is time to take out all but a liquid from your slow cooker & shred your pork when it is done cooking. Serve.

Nutrition Information
Calories: 321 kcal, Carbohydrates: 5 g, Protein: 52 g, Fat: 10g

94. Oven Baked Apple Pork Chops
Prep Time: 10 Mins, Cook Time: 20 Mins, Servings: 1
Ingredients
- 4 center fat pork chops
- 1 tsp oil olive
- to taste kosher salt
- black pepper ground
- 1 tsp thyme leaves dried
- 2 cored & sliced apples
- 1 tbsp sugar brown
- 1 tsp cinnamon ground

Instructions
- The oven should be preheated at 425 degrees Fahrenheit. Spray your baking pan using nonstick spray & line it with Al foil.
- Your pork chops should be equally distributed on a baking sheet. Use olive oil to coat the chicken, then season with salt, pepper & thyme before cooking. The pork chops should be topped with apple slices with cinnamon & brown sugar.
- Pork & apples should be cooked thoroughly in around 20-25 Mins. Serve warm.

Nutrition Information
Calories: 240 kcal, Carbohydrates: 16 g, Protein: 30 g, Fat: 6g

95. Maple Mustard Chicken Thighs
Prep Time: 5 Mins, Cook Time: 40 Mins, Servings: 6
Ingredients
- 2 lb chicken thighs boneless & skinless

- ½ cup mustard yellow
- ½ cup syrup maple
- 1 cup low sodium chicken broth
- ½ tsp salt kosher

Instructions
- The oven should be preheated at 375°F. Mix maple syrup, yellow mustard, & salt in a large mixing bowl. Mix well until all ingredients are incorporated.
- Pour your chicken broth into a baking dish that can go into the oven. Place the chicken thighs inside a baking dish and bake for 30 Mins at 350 degrees. Chicken should be uniformly coated with a combination of maple syrup and mustard before serving.
- Bake for around 35-40 Mins, depending on the size of your pan. As just a sandwich, either shredded or whole may be served.

Nutrition Information
Calories: 268 kcal, Carbohydrates: 19 g, Protein: 30 g, Fat: 7g

96. The Perfect Turkey and Gravy
Prep Time: 1 day, Cook Time: 4 hrs, Servings: 6
Ingredients
- 1 thawed whole turkey
- coconut oil melted olive oil
- rub dry
- 2 cups chicken broth low sodium

Turkey Gravy
- gizzards, giblets, neck
- 3 & ½ cups of chicken broth low sodium
- 1 tsp rub dry
- ¼ cup of flour

Instructions
- Preheat your oven at 450°F.
- While your oven is heating up, remove the turkey from the fridge. You might use the turkey's giblets, neck, & gizzards to make gravy & stock if you did not brine it.
- The roasting rack within the roasting pan should be used to cook the turkey. Tuck the turkey's wings underneath it and bind the legs together to ensure consistent cooking.
- Liquefied olive oil may be used to coat the turkey's skin, and a dry rub may be used to season the turkey to your liking. If you were using brine, there is no need to add more salt. Before roasting, add some orange or lemon slices, garlic, or the onion quarter to the bird cavity.
- Promptly wiggle a probe thermometer into the deepest portion of the turkey's thigh or breast to be sure it doesn't strike bone.
- A large roasting pan should have a layer of vegetables on the bottom, including onion, carrots, and celery.
- Get your oven ready for Thanksgiving by placing the turkey leg-side-up in the oven. The rear of the oven is usually warmer, allowing the dark meat to attain its higher temperatures more quickly.
- Lower the temperature to 325°F. Based on the scale of the turkey and its cooking time, roast for 3-4 hrs, or unless the probe thermometer inserted into the breast flesh registers 170°F.
- While your turkey is baking, resist the impulse to peek inside the oven. Leaving the oven door open will allow the heat to escape, resulting in a longer cooking time.
- Make gravy using turkey drippings & let the bird rest almost 30 mins before cutting.

Turkey Gravy
- Add the ingredients to a saucepan and boil for 1 hr while the turkey cooks.
- Gizzards should be discarded, as well as the neck.
- Make 4 cups of stock from the turkey drippings when it's finished cooking. If necessary, top it with extra broth.
- Whisk in the flour until it is completely incorporated and there are no lumps left.
- Bring the pot up to a boil by putting it back on the heat. Add water if necessary to get the required consistency.

Nutrition Information
Calories: 357 kcal, Carbohydrates: 7 g, Protein: 51 g, Fat: 13g

97. Loaded Greek Sweet Potato Fries
Prep Time: 10 Mins, Cook Time: 30 Mins, Servings: 4
Ingredients
- 2 large, sweet potatoes
- 2 tsp oil olive
- Kosher salt
- black pepper ground
- ½ cup Greek yogurt plain
- 1 minced garlic clove
- ½ tsp juice lemon
- 2 tbsp grated cucumber
- 1 tsp dill dried
- ½ cup diced small Roma tomato
- ¼ cup diced small red onion
- ¼ cup feta cheese fat-free

Instructions
- The oven should be preheated at 425 degrees Fahrenheit. Set aside the baking sheet that has been sprayed using a nonstick spray.
- Gather all of the ingredients in a big bowl and mix well. Toss the potatoes thoroughly to coat them with the oil. Spread out evenly on a baking sheet that has been prepared. Once soft, remove from the oven and let cool for a few Mins.
- Mix all of the ingredients for the Greek yogurt dip while potato fries are baking. Set aside to cool.
- Remove your fries from the oven and allow them to cool. Top with onion, tomato, and feta, then drizzle with cucumber yogurt mix. Serve warm.

Nutrition Information
Calories: 125 kcal, Carbohydrates: 17 g, Protein: 5 g, Fat: 4g

98. Plant-Based Cheese Spread that Tastes Great on Everything
Prep Time: 10 Mins, Cook Time: 10 Mins, Servings: 2
Ingredients
- 1 & ½ cups raw cashews
- 2 tbsp yeast nutritional
- 1 minced garlic clove
- ½ tsp salt
- 1 zest & juice lemon
- ½ cup of water
- 8 finely diced chives
- ¼ cup finely chopped parsley

Instructions
- Blend everything except the chives & parsley in a blender until smooth and creamy.
- Blend all ingredients in the food processor or blender until they reach a smooth, creamy consistency.
- Add the chopped chives & parsley to a spread in the bowl.
- Before serving, cover & refrigerate for almost two to three hrs.

Nutrition Information
Calories: 146 kcal, Carbohydrates: 10 g, Protein: 6 g, Fat: 11g

99. Instant Pot Apple-Cinnamon Chicken
Prep Time: 5 Mins, Cook Time: 40 Mins, Servings: 4
Ingredients
- 1 tbsp oil olive
- 1 sliced thin yellow onion
- 2 cored & sliced thin apples
- 3 lb chicken breasts boneless, skinless
- 1 tsp cinnamon
- ½ tsp powder garlic
- ½ tsp salt
- ½ tsp pepper black
- 1 cup broth chicken

Instructions
- Select "sauté" in the Instant Pot. Add some olive oil & the chicken when the pan is hot. Make sure the chicken is well-browned on both sides before serving. To save time, remove your chicken from the pot. For one Min, sauté the onions & apples within a pot. Remove the lid from Instant Pot & add the chicken, seasonings, salt, & pepper to taste.
- Cook for around 22 Mins at high pressure within Instant Pot on manual mode. It's best to let the pressure gradually dissipate for around 10 Mins before using the rapid release technique to finish. Serve your chicken, shredded with 2 forks.

Nutrition Information
Calories: 318 kcal, Carbohydrates: 10 g, Protein: 49 g, Fat: 8g

100. Easy 2-Ingredient Sweet Potato Pancakes
Prep Time: 10 Mins, Cook Time: 10 Mins, Servings: 2
Ingredients
- 1 cup mashed sweet potatoes
- 2 large eggs

Instructions
- Both sweet potato & egg should be mixed. Stir well. You can also add cinnamon if you'd like.
- Add some non-stick spray to a pan & heat it up over medium-high heat. A quarter of the batter should be put in. To get the best results, cook pancakes for 3-4 minutes or until they bubble inside the middle. Flip & cook for the next 2-3 mins, or until the meat is done. Remove your pancake from the pan & continue the procedure until all of the batter has been utilized. In between batches of pancakes, coat the skillet using non-stick spray.
- Serve warm. A variety of sweeteners and jams may be used to customize this dish.

Nutrition Information
Calories: 79 kcal, Carbohydrates: 9 g, Protein: 4 g, Fat: 3g

101. Best Creamy Slow Cooker Broccoli Cheddar Soup
Prep Time: 10 Mins, Cook Time: 6 hrs, Servings: 1
Ingredients
- 3 tbsp flour whole wheat
- 1 cup of low-fat organic preferred milk
- 3 tbsp oil olive
- 4 cups broth chicken
- 1 lb thawed & chopped broccoli frozen
- 3 cups shredded cheddar cheese
- 1 minced garlic clove

Instructions
- The oil should be heated but not so hot that it smokes in a frying pan. Stir in flour a bit at a time with a whisk until the flour & oil are well combined, the oil begins to bubble, & the mixture becomes golden and aromatic.
- When adding the milk, constantly whisk to ensure that a thick cream forms. Remove from the heat after the vegetable stock or chicken has been entirely absorbed.
- Add your thawed broccoli to a slow cooker after you've added the rest of the ingredients. We like to use frozen broccoli to hold up better into the slow cooker. However, you may instead use green broccoli florets. Toss in the seasonings of your choice, including salt, pepper, & garlic.
- On medium for around 4-6 hrs, or unless your broccoli is tender, the cheese should be added in a cupful at a time, stirring until melted after each addition.
- Blend the soup in stages, filling the blender halfway each time until smooth. As an alternative, you may use a hand mixer. Make careful to scrape any residual cheese from the slow cooker in the soup to ensure a smooth and creamy consistency. Make the soup as smooth or chunky as desired by blending as much according to your preference.

Nutrition Information
Calories: 360 kcal, Carbohydrates: 10 g, Protein: 20 g, Fat: 27g

102. Sweet Potato Crunchies
Prep Time: 10 Mins, Cook Time: 30 Mins, Servings: 3
Ingredients
- 1 potato sweet
- 1 tbsp oil olive

Instructions
- Cut your sweet potato in julienne strips after peeling it.
- Preheat your oven to 375°F.
- Pour olive oil over the strings & toss to cover them. Spread the strings out on a cookie sheet in an equal layer. Bake for 30 Mins, stirring every 10 mins, unless crispy. After taking it out of your oven, the strings would proceed to crisp up a little more. Remove all brown potato threads from the dish. Allow it to cool around room temp. Ziplock bags or other sealed containers are ideal for storing.

Nutrition Information
Calories: 117 kcal, Carbohydrates: 13 g, Protein: 1 g, Fat: 7g

103. Instant Pot Everything Shredded Chicken
Prep Time: 5 Mins, Cook Time: 28 Mins, Servings: 5
Ingredients
- 3 lb chicken breasts boneless, skinless
- 1 peeled, halved onion medium
- 3 celery stalks
- 2 peeled & crushed garlic cloves
- 1 tsp salt kosher
- ½ tsp black pepper ground
- 2 tsp turmeric ground
- 1 & ½ cups of low-sodium chicken broth

Instructions
- Make a soup in the Instant Pot by adding onion, celery, & cloves of garlic.
- Salt, pepper, & turmeric should be properly combined in a medium mixing bowl.
- Apply a variety of spices to the chicken breasts.
- In the Instant Pot, place the chicken breasts over the top of the veggies.
- Seal the Instant Pot with the chicken broth & cook on high pressure for 30 Mins.
- Set the pressure to "High" and the timer to "Manual" for 18 Mins.
- Allow the pressure to naturally dissipate for 10 mins, then actively release the pressure until the pressure gauge's indication lowers.
- Make a forkful of chicken schnitzel out of the chicken breasts. Cooked veggies may be discarded, or they can be pureed and frozen for future use.

Nutrition Information
Calories: 187 kcal, Carbohydrates: 2 g, Protein: 33 g, Fat: 4g

104. Cheesy Scalloped Zucchini
Prep Time: 15 Mins, Cook Time: 45 Mins, Servings: 5
Ingredients
- 1 cup cottage cheese low-fat
- 4 large egg white
- 2 tbsp milk skim
- ½ tsp salt kosher
- 1 tbsp mustard Dijon
- 2 tsp chopped thyme leaves
- 1 tbsp flour
- 6 zucchinis
- 2 cup shredded cheddar cheese fat-free

Instructions
- Preheat the oven to 375°F. Set aside the casserole dish that has been sprayed using non-stick spray.
- Combine all ingredients in a large mixing basin, excluding the cheddar cheese & zucchini, then stir until evenly distributed.
- Layer the casserole dish with zucchini. Sprinkle some cheddar cheese on top of your cottage cheese mix. Once all ingredients have been utilized, finish with the cheddar cheese.

- Cover your zucchini with the nonstick layer of foil. Take it out of the oven after 30 Mins. Continue baking for 15-20 more Mins or till golden and bubbling after removing the lid. Before serving, let it settle for ten Mins.

Nutrition Information
Calories: 112 kcal, Carbohydrates: 9 g, Protein: 14 g, Fat: 2g

105. Vegan Coconut Curry in as Little as 30 Mins!
Prep Time: 20 Mins, Cook Time: 30 Mins, Servings: 2
Ingredients
- 2 tbsp olive oil extra-virgin
- 1 diced small onion
- 2 minced cloves garlic
- 1 large chopped sweet potato
- 2 cups florets broccoli
- 4 tsp curry spices curry powder
- ½ tsp salt
- ½ tsp pepper black
- 1 coconut milk canned
- 2 tbsp water
- 1 & 15 oz can of tomatoes diced

Instructions
- Add coconut oil to a big saucepan that has been heated.
- Toss in some chopped onion and minced garlic. Cook for approximately one Min.
- Salt and pepper to taste before adding the potatoes, vegetables, and curry powder Stir regularly until all ingredients have melted and become pliable.
- A few Mins later, add the coconut milk & water, then simmer for the next 10-15 mins.
- Allow the tinned tomatoes to simmer for the additional 5 Mins before serving. Turn off the burner and let the curry cool down. Serve with quinoa.

Nutrition Information
Calories: 263 kcal, Carbohydrates: 19 g, Protein: 4 g, Fat: 21g

106. Roasted Spicy Maple Pecans
Prep Time: 5 Mins, Cook Time: 20 Mins, Servings: 3
Ingredients
- 1 tsp. oil olive
- 2 cups halves shelled pecan
- ¼ cup syrup maple
- ½ tsp. salt
- 1 tsp. cinnamon
- ¼ tsp. pepper cayenne
- ¼ tsp. nutmeg ground
- ¼ tsp. cloves ground

Instructions
- The oven should be preheated to 350°F.
- A big baking sheet is ideal for tossing the pecans and the rest of the ingredients together. Place on a flat surface and spread evenly.
- Check after every 10 mins to ensure the nuts don't burn. Roast for around 15-20 Mins.
- In a thin layer, transfer pecans out of the oven & onto wax paper to cool.
- Ensure that the container is airtight.

Nutrition Information
Calories: 241 kcal, Carbohydrates: 11 g, Protein: 3 g, Fat: 22g

107. Juicy Faux Fried Chicken
Prep Time: 20 Mins, Cook Time: 15 Mins, Servings: 1
Ingredients
- ½ cup buttermilk non-fat
- 1 & ½ tbsp mustard Dijon
- 2 minced garlic cloves
- 2 tsp sauce hot
- 2-2 & ½ lb chicken breasts split
- 1 cup whole wheat flour white
- 1 tsp paprika
- 1 tsp thyme dried
- 1 tsp powder baking
- 1/8 tsp sea salt or kosher
- ½ tsp pepper black

Instructions
- The oven should be preheated at 425°F.
- Whisk together all the mustard, garlic, buttermilk, & spicy sauce in a large and deep bowl. Chicken should be added to the pan and flipped over to coat all sides.
- Use parchment paper to cover a baking pan.
- Salt & pepper to taste are all that's needed for this recipe.
- Seasoned flour should be stored in an airtight container. Shake the container vigorously while adding the chicken to two pieces at once. Place your chicken on the baking sheet after shaking off any leftover flour.
- The cooking spray may be used to coat your chicken's top & sides. The chicken should be golden brown over the outside and no pinker inside the middle during this time.

Nutrition Information
Calories: 262 kcal, Carbohydrates: 10 g, Protein: 42 g, Fat: 5g

108. Easy Plant-Based Mayonnaise Recipe
Prep Time: 10 Mins, Cook Time: 10 Mins, Servings: 1
Ingredients
- 1 cup of cashews
- ¾ cup of water
- 2 tbsp vinegar white
- 2 tbsp freshly squeezed lemon juice
- 1 tsp powder garlic
- ½ tsp powder onion
- ½ tsp salt
- ½ tsp Mustard Dijon
- ¼ tsp paprika

Instructions
- A blender may combine all ingredients until they reach the desired consistency.
- Refrigerate for at least 8 hrs before serving in an airtight container. This will give the

mayo enough time to stiffen before serving.

Nutrition Information
Calories: 46 kcal, Carbohydrates: 3 g, Protein: 2 g, Fat: 4g

109. Super Easy Skillet-Pizza Made with On-Hand Ingredients
Prep Time: 2 Mins, Cook Time: 6 Mins, Servings: 6
Ingredients
- 1 8" tortilla flour
- 2 tbsp sauce marinara
- 3 tbsp shredded mozzarella cheese
- ¼ cup mushrooms sliced
- 1 tbsp onion diced

Instructions
- For approximately 2-3 Mins, or till gently browned, lay the tortilla within the pan that has been heated. To toast the other side, just flip your tortilla over.
- Whereas the other side is browning, add marinara on it & top it using mozzarella and any other toppings you choose. The cheese should melt by the time it's done cooking.
- Pizza may be cooked in an oven-safe pan in the oven or transferred to the baking sheet & broiled for approximately 30-60 mins, or unless the cheese is browned.

Nutrition Information
Calories: 231 kcal, Carbohydrates: 18 g, Protein: 13 g, Fat: 12g

110. Stuffed Peppers make a Great Budget-Friendly Family Meal
Prep Time: 20 Mins, Cook Time: 40 Mins, Servings: 6
Ingredients
- 6 bell peppers whole
- ½ cup rinsed & strained dry quinoa
- 1 lb lean cooked ground turkey
- 1 cup of salsa

- 1.5 cup cheddar low fat

Instructions
- Preheat the oven to 350°F. Peppers may be prepared by removing & discarding the top & insides while retaining the peppers as they are.
- To make 1 cup of boiling water, put 1 cup of water in a pot. Pour in the quinoa and lower the heat. Simmer, covered, for 15 mins, or until all the water evaporates.
- Serve with 1 cup cheese on top of a plate of quinoa mixed with ground turkey, salsa, and seasonings. The mixture may be stuffed into each pepper.
- When finished cooking, top every pepper with the leftover cheese & any extra toppings you'd like.

Nutrition Information
Calories: 183 kcal, Carbohydrates: 11 g, Protein: 27 g, Fat: 4g

111. Simple and Delicious Fajita Chicken Bake
Prep Time: 15 Mins, Cook Time: 1 hr, Servings: 6
Ingredients
- 5 chicken breasts boneless & skinless
- 2 tsp Seasoning Skinny Taco
- ½ tsp salt Kosher
- ½ tsp black pepper ground
- 3 whole sliced bell peppers
- 1 small thinly sliced red onion
- 1.5 tbsp oil olive
- ½ cup cheddar cheese shredded fat-free

Instructions
- Preheat your oven to 375°F. Slice the peppers & onion into small slices, then toss them within olive oil before serving. Remove from consideration.
- Make an even layer of chicken breasts in a baking dish & season with taco seasoning before adding salt & pepper.
- Sliced onion & peppers should be sprinkled evenly over your chicken breasts. Add a few more drops of olive oil to the mix (optional).
- Finally, sprinkle the cheese over the meat and vegetables, then bake for 45-60 Mins, unless the meat is cooked through & reaches a core temp of 165 degrees Fahrenheit, depending on your oven.

Nutrition Information
Calories: 217 kcal, Carbohydrates: 7 g, Protein: 28 g, Fat: 8g

112. Easy Three-Ingredient Pancakes are Chock-Full of Flavor and Nutrients
Prep Time: 5 Mins, Cook Time: 3 Mins, Servings: 2
Ingredients
- 1 tbsp oil coconut
- 1 banana ripe
- 2 lightly beaten large eggs
- 1 tsp cinnamon ground

Instructions
- Make a creamy pudding-like sauce by mashing ripe bananas.
- Stir in eggs till they are completely incorporated into the banana mush.
- If you want your pancakes a little fluffier, you may add a little salt & baking powder to the mix.
- Drop approximately batter onto griddle or frying pan, spacing every drop of the batter by some inches.
- Cook for a Min, or until the edges begin to brown. Add any extra garnishes of your choosing to the dish (berries, nuts, chocolate chips semi-sweet, etc.)
- Once the edges become crisp & the pancakes are equally browned on both sides, flip them over, then cook for additional 30 seconds to a Min.
- Serve with your favorite dipping sauce and garnishes.

Nutrition Information
Calories: 89 kcal, Carbohydrates: 7 g, Protein: 3 g, Fat: 6g

113. Garlic Braised Greens and Chickpea Salad
Prep Time: 5 Mins, Cook Time: 15 Mins, Servings: 3
Ingredients
- 1 tbsp oil olive
- 1 cup stems removed & roughly chopped kale
- 2 cups stem removed & roughly chopped collard greens
- 2 cups stem removed & roughly chopped mustard greens
- 1 cup stems removed & roughly chopped Swiss chard
- 3 minced cloves garlic
- 1 cup cooked & rinsed chickpeas
- ½ tsp salt kosher
- ¼ tsp black pepper ground

Instructions
- A big pan with olive oil heated over medium-high heat may be used for this purpose. Add the mustard greens, collard greens, kale, & Swiss chard to the pot after it's warmed through.
- Stir in chickpeas, salt, garlic, & pepper as soon as your greens start to wilt. Serve with a drizzle of olive oil and a sprinkle of salt & pepper. Clear away any remaining liquids.

Nutrition Information
Calories: 125 kcal, Carbohydrates: 16 g, Protein: 6 g, Fat: 5g

114. Egg Roll Salad with Asian Style Dressing
Prep Time: 10 Mins, Cook Time: 10 Mins, Servings: 7
Ingredients
- 1 lb turkey breast ground
- 3 minced garlic cloves
- 1 tbsp grated ginger fresh
- 4 cups shredded Napa cabbage
- 2 cups stem removed & roughly chopped kale
- 1 shredded carrot large
- 1/3 cup sliced thinly red onion
- ¼ cup vinegar rice
- 1 tbsp low-sodium soy sauce
- 2 tbsp oil sesame
- 1 tbsp honey
- ¼ cup roughly chopped cilantro fresh
- ¼ cup roughly chopped green onion

Instructions
- Cook your ground turkey in a big pan over medium heat, breaking it up into tiny bits as you go. Add half of the garlic & half of the ginger to your turkey when it's halfway done cooking. Continue cooking the turkey till it reaches the desired doneness. Take out of the pan.
- Mix Napa cabbage, carrots, kale, & red onion are all in a big bowl.
- Combine the honey, rice vinegar, sesame oil, soy sauce, garlic & ginger in a mixing bowl. In a large bowl, add all ingredients and whisk until smooth. Make sure the ingredients are well-coated in the dressing before serving. The Napa combination should be served in four separate bowls.
- Cooked turkey should be added to the top of each bowl. Top with fresh cilantro & green onion.

Nutrition Information
Calories: 257 kcal, Carbohydrates: 14 g, Protein: 30 g, Fat: 10g

115. One Pan General Tso's Chicken with Broccoli
Prep Time: 15 Mins, Cook Time: 25 Mins, Servings: 1
Ingredients
- 1 tbsp oil sesame
- ½ tsp salt Kosher
- ¼ tsp black pepper ground
- 2 minced cloves garlic
- 3 tbsp soy sauce low sodium
- 1 tbsp honey
- 1 tbsp vinegar rice
- 1 tsp red pepper crushed
- 1 tbsp ginger grated fresh
- 1 lb chicken breast boneless & skinless
- 4 cups florets broccoli

Instructions
- The oven should be preheated at 400°F.
- Add the rest of the ingredients to a mixing bowl, except for the chicken & broccoli. Mix thoroughly.
- Spread your chicken on a baking sheet & the broccoli over the other half of this baking sheet. Season the chicken & broccoli with the spice combination. Gently toss the chicken & broccoli to coat them in the marinade, being sure to coat them evenly.
- Remove from your oven & stir after 8 Mins of baking. To finish cooking the chicken & broccoli, return them to your oven for another 8 mins or so.

Nutrition Information
Calories: 217 kcal, Carbohydrates: 12 g, Protein: 27 g, Fat: 7g

116. Simple One-Pan Lemon Salmon with Roasted Asparagus
Prep Time: 10 Mins, Cook Time: 15 Mins, Servings: 1
Ingredients
- 1 lb salmon fresh
- 1 lb bottoms trimmed asparagus
- 1 tbsp oil olive
- 1 tsp oil Kosher salt
- ½ tsp black pepper ground
- 2 tsp powder garlic
- 1 tsp zest lemon
- 1 tbsp juice lemon
- 1 sliced lemon

Instructions
- The oven should be preheated at 400 degrees Fahrenheit. Spray nonstick spray on a baking pan after lining it with foil.
- Place your salmon fillets on the single side of a baking sheet and bake. Make sure to distribute the asparagus beside the fish evenly.
- Add some olive oil to the fish & asparagus, then toss to coat. Salt, pepper, & garlic powder are all you need to season, and lemon zest & lemon juice should be sprinkled on top. Finally, serve the salmon topped with lemon wedges.
- Asparagus & salmon should be cooked until they are firm yet flaky, around 15 mins. Serve.

Nutrition Information
Calories: 458 kcal, Carbohydrates: 17 g, Protein: 51 g, Fat: 22g

117. Roasted Brussels Sprouts with Spicy Charred Corn
Prep Time: 10 Mins, Cook Time: 30 Mins, Servings: 5
Ingredients
- 1 lb stems removed Brussels sprouts
- 2 tbsp oil olive
- ½ tsp salt kosher
- 2 cups kernels corn
- 1 minced shallot
- ½ tsp seasoning Cajun

Instructions
- The oven should be preheated at 400 degrees Fahrenheit. On the baking sheet, sprinkle olive oil over your Brussels sprouts. Bake for 30 Mins, or until the sprouts are tender. Toss the kosher salt into the salad and taste for seasoning. Roast for around 20-25 mins, or unless softened and starting to brown, when spread out in a thin layer.
- Heat the oil to medium heat & add some Brussels sprouts. Add the rest of the olive oil & the onions. The onion should be mellow and aromatic in 2 to 3 Mins. Toss in corn kernels & Cajun spice to your liking. Stir often and continue to cook for the next 8 to 10 mins. A few Mins later, add your roasted Brussels.

Nutrition Information
Calories: 120 kcal, Carbohydrates: 17 g, Protein: 4 g, Fat: 6g

118. Open-Faced Tomato Parmesan Toast with Arugula
Prep Time: 10 Mins, Cook Time: 10 Mins, Servings: 1

Ingredients
- 2 rolls Ciabatta
- 2 tsp oil olive
- 1 tsp salt kosher
- ½ tsp black pepper ground
- 1/3 cup cream cheese fat-free
- 2 tbsp grated cheese Parmesan
- 1 large tomato Roma
- 2 cups arugula fresh
- 1 tsp vinegar apple cider

Instructions
- Set the oven temperature to broil.
- Make a top & a bottom for each ciabatta by cutting it along the middle, as if creating a sandwich. The baking sheet is ideal for this step. Use olive oil to coat each piece. Use pepper and salt. About 5 minutes in the oven will be enough, or until the ciabatta starts to brown.
- While the ciabatta is broiling, mix some cream cheese with Parmesan cheese & spread it over the toast. Mix until a homogeneous mixture is achieved. Remove your ciabatta from the oven & smear each piece with the cream cheese mixture. Add a layer of cream cheese on top of the tomatoes, then sprinkle the rest of the Parmesan cheese on top. To finish, broil for another 5 mins or more unless the tops bubble & become golden brown.
- Take out ciabatta from the oven and cool down a little before serving. Toss the pepper, oil, arugula, salt, & vinegar into a salad bowl. Top every ciabatta with a few sprigs of a dressed arugula. It's time to eat!

Nutrition Information
Calories: 138 kcal, Carbohydrates: 16 g, Protein: 5 g, Fat: 6 g

119. One-Pot Skinny Sloppy Joes
Prep Time: 10 Mins, Cook Time: 15 Mins, Servings: 1
Ingredients
- 1 lb turkey breast ground
- ½ cup diced small yellow onion
- ½ cup diced small bell pepper green
- 2 minced cloves garlic
- 2 tbsp sauce Worcestershire
- 2 tsp powder chili
- ¼ tsp pepper flakes red
- 6 oz tomato paste canned
- ½ cup of water

Instructions
- A big skillet over medium heat should be warmed up. Cook your turkey, breaking it up into little pieces as it cooks until it is cooked through.
- After approximately 5 mins, or once your turkey is half done, add the green pepper, onion, & garlic to the pot. When the turkey is done, and the onions are starting to soften, continue cooking for another 5-10 mins.
- Add the rest of the ingredients & bring it to a boil. Simmer for approximately 10 Mins, or unless the appropriate consistency is achieved. Make a wheat bun out of it or eat it hot.

Nutrition Information
Calories: 173 kcal, Carbohydrates: 8 g, Protein: 28 g, Fat: 3 g

120. Ultimate Skinny BLT with Dill Mayo
Prep Time: 10 Mins, Cook Time: 5 Mins, Servings: 1
Ingredients
- ¼ cup mayonnaise clean
- 2 tsp juice lemon
- ½ tsp zest lemon
- 1 tsp dill dry
- pinch pepper flakes red
- 4 slices bread toasted whole grain
- 6 bacon cooked strips of turkey
- 4 large butter lettuce leaves
- 1 tomato large

Instructions
- Combine all of the ingredients for the dressing in a medium bowl and mix well. Using a knife, spread mayonnaise over each piece of bread.
- Top your bread with some lettuce & tomato, then divide your bacon across the two pieces. Finish up with the last piece of bread & a plate of soup.

Nutrition Information
Calories: 183 kcal, Carbohydrates: 6 g, Protein: 14 g, Fat: 12 g

121. Spicy Lentil Salad
Prep Time: 10 Mins, Cook Time: 25 Mins, Servings: 2
Ingredients
- ½ cup peeled & diced small cucumber
- ½ cup diced small bell pepper red
- 3 minced cloves garlic
- 1 & ½ cups fat-free plain Greek yogurt
- ½ tsp pepper cayenne
- ½ tsp cumin ground
- ½ tsp salt Kosher
- ¼ cup chopped cilantro fresh
- 2 tsp juice lemon
- 2 cups cooked red lentils

Instructions
- Excluding the lentils, combine all the ingredients in a large bowl. Mix thoroughly. Add the lentils and give them a little swirl. Before serving, chill the dish in the refrigerator for approximately 20 Mins.

Nutrition Information
Calories: 81 kcal, Carbohydrates: 7 g, Protein: 12 g, Fat: 1g

122. Cool Down with Our Easy Watermelon Spritzer
Prep Time: 3 Mins, Cook Time: 5 Mins, Servings: 2
Ingredients
- 2 cups watermelon cubed seedless
- ½ ice cup
- 1 tsp juice lime
- 2 tsp honey
- 2 cup soda club
- 1 lime wedges

Instructions
- A blender is all that is needed to make this cocktail. Blend until smooth and creamy.
- Slowly add your club soda till it is completely incorporated into the mixture. If the slushier spritzer required, add additional ice.
- In the serving glass, top with lime juice and serve.

Nutrition Information
Calories: 52 kcal, Carbohydrates: 14 g, Protein: 1 g, Fat: 1g

123. Spicy Grilled Pork Kebabs for the Perfect Summer Meal
Prep Time: 15 Mins, Cook Time: 15 Mins, Servings: 2
Ingredients
- 3 tsp zest lime
- 1 tbsp juice lime
- ½ cup diced yellow onion
- ½ cup no sugar orange juice
- ¼ cup minced fresh cilantro
- 2 tbsp oil olive
- 1 tsp salt kosher
- 1 tsp red pepper crushed
- 1 minced jalapeno
- 1-lb chops thick boneless pork
- 1 bell pepper red
- 1 bell pepper yellow

Instructions
- Combine all the ingredients except pork & bell peppers in a mixing bowl. Add pork to the mixture and mix well. Toss the mixture with the pork to coat it. Refrigerate for at least 30 Mins, or possibly to several hrs.
- Grill at medium heat or bake at 450°F. Place pork, red pepper, & yellow pepper on the skewer. Re-fill the skewer till it's full. ' Re-use the rest of the ingredients on the remaining skewers.
- Then cook for around 10 Mins on a hot grill until done.

Nutrition Information
Calories: 281 kcal, Carbohydrates: 10 g, Protein: 26 g, Fat: 15g

124. Light and Sweet Whipped Coffee
Prep Time: 5 Mins, Cook Time: 5 Mins, Servings: 1
Ingredients
- 1 tbsp coffee crystals instant
- 1 ½ tsp sugar coconut
- Ice
- 1 tbsp water hot
- ¾ cup milk fat-free

Instructions
- Coconut sugar, Instant coffee, and boiling water are combined in the bowl. Whip the coffee on high with an electric mixer until it reaches the creamy texture, and then serve.
- Over ice, pour some milk into the glass. Serve with a dollop of whipped coffee over the top!

Nutrition Information
Calories: 100 kcal, Carbohydrates: 18 g, Protein: 7 g, Fat: 1g

125. Chickpea Avocado Toast
Prep Time: 5 Mins, Cook Time: 2 Mins, Servings: 1
Ingredients
- 1 peeled & pit removed avocado
- ½ cup chickpeas cooked
- ¼ tsp salt kosher
- 1 tsp juice lemon
- 4 slices bread toasted whole grain
- 3 tbsp roughly chopped fresh cilantro

Instructions
- Chickpeas & avocado should be combined in a bowl. Leave some lumps within the mixture after mashing. Lastly, add a dash of salt and some fresh lemon juice.
- Toast your bread and then spread it with the avocado mix. Serve garnished with chopped fresh cilantro.

Nutrition Information
Calories: 117 kcal, Carbohydrates: 11 g, Protein: 3 g, Fat: 8g

126. Easy Peanut Butter Banana Cookies
Prep Time: 5 Mins, Cook Time: 8 Mins, Servings: 2
Ingredients
- 1 peeled & pit removed small avocado
- 1 banana small
- 2 large eggs
- 1 cup peanut butter creamy
- 1 tsp extract vanilla
- 1 cup chocolate chips semi-sweet

Instructions
- Preheat the oven to around 350 degrees Fahrenheit. Line the baking sheet using parchment paper or coat it using non-stick spray.
- Remove chocolate chips & combine till smooth in the food processor with all other ingredients except for them. By hand, add some chocolate chips.
- Drop roughly 2 tsp of cookie batter each cookie onto that baking sheet. Bake for ten to twelve Mins. As they chill, the cookies would harden up a little more.

Nutrition Information
Calories: 288 kcal, Carbohydrates: 18 g, Protein: 8 g, Fat: 22g

127. Healthy Teriyaki Slow Cooker Roasted Pulled Pork
Prep Time: 10 Mins, Cook Time: 6 hrs, Servings: 2
Ingredients
- 2 lb Fat trimmed Lean Pork
- ½ cup wine vinegar rice
- 1 cup of water
- ¼ cup soy sauce low sodium

- ¼ cup of honey
- 2 tbsp minced fresh ginger
- 4 minced cloves garlic
- ¼ tsp pepper flakes red crushed
- 2 tbsp roughly chopped fresh cilantro
- ¼ cup onion chopped green

Instructions
- In a slow cooker, combine the other ingredients, except for the cilantro & green onion. 4-5 hrs on high, or 8 hrs on low, is the recommended time.
- When done cooking, take pork loin out of the oven and serve. Slice the pork with two forks and serve. Remove the meat from the slow cooker and shred it. Add the chopped fresh cilantro & green onion before serving. Serve.

Nutrition Information
Calories: 168 kcal, Carbohydrates: 10 g, Protein: 24 g, Fat: 3g

128. Peanut Butter Banana Cups
Prep Time: 10 Mins, Cook Time: 1 hr, Servings: 1
Ingredients
- ¾ cup chips chocolate
- 1 medium banana
- ¼ cup all-natural peanut butter
- 1 tbsp oil melted coconut oil melted

Instructions
- Lay down a piece of wax paper over a counter to begin the preparation process. On top of it, put your baking cups in place.
- Set your double boiler at low heat and begin melting the chocolate. Cool gently before using. Melt the coconut oil & peanut butter together as you wait.
- Make a layer of melted chocolate, followed by the banana slice, peanut butter mix, and a final layer of melted chocolate in all the cups. Using a casserole pan, carefully put the cups. Put it within the freezer for about an hr & a half to harden up.

Nutrition Information
Calories: 80 kcal, Carbohydrates: 8 g, Protein: 1 g, Fat: 5g

129. 20-Min Easy Pesto Salmon Recipe
Prep Time: 5 Mins, Cook Time: 15 Mins, Servings: 1
Ingredients
- 2 lb salmon fresh
- 2 tbsp pesto basil

Instructions
- If a broil setting is not accessible, heat the oven to around 450 degrees Fahrenheit.
- Spray a baking pan with nonstick spray and line it with Al foil. Each salmon fillet should be placed on a baking sheet that has been coated with parchment paper and slathered with basil pesto.
- To get a crisp & flaky salmon, bake for around 15-20 mins, flipping the pan halfway during cooking.

Nutrition Information
Calories: 351 kcal, Carbohydrates: 1 g, Protein: 45 g, Fat: 17g

130. Jalapeno Popper Zucchini Boats
Prep Time: 30 Mins, Cook Time: 15 Mins, Servings: 4
Ingredients
- 4 halved lengthwise zucchinis
- 1 tbsp oil olive
- 1 tsp salt Kosher
- 8 oz softened cream cheese
- 1 cup shredded fat-free cheddar cheese
- 6 turkey bacon crumbled strips cooked
- 2 jalapeños minced seeds removed
- 2 fresh minced garlic cloves

Instructions
- Set the oven to 375°F. Apply olive oil & salt to the zucchini. Nonstick spray may coat a baking sheet using nonstick spray before placing. Just before the zucchini starts to soften, put it in the oven for approximately 10 Mins.
- Let the zucchini cool once you remove it from the oven. Once zucchini has cooled to the touch, use a spoon to scoop out the center to make a boat. The bit that was scooped out should be saved.
- Add some cream cheese to a bowl and whisk well. Soften and fluff the mixture at a medium-high speed. Make sure to squeeze out all the extra moisture from the zucchini before adding it to the cream cheese. Stir in the rest of the ingredients with a whisk.
- Spread a layer of cream cheese mix in the middle of zucchini boats & bake for approximately 15 Mins till the cheese is melted & the zucchini is tender. Before eating, let the food cool down a little.

Nutrition Information
Calories: 228 kcal, Carbohydrates: 5 g, Protein: 10 g, Fat: 19g

131. Greek Chicken Kebabs
Prep Time: 25 Mins, Cook Time: 10 Mins, Servings: 2
Ingredients
- 4 minced garlic cloves
- 1 tbsp olive oil
- ¼ cup lemon juice
- 1 tbsp minced oregano fresh
- 1 tsp salt kosher
- 2 boneless & skinless chicken breasts
- 1 onion red
- 1 cup tomatoes grape
- 1 zucchini chunks

Instructions
- Mix the garlic, lemon juice, olive oil, & oregano.
- In a small bowl, combine the chicken breasts with garlic-lemon juice mixture. Refrigerate for almost 30 Mins after tossing the chicken with the marinade. The rest of the marinade may be stored in a separate container.
- Grill over medium heat for a few Mins. Preheat the oven to 400°F if you don't have access to a grill.
- Put chicken and one slice of onion over a skewer. Add a sec piece of chicken, followed by a tomato, on the skewer. Add a third cube of chicken and a slice of zucchini to the skewer. Re-fill the skewer till it's full. Skewers may be utilized for this procedure until all ingredients have been used.
- Set the skewers on the hot grill one at a time. Turn the kebabs after 5 Mins of cooking. Cook your kebabs for a further 5 mins on the other side, or until the chicken is well cooked. Reserving the marinade, brush the meat before removing it from your grill. Serve.

Nutrition Information
Calories: 197 kcal, Carbohydrates: 8 g, Protein: 26 g, Fat: 7g

132. Balsamic Asparagus and Blistered Tomatoes
Prep Time: 5 Mins, Cook Time: 25 Mins, Servings: 8
Ingredients
- 1-pint halved grape tomatoes
- ½ tbsp divided olive oil
- 1 lb trimmed asparagus
- 1 Tbsp balsamic vinegar aged
- ½ tsp salt
- ¼ tsp black pepper ground

Instructions
- The oven should be preheated to 400°F before you begin baking.
- Combine the tomatoes with 2 tbsp of olive oil in a baking dish.
- Tomatoes should be "burst" & slightly charred after baking for 15-20 mins.
- Toss the trimmed asparagus with the leftover salt, olive oil, and pepper in a large mixing bowl.
- Toss the asparagus into the baking dish once the tomatoes have blistered. Toss the tomatoes using balsamic vinegar before serving.

- Bake for another 5 Mins, then remove from the oven. Tender-crisp asparagus is ideal.

Nutrition Information
Calories: 63 kcal, Carbohydrates: 10 g, Protein: 4 g, Fat: 2g

133. Chicken Florentine Meatballs
Prep Time: 5 Mins, Cook Time: 20 Mins, Servings: 5
Ingredients
- 2 lightly beaten eggs
- 1 cup chopped & cooked spinach
- ½ cup chopped yellow onion
- 3 minced cloves garlic
- ½ cup grated parmesan fat-free
- ½ cup panko breadcrumbs whole wheat
- 1 lb chicken ground

Instructions
- Preheat the oven to around 400°F. Set aside the baking sheet that has been sprayed using a nonstick spray.
- Mix all of the ingredients well together before serving. Place the 1" balls over the baking tray and bake as directed. Bake for approximately 20 Mins, or till golden brown & cooked through.

Nutrition Information
Calories: 188 kcal, Carbohydrates: 9 g, Protein: 19 g, Fat: 8g

134. White Fish and Vegetables in Parchment Paper
Prep Time: 20 Mins, Cook Time: 20 Mins, Servings: 2
Ingredients
- 4 white fish filets
- 1 large, minced shallot
- ½-lb French sliced green beans
- 3 medium peeled & julienned carrots
- 3 Tbsp divided lemon zest
- 1 Tbsp divided olive oil
- ½ tsp divided kosher salt
- ¼ tsp divided black pepper ground
- 8 parchment paper pieces

Instructions
- Make sure your oven is preheated at 375°F.
- Combine your shallots, carrots, green beans, olive oil, lemon zest, salt & pepper in a mixing bowl.
- Make four stacks of the parchment paper by stacking two sheets together & repeating this process with the rest of the paper.
- Stack two parchment papers together and spread a quarter-portion of the veggie mix in the middle.
- Add a 4-oz chunk of wild cod to the vegetable mixture before serving.
- Brush each fish fillet with the leftover olive oil & lemon zest, then season with the leftover pepper and salt to your taste.
- To seal a package, fold the 2 opposing ends together and wrap them up.
- In a preheated oven, lay the packets on the baking sheet.
- Open the packages after baking for 18 mins. When using a fork, fish must be readily flaked. The package may be resealed and reheated for an additional 2 to 5 Mins if not done.
- Serve.

Nutrition Information
Calories: 237 kcal, Carbohydrates: 10 g, Protein: 36 g, Fat: 7g

135. Slow Cooker Taco Soup
Prep Time: 30 Mins, Cook Time: 3 hrs, Servings: 5
Ingredients
- 1 lb cooked & broken ground turkey
- 1 cup chopped yellow onion
- 1 minced jalapeno seeds & stem removed
- 2 & ½ cups broth chicken
- 15 oz canned tomatoes diced
- 15 oz canned drained & rinsed black beans
- 15 oz canned drained & rinsed kidney beans
- 1 cup frozen, fresh corn kernels
- 2 tbsp Taco Seasoning Skinny

Instructions
- In a crockpot, combine all the ingredients. Cook for six hrs on low or three hrs on high. Pour into serving plates once they've been cooked.

Nutrition Information
Calories: 258 kcal, Carbohydrates: 33 g, Protein: 28 g, Fat: 3g

136. Simple DIY Oat Milk
Prep Time: 10 Mins, Cook Time: 10 Mins, Servings: 8
Ingredients
- 1 cup rolled or quick oats soaked
- 3-4 cups of water

Instructions
- Oats should be rinsed, and a blender is needed for this recipe. Strain your milk through a cheesecloth and remove the oats from the dish. The oat milk may be stored in a closed container for almost a week.

Nutrition Information
Calories: 77 kcal, Carbohydrates: 14 g, Protein: 3 g, Fat: 1g

137. Guilt-Free Migas Recipe
Prep Time: 10 Mins, Cook Time: 5 Mins, Servings: 1
Ingredients
- 8 eggs large
- 2 Tbsp milk skim
- 1 Tbsp oil avocado
- 2 corn tortillas gluten-free
- ½ small chopped fine yellow onion
- 1 chopped fine jalapeno pepper seeds & veins removed
- 1 chopped fine bell pepper red
- ½ tsp salt kosher
- 2 Tbsp cheddar low fat
- 1 Tbsp minced cilantro

Instructions
- Set the skillet on medium-high heat and begin cooking.
- Set aside a medium-sized dish of eggs & skim milk for later use.
- Add tortillas, avocado oil, onions, & peppers to the mix.
- For 2 Mins, cook until the tortillas become golden brown & the onions and peppers have softened to your liking.
- Pour the egg & milk mixture into the sautéed peppers & tortillas. Toss in some salt & continue scrambling the eggs until they are fully cooked, but it's still wet to the touch.
- Top with some cheese & cilantro, then serve on four plates.

Nutrition Information
Calories: 209 kcal, Carbohydrates: 7 g, Protein: 13 g, Fat: 13g

138. Classic Shrimp with Cocktail Sauce
Prep Time: 10 Mins, Cook Time: 5 Mins, Servings: 5
Ingredients
For Cocktail Sauce:
- ½ cup no-sugar ketchup
- ½ tbsp grated horseradish
- ½ tsp juice lemon

For Shrimp:
- 4 cups of water
- 1 whole sliced lemon
- 2 tbsp spice pickling
- 1-lb peeled & deveined raw shrimp

Instructions
For Cocktail Sauce:
- Mix all of the ingredients well. Set away for later.

For Shrimp:
- Bring the lemon slices, water, & pickling spices to a boil in a big saucepan. Pour in some shrimp and bring to a boil. After 5 mins, the shrimp should be pink & firm.

- In a big container of ice, rapidly drain your shrimp & put the shrimp in, making sure the ice has completely covered the shrimps. Remove your shrimp from the pan & let cool completely before patting them dry. Cocktail sauce may be served on the side.

Nutrition Information
Calories: 149 kcal, Carbohydrates: 7 g, Protein: 24 g, Fat: 2g

139. Skinny Smoked Salmon Dip
Prep Time: 30 Mins, Cook Time: 30 Mins, Servings: 3
Ingredients
- 8 oz cream cheese fat-free
- ½ cup Greek yogurt fat-free plain
- ¼ tsp sauce Worcestershire
- ½ tsp Kosher salt
- ¼ tsp red pepper ground
- 2 tsp lemon juice
- ¼ cup chopped green onion
- 2 tsp fresh grated horseradish
- 6 oz salmon flaked smoked

Instructions
- Combine all ingredients, excluding the horseradish, green onion, & salmon, in a large bowl and stir until well combined. The mixture should be completely homogeneous. In a separate bowl, whisk together the other ingredients until well blended. Before serving, cover and chill for 20-30 Mins.
- Serve delicious salmon dip alongside crostini, crackers of your choice, or raw vegetables as you see fit!

Nutrition Information
Calories: 75 kcal, Carbohydrates: 3 g, Protein: 6 g, Fat: 4g

140. Grandma's Homemade Wheat Bread Recipe
Prep Time: 1 hr 45 Mins, Cook Time: 40 Mins, Servings: 2
Ingredients
- 1 ¾ cups of warm water
- 2 tsp dry yeast active
- 2 tbsp honey
- 4 cups all-purpose flour whole-wheat
- 1 tsp salt sea
- 2 tbsp oil olive

Instructions
- The yeast should be sprinkled on top of the water in a big mixing basin and not stirred in. Allow your yeast to 'bloom' for around 10 Mins. Honey should be added after the yeast has "bloomed" (or begun to bubble). Take care while adding the flour. To double in size, cover & let rest for around 30 Mins.
- Add the salt & olive oil once the dough has rested. Knead your dough till it is smooth & elastic, then shape it into a loaf. A 30-Min period of relaxation is required before you can go back to work.
- Apply nonstick spray to a loaf pan. Place the dough in the loaf pan after kneading a second time. Allow rising for the next 30 Mins before removing the lid.
- Set the oven to 375°F. The bread should be baked for 40 minutes, or unless it is golden & hollow when you softly tap it. Remove your bread from the oven and cool after removing it from the heat. Remove your bread from the pan once it has cooled down completely before cutting.

Nutrition Information
Calories: 100 kcal, Carbohydrates: 18 g, Protein: 3 g, Fat: 2g

141. Creamy Sun-Dried Tomato Chicken
Prep Time: 15 Mins, Cook Time: 15 Mins, Servings: 1
Ingredients
- 2 tbsp oil olive
- 3 finely chopped cloves garlic
- salt & pepper
- 4 fillets chicken breasts
- ½ cup of chicken broth
- ¼ cup of sun-dried finely chopped tomatoes
- 1 cup of coconut milk canned
- ¼ cup freshly chopped basil

Instructions
- Add olive oil to a big pan and bring it to a boil over medium-high heat. Cook garlic in oil for 60 seconds to release its scent.
- Sauté the chicken breasts in a pan with a little olive oil and a little salt and pepper. Then add chicken stock & sun-dried tomatoes in the skillet, cover it, and simmer for a further 5 Mins. Transfer the chicken to trays after removing the lid.
- Stir in the coconut milk in the skillet. Serve the chicken with the sauce on the side. Serve and savor the flavor of fresh basil on top!

Nutrition Information
Calories: 480 kcal, Carbohydrates: 8 g, Protein: 51 g, Fat: 27g

142. Turkey Chorizo Meatballs
Prep Time: 10 Mins, Cook Time: 20 Mins, Servings: 3
Ingredients
- 2 lbs ground turkey lean
- ½ cup flour almond
- 3 eggs large
- ¼ cup Greek yogurt plain
- 1 Tbsp paprika smoked
- 2 tsp powder chili
- 2 tsp cumin ground
- 1 tsp coriander
- 1 tsp powder onion
- 2 tsp garlic granulated
- 1 ½ tsp kosher salt
- ½ tsp black pepper ground
- ¼ tsp cayenne pepper

Instructions
- The oven should be preheated at 375°F.
- In a mixing bowl, combine all of the ingredients.
- Using your hands, shape into two "Meatballs are on the menu.
- To bake, place on the baking sheet that has been gently coated using cooking spray "different from each other.
- Bake for about 20 to 22 mins, or until done.

Nutrition Information
Calories: 203 kcal, Carbohydrates: 4 g, Protein: 31 g, Fat: 8g

143. Low-Carb Stuffed Cabbage Enchiladas
Prep Time: 10 Mins, Cook Time: 35 Mins, Servings: 2
Ingredients
- 8 cabbage leaves large
- 1 tbsp olive oil
- ½ cup chopped yellow onion
- ½ chopped bell pepper red
- 3 minced cloves garlic
- 2 tsp cumin ground
- 1 tbsp powder chili
- 1 tsp salt kosher
- ¼ tsp red pepper crushed
- 2 cups of boneless & skinless shredded chicken breasts
- 1 cup enchilada sauce no-sugar
- ½ cup cheddar cheese fat-free

Instructions
- Preheat the oven to 400°F. Set aside a medium casserole dish that has been sprayed with nonstick cooking spray.
- Bring water to your boil in a big saucepan. A few seconds after the water is boiling, drop each cabbage leaf into the pot. Remove, put on a piece of paper towel, then pat dry.
- Add some olive oil to your large pan and sauté the prepared cabbage leaves on moderate flame. Make sure your pan is heated before adding onion, peppers, & garlic. For approximately 5 mins, or unless the onions are transparent, cook the onions. Chicken and spices such as cumin & chili powder should be mixed in at this point.

- Remove the chicken from the heat when it is no longer pink in the middle.
- Flatten out cabbage leaves. Place your chicken mix in a line along the middle of each leaf. Roll each leaf into a burrito form by folding it on the sides. Place within casserole dish that has been prepared. Pour your enchilada sauce on top & sprinkle with cheese.
- The cheese should be melted and bubbling after 15-20 mins of baking. Before serving, allow the food to settle for 5 mins.

Nutrition Information
Calories: 200 kcal, Carbohydrates: 12 g, Protein: 22 g, Fat: 7g

144. Easy Sweet Potato Hashbrown Cakes with Poached Egg
Prep Time: 5 Mins, Cook Time: 5 Mins, Servings: 2
Ingredients
- 1 large, peeled & shredded sweet potato
- 3 lightly beaten egg whites
- 1 tsp Kosher salt
- ½ tsp black pepper ground
- 1 tsp melted coconut oil
- 2 tsp oil olive
- 2 poached eggs
- 2 tbsp roughly chopped fresh parsley

Instructions
- Add the pepper, egg whites, sweet potato, salt, & coconut oil to a small mixing bowl.
- Your olive oil should be heated to medium-high heat in the skillet. Form patties out of the potato mix and fry them in hot oil. When golden brown, remove from the heat and serve.
- Serve two hashbrown patties with each dish, with a poached egg over the top, on the serving platter. Serve with a sprinkle of fresh parsley on top.

Nutrition Information
Calories: 198 kcal, Carbohydrates: 14 g, Protein: 12 g, Fat: 10g

145. Cauliflower-Parsnip Puree
Prep Time: 5 Mins, Cook Time: 35 Mins, Servings: 10
Ingredients
- 1 tsp oil olive
- 1 minced small shallot
- 2 minced cloves garlic
- 16 oz frozen cauliflower florets
- 1-lb parsnips peeled, removed the woody core
- 3 cups chicken broth low sodium
- ½ tsp salt
- ¼ tsp black pepper ground

Instructions
- Medium-high heat is ideal for cooking soup.
- In a small saucepan, heat the olive oil over medium heat until it shimmer.
- Sauté the shallots & garlic for a further Min, till they begin to brown.
- Pour in the chicken broth, then add the cauliflower & parsnip.
- Boil the mixture over high heat for a few Mins.
- Let it simmer for around 30 Mins, till the parsnips & cauliflower are soft enough to be mashed using a fork, then remove from the heat and serve.
- Reserve 14 cups of the broth before draining.
- Immersion blenders or food processors may blend the mixture until it reaches the desired smoothness. It should have the consistency of gummy texture mashed potatoes. If you pour too many liquids, you'll wind up with a soup-like dish instead of a dessert.
- Season to your liking with salt and pepper.

Nutrition Information
Calories: 105 kcal, Carbohydrates: 20 g, Protein: 5 g, Fat: 2g

146. Instant Pot Spiced Orange Carrots
Prep Time: 7 Mins, Cook Time: 3 Mins, Servings: 3
Ingredients
- 1-lb peeled carrots
- 1 cup juice orange
- ½ tsp kosher salt
- ½ tsp ground cinnamon
- ½ tsp ginger ground
- 2 tbsp honey

Instructions
- Within Instant Pot, add the rest of the ingredients, excluding honey. Place your pot cover on, making the valves in a closed position. Ensure that the timer is set for 3 minutes, and that Instant Pot is on Manual Mode at high pressure. Allow time to run its course before reducing pressure manually & removing the lid with extreme care. Carrots should be drained of their water, and honey should be drizzled on top. Serve warm.

Nutrition Information
Calories: 72 kcal, Carbohydrates: 18 g, Protein: 1 g, Fat: 1g

147. Easy 5-Ingredient Garlic Herb Sauteed Mushrooms
Prep Time: 5 Mins, Cook Time: 10 Mins, Servings: 4
Ingredients
- 1 tbsp oil olive
- 1-lb button mushrooms whole small
- 3 minced cloves garlic
- 2 tbsp roughly chopped fresh thyme
- 1 tbsp roughly chopped fresh tarragon

Instructions
- Set a big sauté pan over medium-high heat and warm your olive oil. Add mushrooms to the pan after it's heated through. The mushrooms may leak liquid as you cook them, so heat just unless the tops of the mushrooms start to turn brown.
- Cook for approximately a Min after adding the garlic.
- Add fresh thyme & tarragon to the mushrooms once removed from the fire. Toss your mushrooms with the herbs unless they are well-coated. Serve warm.

Nutrition Information
Calories: 62 kcal, Carbohydrates: 5 g, Protein: 4 g, Fat: 4g

148. Instant Pot Coq Au Vin
Prep Time: 10 Mins, Cook Time: 50 Mins, Servings: 3
Ingredients
- 1 Tbsp oil olive
- 2 garlic cloves
- 1 small diced yellow onion
- 1 cup diced carrots
- 2 cups sliced mushrooms
- 2 Tbsp thyme leaves fresh
- 2 lbs chicken breasts boneless skinless
- 1 cup red wine dry
- 1 cup chicken broth low sodium
- 2 tsp salt kosher
- ¼ tsp black pepper ground
- 1 Tbsp arrowroot or cornstarch
- 3 Tbsp chicken broth

Instructions
- Add olive oil to the Instant Pot and put it to sauté mode.
- Heat the inner pot & add the olive oil.
- Add the thyme, carrot, onion, and garlic to the pot.
- Sauté for two Mins.
- Sauté chicken pieces for another 3 to 5 Mins, then remove from the heat and set aside.
- Wine & chicken broth should be poured in.
- Add salt and pepper to your taste.
- Set a timer for around 20 Mins and switch the setting to a Manual Higher Pressure.
- The release valve must be closed to seal the pot.
- Wait 10-15 mins for the normal pressure release before using a rapid release procedure to complete the process.

- When reducing pressure, be careful not to injure yourself.
- Stir together 3 tbsp of chicken broth & arrowroot in a shallow dish until smooth.
- Stirring continually, add to chicken mix till thickened.
- Serve on boiled squash noodles or egg noodles with more pepper and salt to taste.

Nutrition Information
Calories: 398 kcal, Carbohydrates: 13 g, Protein: 52 g, Fat: 10g

149. 3-Ingredient Chocolate Cake | Gluten-Free Recipe
Prep Time: 15 Mins, Cook Time: 30 Mins, Servings: 1
Ingredients
- 8 large Eggs
- 1 lb chocolate chips semi-sweet
- 1 cup butter whole

Instructions
- A 325-degree oven is ideal for baking. Set the parchment paper within the form pan, ensuring that it is the same diameter as your pan. The springform pan should be sprayed using nonstick spray & Al foil should be wrapped around the pan. Set aside the coated pan in a high-sided roasting pan.
- Whip your eggs till they have doubled in volume in a mixer bowl fitted with the whisk attachment. Approximately six to eight Mins. Meanwhile, combine the chocolate & butter to warm in a medium dish when the eggs whisk.
- Once the chocolate has melted, mix in egg mixture. Gently press the egg mixture into chocolate unless it is completely integrated. When all of the egg mixes have been incorporated into chocolate, repeat this process 2 more times. Prepare the pan by lining the bottom and sides with parchment paper.
- Pour boiling water into the roasting pan unless the water hits 1/3 up the edge of the pan. Bake for 25-30 Mins, depending on the size of your oven. The oven should be cooled before removing the sides. Using a plate, delicately "flip" the cake out of the pan & parchment paper.
- Fresh fruit may be sprinkled on top if needed.

Nutrition Information
Calories: 196 kcal, Carbohydrates: 15 g, Protein: 4 g, Fat: 13g

150. 3-Ingredient Spicy Roasted Broccoli
Prep Time: 5 Mins, Cook Time: 15 Mins, Servings: 3
Ingredients
- 1 broccoli head
- 1 tbsp oil olive
- 1 tsp red pepper crushed

Instructions
- The oven should be preheated at 425 degrees Fahrenheit.
- Toss all ingredients together and coat your broccoli with oil & red pepper. Spread out on the baking sheet in an equal layer. Toss the broccoli in the oven for approximately 15 mins, or until it starts to brown slightly and char.

Nutrition Information
Calories: 33 kcal, Carbohydrates: 1 g, Protein: 1 g, Fat: 4g

151. Caprese Stuffed Chicken Breast
Prep Time: 5 Mins, Cook Time: 15 Mins, Servings: 1
Ingredients
- 4 oz boneless & skinless chicken breasts
- 2 sliced Roma tomatoes medium-sized
- ¾ cup shredded mozzarella cheese low-fat
- 1 tsp Kosher salt
- ½ tsp black pepper crushed
- 2 tbsp olive oil
- ¼ cup chopped fresh basil
- 2 tbsp balsamic vinegar dark

Instructions
- Preheat your oven to 400°F.
- Using a sharp knife, cut a small pocket within the middle of each chicken breast. Tomatoes should be uniformly distributed throughout your chicken breasts & placed within the breast's pocket. Tomatoes, cheese, and a small number of breadcrumbs should be placed within a pocket. Salt & pepper the exterior of your chicken breast.
- Olive oil should be heated to a high temperature on a nonstick pan that may be placed in an oven. When the pan is heated, sear the filled breasts for 5 Mins on one side until they brown. The breasts should be turned over with care. Cook chicken for a final 10 mins within the oven using the same skillet.
- Remove Chicken from your oven & sprinkle this with fresh basil. Before serving, drizzle some balsamic vinegar over every chicken breast.

Nutrition Information
Calories: 258 kcal, Carbohydrates: 3 g, Protein: 30 g, Fat: 13g

152. Smoky Maple Brussels Sprouts
Prep Time: 10 Mins, Cook Time: 25 Mins, Servings: 4
Ingredients
- 1 lb outer leaves & stems removed Brussels sprouts
- 1 Tbsp olive oil
- 2 tsp smoked paprika
- ½ tsp chili powder ancho
- ½ tsp sea salt or kosher
- ¼ tsp black pepper ground
- 2 Tbsp maple syrup

Instructions
- The oven should be preheated at 375 degrees Fahrenheit.
- Salt, pepper & maple syrup are all you need to add to a small dish of olive oil.
- Spread out the brussels sprouts on a baking sheet and bake until tender.
- Toss the brussels sprouts with the spice mixture once poured over them.
- For 20 to 25 Mins, roast the brussels sprouts inside a preheated oven at 350 degrees Fahrenheit.

Nutrition Information
Calories: 111 kcal, Carbohydrates: 18 g, Protein: 4 g, Fat: 4g

153. Coconut Curry Cauliflower
Prep Time: 5 Mins, Cook Time: 30 Mins, Servings: 6
Ingredients
- 2 minced cloves garlic
- 2 tsp extra-virgin olive oil
- 4 cups florets cauliflower
- 2 cups of light canned coconut milk
- 1 & ½ tsp yellow curry powder
- ½ tsp black pepper
- ½ tsp crushed pepper flakes red
- sea salt or Kosher

Instructions
- Preheat your oven to 375°F.
- Using moderate heat, sauté the garlic in the oil for one Min. Add the rest of the ingredients to a medium-sized casserole dish & mix well. About 25-30 mins in the oven should be enough time for the cauliflower to soften. Serve at once. If desired, garnish with some chopped cilantro.

Nutrition Information
Calories: 88 kcal, Carbohydrates: 6 g, Protein: 1 g, Fat: 6g

154. 3-Ingredient Tender Broiled Salmon
Prep Time: 2 Mins, Cook Time: 18 Mins, Servings: 1
Ingredients
- 2 6-oz skins on salmon filet
- ¼ tsp red pepper crushed
- ½ tsp Kosher salt

Instructions
- The oven should be preheated to moderate broil. The oven should be preheated to 500°F if it doesn't have a broiler setting.

- A frying pan should be placed within the oven after being warmed for approximately 10 Mins. Using a pan is recommended.
- After removing the pan from the oven, gently lay the salmon within the pan & cook for about 5 Mins. Salt & red pepper flakes should be added to the mixture. After 8 Mins, remove the pan from the oven & allow it to cool completely before slicing.
- Take it out of the oven. Lemon juice may be added to the dish if desired.

Nutrition Information
Calories: 242 kcal, Carbohydrates: 1 g, Protein: 34 g, Fat: 11g

155. Orange Ginger Sesame Salad Dressing
Prep Time: 5 Mins, Cook Time: 5 Mins, Servings: 2
Ingredients
- 2 large zested & juiced navel oranges
- 2 tsp peeled & finely grated fresh ginger
- 1 tbsp honey raw
- ¼ cup sesame oil toasted
- 2 tbsp low sodium coconut aminos or soy sauce

Instructions
- In a mixing bowl, add all of the ingredients & whisk until well combined.
- Alternative method: Combine all the ingredients, cover tightly, & shake briskly until well blended.
- Refrigerate any remaining dressing in an airtight container.

Nutrition Information
Calories: 88 kcal, Carbohydrates: 7 g, Protein: 1 g, Fat: 7g

156. Instant Pot Sunday Pot Roast
Prep Time: 15 Mins, Cook Time: 1 hr 5 Mins, Servings: 8
Ingredients
- 1 tbsp oil olive
- 2 lbs roast beef chuck
- 3 tsp powder garlic
- 2 tsp powder onion
- 2 tsp dried thyme
- 2 tbsp paste tomato
- 1 & ½ cups broth beef

Instructions
- Turn on your Instant Pot's sauté option at a very high temperature. Warm up the olive oil.
- Sprinkle thyme, garlic powder, and onion powder over the whole chuck roast. In a skillet over medium-high heat, sear the roast on both sides with a little olive oil until crispy. Add the broth once the meat has been removed. Stir until the broth starts to boil, scraping Instant Pot as necessary. Stop Instant Pot.
- Place your beef on Instant Pot & cook according to the manufacturer's instructions. Tomato paste should be smeared on top of it. Check whether the pot's valve is shut before putting the lid on it. Set your Instant Pot for around 90 Mins on Manual, Maximum Pressure.
- After the allotted time has passed, allow the steam to escape naturally for around ten Mins before letting it manually. Slice & serve the roast.

Nutrition Information
Calories: 464 kcal, Carbohydrates: 4 g, Protein: 45 g, Fat: 30g

157. Low-Carb Eggplant Pizza Recipe
Prep Time: 10 Mins, Cook Time: 25 Mins, Servings: 10
Ingredients
- 1 eggplant large
- 1 tbsp oil olive
- ½ tsp Kosher salt
- ½ cup marinara sauce no-sugar
- 1 cup of fat-free shredded mozzarella cheese
- ¼ cup roughly chopped fresh basil

Instructions
- Spray the baking sheet using nonstick spray & preheat the oven to 400°F. Prepare the baking sheet by slicing the eggplant & brushing every slice with some olive oil. Bake for around 15 Mins, then season with salt if desired.
- Using a spoon, spread your marinara sauce over the eggplant, being sure to cover all of its surfaces. Return to your oven and top with mozzarella. After 7-10 Mins, or when the cheese is starting to brown, remove from the oven and let to cool. Serve with fresh basil sprinkled over the top.

Nutrition Information
Calories: 143 kcal, Carbohydrates: 13 g, Protein: 14 g, Fat: 5g

158. 5-Ingredient Egg Stuffed Peppers
Prep Time: 10 Mins, Cook Time: 35 Mins, Servings: 1
Ingredients
- 4 whole seeds removed bell peppers cut off tops
- 4 lightly beaten eggs
- 1 tsp salt kosher
- 1 cup of fat-free shredded cheddar cheese
- ¼ cup chopped green onions

Instructions
- Preheat your oven to around 375°F. Spray your baking pan using a nonstick spray, then line it using Al foil. On the baking pan, place your peppers.
- Add salt & cheddar cheese to the eggs in a mixing bowl. Toss chopped green onion over the top before serving within pepper "bowls." Bake for approximately 30 mins, or unless the tops become golden brown, on the baking sheet. Before serving, let the food rest for approximately five Mins. The peppers must be let to sit for a few Mins for the eggs to set.

Nutrition Information
Calories: 151 kcal, Carbohydrates: 8 g, Protein: 14 g, Fat: 5g

159. Herb-Roasted Nuts
Prep Time: 15 Mins, Cook Time: 20 Mins, Servings: 2
Ingredients
- ½ cup of pecan halves
- ½ cup of raw cashews
- ½ cup of walnut halves
- ½ cup of hazelnuts
- ½ cup of Brazil nuts
- ½ cup of almonds raw
- 1 Tbsp rosemary leaves fresh
- 1 Tbsp thyme leaves fresh
- ½ Tbsp finely chopped parsley
- 1 tsp granules garlic
- ½ tsp paprika
- ½ tsp kosher salt
- ¼ tsp black pepper ground
- ½ Tbsp olive oil

Instructions
- The oven should be preheated at 375°F.
- Spread out the ingredients on a baking sheet in an equal layer.
- Stir and re-spread in a thin layer after 10 Mins of roasting.
- Check whether the nuts are burning after every 5 Mins of roasting.
- Roast for a further 3-5 mins, often monitoring to avoid overcooking.
- Serve at room temperature after cooling somewhat.

Nutrition Information
Calories: 204 kcal, Carbohydrates: 6 g, Protein: 5 g, Fat: 19g

160. 3-Ingredient Broiled Asparagus with Balsamic Brown Butter
Prep Time: 5 Mins, Cook Time: 10 Mins, Servings: 4
Ingredients
- 1-lb fresh ends removed asparagus hard
- 2 tbsp melted butter

- 1 tbsp balsamic vinegar dark

Instructions
- The oven should be preheated at 425 degrees. Add the butter & balsamic vinegar to the asparagus and toss to coat. Spread out on the baking sheet in an equal layer. Depending on how brown and blistered you want your asparagus, this may take as little as 10 mins in the oven.

Nutrition Information
Calories: 76 kcal, Carbohydrates: 5 g, Protein: 3 g, Fat: 6g

161. Easy Zucchini Ravioli
Prep Time: 15 Mins, Cook Time: 30 Mins, Servings: 3

Ingredients
- 1 cup ricotta cheese fat-free
- 1 lightly beaten large egg
- ¼ cup chopped fresh basil
- 2 minced cloves garlic
- 4 zucchinis shaved medium
- 1 jar marinara no-sugar

Instructions
- Preheat your oven to 375°F. Nonstick spray a baking dish & put it away.
- Combine the egg, basil, ricotta, & garlic in a mixing bowl. In a large bowl, combine all of the ingredients and whisk vigorously until completely
- Spread out 2 zucchini strips at a level surface. Create an "X" by stacking two strips, right angles to the 1st one. One spoonful of ricotta mixture should be scooped into the "X." When you finish one side of zucchini strips, switch to the next. Place the ravioli in a baking dish. Repeat the process with the leftover zucchini & filling.
- Bake for approximately 30 mins, or unless the zucchini is fork-tender, before serving. Serve warm.

Nutrition Information
Calories: 101 kcal, Carbohydrates: 12 g, Protein: 9 g, Fat: 2g

162. 5-Ingredient Apple Cider Braised Chicken
Prep Time: 10 Mins, Cook Time: 20 Mins, Servings: 1

Ingredients
- 1 & ½ cups of apple cider
- 3 tbsp mustard whole-grain
- ¾ cup diced yellow onion
- 24-32 oz chicken breasts boneless & skinless
- 1 tsp salt kosher

Instructions
- Make a sauce into Instant Pot by combining both apple cider & mustard. Add the onion to the mix. Place your chicken within the cider mixture & season it with salt. Set a timer for 20 Mins on the Instant Pot's setting & seal the lid. You may manually depressurize & remove its lid at this point. Serve the chicken hot.

Nutrition Information
Calories: 263 kcal, Carbohydrates: 14 g, Protein: 39 g, Fat: 5g

163. Spicy Broiled Green Beans
Prep Time: 5 Mins, Cook Time: 10 Mins, Servings: 4

Ingredients
- 2 tsp oil olive
- 2 tsp soy sauce low-sodium
- 1 tsp powder garlic
- ½ tsp cayenne pepper
- ½ tsp red pepper crushed
- ¼ tsp salt Kosher
- 1-lb fresh ends trimmed green beans

Instructions
- The oven should be preheated to a low boil.
- All ingredients, excluding green beans, should be combined & well mixed. Toss the beans with the spice mix in a big bowl and set aside. Toss your green beans well to coat them within the sauce.
- On a large baking sheet, spread your beans out evenly. The beans should be browned and crispy after 10 Mins of broiling.

Nutrition Information
Calories: 58 kcal, Carbohydrates: 9 g, Protein: 2 g, Fat: 2g

164. Moo Shu Chicken Skillet Recipe
Prep Time: 20 Mins, Cook Time: 20 Mins, Servings: 1.5

Ingredients
- 1 Tbsp oil sesame
- 1 cup white mushrooms sliced
- ½ cup thinly sliced green onion
- 2 cups cabbage shredded
- 3 cups pre-cooked chicken shredded
- 2 lightly beaten large eggs
- ¼ cup of sauce hoisin
- 2 tbsp coconut aminos
- 2 tsp chili sauce sriracha

Instructions
- Set moderate heat on a skillet. Add a few drops of extra virgin olive oil to the mix.
- Cook for 5-6 Mins, or unless the mushrooms are browned & the liquid from them has evaporated.
- Cook for a further 2 Mins after adding the cabbage & scallions.
- Simmer for another 3 to 5 Mins, unless the chicken is cooked through.
- To make scrambled eggs, add eggs & heat until they're done. Eggs that have been browned are fine.
- Serve with sriracha sauce on the side for an extra kick.
- Turn down the heat and let the sauce warm through completely.

Nutrition Information
Calories: 378 kcal, Carbohydrates: 15 g, Protein: 23 g, Fat: 25g

165. Greek Yogurt Chicken Salad with Toasted Pecans and Apples
Prep Time: 15 Mins, Cook Time: 15 Mins, Servings: 4

Ingredients
- 2 boneless & skinless cooked & shredded chicken breasts
- 1 medium diced small apple Granny Smith
- 2 tbsp minced red onion
- 1 tbsp lemon juice
- ½ cup Greek yogurt plain
- 2 tbsp mayonnaise clean eating
- 1 cup lightly toasted pecans
- ½ tsp Kosher salt
- ¼ tsp cumin ground

Instructions
- Mix all of the ingredients well. Allow the flavors to meld for approximately 15 mins in the refrigerator before serving.

Nutrition Information
Calories: 215 kcal, Carbohydrates: 8 g, Protein: 11 g, Fat: 16g

166. Quick and Easy Roasted Veggie Kebabs
Prep Time: 15 Mins, Cook Time: 15 Mins, Servings: 4

Ingredients
- 1 bell pepper green
- 1 squash zucchini
- 1 onion red
- 2 cups cherry tomatoes or grape
- 2 cups mushrooms button
- 2 tbsp oil olive
- 1 tsp basil dried
- ½ tsp oregano dried
- 2 minced cloves garlic
- ¼ tsp ground thyme dried

Instructions
- Preheat the oven to 425°F. Set aside the baking sheet that has been linked with Al foil.
- Assemble the skewers with a slice of bell pepper (top), zucchini (bottom), red onion (top), tomato, & mushroom (bottom). Re-fill the skewer till it's full. Place each skewer on your baking sheet in its entirety.

- Add the oregano, garlic, basil, olive oil, and thyme to a medium bowl and mix well. Apply olive oil mix to all sides of the skewers.
- When they're done baking, remove them from the oven. Remove from oven and flip the dish over before serving. After 5-6 Mins of baking, remove from oven. Serve warm.

Nutrition Information
Calories: 57 kcal, Carbohydrates: 5 g, Protein: 2 g, Fat: 4g

167. Cracker Barrel "Copycat" Hashbrown Casserole
Prep Time: 5 Mins, Cook Time: 30 Mins, Servings: 4
Ingredients
- 1 tbsp oil olive
- 1/3 cup diced yellow onion
- 2 minced cloves garlic
- ½ tsp black pepper ground
- 1 tsp salt kosher
- ½ cup Greek yogurt plain
- ¼ cup milk skim
- 1 cup of sharp fat-free shredded cheddar cheese
- 1-lb hashbrown potatoes frozen

Instructions
- Preheat the oven to 400°F. Set aside the casserole dish sprayed using non-stick spray & ready for use.
- Olive oil should be heated to medium-high in a big skillet. Add both garlic and onions when the oil is heated. Just until the onions start to turn transparent, stir often. Stir in the yogurt & skim milk, then turn the heat down to a simmer. Bring to a boil, lower the heat, then add the hashbrowns & cheddar cheese.
- Using a spatula, pour the mixture evenly into a casserole dish. It should be baked for about 20 Minutes, or unless the top starts to brown, and the dish should rest for at least ten minutes before it's ready to be served.

Nutrition Information
Calories: 100 kcal, Carbohydrates: 12 g, Protein: 6 g, Fat: 2g

168. Vegetable Egg Roll Skillet
Prep Time: 10 Mins, Cook Time: 10 Mins, Servings: 1.5
Ingredients
- 3 cups green cabbage shredded
- ¼ medium sliced thin yellow onion
- 1 cup florets broccoli
- 1 bell pepper red
- 1 cup snap sugar
- ¼ cup green onions chopped
- 2 tbsp aminos coconut
- 1 tbsp vinegar rice
- 1 tbsp sesame oil toasted

Instructions
- Heat a nonstick frying pan to a high temperature before cooking the meat.
- Add snow peas/sugar snap, broccoli slaw, red pepper, onion, broccoli, & scallions to the mixture.
- Add rice vinegar & coconut aminos to the mixture.
- Vegetables should be tender but still crunchy after 5-6 mins of stir-frying.
- Sprinkle with sesame oil & serve immediately.

Nutrition Information
Calories: 84 kcal, Carbohydrates: 11 g, Protein: 2 g, Fat: 4g

169. Paleo Maryland Crab Cakes
Prep Time: 10 Mins, Cook Time: 25 Mins, Servings: 2
Ingredients
For crab cakes
- 8 oz crab meat jumbo lump
- ¼ cup finely diced bell pepper green
- ¼ cup finely diced bell pepper red
- ¼ cup finely diced celery
- 2 Tbsp minced green onions
- ¼ cup breadcrumbs gluten-free
- ¼ cup mayonnaise paleo
- 1 Tbsp brown mustard spicy
- 2 tsp seasoning Cajun
- 1 Tbsp finely chopped parsley

For remoulade
- 1/3 cup mayonnaise paleo
- 2 tsp mustard spicy brown
- 1 tsp sauce hot
- 1 Tbsp drained & rinsed capers
- 1 Tbsp finely chopped celery
- 1 Tbsp red finely chopped bell pepper
- 2 tsp seasoning Cajun
- 1 Tbsp finely chopped parsley

Instructions
Make crab cakes:
- Preheat your oven to 400°F. Apply cooking spray to a baking sheet and set it aside.
- In a medium bowl, combine all ingredients, taking good care to separate the crab meat's shell.
- Place patties on the baking sheet & bake for 20 Mins.
- Make sure all sides become golden brown & crispy by turning halfway through the cooking time.
- Serve with a remoulade sauce.
- Make your remoulade sauce while your crab cakes continue baking.
- In a medium mixing dish, combine all of the ingredients.
- Crab cakes are a good accompaniment.

Nutrition Information
Calories: 165 kcal, Carbohydrates: 11 g, Protein: 12 g, Fat: 8g

170. Instant Pot Barbecue Ribs
Prep Time: 2 hrs, Cook Time: 30 Mins, Servings: 1
Ingredients
- 1 tsp powder onion
- 1 tsp powder garlic
- 1 tbsp powder chili
- 1 tbsp sugar brown
- 1 tsp black pepper ground
- 1 tsp paprika smoked
- 1 tsp salt Kosher
- 1 cup of water
- 4 lbs back ribs baby bone-in
- 1 cup BBQ Sauce no-sugar

Instructions
- Combine all spices in a medium bowl and mix well until the mixture resembles a fine powder. Make sure everything is mixed well. Season the ribs on both sides with seasoning mix, then gently massage the mix into ribs. Refrigerate your ribs for almost 2 hrs, preferably overnight.
- Please take out a trivet rack & place it inside Instant Pot, then fill it with water. The ribs should not be stacked in the pot. If you want, you may stand them upright in the Instant Pot. Make sure the saucepan is sealed by putting the lid on.
- High-pressure cooking for 23 mins is recommended. Before removing the steam, allow the pot to rest for five Mins to cool down. BBQ sauce may be used in BBQ sauce to coat the ribs. Serve.

Nutrition Information
Calories: 393 kcal, Carbohydrates: 17 g, Protein: 28 g, Fat: 24g

171. Cold Sesame Shrimp Zoodles
Prep Time: 10 Mins, Cook Time: 5 Mins, Servings: 15
Ingredients
For shrimp:
- ½ Tbsp oil olive
- 1-lb extra-large peeled & deveined wild shrimp
- 1 Tbsp soy sauce low-sodium
- spiral salad veggie
- 4 cups spirals zucchini
- 1 & ½ cups halved lengthwise seedless cucumber

For dressing:

- 2 Tbsp soy sauce low-sodium
- 1 Tbsp sesame oil toasted
- 2 Tbsp cider vinegar apple
- 2 tsp chili flakes red
- 1 Tbsp sesame seeds toasted

Instructions
Cook shrimp:
- A medium-sized skillet should be heated to medium-high.
- Add the olive oil & shrimp that have been cleaned.
- When the shrimp is opaque but not overdone, add the soy sauce & continue to simmer for another 5-6 Mins.
- To cool down, remove from the heat source.

Prepare Your salad dressing:
- Whisk together the soy sauce, rice vinegar, sesame oil, & red chili flakes in a medium dish or liquid glass container.

Assemble salad:
- Cucumber and zucchini spirals should be combined in a big basin.
- Toss in the shrimp.
- Sprinkle sesame seeds on top of the salad dressing. Toss to distribute the ingredients evenly.
- Eat it right now or store it in the fridge for later use.

Nutrition Information
Calories: 228 kcal, Carbohydrates: 11 g, Protein: 27 g, Fat: 9g

172. Tomato, Mozzarella, & Basil Panini
Prep Time: 5 Mins, Cook Time: 5 Mins, Servings: 2
Ingredients
- 2 slices whole bread wheat
- ½ cup part-skim mozzarella shredded
- 1 thinly sliced Roma tomato
- 1 red onion thin slice
- 8 fresh basil leaves
- sea salt or kosher
- 1/8 tsp pepper
- 1 tbsp olive oil extra-virgin

Instructions
- 2 slices of the bread are brushed with olive oil using a basting brush. Salt & pepper to taste.
- Basil leaves, onion slices, tomato slices, & mozzarella cheese should be layered on top of bread pieces with the oil-side down. Top with another slice of bread, with olive oil side facing up.
- A skillet may be used to cook this dish.
- Press your sandwich down using the cover of a pan to make it a little flatter. Flip after 2 Mins of cooking when the bottom is golden brown. Do it on the opposite side, too!
- Two servings may be made by cutting the sandwich in half. Enjoy!

Nutrition Information
Calories: 231 kcal, Carbohydrates: 15 g, Protein: 10 g, Fat: 13g

173. Chicken with Onions
Prep Time: 2 hrs 15 Mins, Cook Time: 30 Mins, Servings: 1
Ingredients
- 2 lbs chicken breast boneless & skinless
- 5 divided & sliced thin garlic cloves
- 2 sliced thin onions medium
- 1 tsp oregano dried
- 1 tbsp chopped cilantro fresh
- ½ cup orange citrus juice
- ½ tsp pepper black
- 1 tsp salt kosher
- 3 tbsp oh Ghee butter
- 1/3 cup of water
- for garnish cilantro chopped

Instructions
- Place the chicken breasts in a container & pat them dry with a towel. Mix the garlic, oregano, sliced onions, cilantro, lemon juice, and a pinch of salt & pepper in a medium bowl to make the marinade. Spritz the chicken breasts with the mixture before cooking.
- For 2 hrs, cover and chill. Remove & discard the marinade from the chicken.
- In a big pan, melt the butter on medium heat. Cook for around 5 Mins, occasionally stirring, until the butter has browned.
- In about 5 Mins, flip the chicken over & cook the opposite side for another 5 Mins.
- Reducing the heat to medium, add the rest onions & 2 cloves of chopped garlic to the pan. For 5 Mins, swirl, then cover & simmer on a moderate to low heat level.
- Adding extra liquid, if necessary, simmer for a further 10 Mins with the lid on until your chicken has cooked through.
- Toss in a little coarsely diced cilantro if you want.

Nutrition Information
Calories: 324 kcal, Carbohydrates: 3 g, Protein: 32 g, Fat: 20g

174. Plant-Based Cashew Flat Bread
Prep Time: 10 Mins, Cook Time: 25 Mins, Servings: 1
Ingredients
- 1 cup raw cashews
- ¾ cup of water

Additional
- 1 tsp syrup maple
- ¼ tsp pepper black
- ¼ tsp salt
- ¼ tsp garlic powder
- ½ tsp oregano dried

Instructions
- The oven should be preheated to 410°F. Put two sheets of parchment paper on top of each other on a baking sheet or stone and leave them aside.
- After 15 Mins of soaking in water, the cashews should be rinsed and dried carefully. Pat the cashews with a paper towel to remove any remaining water.
- Add the cashews and the leftover water to a food processor & pulse until the mixture resembles pancake batter.
- Whisk in the extra ingredients to the batter.
- Bake for about by pouring the mixture in the middle of the baking pan. Allow it cool for 15 minutes before removing the bread & parchment paper and then flipping it over to the 2nd sheet.
- Bake for another 15 Mins within the oven. Check the bread to see whether it's cooked all the way through. Cook for another 1-2 Mins if necessary. Keep a close eye on the bread to prevent it from burning. Place the bread on the cooling rack after carefully flipping it over. Wait until the dough has cooled before slicing.

Nutrition Information
Calories: 159 kcal, Carbohydrates: 10 g, Protein: 5 g, Fat: 12g

175. Quinoa and Egg Protein Breakfast Bites
Prep Time: 10 Mins, Cook Time: 20 Mins, Servings: 3
Ingredients
- 1 cup cooked white quinoa
- 3 lightly beaten egg whites
- ½ tsp kosher salt
- ¼ cup diced bell peppers red
- ¼ cup chopped spinach
- ½ cup shredded fat-free mozzarella cheese

Instructions
- Set the oven's temperature to 350°F and prepare the oven for baking. Using a nonstick spray, coat the inside of a tiny muffin pan.
- In a large bowl, combine all ingredients and thoroughly mix them. Spoon approximately 3 tsp of quinoa & egg

mixture into each muffin cup within a small muffin tray that has been prepped. About 20 Mins in the oven should be enough to make the bites stiff & slightly browned on top.
- Before taking the breakfast bits from the pan, allow them to cool somewhat.

Nutrition Information
Calories: 114 kcal, Carbohydrates: 11 g, Protein: 7 g, Fat: 4g

176. Slow Cooker Everything Chicken
Prep Time: 5 Mins, Cook Time: 4 hrs, Servings: 2
Ingredients
- 3 lbs chicken breasts boneless & skinless
- ¼ cup olive oil extra-virgin
- 1-2 tbsp chopped garlic
- 1 & ½ tsp sea salt kosher
- 1 tsp pepper
- ½ cup low sodium vegetable broth

Instructions
- In your slow cooker, put the chicken. Olive oil should be dripped on both sides to provide an even coating. Salt & pepper to taste. Pour the broth all over the chicken's exterior. In a slow cooker, simmer the chicken for around 6 to 8 hrs until it reaches a core temperature of 170°F, or until it is done.
- Using a fork, take the chicken from the slow cooker once it is fork tender.
- It may be used in tacos and soups, topped with gravy and mashed potatoes, or on brown rice with teriyaki sauce for an Asian touch. Enjoy!

Nutrition Information
Calories: 228 kcal, Carbohydrates: 1 g, Protein: 32 g, Fat: 10g

177. Turkey and Avocado Roll-Ups
Prep Time: 10 Mins, Cook Time: 10 Mins, Servings: 2
Ingredients
- 8 thin fat-free turkey slices deli
- ¼ cup pesto basil
- ½ avocado peeled & sliced pit removed
- 1 cup sprouts bean

Instructions
- Spread pesto roughly on every turkey slice and place it on the flat surface. Place 2 or 3 avocado slices on one side of your turkey & top with bean sprouts. Roll each one carefully. Serve.

Nutrition Information
Calories: 333 kcal, Carbohydrates: 5 g, Protein: 37 g, Fat: 18g

178. Zucchini Crusted Pizza
Prep Time: 10 Mins, Cook Time: 15 Mins, Servings: 3
Ingredients
- 2 cups shredded zucchini
- 2 tsp coarse sea salt or kosher salt
- ¼ cup of flour
- 2 tbsp grated parmesan cheese
- 1 large egg
- ¼ tsp black pepper ground
- 1 tsp dried oregano
- 1 tbsp olive oil extra virgin
- ½ cup sauce marinara
- 1 cup grated mozzarella skim

Instructions
- Combine chopped zucchini & coarse salt in a small bowl and set aside for around 30 Mins.
- Preheat oven to 450°F.
- Drain your liquid from zucchini after 30 mins, then crush your zucchini inside a strainer to drain any excess liquid.
- Combine your zucchini, flour, Parmesan, pepper, egg, & oregano in a small mixing basin. Spray a small coating of olive oil over the baking sheet. Pour your zucchini batter inside the middle of a baking pan & smooth it out evenly.
- Bake for around 15 Mins, or unless the crust is brown around the edges, in a preheated oven. Reduce heat to 400°F after removing the crust.
- Pour some marinara sauce onto the crust's center and evenly distribute it out to the edges. Distribute your mozzarella evenly over the top, then finish with the leftover Parmesan.
- 5 Mins in the oven, or until mozzarella fully melted. Serve with a drizzle of olive oil extra-virgin.

Nutrition Information
Calories: 241 kcal, Carbohydrates: 16 g, Protein: 17 g, Fat: 13g

179. Low-Carb Turkey Club Lettuce Cups
Prep Time: 20 Mins, Cook Time: 20 Mins, Servings: 2
Ingredients
- 14 oz turkey ground
- ½ tsp kosher salt
- ¼ tsp black pepper ground
- 6 bibb lettuce leaves
- 3 slices diced & cooked turkey bacon
- 1 diced small Roma tomato
- 2 tbsp diced small red onion
- ½ cup of fat-free cheddar cheese shredded
- 2 tbsp mayonnaise clean eating
- 1 tsp juice lemon

Instructions
- In a wide pan over medium heat, brown your ground turkey. Season your turkey with pepper and salt while it cooks, breaking it up into little pieces.
- On a level surface, arrange lettuce leaves. 2 tbsp sauteed ground turkey, stuffed into each. Bacon, onion, tomato, & cheese go on top of each.
- Combine both mayonnaise & lemon juice in a mixing bowl. Drizzle the dressing over the lettuce cups.

Nutrition Information
Calories: 382 kcal, Carbohydrates: 2 g, Protein: 33 g, Fat: 27g

180. Vegetable Skewer Cocktail Recipe
Prep Time: 20 Mins, Cook Time: 20 Mins, Servings: 2
Ingredients
- 5 oz low-fat cream cheese
- 1 diced celery stalk
- 1/8 cup olive oil extra virgin
- 1 tsp vinegar or lemon juice
- ¼ tsp salt
- 1/8 tsp pepper ground
- 8 small cherry tomatoes
- 4 halved baby carrots
- 2 thinly sliced zucchinis

Instructions
- Puree your celery, cream cheese, olive oil, lemon, vinegar, salt, & pepper in a blender.
- Divide the mixture into four equal parts and put in a tiny serving dish or glass.
- Using four skewers, alternately skewer the carrots, tomatoes, and zucchini. Before skewering your zucchini, roll it out first.
- In each purée glass, place two skewers. Serve & have fun.

Nutrition Information
Calories: 151 kcal, Carbohydrates: 7 g, Protein: 4 g, Fat: 12g

181. 5-Ingredient Vegan "Chicken" Salad Recipe
Prep Time: 15 Mins, Cook Time: 15 Mins, Servings: 3
Ingredients
- 2 cups cooked & diced chicken plant-based
- ½ cup mayonnaise vegan
- ½ cup halved or pecans diced
- ½ cup diced onion
- 1 cup chopped apples

Instructions
- In a mixing bowl, combine all of the ingredients. Freeze for at least two hrs before serving.

Nutrition Information
Calories: 237 kcal, Carbohydrates: 6 g, Protein: 11 g, Fat: 19g

182. Skinny Peanut Butter Yogurt Dip
Prep Time: 5 Mins, Cook Time: 5 Mins, Servings: 2
Ingredients
- ½ cup of Greek yogurt plain fat-free
- ¼ cup natural peanut butter

Instructions
- In a medium mixing dish, combine all of the ingredients.
- Refrigerate till ready to be served, covered.

Nutrition Information
Calories: 73 kcal, Carbohydrates: 3 g, Protein: 4 g, Fat: 5g

183. Balsamic-Glazed Whole Roasted Cauliflower
Prep Time: 10 Mins, Cook Time: 45 Mins, Servings: 3
Ingredients
- 1 cauliflower head
- 2 tbsp oil olive
- 2 tbsp vinegar balsamic
- 1 tsp seasoning Italian
- ½ tsp powder garlic
- ¼ tsp salt
- 1/8 tsp black pepper ground
- 1 zested lemon
- freshly chopped parsley

Instructions
- Preheat oven to 400°F. Trim your cauliflower by cutting the lowest green stems. Remove your stem & the stiff core with care, careful not to damage the head. In a cast-iron skillet, place this cut side down.
- Combine the salt, pepper, olive oil, Italian seasoning, balsamic vinegar, garlic powder, & lemon zest in a mixing bowl. Cover your cauliflower with Al foil after brushing the mixture on top.
- Preheat oven to 350°F and bake for around 30 Mins. Take off the foil & bake for another 15 Mins, or unless the cauliflower pierces easily using a knife. Cook the cauliflower for a further 15-30 Mins, uncovered if you want it softer.
- Carefully place the cooked cauliflower on a platter and top with chopped parsley. Serve right away.

Nutrition Information
Calories: 107 kcal, Carbohydrates: 10 g, Protein: 3 g, Fat: 7g

184. No-Bread Italian Sandwiches
Prep Time: 10 Mins, Cook Time: 20 Mins, Servings: 1
Ingredients
- 1 large eggplant
- ½ tsp salt kosher
- 1 tbsp oil olive
- 4 slices nitrate-free & low-sodium deli ham
- 4 slices nitrate-free & low-sodium salami
- 12 slices nitrate-free & low-sodium pepperoni small
- 4 leaves large romaine lettuce
- 1 sliced tomato large
- ½ cup sliced rings banana pepper
- ¼ cup dressing Italian

Instructions
- Cut the eggplant crosswise into thin slices. These will serve as the sandwich's "bread." You'll need a total of 8 slices. Season each slice with salt and set aside for 5 Mins.
- Brush your eggplant slices using olive oil on both sides. In a large skillet, heat the oil over high heat. Place your eggplant within skillet once it is extremely hot and sear each side for approximately 2 mins or till browned. The eggplant should be firm but not mushy. Allow cooling once both sides have been seared.
- Place 4 eggplant slices on the flat surface. On top of each, place one slice of ham, one slice of salami, and three pepperonis. Lettuce, tomato, & banana peppers go on top. Drizzle each with Italian dressing. Top with a 2nd eggplant slice.

Nutrition Information
Calories: 232 kcal, Carbohydrates: 15 g, Protein: 10 g, Fat: 15g

185. Thai Chicken Veggie Salad with Peanut Dressing
Prep Time: 15 Mins, Cook Time: 15 Mins, Servings: 1
Ingredients
- 1 tbsp peanut butter creamy
- ¼ cup sauce hoisin
- 2 tsp sriracha
- 1 tbsp minced ginger fresh
- ¼ cup low-sodium soy sauce
- ¼ cup no sugar orange juice
- 1 tsp oil sesame
- 2 cups chopped romaine lettuce
- 2 cups spinach baby
- 3 peeled & sliced thin carrots medium
- 1 cup halved snap peas
- ½ cup sliced radishes
- ¼ cup sliced thin cucumber
- 4 boneless & skinless cooked & sliced thin chicken breasts
- ¼ cup chopped peanuts
- ¼ cup chopped green onion
- 2 tbsp chopped cilantro fresh
- 2 tbsp chopped parsley fresh

Instructions
- Combine the orange juice, peanut butter, ginger, hoisin, sriracha, & sesame oil in a small bowl. Set aside after whisking until smooth.
- Toss romaine & baby spinach with radishes, sugar snap peas, sliced carrots, & cucumber slices in a big mixing bowl. Top with cut chicken breast & divide among 4 plates.
- Peanut vinaigrette, chopped peanuts, cilantro, green onions, & mint are served on top.

Nutrition Information
Calories: 311 kcal, Carbohydrates: 22 g, Protein: 31 g, Fat: 11g

186. Melt in Your Mouth" Italian Baked Chicken
Prep Time: 15 Mins, Cook Time: 15 Mins, Servings: 1
Ingredients
- 2 tbsp oil olive
- 1 tbsp seasoning Italian
- ½ tsp salt kosher
- 1 tbsp balsamic vinegar dark
- 3 minced garlic cloves
- 4 boneless & skinless chicken breasts
- 2 cups tomatoes cherry
- ¼ cup roughly chopped basil fresh

Instructions
1. Preheat the oven to 400°F. Combine your olive oil, balsamic vinegar, salt, Italian seasoning, and garlic in a mixing bowl. Olive oil mix should be set aside for the tomatoes.
2. Pour roughly olive oil mix over your chicken into a mixing bowl. Toss the chicken within the oil & vinegar mixture to coat it.
3. Place your chicken on the baking sheet that hasn't been oiled. Drizzle any remaining oil mixture over the top of the chicken bowl.
4. In a clean dish, combine the extra oil mix with grape tomatoes. Cover the chicken with the mixture and place it on the baking pan.
5. Bake for around 15-20 Mins, or till meat is cooked through & tender. Serve with a sprinkling of fresh basil on top.

Nutrition Information
Calories: 323 kcal, Carbohydrates: 5 g, Protein: 46 g, Fat: 12g

187. Easy Skillet Cilantro Lime Chicken
Prep Time: 20 Mins, Cook Time: 15 Mins, Servings: 1
Ingredients
- 1 tbsp oil olive
- 4 chicken breasts boneless & skinless
- 1 tsp salt kosher
- ½ tsp black pepper ground
- ¼ tsp pepper flakes red
- 4 minced garlic cloves
- ¼ cup minced yellow onion
- ½ cup low-sodium chicken broth
- 2 tbsp juice lime
- 2 tsp zest lime
- 2 tbsp chopped cilantro fresh

Instructions
- Heat some olive oil in a pan over medium heat. Season your chicken breast with pepper and salt once the pan is heated. Cook for 3-5 Mins on each side, or golden brown. Remove your pan from the heat and put it aside.
- Add garlic, red pepper, & onion to the same pan where the chicken was cooked. Cook for 2 Mins, or unless the onion becomes transparent.
- Combine the lime juice, chicken broth, & lime zest in a mixing bowl. Return your chicken to a pan & reduce the heat to maintain a low simmer. Cook for around 5 Mins, or unless your chicken is fully cooked & the liquid has been absorbed.
- Serve with a garnish of fresh cilantro.

Nutrition Information
Calories: 285 kcal, Carbohydrates: 3 g, Protein: 46 g, Fat: 9g

188. Korean BBQ Cabbage Cups
Prep Time: 5 Mins, Cook Time: 25 Mins, Servings: 2
Ingredients
- 1 lb lean beef ground
- 1 yellow chopped onion small
- 4 minced garlic cloves
- 2 tsp minced ginger fresh
- 1 tbsp oil sesame
- 3 tbsp low-sodium soy sauce
- 1 tsp paste red chili
- 2 tbsp vinegar rice wine
- 8 large cabbage leaves
- ¼ cup chopped green onion
- ¼ cup chopped cilantro fresh

Instructions
- Cook your ground beef in a big pan over high heat, breaking it up into little pieces as this cook. Drain any surplus liquid after the food is thoroughly cooked. Reduce heat to moderate & return your pan to fire. Toss your ground beef with onion, garlic, ginger, and sesame oil. Cook for 3 to 5 Mins, or until the onion becomes translucent. Bring to the boil with soy sauce, chili paste, & vinegar. Cook for around 3 Mins at a low temperature.
- Fill every cabbage cup with 2-3 tbsp of beef and garnish with green onion & cilantro.

Nutrition Information
Calories: 268 kcal, Carbohydrates: 8 g, Protein: 25 g, Fat: 15g

189. Instant Pot Chicken Cordon Bleu Chowder
Prep Time: 10 Mins, Cook Time: 20 Mins, Servings: 1
Ingredients
- 1 tbsp oil olive
- 2 lbs chicken breasts boneless & skinless
- ½ lb ham cubed low sodium
- 1 yellow diced small onion small
- 3 diced celery ribs
- 2 peeled & diced carrots large
- 1 lb peeled & diced russet potatoes
- 2 tsp fresh thyme
- 2 minced garlic cloves
- 4 cups low-sodium chicken broth
- ½ tsp kosher salt
- ¼ tsp black pepper ground
- 1 cup coconut cream
- 1 tbsp mustard Dijon
- ¼ cup of Swiss cheese shredded fat-free
- ½ cup of croutons
- 2 tbsp finely chopped parsley fresh

Instructions
- Set the Instant Pot to "sauté" mode.
- Add the cubed chicken breast and olive oil to the pan. Cook, regularly flipping, for approximately 5 Mins, or till golden brown on both sides.
- Combine the chopped ham, onion, garlic, salt, celery, carrots, chicken broth, potatoes, thyme, & pepper in a large mixing bowl.
- Set your Instant Pot to High Pressure & 30 Mins on the timer. The cooker must be sealed.
- Set aside coconut cream & Dijon mustard while the chowder is heating.
- Allow 10 mins for your cooker to gradually release pressure before manually releasing steam till the pressure is removed.
- Remove the cover with care. One cup of the veggies, potatoes, & broth should be blended or processed. Process the Dijon mustard mix until it is smooth.
- Return to the chowder & whisk until everything is well combined. If using, stir in the shredded cheese. The texture of the chowder should be creamy.
- Serve in serving dishes with croutons & parsley over the top.

Nutrition Information
Calories: 332 kcal, Carbohydrates: 19 g, Protein: 38 g, Fat: 12g

190. Crispy Broiled Green Beans for Snacking
Prep Time: 5 Mins, Cook Time: 10 Mins, Servings: 3
Ingredients
- 1 lb ends trimmed green beans
- 1 tbsp melted coconut oil
- ½ tsp salt kosher
- 1 tsp powder garlic

Instructions
- Preheat the oven to 425°F for ovens that don't have a broil option. Set aside the baking sheet lined with foil.
- Combine all the ingredients in a mixing dish & toss to cover the beans with oil & spices; spread in 1 equal layer on a baking sheet. The beans must be evenly distributed on the baking pan and use 2 sheets as necessary.
- Broil your beans for 10 mins, or till crispy and not charred, flipping halfway through. Keep in mind that the beans would crisp up as they cool and allow to cool before serving. Serve with spicy sauce.

Nutrition Information
Calories: 67 kcal, Carbohydrates: 8 g, Protein: 2 g, Fat: 4g

191. Slow Cooker Easy Italian Meatballs
Prep Time: 15 Mins, Cook Time: 4 hrs 5 Mins, Servings: 3
Ingredients
- 1 lb chicken or ground turkey
- ¼ cup finely minced yellow onion
- 2 minced garlic cloves
- ½ cup panko breadcrumbs whole-wheat
- 2 large egg whites
- ½ tsp kosher salt
- ¼ tsp black pepper ground
- ¼ tsp red pepper crushed
- 2 tsp seasoning Italian
- 24 oz no sugar marinara jar
- ½ cup broth chicken
- ½ cup of parmesan cheese shredded fat-free

Instructions
- Spray the baking sheet using non-stick spray & preheat the oven to medium broil.

- In a large mixing basin, combine all the ingredients (excluding marinara, chicken stock, & parmesan) and stir thoroughly. Form into 1" balls & put on the baking sheet that has been prepped. 5 Mins under the broiler, or until golden brown.
- Add your marinara and stock to the browned meatballs within the slow cooker. Cook for around 4 hrs on low. Serve with the parmesan cheese garnish.

Nutrition Information
Calories: 284 kcal, Carbohydrates: 11 g, Protein: 31 g, Fat: 13g

192. Coconut Fried Shrimp, Red Lobster Style
Prep Time: 10 Mins, Cook Time: 30 Mins, Servings: 4
Ingredients
For Sauce
- ½ cup yogurt coconut
- ¼ cup well-drained crushed pineapple
- 2 tbsp crushed pineapple juice
- ½ tsp freshly squeezed lime juice
- salt & pepper

For Shrimp
- nonstick cooking spray
- 1 large egg
- 2 tbsp coconut milk
- ½ cup panko breadcrumbs whole-wheat
- ½ cup unsweetened shredded coconut
- 1 lb peeled & deveined shrimp large

Instructions
- A tiny bowl is all that is needed to make the sauce. Refrigerate the sauce until you are ready to dish it out.
- The oven should be preheated at 450°F. An oven wire rack should be placed on a baking sheet and set aside with a little coating of nonstick frying oil.
- Egg & coconut milk may be mixed in a small dish to create an egg wash. The mixture should be well-combined after a few Mins of whisking.
- Combine the panko breadcrumbs with the unsweetened grated coconut in a medium bowl and stir well.
- A shrimp should be coated in bread crumb mix one at a time after being dipped in egg wash. To ensure that the shrimp are well-coated, gently press them into the breadcrumbs.
- Once you have dredged all of the shrimp, place them on the lined baking sheet. Apply a little coat of cooking oil to the shrimp as soon as they are all on the sheet.
- During this time, the shrimp should be cooked to a lightly browned.

Nutrition Information
Calories: 258 kcal, Carbohydrates: 14 g, Protein: 20 g, Fat: 14g

193. Slow Cooker Broccoli and Cheddar Soup
Prep Time: 10 Mins, Cook Time: 2 hrs 10 Mins, Servings: 1.5
Ingredients
- 5 cups florets broccoli
- 1 diced medium yellow onion
- 3 minced garlic cloves
- 1 cup grated carrots
- 2 oz reduced-fat cream cheese
- 1 tsp kosher salt
- ½ tsp black pepper
- ¼ tsp nutmeg
- 4 cups of low-sodium vegetable broth
- 1 tbsp water
- 1 tbsp cornstarch
- ¼ cup plain Greek yogurt
- ¼ cup of warm water
- 1 cup of cheddar cheese shredded low-fat

Instructions
- Simmer for a few hrs until the vegetables are tender. Remove from heat and serve garnished with chopped parsley or parsley sprigs. Mix thoroughly. Cook for 4-5 hrs on low & 2-3 hrs on high, depending on your preference. In the saucepan, combine the cornstarch & water, then add the Greek yogurt & heated water. Mix in the cheddar cheese over low heat till it's creamy & melted. Pour the mixture into a slow cooker & serve.

Nutrition Information
Calories: 160 kcal, Carbohydrates: 10 g, Protein: 8 g, Fat: 11g

194. Easy 3-Ingredient Chicken Tacos
Prep Time: 5 Mins, Cook Time: 10 Mins, Servings: 3
Ingredients
- 4 cups boneless & skinless cooked & shredded chicken breasts
- 16 oz no sugar salsa jar
- 1 tbsp seasoning taco

Instructions
- Combine all the ingredients in a wide skillet. Bring the ingredients to the simmer & cook for 5–10 Mins in a saucepan, depending on your stove.
- You may use it in your favorite taco shells & top it with your favorite toppings!

Nutrition Information
Calories: 215 kcal, Carbohydrates: 4 g, Protein: 24 g, Fat: 11g

195. Chicken Zucchini Roll-Ups
Prep Time: 15 Mins, Cook Time: 15 Mins, Servings: 1
Ingredients
- 2 chicken breasts boneless & skinless
- ½ tsp salt
- ¼ tsp pepper ground
- 2 sliced zucchinis thinly
- 4 slices fat-free provolone cheese
- ½ cup of breadcrumbs
- 2 tbsp oil sunflower

Instructions
- Salt & pepper your chicken on a serving platter.
- Pieces of zucchini & cheese go on top of your chicken when served. Close using a toothpick by rolling the mixture into a log. Continue in the same manner with the rest of the items.
- Breadcrumbs should be dipped into the chicken wraps before cooking. Get rid of the extra.
- Oil should be heated to medium-high heat in a big pot. Brown your chicken rolls evenly in the heated oil.
- Your chicken rolls may either be cut into small pieces or left whole, depending on how you like your meal to be served.
- Serve it while it's still piping hot.

Nutrition Information
Calories: 297 kcal, Carbohydrates: 13 g, Protein: 23 g, Fat: 17g

196. Slow Cooker Creamy Chicken and Mushrooms
Prep Time: 10 Mins, Cook Time: 3 hrs 20 Mins, Servings: 1
Ingredients
- 4 chicken breasts boneless & skinless
- 1 & ½ cups broth chicken
- 2 cups sliced mushrooms
- 1 tsp kosher salt
- ½ tsp black pepper ground
- ½ tsp dried thyme
- 1 tsp powder garlic
- 2 tsp sauce Worcestershire
- ¼ cup fat-free cream cheese
- ½ cup fat-free plain Greek yogurt

Instructions
- Put the rest of the ingredients into a cooker, but don't add cream cheese or Greek yogurt. Cook for six hrs on low & three hrs on high.
- To serve, remove and discard your chicken from the slow cooker. Whisk in some cream cheese & yogurt till a smooth paste is formed. Turn on your slow cooker and put the chicken back in. Add additional 15 mins to the cooking time on the stove.

- Ensure that the food is served at the correct temperature.

Nutrition Information
Calories: 291 kcal, Carbohydrates: 8 g, Protein: 48 g, Fat: 6g

197. Instant Pot Cinnamon Apples
Prep Time: 5 Mins, Cook Time: 10 Mins, Servings: 2
Ingredients
- 1 tbsp butter
- 4 peeled, cored, & sliced apple medium
- 1 tsp cinnamon
- 1 tbsp maple syrup
- ¼ cup of water

Instructions
- Sauté on low within Instant Pot. Add the apples to the melted butter and mix well. Cook for 5 Mins at the most. Mix the cinnamon & maple syrup until the apples are well-coated, but do not overdo it.
- Using low pressure, go to Manual mode. When filling the pot, be careful to shut the vent before adding water and covering the pot tightly. Allow for 4 Mins of the heating period. Remove the lid & manually remove the steam after the timer expires. You want the apples to be mushy but yet retain some chew. Ensure that the food is served at the correct temperature.

Nutrition Information
Calories: 90 kcal, Carbohydrates: 19 g, Protein: 1 g, Fat: 2g

198. Slow Cooker Greek Lemon Chicken
Prep Time: 10 Mins, Cook Time: 4 hrs, Servings: 1
Ingredients
- 24-32 oz chicken breast boneless & skinless
- 4 minced garlic cloves
- 1 tsp salt kosher
- 3 tsp oregano dried
- ¼ cup fresh squeezed lemon juice
- 1 tbsp zest lemon
- 1 cup broth chicken
- 3 tbsp chopped parsley fresh

Instructions
- Put all of the ingredients, excluding parsley, into a slow cooker and simmer for a few hrs.
- Slow-cooker for 6 hrs or high-heat for 4 hrs. Serve with parsley sprinkled on top.

Nutrition Information
Calories: 237 kcal, Carbohydrates: 5 g, Protein: 40 g, Fat: 5g

199. Mediterranean Greek Salmon with Orzo Recipe
Prep Time: 5 Mins, Cook Time: 20 Mins, Servings: 1
Ingredients
- 1 tbsp zest lemon
- 2 tsp oregano dried
- 1 tbsp divided olive oil
- 16 oz filets salmon
- 1 tsp salt
- ½ tsp pepper black
- 2 cups broth vegetable
- ½ cup orzo whole-wheat
- 1 cup halved cherry tomatoes
- 2 cups roughly chopped baby spinach
- ¼ cup crumbles feta cheese

Instructions
- Spray the baking sheet using non-stick spray before placing it in the oven at 375°F for around 15 Mins.
- Lemon zest, oregano, dried & olive oil should be mixed in a mixing bowl before adding to a pizza.
- Prepare the baking dish by laying out salmon fillets and brushing each one with olive oil & lemon juice.
- Use salt & pepper to season the fish.
- To get a flaky & firm salmon fillet, cook it for around 15-20 mins.
- Bring a vegetable stockpot to a boil while the salmon is frying. Add the orzo & bring the mixture to a boil. Take off the lid and simmer for approximately 10 Mins, or until the meat is fork tender.
- Spray the medium-sized pan using non-stick spray & heat it over medium-high heat, stirring occasionally. Tomatoes & spinach should be added to the pan as soon as it's heated, and the spinach should be wilted in 5-10 mins. Stir in some orzo after taking the dish from the heat.
- Serve the orzo & veggies along with the salmon over a serving platter. Add some feta cheese to finish it off.

Nutrition Information
Calories: 347 kcal, Carbohydrates: 13 g, Protein: 27 g, Fat: 21g

200. Slow Cooker Spinach Artichoke Chicken
Prep Time: 15 Mins, Cook Time: 4 hrs, Servings: 1
Ingredients
- 8 cups chopped loosely packed spinach
- 1 cup broth chicken
- 4 filets chicken breast
- 3 garlic chopped cloves fresh
- ¼ finely chopped sweet onion
- 4 tbsp reduced-fat cream cheese
- 4 tbsp shredded parmesan cheese
- 14 oz hearts artichoke
- 1 cup chopped cherry tomatoes or grape tomatoes
- salt & pepper

Instructions
- Combine chicken broth, spinach, & chicken breasts. Use salt & pepper in addition to the garlic and onions. Alternatively, cook on high for around 4-6 hrs.
- Remove your chicken breast from the slow cooker well before serving & arrange it on serving plates. Add the parmesan cheese, cream cheese, & artichokes to the mixture and mix well. Cream the mixture for a few Mins, and chicken should be doused with sauce.
- Then add some tomatoes. If desired, top with more parmesan cheese.

Nutrition Information
Calories: 246 kcal, Carbohydrates: 14 g, Protein: 35 g, Fat: 6g

201. 5-Ingredient Bacon Cauliflower Slow Cooker Soup
Prep Time: 10 Mins, Cook Time: 3 hrs, Servings: 2
Ingredients
- 1 head chopped cauliflower
- 3 minced garlic cloves
- 1 chopped yellow onion
- 4 cups broth vegetable
- 4 strips cooked & chopped turkey bacon

Instructions
- In the slow cooker, combine all the ingredients except the bacon; stir well to combine. Cook on high heat for around 3 hrs.
- Small amounts of soup may be blended in the blender, then ladled into bowls to serve. Add the fried bacon on the top to complete the dish.

Nutrition Information
Calories: 173 kcal, Carbohydrates: 11 g, Protein: 7 g, Fat: 12g

202. Instant Pot Healthy Chicken and Spinach Ramen Noodle Bowl
Prep Time: 10 Mins, Cook Time: 15 Mins, Servings: 3
Ingredients
- 1 tbsp minced ginger fresh
- 2 minced garlic cloves
- 4 cups low-sodium chicken broth
- 2 tbsp low-sodium soy sauce
- ¼ cup of vinegar rice
- 1 tsp powder curry
- 8-12 oz chicken breasts boneless & skinless
- 1 cup sliced mushrooms fresh
- 1 tbsp oil sesame
- 1 pack seasoning ramen noodle

- 3 cups fresh baby spinach
- ¼ cup shredded carrots
- ¼ cup chopped green onions
- 1 sliced jalapeno pepper
- 2 tbsp chopped cilantro fresh

Instructions
- Make sure your Instant Pot is set to manual. This dish is made by combining all ingredients except for the sesame oil in a large saucepan and cooking over medium-high heat. Set the timer for 10 Mins set pressure to medium. Check whether the pot's valve is shut before putting the lid on it. Open the cover when the 10 mins are up & manually removing the steam.
- Ramen & spinach are mixed in at this point. For approximately 5-8 mins, or when the noodles have cooked & the spinach has wilted, place the pot within heated soup and cover. Serve in dishes by ladling into them.
- Carrots, jalapenos, green onions, & cilantro should be placed in each bowl. Ensure that the food is served at the correct temperature.

Nutrition Information
Calories: 275 kcal, Carbohydrates: 20 g, Protein: 25 g, Fat: 11g

203. Slow Cooker French Toast Casserole
Prep Time: 15 Mins, Cook Time: 3 hrs, Servings: 2
Ingredients
- 2 eggs whole
- 2 large egg white
- 1 & ½ cups of milk 1%
- 2 tbsp honey
- 1 tsp vanilla extract
- ½ tsp cinnamon
- 9 bread slices whole grain

Filling
- 3 cups of apple pieces uncooked finely diced
- 3 tbsp honey
- 1 tsp juice lemon
- 1/3 cup diced pecans raw
- ½ tsp cinnamon

Instructions
- In a small bowl, whisk together the first six ingredients. Apply a little coat of cooking spray to the interior of your slow cooker.
- Incorporate all of the fillings. Stir together all ingredients into a mixing bowl until they are evenly coated with the apple slices and put aside.
- Make triangles out of bread pieces. Once you have 3 levels of bread & one-fourth of the filling within the slow cooker, please turn it on. Top with the remainder of the filling.
- Pour the egg mixture on top of the bread slices on high for 2 to 3 hrs, or unless your bread has absorbed the liquid, cover & cook.
- 3 Bananas may be used in place of apples in this recipe.

Nutrition Information
Calories: 121 kcal, Carbohydrates: 19 g, Protein: 4 g, Fat: 4g

204. Anti-Inflammatory Broccoli Turmeric Slow-Cooker Soup
Prep Time: 15 Mins, Cook Time: 4 hrs, Servings: 1
Ingredients
- 2 cups chopped leeks
- 1 cup diced small carrots
- 2 tbsp chopped ginger fresh
- 4 cups of broccoli
- 1 tsp turmeric ground
- ½ tsp cumin ground
- ½ tsp salt kosher
- ¼ tsp red pepper crushed
- 2 minced garlic cloves
- 3 cups of vegetable broth

Instructions
- In the slow cooker, combine all the ingredients. Cook for around 4 hrs on high. Blend your soup in stages in a blender till it is smooth. Ensure that the food is served at the correct temperature.

Nutrition Information
Calories: 77 kcal, Carbohydrates: 16 g, Protein: 4 g, Fat: 1g

205. Smoked Salmon with Asparagus and Egg Salad
Prep Time: 10 Mins, Cook Time: 30 Mins, Servings: 2
Ingredients
- 8 cups of water
- 2 tbsp salt coarse
- 1 & ½ lbs hard ends asparagus
- 8 large eggs
- 1 lb salmon smoked
- 2 tsp untreated lemon zest
- 2 tsp chopped chives fresh
- 2 tsp olive oil extra virgin
- 1/8 tsp black pepper ground
- ½ juice lemon

Instructions
- Bring water to your boil on high heat in a medium-sized cooking pot. Cook for around 4-5 Mins based on thickness after adding all coarse salt to a pot that's already boiling. Cooking your eggs will necessitate keeping the water within the saucepan at a simmer.
- When they're done cooking, remove them using a slotted spoon & immediately place them in the ice bath. Simply allow your drained asparagus to come to room temperature before placing it in the ice bath. An ice treatment keeps the asparagus's green color more vivid.
- You may cook your eggs for 5-6 Mins in the boiling water, based on how watery you want your egg yolks to be. This photo shows six-Min-cooked eggs.
- Drain the water from the eggs, then allow them to cool completely before shelling.
- Place the chives, pepper, salmon, lemon zest, asparagus, eggs, olive oil, & lemon juice on a big platter or separate plates.

Nutrition Information
Calories: 312 kcal, Carbohydrates: 8 g, Protein: 35 g, Fat: 16g

206. Paleo Zucchini and Turkey Skillet Dinner
Prep Time: 5 Mins, Cook Time: 15 Mins, Servings: 1
Ingredients
- 1 lb turkey ground
- 4 minced garlic cloves
- 1 chopped small yellow onion
- 1 tbsp oil olive
- 2 medium-sized zucchinis
- 4 diced small Roma tomatoes
- ¼ cup chopped basil fresh

Instructions
- Large skillet over medium heat, breaking up turkey into tiny pieces while cooking

your ground turkey. Add both onion and garlic, then simmer for approximately 3-4 Mins, till the onion is transparent. Any remaining liquid should be drained.
- Add some olive oil into a turkey mix, raise the heat to medium, and then cook for a few Mins. Add both zucchini & tomatoes to oil once it's heated. Zucchini should begin to soften after around 5 Mins of cooking time, during which time you should stir often. The basil should be added at this point after the dish has cooled and eaten while it's still warm.

Nutrition Information
Calories: 237 kcal, Carbohydrates: 8 g, Protein: 24 g, Fat: 13g

207. Easy Stuffed Mushrooms Recipe
Prep Time: 15 Mins, Cook Time: 15 Mins, Servings: 2
Ingredients
- 1 tbsp oil olive

- 12 mushrooms baby Bella
- ½ cup diced sweet onion
- 2 minced garlic cloves
- ¼ cup finely diced tomatoes sun-dried
- 2 cups torn baby spinach
- 1/3 cup breadcrumbs panko
- 4 oz low-fat feta cheese
- ¼ cup cheese parmesan

Instructions
- The oven should be preheated to 350°F.
- Remove the mushrooms' stems, then chop them into little pieces.
- Sauté mushroom stems, onion, & sun-dried tomatoes in a large pan for approximately 4 mins on medium heat. One Min later, add chopped garlic to the pan & proceed to sauté. Toss in the spinach and cook for a few Mins until wilted. Then, remove the pan and whisk in the feta cheese, breadcrumbs, & parmesan.
- Bake at 350 degrees for approximately 15 minutes till the cheese melts & the mushrooms are cooked through, then remove from the oven and serve.

Nutrition Information
Calories: 146 kcal, Carbohydrates: 10 g, Protein: 8 g, Fat: 9g

208. Chicken Piccata Dinner
Prep Time: 15 Mins, Cook Time: 20 Mins, Servings: 1
Ingredients
- 4 chicken breasts boneless & skinless
- ½ tsp salt
- ¼ tsp ground pepper
- ½ cup of flour
- 1 tbsp softened butter
- 2 tbsp olive oil
- ¼ cup low-salt chicken broth
- ¼ cup freshly squeezed lemon juice
- 4 tbsp rinsed & drained capers
- 3 tbsp finely chopped parsley
- 3 tbsp organic lemon zest

Instructions
- Using two pieces of plastic wrap, pound every chicken breast until it is pliable.
- Use the pepper and salt to season them.
- Chicken should be dredged in half a cup of flour before cooking. Get rid of the extra.
- A tiny bowl of butter & flour should be whisked together until smooth. Dispose of.
- Some olive oil heated in a wide nonstick saucepan on medium heat is used to brown your chicken on every side for 4 mins or till it is cooked through. Cover the platter with the chicken to keep it warm.
- Wipe away any remaining oil & flour within the same pot. Pour your chicken stock & lemon juice into a saucepan, bring it to a boil, add the butter & flour combination and the rest of the salt, oil, & pepper, then whisk till the mix is smooth. Combine all ingredients in the bowl of a stand mixer and whisk until smooth. You may want to experiment with other flavors. Toss the capers in there. Return your cooked chicken to the pan and drizzle with the remaining sauce. Turn the heat down and add the parsley & lemon zest.
- Serve it while it's still piping hot.

Nutrition Information
Calories: 362 kcal, Carbohydrates: 16 g, Protein: 41 g, Fat: 17g

209. Sicilian Caponata
Prep Time: 30 Mins, Cook Time: 1 hr, Servings: 1
Ingredients
- 2 lbs diced eggplants
- 2 tbsp salt coarse
- ¼ cup of sunflower
- 1/3 cup of capers
- 3 tbsp oil olive
- 1 white sliced thinly onion big
- ½ cup pitted & quartered green olives
- 1 cup pomodoro passata di
- 1 cleaned & diced celery stalk
- 2 tbsp sugar raw cane
- ¼ cup vinegar white wine
- ¼ cup fresh basil leaves

Instructions
- Mix some coarse salt into a big bucket of water, then add the eggplants. To remove the extra liquid, wait for 15 minutes, then drain entirely and softly squeeze.
- In a large saucepan, heat the sunflower oil over moderate heat and cook the eggplants until golden brown. Avoid overloading the pot by doing this in batches. After cooking, transfer to some big dish lined with paper towels to remove any excess oil accumulated. Dispose of.
- For 10 min, soak your capers in a pan of water, then drain, & squeeze gently to remove any remaining liquid. Dispose of.
- Using a medium-sized saucepan, sauté chopped onions with water over medium-high heat. Sauté them for a few Mins until they're a golden-brown color, then remove them from the pan and allow them to cool. Cook for around 15 Mins with passata di Pomodoro. Switch off the stove and then put it away.
- Cook your celery for around 10 minutes in a boiling water saucepan on medium heat. Drain.
- Set aside the sugar & vinegar in a shallow dish and combine well.
- Heat the rest of the olive oil over high heat in a medium saucepan and sauté the celery for approximately 3 Mins. It is time to add the onions to the sauce and the passata di pomodoro & the rest of the ingredients: olives, capers, and basil.
- Add both sugar & vinegar mix after approximately 10 mins. Adding extra vinegar and sugar might change the flavor to suit your preference. Allow it to cook for the next 20 Mins.
- Serve hot or cold, as desired. Cooking Caponata in advance enhances its flavor, and it tastes much better the next day. Keep the food in the refrigerator at all times.

Nutrition Information
Calories: 180 kcal, Carbohydrates: 15 g, Protein: 2 g, Fat: 14g

210. Low-Carb Loaded Cauliflower Casserole
Prep Time: 10 Mins, Cook Time: 30 Mins, Servings: 1
Ingredients
- 1 lb large cauliflower head
- 2 tbsp oil olive
- ¼ tsp salt kosher
- ¼ tsp powder garlic
- 1/8 tsp black pepper ground
- 1 cup yogurt Greek
- 1 tbsp juice lemon
- 1 cup cheese grated cheddar
- 2 slices cooked & crumbled bacon
- 1 chopped green onion

Instructions
- The oven should be preheated at 450°F.
- The cauliflower florets should be placed in a baking pan. Grind both black pepper & garlic powder into the olive oil. Toss to distribute the ingredients evenly.
- It should be roasted for around 20 Mins till it's soft and pliable.
- In the meantime, mix the lemon juice, Greek yogurt, cheddar cheese, & the diced bacon in a small bowl. Stir well.
- Toss the roasted cauliflower with the yogurt mixture after it has finished roasting.
- Top your cauliflower with the leftover cheese and bake it again.

- The cheese should be melted & bubbling after baking for 10 mins at 350°F.
- Before serving, sprinkle chopped green onions over the top.

Nutrition Information
Calories: 163 kcal, Carbohydrates: 5 g, Protein: 8 g, Fat: 13g

211. Creamy Vegan Spinach Dip
Prep Time: 15 Mins, Cook Time: 10 Mins, Servings: 2
Ingredients
- 1-½ cups raw cashews
- 2 tbsp yeast nutritional
- 1 tsp powder onion
- ½ tsp powder garlic
- ½ tsp salt kosher
- 3 tbsp juice lemon
- ½ cup almond milk unsweetened
- 10 oz frozen & thawed spinach packaged
- 3 chopped green onions
- black pepper ground

Instructions
- Cover your cashews in cold water for the creamiest dip. Drain and rinse them after resting for approximately four hrs if you have got a powerful blender.
- Combine the kosher salt, cashews, garlic powder, onion powder, nutritional yeast, & lemon juice. Using a spatula, scrape down the bowl as required and blend the ingredients until a homogeneous paste is formed.
- Blend in the water till the mixture is creamy & smooth.
- Squeeze out the spinach's excess water. Combine it with some green onions in a blender and mix until smooth. Pulse your mixture until it's well incorporated before moving on to the next step. Process till its dip is vivid green or stop once there are huge bits of spinach in it.
- Add salt & pepper to the dip before serving. Add more nutritional yeast if you'd like the cheese taste to be even stronger.
- Allow the flavors to mingle for an hr before serving.
- If you want to serve it warm, put it in the oven for around 5-10 mins at 375°F and serve.

Nutrition Information
Calories: 58 kcal, Carbohydrates: 4 g, Protein: 3 g, Fat: 4g

212. Curried Salmon and Roasted Sweet Potatoes
Prep Time: 15 Mins, Cook Time: 30 Mins, Servings: 3
Ingredients
For Sweet Potatoes
- 2 sweet, peeled potatoes large
- 1 tbsp olive oil
- ½ tsp salt kosher
- 1 tsp thyme leaves dried

For Salmon
- 1 tsp powder curry
- 1 tsp honey
- ½ tsp zest lime
- 1 tsp olive oil
- crushed pepper flakes red
- 16 oz filets salmon

Instructions
For Potatoes
- The oven should be preheated at 400°F.
- A big bowl should mix the potatoes, salt, olive oil, & thyme. Bake your potatoes for approximately 20 mins, or till they're fork-tender, tossing the potatoes midway through.

For Salmon
- To prevent the potatoes from sticking to the pan, spray nontoxic spray over foil & line the baking sheet. Keep your oven temperature at 400 degrees.
- The salmon may be added at this point if desired. Lay your salmon on a baking pan and brush your curry mix over. Bake for about 20 Mins. For best results, allow the salmon to marinate for approximately 5 Minutes before baking for 10-15 minutes, or unless the fish becomes flaky & firm. Potatoes may be served as a side dish.

Nutrition Information
Calories: 353 kcal, Carbohydrates: 18 g, Protein: 25 g, Fat: 20g

213. Skinny Mississippi Pot Roast
Prep Time: 3 Mins, Cook Time: 4 hrs 15 Mins, Servings: 6
Ingredients
- 4 lbs chuck roast lean beef
- 1 tsp kosher salt
- ¼ cup paste tomato
- 1 tbsp powder onion
- 1 tbsp powder garlic
- 1 tsp chives dried
- 2 tbsp parsley dried
- 1 tsp thyme leaves dried
- 1 tsp dill dried
- 1 cup broth beef
- 2 tbsp cornstarch
- 3 tbsp water

Instructions
- Place your roast in a crockpot.
- Salt, dried chives, tomato paste, garlic powder, onion powder, parsley, thyme & dill are all good additions to a shallow dish. Spread the mixture evenly on the roast. All around roast, ladle some beef broth. Once it's cooled down enough, remove the lid, and set the timer to either high or low.
- Remove your roast from the slow cooker & place it on a cutting board. Corn starch & water should be dissolved in a blender or food processor until they form a homogeneous paste. Stir the mix into the slow cooker's remaining liquid. Cook the mix for approximately 10 mins on high, till it becomes thick.
- The sauce should be drizzled over the meat before serving. Enjoy!

Nutrition Information
Calories: 328 kcal, Carbohydrates: 6 g, Protein: 49 g, Fat: 12g

214. Easy Classic Bruschetta
Prep Time: 15 Mins, Cook Time: 15 Mins, Servings: 2
Ingredients
- 6 diced Roma tomatoes
- ¼ cup diced red onion
- 3 minced garlic cloves
- ¼ cup chopped basil fresh
- 2 tsp oil olive
- 2 tsp balsamic vinegar dark
- ½ tsp salt kosher

Instructions
- Make a mixture by combining all of the ingredients. When serving, let the flavors meld for approximately 5-10 minutes. Mix into grains like rice and quinoa, or drizzle over meats like chicken or beef that have been grilled.

Nutrition Information
Calories: 31 kcal, Carbohydrates: 4 g, Protein: 1 g, Fat: 2g

215. 4-Ingredient Peanut Butter Cookies
Prep Time: 15 Mins, Cook Time: 12 Mins, Servings: 1
Ingredients
- 1 cup natural peanut butter
- 1 large beaten egg
- ½ cup palm sugar coconut
- 1 tsp extract vanilla

Instructions
- The oven should be preheated to 350°F.
- Add peanut butter, beaten egg, coconut sugar, & vanilla extract. You'll need around 14 1" balls of cookie dough for this recipe.
- A parchment sheet is required for this step.

- When you've dipped a fork within leftover coconut sugar, use it to push the balls to flatten them.
- Using the central oven rack, bake cookies for around 6 mins, rotate your baking sheet 180 degrees & bake for an extra 5-6 mins. Remove with a spatula after cooling for 25-30 mins on the baking sheet. Enjoy!

Nutrition Information
Calories: 136 kcal, Carbohydrates: 9 g, Protein: 5 g, Fat: 10g

216. Super Easy Pork Tenderloin with Garlic and Rosemary
Prep Time: 2 hrs 15 Mins, Cook Time: 45 Mins, Servings: 4
Ingredients
- 1 tsp kosher salt
- ½ tsp black pepper ground
- 5 minced garlic cloves
- 2 tsp ground rosemary dried
- 2 tbsp oil olive
- 1 & ½ lbs pork tenderloin lean

Instructions
- Combine 1 tbsp olive oil, pepper, garlic, salt, & rosemary in a mixing bowl. Spread your tenderloin with the mixture. Freeze for at least two hrs, if not all night.
- Make sure the oven temperature is 400°F. Spray a nonstick spray on a baking pan after lining it using foil.
- Remove the majority of the spice from the tenderloin. ' In a large skillet, heat any remaining oil over high heat. The tenderloin should be cooked on both sides until golden brown in the heated oil. Bake sliced pork tenderloin for around 45 mins, till it reaches an internal temperature of 145 degrees. The tenderloin would remain juicy if you let it rest for 15 mins before slicing & serving.

Nutrition Information
Calories: 271 kcal, Carbohydrates: 21 g, Protein: 35 g, Fat: 13g

217. Asian Chicken Wraps
Prep Time: 10 Mins, Cook Time: 15 Mins, Servings: 1
Ingredients
For Stir-Fry Sauce
- 2 tbsp honey
- ½ tsp vinegar rice wine
- 2 tbsp soy sauce lite

For Dipping Sauce
- ¼ cup of honey
- ½ cup of water warm
- 2 tbsp soy sauce lite
- 2 tbsp vinegar rice wine
- 2 tbsp ketchup
- 1 tbsp freshly squeezed lemon juice
- 1/8 tsp oil sesame
- 1 tbsp mustard Dijon

For Chicken
- 1 tbsp oil canola
- 1 tbsp oil sesame
- 3 chicken breasts boneless & skinless
- 1 cup lightly roasted cashews diced
- ½ cup diced button mushrooms
- ½ cup finely diced yellow onion
- 2 minced garlic cloves
- 6 Napa large cabbage leaves

Instructions
For Stir-Fry Sauce
- Mix the ingredients in a medium bowl.

For Dipping Sauce
- In a small saucepan, combine honey & warm water. Simmer the mixture for a few Mins, then remove from the heat & stir in the other ingredients. 5 Mins later, remove from the heat and let it cool. Set up a serving dish for a dipping sauce.

For Chicken
- Canola and sesame oils should be heated together in a large pan or wok before using. Diced chicken breast should be cooked for 8-10 mins at high heat till it has shed its pink hue. Remove chicken from liquid and pat dry. Continue to cook the chicken while stirring the pre-prepared ingredients in the pan. Add the chicken, mushrooms, onion, water chestnuts, & garlic to the stir-fry sauce. Cook for around 4-5 Mins over medium heat, stirring occasionally.
- Pour dipping sauce over cooked chicken on each cabbage leaf. Allow for the addition of extra dipping sauce by each guest. When eating, gently fold the wrapping in half. Even if some sauce leaks out, don't worry; there's enough left over. Enjoy!!!

Nutrition Information
Calories: 123 kcal, Carbohydrates: 13 g, Protein: 11 g, Fat: 3g

218. Slow Cooker Chai Tea
Prep Time: 5 Mins, Cook Time: 2 hrs 45 Mins, Servings: 1
Ingredients
- 3 cups water hot
- 2 tbsp leaves chai tea
- 4 sticks cinnamon
- 1 tsp allspice whole
- 1 tsp cloves whole
- 6 thin slices of ginger root
- 1/3 cup of honey
- 5 cups milk coconut

Instructions
- In your slow cooker, combine the heated water & tea. Cook for approximately 15 Mins on high in a large pot.
- On lower for around 4 hrs, add the rest of the ingredients, except the coconut milk. After 30 Mins, add some coconut milk & continue cooking on high for another 30 mins.

Nutrition Information
Calories: 271 kcal, Carbohydrates: 16 g, Protein: 2 g, Fat: 24g

219. Slow Cooker Fudge
Prep Time: 5 Mins, Cook Time: 35 Mins, Servings: 1
Ingredients
- 2 & ½ cups chips chocolate
- ½ cup of coconut milk
- ¼ cup of coconut sugar
- sea salt dash
- 2 tbsp oil coconut
- 1 tsp extract pure vanilla

Instructions
- Toss in the cocoa powder & chocolate chips, then whisk in the sugar, salt, milk, & oil. After that, cover, and simmer on low for two hrs without stirring, and the lid must be kept on for the whole two-hr period.
- After two hrs, remove the lid, stir in the vanilla, & turn your cooker off. At this time, you mustn't stir the fudge mixture. Allow the mixture to cool at room temp.
- Use a big spoon to aggressively swirl for 5 to 10 Mins after cooling until some of the shine has been lost.
- Grease an eight-by-eight-inch square baking dish with a little vegetable oil. Refrigerate for at least four hrs, or until hard, before pouring into the pan. This fudge seems very indulgent and should only be consumed on special occasions.
- Most supermarkets have canned coconut milk in organic aisles.

Nutrition Information
Calories: 114 kcal, Carbohydrates: 17 g, Protein: 1 g, Fat: 8g

220. Skinny Cheesy Chicken Sweet Potato Skins
Prep Time: 15 Mins, Cook Time: 20 Mins, Servings: 1
Ingredients
- 2 sweet baked potatoes
- ½ cup of boneless & skinless shredded chicken breast
- 1 tsp oregano dried
- 1 tsp cumin ground
- 2 tsp powder chili

- 1 tsp oil olive
- 2 minced garlic cloves
- 1 tbsp juice lime
- 2 cups fresh baby spinach
- ½ cup shredded mozzarella cheese
- ¼ cup chopped cilantro fresh

Instructions
- Make sure you've got your oven on. Apply nonstick spray on a baking sheet.
- Create a boat out of the potato skins by scooping out the center of the sweet potato. The boat will keep its form if some potato is left around the edges. On a baking sheet, put the boats.
- Chicken, cumin, oregano, and chili powder are mixed with mashed sweet potato centers.
- Meanwhile, in a medium pan, heat the olive oil. Add the lime juice, garlic, & spinach to the pan once heated. Add the spinach to a potato mix & cook till wilted. Once the mix has been combined, put it into potato skins, then top with some cheese.
- When the cheese melts and faintly browned, bake for around 15-20 Mins. Cilantro should be topped on each of the 4 pieces. Ensure that the food is served at the correct temperature.

Nutrition Information
Calories: 171 kcal, Carbohydrates: 19 g, Protein: 12 g, Fat: 3g

221. Slow Cooker Turkey Sloppy Joes
Prep Time: 15 Mins, Cook Time: 2 hrs, Servings: 1
Ingredients
- 1 lb ground raw turkey breast
- 1 cup diced onion
- ½ cup diced green pepper
- 3 minced garlic cloves
- 1 tbsp yellow mustard
- ¼ cup natural ketchup
- 8 oz no-salt tomato sauce
- 1 tbsp sauce BBQ
- 1-2 Stevia packets

Instructions
- Sauté onions, raw turkey, & green peppers in a pan with a little oil.
- Combine onions, turkey meat, and green peppers in a slow cooker. Take a large bowl & add other ingredients.
- It's best to keep it covered and cook it on low or medium-high for about 3-4 hrs.
- The whole grain bread should be toasted before serving.

Nutrition Information
Calories: 183 kcal, Carbohydrates: 11 g, Protein: 28 g, Fat: 3g

222. Souffle Omelets with Mushrooms
Prep Time: 10 Mins, Cook Time: 15 Mins, Servings: 1
Ingredients
- 1 tsp oil olive
- 1 minced clove garlic
- 8 oz sliced mushrooms
- 1 tbsp minced parsley
- 3 separated large eggs
- ¼ cup of cheddar cheese shredded fat-free

Instructions
- In a pan, heat olive oil on medium heat & cook the garlic.
- Sauté your mushrooms for ten Mins. Remove from heat and add the parsley.
- In a bowl, beat your egg yolks till they are pale yellow and thick. To begin with, whip the egg whites until they're foamy white. A blender was used for egg whites. Add salt, cheese, & pepper to the yolks before folding within whites.
- Use nonstick spray to coat a big skillet. Cover and let the egg mix sit for a few Mins. In other words, don't stop cooking until you have a golden-brown crust on the top & bottom. Using a spatula, gently loosen it. To make an omelet, add mushrooms and then fold the omelet over.

Nutrition Information
Calories: 329 kcal, Carbohydrates: 10 g, Protein: 31 g, Fat: 19g

223. Mushroom Parmesan Bites
Prep Time: 15 Mins, Cook Time: 15 Mins, Servings: 2
Ingredients
- 1 lb button mushrooms washed & stem removed bite-sized
- 2 tbsp olive oil
- ¼ cup fat-free parmesan cheese
- 2 minced garlic cloves
- ¼ cup fat-free cream cheese
- ¼ cup panko breadcrumbs whole-wheat

Instructions
- Preheat your oven to 375°F. Set aside the baking sheet sprayed using non-stick spray.
- Place your mushrooms on a baking pan & brush them with olive oil.
- Combine the garlic, cream cheese, & parmesan in a large mixing bowl. The mixture should be completely homogeneous, and each mushroom should have cheese filling. The leftover olive oil & panko should be combined in a separate mixing bowl. A panko topping should be applied to every mushroom that was stuffed.
- Tops should be golden brown after 15-20 Mins of baking time.

Nutrition Information
Calories: 117 kcal, Carbohydrates: 7 g, Protein: 7 g, Fat: 7g

224. Slow Cooker Pork Tenderloin
Prep Time: 20 Mins, Cook Time: 6 hrs 10 Mins, Servings: 4
Ingredients
1 ½ to 2 lbs lean pork tenderloin
Marinade
- 1 cup of chicken broth low-sodium fat-free
- 1 tbsp mustard Dijon
- 1 tbsp vinegar rice wine
- 1 tbsp low sodium soy sauce lite
- 2 tbsp honey
- 2 tsp freshly grated ginger
- 2 minced garlic cloves
- 1 tsp powder curry
- ½ tsp pepper black
- sea salt or kosher

Instructions
- Combine all the marinade ingredients in a mixing bowl. Remove all of the visible fat from the tenderloin & discard it. Ensure both sides of the tenderloin are covered in the marinade before putting it in the oven. Overnight, cover & refrigerate tenderloin within the fridge to marinate.
- In a slow cooker, combine the tenderloin & marinade; simmer for 4 to 6 hrs on low heat, or till meat readily shreds. Serve on a serving plate after removing from slow cooker.

Nutrition Information
Calories: 210 kcal, Carbohydrates: 14 g, Protein: 26 g, Fat: 5g

225. Cauliflower Holiday Stuffing
Prep Time: 10 Mins, Cook Time: 30 Mins, Servings: 3
Ingredients
- 1 lb head cauliflower
- 1 medium thinly sliced red onion
- 2 small, diced celery stalk
- 1 cup finely chopped cremini mushrooms
- 3 tbsp oil olive
- ¼ tsp powder garlic
- 1 tsp seasoning Italian
- ½ tsp salt kosher
- 1/8 tsp black pepper ground
- 2 tbsp freshly chopped parsley

Instructions
- The oven should be preheated at 450°F. Set aside the baking sheet that has been lined using parchment paper.
- Gather all of the ingredients for the Cauliflower Casserole in a big bowl and mix them. The veggies should be well covered in the spices when the mixture has been stirred.
- Pour the mixture on a sheet pan in a thin layer, if necessary, using 2 pans.
- Cauliflower & onions should be caramelized & golden brown after 30 Mins of roasting.
- Before serving, garnish the filling with the parsley.

Nutrition Information
Calories: 55 kcal, Carbohydrates: 4 g, Protein: 1 g, Fat: 4g

226. Instant Pot Apple Cider Glazed Chicken
Prep Time: 10 Mins, Cook Time: 15 Mins, Servings: 8
Ingredients
- 4 lbs chicken whole
- 1 tsp salt kosher
- 1 tsp black pepper ground
- 1 tbsp oil olive
- 1 cup of cider apple
- 2 tbsp honey
- 2 tbsp coconut aminos
- ¼ tsp flakes red pepper

Instructions
- Before seasoning the chicken with salt & pepper, pat it dry. Check to see whether it's seasoned on all four corners.
- Press to Sauté button on your Instant Pot.
- In a small bowl, add some olive oil & cook the chicken till it's nicely browned on both sides. The chicken should be taken out of the saucepan and placed aside.
- Pour the coconut aminos, honey, apple cider, and pepper flakes into a medium bowl, then mix well. Stir your apple cider mix into an Instant Pot & scrape the pot to remove any chicken remains. Cancel this Sauté function by pressing the Cancel button.
- Incorporate your chicken back into an Instant Pot & close the cover. Ensure the lid is shut & the vent is pushed back in.
- To raise the cooking time to 25 mins, press on Poultry button & the plus button simultaneously. As a general rule, you should allow an additional 6 Mins per lb of chicken that weighs more than 4 lbs.
- It will sound when the timer has run out. Carefully vent your Instant Pot to disburse the steam. It's going to be a lot of steam! Your hand should not be directly above the vent. Remove the cover after the steam has dissipated. Ensure that the temperature of the chicken is at least 165°F. The chicken should rest for at least five Mins before being carved.

Nutrition Information
Calories: 396 kcal, Carbohydrates: 12 g, Protein: 29 g, Fat: 25g

227. Skinny Slow Cooker Italian Beef
Prep Time: 10 Mins, Cook Time: 4 hrs, Servings: 2
Ingredients
- 1 tsp salt kosher
- ½ tsp black pepper ground
- 1 tsp powder garlic
- 1 tsp powder onion
- 2 tsp seasoning Italian
- 6 oz paste tomato
- 2 lbs sirloin roast beef
- 1 sliced thin yellow onion
- 1 green sliced thin bell pepper
- 1 sliced thin banana pepper
- ½ cup low-sodium beef broth

Instructions
- Combine the Italian seasoning, salt, pepper, onion powder, garlic powder, & tomato paste in a mixing bowl. Make sure everything is well-combined. Place your roast within a slow cooker after being well coated with the mixture. Pour hot beef broth on the peppers and onions before serving.
- Cook for around 4 hrs on high. Shred your roast once it has been removed from the pan. Add the shredded meat, peppers, & broth back to a slow cooker. Make a sandwich with shredded beef or give it with some BBQ sauce.

Nutrition Information
Calories: 270 kcal, Carbohydrates: 6 g, Protein: 24 g, Fat: 16g

228. Super Easy 3-Ingredient Chicken for Two
Prep Time: 5 Mins, Cook Time: 4 hrs, Servings: 4
Ingredients
- 1 chicken breast boneless & skinless
- 1 cup sugar-free chunky salsa
- ¼ cup vinegar balsamic

Instructions
- Pour both salsa & balsamic vinegar over chicken breasts in a slow cooker.
- Cover & cook for around 6 hrs. Make sure to mash the salsa using a fork before adding your cooked chicken.

Nutrition Information
Calories: 130 kcal, Carbohydrates: 14 g, Protein: 14 g, Fat: 2g

229. Stuffed Philly Chicken Peppers
Prep Time: 10 Mins, Cook Time: 45 Mins, Servings: 1
Ingredients
- 1 tbsp olive oil extra virgin
- 1 diced yellow onion
- 1 minced garlic clove
- 2 boneless & skinless sliced chicken breasts
- ¼ tsp sea salt or kosher
- ¼ tsp pepper cayenne
- 1 tbsp vinegar balsamic
- 2 seeds removed bell peppers
- 2 provolone reduced-fat cheese slices

Instructions
- Set the oven temperature to 350°F.
- In a big skillet, heat some olive oil to medium-high heat. Make sure that the onion is cooked through. Remove from heat when it's done browning. Add the salt, cayenne pepper, and Balsamic vinegar. Continue to cook the chicken until it is done.
- Split fresh bell peppers, then remove both seeds & core. Place the peppers into the baking dish with some chicken mixture & bake at 350 degrees Fahrenheit for 30 Mins. Make sure the dish is completely covered with Al foil by adding water. Take the cake out of the oven after 35 Mins of baking time.
- Remove the lid and top bell pepper with provolone cheese. Bake until the cheese has browned and bubbled, about 5 to 10 minutes longer.

Nutrition Information
Calories: 259 kcal, Carbohydrates: 7 g, Protein: 23 g, Fat: 15g

230. Crock Pot 3-Ingredient Balsamic Chicken
Prep Time: 2 Mins, Cook Time: 4 hrs, Servings: 3
Ingredients
- 2 lbs chicken breasts boneless & skinless
- 16 oz salsa jar chunky
- ½ cup vinegar balsamic

Instructions
- Pour salsa & balsamic over chicken breasts in the slow cooker. For a low of 6 hrs, cover & cook. Using a fork, shred your chicken, then combine it with some salsa.

Nutrition Information
Calories: 263 kcal, Carbohydrates: 8 g, Protein: 35 g, Fat: 5g

231. Chocolate Hazelnut and Berry Puff Pastry Tart
Prep Time: 10 Mins, Cook Time: 20 Mins, Servings: 4
Ingredients
- 1 puff pastry whole-wheat

- ¼ cup hazelnut spread chocolate
- ¼ cup fresh raspberries
- ¼ cup fresh blueberries
- ½ cup sliced strawberries

Instructions
- Set the oven temperature to 425°F. On the baking sheet, place your puff pastry. Make a crust by rolling up a little part of each edge. Prick your pastry all over the bottom with a fork. A beautiful brown crust should form after baking for around 20-30 Mins. Let it cool down a little.
- Spread some chocolate hazelnut butter on top of the chilled puff pastry. If your chocolate hazelnut butter is too firm to spread on the crust, warm it up a little. The berries may be sprinkled on top. Cool completely before serving.

Nutrition Information
Calories: 151 kcal, Carbohydrates: 14 g, Protein: 2 g, Fat: 10g

232. Parmesan Eggplant and Spinach Dip | Healthy Dip Recipe
Prep Time: 15 Mins, Cook Time: 30 Mins, Servings: 2
Ingredients
- 1 peeled & cubed eggplant large
- 1 tbsp oil olive
- ¼ tsp salt kosher
- 2 cups spinach baby
- 3 minced garlic cloves
- 1/3 cup of parmesan cheese shredded fat-free

Instructions
- Line the baking pan with Al foil and place it in your oven.
- Salt and pepper the eggplant mixture. Spread your eggplant out evenly on your baking sheet & toss to cover it with the oil. The eggplant should be baked for 10-15 Mins, or until it starts to color.
- The leftover olive oil may be heated in a pan on medium heat while your eggplant is being roasted. Stir in some spinach & garlic after it's warmed through. Cook until the spinach is completely wilted.
- In your food processor, puree the eggplant till smooth, adding some water as required if eggplant is thick to mix. In your food processor, pulse together the spinach & parmesan cheese.
- Apply nonstick spray to a casserole dish & spread the eggplant mixture evenly. On top, scatter the remaining shaved cheese. Just 10 Mins in the oven should do the trick. Serve with veggies, pita bread, crusty bread, or your favorite crackers while it's still hot!

Nutrition Information
Calories: 58 kcal, Carbohydrates: 6 g, Protein: 3 g, Fat: 3g

233. Plant-Based Avocado Mayonnaise
Prep Time: 2 Mins, Cook Time: 5 Mins, Servings: 1
Ingredients
- ½ cup plain soy milk
- 2 tsp juice lemon
- 1 tsp vinegar apple cider
- 1 pit removed & roughly chopped avocado peeled
- ½ tsp salt kosher
- ½ cup oil olive

Instructions
- All ingredients save the oil should be blended in a blender, excluding the oil. Mix on high speed until smooth.
- Turn your blender on & scrape all sides. Add oil slowly while combining and keep blending till the mixture becomes thick. Blend for another two Mins.
- Before serving, let the food sit in the refrigerator for at least an hr. For up to a week, keep it in a sealed container.

Nutrition Information
Calories: 57 kcal, Carbohydrates: 1 g, Protein: 5 g, Fat: 6g

234. Chicken Tikka Masala Slow Cooker Recipe
Prep Time: 5 Mins, Cook Time: 6 hrs, Servings: 2
Ingredients
- 1 lb chicken breasts boneless & skinless
- 15 oz diced can tomatoes
- 1 diced yellow onion
- 3 minced garlic cloves
- 1 tbsp minced ginger
- 1 minced jalapeno pepper
- ½ tsp turmeric
- 1 tsp coriander ground
- 1 tsp cumin ground
- 3 tsp paprika
- 3 tsp powder chili
- 2 tsp masala garam
- ¼ cup chicken water or broth
- 15 oz milk coconut
- 1 tbsp paste tomato
- ¼ cup fresh, chopped cilantro

Instructions
- A slow cooker may mix all of the above ingredients except for coconut milk, tomato sauce, and cilantro. Cook for around 4 hrs on high.
- Stir in some coconut milk & tomato paste after the dish has cooked. Garnish with chopped cilantro & serve with quinoa.

Nutrition Information
Calories: 271 kcal, Carbohydrates: 10 g, Protein: 20 g, Fat: 18g

235. Apple Cider Vinegar and Cranberry Detox Drink
Prep Time: 2 Mins, Cook Time 2 Mins, Servings: 8
Ingredients
- ¼ cup no sugar cranberry juice
- ½ cup water cold
- 2 tbsp vinegar apple cider
- 1 tsp lime juice or lemon juice

Instructions
- Combine the ingredients in a large mixing bowl. Serve at room temperature!

Nutrition Information
Calories: 41 kcal, Carbohydrates: 9 g, Proteins: 10 g, Fat: 3 g

236. Steamed Salmon with Sweet Ginger Soy Glaze
Prep Time: 10 Mins, Cook Time: 10 Mins, Servings: 4
Ingredients
- 16 oz salmon fillets skinless & boneless
- ½ tsp salt kosher
- ¼ tsp black pepper ground
- 2 tsp ginger ground
- 1 tsp powder garlic
- ¼ cup low-sodium soy sauce
- ¼ cup honey pure
- ½ tsp red pepper crushed

Instructions
- Season your salmon with pepper, salt, ginger, & garlic powder.
- Fill a pan with approximately 1" of water. A steaming basket can only be used in a pan or saucepot. Begin heating up. Once boiling, gently lay your seasoned salmon into the steaming basket. Place your basket into a pot, so this lies just over the water. Cover & steam for around 8-10 Mins or till salmon becomes firm & cooked through.
- Add soy sauce & honey to a pot over low heat when the salmon is cooking. Stir the honey frequently until it is completely dissolved, then remove it from the heat. Crush the leftover ginger, red pepper, garlic, & add them to the mixture. Bring the mixture to a boil, lower the heat, and let it simmer for a few Mins.
- Enjoy with steamed salmon & a spicy sauce.

Nutrition Information
Calories: 316 kcal, Carbohydrates: 20 g, Protein: 25 g, Fat: 15g

237. Best Ever Spinach and Artichoke Stuffed Chicken
Prep Time: 5 Mins, Cook Time: 15 Mins, Servings: 1
Ingredients
- 6 oz fat-free cream cheese
- 15 oz drained & chopped artichoke hearts
- 1 cup cooked & liquid squeezed baby spinach
- 3 minced garlic cloves
- ½ cup of parmesan cheese shredded fat-free
- 1 tsp salt kosher
- ½ tsp black pepper ground
- 24 oz chicken breasts boneless & skinless
- 1 tbsp oil olive

Instructions
- Make sure the oven temperature is 400°F.
- Whip your cream cheese over high in a small bowl till it is light and frothy. Toss in the artichokes & spinach, garlic, salt, and pepper. In a low-speed blender, mix the ingredients.
- Make a pocket by carefully slicing your chicken breast. To make the filling, spread your cream cheese mixture over each. Chicken breasts should have around 3-4 tsp of sauce.
- Warm the olive oil in a big skillet. Take care not to let the filling drop out of the chicken when you put it to the oil. The golden-brown color should appear on both sides after roughly a Min of cooking. After approximately 10 Mins in the oven, remove the chicken from the pan & let it rest.
- For best results, let the dish rest in your oven for at least five mins before serving it.

Nutrition Information
Calories: 389 kcal, Carbohydrates: 16 g, Protein: 54 g, Fat: 12g

238. Sweet Potato Breakfast Hash
Prep Time: 10 Mins, Cook Time: 30 Mins, Servings: 4
Ingredients
- 2 sweet peeled & diced small potatoes large
- 3 tbsp oil olive
- ½ tsp salt kosher
- ¼ tsp white pepper ground
- 1 tbsp vinegar apple cider
- 2 minced garlic cloves
- 1 tsp honey
- ¼ cup diced small yellow onion
- ¼ cup diced small bell pepper green
- 8 oz ham diced small sulfate-free low-sodium
- 1 tbsp juice lemon
- 1 pit removed & diced small avocado peeled

Instructions
- Make sure you've got your oven on. Make a foil-lined baking sheet and place it in the oven.
- Toss your chopped sweet potatoes, salt, olive oil, & pepper in a bowl, then spread them evenly on a baking sheet. Bake for 30 Mins. Put the potatoes within the oven for approximately 15 Mins or till they're just starting to brown & are soft.
- Small bowl: Add honey & apple vinegar to a mixing bowl. Add some olive oil, stirring constantly. Mix well with a whisk.
- The leftover olive oil should be heated in a big pan over medium-high heat. Add onion & green pepper after the oil is heated. Add your ham & potatoes when the onions start to soften. It's time to brown your ham, so keep cooking. Remove from the stove and mix in some apple vinegar sauce after cooling.
- Avocado & lemon juice should be combined. Gently incorporate the hash into the mixture. Serve it hot!

Nutrition Information
Calories: 186 kcal, Carbohydrates: 14 g, Protein: 8 g, Fat: 11g

239. Cheesy Summer Squash Stuffed Chicken
Prep Time: 15 Mins, Cook Time: 20 Mins, Servings: 1

Ingredients
- 24-32 oz chicken breasts boneless & skinless
- 1 squash small yellow summer
- 1 small zucchini
- 2 small Roma tomatoes
- 1 tbsp oil olive
- 3 minced garlic cloves
- ½ tsp salt kosher
- ¼ tsp black pepper ground
- ½ cup of mozzarella cheese shredded fat-free

Instructions
- The oven should be preheated at 400°F. Spray nonstick spray on the baking pan after lining this with foil.
- To form pockets within the chicken breast, cut 3-4 slits in the meat. Place 1 slice of yellow squash, 1 slice of zucchini, & 1 slice of tomato in every one of the pockets.
- Olive oil & garlic should be mixed in a shallow dish to make an aromatic dressing. Sprinkle salt & pepper over the chicken before brushing it with some olive oil mix. Remove the food from your oven after 10 mins of baking.
- Return your chicken to the oven & top this with your mozzarella, then bake for another 10 Mins. If you want the cheese to become nice and melted, bake for the next 10 mins. Enjoy your meal while it's still piping hot!

Nutrition Information
Calories: 333 kcal, Carbohydrates: 5 g, Protein: 49 g, Fat: 12g

240. Spinach Parmesan Baked Eggs Recipe
Prep Time: 10 Mins, Cook Time: 25 Mins, Servings: 2
Ingredients
- 2 tsp oil olive
- 2 minced garlic cloves
- 4 cups spinach baby
- ½ cup of parmesan cheese grated fat-free
- 4 large eggs
- 1 diced small tomato small

Instructions
- The oven should be preheated to 350°F. Apply nonstick spray to a casserole dish.
- Olive oil should be heated over medium-high heat in a big pan. Toss in some spinach & garlic when the pan has a nice smoky flavor. In a hot pan, add the spinach and cook until it has wilted. Remove from the heat & let any remaining liquid drip away. Some parmesan cheese should be added at this point, and then the mixture should be spooned evenly into a casserole dish.
- Divvy up the spinach into four little nooks. Each divot should contain an egg. Take them out of the oven when egg whites have been almost set, around 15-20 Mins. Approximately 5 Mins after removing from oven, garnish with tomatoes. Prepare the food and serve it to your guests.

Nutrition Information
Calories: 149 kcal, Carbohydrates: 3 g, Protein: 12 g, Fat: 10g

241. Individual Egg & Spinach Bowls
Prep Time: 5 Mins, Cook Time: 20 Mins, Servings: 1
Ingredients
- 8 large egg whites
- 1 egg whole
- 1 cup torn baby spinach
- ½ cup tomatoes diced
- ¼ cup fat-free feta cheese
- ½ tsp pepper black
- sea salt or kosher

Instructions
- The oven should be preheated to 350°F.
- In a medium-sized mixing bowl, combine all of the ingredients. Use nonstick spray to lightly spritz 4 ramekins & equally divide the egg mixture into each one.
- Bake your ramekins for 20 minutes unless the eggs have puffed up and are nearly set within the middle.

Nutrition Information
Calories: 84 kcal, Carbohydrates: 6 g, Protein: 11 g, Fat: 2g

242. Baked Chicken and Vegetable Spring Rolls
Prep Time: 20 Mins, Cook Time: 40 Mins, Servings: 4
Ingredients
- 3 tbsp extra virgin divided olive oil
- 1 finely chopped garlic clove
- 1 finely chopped onion small
- 4 oz chicken breasts boneless & skinless
- 1 cup julienned carrots
- 1 cup sliced diagonally string beans
- 1 cup julienned cabbage
- 3 tbsp low salt soy sauce
- ¼ tsp salt
- ¼ tsp pepper ground
- 8 wrappers spring roll

Instructions
- The oven should be preheated at 400 deg F.
- Sauté both garlic & onion in olive oil on medium heat in a big saucepan for around 1 Min.
- Add chicken & cook for approximately five Mins.
- Sauté the veggies for around 15 Mins before adding the meat.
- Toss with the salt, soy sauce, & pepper for 1 Min.
- Place two filo squares over the work surface and begin rolling. Place a dollop of chicken & vegetable sauté on the section closest to you. Tuck all sides in and keep rolling till you get to the finish. To seal the edges of the filo, moisten your fingers with water and softly dab them. The rest of the spring rolls can wait.
- Place your spring rolls over a parchment-lined baking sheet.
- Using the leftover 1 tbsp of olive oil, brush every spring roll.
- When they are golden brown, they are done baking.
- Serve with a dipping sauce of your choice, sweet & sour, or anything else.

Nutrition Information
Calories: 127 kcal, Carbohydrates: 12 g, Protein: 4 g, Fat: 7g

243. Slow Roasted Tomatoes
Prep Time: 10 Mins, Cook Time: 3 hrs, Servings: 5
Ingredients
- ¼ tsp salt
- 1 & ½ tbsp oregano dried
- 1 tsp sugar coconut
- 1 lb tomatoes cherry
- 1 tbsp capers
- 2 tbsp olive oil extra virgin

Instructions
- The oven should be preheated at 275°F.
- Salt & oregano should be mixed in a shallow bowl. Dispose of.
- Tomatoes should be spread out on the baking pan, then coated with salt and sugar mixture. Mix in some capers and then drizzle the olive oil over the whole thing.
- Bake 3 hrs in the oven, and they're ready.
- Slow-roasted tomatoes may be utilized in various ways after they've been browned and softened. Place a container within the refrigerator may keep the food fresh for four days.

Nutrition Information
Calories: 103 kcal, Carbohydrates: 11 g, Protein: 1 g, Fat: 7g

244. Grilled Chicken and Zucchini Salad
Prep Time: 5 Mins, Cook Time: 16 Mins, Servings: 3
Ingredients
- 4 sliced thinly & vertically zucchini medium
- 1 lb chicken breasts boneless & skinless
- 1 tsp mustard
- 3 tbsp vinegar cider
- lettuce
- 3 tbsp olive oil extra virgin
- ½ tsp salt
- 2 sliced apricots
- leaves basil
- walnuts

Instructions
- Add an oil spray to the pan before cooking.
- Grill both zucchini & chicken for approximately 8 Mins from all sides on a skillet over medium heat.
- Preparation: While your chicken & zucchinis continue cooking, mix the mustard, vinegar & olive oil in a shallow dish. Seasoning: Dispose of it.
- Slice the chicken into strips and add it to a bowl with zucchini after it's done cooking.
- Pour your vinaigrette over the zucchini & chicken and stir well. Leave a little for the lettuce as well.
- If desired, apricots & walnuts may be used in lieu of the walnuts.

Nutrition Information
Calories: 178 kcal, Carbohydrates: 5 g, Protein: 18 g, Fat: 9g

245. Plant-Based Ranch Dressing Recipe
Prep Time: 35 Mins, Cook Time 35 Mins, Servings: 6
Ingredients
- 1 cup raw cashews
- 2 cups soaking water
- 1 tsp powder garlic
- ½ tsp powder onion
- ½ tsp salt sea
- ¼ tsp pepper black
- 2 tbsp vinegar apple cider
- 2 tbsp freshly squeezed lemon juice
- ¼ cup finely diced chives
- ¾ cup water purified
- ¼ cup freshly chopped parsley

Instructions
- Drain & rinse your cashews after soaking them for 30 mins within 2 cups of water.
- A blender is all that is needed to combine cashews, the rest of the ingredients, and the herbs. Once you've reached a creamy texture, give it one more pulse.
- Pour the mix into the glass container & seal it with the lid. Overnight refrigeration is preferable.

Nutrition Information
Calories: 25 kcal, Carbohydrates: 2 g, Protein: 1 g, Fat: 2g

246. Grilled Honey Lime Cilantro Chicken Skewers
Prep Time: 10 Mins, Cook Time: 25, Servings: 3
Ingredients
- 24-32 oz chicken breast boneless & skinless
- 1 bell pepper red
- 1 bell pepper green
- ½ cup fresh lime juice
- 1 tsp zest lime
- 1 tbsp melted coconut oil
- 3 minced garlic cloves
- ½ tsp salt kosher
- 1 tsp honey
- 1 tsp red pepper crushed
- ½ cup fresh, chopped cilantro

Instructions
- Chicken cubes, green and red bell peppers, and then wooden skewers are arranged in the following order: bell pepper cubes & bell pepper cubes.
- Only fresh cilantro should be used in this recipe. Combine all other ingredients in a mixing dish, and make sure everything is well-combined.
- In a small bowl, pour the lime mixture over the skewers & toss to coat. For 30 mins, place the covered skewers in the refrigerator.

- Prepare a medium-high grill by preheating it. Place your skewers over the grill after it has heated up. Chicken should be firm, and veggies should be tender after approximately 10 Mins of cooking.
- To serve, remove off the grill, spray the leftover marinade on the top, & sprinkle with the rest of the cilantro; serve it hot!

Nutrition Information
Calories: 129 kcal, Carbohydrates: 4 g, Protein: 19 g, Fat: 4g

247. 30-Min Buffalo Cauliflower Bites
Prep Time: 10 Mins, Cook Time: 20 Mins, Servings: 7
Ingredients
- 4 cups fresh cauliflower florets
- 1 tbsp melted coconut oil
- 1 tbsp sauce hot
- 1 tbsp sauce sriracha
- 1 tbsp juice lime

Instructions
- Make sure you've got your oven on. Apply nonstick spray over the baking sheet.
- Pour coconut oil over the cauliflower & smooth it out evenly. Cauliflower should be roasted for approximately 10 Mins, or unless it is browned and tender. Meanwhile, combine the other ingredients in a bowl and roast your cauliflower.
- Serve with the cauliflower tossed within the sauce mix when cooled down. Roast for a further 10 mins, stirring as necessary, on a baking sheet. Before serving, allow the food to cool somewhat.

Nutrition Information
Calories: 57 kcal, Carbohydrates: 6 g, Protein: 2 g, Fat: 4g

248. 15-Min Spicy Garlic Ginger Shrimp
Prep Time: 20 Mins, Cook Time: 15 Mins, Servings: 4
Ingredients
- 1 tbsp oil coconut
- 3 minced garlic cloves
- 1 tbsp fresh, minced ginger
- 1 lb peeled & deveined shrimp raw
- ½ tsp red pepper crushed
- 2 tbsp juice lime
- ½ tsp salt kosher

Instructions
- Your coconut oil should be heated in a large pan over medium-high heat. Adding the garlic & ginger is done when the oil is heated enough to incorporate them. Cook for approximately 30 seconds or until aromatic. Add your shrimp and boil them until they are pink & firm. Add lime juice, red pepper, & salt to the mix. For approximately 30 seconds, stir & simmer.
- Serve over quinoa while it's still warm.

Nutrition Information
Calories: 133 kcal, Carbohydrates: 2 g, Protein: 23 g, Fat: 4g

249. Skinny Spinach Stuffed Chicken Breast
Prep Time: 10 Mins, Cook Time: 25 Mins, Servings: 5
Ingredients
- 24-32 oz chicken breasts boneless & skinless
- 1 tbsp oil olive
- 1 tsp paprika
- 1 tsp kosher salt
- ¼ tsp garlic powder
- ¼ tsp powder onion
- 2 tbsp fat-free cream cheese
- 2 tbsp fat-free, plain Greek yogurt
- ¼ cup grated parmesan cheese
- 2 cups fresh, chopped spinach
- 2 minced garlic cloves
- ½ tsp pepper flakes red

Instructions
- Set the oven to 375°F. Spray the baking sheet using a non-stick spray, then line it with Al foil.
- Carve a small pocket onto each chicken breast's longest side using a knife. Apply olive oil to each & coat well.
- Garnish the chicken breasts with paprika mixed with garlic powder, salt, & onion powder. Dispose of.
- The yogurt, Parmesan, cream cheese, & salt go into a small bowl with the red pepper, spinach, garlic, & Greek yogurt. The mixture should be completely homogeneous. Place the packed chicken breasts over a baking sheet after stuffing them with the spinach mix.
- Remove foil & bake for another 30 mins to get a nice golden crust on the chicken. Before serving, allow the food to cool somewhat. Enjoy!

Nutrition Information
Calories: 371 kcal, Carbohydrates: 3 g, Protein: 41 g, Fat: 21g

250. Peach Salsa Recipe
Prep Time: 5 Mins, Cook Time: 15 Mins, Servings: 5
Ingredients
- 4 peaches peeled, pit removed fresh, ripe,
- 6 diced small Roma tomatoes
- ¼ cup diced small red onion
- 1 tbsp juice lime
- 1 seed removed & minced jalapeno
- ¼ cup fresh, chopped cilantro
- 1 tsp salt kosher

Instructions
- In a medium-sized mixing bowl, combine all of the ingredients. Serve after almost 15 Mins of chilling in the refrigerator. Use your favorite pita chips and tortilla to accompany this dish.

Nutrition Information
Calories: 21 kcal, Carbohydrates: 5 g, Protein: 1 g, Fat: 3 g

251. Easy Thai Beef Salad Recipe
Prep Time: 15 Mins, Cook Time: 10 Mins, Servings: 4
Ingredients
- 2 chopped green onions
- 1 cup fresh, chopped cilantro
- ½ cup fresh, chopped mint leaves
- ¼ cup fresh, chopped basil
- 1 cup juice lime
- ¼ cup low-sodium soy sauce
- ½ tsp pepper flakes red
- 2 tbsp honey
- 1 lb flank steak lean
- 1 tbsp oil olive
- 1 tsp salt kosher
- ½ tsp black pepper ground
- 3 cups chopped romaine lettuce
- 2 cups arugula baby
- 2 cups spinach baby
- 1 medium, sliced cucumber
- 1 cup cherry tomatoes or grape tomatoes

Instructions
- Make a big mixing basin and combine the cilantro, green onion, & mint with the honey & lime juice. Set aside once you've thoroughly mixed everything.
- Prepare a hot grill for cooking. Season your flank steak using pepper and salt before cooking. Cook your steak to your preferred degree of doneness. Cooking your steak to medium-rare, or 5 minutes on each side, is recommended. Allow the steak to rest for five Mins after removing it from the grill.
- When your steak is cooling, add all of the salad ingredients and toss thoroughly. Serve in separate bowls. Cucumbers & tomatoes go well on top of the lettuce.
- Lay your steak on top of the lettuce & slice it into thin slices. Add the cilantro sauce to the salad and toss to combine. Prepare the food and serve it to your guests.

Nutrition Information
Calories: 155 kcal, Carbohydrates: 11 g, Protein: 14 g, Fat: 7g

252. Instant Pot Creamy Salsa Verde Chicken
Prep Time: 5 Mins, Cook Time: 25 Mins, Servings: 1.5
Ingredients
- 2 lbs chicken breasts boneless & skinless
- 16 oz jar salsa Verde
- 1 deseeded, deveined, & diced jalapeno
- 1 tsp powder chili
- 1 tsp salt kosher
- ½ tsp pepper black
- 1 cup plain Greek yogurt

Instructions
- All ingredients should be placed in your Instant Pot, excluding the yogurt. Ensure that the pot's vent is completely shut by putting the lid on it. Manual high pressure within Instant Pot. After 15 minutes of cooking, let the steam escape normally for around 5 minutes before releasing it manually and opening the pot.
- Remove the chicken from the bones and pulverize it. Stir both yogurt & chicken back into the Instant Pot unless everything is well combined. Simmer your mixture after switching the Instant Pot's sauté function to "off" to prevent it from burning. 5 Mins of simmering time. Enjoy your meal while it's still piping hot!

Nutrition Information
Calories: 254 kcal, Carbohydrates: 7 g, Protein: 38 g, Fat: 7g

253. Apple and Endive Salad with Apple Cider Vinaigrette
Prep Time: 15 Mins, Cook Time: 15 Mins, Servings: 6
Ingredients
For Salad
- 4 heads stem cut & roughly chopped Belgian endive
- 2 cored & thinly sliced apples
- ¼ cup chopped walnuts
- ¼ cup crumbles fat-free feta cheese

For Vinaigrette
- 2 tsp vinegar apple cider
- ½ tsp honey
- 1 tsp fresh lemon juice
- 1 minced garlic clove
- 2 tsp oil olive

Instructions
For Salad
- Add chopped endive to a medium bowl. Add walnuts, apples, & feta cheese to taste.

For Vinaigrette
- Whisk the lemon juice, honey, & garlic into a mixing bowl. Whisk in some olive oil till the mixture is well emulsified.
- Pour the dressing on the salad & gently stir. Prepare the food and serve it to your guests.

Nutrition Information
Calories: 148 kcal, Carbohydrates: 17 g, Protein: 4 g, Fat: 9g

254. Easy Plant-Based Recipes: Dijon Roasted Garlic Asparagus
Prep Time: 5 Mins, Cook Time: 10 Mins, Servings: 4
Ingredients
- 2 minced garlic cloves
- 3 tbsp mustard Dijon
- 1 tsp oil olive
- 1 tsp juice lemon
- 1 lb ends trimmed asparagus fresh

Instructions
- Make sure the oven temperature is 400°F. Apply nonstick spray over a baking sheet.
- Garlic, Dijon mustard, olive oil, & lemon juice should be combined in a dish. Make sure everything is well-combined.
- Make sure to distribute the asparagus onto your baking sheet evenly, then sprinkle the Dijon mix over it and gently stir. Asparagus should be cooked for around 10 mins in the oven.

Nutrition Information
Calories: 42 kcal, Carbohydrates: 6 g, Protein: 3 g, Fat: 2g

255. Avocado Stuffed Deviled Eggs
Prep Time: 20 Mins, Cook Time 20 Mins, Servings: 2
Ingredients
- 6 eggs hard-boiled
- ½ pit removed, & mashed avocado peeled
- ½ tsp juice lemon
- 1 tbsp mustard Dijon
- 1 minced garlic clove
- ½ tsp salt kosher
- 1 tsp paprika smoked
- ¼ cup chopped green onion

Instructions
- Remove your yolks from hardboiled eggs with great care. In a medium basin, combine egg yolks & egg halves.
- Squeeze in some lemon juice & mix it all until you have a smooth paste. Fill each side of an egg with a piping or spoon bag.
- Indulge your taste buds by sprinkling chopped green onion over the top. It is best served chilled.

Nutrition Information
Calories: 94 kcal, Carbohydrates: 3 g, Protein: 6 g, Fat: 7g

256. Celebrity Salad
Prep Time: 10 Mins, Cook Time: 10 Mins, Servings: 1
Ingredients
- 2 red tomatoes beefsteak
- ½ cup tomatoes sliced yellow grape
- 1 sliced thinly green onion
- 6 fresh basil leaves
- 1 tbsp olive oil extra virgin
- 2 tbsp vinegar balsamic
- ½ tsp salt sea
- ¼ tsp freshly ground black pepper

Instructions
- Add green onions, yellow tomatoes, red tomatoes, & basil on a wide serving plate.
- Salt & pepper the salad before drizzling it with some oil & vinegar. Enjoy!

Nutrition Information
Calories: 107 kcal, Carbohydrates: 10 g, Protein: 2 g, Fat: 7g

257. Red, White, and Blueberry Lemonade
Prep Time: 10 Mins, Cook Time: 10 Mins, Servings: 8
Ingredients
- 12 oz white frozen, organic preferred grape juice
- 1 cup freshly squeezed lemon juice
- 1-gallon water & ice & cold water
- 2 cut across apples
- 1 washed pint blueberries
- 1 stem removed & halved pint strawberries

Instructions
- Combine your grape juice concentrate, water, & lemon juice. Using a cookie cutter, cut off apple shapes. You may cut the apple rounds into half before adding them if you like. The lemonade should be made using all fruit. Serve as a punch with a spoon.

Nutrition Information
Calories: 47 kcal, Carbohydrates: 11.1 g, Protein: 0.4 g, Fat: 0.2g

258. Cheesy Spinach Vegetable Bake
Prep Time: 15 Mins, Cook Time: 20 Mins, Servings: 3
Ingredients
- 2 tbsp oil olive
- 3 cups chopped small cauliflower

- 1 cup chopped mushrooms
- 4 cups spinach baby
- 15 oz drained & chopped artichoke hearts
- 4 minced garlic cloves
- ½ tsp salt kosher
- ¼ tsp black pepper ground
- 1 tsp thyme dry
- ½ cup milk skim
- ¾ cup of mozzarella cheese shredded fat-free
- ½ cup of cheddar cheese shredded fat-free
- ¼ cup of parmesan cheese grated fat-free
- 1 cup panko breadcrumbs whole-wheat

Instructions
- Make sure the oven temperature is 400°F. Set aside a nonstick pan by spraying it using a nonstick spray.
- Olive oil should be heated over medium-high heat in a big pan. Add both cauliflower & mushrooms after they're heated. Cook both cauliflower & mushrooms till tender and the liquid has evaporated, stirring often. It should take between six and eight Mins. Salt, pepper & thyme are added to the spinach & artichoke mixture. Cook for 3 Mins or till the spinach has wilted.
- Bring milk to a boil, then add the cheeses and stir until they're melted. Keep stirring until the chocolate is completely melted. Prepare the casserole dish by putting the contents in it.
- Combine the panko and parmesan in a small bowl. Add the toppings to the spinach mixture and toss well. Place in oven & bake for around 15-20 mins, or until browned on the edges and crisp on the top. Ten Mins after taking it from your oven, allow the dish to cool before serving.

Nutrition Information
Calories: 118 kcal, Carbohydrates: 10 g, Protein: 6 g, Fat: 7g

259. Homemade Avocado and Onion Chip Dip
Prep Time: 5 Mins, Cook Time: 5 Mins, Servings: 2
Ingredients
- 1 tbsp juice lemon
- 1 pit removed, & mashed avocado peeled
- 1 tsp powder onion
- 1 minced garlic clove
- 3 sliced thin large green onions
- ½ tsp salt kosher
- ¾ cup fat-free, plain Greek yogurt

Instructions
- In a small bowl, combine lemon juice & avocado. Make sure everything is well-combined.
- Add the rest of the ingredients and mix until they're all incorporated. Allow at least 15 Mins for the flavors to mingle before serving.
- Serve with pita bread, tortilla chips, or a salad of your choice.

Nutrition Information
Calories: 28 kcal, Carbohydrates: 2 g, Protein: 1 g, Fat: 2g

260. Skinny Turkey Meatloaf
Prep Time: 5 Mins, Cook Time: 45 Mins, Servings: 1
Ingredients
- 1-lb ground turkey lean
- 1 whipped egg lightly
- 1/3 cup uncooked rolled oats
- ¼ tsp salt
- 1/3 cup no sugar chunky salsa
- ½ cup diced onion
- ½ tsp pepper black
- 1/3 cup of ketchup

Instructions
- Set the oven to 375°F.
- In a large dish, combine all of the ingredients, excluding ketchup. Press the mixture into a 5-by-7-inch loaf pan. Bake uncovered for 35 Mins.
- Ketchup should be slathered from the top once the pan has been removed. Bake for another ten Mins.
- Give 5 Mins of relaxation time. Slice bread loaf or take it from the pan and set it over a serving dish.

Nutrition Information
Calories: 124 kcal, Carbohydrates: 7 g, Protein: 12 g, Fat: 6g

Chapter 5: Snacks and Desserts

1. Skinny Mini Desserts - Banana Pudding
Prep Time: 20 Mins, Cook Time: 15 Min, Servings: 6
Ingredients
- 10 whole almonds
- 2 tbsp cornstarch
- sea salt or kosher
- 3 tbsp palm sugar coconut
- 1 slightly beaten egg yolk
- ¾ cup milk 1-2%
- ½ tsp vanilla
- 2 thinly sliced bananas

Instructions
- Preheat your oven to 325°F. Allow the almonds to cool while you prepare the pudding. After the almonds have cooled, use the food blender or a knife to pulverize them.
- Add the cornstarch, salt, & sugar to a pot and bring it to a boil. Combine dry ingredients with egg yolk. Add the milk gradually & keep stirring until the mixture is well incorporated. Cook over medium-low heat, often stirring, for about an hr and a half. Continue to heat until it reaches a pudding-like texture.
- Remove from the heat and mix in the vanilla. – Bananas and pudding may be served together on dessert plates when they are still warm. Top the pudding with a layer of finely chopped almonds. If preferred, garnish with a dollop of whipped cream.

Nutrition Information
Calories: 102 kcal, Carbohydrates: 19 g, Protein: 2 g, Fat: 2 g

2. Paleo Angel Food Cake
Prep Time: 15 Mins, Cook Time: 40 Mins, Servings: 1
Ingredients
- 12 large egg whites
- 1 tsp tartar cream
- 3 tsp extract almond
- ½ tsp juice lemon
- 1 tsp zest lemon
- ¾ cup sugar coconut
- 1 cup flour arrowroot

Instructions
- The oven should be preheated to 350°F. Set aside a bunt pan that has been sprayed using a nonstick spray.
- At fast speed, beat egg whites & tartar cream together in a wide mixing bowl until frothy. Using an electric mixer, whip your egg whites unless they form firm peaks, add powdered almond essence, lemon juice, & lemon zest, then whip again.
- Add sugar to the mixer at medium-high speed and mix just until it's a homogeneous mixture. In another dish, combine the leftover flour and sugar and sift. Add flour gradually by lowering the speed of the mixer. Switch off the mixture, then gently pour your batter into the pan when the flour has been combined. It's important to avoid jolting or bumping the pan when cooking.
- Place the cake in the oven for 35-40 Mins to bake.
- Please wait at least an hour until it is totally cold before removing the pan from the cooling rack.
- Fresh berries and coconut cream may be added to the top of your cake for decoration.

Nutrition Information
Calories: 90 kcal, Carbohydrates: 19 g, Protein: 3 g, Fat: 1 g

3. Fried Apple Pies that Anyone Can Make in Mins
Prep Time:5 Mins, Cook Time: 5 Mins, Servings: 1

Ingredients
- ½ tsp oil olive
- 1 8" tortilla flour
- 1/3 cup of applesauce
- 1 tsp sugar cinnamon

Instructions
- Melt the butter in a large pan over medium heat, then add olive oil. Once your tortilla is heated, cook it for approximately 2 Mins, or till it's browned and crispy on the outside and soft within.
- When you flip your tortilla, distribute the applesauce over the browned side of the tortilla. A Min or two on the opposite side is all it takes.
- Remove your tortilla from the pan & fold it in half. Serve it hot with a generous dusting of cinnamon sugar!

Nutrition Information
Calories: 158 kcal, Carbohydrates: 29 g, Protein: 3 g, Fat: 4 g

4. Easiest Ever Oatmeal Cookie Recipe
Prep Time:5 Mins, Cook Time: 15 Mins, Servings: 3
Ingredients
- ½ cups rolled oats quick
- 2 bananas ripe
- ½ tsp extract vanilla
- 1 tsp cinnamon
- ¼ cup chocolate chips semi-sweet

Instructions
- The oven should be preheated at 350°F. Use parchment paper to cover a baking pan.
- Use a fork to mash ripe bananas into a smooth, creamy paste.
- Stir in cinnamon, oats, & vanilla extract and mix well.
- You may add raisins, chocolate chips, walnuts, or any other flavorings of your preference. Let your creative juices flow and use as many as you want!
- A sum of 8-10 1" balls should be formed from the batter. A few inches apart, put every scoop in the middle of the plate.
- Bake for around 12-15 mins unless the cookies are light brown and somewhat crunchy. Enjoy!

Nutrition Information
Calories: 129 kcal, Carbohydrates: 21 g, Protein: 3 g, Fat: 4 g

5. Clean-Eating Apple Pecan Crumble
Prep Time:10 Mins, Cook Time: 30 Mins, Servings: 5
Ingredients
- 8 peeled, cored apples
- 3 tsp cinnamon ground
- ½ tsp nutmeg ground
- 1/3 cup sugar coconut
- 1 juiced & zested lemon
- ½ cup chopped pecans
- ½ cup chopped almonds
- ½ cup shredded & unsweetened coconut
- ¼ cup oats quick
- 2 tbsp melted coconut oil
- ½ tsp salt kosher

Instructions
- The oven should be preheated at 350°F.
- A big bowl should include apples, nutmeg, cinnamon, & sugar. Set aside to cool.
- In a separate mixing bowl, combine the other ingredients & thoroughly combine them.
- Nonstick spray the baking sheet and bake according to the manufacturer's instructions. Crumble the crumble on top of the apple mix in a baking dish. The dish should

be baked for 25-30 minutes unless the top is golden and bubbling. Serve at room temperature.
Nutrition Information
Calories: 274 kcal, Carbohydrates: 38 g, Protein: 4 g, Fat: 15 g

6. Sweet and Salty Chocolate Covered Pretzels
Prep Time:1 hr, Cook Time: 50 Mins, Servings: 5
Ingredients
- 10 oz chips dark chocolate
- 1 lb whole-wheat unsalted mini pretzels
- 2 tsp flakes sea salt

Instructions
- Using wax paper, cover two baking sheets
- Melt chocolate within a double boiler set over a pan of simmering water.
- Put a heat-resistant glass dish or saucepan on top of a pot of boiling water. There should be no contact between the bowl or pot on top and simmering water.
- Constantly stir. Remove from the heat as soon as it has melted. You may also melt the chocolate by heating it in a microwave-safe dish for around 30 seconds at a time and stirring every time. Ensure there is no water inside the chocolate; otherwise, it will harden and become unusable.
- Remove the chocolate from the heat source and allow it to cool.
- Put a handful of pretzels at the moment into the melted chocolate. Using a fork, remove the pretzels one at the moment, brushing off any excess chocolate & laying the pretzel over a wax paper. Before placing each piece on wax paper, season it with some sea salt as it is still hot.
- Finish all your pretzels one at a time. For the chocolate to firm, put your baking sheet inside the refrigerator for almost an hr.

Nutrition Information
Calories: 271 kcal, Carbohydrates: 43 g, Protein: 6 g, Fat: 8 g

7. Melt-in-Your-Mouth Sweet Potato Fudge Brownies
Prep Time:15 Mins, Cook Time: 30 Mins, Servings: 6
Ingredients
- 12 pitted Medjool Dates
- 1 large, baked & peeled sweet potato
- ¼ cup butter almond
- ½ cup flour oat
- 1 tsp vanilla
- 2/3 cups chocolate chips vegan
- 3 tbsp powder cocoa

Instructions
- The oven should be preheated to 350°F.
- Using parchment paper, cover the baking dish with the material.
- Pulse dates in a blender until finely ground. Make a ball out of the minced dates by pulsing them in a food processor.
- Adding chocolate chips & pluses, add the rest of the ingredients until they are well-combined.
- Bake for 25-30 Mins in a baking dish.
- The food should be cooled before serving.

Nutrition Information
Calories: 296 kcal, Carbohydrates: 52 g, Protein: 5 g, Fat: 10 g

8. Best-Ever Strawberry Rhubarb Crisp
Prep Time:15 Mins, Cook Time: 30 Mins, Servings: 5
Ingredients
- 4 cups sliced strawberries
- 2 cups sliced rhubarb
- 2 tbsp cornstarch
- ¼ cup sugar granulated
- ½ tsp cinnamon ground
- ½ cup flour all-purpose
- 1 cup oats rolled
- ¼ cup diced whole butter
- ¼ cup sugar brown

Instructions
- The oven should be preheated at 375 degrees Fahrenheit, and one casserole dish should be sprayed using non-stick spray.
- Strawberry, rhubarb, & sugar are combined in a mixing dish. Spread it evenly within the casserole dish after mixing well.
- Second, add the rest of the ingredients to a separate bowl and mix well. Carefully combine all ingredients until they resemble sand, using a pastry blender with some bigger pea-sized pieces. Over strawberry mix, spread it out evenly.
- A light golden top should be achieved in around 20-30 Mins of baking time. Serve at room temperature or cooled, if desired.

Nutrition Information
Calories: 205 kcal, Carbohydrates: 35 g, Protein: 3 g, Fat: 7 g

9. Chocolate Chip Cookies
Prep Time:10 Mins, Cook Time: 10 Mins, Servings: 8
Ingredients
- 3 avocados
- ¼ cup of honey
- 1 large egg
- ½ cup powder cocoa
- ½ cup butter almond
- ½ tsp extract almond
- ½ cup of semi-sweet Vegan chocolate chips

Instructions
- The oven should be preheated to 350°F. Set aside one baking sheet that has been lined using parchment paper.
- Avocado & honey should be processed in the food processor. Blend until completely smooth.
- Except for the chocolate chips, combine the remaining ingredients. Pulse your food processor till the mixture is smooth and creamy. You may add your chocolate chips one at a time.
- Drop some batter over the cookie sheet. Bake for 10-12 mins. Set aside for approximately 10 mins before slicing and serving.

Nutrition Information
Calories: 254 kcal, Carbohydrates: 23 g, Protein: 6 g, Fat: 18 g

10. Gluten-Free Orange Creamsicle Cake
Prep Time:20 Mins, Cook Time: 30 Mins, Servings: 3
Ingredients
- ¾ cup of almond flour
- ¼ cup of all-purpose flour gluten-free
- ½ cup potato starch gluten-free
- ¼ cup corn starch gluten-free
- 1 tsp powder baking
- 1 & ¼ cup sugar coconut
- 1/3 cup coconut milk unsweetened
- 2 large eggs
- ½ cup orange juice fresh
- 1 tbsp zest orange
- 2 tsp extract vanilla
- ½ tsp extract almond

Instructions
- Set the oven temperature to 325°F. Apply non-stick spray to a parchment-lined cake pan before placing the cake in the pan for baking. Set away for a later time.
- Almond flour, baking powder/potato starch/cornstarch, all-purpose flour, and sugar are sifted into a large bowl.
- In a mixing bowl, beat together coconut milk, vanilla extract, eggs, orange zest, orange juice, & almond extract. Make sure to mix well.
- Add your coconut milk mixture to a flour mixture in small amounts. Indent your cake pan with the batter. To

test whether the center is done, stick a toothpick and bake for 30-40 Mins till the toothpick falls out clean. Once the cake has cooled, cover this with your favorite vanilla frosting.

Nutrition Information
Calories: 170 kcal, Carbohydrates: 28 g, Protein: 3 g, Fat: 6 g

11. Dairy-Free Pumpkin Pie with Coconut Milk
Prep Time:5 Mins, Cook Time: 1 hr, Servings: 6
Ingredients
- 1 9" gluten-free pie crust
- 2 large eggs
- 15 oz puree canned pumpkin
- 1 tsp extract vanilla
- ¾ cup sugar brown
- ½ tsp salt kosher
- 1-½ tsp spice pumpkin pie
- 1 cup milk coconut

Instructions
- The oven should be preheated at 425°F.
- A big bowl should be used to blend the eggs & pumpkin puree with the vanilla essence & brown sugar, salt & pumpkin spice.
- Add fresh coconut milk & continue swirling until well blended.
- Bake your pie for around 15 Mins after adding the contents to the crust.
- To bake your pie for a further 35-50 Mins, lower the oven temperature to 350°F. You may use a thermometer to measure the filling's temperature. Whenever it hits a core temp of 175°C, it is done.
- For almost two hrs, allow your pie to chill on a cooling rack before placing it within the refrigerator.
- Keep it in the fridge if you're not ready to serve it right away.

Nutrition Information
Calories: 249 kcal, Carbohydrates: 32 g, Protein: 3 g, Fat: 13 g

12. Chocolate Banana Bread with Hot Fudge Sauce
Prep Time:25 Mins, Cook Time: 55 Mins, Servings: 4
Ingredients
- 1 & ½ cups of white flour whole-wheat
- ½ cup unsweetened cocoa
- 1 & ½ tsp powder baking
- ½ tsp soda baking
- ½ tsp sea salt or kosher
- 4 overly ripe bananas
- 2 large eggs
- 1 & ¼ cups sugar coconut
- ½ cup melted unrefined coconut oil
- ½ cup low-fat buttermilk
- 1 tsp vanilla pure
- ½ cup dark chips chocolate
- ½ cup pieces walnut

Fudge Sauce
- ½ cup chips chocolate
- ¼ cup of lite canned coconut milk
- 1 tbsp sugar coconut
- ½ tsp vanilla pure

Instructions
- The oven should be preheated at 325°F. Roast walnuts for 12 mins in a preheated oven. Set aside for a Min or two while you prepare the batter. Adjust 350°F to the oven's temperature. A loaf pan should be greased and floured before use.
- Combine the baking soda, baking powder, flour, cocoa, & salt in a large mixing bowl. Set away for a later time.
- To get mashed bananas, you'll need about 3 bananas. Dice the remainder of the banana finely. Set away for a later time.
- Beat eggs in a medium bowl until they are slightly beaten. To mix the eggs & sugar, add them to a bowl & whisk until smooth. Whisk in the heated coconut oil, mashed, buttermilk, sliced bananas, & vanilla extract. Stir in some flour mix until it's barely wet, then remove from the heat. Make a paste by sprinkling in the almonds & chocolate. Bake for around 55 Mins, till a fork stabbed into the middle comes out clean. Try again when the fork strikes the chocolate chip.
- After 15 Mins of cooling, invert onto the wire rack to finish cooling. Allow it cool to room temperature before flipping & adding the hot fudge.

Fudge Sauce
- Cook over low heat, occasionally stirring, until chips have melted & smooth, about five Mins. Stir the chips as they're about to be melted.
- To serve, remove from the heat & let cool somewhat before dripping over the bread.

If desired, more hot fudge may be drizzled over individual pieces.
- Refrigerate any remaining hot fudge. Fudge would harden & may need to be reheated before the next serving.

Nutrition Information
Calories: 386 kcal, Carbohydrates: 58 g, Protein: 6 g, Fat: 17 g

13. Fruit and Oat Cookies
Prep Time:5 Mins, Cook Time: 15 Mins, Servings: 3
Ingredients
- 1 mashed banana
- 1 cup butter almond
- 1/3 cup unsweetened applesauce
- ¼ cup syrup maple
- 2 cups oats quick
- 1 tsp cinnamon ground
- ¼ tsp nutmeg ground
- ½ tsp salt
- 1 cup raisins cran
- ¼ cup lightly toasted sunflower seeds
- 2 tbsp flax seeds ground

Instructions
- Preheat your oven to 325°F.
- Apply parchment paper to the cookie sheets to ensure they are ready to bake.
- Stir together the first four ingredients in a big bowl until they are well incorporated.
- A different bowl should be used to mix the rest of the ingredients.
- In a large bowl, mix the wet and dry ingredients.
- On a parchment-lined cookie sheet, scoop out a heaping tbsp of dough.
- Bake at 325°F for around 15-20 Mins till golden brown & a solid dough has been formed. Make sure you don't get burned by checking often.
- After cooling, keep in a sealed jar at room temp.

Nutrition Information
Calories: 174 kcal, Carbohydrates: 20 g, Protein: 5 g, Fat: 10 g

14. 5-Ingredient Slow Cooker Spiced Poached Pears
Prep Time: 40 Mins, Cook Time: 4 hrs, Servings: 1
Ingredients
- 1 & ½ cups cranberry juice no-sugar
- ¼ cup of honey
- 2 tbsp lightly chopped dried cherries
- 1 tbsp cinnamon ground
- 4 peeled large pears

Instructions
- Cook for four hrs on low into your slow cooker with all the ingredients. Pears should be gently removed from the liquid with a slotted spoon. Before serving, let the food cool down a little.

Nutrition Information
Calories: 119 kcal, Carbohydrates: 32 g, Protein: 1 g, Fat: 1 g

15. Skinny Strawberry Sorbet
Prep Time: 25 Mins, Cook Time: 10 Mins, Servings: 1
Ingredients
- 2 & ½ cups quartered strawberries
- 1 & ½ cups no sugar orange juice
- 2 zested & juiced navel oranges
- 1/3 cup of honey

Instructions
- In a medium saucepan, heat honey & orange juice on moderate flame till honey is hot but not boiling and can be easily stirred approximately 3-5 Mins.
- Add orange juice & orange zest to the mixture. Set aside for a few Mins to cool off.
- Pulse the strawberries in the food processor for approximately 5 Mins to get a smooth paste.
- Combine orange honey, strawberries, and agave nectar in a large bowl.
- Churn as per the instructions on an ice cream maker's manual.
- Freeze till ready to serve inside a freezer-safe jar.

Nutrition Information
Calories: 128 kcal, Carbohydrates: 33 g, Protein: 1 g, Fat: 0 g

16. Slow Cooker Cranberry Nut Stuffed Baked Apples
Prep Time: 20 Mins, Cook Time: 5 hrs, Servings: 3
Ingredients
- 6 medium tart apples
- ½ cup dried cranberries
- ½ cup roughly chopped walnuts
- 2 tbsp sugar brown
- 1 tbsp zest orange
- 1 cup of water

Instructions
- Remove the apple's skin & core it.
- A tiny bowl is all that is needed to make this recipe. Once the ingredients have been blended, insert the mix into the apple's core, remove. In your slow cooker, add the filled apples & the water, then simmer on low for 8 hrs. On low, cook for around 4-5 hrs with the lid closed.

Nutrition Information
Calories: 206 kcal, Carbohydrates: 39 g, Protein: 2 g, Fat: 7 g

17. Bananas Brule with Vanilla Cream
Prep Time: 15 Mins, Cook Time: 5 Mins, Servings: 2
Ingredients
- 4 ripe peeled & halved lengthwise medium bananas
- ¼ cup sugar coconut
- ½ cup cream coconut
- 2 tsp syrup maple
- ½ tsp vanilla bean or vanilla paste

Instructions
Bananas Brule:
- On a baking sheet, place the banana halves.
- Sugar-coated coconut is sprinkled liberally over the surface.
- A cooking torch may be used to caramelize the sugar. Allow the sugar to solidify by letting it cool.
- The sugar may also be caramelized by broiling it in an oven at a high temperature.

Keep an eye on the sugar to ensure it does not burn too quickly. The sugar will harden if it is allowed to cool.
- Top with some vanilla cream.

Vanilla Cream:
- The hand mixer may blend the maple syrup, coconut cream, & vanilla paste.

Assemble:
- Pour vanilla cream over 2 banana halves & serve.

Nutrition Information
Calories: 249 kcal, Carbohydrates: 40 g, Protein: 2 g, Fat: 11 g

18. Gluten Free Apple Crumble
Prep Time: 10 Mins, Cook Time: 35 Mins, Servings: 5

Ingredients
- 6 large peeled, core apples
- ½ cup sugar coconut
- 2 Tbsp syrup maple
- 2 tsp cinnamon ground
- ½ tsp nutmeg ground
- 1 tsp cardamom ground
- ½ tsp salt
- 2 tsp juice lemon
- ½ cup finely chopped pecans
- ½ cup finely chopped walnuts
- 2 Tbsp coconut oil refined
- ¼ cup sugar coconut
- 1 tsp cinnamon ground

Instructions
- Set the oven temperature to 375 degrees.
- A large bowl should combine the diced apples with the following ingredients: coconut sugar, cardamom, salt, cinnamon, nutmeg, maple syrup, & lemon juice. Take your time and mix well.
- Put chopped nuts & oil in a separate dish and stir until the mix resembles coarse crumbs. Stir in coconut sugar & cinnamon.
- Top the apple mix with the crumble mix and bake.
- During this time, the apples should be soft, and the crumble should be golden brown. Temps should be reduced to 350°F. You may also use foil to keep the top from burning when it's cooking too rapidly.

Nutrition Information
Calories: 344 kcal, Carbohydrates: 51 g, Protein: 3 g, Fat: 17 g

19. Clean Lemon Yogurt Cake Recipe
Prep Time: 20 Mins, Cook Time: 15 Mins, Servings: 1
Ingredients
- 1 & ½ cups unbleached flour all-purpose
- 2 tsp powder baking
- ¼ tsp baking soda
- ½ tsp kosher salt
- 1 cup of Greek yogurt fat-free plain
- ¾ cup sugar coconut
- 2 tbsp honey
- 3 large eggs
- 2 tbsp zest lemon
- ½ tsp almond extract
- ½ cup melted coconut oil

Glaze
- ½ cup sugar powdered
- 1 tsp juice lemon

Instructions
- The oven should be preheated to 350°F. Set aside a loaf pan that has been sprayed using a nonstick spray.
- Add the flour, baking soda, baking powder, & salt to a medium mixing bowl.
- Add the other ingredients to a large bowl and whisk well until the mixture is completely smooth. Sift this flour mix into the yogurt mixture using a sifter. Carefully mix yogurt and sifted flour with a spoon or spatula until smooth. Overmixing will result in a thick, crumbly cake, so be careful not to do so.
- Pour the mixture into a prepared pan & bake in the preheated oven for about an hr. Using a toothpick, test your cake for doneness after 45 Mins. Once it's cooled, slice
and serves.

Glaze
- Mix both powdered sugar & lemon juice until they are completely dissolved.
- When your lemon cake is hot, drizzle the syrup over it once it's cooled, slice, and serve.

Nutrition Information
Calories: 347 kcal, Carbohydrates: 56 g, Protein: 10 g, Fat: 23 g

20. Classic Hot Chocolate Recipe
Prep Time: 5 Mins, Cook Time: 5 Mins, Servings: 1
Ingredients
- ¼ cup unsweetened cocoa powder
- ½ cup palm sugar coconut
- ¼ cup chips dark chocolate
- 4 & ½ cups unsweetened almond milk
- 1 tsp vanilla extract pure

Instructions
- Pour the milk into a medium saucepan and bring it to a boil on medium-low heat. Ensure that all ingredients are mixed before adding the chocolate chips & sweetener.
- In a medium-sized saucepan, mix all of the ingredients & bring to a boil on medium-low heat, stirring often. Stir in some vanilla and mix well.
- With a spoon and a sprinkling of cocoa powder or dark chocolate, serve in cups
- Adding a peppermint essence in place of the vanilla might give your recipe a festive flare.

Nutrition Information
Calories: 182 kcal, Carbohydrates: 32 g, Protein: 7 g, Fat: 4 g

21. Peanut Butter Swirl Fudge
Prep Time: 25 Mins, Cook Time: 35 Mins, Servings: 1
Ingredients
- 20 oz bags chocolate chips
- 1 cup canned coconut milk
- ¼ cup sugar coconut
- salt pinch
- 1 & ½ tsp vanilla
- 1 tbsp oil coconut
- 1 cup crunchy peanut butter

Instructions
- Chop up the chocolate chips & put them in a large pot with the coconut milk, sugar & salt, then mix it all.
- Stir the chocolate chunks until they are fully melted on low heat.
- Make a paste by combining vanilla extract and coconut oil. In a pan, spread the fudge.
- Add some peanut butter over the top and swirl it into chocolate with a toothpick. This swirling effect may be achieved without going overboard.
- Chill for at least two and a half hrs before serving.

Nutrition Information
Calories: 214 kcal, Carbohydrates: 21 g, Protein: 4 g, Fat: 14 g

22. Triple Chocolate Cheesecake
Prep Time: 20 Mins, Cook Time: 30 Mins, Servings: 1
Ingredients
Crust
- 2 oz chocolate semisweet
- 1 cup raw almonds
- 1 cup, not instant oats
- salt pinch
- 3 tbsp melted coconut oil

Filling
- 6 oz chocolate semisweet
- 16 oz reduced-fat cream cheese
- 1 cup low-fat ricotta cheese
- ¾ cup palm sugar coconut
- 4 large eggs
- ½ cup of Greek yogurt fat-free plain
- 1 tsp vanilla extract pure

Chocolate Sauce
- ½ cup chocolate semisweet
- ¼ cup lite canned coconut milk
- 1 tbsp palm sugar coconut
- ½ tsp vanilla extract pure

Berries
- 1 cup fresh raspberries

Instructions
- Preheat your oven to 350 deg F.

For Crust
- Melt chocolate in a double boiler or a saucepan over low heat.
- Food processor: Add the almonds, oats, & salt, then pulse until the mixture resembles fine crumbs. A small bowl of almond-oat mix melted chocolate & coconut oil should be stirred together well.
- A springform pan should be filled with crumbs, which should be pressed uniformly on the pan & up to the edges.

For Filling
- Because when chocolate has melted, remove it from the heat source and let it cool. While you're making the filling, keep the pan covered and the stove on. When pouring the chocolate into a filling, make sure it is still warm.
- In a large mixing bowl, combine the cream cheese & ricotta cheeses.
- Beat the cheeses until they are light and frothy, using your electric mixer, & lumps aren't any longer visible.
- Continue beating for approximately 30 seconds after adding the coconut palm sugar. Once you've added each egg, just beat them in until they're well combined. Beat in the yogurt and vanilla extract until well mixed.
- Mix in the heated chocolate till it is well incorporated.
- In the Oven and Freeze
- Bake for 45-60 Mins on the middle oven rack, or unless the top is set, there is still some jiggle in the center.
- About 3-4 hrs after placing the cheesecake on the cooling rack, let it cool completely.
- Cracks in the cheesecake won't be noticeable because of their topping cover.
- Refrigerate this pan, covered with plastic wrap, for at least one night or till it has reached room temperature. Set aside for approximately five Mins after you've removed it from the refrigerator. Using a heated knife, carefully loosen the springform pan's sides before serving the cheesecake. The springform pan should be used to serve the cheesecake.
- The Purpose of - Berries & Chocolate Sauce adorns the dessert.
- In a medium saucepan on low heat, combine all the ingredients for the chocolate sauce and stir until the chocolate has dissolved. Pour over some cheesecake when it has cooled down a little.
- Add berries over the top. Enjoy!

Nutrition Information
Calories: 383 kcal, Carbohydrates: 32 g, Protein: 10 g, Fat: 26 g

23. Nutella Banana Espresso Shake
Prep Time: 5 Mins, Cook Time: 5 Mins, Servings: 1
Ingredients
- ¼ cup espresso brewed
- 1 frozen banana
- 2 tbsp Nutella Homemade
- 1 cup unsweetened almond milk
- ½ cup of ice

Instructions
- Blend all the ingredients in a blender unless they're smooth.

Nutrition Information
Calories: 345 kcal, Carbohydrates: 52 g, Protein: 5 g, Fat: 14 g

24. Slow Cooker Bananas Foster
Prep Time: 5 Mins, Cook Time: 1 hr 30 Mins, Servings: 3
Ingredients
- 1 tbsp melted coconut oil
- 3 tbsp honey
- ½ lemon juiced
- ¼ tsp cinnamon
- 5 medium firmness bananas

- ½ tsp rum extract 100%

Instructions
- Add the first 4 ingredients to your slow cooker & mix them. Incorporate the honey mixture by gently tossing in the banana slices on low for 2 hrs, cover & cook. Toss the bananas with the rum essence and mix until smooth.

Nutrition Information
Calories: 110 kcal, Carbohydrates: 28 g, Protein: 2 g, Fat: 2 g

25. Gingerbread Scones
Prep Time: 20 Mins, Cook Time: 10 Mins, Servings: 1
Ingredients
- 2-3 cups white flour whole-wheat
- 1 tbsp powder baking
- 1/3 cup sugar coconut
- 1 tsp ginger ground
- ½ tsp ground cinnamon
- ¼ tsp cloves ground
- 5 tbsp butter cold unsalted
- 1/3 cup molasses black strap
- ½ cup plain, divided nonfat Greek yogurt
- ½ cup milk skim
- 1 tsp syrup maple
- ¼ tsp extract vanilla

Instructions
- The oven should be preheated at 425°F. Set aside one baking sheet that has been lined using parchment paper.
- Combine the ginger, cinnamon, flour, coconut sugar, baking powder, & cloves in a medium bowl and whisk until well combined.
- Using a box grater, shred the butter into the flour till it resembles lumpy sand.
- Gently incorporate the molasses, yogurt, and milk into the dough. To form a dough, carefully knead the ingredients with your hands over floured surface till it clumps together.
- The dough is formed into a 1-inch-thick circular. It's time to split the circle into eight equal halves.
- Bake your slices for around 15 Mins or till they're just beginning to the brown exterior. Scone should be clean when a toothpick is poked in the middle.
- Add maple syrup & vanilla essence to a small dish with the leftover Greek yogurt for drizzle while you're waiting for it to cool. The pastry bag may be used to transfer this mixture.
- Ten Mins before serving, let the scones cool completely before spreading the glaze over them.

Nutrition Information
Calories: 259 kcal, Carbohydrates: 43 g, Protein: 7 g, Fat: 8 g

26. Grandma's Applesauce Spice Cake
Prep Time:15 Mins, Cook Time: 45 Mins, Servings: 1
Ingredients
- 2 & ½ cups of flour
- 1 & 2/3 cups of palm sugar coconut
- 1 ½ tsp soda baking
- 1 tsp sea salt kosher
- ¼ tsp powder baking
- 1 tsp cinnamon
- ½ tsp cloves
- ½ tsp allspice
- 1 peeled & chopped sweet apple
- 1 cup chopped walnuts
- 1 cup optional raisins
- 2 large eggs
- ½ cup of water
- 1 & ½ cups natural applesauce
- 1 tsp vanilla extract pure
- ¼ cup of oil

Instructions
- The oven should be preheated to 350°F. A cake pan should be greased and floured.
- The dry ingredients should be whisked together well in a mixing dish. If adding walnuts or raisins, add them to the dry ingredients & stir them in. Set aside all of the dry ingredients for later use. Whisk together the rest of the ingredients in a medium-sized bowl.
- Using a big spoon, combine the dry and wet ingredients. A toothpick put into the middle of the cake should come out clear after baking for 45-50 Mins.
- The cake is at its finest when cooled, and it tastes even greater the following day.

Nutrition Information
Calories: 307 kcal, Carbohydrates: 40 g, Protein: 3 g, Fat: 12 g

27. Apple Cardamom Bread Pudding
Prep Time:15 Mins, Cook Time: 45 Mins, Servings: 4
Ingredients
- 6 slices bread whole-wheat
- 1 & ½ cups reduced-fat coconut milk
- 3 lightly beaten eggs large
- 1 cup unsweetened applesauce
- ¾ tsp cardamom ground
- 1 tsp cinnamon ground
- ¼ tsp nutmeg ground
- 1 cup cored, & chopped apples peeled

Instructions
- The oven should be preheated at 325 degrees Fahrenheit. Use nonstick spray to grease the baking dish and put it aside.
- Bread cubes, cut to 1", should be placed within the baking dish.
- Gather all the ingredients for the batter in a medium bowl and whisk until smooth. Combine all the ingredients using a whisk until they're completely incorporated.
- Make sure you stir with apples before spreading over bread pieces. To ensure that all of the cubes have absorbed the liquid, push them down into the mixture.
- To get the pudding to firm and not wobble, bake it for 45 Mins. Ensure the pudding falls out clean by inserting a knife in the center.
- At least 20 Mins before slicing, place the pan over a cooling rack.
- Whether served cold or hot, this pudding will be a hit.

Nutrition Information
Calories: 256 kcal, Carbohydrates: 23 g, Protein: 8 g, Fat: 16 g

28. Chocolate Hazelnut and Berry Puff Pastry Tart
Prep Time:10 Mins, Cook Time: 20 Mins, Servings: 5
Ingredients
- 1 whole-wheat sheet puff pastry
- ¼ cup spread chocolate hazelnut
- ¼ cup of raspberries fresh
- ¼ cup of blueberries fresh
- ½ cup sliced strawberries fresh

Instructions
- Preheat your oven to 425°F. On a baking sheet, place your puff pastry. Create a crust by rolling up a little part of each edge. Prick the pastry many times with a fork. Bake for 20-30 Mins, or till puffed & golden brown on the outside. Let it cool down.
- Spread some chocolate hazelnut butter on top of the chilled puff pastry. If your chocolate hazelnut spreading is too firm to spread on the crust, warm it up a little. The berries may be sprinkled on top. Place in the refrigerator until ready to use.

Nutrition Information
Calories: 151 kcal, Carbohydrates: 14 g, Protein: 2 g, Fat: 10 g

29. Panko Crusted Brownie Pie Recipe
Prep Time: 20 Mins, Cook Time: 25 Mins, Servings: 3
Ingredients
Panko Crust
- 2 cups of panko
- ¼ cup of coconut sugar
- ¼ cup butter pure

Brownie Mixture
- ½ cup butter pure
- 2 tsp extract vanilla
- 2 lightly whipped eggs large
- ½ cup of flour
- ¼ tsp salt sea
- 1 cup sugar coconut
- ½ cup powder cocoa
- 1 cup chips chocolate

Instructions
- The oven should be preheated to 350°F.
- Pour the ingredients of panko crust into a pie pan. Spread some crumbs along the edges of the pie pan. Using your fingers, press crumbs into the bottom & edges of the pan. Set away for a later time.
- Melt the butter in a medium saucepan over medium heat. On low heat, add the coconut sugar & stir to combine. Remove from the heat and mix in the vanilla & eggs.
- Combine cocoa powder, flour, & salt, then mix well. Whisk the dry ingredients to the butter mix using a wooden spoon until they are completely incorporated. Toss in the chocolate chunks until evenly distributed.
- Pour your brownie mixture into the pie dish. Bake at 375 degrees Fahrenheit for about 25 Mins. Before slicing, allow the meat to cool over the wire rack.

Nutrition Information
Calories: 370 kcal, Carbohydrates: 47 g, Protein: 4 g, Fat: 20 g

30. Vegan Chocolate Strawberry Coconut Butter Cups
Prep Time: 30 Mins, Cook Time: 30 Mins, Servings: 5
Ingredients
- ¼ cup unsweetened shredded coconut
- ¼ cup fresh, sliced strawberries
- 1 tbsp syrup maple
- 1 tbsp flour coconut
- 2 cups chocolate chips semisweet
- 2 tbsp oil coconut

Instructions
- Blend your shredded coconut at high in the food processor, pausing to scrape the sides if required. Blend in the strawberries & maple syrup till they are completely dissolved. Add some coconut flour & pulse until it's all incorporated. Set away for a later time.
- Using paper liners, fill each muffin cup to the brim. Melt both chocolate chips & coconut oil in a saucepan over low heat until smooth, stirring often. Using melted chocolate, spread it evenly on the paper cups. Ten Mins within the fridge should do the trick.
- Frozen candy should be removed from the fridge. Use your fingers to distribute approximately half a spoonful of a strawberry filling over chocolate, if necessary.

Cover your strawberry filling with roughly melted chocolate.
- After approximately 10-15 Mins within the fridge, remove your chocolate cups and let them harden. To eat, just take it out of the freezer. In a sealed jar, keep it in the refrigerator.

Nutrition Information
Calories: 178 kcal, Carbohydrates: 21 g, Protein: 1 g, Fat: 12 g

31. Chocolate Chip Pumpkin Bread
Prep Time: 15 Mins, Cook Time: 1 hr, Servings: 6
Ingredients
- ½ cup of applesauce
- ½ cup maple syrup pure
- 2 lightly beaten eggs
- 1 cup puree pumpkin
- 2 tsp spice pumpkin pie
- 1 tsp extract vanilla
- ¼ tsp salt
- 1 tsp soda baking
- 1 & ¾ cups white flour whole-wheat
- ¾ cup of mini chocolate chips semi-sweet

Instructions
- The oven should be preheated at 325°F before starting. To begin, prepare a loaf pan by coating it with cooking spray.
- Mix maple syrup, applesauce, & eggs in a medium bowl with the whisk unless well combined.
- Make sure that all ingredients are mixed before adding the pumpkin puree.
- A flexible spatula may be used to include the flour & mix it into the batter unless it is barely wet. Don't go overboard with the mixing!
- Fold in micro chocolate chips before putting the batter in the loaf pan.
- Using a toothpick, check the middle of the bread after an hr.
- Wait until the bread has cooled fully before slicing.

Nutrition Information
Calories: 174 kcal, Carbohydrates: 33 g, Protein: 4 g, Fat: 5 g

32. 3-Ingredient Coconut Mango Ice Cream
Prep Time: 5 Mins, Cook Time: 5 Mins, Servings: 5
Ingredients
Ice Cream
- 1 cup canned coconut milk
- 3 cups diced: organic mango frozen
- 1 tbsp honey

Raspberry Sauce
- 1/3 cup of raspberries
- 3 tbsp honey
- 1 tsp chia

Instructions
Ice Cream
- Blend frozen mango, coconut milk, & honey in a high-speed blender or big food processor till it resembles ice cream. Scoop the ice cream in the serving bowls.

Raspberry Sauce
- In a tiny food processor, combine the ingredients for the raspberry sauce.

Nutrition Information
Calories: 189 kcal, Carbohydrates: 30 g, Protein: 2 g, Fat: 9 g

33. Glazed Coconut Lime Cupcakes
Prep Time: 10 Mins, Cook Time: 20 Mins, Servings: 1
Ingredients
For Cupcakes
- 2 large eggs
- ½ cup milk coconut
- 3 tbsp honey
- 1 tsp extract vanilla
- ¼ cup juice lime
- 1 tbsp zest lime
- 2 & ¼ cups flour almond
- 1 tsp soda baking
- ½ cup unsweetened shredded coconut

For Glaze
- ½ cup coconut sugar powdered
- 1 tbsp juice lime
- 1 tsp zest lime

Instructions
For Cupcakes
- The oven should be preheated to 350°F. Cover a muffin tray using cupcake liners before baking.
- Pour the eggs, lime juice, honey, vanilla, coconut milk, & lime zest into a large bowl. As soon as the mixture

becomes frothy & thick, increase the speed to high. There is no better way to get more air into a mixture than to mix it!
- Before serving, stir in the baking soda, almond flour, & coconut with hand. Bake for 15-20 Mins, till a toothpick poked into the middle of a cupcake, falls out clear. Scoop your batter into prepared muffin cups. Allow the cake to cool somewhat before adding the glaze.

For Glaze
- Mix all the ingredients well. Put a dollop on cooled cupcakes.

Nutrition Information
Calories: 321 kcal, Carbohydrates: 23 g, Protein: 9 g, Fat: 23 g

34. Coconut Blackberry Cake
Prep Time: 10 Mins, Cook Time: 15 Mins, Servings: 1 slice
Ingredients
For Cake
- 4 large, separated eggs
- 1 tsp tartar cream
- ¼ cup oil coconut
- ¼ cup of coconut sugar
- ¼ cup of sifted coconut flour
- 1 tsp extract almond
- ½ tsp soda baking
- 1 cup finely shredded coconut unsweetened
- ½ cup fresh blackberries

For Blackberry Frosting
- 2 cups plain Greek yogurt
- 3 tbsp honey
- ½ tsp extract almond
- 1 tsp zest lemon
- ¾ cup fresh blackberries

Instructions
For Cake
- The oven should be preheated at 350°F. Set aside 2 9" cake pans that have been sprayed using a nonstick spray.
- Set aside your egg whites & tartar cream in a large dish and whisk fast until firm peaks form.
- Coconut oil, sugar, & egg yolks are mixed in a separate dish. Add the almond extract, flour, & baking soda, then stir until the mixture is completely smooth & free of lumps. Add your shredded coconut to the mixture and mix till your flakes are evenly dispersed throughout.
- The leftover coconut sugar & blackberries should be mixed in a mixing bowl, and the berries should be somewhat chunky after a gentle mash. Toss the blackberries and whisked egg whites into the batter with a spatula. Place the cake pan within the oven and bake the batter according to the manufacturer's instructions.
- Make sure the toothpick poked comes out clear after baking for 20-25 Mins. Before icing, allow the cake to cool fully in the fridge.

For Blackberry Frosting
- Mix the yogurt, almond extract, honey, & lemon zest in a medium-sized mixing bowl until well incorporated and smooth. Mash your blackberries into a small dish and toss them into the yogurt until barely mixed. Chill for at least one hr before serving.
- Carefully arrange the cake with the yogurt icing. The second cake should be frosted. The sides should not be frosted. Wait until you are willing to refrigerate & serve.

Nutrition Information
Calories: 202 kcal, Carbohydrates: 15 g, Protein: 7 g, Fat: 14 g

35. Flourless Peach Cobbler
Prep Time: 20 Mins, Cook Time: 35 Mins, Servings: 3
Ingredients
For Peach Filling
- 5 peeled, pitted & sliced peaches fresh
- 3 tbsp sugar coconut
- 1 tsp flour coconut
- ¼ tsp cinnamon
- 1/8 tsp nutmeg ground

For Cobbler Topping
- ½ cup flour almond
- 1 cup ground fine oats
- 1 ½ tsp powder baking
- ¼ cup milk almond
- 1 tsp extract almond
- 2 tbsp honey

Instructions
For Peach Filling
- Use nonstick spray to coat your baking pan.
- Toss sliced peaches with the other ingredients in a large bowl until well-coated. Pour the batter into the baking dish and put it aside for later.

For Cobbler Topping
- The oven should be preheated to 350°F.
- Gently mix all of the ingredients until they are completely incorporated. Add a tbsp at a time to the peaches. Bake in the oven for 35-45 minutes unless the tops are a light brown. Serve hot.

Nutrition Information
Calories: 256 kcal, Carbohydrates: 44 g, Protein: 8 g, Fat: 7 g

36. Lemon Blueberry Cake Recipe
Prep Time: 15 Mins, Cook Time: 30 Mins, Servings: 3
Ingredients
- 1 & ½ cups flour whole-wheat
- ¾ cup sugar coconut
- 3 tsp powder baking
- ½ tsp salt kosher
- 1/3 cup juice lemon
- 1 tsp zest lemon
- 1 & ¼ cups milk coconut
- 1 tsp extract vanilla
- 1 cup fresh blueberries

Instructions
- The oven should be preheated at 350 degrees. Set aside a 9-inch cake pan that has been sprayed with nonstick spray.
- Mix flour, baking powder, sugar, & salt in a medium-sized bowl. Add milk & vanilla to a second big dish with the lemon zest and juice. Add dry ingredients to your wet ingredients in a slow, steady stream, mixing till the dry ingredients are well combined.
- Toss your blueberries with flour in a mixing bowl. Pour batter over berries and gently fold until berries are evenly distributed. Bake for 30-40 Mins, till a toothpick stabled in the center, comes out clean. Before removing the cake from the pan, let it cool for around 20 Mins.

Nutrition Information
Calories: 207 kcal, Carbohydrates: 40 g, Protein: 4 g, Fat: 5 g

37. Chocolate Peanut Butter Oatmeal Bars
Prep Time: 10 Mins, Cook Time: 30 Mins, Servings: 7
Ingredients
- 2 cups oats rolled
- 2 cups milk coconut
- ½ cup very ripe, mashed banana
- ¼ cup no sugar peanut butter
- ¼ cup of almond meal or almond flour
- ¼ cup unsweetened cocoa powder
- 2 tbsp flaxseed ground
- ¼ cup chopped peanuts
- 1 tbsp vanilla protein powder clean

Instructions
- The oven should be preheated to 350°F. Apply nonstick spray to a casserole dish.
- Using a large mixing basin, stir together all ingredients until evenly distributed. Spread the mix into a casserole dish in a uniform layer, gently pushing it into the dish.

- To firm up, bake for an additional 20-30 Mins. Preparation is required before serving.

Nutrition Information
Calories: 217 kcal, Carbohydrates: 17 g, Protein: 7 g, Fat: 15 g

38. Dairy-Free Crepes
Prep Time: 10 Mins, Cook Time: 40 Mins, Servings: 5
Ingredients
- 1 cup of flour
- 1 & ¼ cups water
- 2 large eggs
- 1 tsp sugar
- salt pinch
- 1 & ¼ tbsp divided olive oil

Instructions
- Gather all ingredients into a large bowl and whisk them together until they form a homogeneous paste. 30 Mins in the fridge is enough time.
- After almost 30 Mins, use the leftover olive oil to coat a saucepan. You may use a paper towel to remove any excess.
- Pour a bit of crepe batter onto a crepe pan and tilt it back and forth to spread the batter evenly. It's time to flip and cook the other side once it's done.

Nutrition Information
Calories: 190 kcal, Carbohydrates: 25 g, Protein: 6 g, Fat: 7 g

39. Banana Pudding Ice Cream
Prep Time: 5 Mins, Cook Time: 5 Mins, Servings: 1
Ingredients
- 2 ripe bananas large
- ½ cup unsweetened almond milk
- ¼ cup chopped walnuts

Instructions
- Blend almond milk with bananas in a blender until smooth. If extra milk is required, add it in small increments.
- Serve and savor the walnuts!

Nutrition Information
Calories: 249 kcal, Carbohydrates: 37 g, Protein: 6 g, Fat: 11 g

40. No-Bake Chocolate-Covered Cookie Dough Bars (Vegan)
Prep Time: 15 Mins, Cook Time: 15 Mins, Servings: 1
Ingredients
For Cookie Dough
- 1 cup flour almond
- 2 tbsp flour coconut
- ¼ tsp salt kosher
- 1/3 cup maple syrup pure
- 1/3 cup butter almond
- ½ tsp extract vanilla
- ¾ cup chocolate chips semisweet

For Chocolate Topping
- 1 cup chocolate chips semisweet Vegan
- 2 tbsp butter almond

Instructions
For Cookie Dough
- Set aside a pan sprayed using a nonstick spray. Mix all of the ingredients, excluding chocolate chips. Your chocolate chips may now be added and combined. Make a uniform layer of the dough by pressing it onto the pan & refrigerating it until it is solid. Slice & serve with a drizzle of chocolate on top.

For Chocolate Topping
- Blend unless smooth by melting the chocolate chunks with almond butter. Cover and distribute evenly on top of the bars that have been set. When ready to cut and serve, let harden.

Nutrition Information
Calories: 316 kcal, Carbohydrates: 32 g, Protein: 6 g, Fat: 21 g

41. Oil-Free Chocolate Muffins | Plant-Based Desserts
Prep Time: 10 Mins, Cook Time: 30 Mins, Servings: 1
Ingredients
- 15 oz beans black
- ¾ cup powder cacao
- ½ cup palm sugar coconut
- 1 small banana
- ¼ cup applesauce unsweetened
- 6 tbsp water
- 2 tbsp flax seed ground
- 1 ½ tsp powder baking
- 1 tsp powder arrowroot
- 1 tsp extract vanilla
- ¼ tsp salt

Instructions
- Preheat your oven to 350 degrees Fahrenheit.
- After pureeing all ingredients, the consistency might be thinner than frosting but not sloppy.
- Fill each of the 12 muffin cups approximately halfway with the batter, then divide the batter evenly among the liners in the pan.
- Bake for 30 Mins at 350°F — the muffin tops must be dry, slightly risen, & slightly cracked after this period.
- Cool for around 30 Mins before serving.

Nutrition Information
Calories: 105 kcal, Carbohydrates: 23 g, Protein: 5 g, Fat: 1 g

42. Epic Clean Eating Blueberry Cheesecake Bars
Prep Time: 10 Mins, Cook Time: 30 Mins, Servings: 7
Ingredients
- 2 cups fat-free crumbs graham cracker
- 3 tbsp melted coconut oil
- 8 oz cream cheese softened fat-free
- ¾ cup plain Greek yogurt
- ¼ cup sugar coconut
- 1 tbsp honey
- 2 tbsp flour
- 2 large egg whites
- 1 tsp juice lemon
- 1 tsp zest lemon
- 1 tsp extract vanilla
- ½ cup fresh blueberries

Instructions
- The oven should be preheated to 350°F. Set aside an 8-by-8-inch baking sheet sprayed with nonstick spray.
- Combine your cracker crumbs & coconut oil in a medium mixing bowl. Stir gently until your graham crackers resemble wet sand in appearance. Make a crust by squeezing the mixture into the pan and pressing down.
- Combine your cream cheese, yogurt, & sugar in a mixing bowl. Stir vigorously until the mixture is light and fluffy. In a large mixing bowl, whisk together the honey & flour until smooth. Simply blend at low speed. Pour your batter over the prepared crust & gently mix in the blueberries.
- Remove the bars from the oven & cover them with foil after 15 Mins of baking. Continue baking for another 15 Mins until the cheesecake is done. Cheesecake may still be wobbly in the pan, but that's just OK! At least three hrs before serving, allow the mixture to cool at room temp before refrigerating. Take a slice and savor it!

Nutrition Information
Calories: 210 kcal, Carbohydrates: 27 g, Protein: 8 g, Fat: 8 g

43. No-Bake Oatmeal Chocolate Cookies
Prep Time: 10 Mins, Cook Time: 5 Mins, Servings: 3
Ingredients
- ¼ cup milk almond
- 2 tbsp unsalted butter
- 1 cup sugar coconut
- 2 tbsp powder cocoa

- 3 tbsp almond butter or peanut butter
- ¼ tsp vanilla
- 1 & ¼ cups oats quick

Instructions
- Pour the coconut sugar, butter, almond milk, & cocoa into a medium saucepan & stir to combine. Bring the mixture to a boil, then reduce the heat to a simmer. Remove from the heat after 2 Mins of boiling, stirring constantly.
- Combine the chocolate chips, peanut butter, vanilla extract, and oats in a large bowl. Stir until all of the ingredients are covered.
- Take a spoonful and place it on a piece of parchment paper to cool. Enjoy!

Nutrition Information
Calories: 103 kcal, Carbohydrates: 17 g, Protein: 2 g, Fat: 4 g

44. Honey Cupcakes with Vanilla Frosting
Prep Time:15 Mins, Cook Time: 30 Mins, Servings: 4

Ingredients
Cupcakes
- 1 & ½ cups white flour whole-wheat
- 1 tsp powder baking
- ½ tsp soda baking
- 3 tbsp honey
- ½ tsp vanilla
- 1 large egg
- ½ cup plain Greek yogurt
- 2 & ½ tbsp olive oil
- ½ cup milk almond
- 1 tbsp juice orange
- ½ cup finely diced apples

Frosting
- ½ cup of cream cheese softened reduced fat
- 2 tbsp raw honey
- 1 tsp vanilla pure

Instructions
Cupcakes
- Preheat the oven to 375°F.
- Set aside the dry ingredients.
- Make a honey-vanilla-egg-yogurt-oil concoction. Whisk in some almond milk & orange juice.
- Combine the wet & dry ingredients in a large bowl. Bake for 30 mins until a toothpick comes out clear in eight muffin pans. Before putting on the icing, let the cupcakes cool fully.

Frosting
- Pour in all of the ingredients & mix well.

Nutrition Information
Calories: 237 kcal, Carbohydrates: 30 g, Protein: 6 g, Fat: 12 g

45. 3-Ingredient Vanilla Frosting
Prep Time: 5 Mins, Cook Time: 5 Mins, Servings: 4

Ingredients
- 8 oz cream cheese reduced-fat package
- ¼ cup of honey
- 1 tsp vanilla pure

Instructions
- In a small bowl, combine all of the ingredients & beat for 3-5 Mins.
- Wait until you're ready to use it on your favorite cupcakes before refrigerating.

Nutrition Information
Calories: 53 kcal, Carbohydrates: 4 g, Protein: 1 g, Fat: 4 g

46. No-Bake Oatmeal Raisin Energy Bites
Prep Time: 10 Mins, Cook Time: 30 Mins, Servings: 2

Ingredients
- 1 cup oats dry
- ¼ cup butter peanut
- 2 tbsp honey
- ¼ cup chocolate chips semisweet mini
- ¼ cup of raisins
- ¼ cup of chopped peanuts
- ½ tsp cinnamon ground
- 1 tbsp powder vanilla protein

Instructions
- Mix all ingredients well until they form a smooth & sticky paste.
- Roll the dough into 1" balls on a baking sheet and lay them on it. About 30 Mins before serving, place within the fridge to harden. Refrigerate in a sealed jar & keep covered and chilled.

Nutrition Information
Calories: 152 kcal, Carbohydrates: 20 g, Protein: 6 g, Fat: 6 g

47. Ooey Gooey Skillet Chocolate Chip Cookie
Prep Time:15 Mins, Cook Time: 20 Mins, Servings: 5

Ingredients
- ¼ cup solid coconut oil
- 1/3 cup sugar coconut
- 1 room temperature egg
- 1 tsp extract vanilla
- ¼ tsp soda baking
- ¼ tsp salt kosher
- 1 cup flour almond
- 1 cup chocolate chips semisweet

Instructions
- The oven should be preheated at 350°F. Take the skillet out of the oven and coat it with nonstick spray. This meal is best served in a frying pan!
- In a small bowl, beat the oil & sugar together till frothy using an electric mixer set to low speed. The egg & vanilla should be mixed in at a moderate speed until they are barely incorporated and smooth. Add the baking soda, salt, & flour to the mixture and mix well. Some chocolate chips may now be added and combined.
- Using a rolling pin, flatten the dough in the pan. A cookie should be baked for around 15-20 Minutes, or unless the edges turn brown. Serve hot from the oven after removing from the heat source.

Nutrition Information
Calories: 378 kcal, Carbohydrates: 33 g, Protein: 6 g, Fat: 28 g

48. Yam Balls with Coconut & Pecans Recipe
Prep Time:1 hr, Cook Time: 15 Mins, Servings: 2

Ingredients
- 4 sweet potatoes or yams
- ¼ cup syrup maple
- 2 tsp zest orange
- 1 tsp ginger ground
- 1 tsp cinnamon
- 1 large egg white
- ¼ tsp salt kosher
- 2 & ½ cups of shredded coconut unsweetened
- ¾ cup chopped pecans

Instructions
- Preheat your oven to around 400°F. Set aside the baking sheet that has been lined using parchment paper.
- The yams should be washed and dried. Prick the surface using a fork & pat dry. Bake for 40-50 Mins, or till tender, over a baking sheet. Yams should be cold enough to handle after being taken out of the oven.
- Preheat the oven to 350°F and prepare a separate baking sheet using parchment paper on top of it.
- Cut your yams in half & scoop out the flesh into a medium bowl after they have cooled enough to handle. Mash to a pulp. In a medium saucepan, combine maple syrup with orange zest, cinnamon, ginger root, & egg white.
- Coconut, pecans & maple syrup in a 2nd bowl are combined. Gently roll your yam balls within coconut pecan mix before forming them into two-inch balls. As

required, gently push the coconut into the ball. Please make sure they're at least an inch apart on the second layer of baking paper.
- Bake for around 15 mins. Cool down before serving.

Nutrition Information
Calories: 222 kcal, Carbohydrates: 19 g, Protein: 3 g, Fat: 16 g

49. Greek Yogurt Orange Lb Cake
Prep Time:15 Mins, Cook Time: 30 Mins, Servings: 5
Ingredients
- 2 & ¾ cups of white flour whole-wheat
- 1 tsp powder baking
- 1 tsp soda baking
- ¼ cup zest orange
- 1 tbsp melted coconut oil
- 2 large eggs
- 1/3 cup juice orange
- 1 tsp extract almond
- ¼ cup sugar coconut
- 1 cup of Greek yogurt
- 2/3 cup milk almond
- ¼ cup of honey

Instructions
- The oven should be preheated at 350°F. Set aside 2 loaf pans that have been sprayed using a nonstick spray.
- Mix the baking powder, flour, & baking soda in a mixing bowl. Set away for a later time.
- Combine the yogurt, juice, zest, extract, sugar, oil, eggs, & milk in a medium bowl. Stir in some flour mixture slowly and carefully till its mixture is smooth after you've mixed everything well. Pour the batter into loaf pans, filling each approximately three-quarters of the way.
- If a toothpick falls out clean after 30-45 Mins of baking, the cake is made. Immediately after removing the cake from the oven, pour the honey on the top. Make sure to chill before cutting & serving your meal.

Nutrition Information
Calories: 92 kcal, Carbohydrates: 13 g, Protein: 3 g, Fat: 3 g

50. Avocado Fudge Brownie Recipe
Prep Time: 10 Mins, Cook Time: 45 Mins, Servings: 4
Ingredients
- 3 overly ripe bananas large
- 1 medium, ripe avocado
- 1 cup natural, smooth, or crunchy peanut butter
- 1 tsp vanilla
- ½ cup powder raw cacao
- ¼ cup of almond meal or almond flour
- ½ cup of millet
- ¼ cup of cacao nibs
- ½ cup of walnut pieces

Instructions
- The oven should be preheated to 350°F.
- Use a fork to mash the bananas & avocado thoroughly. It's recommended that you use banana & avocado mixture per serving. Add a mashed banana if you're short. Add both peanut butter & vanilla, then mix with a big spoon or beater until well incorporated.
- If used, combine cacao, cacao nibs, millet, almond meal, & walnuts in a large mixing bowl. Beat or whisk the wet ingredients into the dry ingredients till they are completely incorporated.
- Beat or whisk the wet ingredients until they are completely incorporated. The baking pan should be lightly greased or coated with parchment paper. Pour the brownie mix into the pan. Make sure the top of the cake isn't wet within the center after cooking for 30-35 Minutes. Completely cool down.
- Cut the cake after it has been refrigerated for at least three hrs. Store in the refrigerator for up to five days.

Nutrition Information
Calories: 240 kcal, Carbohydrates: 23 g, Protein: 8 g, Fat: 16 g

51. No-Bake Almond Energy Balls
Prep Time:35 Mins, Cook Time: 35 Mins, Servings: 4
Ingredients
- 1 cup dry oats old-fashioned
- ¼ cup natural almond butter
- ¼ cup honey agave syrup
- ¼ cup finely diced almonds
- ½ tsp vanilla extract pure
- ¼ cup chocolate chips mini

Instructions
- In a mixing bowl, add all of the ingredients & stir well.
- Around 30 Mins before serving, chill the mixture within the refrigerator to make it easier to handle. Place the balls on a baking sheet & bake for 15 Mins.
- Serve right away or keep in a sealed jar in the refrigerator.

Nutrition Information
Calories: 139 kcal, Carbohydrates: 18 g, Protein: 4 g, Fat: 6 g

52. Chocolate Chip Coconut Cookies
Prep Time: 30 Mins, Cook Time: 25 Mins, Servings: 4
Ingredients
- 2 tsp extract vanilla
- 1 large egg
- 1/3 cup sugar coconut
- ½ cup melted & cooled coconut oil
- 1 cup of white flour whole-wheat
- ½ tsp soda baking
- ½ cup chocolate chips semisweet
- ½ cup unsweetened shredded coconut

Instructions
- The oven should be preheated to 350°F.
- Mix the egg, sugar, vanilla, & oil in a bowl. Stir the mixture until it is completely smooth. Mix in the flour & baking soda until mixed before adding the rest of the ingredients. Stir in some coconut & chocolate chips after adding the ingredients to a large bowl.
- Drop your batter by the tbsp onto a baking sheet that has not been coated with cooking spray. Bake for around 7-8 Mins unless the cookies brown on the edges. Before serving, allow the food to come to room temperature.

Nutrition Information
Calories: 198 kcal, Carbohydrates: 18 g, Protein: 2 g, Fat: 14 g

53. Easy Coconut Cake
Prep Time:15 Mins, Cook Time: 20 Mins, Servings: 3
Ingredients
- 4 separated eggs large
- 1 tsp tartar cream
- ¼ cup oil coconut
- 3 tbsp sugar coconut
- ¼ cup sifted coconut flour
- 1 tsp extract almond
- ½ tsp soda baking
- 1 cup finely shredded coconut unsweetened
- 8 oz cream cheese reduced-fat package
- ¼ cup raw honey
- 1 tsp vanilla pure

Instructions
- Preheat your oven to 350 deg Fahrenheit. Set aside a 9" cake pan sprayed using a nonstick spray.
- Set aside your egg whites & tartar cream in a mixing dish and whisk at max speed till firm peaks form.
- Combine the sugar, coconut oil, & egg yolks in a separate mixing dish. Add the almond extract, flour, & baking soda, then stir until the mixture is completely smooth and free of lumps. Make sure to incorporate the grated coconut into the batter well. When all the

- ingredients have been combined, mix in the beaten egg whites & pour the batter into the cake pan.
- Take it out of the oven and let it cool for a few Mins before slicing. The food should be cooled before serving.
- You may top the cake with fruit or Vanilla Frosting.
- Vanilla Frosting uses only three ingredients.
- A mixer should be used to whip everything together until it's smooth and creamy. Stir in shredded coconut into the frosting if desired; otherwise, serve with a coconut sprinkle over the top, if desired.

Nutrition Information

Calories: 199 kcal, Carbohydrates: 10 g, Protein: 4 g, Fat: 17 g

54. Slow Cooker Roasted Sugared Pecans

Prep Time:5 Mins, Cook Time: 3 hrs, Servings: 5

Ingredients

- 1 lb pecan halves
- ½ cup of butter melted
- ¼ cup sugar coconut
- 2 tbsp honey
- 1 & ½ tsp cinnamon ground
- ¼ tsp clove ground
- ¼ tsp nutmeg ground

Instructions

- Prepare your slow cooker and add the pecans to it. Toss the pecans in the melted butter and mix until evenly coated. The other ingredients should be mixed with the pecans to ensure they are well-coated.
- Stirring periodically, cook for around 3 hrs on high with the cover OFF.
- To cool, spread the baked goods out in a uniform layer on the baking sheet lined using parchment paper. Completely cool down. Refrigeration is not necessary; instead, stored in a jar within the pantry.

Nutrition Information

Calories: 267 kcal, Carbohydrates: 9 g, Protein: 3 g, Fat: 26 g

55. Gingerbread "Breakfast" Cookie

Prep Time:15 Mins, Cook Time: 10 Mins, Servings: 2

Ingredients

- ½ cup butter almond
- 2 tbsp maple syrup pure
- 2 tbsp molasses
- 1 mashed banana
- 1 egg
- ½ cup oats
- ¼ cup cooked quinoa
- ¼ cup flour whole-wheat
- 1 tsp powder baking
- 1 tsp ginger ground
- ½ tsp nutmeg ground
- ½ tsp cinnamon ground
- ¼ tsp clove ground

Instructions

- The oven should be preheated to 350°F. Place parchment paper on a baking pan and put it aside.
- Mix the syrup, molasses, almond butter, & banana in a bowl. Mix thoroughly. Add the egg and mix.
- Add the dry ingredients to wet ones and mix well. Take care not to overdo it.
- Drop by the tbsp onto the baking dish that has been lined with parchment paper. Each drop should have around 2 tsp of dough in it. Bake for 10-15 Mins at a temperature of 350 degrees Fahrenheit. Remove from the pan and let cool for around 5 Minutes before slicing into serving pieces. Enjoy!

Nutrition Information

Calories: 272 kcal, Carbohydrates: 32 g, Protein: 9 g, Fat: 14 g

56. Dark Chocolate Cranberry Oatmeal Cookies

Prep Time:15 Mins, Cook Time: 10 Mins, Servings: 4

Ingredients

- 1 & ½ cups of oats
- ¾ cup flour whole-wheat
- ¼ cup powder cocoa
- 1 tsp powder baking
- ½ tsp soda baking
- ¼ tsp salt kosher
- 2 tbsp melted coconut oil
- 2 large egg whites
- 1 tsp extract vanilla
- ½ cup honey pure
- ½ cup frozen or fresh, chopped cranberries
- ½ cup chocolate chips semisweet

Instructions

- Preheat your oven to around 350°F. Set aside any baking pan that has been lined using parchment paper.
- The following ingredients should be combined in a mixing bowl: baking soda, oats; flour; powder; & cocoa powder. Set away for later. Mix the vanilla, egg whites, & honey with the coconut oil in a separate large basin. Then whisk it all together again. When all of the flour has been mixed, remove the pan from the heat. Toss the cranberries & chocolate chips into the batter with a fork.
- Drop your cookie dough by a spoonful over the baking sheet, being sure to spread it out evenly. The cookie may be flattened by softly pressing it. 7-8 Mins should be enough time to cook your cookie's middle to a soft set. Remove all cookies from the baking pan after cooling for approximately five Mins.

Nutrition Information

Calories: 201 kcal, Carbohydrates: 33 g, Protein: 5 g, Fat: 7 g

57. Gingerbread Cake

Prep Time:15 Mins, Cook Time: 35 Mins, Servings: 6

Ingredients

- 2 cups flour whole-wheat
- 1 tsp powder baking
- ½ tsp soda baking
- 2 tsp ginger ground
- ½ tsp ground cinnamon
- ¼ tsp ground nutmeg
- ¼ tsp cloves ground
- 1 tbsp melted coconut oil
- 2 large egg whites
- 1 tsp extract vanilla
- ¾ cup plain Greek yogurt
- ¼ cup of molasses
- ¼ cup maple syrup pure
- ¼ cup milk coconut

Instructions

- Preheat your oven to 350 degrees Fahrenheit. Set aside the loaf pan and coat it using a nonstick spray.
- Flour, cinnamon, baking powder, baking soda, & allspice should be mixed in a large mixing dish. Set away for later.
- The remainder Ingredients should be combined in a mixing bowl. Combine the flour, baking powder, sugar, and salt in a small bowl. Pour the batter into the loaf pan and bake as directed. Take it out of the oven when a toothpick pierced comes out clear and bake for another 15 Mins. Before slicing & serving, let the cake cool fully. Drizzle some honey or any favorite glaze over the top if desired.

Nutrition Information

Calories: 220 kcal, Carbohydrates: 39 g, Protein: 7 g, Fat: 6 g

58. Chocolate Peanut Butter Popcorn

Prep Time: 15 Mins, Cook Time: 15 Mins, Servings: 0.5 cup

Ingredients

For Popcorn

- 8 cups unseasoned popped popcorn
- 1 tbsp oil coconut

- ¼ cup butter peanut
- 2 tbsp syrup maple

For Chocolate Drizzle
- 1 & ½ tbsp coconut oil
- ¼ cup chocolate chips semisweet

Instructions
For Popcorn
- On a baking sheet, evenly distribute the popped popcorn.
- Melt the peanut butter, coconut oil, & maple syrup in a medium saucepan over low heat. Pour the warm peanut butter on the popped kernels & gently toss till every kernel is covered. Let it cool down.

For Chocolate Drizzle
- Melt your chocolate chips & coconut oil together unless smooth in a medium saucepan. Let your popcorn cool before drizzling some peanut butter over it.

Nutrition Information
Calories: 164 kcal, Carbohydrates: 13 g, Protein: 3 g, Fat: 12 g

59. Chocolate Pumpkin Filled Cookies
Prep Time: 30 Mins, Cook Time: 25 Mins, Servings: 3
Ingredients
For Cookies
- ½ cup powder cocoa
- 1/3 cup syrup maple
- 1 cup flour whole-wheat
- 1/3 cup oil coconut
- 1 tsp soda baking
- 1 tsp extract almond
- ½ tsp salt

For Filling
- ¼ cup fat-free cream cheese
- ¼ cup puree pumpkin
- ½ cup sugar powdered
- ½ tsp cinnamon ground
- ¼ tsp clove ground

Instructions
For Cookies
- The oven should be preheated to 350°F. Place parchment paper on a baking pan and put it aside.
- Mix all ingredients in a medium bowl until they are well incorporated. Using a floured surface, roll out a thick rectangle. Cut the cookies into circles using a 2" round cookie cutter & set them on a baking sheet that has been prepped. Take it out of the oven after 10 Mins. Remove from the oven & let cool to room temperature before serving.

For Pumpkin Filling
- In a blender, combine the ingredients & whisk at moderate speed until they form a smooth, creamy texture. One spoonful of filling should be spooned onto the cookies. To create a cookie sandwich, place the 2nd cookie over the top. One hr or so, or unless the filling starts to harden in the fridge. To preserve freshness, keep it in the fridge in an airtight container.

Nutrition Information
Calories: 146 kcal, Carbohydrates: 21 g, Protein: 3 g, Fat: 7 g

60. Carrot Spice Oatmeal Cookies
Prep Time: 20 Mins, Cook Time: 10 Mins, Servings: 5
Ingredients
- 1 cup of oats
- ¾ cup flour whole-wheat
- 1 ½ tsp powder baking
- 1 tsp cinnamon ground
- ½ tsp cloves ground
- 2 tbsp melted coconut oil
- ½ cup milk coconut
- ½ cup of applesauce
- 1 tsp extract almond
- 1 cup coconut sugar granulated
- 1 cup finely grated carrots

Instructions
- Preheat your oven to 325°F. Place parchment paper on a baking pan and put it aside.
- Mix the cinnamon, baking powder, oats, flour, and cloves in a medium bowl. Set

aside for later use after thoroughly combining all of the ingredients. Combine the almond extract, coconut oil, applesauce, coconut milk, & coconut sugar in a mixing basin. Add flour mix gradually after the mixture has been well mixed. Continue mixing until the mixture is well incorporated. Add the carrot to the mix.
- Add batter on a baking sheet and spread it out evenly. Bake for 8-10 Mins, unless the bread is golden brown and crispy outside. Cool down before serving.

Nutrition Information
Calories: 181 kcal, Carbohydrates: 31 g, Protein: 4 g, Fat: 5 g

61. Strawberry Cream Cheese Stuffed Crepes
Prep Time: 10 Mins, Cook Time: 25 Mins, Servings: 5
Ingredients
For Crepes
- 2 large eggs
- 1 cup flour whole-wheat
- ¾ cup milk almond
- ½ cup of water
- 3 tbsp melted coconut oil

For Filling
- ½ cup fat-free cream cheese
- ¼ cup fresh, sliced strawberries
- 1 tbsp honey

Instructions
For Crepes
- Blend all the ingredients in a blender till they are completely smooth. The batter must be light.
- Set medium heat to a pan. A ladle should be used to spread a narrow circle of batter over the heated pan. Cook the first side for approximately a Min before quickly and gently flip it over. Remove from pan after a further Min of cooking. Repeat the same with the rest of the batter.

For Filling
- Mix all of the ingredients until they are completely incorporated.
- Make a line through the center of the cooked crepe with 1-2 tsp of the filling. Serve the burrito-shaped crepe to your guests. Enjoy!

Nutrition Information
Calories: 283 kcal, Carbohydrates: 30 g, Protein: 13 g, Fat: 14 g

62. Paleo Chocolate Cupcakes
Prep Time: 15 Mins, Cook Time: 25 Mins, Servings: 3
Ingredients
For Cupcakes
- ¾ cup powder cocoa
- 1 cup flour almond
- 1 & ½ tsp powder baking
- ¼ tsp salt kosher
- ½ cup melted coconut oil
- ½ cup unsweetened applesauce
- ½ cup sugar coconut
- 4 large egg whites
- ¼ cup brewed coffee strong
- 1 tbsp extract vanilla

For Frosting
- 2 cups chocolate chips semisweet
- ½ cup canned coconut milk
- ½ tsp extract almond

Instructions
For Cupcakes

- The oven should be preheated at 350 degrees Fahrenheit & a muffin tin should be lined or sprayed using a nonstick spray. Set away for later.
- Add the baking powder, almond flour, cocoa powder, & salt to a medium-sized mixing bowl & mix well until the mixture is smooth. Set away for later.
- Pour the eggs, coffee, coconut oil, coconut sugar, applesauce, & vanilla into a large mixing bowl. Add the dry ingredients one at a time to a wet & mix until they are completely incorporated. Add more almond flour if the batter is just too runny. Dollop the batter into muffin tins approximately three-quarters full.
- Bake for around 25-30 Mins is a good amount of time to bake. Using a toothpick, poke it into the center, and it ought to come out largely clean. It's expected that the toothpick will be covered with some crumbs.
- Remove to the wire rack for cooling entirely after cooling for 5 mins. About two hrs or until cooled is the ideal time for this.

For Frosting
- Melt chocolate chips in a medium saucepan with the rest of the ingredients over low heat, stirring constantly. Wait until the frosting has cooled before using it on cupcakes. Frosted cupcakes may be stored in the fridge in a sealed jar.

Nutrition Information
Calories: 333 kcal, Carbohydrates: 30 g, Protein: 4 g, Fat: 24 g

63. 4-Ingredient Peanut Butter Fudge Bars
Prep Time: 10 Mins, Cook Time: 25 Mins, Servings: 2
Ingredients
- 2 cups creamy, natural peanut butter
- ½ cup syrup agave
- 1 & ½ cups oats ground
- 1 cup chocolate chips semisweet

Instructions
- Set aside a baking pan by lining it using parchment paper.
- Add peanut butter & agave syrup to a medium saucepan and bring to a boil. Oats may be added at this point after the dish has been taken from the stove, and a little water may be added if the mix is too dry. Chill for around 30 Mins after pressing into the prepared baking tray.
- Before serving, melt chocolate chips & drizzle over peanut butter bars. Freeze for the next 20 mins, or unless chocolate has hardened, to ensure a uniform coating.
- Cut the meat into slices and put them on a plate.

Nutrition Information
Calories: 323 kcal, Carbohydrates: 29 g, Protein: 10 g, Fat: 21 g

64. Fudgy Chocolate Zucchini Cookies
Prep Time: 15 Mins, Cook Time: 12 Mins, Servings: 3
Ingredients
- 1 & ¼ cups of white flour whole-wheat
- ½ tsp soda baking
- ¼ tsp salt kosher
- ½ cup unsweetened cocoa powder
- ½ cup coconut sugar
- ¼ cup oil coconut
- 1/3 cup unsweetened applesauce
- 1 tsp extract vanilla
- 1 egg large
- ½ cup finely grated zucchini
- ½ cup chocolate chips semisweet

Instructions
- The oven should be preheated to around 350°F. Place parchment paper on a baking pan and put it aside.
- Mix the cocoa powder, flour, baking soda, salt, & sugar in a bowl. Set the mixture aside to cool down.
- Add it to a mixing bowl once you've grated and drained the zucchini.
- The vanilla, egg, oil, applesauce, & zucchini are all mixed in a big mixing dish. After blending well, slowly add some flour mixture until it's completely incorporated.
- Drop onto the baking sheet. Flatten the mounds gently using a fork & bake them for around 12 Mins or till they're hard enough to handle. Allow to cool & take pleasure in!

Nutrition Information
Calories: 169 kcal, Carbohydrates: 25 g, Protein: 3 g, Fat: 8 g

65. No-Bake Carrot Cake Bites
Prep Time: 15 Mins, Cook Time: 15 Mins, Servings: 2
Ingredients
Cake
- 15 pitted dates
- 1 & ½ cups of pecan halves
- 1/3 cup of raisins
- 1 & ½ cups grated carrots
- 1 cup finely shredded coconut
- 1 tsp cinnamon
- 1/8 tsp salt sea
- 1 tsp vanilla

Frosting
- 4 oz fat-free cream cheese
- 2 tbsp butter
- 2 cups sugar powdered
- 1 tsp vanilla

Instructions
Cake
- Add the dates to a blender & pulse till they make a dough-like ball. Take out the dates & set them in a medium-sized mixing bowl. The food processor may be used to grind pecans into a fine crumb. Take care not to grind or fluoride the nuts.
- Use paper towels to remove as much moisture as possible from shredded carrots.
- In a large mixing basin, combine all the cake ingredients, including the dates, using the wooden spoon, then mix well. In a square pan, firmly press the cake dough. At the same time, create the icing, cover, and chill the cake.

Frosting
- Beat the ingredients together in a bowl once they're smooth and well-combined.
- Cut the cake into 20 little squares & frost them.

Nutrition Information
Calories: 180 kcal, Carbohydrates: 30 g, Protein: 1 g, Fat: 7 g

66. Sweet Potato Cookies
Prep Time: 10 Mins, Cook Time: 15 Mins, Servings: 3
Ingredients
- 1 cup mashed sweet potato
- ½ cup butter almond
- 2 tbsp honey
- ¼ cup of flour
- 1 tsp baking soda
- ½ tsp extract vanilla

Instructions
- The oven should be preheated to 350°F.
- All ingredients should be mixed in a medium-sized bowl before being stored in an airtight container. Dollop onto a nonstick baking sheet.
- Allow baking for 15 Mins, or till golden brown. Allow 10 Mins for cooling before enjoying!

Nutrition Information
Calories: 188 kcal, Carbohydrates: 18 g, Protein: 5 g, Fat: 12 g

67. Cardamom Pecan Pie
Prep Time: 20 Mins, Cook Time: 35 Mins, Servings: 2

Ingredients
For the Crust
- 2 cups flour almond
- 2 tbsp flour coconut
- ½ tsp salt kosher
- 3 tbsp cold coconut oil
- 1 large egg
- 1 tbsp water

For the Filling
- ¾ cup maple syrup pure
- 1/3 cup of molasses
- ½ cup sugar coconut
- 2 tbsp butter unsalted
- 3 large eggs
- 1 tsp vanilla extract
- ½ tsp salt kosher
- 1 tsp cardamom ground
- ½ tsp cinnamon
- ¼ tsp nutmeg ground
- 1 & ½ cups chopped pecans

Instructions
For Crust
- Gather all of the ingredients into a food processor & mix until smooth. Using a food processor, slowly add water till the mixture forms a ball, then pulse again.
- Roll out the dough on a floured surface & press it into a pie plate. Chill till ready for use, store in the fridge.

For Filling
- The oven should be preheated at 375 degrees Fahrenheit.
- Maple syrup & molasses should be mixed in a saucepan. Simmer for approximately 10 Mins after bringing to a boil. Take caution while handling the syrup since it will be quite hot. Remove from the heat & stir in butter and sugar until smooth and melted. Remove from the heat and serve immediately.
- Egg, cardamom, cinnamon, vanilla, salt, & nutmeg are whisked together in a small basin. Add this in your syrup mixture as fast as possible while whisking vigorously. Pour the pecan mixture into the cold crust and bake.
- Allow baking for around 20-30 Mins. Set on the sides, the pie would be somewhat jiggly in the center, but the crust will remain solid. Before slicing, allow the cake to cool fully, ideally overnight. Prepare the food by chopping it up and serving it immediately.

Nutrition Information
Calories: 385 kcal, Carbohydrates: 35 g, Protein: 7 g, Fat: 26 g

68. Cran-Apple Coffee Cake
Prep Time: 20 Mins, Cook Time: 30 Mins, Servings: 5
Ingredients
For Cake
- 1 & ¾ cups flour whole-wheat
- 1 & ½ tsp powder baking
- ½ tsp soda baking
- 2 tsp cinnamon ground
- 1 tbsp melted coconut oil
- 1 large egg
- 1 tsp extract almond
- ½ cup fat-free sour cream
- 1/3 cup maple syrup pure
- 1/3 cup milk almond
- 1/3 cup applesauce unsweetened
- ¾ cup peeled & chopped small green apple
- ¾ cup frozen or fresh, roughly chopped cranberries

For Topping
- ½ cup flour whole-wheat
- ¼ cup of oats
- 1 tsp cinnamon ground
- 2 tbsp cold coconut oil
- 2 tbsp maple syrup pure

Instructions
For Cake
- Pre-heat the oven to 350 degrees Fahrenheit. Set aside a cake pan that has been sprayed using non-stick spray.
- Mix the flour, baking soda, baking powder, & cinnamon in a medium basin. Mix everything with a spoon.
- Sift together the dry ingredients in a third big basin and add the wet ingredients in a fourth large bowl. Add flour mix to applesauce mix in a slow, steady stream, stirring until incorporated after each addition. It's okay if there are a few lumps! Incorporate the apples & cranberries into the mixture. To make a uniform layer, pour your batter into the pan & level it out.

For Topping
- All ingredients should be put into a small bowl and mixed. Press some oil within dry ingredients with your hands to form crumbs the size of peas. Sprinkle the batter with a light dusting of powdered sugar.
- When a toothpick pierced comes out clear, the dish is done baking. Ensure that the food is at room temperature before serving.

Nutrition Information
Calories: 263 kcal, Carbohydrates: 46 g, Protein: 7 g, Fat: 7 g

69. Baked Apple Pecan Crisp
Prep Time: 15 Mins, Cook Time: 30 Mins, Servings: 3
Ingredients
For Filling
- 5 peeled & diced small apples
- 2 tbsp sugar coconut
- 2 tsp cinnamon
- 1 tbsp flour almond

For Topping
- 1 cup oats old-fashioned
- ½ cup flour almond
- ½ cup roughly chopped pecans
- ¾ tsp cinnamon
- ¼ tsp salt
- ¼ cup melted coconut oil
- ¼ cup of honey

Instructions
- Preheat the oven to around 350 degrees Fahrenheit. Set aside a casserole dish that has been sprayed using a nonstick spray.
- Toss the apples with the cinnamon, sugar, & flour in a big bowl to coat them. Then pour it into the prepared dish. Make a space for it
- When it comes to toppings
- Combine all the ingredients in a big bowl. Rub all ingredients together with your hands until they resemble fine crumbs. Pour over the fruit.
- Apples should be cooked for 30-40 Mins before the coating is golden brown. Before serving, let the food cool down a little. Enjoy!

Nutrition Information
Calories: 279 kcal, Carbohydrates: 33 g, Protein: 4 g, Fat: 16 g

70. Pecan Pie Cheesecake Bars
Prep Time: 10 Mins, Cook Time: 30 Mins, Servings: 2
Ingredients
- 2 cups crumbs fat-free graham cracker
- 3 tbsp melted coconut oil
- 8 oz cream cheese softened fat-free
- ¾ cup plain Greek yogurt
- ¼ cup sugar coconut
- ¼ cup of flour
- 3 large egg whites
- 1 tsp juice lemon
- 2 tsp extract vanilla
- 3 tbsp honey
- 2/3 cups diced pecans

- 1 tsp of cinnamon

Instructions
- The oven should be preheated to 350°F. Set aside a baking pan sprayed using a nonstick spray.
- Combine a cracker crumb & coconut oil in a mixing bowl. The graham cracker should resemble wet sand when they've been sifted together. Make a crust by squeezing the mixture into the pan and pressing down.
- Combine the yogurt, cream cheese, & sugar in a mixing bowl. High-speed whipping produces the fluffiest results. Add flour, lemon juice, egg whites, and vanilla extract to the mixture. Pour batter over prepared crust & blend at lower speed unless it's just combined.
- A bowl is needed to combine the leftover flour, egg white with the rest of the ingredients: the leftover honey, vanilla, pecans & cinnamon. Press the mixture gently onto the cheesecake.
- Bake your bars for between 25 and 30 Mins, depending on the size of the pan. Cheesecake may still be wobbly in the pan, but that's perfectly fine! Put it in the fridge for three hrs, loosely covered, after cooling to room temp.

Nutrition Information
Calories: 279 kcal, Carbohydrates: 32 g, Protein: 9 g, Fat: 13 g

71. Pumpkin Spice Cake
Prep Time:15 Mins, Cook Time: 45 Mins, Servings: 5
Ingredients
- 2 & ½ cups flour whole-wheat
- 1 ¾ cups sugar coconut
- 1 ½ tsp soda baking
- 1 tsp salt kosher
- ¼ tsp powder baking
- 1 tsp cinnamon ground
- ½ tsp cloves ground
- ½ tsp nutmeg ground
- 2 large eggs
- 1 & ½ cups puree pumpkin
- 1 tsp vanilla extract pure
- ¼ cup melted coconut oil

Instructions
- The oven should be preheated to 350°F. A cake pan should be greased and floured.
- Incorporate the dry ingredients into a mixing bowl & whisk thoroughly to combine. Whisk together the other ingredients inside another medium bowl.
- With a big spoon, mix the wet & dry ingredients. A toothpick put into the middle of the cake should come out clear after baking for 45-50 Mins.

Nutrition Information
Calories: 369 kcal, Carbohydrates: 71 g, Protein: 7 g, Fat: 9 g

72. Best Ever Pumpkin Cheesecake
Prep Time:25 Mins, Cook Time: 1 hr, Servings: 2
Ingredients
Crust
- 1 cup almonds whole
- 1 cup oats rolled
- 1/8 tsp salt sea
- ½ tsp pie spice pumpkin
- ¼ cup sugar coconut
- ¼ cup melted butter

Cheesecake Filling
- 16 oz reduced-fat, packages cream cheese
- 1 cup reduced-fat ricotta cheese
- 3 whole large eggs
- 1 large egg yolk
- ¼ cup of sour cream
- 15 oz puree pumpkin
- 1 & ½ cups sugar coconut
- 1 tsp spice pumpkin pie
- 2 tbsp flour all-purpose
- 1 tsp vanilla

Instructions
- The oven should be preheated to 350°F.
- Add oats, salt, almonds, & pumpkin spice to a high-powered blender & pulse until finely ground. Pulse until the mixture resembles crumbs.
- Using your hands, press the mixture into an 8-inch square baking dish. Crumbles should cover the springform pan & the edges by about half an inch. To speed things up, wrap your fingers in Saran Wrap & press your crumbs together. Set away for later.
- Filling: In a mixing bowl, combine cream cheese & ricotta cheese. Using the electric mixer, blend until smooth. Add the eggs, sugar, cornstarch, pumpkin puree, sour cream, vanilla, and pumpkin spice to continue creaming with the electric mixer.
- Prepared crust: Pour & distribute filling evenly over it. Place one baking sheet in the middle of the oven & springform pan over top of it for baking. One hr in the oven is enough time for the sides of the cheesecake to firm, but the middle still jiggles slightly. It will bake even after it is taken out of the oven. Remove from heat and let it reach room temperature before storing.
- Cover and chill for 4-6 hrs to cool. Remove the cheesecake from the pan by running a knife around the edges. Slicing your cheesecake will be easier if you peel the pan's edges first.

Nutrition Information
Calories: 383 kcal, Carbohydrates: 35 g, Protein: 9 g, Fat: 25 g

73. Pumpkin Cornbread with Whipped Honey Butter
Prep Time:15 Mins, Cook Time: 25 Mins, Servings: 3
Ingredients
For Cornbread
- 1 cup flour whole-wheat
- 1 cup of cornmeal
- 1 tsp baking powder
- ½ tsp baking soda
- ½ tsp salt
- ½ tsp ground cinnamon
- ½ tsp ground ginger
- ¼ tsp ground nutmeg
- ¼ tsp ground cloves
- ½ cup coconut sugar
- ¼ cup olive oil
- 1 cup puree pumpkin
- ½ cup plain Greek yogurt
- 2 large eggs

For Butter
- ½ cup of butter
- 2 tbsp honey
- ½ tsp cinnamon ground
- ¼ tsp salt kosher

Instructions
For Cornbread
- The oven should be preheated at 375°F. Set aside a casserole dish that has been sprayed with nonstick cooking spray.
- A small mixing bowl should combine the cornmeal, flour, and cornstarch with baking powder & baking soda, salt, or spices such as nutmeg & cloves. The mixture should be stored in an airtight container.
- Make sure to whisk all of these ingredients together well into a large bowl before adding them to the batter. Using your rubber spatula, stir the mixture into flour till it's evenly distributed.
- Pour the batter into the baking dish and level it out evenly. Bake for approximately 25-30 Mins, till a toothpick incorporated into the middle, comes out clear. Cut into cubes after cooling somewhat on the wire rack. Serve with honey butter beaten to a spreadable consistency.

For Honey Butter
- Beat the butter with a hand mixer till it is creamy & light in color in a large basin. Whip on high speed till light & fluffy, approximately 2 - 3 Mins, after adding honey & cinnamon to the mix.

Nutrition Information
Calories: 391 kcal, Carbohydrates: 46 g, Protein: 7 g, Fat: 21 g

74. Apple Pie Cinnamon Cookies
Prep Time: 20 Mins, Cook Time: 25 Mins, Servings: 4
Ingredients
- 1 tbsp olive oil
- 3 large apples
- ¼ cup sugar coconut
- 2 tsp cinnamon ground
- 1 tsp juice lemon
- 2 pie crusts whole-wheat
- 1 lightly beaten egg white

Instructions
- Preheat the oven to 375°F
- Some olive oil should be heated to medium-high heat in a medium skillet. Cook the apples for approximately 5 Mins, often stirring, until they're soft. Cinnamon, sugar, & lemon juice are all that is needed. Stir often and continue cooking for another 5 Mins. Remove from the stove and let it cool before serving.
- For around 15 Mins, remove the pie crusts & let them soften. On the flat surface, unroll your crusts. Cutting roughly 14 circles out of a single crust using the circle cutter. Scraps may be re-rolled into new circles if needed. Slice the other crust into ¼-inch-wide pieces.
- Each circle should have 1 heaping spoonful of pie stuff on it. A crisscross or lattice design may be created by placing pastry strips over the top and weaving them over each circular. Remove any extra dough from the edges with the same circle cutter used before. Finally, use a fork & tongs to glue the dough parts together & form a "crust" around the borders.
- Place each cookie on the baking sheet & brush its tops with egg white. Allow baking for around 10-15 minutes, unless gently browned the tops. Serve hot or cold and keep in a sealed jar in the refrigerator.

Nutrition Information
Calories: 194 kcal, Carbohydrates: 27 g, Protein: 1 g, Fat: 9 g

75. Slow Cooker Pumpkin Pecan Cobbler
Prep Time:15 Mins, Cook Time: 2 hrs 15 Mins, Servings: 6
Ingredients
Filling
- 1 cup all-purpose white flour
- 2 tsp powder baking
- ½ tsp sea salt
- ¾ cup sugar coconut
- 1 & ½ tsp spice pumpkin pie
- 2/3 cup of puree pumpkin
- ¼ cup canned coconut milk
- ¼ cup butter
- 2 tsp vanilla

Topping
- 1 cup sugar coconut
- ½ tsp vanilla
- ¼ tsp cinnamon
- 1/3 cup diced pecans
- 1 & ¾ cups water boiling

Instructions
- Use nonstick spray to coat the interior of a slow cooker.
- Whisk together all the dry ingredients in a large bowl. Combine pumpkin puree, butter, coconut milk, & vanilla extract. Whisk together the dry & wet ingredients until the filling has a slightly thicker consistency. Spread the batter equally in a slow cooker with a capacity of 3-4 quarts.
- Slowly pour all topping ingredients on the batter after whisking them together. On high for 2-3 hrs, or unless the top is done, cover & cook. Allow the cake to cool for 15 mins before dishing it out of the slow cooker.
- Add a dollop of ice cream to your cobbler for an extra dose of sweetness.

Nutrition Information
Calories: 318 kcal, Carbohydrates: 56 g, Protein: 2 g, Fat: 10 g

76. Paleo Fudge Brownies
Prep Time:15 Mins, Cook Time: 35 Mins, Servings: 12
Ingredients
- 2 cups of ripe, mashed bananas
- 1 cup natural almond butter
- ¼ cup almond meal or almond flour
- ½ cup powder cocoa
- ½ cup chocolate chips paleo-friendly

Instructions
- The oven should be preheated to 350°F.
- Whisk together mashed bananas & almond butter. Pour your ingredients into a casserole pan that has been gently greased.
- Bake for 35-40 mins, till a toothpick inserted into the center, comes out clear.
- Before slicing, allow the meat to cool. For almost four days, keep it within the fridge covered.

Nutrition Information
Calories: 246 kcal, Carbohydrates: 24 g, Protein: 7 g, Fat: 16 g

77. Pecan Stuffed Baked Apples
Prep Time:20 Mins, Cook Time: 40 Mins, Servings: 3
Ingredients
- 4 apples large, gala or fuji apples work great!!
- ½ cup pecans roughly chopped
- ¼ cup coconut sugar
- 2 tbsp coconut oil
- 1 tbsp molasses
- ½ tsp ground cinnamon
- ½ cup water

Instructions
- The oven should be preheated at 350°F.
- Remove the core & seeds from the middle of the apples. The apples should be placed in a small baking dish using a high perimeter.
- Coconut oil, some molasses & cinnamons are all you need in this recipe for pecan pie. Spoon the filling into the hollowed-out apples' centers. Fill the apples to the brim, but don't worry about spilling out. Place a layer of water on the apples in a small baking dish.
- Bake for 40-45 Mins, uncovered. There will be a lot of wiggle room. Before serving, let them cool somewhat, but keep them warm! Enjoy!

Nutrition Information
Calories: 329 kcal, Carbohydrates: 49 g, Protein: 2 g, Fat: 17 g

78. 4-Ingredient Protein Fudge Brownies
Prep Time:10 Mins, Cook Time: 25 Mins, Servings: 4
Ingredients
- 2 cups ripe, mashed bananas
- 1 cup extra-crunchy peanut butter
- 1 cup clean protein powder dark chocolate
- 2/3 cup chocolate chips mini

Instructions
- The oven should be preheated to 350°F.
- Add the mashed banana & peanut butter to a bowl and stir with a blender until they're well-combined. Make a smoothie by combining the protein powder & chocolate chips. Pour the mix into a casserole dish that has been gently greased.
- Bake for 25 to 30 Mins. Before slicing, let it cool fully. Before slicing the brownies, immerse the butter knife

into water and wipe it clean after every slice. To preserve freshness, keep it in the fridge in an airtight container.
- Diced pecans or walnuts may be used as an optional ingredient.

Nutrition Information
Calories: 287 kcal, Carbohydrates: 28 g, Protein: 17 g, Fat: 14 g

79. Caramel Pear Ice Cream
Prep Time: 10 Mins, Cook Time: 35 Mins, Servings: 3
Ingredients
- 6 peeled, sliced & core removed pears ripe
- 8 cups no sugar apple juice
- 1 tsp juice lemon
- 32 oz Greek yogurt plain

Instructions
- Sliced pears may be frozen in the freezer until they are totally solid.
- Bring the apple juice to a boil in a medium saucepan. Stir often while cooking at a low simmer. Simmer the liquid until it achieves a caramel-like consistency, then remove from the heat and strain. Remove and let cool.
- Put frozen pears in a small blender with lemon juice, yogurt, & caramel that has been allowed to cool. Blend until smooth. Place in an airtight jar in the freezer till ready to use; then take from the blender when smooth.
- Sprinkle apple juice caramelized on top of the sorbet before serving. Enjoy!

Nutrition Information
Calories: 281 kcal, Carbohydrates: 68 g, Protein: 5 g, Fat: 2 g

80. Papaya Boat Parfait
Prep Time: 10 Mins, Cook Time: 10 Mins, Servings: 1
Ingredients
- 1 papaya whole
- 1 cup plain Greek yogurt
- 2 tsp honey
- 2 tbsp seeds pomegranate
- 1 peeled kiwi
- ½ tsp seeds chia
- 2 tbsp slivered almonds

Instructions
- Cut your papaya fruit into half lengthwise, removing the skin but keeping the fruit within. To construct a boat, remove the seeds & pulp from the middle of the fruit.
- Using the hollowed-out core of the papaya as a guide, divide your Greek yogurt among each boat. Mix the honey & pomegranate seeds, then sprinkle them on top of each boat. It's time to eat!

Nutrition Information
Calories: 313 kcal, Carbohydrates: 43 g, Protein: 13 g, Fat: 12 g

81. Blackberry and Chia Breakfast Pudding
Prep Time: 10 Mins, Cook Time: 30 Mins, Servings: 3
Ingredients
- ½ cup fresh blackberries
- 3 tbsp seeds chia
- 1 cup unsweetened coconut milk
- ½ cup plain Greek yogurt
- ¼ tsp extract almond
- 2 tbsp honey
- 1 tbsp unsweetened shredded coconut
- ¼ cup sliced almonds toasted

Instructions
- Using a fork, mash the blackberries in a large bowl until they're completely smooth. Chia seeds, honey, coconut milk, almond extract, yogurt, & shredded coconut should be added. Cover and chill overnight for best results. The mixture would thicken as this sets, so don't panic if it's just a bit runny!
- When ready to eat, take it from the fridge and mix well. Add more Greek yogurt if your pudding is still sloppy for your liking. Coconut milk may be added if it's too stiff. Sliced almonds may be added to the top of the serving dishes. Enjoy!

Nutrition Information
Calories: 211 kcal, Carbohydrates: 19 g, Protein: 8 g, Fat: 12 g

82. Apple Cream Cheese Tarts
Prep Time: 20 Mins, Cook Time: 40 Mins, Servings: 3
Ingredients
- 2 tsp oil olive
- 1 large, peeled apple
- 1 tbsp juice lemon
- 2 sheets puff pastry whole-wheat
- ¼ cup fat-free softened cream cheese
- 3 tbsp sugar coconut
- 1 tsp cinnamon
- 1 tsp honey

Instructions
- The oven should be preheated at 375°F. Apply non-stick spray to the muffin pan and put it aside.
- Add olive oil to a small pan and heat it over medium-high heat. Afterward, sauté the apples with lemon juice for around five Mins. Allow cooling before storing in an airtight container.
- To make four equal strips from each puff pastry sheet, cut in half. Spread some cream cheese over each strip & top with sugar. Apply the apple & lemon juice mix on top of the cake. Each strip should be rolled into a cinnamon roll-like form by folding half along its long axis. Each roll should be placed in a muffin cup with the spiral side up.
- Use a pastry brush to apply a little coating of cinnamon & honey over the top of every tart.
- Bake for around 40 Mins, or unless the top is golden. Before serving, let the dish cool down a little.

Nutrition Information
Calories: 384 kcal, Carbohydrates: 36 g, Protein: 6 g, Fat: 25 g

83. Raspberry Kiwi Lime Cake
Prep Time: 10 Mins, Cook Time: 50 Mins, Servings: 7
Ingredients
For Crust
- ½ cup ground fine walnuts
- 1 cup of whole-wheat crumbs graham cracker
- 1 whisked egg white
- 1 tbsp honey
- ¼ tsp salt kosher
- 1 tbsp melted butter
- 1 tbsp melted coconut oil

For Filling
- 2 cups fresh raspberries
- 1 medium, mashed banana
- 2 cups plain Greek yogurt
- 2 tbsp honey
- 3 tbsp juice lime
- 2 peeled & sliced kiwis

Instructions
For Crust
- The oven should be preheated at 325 degrees Fahrenheit.
- Mix all of the ingredients well. The final product should resemble wet sand in appearance. A pie plate is perfect for this step. When the crust is browned and dry, it's done baking. Before filling, make sure it's cooled down to room temperature. Keep the pan in the oven.

For Filling
- Top your cooled crust with raspberries. Set away for later.
- Mix the banana, yogurt, honey, & lime juice in a large mixing bowl. Pour the mixture over raspberries into an equal layer & whisk well on top, place kiwi slices.

- Three hrs in the freezer should be enough time to freeze totally. It's time to eat! Keep in the freezer, sealed, for up to a month.

Nutrition Information
Calories: 313 kcal, Carbohydrates: 37 g, Protein: 10 g, Fat: 16 g

84. Strawberry Rhubarb Buckwheat Bars
Prep Time: 30 Mins, Cook Time: 55 Mins, Servings: 10
Ingredients
For Crust
- 2 ¼ cups flour whole-wheat
- ¾ cup flour buckwheat
- ½ cup sugar coconut
- 1 tsp salt kosher
- 1 tsp powder baking
- 1 cup butter cold unsalted
- 1 large egg
- 2 tbsp honey
- 3 tbsp molasses

For Filling
- 2 cups of strawberries
- 2 cups of chopped rhubarb
- 12 oz strawberry no sugar preserves jar
- 1 tbsp cornstarch
- 2 tsp juice lemon

Instructions
For Crust
- Preheat the oven to 370°F. The pan should be lightly sprayed with cooking spray.
- Whole wheat, coconut sugar, and buckwheat are pulsed in the food processor with salt & baking powder till thoroughly blended. Pulse in the butter cubes till the mix is crumbly & add the flour. Pulse in the egg, honey, & molasses till they form huge clusters. Only half of the mix should be kept aside, so pour the rest into a baking pan & press it down to produce a crust that extends slightly higher on the edges.
- Then, take from the oven and let cool for around 10 Mins.

For Filling
- In your food processor, add all ingredients & pulse just enough to blend them. When the preserves have melted, pour into the small saucepan & warm over medium heat till a sauce has formed. Sprinkle saved crust mix on top when it has cooled.
- The filling should bubble, and the top should brown after approximately 20 Mins of baking. Before slicing and serving, allow the meat to cool fully. Sprinkle with some powdered sugar, if desired.

Nutrition Information
Calories: 186 kcal, Carbohydrates: 30 g, Protein: 3 g, Fat: 8 g

85. Spiced Green Tea Smoothie
Prep Time: 5 Mins, Cook Time: 5 Mins, Servings: 6
Ingredients
- ¾ cup of brewed strong green tea
- 1/8 tsp pepper cayenne
- ¼ tsp cinnamon ground
- 3 tsp honey
- ½ peeled & sliced thin pear
- ½ peeled & sliced thin apple
- ½ peeled & segmented orange
- ¼ cup plain Greek yogurt
- 6 cubes ice

Instructions
- Blend all of the ingredients until smooth. Blend on fast speed until smooth.

Nutrition Information
Calories: 214 kcal, Carbohydrates: 42 g, Protein: 7 g, Fat: 4 g

86. Skinny Lemon Muffins
Prep Time: 15 Mins, Cook Time: 20 Mins, Servings: 10
Ingredients
- 1 cup of flour
- 1 tsp powder baking
- ½ tsp soda baking
- ¼ tsp salt sea
- ½ cup melted coconut oil
- 2 large eggs
- 2 tbsp palm sugar coconut
- ¼ cup raw honey
- 1 cup low-fat Greek yogurt
- 1 tsp extract vanilla
- 3 tbsp freshly squeezed lemon juice
- 1 tsp zest lemon

Instructions
- The oven should be preheated at 355 degrees Fahrenheit. To begin, prepare a 12-cup muffin tray by spraying it with nonstick cooking spray.
- Sift the baking soda, baking powder, flour, and salt in a big mixing bowl & put it aside.
- In a second large bowl, whisk the eggs & coconut oil till they form a homogeneous mixture. Mix in raw honey, coconut sugar, & Greek yogurt. Lemon juice & zest should be included in the mixture before being whisked thoroughly.
- Add the ingredients to this mixture and stir well. Fold them with a spatula till they're the same thickness and texture. Bake at 355°F for around 18-20 Mins, till the toothpick inserted, falls out clear, then divide all batter into muffin pans. Cool on the wire rack once you remove it from the oven. Enjoy!

Nutrition Information
Calories: 180 kcal, Carbohydrates: 17 g, Protein: 4 g, Fat: 11 g

87. Trail Mix Cookie Bars
Prep Time: 20 Mins, Cook Time: 15 Mins, Servings: 7
Ingredients
- 2 cups flour whole-wheat
- ¼ cup flour almond
- 1 tsp soda baking
- ½ tsp salt kosher
- ½ cup cold coconut oil
- ½ cup sugar coconut
- 2 tbsp of honey
- 2 large eggs
- 1 tsp extract vanilla
- 2 cups oats rolled
- 1 & ½ cups chocolate chips mini
- 1 cup unsweetened shredded coconut
- ¾ cup raisins golden
- 1 cup chopped almonds
- 2 tbsp seeds sunflower

Instructions
- The oven should be preheated to 350°F. With an overhang of 2 inches, cover the bottom of a pan with parchment paper.
- Baking soda & salt go into a small bowl with the whole wheat & almond flour. Set away for later. Coconut oil, honey, and sugar are mixed in a small bowl. Beat for approximately 4 Mins till the mixture is light & fluffy. To finish blending, add the eggs & vanilla extract and stir until well-combined. Add the flour mixture gradually to an egg & oil mixture. Mix until the flour is completely integrated. Add the rest of the ingredients & mix till just blended, using a wooden spoon.
- Pour the mixture into the dish and gently press it into the pan & along the edges to form a crust. Bake for 15-20 Mins, unless the top is just beginning to turn golden brown. Cut and serve after entirely cooling from the oven. Dark chocolate ganache may be drizzled over the bars if desired.

Nutrition Information
Calories: 277 kcal, Carbohydrates: 33 g, Protein: 5 g, Fat: 15 g

88. Morning Glory Muffin
Prep Time: 15 Mins, Cook Time: 15 Mins, Servings: 4
Ingredients
- 1 cup flour almond
- ½ cup flour whole-wheat
- 2 tsp flour coconut
- ½ tsp salt
- ½ tsp soda baking
- 1 tsp cinnamon
- 1 tbsp coconut oil
- 2 large eggs
- 2 tbsp honey
- 1 tbsp molasses
- 1 tsp vanilla extract
- ¼ cup unsweetened applesauce
- ¼ cup unsweetened shredded coconut
- ¼ cup raisins golden
- ½ cup chopped apple
- ¼ cup grated carrot
- ¼ cup walnuts chopped
- ¼ cup crushed pineapple

Instructions
- The oven should be preheated to 350°F. Line the muffin pan with some liners or gently coat it using a non-stick spray, depending on how you choose to prepare your muffins.
- Sift the almond flour, baking soda, wheat flour, salt, coconut flour, & cinnamon in a large bowl before adding the milk and oil & mixing well. Set away for later.
- Gather all of the ingredients for the cake in a different bowl and mix them. Mix thoroughly. Add the flour mix to this egg mixture in stages, mixing well after each addition. Gently mix until the mixture is smooth. Using a rubber spatula, gently fold in the remainder of the ingredients. Scoop in muffin tins that have been prepped.
- Using a toothpick, place it into the middle and bake for around 15 Mins. Make sure it's cooled down before serving. Put it in the fridge to keep it fresh.

Nutrition Information
Calories: 155 kcal, Carbohydrates: 15 g, Protein: 4 g, Fat: 9 g

89. Sweet Potato Brownies
Prep Time: 15 Mins, Cook Time: 15 Mins, Servings: 9
Ingredients
- ¾ cup butter almond
- 3 tbsp maple syrup pure
- 1 & ¼ cup cooked & mashed sweet potatoes
- ½ cup powder cocoa
- ¾ cup flour whole-wheat
- ½ tsp salt kosher
- ¼ cup chocolate chips semisweet

Instructions
- The oven should be preheated to 350°F. Using a non-stick spray, lightly coat an 8-by-8-inch pan with it.
- Over moderate flame, combine almond butter & maple syrup in a medium saucepan and whisk regularly until smooth. Remove from the heat & whisk in mashed potato, flour, cocoa powder, & salt until it is a smooth consistency. Gently include chocolate chunks into the mixture.
- Bake for around 15-20 Mins, till a toothpick in the middle, comes out clear. Pour batter into the pan. Before slicing, allow the brownies to chill fully. In a sealed jar, keep it in the refrigerator.

Nutrition Information
Calories: 155 kcal, Carbohydrates: 17 g, Protein: 5 g, Fat: 9 g

90. Instant Pot Applesauce
Prep Time:10 Mins, Cook Time: 10 Mins, Servings: 10
Ingredients
- 6-8 medium apples
- 1 cup of water
- 1 tsp juice lemon
- 2 tsp cinnamon

Instructions
- Cut the apples into 2″ pieces after peeling and slicing them in half. In your Instant Pot, add the apples & the rest of the ingredients.
- Ensure that the vent just on the cover of your Instant Pot has been pushed in. Adjust pressure to maximum & set a timer for 8 Mins by pressing the "manual" button. Before commencing the cooking time, your Instant Pot should preheat.
- Allow at least two and a half to three Mins after the timer has gone off. Remove the lid by turning the steam vent to the open position and gradually releasing the steam.
- Drain the remaining water. Blend on low till desired applesauce texture is achieved; chunky or smooth, it's up to you! Before serving, let the dish cool down a little.

Nutrition Information
Calories: 177 kcal, Carbohydrates: 42 g, Protein: 1 g, Fat: 1g

91. Blueberry Tart with Walnut Crust
Prep Time: 25 Mins, Cook Time: 45 Mins, Servings: 4
Ingredients
For Crust
- ½ cup ground fine walnuts
- 1 cup of whole-wheat crumbs graham cracker
- 1 whisked egg white
- 1 tbsp honey
- ¼ tsp salt kosher
- 1 tbsp melted butter
- 1 tbsp melted coconut oil

For Blueberry Filling
- 8 oz cheese cream
- ¼ cup plain Greek yogurt
- ¼ cup of honey
- 1 tsp extract almond
- 1 tbsp zest lemon
- 2 cups fresh blueberries

Instructions
For Crust
- The oven should be preheated at 325 degrees Fahrenheit.
- Mix all of the ingredients well. Ideally, the mixture will resemble wet sand. Pour the mixture into a cheesecake pan with a detachable bottom. When the crust is browned and dry, it's done baking. Before filling, make sure it's cooled down to room temperature. Keep the pan in the oven.

For Filling
- Whip both yogurt and cream cheese together till they are light and fluffy. Other ingredients (excluding blueberries) should be added now. Pour into the prepared crust, being sure to spread it out evenly. Make sure you don't damage the outer layer. Top the filling with a layer of blueberries. The tart should be refrigerated for at least an hr, or overnight if feasible, to set. Cut, serve!

Nutrition Information
Calories: 208 kcal, Carbohydrates: 28 g, Protein: 7 g, Fat: 8 g

92. Baked Almond Peaches
Prep Time: 10 Mins, Cook Time: 30 Mins, Servings: 5
Ingredients
- ½ cup flour whole-wheat
- 1/3 oats cup
- 1/3 cup lightly chopped almonds

- ¼ cup sugar coconut
- ¼ cup maple syrup pure
- ½ tsp extract almond
- ½ tsp salt
- ¼ tsp nutmeg ground
- ¼ tsp ginger ground
- ½ tsp cinnamon ground
- ¼ cup cold coconut oil
- 4 large, ripe peaches

Instructions
- The oven should be preheated to 350°F. Spritz the casserole dish using non-stick spray & put it away.
- Add the other ingredients to the food processor, excluding the peaches. Pulse the ingredients until it is crumbled and resemble coarse crumbs. Skin-side down put peaches into the casserole dish that has been prepared. 2-3 tsp of the oatmeal mixture should be poured into a gaping hole left by the pit.
- Serve warm with a dollop of sour cream or ice cream. Serve hot. Dollop on honey or whipped sweetened coconut cream, if preferred.

Nutrition Information
Calories: 223 kcal, Carbohydrates: 31 g, Protein: 4 g, Fat: 11 g

93. Banana Nut Coconut Clusters
Prep Time: 10 Mins, Cook Time: 25, Servings: 1
Ingredients
- ½ cup sugar coconut
- 2 tbsp milk almond
- 3 tbsp oil coconut
- 2 tbsp powder cocoa
- 1/3 cup unsweetened shredded coconut
- 1 cup of oats
- ½ cup peanut butter or almond butter
- ¼ cup mashed banana
- ¼ cup chopped almonds
- ¼ tsp cinnamon ground
- 2 tbsp seeds sunflower

Instructions
- Bring sugar, oil, milk, & cocoa to your boil in a saucepan. One Min of boiling time. After removing from the heat, add the other ingredients and thoroughly combine.
- Spoon onto a parchment-lined baking sheet or the nonstick baking tray. Allow the mixture to come to room temperature before refrigerating or freezing it for longer periods. Refrigerated storage is recommended.

Nutrition Information
Calories: 221 kcal, Carbohydrates: 22 g, Protein: 6 g, Fat: 14 g

94. No-Bake Almond Joy Bars
Prep Time: 25 Mins, Cook Time: 20 Mins, Servings: 10
Ingredients
For Crust
- 2 cups raw almonds
- ¼ cup melted coconut oil
- 2 tbsp honey

For Filling
- 1 cup unsweetened shredded coconut
- 2 tbsp syrup maple
- 2 tbsp coconut oil
- ½ tsp extract almond
- 1 tbsp water

For Topping
- 8 oz chopped dark chocolate
- 1 tbsp oil coconut
- ¼ cup unsweetened, toasted shredded coconut
- 2 tbsp chopped almonds

Instructions
- Apply nonstick spray to a 9x13-inch pan.

To get the best crust
- Grind all nuts in your food processor to a fine powder. A few big pieces are Still ok but avoid over-processing the nuts. Add some honey & coconut oil. Pulse your processor till the mixture is smooth and creamy. Pour the mixture into the pan and spread it out evenly.
- Mix all of the ingredients well. Overlay the crust with a layer of coconut. Make sure that the stuffing is as even as possible. While your topping has been made, put the pizza in the fridge.

When it comes to toppings
- Stir your chocolate often while it melts. Whisk within coconut oil after the chocolate has melted to combine the two ingredients. To finish the dessert, remove the crust & filling layers from the refrigerator, then drizzle chocolate evenly over the surface of your filling. Add a layer of coconut & almonds. Chill for at least an hr to set the chocolate. It's time to slice, dice, and serve.

Nutrition Information
Calories: 286 kcal, Carbohydrates: 19 g, Protein: 5 g, Fat: 24 g

95. Roasted Banana Smash
Prep Time: 3 Mins, Cook Time: 12 Mins, Servings: 6
Ingredients
- 1 very ripe banana medium

Instructions
- 400°F is a good starting point.
- Bananas should be peeled and placed on the baking pan coated with parchment paper. A fork may be used to mash up a banana.
- 12 Mins in your preheated oven, or unless the top is gently browned.
- Use as a garnish on your favorite dishes or as a delicious treat on its own.

Nutrition Information
Calories: 105 kcal, Carbohydrates: 27 g, Protein: 1.3 g, Fat: 0 g

96. Lemon Meringue Pie Parfait
Prep Time: 10 mins, Cook Time: 25 Mins, Servings: 10
Ingredients
- 2 large egg whites
- ¼ cup of honey
- pinch tartar cream
- kosher salt pinch
- ½ tsp extract vanilla
- 14 oz cold coconut milk
- 2 cups Greek yogurt lemon
- ½ cup of granola

Instructions
- Pour in both egg whites & honey, along with the tartar cream and salt, into your double boiler over medium heat. Whisk frequently until the honey has dissolved & the whites have frothed up.
- Add the egg & honey mixture to the bowl & whisk well. Add the vanilla extract using the electric mixer, beginning on low & working your way up to high. Eggs should be whipped until they form firm peaks, and the mixture is white & shiny.
- Remove the coconut juice from the fat. You may save some of the liquid for later use.
- Coconut fat should be placed in a mixing dish and beaten till it reaches a whipped cream-like consistency. Incorporate the lemon yogurt with care.
- Add granola to a food processor. Granola should be finely ground.
- Begin putting together the parfaits. Layer granola, meringue, and yogurt in a big glass with meringue as the last layer. Serve.

Nutrition Information
Calories: 115 kcal, Carbohydrates: 12 g, Protein: 13 g, Fat: 2 g

97. Dark Chocolate Avocado Brownies
Prep Time: 15 Mins, Cook Time: 20 Mins, Servings: 3

Ingredients
- ¾ cup flour whole-wheat
- ¾ cup powder cocoa
- 1 tsp powder baking
- ½ tsp salt kosher
- 1 large egg
- 1 peeled, pitted avocado ripe
- ½ cup melted coconut oil
- 1 tsp extract vanilla
- ¾ cup maple syrup pure
- 1 cup chocolate chips dark

Instructions
- Preheat the oven to around 350 degrees Fahrenheit. Using the non-stick spray, lightly coat an 8-by-8-inch pan with it.
- Mix flour, baking powder, cocoa powder, & salt in a medium bowl. Set away for later. Mix the egg, avocado, vanilla extract, coconut oil, & maple syrup in a small bowl. Mix well till the mixture is completely smooth. Blend in the flour mix gradually to add it to the avocado mix. Then, using a spoon or spatula, stir in the chocolate chips & pour them into the pan.
- When a toothpick pushed into the middle of the cake comes out clear, baking the cake. After it's cooled down, slice it into squares. In a sealed jar, keep it in the refrigerator.

Nutrition Information
Calories: 294 kcal, Carbohydrates: 36 g, Protein: 4 g, Fat: 17 g

98. Chocolate Chip Protein Cupcakes
Prep Time:15 Mins, Cook Time: 15 Mins, Servings: 6
Ingredients
Muffins
- ¼ cup flour almond
- ¼ cup flour coconut
- ¼ cup of oats
- 2 tsp powder baking
- ½ tsp salt kosher
- 1 cup mashed banana
- 1 tbsp melted coconut oil
- 2 tbsp of honey
- 1 whole egg
- 1 large egg white
- 1 tsp extract vanilla
- ½ cup chocolate chips mini semisweet

For Icing Peanut Butter
- ¼ cup of peanut butter no sugar creamy
- 1 tbsp honey
- 1 tbsp coconut oil

Instructions
Muffins
- The oven should be preheated to 350°F. Line the muffin pan with a muffin liner and lightly coat the tin using non-stick spray.
- Almond, coconut flour, baking powder, oats, & salt are all combined in a bowl. Set away for later.
- A medium-sized mixing basin should be filled with bananas, coconut oil, one egg, honey, and vanilla extract. Whisk the mixture well. Add dry ingredients into the banana mix one at a time, mixing well after each addition. Make sure you don't over-mix; some lumps are Still ok! Gently mix the chocolate chunks into the batter.
- Fill three-quarters of the muffin cups. It should take around 15-20 Mins for the toothpick to fall out clear. Peanut butter frosting may be drizzled over the cake.

For Icing Peanut Butter
- While on lower heat, mix all the ingredients in a medium saucepan until they are melted & blended. If the mixture doesn't flow readily off a spoon, add water to get it to the right consistency. Sprinkle the Protein Chocolate Chip Cupcakes with a spoonful of the glaze.

Nutrition Information
Calories: 171 kcal, Carbohydrates: 19 g, Protein: 4 g, Fat: 10 g

99. Honey Mint Fruit Salad
Prep Time: 20 Mins, Cook Time: 20 Mins, Servings: 4
Ingredients
- ¼ cup sliced honeydew melon
- ¼ cup fresh blueberries
- ¼ cup fresh, sliced strawberries
- 1 fresh, peeled & sliced peach
- 1 tbsp juice lime
- 1 tbsp honey
- 2 tbsp fresh, chopped mint

Instructions
- A fruit salad with lime juice & honeydew melon is ready. Put honey over the top & garnish with mint. Once again, lightly toss. It's time to eat!

Nutrition Information
Calories: 91 kcal, Carbohydrates: 23 g, Protein: 8 g, Fat: 1 g

100. Workout Banana Bites
Prep Time: 15 Mins, Cook Time: 25 Mins, Servings: 5
Ingredients
- 1 medium, mashed banana
- ¼ cup powder protein
- ¼ cup of nut butter
- ¼ cup chopped dark chocolate
- 2 cups oats old-fashioned
- 1/3 cup no sugar dried currants
- ¼ cup of honey
- 2 tbsp seed flax
- 1 tbsp seeds chia
- ¼ cup sliced almonds

Instructions
- Mix all the ingredients in a blender. Make sure all the nuts and seeds are evenly dispersed throughout the mixture over low heat.
- If the mix is too dry or crumbly, add honey & nut butter. Adding oats, one spoonful at the moment, if the mix is too moist, will help it come together.
- Make roughly 2 tbsp-sized balls out of the mixture. Line your cookie sheet with parchment paper. Refrigerate for at least 12 hrs to set.
- Refrigerate after storing in a sealed jar.

Nutrition Information
Calories: 183 kcal, Carbohydrates: 26 g, Protein: 7 g, Fat: 7 g

101. Herb Barley Salad
Prep Time: 10 Mins, Cook Time: 25 Mins, Servings: 4
Ingredients
- 2 cups cooked & cooled barley
- 1 tbsp olive oil extra virgin
- 2 cups chopped mushrooms
- ½ tsp salt kosher
- ½ tsp black pepper ground
- 1 small, sliced red onion
- 1 tsp fresh, chopped thyme
- 2 minced garlic cloves
- ½ cup fresh, chopped cilantro
- ½ cup fresh, chopped parsley
- 2 tbsp juice lemon
- ½ cup low-fat, shredded parmesan

Instructions
- Medium-high heat olive oil in a big pan. Mushrooms should be added to the oil after it reaches a high temperature. Make sure the mushrooms are arranged in a thin layer in the pan. Mushrooms should be cooked without stirring till they are browned and crispy. Add pepper, salt, & red onion to the pot & continue to simmer over medium-low heat. To get the golden color, stirring often.

- Ensure the mushrooms are well covered with thyme & garlic as you continue to roast. Excess oil should be drained and saved for later use.
- You can make this dish in advance and store it in an airtight container in the fridge for up to three days or freeze it for up to three months. Toss in some reserved mushrooms one more time, just to ensure everything is well combined. Top with the rest of the Parmesan cheese. Enjoy!

Nutrition Information
Calories: 218 kcal, Carbohydrates: 37 g, Protein: 9 g, Fat: 5 g

102. Cookie Dough Energy Bites
Prep Time: 20 Mins, Cook Time: 20 Mins, Servings: 2 bites
Ingredients
- 1 cup flour oat
- ½ cup almond flour or almond meal
- ½ cup unsweetened shredded coconut
- 1 cup creamy almond butter
- ¼ cup maple syrup pure
- 1 tsp extract vanilla
- ¼ cup chocolate chips mini semisweet

Instructions
- All except the chocolate chips should be mixed. Add a spoonful of almond butter at a moment if the mixture seems too dry. The dough should be well-mixed before adding the chocolate chips.
- Bake on a baking sheet after being rolled into 1″ balls using a spoonful of dough for each ball. Refrigerate for at least one hr before serving. In a sealed jar, keep it in the refrigerator.

Nutrition Information
Calories: 255 kcal, Carbohydrates: 19 g, Protein: 7 g, Fat: 18 g

103. Carrot and Honey Muffins
Prep Time: 15 Mins, Cook Time: 25 Mins, Servings: 12
Ingredients
- 1 & ¾ cup of white flour whole-wheat
- 1 & ½ tsp powder baking
- ½ tsp soda baking
- 1 tsp ginger ground
- 2 large eggs
- ½ cup of honey
- ¼ cup oil olive
- 1 tbsp extract vanilla
- 1 cup plain Greek yogurt
- 2 cups peeled & grated carrots

Instructions
- Preheat your oven to around 325 deg F. You'll need to lubricate your muffin pans. The baking soda, flour, & ginger should be shifted into a large bowl. Combine the rest of the ingredients in a separate bowl. Mix both wet and dry ingredients in a slow, steady stream.
- A toothpick should come out clear after baking for 25-30 Mins. Before serving, allow the food to come to room temperature.

Nutrition Information
Calories: 185 kcal, Carbohydrates: 27 g, Protein: 5 g, Fat: 7 g

104. Chia Seed Berry Yogurt Smoothie
Prep Time: 10 Mins, Cook Time: 25 Mins, Servings: 3
Ingredients
- 2 tbsp chia seeds
- 1 cup no sugar orange juice
- ½ cup fresh strawberries
- ½ cup fresh blueberries
- ½ cup fresh raspberries
- ½ cup fresh blackberries
- 1 large banana
- 2 tbsp of honey
- ¼ tsp cinnamon
- 2 cups plain Greek yogurt

Instructions
- Add the chia seeds to a small dish & mix well with the orange juice. Then freeze the mixture.
- In your blender, combine the other ingredients chia while seeds set. Blend till completely smooth. Get rid of chia seeds in the fridge. Blend the ingredients in a food processor or blender till smooth. It's time to eat!

Nutrition Information
Calories: 277 kcal, Carbohydrates: 38 g, Protein: 13 g, Fat: 10 g

105. Slow Cooker Lemon Bars
Prep Time: 30 Mins, Cook Time: 25 Mins, Servings: 5
Ingredients
Crust
- 1 & ½ cups pastry flour whole-wheat
- ½ cup flour oat
- 1 tbsp sugar coconut
- 1 tbsp zest lemon
- ½ tsp salt
- 2/3 cup cold coconut oil
- ice-cold water

Filling
- 8 oz reduced-fat cream cheese
- 2 large eggs
- ½ cup sugar coconut
- ½ tsp extract vanilla
- 5.3 oz Greek yogurt lemon
- 1 tbsp zest lemon
- 2 tbsp freshly squeezed lemon juice
- ¼ tsp salt
- ½ cup white flour whole-wheat
- 3 cups frozen or fresh, unthawed blueberries

Instructions
Crust
- Combine the lemon zest, wheat flour, sugar, oat flour, and salt in a big bowl. Then, form a crust by kneading the mixture. Using your hands, incorporate the coconut oil/butter combination into the flour until crumbly dough forms.
- To make a dough, gradually add some ice water, 2 tsp at the moment, until you get the desired consistency.
- Form your dough into a ball, cover in plastic, & chill for a ½ hr until it's firm.

Filling
- High-speed whipping of the cream cheese will achieve this goal. Beat in the eggs at
this point. Then, add lemon juice, sugar, lemon zest, Greek yogurt, vanilla extract, & salt to the mixture, and stir. Beat the ingredients together until they're completely incorporated. Beat within flour till the mixture is smooth, but don't over-beat it. Using the rubber spatula, incorporate the blueberries.
- Slow cookers should be sprayed using cooking spray before use. After placing the dough in the slow cooker, you may put the filling over the top. Cook for around 2-3 hrs on low, till the edges, start to brown. Remove individual squares from your slow cooker when they have cooled.

Nutrition Information
Calories: 319 kcal, Carbohydrates: 33 g, Protein: 7 g, Fat: 19 g

106. Chocolate Covered Cheesecake Bites
Prep Time: 20 Mins, Cook Time: 30 Mins, Servings: 4
Ingredients
- 8 oz reduced-fat cream cheese
- 1 cup plain Greek yogurt
- 1 tsp extract vanilla
- ¼ cup sugar coconut
- 1 large egg
- 12 oz chocolate dark
- 3 tbsp oil coconut

Instructions
- Preheat your oven to around 325 degrees. Apply cooking spray to an 8-by-8-inch square pan. Whisk together coconut sugar, yogurt, vanilla, cream cheese, & extract. Cheesecake should be baked for 55-60 Mins or till it's set. Cut into squares after cooling.
- At low flame over the stove, melt the dark chocolate & coconut oil. Switch off the heat when it's completely melted. Dip chocolate-covered cheesecake pieces into the mixture. Once all of the bites have been coated in chocolate, store them in the refrigerator to set.

Nutrition Information
Calories: 272 kcal, Carbohydrates: 24 g, Protein: 5 g, Fat: 20 g

107. Caramel Apple Bread Pudding
Prep Time: 20 Mins, Cook Time: 30 Mins, Servings: 6
Ingredients
- 1 cup unsweetened applesauce
- 1 cup milk almond
- ½ cup of molasses
- 3 large eggs
- 1 tsp extract vanilla
- 1 tsp cinnamon ground
- ¼ tsp nutmeg ground
- 5 cups bread whole-wheat
- 1 cup fresh, peeled apples

Instructions
- Pre-heat your oven to 325°F. Use nonstick spray to coat a casserole dish lightly.
- Pour everything into a large mixing basin, save for the bread and apple. Top the bread pieces with diced apples on the plate. Overlay the bread & apples with an applesauce mixture. Add extra liquid after 5 Mins of sitting. Once liquid & bread mix is ¼" from the top of your casserole dish, repeat this procedure until it is done.
- The rack of your oven should be filled with water. Your bread pudding mixture should be placed on the rack above the water dish. 'Make sure a toothpick put into the middle comes out clean after 30-40 Mins of baking time. Golden brown is the perfect color for the top. Add extra water to the pan if it gets low. Serve at room temperature after allowing it to settle for around 10 Mins.

Nutrition Information
Calories: 199 kcal, Carbohydrates: 37 g, Protein: 7 g, Fat: 3 g

108. Superfood Chocolate Bark
Prep Time: 30 Mins, Cook Time: 45 Mins, Servings: 5
Ingredients
- 1 lb dark chocolate
- 3 tbsp coconut oil
- ¼ cup chopped dried blueberries
- ¼ cup chopped dried cranberries
- ¼ cup chopped almonds

Instructions
- Put parchment paper on a baking pan and set it aside.
- Melt chocolate in your heavy saucepan at low heat. Quickly add chopped almonds & dried blueberries to your heated coconut oil when it's done melting. Spread the batter evenly on the cookie sheet.
- Allow your bark to cool before placing it in the fridge to solidify. Make big pieces and keep them in an airtight jar until solid.

Nutrition Information
Calories: 185 kcal, Carbohydrates: 22 g, Protein: 2 g, Fat: 12 g

109. Cranberry Apricot Fruit Cake
Prep Time: 20 Mins, Cook Time: 25 Mins, Servings: 2
Ingredients
- ½ cup chopped dried cranberries
- ½ cup chopped dried apricots
- 3 tbsp brandy
- ¼ cup of water
- 1 tbsp honey
- 2 cups flour whole-wheat
- 1 & ½ tsp powder baking
- ½ tsp soda baking
- 1 ½ tsp cinnamon ground
- ½ tsp allspice
- ¼ tsp salt kosher
- 1 tbsp melted coconut oil
- 1 tbsp zest lemon
- 1 large egg
- 2 tsp extract almond
- ½ cup plain Greek yogurt
- 2 tbsp molasses
- ½ cup maple syrup pure
- ½ cup milk almond

Instructions
- In a jar with a fitting cover, combine brandy, water, cranberries, apricots, & honey. Keep it in the fridge for almost 2 hrs. Dehydration makes the taste of dried fruit better.
- The oven should be preheated to 350°F. Apply nonstick spray to your bread pan. Set away for later.
- A large bowl should be emptied of the flour mixture & the baking powder & baking soda, along with cinnamon, allspice, & salt. Whisk the rest of the ingredients in a second dish. Whisk until there are no more lumps. Before serving, add the flour mix and whisk until it's evenly distributed. Drain and combine dried fruit with the batter.
- Bake for around 40-45 Mins unless a toothpick into the middle comes out clear. Remove from the pan after cooling for 15 mins. Before slicing & serving, let the cake cool fully.

Nutrition Information
Calories: 303 kcal, Carbohydrates: 61 g, Protein: 7 g, Fat: 5 g

110. Chocolate Peppermint Cookies
Prep Time: 15 Mins, Cook Time: 15 Mins, Servings: 8
Ingredients
- 4 tbsp butter
- 1 cup sugar coconut
- 2 large eggs
- 1 & ½ cups white flour whole-wheat
- ½ cup powder cocoa
- 1 tsp cornstarch
- 1 tsp soda baking
- 1 tsp extract vanilla
- ½ tsp extract peppermint
- 4 crushed candy canes

Instructions
- The oven should be preheated to 350°F. Butter & sugar should be well mixed in a bowl. Fold in the rest of the ingredients, excluding candy canes.
- Each cookie should be scooped onto a prepared baking tray, one heaping spoonful of cookie batter. Baking time should be between 10 and 12 mins; however, the cookie doesn't need to be cooked in the center to be done. After 5 Mins, garnish with some candy canes. Enjoy!

Nutrition Information
Calories: 197 kcal, Carbohydrates: 35 g, Protein: 4 g, Fat: 6 g

111. Eggnog Macaroons
Prep Time: 15 Mins, Cook Time: 15 Mins, Servings: 2
Ingredients
- 3 cups shredded coconut unsweetened
- ½ cup of eggnog
- 4 large egg whites
- 2 tbsp honey
- ¼ cup flour whole-wheat
- 1 tsp nutmeg ground

Instructions
- The oven should be preheated to 350°F. Line the cookie sheet using parchment paper and lightly coat it using a nonstick spray.
- In a mixing bowl, mix all of the ingredients. Add flour if the batter is too moist to shape into cookies. Place roughly cookie dough on each cookie sheet after reaching the desired consistency.
- Take them out of the oven when they are just beginning to brown. Take out of the oven and wait for it to cool down before serving. If you choose, you may add more ground nutmeg to the dish. Enjoy!

Nutrition Information
Calories: 174 kcal, Carbohydrates: 11 g, Protein: 3 g, Fat: 14 g

112. Gingerbread Brownies
Prep Time:15 Mins, Cook Time: 25 Mins, Servings: 8
Ingredients
- 1 cup white flour whole-wheat
- ¼ cup powder cocoa
- 1 cup sugar coconut
- 1 tsp salt
- 1 tsp soda baking
- 1 tsp cinnamon
- 1 tsp nutmeg
- 1 tsp ginger ground
- ½ tsp ground clove
- ½ tsp allspice
- 2 large eggs
- ½ cup softened butter
- 1/3 cup of molasses

Instructions
- The oven should be preheated to 350°F. Combine the baking soda, flour, sea salt, coconut sugar, cocoa powder, & spices in a large bowl. Combine the butter & eggs in a different dish before adding them to dry ingredients. Mix in molasses until it is well incorporated.
- To bake: Pour into the baking dish. If you can insert a fork into the center & it falls out clear, you've baked it long enough.

Nutrition Information
Calories: 205 kcal, Carbohydrates: 32 g, Protein: 3 g, Fat: 9 g

113. Cinnamon Cookies
Prep Time:20 Mins, Cook Time: 10 Mins, Servings: 10
Ingredients
- 2 cups flour whole-wheat
- 1 tsp soda baking
- ½ tsp baking powder
- ½ tsp salt kosher
- 1 & ½ tsp cinnamon ground
- 1 cup palm sugar coconut
- 2 large eggs
- ½ cup oil coconut
- 1 tsp extract almond
- 1 tbsp cinnamon

Instructions
- The oven should be preheated to 350°F. Two cookie sheets should be lined using parchment paper and sprayed with cooking spray.
- Sift the salt, flour, baking powder, baking soda, & cinnamon in a mixing bowl before adding the milk. Set away for later.
- Gather all of the ingredients into a bowl and stir well. Add flour mix gradually till ball forms. It's best to break it into 24 equal pieces and form each into a ball. Prepare two baking sheets by lining them with parchment paper and arranging the balls 2" apart on each sheet.
- Bake for 8-10 Mins, or unless the edges of the cookies start to brown. Before serving, allow the food to come to room temperature.

Nutrition Information
Calories: 208 kcal, Carbohydrates: 27 g, Protein: 4 g, Fat: 10 g

114. No-Bake Chocolate Peanut Butter Cheesecake
Prep Time: 10 Mins, Cook Time: 35 Mins, Servings: 9
Ingredients
Crust
- 2 oz melted dark chocolate
- 1 cup with skins almonds
- 1 cup oats old-fashioned
- 1/8 tsp salt sea
- 3 tbsp melted coconut oil

Filling
- 13 & ½ oz milk coconut
- 8 & ½ oz cream cheese softened low-fat
- 2/3 cup sugar coconut
- 1 cup natural peanut butter
- 1 tbsp melted coconut oil
- 1 tsp vanilla extract pure

Topping
- 13 & ½ oz milk coconut
- 2 cups of chocolate chips
- ¼ tsp sugar coconut
- 1 tsp vanilla

Instructions
- Preheat oven to 350 degrees.

Crust
- Melt chocolate in a double boiler. Pulse in a food processor till crumbs. Add oats, almonds & salt. A large bowl should combine the toasted almonds, chocolate, & coconut oil. One tbsp of crumbs should be saved for later.
- In a pie pan, combine the crumbs and butter. Crush the bottom & sides of a springform pan equally or use a pan and push crumbs along with the bottom & approximately 0.5 inches up the edges. Remove from the oven after 8-10 Mins & let cool fully.

Filling
- Using an electric mixer, beat the coconut milk in a small bowl unless it's thickened, about 5-6 Mins. When sugar dissolves, add the cream cheese & continue beating for another 2 Mins.
- Beat in the coconut oil, peanut butter, & vanilla till smooth. In a chilled crust, pour the filling and chill for at least 5-6 hrs till it is set.

Topping
- A medium pot should be filled with chocolate chunks, coconut milk, & coconut nectar. Cook on low heat till the chocolate chunks & coconut sugar have melted, and the mixture is smooth. Add the vanilla extract after mixing everything. Cool to room temp before serving. Pour the chocolate topping on the cold pie filling & refrigerate for about two hrs.

Nutrition Information
Calories: 416 kcal, Carbohydrates: 37 g, Protein: 9 g, Fat: 28 g

115. Peppermint Chocolate Fudge
Prep Time: 30 Mins, Cook Time: 40 Mins, Servings: 8
Ingredients
- 3 cups chopped & divided dark chocolate
- 1 & ½ cups chocolate white
- ½ cup divided almond milk
- 2 tbsp divided coconut oil
- 1 tsp oil peppermint

Instructions
- Using parchment paper, line a casserole dish. Add almond milk & coconut oil to melted dark chocolate. Pour into the bottom of the dish that has been pre-made. One hr in the fridge is enough time.
- White chocolate can be melted while you're waiting. Mix the leftover coconut oil, almond milk, & peppermint oil. Evenly spread over the initial layer of chocolate. 1 hr in the fridge

- The leftover dark chocolate should be melted. Pour on top of the chocolate white fudge layer. It's up to you. Let it cool before cutting into squares.

Nutrition Information
Calories: 233 kcal, Carbohydrates: 27 g, Protein: 2 g, Fat: 15 g

116. Poached Pear with Coconut Cream
Prep Time: 20 Mins, Cook Time: 25 Mins, Servings: 5
Ingredients
For Pears
- 2 cups no sugar apple juice
- 2 cups of water
- 2 cups of white wine sweet
- 2 sticks cinnamon
- ½ inch fresh, peeled ginger root
- 1 tsp extract vanilla
- ½ cup of honey
- ½ cup of brandy
- 4 firm, ripe, & peeled pears

For Coconut Cream
- 14 oz cold coconut milk
- 2 tbsp organic powdered sugar
- ½ tsp extract vanilla

Instructions
For Pears
- All ingredients excluding pears should be placed in a big saucepan and brought to a boil. Bring the mixture to a simmer. Put it back on the stove for five more Mins, then lower the heat to a simmer. Take care while adding the pears. Simmer the pears for around 15-20 Mins, stirring periodically, until they are soft and mushy. Remove from the liquid with a spoon & let cool.

For Coconut Cream
- Make sure you don't shake your coconut milk can before opening it. Place coconut solids in a chilled mixing basin & gently scoop them out. Keep the leftover milk within the refrigerator for future use.
- Sugar & vanilla extract should be added to the whipped cream and whipped at a fast speed till the mixture is light & fluffy. Serve with a pear on the side.

Nutrition Information
Calories: 268 kcal, Carbohydrates: 42 g, Protein: 1 g, Fat: 11 g

117. Cinnamon Bun Pancakes
Prep Time: 10 Mins, Cook Time: 20 Mins, Servings: 2
Ingredients
- ¼ cup of coconut flour
- ¼ tsp salt
- 1 tsp soda baking
- 2/3 cup plain Greek yogurt
- 2 large egg whites
- 3 tbsp honey
- 1 tsp extract vanilla
- ¼ cup milk coconut
- 1 tbsp cinnamon

Instructions
- Combine the flour, salt, & baking soda in a medium mixing bowl, then whisk until
- well blended.
- Combine yogurt, honey, vanilla, egg whites, & coconut milk in a second dish. Add flour milk gradually to the yogurt mixture. The batter should be well mixed; add coconut milk to soften it down if it's too thick. Combine batter and cinnamon in a mixing bowl.
- Snip a Ziploc bag & put aside your cinnamon batter.
- Pour nonstick spray into a medium-sized pan and heat over medium-high heat. As soon as the pan is hot, spoon batter onto the skillet and flatten it into a pancake. Use the cinnamon batter to pipe the spiral over the pancake, beginning from the middle and working outwards.
- Immediately but gently turn the pancake once the edges start to dry out & bubbles start to burst in the middle. Cook till the reverse side is a deep golden-brown color. Repeat the same with the rest of the batter.
- For a sweet treat, top with cream cheese icing and some maple syrup, fresh fruit, or honey!

Nutrition Information
Calories: 192 kcal, Carbohydrates: 22 g, Protein: 8 g, Fat: 9 g

118. Chocolate Truffles
Prep Time: 15 Mins, Cook Time: 25 Mins, Servings: 2
Ingredients
- 8 oz chocolate dark
- ¼ cup oil coconut
- 3 tbsp milk coconut
- 1 tsp extract vanilla
- ¼ cup powder cocoa

Instructions
- Mix chocolate, oil, & coconut milk in a boiler & constantly stir until smooth and creamy. Add vanilla once the chocolate has melted & removed from heat. Serve in an 8" baking dish & chill until the chocolate could be shaped into a circle, approximately two hrs.
- Scoop into 1" balls when pliable. Toss in chocolate chips. Refrigerate in the airtight container.

Nutrition Information
Calories: 142 kcal, Carbohydrates: 13 g, Protein: 1 g, Fat: 11 g

119. Orange Spice Cookies
Prep Time: 10 Mins, Cook Time: 20 Mins, Servings: 2
Ingredients
- 1 cup flour whole-wheat
- 1/3 cup flour almond
- 1 tsp powder baking
- 1 tsp soda baking
- 1 tsp ginger ground
- ½ tsp cinnamon ground
- ½ tsp clove ground
- ¼ tsp cardamom ground
- ½ tsp salt kosher
- 2 tbsp melted coconut oil
- 1 large egg
- ½ tsp extract almond
- ¼ cup of molasses
- ¼ cup palm sugar coconut
- 3 tbsp zest orange

Instructions
- Preheat your oven to 325°F. To prevent your cookies from sticking to the pan, use parchment paper.
- If you're using cardamom or cloves (if you're not), you may also add them to the flour mixture. Set away for later. Combine the egg, oil, & almond essence in a separate dish. Once the palm sugar, molasses, & orange zest have been blended, whisk them in. Add flour mixture one tbsp at a time, mixing well after each addition. Refrigerate for one hr, covered.
- On a cookie sheet that has been preheated, drop a spoonful of cookie dough (approximately 1 tbsp). It's done when the edges start to brown. To remove the cookies from the baking pan, allow them to cool for approximately 10 mins before doing so.

Nutrition Information
Calories: 150 kcal, Carbohydrates: 22 g, Protein: 3 g, Fat: 8 g

120. White Chocolate Pomegranate Bark
Prep Time: 10 Mins, Cook Time: 25 Mins, Servings: 2
Ingredients
- 2 cups chopped white chocolate
- 1 tbsp melted coconut oil
- ½ cup seeds pomegranate
- 2 tbsp finely chopped pistachios

Instructions
- Set aside a parchment-lined cookie sheet.
- White chocolate may be melted in a heavy saucepan on low heat. Gently whisk in the pomegranate seeds, coconut oil, & chopped pistachios, being sure to avoid breaking apart pomegranate seeds. Spread the mixture evenly on the cookie sheet.
- Allow solidifying for a few Mins before moving on. Store big chunks in the airtight container. Enjoy!

Nutrition Information
Calories: 145 kcal, Carbohydrates: 15 g, Protein: 2 g, Fat: 9 g

121. Slow Cooker Hot Fudge Cake
Prep Time: 20 Mins, Cook Time: 2 hrs 15 Mins, Servings: 3
Ingredients
Cake
- 1 cup of flour
- ¾ cup sugar coconut
- ¼ cup of cocoa
- 2 tsp powder baking
- ¼ tsp sea salt or kosher
- ½ cup canned coconut milk
- 2 tsp vanilla pure
- ¼ cup melted butter
- ½ cup chocolate chips dark

Fudge Sauce
- ¼ cup powder cocoa
- ¾ cup sugar coconut
- 1 tsp vanilla pure
- 1 & ¾ cups boiling water

Instructions
- Spray the inside of the slow cooker using cooking spray before using it for the first time.
- Dry ingredients should be whisked together in a small mixing basin. Make sure that all of the ingredients are mixed before serving. Place 3-4 quarts of cake batter in the crock pot. The batter would be thick. Add chocolate chips to the batter and mix well.
- Pour the sauce over the cake batter once it has been whipped up. On high for 2-3 hrs, or unless the surface is set, cover & cook. Allow the cake to cool for around 15 mins before dishing it out of the slow cooker.

Nutrition Information
Calories: 320 kcal, Carbohydrates: 58 g, Protein: 3 g, Fat: 11 g

122. Pumpkin Cheesecake Shooters
Prep Time: 30 Mins, Cook Time: 30 Mins, Servings: 1
Ingredients
Crust
- ½ cup of almond
- 2 tbsp sugar coconut
- 1 tbsp oil coconut

Filling
- 4 oz lite softened cream cheese
- ½ cup puree pumpkin
- 1 tsp spice pumpkin pie
- ¼ cup sugar coconut
- 1 & ½ cups of whipped
- 8 sticks cinnamon

Instructions
- Pulse coconut sugar, nuts, & coconut oil in a mini food processor till fine crumbs form. Layer breadcrumbs and fill within shot glasses or pour an equal quantity into each.
- Cream cheese should be smooth & creamy when using a mixer. Pumpkin spice, pumpkin puree, & coconut sugar should be added to the mixture. The sugar should be dissolved and the mixture smooth. Add whipped topping and mix well to combine the two ingredients.
- Using a spatula, divide the mixture evenly among the shot glasses.
- Add a dab of topping to every shot glass to complete the look. Sprinkle with some cinnamon and any leftover crumbs, if desired.

Nutrition Information
Calories: 251 kcal, Carbohydrates: 18 g, Protein: 2 g, Fat: 19 g

123. Grandma's Coconut Cream Pie
Prep Time: 10 Mins, Cook Time: 30 Mins, Servings: 1
Ingredients
Filling
- 1 9" crust pie
- 2 tbsp flour
- 2 tbsp cornstarch
- ½ tsp sea salt or kosher
- 1 cup organic sugar
- 3 large egg yolks
- 2 cups coconut milk regular
- 1 tsp vanilla
- 1 tbsp butter
- ¾ cup freshly shredded coconut

Meringue
- 3 large egg whites
- ¼ cup organic sugar

Instructions
- Before baking, prick the pie crust several times with a fork. When preparing the filling, bake your crust as per the instructions on the box.
- Pour the dry ingredients for the filling into a large pot. Add egg yolks, then gently pour milk and whisk until it's all incorporated. Turn the heat up to medium and constantly whisk until the mixture reaches a pudding-like texture. Remove from the stove and stir in the butter and vanilla extract.
- You should be able to comfortably rest your palm on the pot when the filling is cool enough. Stir & add coconut to complete the dish. Cool crust before adding the filling.
- The oven should be preheated at 375°F.

Meringue
- Using a mixer, whip the egg whites till they are frothy. Continue beating till crisp-tender & the sugar is completely dissolved, one spoonful at a time.
- The meringue should be distributed evenly over your pie filling, ensuring it reaches the crust edges. Sprinkle the additional coconut over the top.
- Place the pie over a baking sheet inside the middle of the oven & bake it for about 12-15 Mins, being careful not to overcook the meringue or the coconut. Leave to cool at room temp before serving. Chilled pie may be served as well as room temp pie.

Nutrition Information
Calories: 313 kcal, Carbohydrates: 34 g, Protein: 3 g, Fat: 19 g

124. Classic Pumpkin Pie with Maple Crust
Prep Time: 10 Mins, Cook Time: 20 Mins, Servings: 6
Ingredients
For Crust
- 2 cups of flour
- ¼ tsp kosher salt
- 1/3 cup cold coconut oil
- 2 tbsp plain Greek yogurt
- 1 tbsp vinegar apple cider
- 1 tbsp maple syrup pure
- ¼ cup cold water

Instructions
- Preheat the oven to around 350 degrees Fahrenheit.
- Pour cool coconut oil and flour into a big basin. Store the oil within the fridge until you're ready to utilize it. Make sure that the oil is broken up into pea-sized pieces using the fork. Add vinegar, maple syrup, & Greek yogurt to the mixture. The dough should be shaped into

a ball after careful mixing. Ideally, the dough must stay together into a ball shape without being too sticky.
- Roll out the dough to ¼" thick on the floured board. Take care while transferring to a pie crust. Apply the fork prick, then cover with Al foil. Remove the foil from the pan and place the weight over the top, including an empty pan or dried beans. Allow cooking for 15 Mins.

Nutrition Information
Calories: 205 kcal, Carbohydrates: 34 g, Protein: 4 g, Fat: 7 g

125. Pumpkin Trifle
Prep Time: 20 mins, Cook Time: 20 mins, Servings: 6
Ingredients
- 12 oatmeal cookies
- 3 cups pumpkin puree
- ½ cup plain Greek yogurt
- 1 tsp cinnamon
- ¼ tsp ginger ground
- ¼ tsp nutmeg ground
- ¼ tsp clove ground
- 2 tbsp honey
- 2 tbsp sugar coconut
- 2 cups Greek yogurt vanilla

Instructions
- Large bits of cookies should be chopped.
- In a big mixing bowl, combine all rest of the ingredients in a large mixing bowl, except the vanilla Greek yogurt.
- Layer cookies in a big, transparent bowl or the trifle dish, then pumpkin mix, then vanilla Greek yogurt on top. Repeat the procedure until there are no more ingredients, or the bowl is filled. Vanilla yogurt will be the topmost part. If desired, sprinkle cinnamon on top.

Nutrition Information
Calories: 259 kcal, Carbohydrates: 39 g, Protein: 8 g, Fat: 9 g

126. Slow Cooker Stuffed Apples
Prep Time: 15 mins, Cook Time: 2 hrs, Servings: 4
Ingredients
- 1 cup oats rolled
- ¼ cup chopped walnuts
- 2 tbsp cranberries dried
- 2 tbsp raw honey
- 2 tbsp oil coconut
- 1 tsp cinnamon
- 1 tsp nutmeg
- 1 tsp allspice
- 5 apples green

Instructions
- Combine the coconut oil, cranberries, honey, oats, walnuts, & spices. Mix until everything is fully blended, and everything is sticking together. Fill the apples halfway with the mixture. Cook for 2 hrs on low.

Nutrition Information
Calories: 254 kcal, Carbohydrates: 44 g, Protein: 3 g, Fat: 8 g

127. Pumpkin Pie Chia Pudding
Prep Time: 10 mins, Cook Time: 8 hrs 10 mins, Servings: 4
Ingredients
- 2 cups canned coconut milk
- 1 cup puree pumpkin
- ¼ cup sugar coconut
- 1 tsp cinnamon
- ½ tsp ginger
- ½ tsp nutmeg
- ¼ tsp allspice
- ½ cup seeds chia
- 4 tbsp topping whipped

Instructions
- Add all the ingredients to a blender, except the chia seeds, and mix till smooth. Pulse till the chia seeds are blended.
- Cover and chill the mix overnight in four mason jars and pastry plates.
- Before serving, garnish with whipped if desired.

Nutrition Information
Calories: 252 kcal, Carbohydrates: 24 g, Protein: 5 g, Fat: 16 g

128. Slow Cooker Cinnamon Apples
Prep Time: 15 mins, Cook Time: 2 hrs, Servings: 4
Ingredients
- 8 peeled & sliced apples cored
- ¼ cup sugar coconut
- 2 tsp freshly squeezed lemon juice
- 2 tsp cinnamon
- ½ tsp nutmeg

Instructions
- In your slow cooker, combine all of the ingredients. Cook for around 3-4 hrs on low, then serve!

Nutrition Information
Calories: 136 kcal, Carbohydrates: 36 g, Protein: 1 g, Fat: 0 g

129. Gluten-Free Pumpkin Apple Muffin
Prep Time: 10 mins, Cook Time: 15 mins, Servings: 6
Ingredients
- 4 large eggs
- ½ cup of applesauce
- ½ cup of pumpkin puree
- ½ cup of coconut flour
- 2 tbsp cinnamon
- ¼ tsp cloves ground
- ¼ tsp ginger ground
- 1/8 tsp nutmeg ground
- ¼ tsp salt sea
- 1 tsp soda baking
- 2 tsp vanilla
- 4 tbsp oil coconut
- 1 tbsp honey

Instructions
- Preheat the oven to around 375°F.
- The cooking spray may be used to line muffin tins. In your blender, combine all of the ingredients. On moderate speed, blend till barely mixed. 8 muffin pans, equally divided muffin batter
- Bake for around 12-15 mins, till a toothpick in the middle, comes out clear. Allow cooling completely before removing & serving.
- Enjoy!

Nutrition Information
Calories: 149 kcal, Carbohydrates: 11 g, Protein: 4 g, Fat: 10 g

130. Almond Crumb Pie Crust
Prep Time: 10 mins, Cook Time: 10 mins, Servings: 4
Ingredients
- 1 cup raw almonds
- 1 cup oats old-fashioned
- sea salt or pinch kosher
- ½ tsp cinnamon
- ¼ cup palm sugar coconut
- ¼ cup melted coconut oil

Instructions
- Preheat the oven to 350°F.
- Combine oats, salt, almonds, & cinnamon in chopping equipment. Pulse until the mixture resembles fine crumbs, taking care not to convert into flour. Combine coconut sugar, crumbs, & melted oil in a large mixing bowl.
- Fill a springform pan halfway with crumb mixture. Crumbs should be pressed into the bottom & edges of the pan.
- Bake for around 8-10 mins on the middle oven rack, then remove & cool fully before pouring the filling.

Nutrition Information
Calories: 149 kcal, Carbohydrates: 14 g, Protein: 4 g, Fat: 9 g

131. Banana Nut Muffins
Prep Time: 15 mins, Cook Time: 15 mins, Servings: 3
Ingredients
Dry
- 1 & ½ cups of flour
- 1 tsp powder baking
- 1 tsp soda baking
- ½ tsp sea salt or kosher
- ½ tsp cinnamon ground
- ¾ cup sugar coconut
- ½ cup pieces walnut

Wet
- 1 large, beaten egg
- 3 overripe, peeled & mashed bananas
- 1/3 cup melted coconut oil
- 1 tsp extract real vanilla

Instructions
- Preheat the oven to 350°F and gently grease or line the muffin tray using cupcake paper.
- Combine flour, salt, baking soda, baking powder, & cinnamon in a mixing bowl.
- Whisk coconut oil, coconut sugar, eggs, bananas, & vanilla in a large dish. Stir in the dry ingredients and walnuts till just mixed. Fill a 12-cup muffin tray halfway with batter.
- Bake for 12 mins, or till golden brown and a probe inserted in the center comes out clear.

Nutrition Information
Calories: 210 kcal, Carbohydrates: 35 g, Protein: 3 g, Fat: 8 g

132. Peanut Butter & Coconut Crunchies
Prep Time: 30 Mins, Cook Time: 40 Mins, Servings: 3
Ingredients
- 1 & ½ cups of old-fashioned gluten-free oats
- ¼ tsp sea salt or kosher
- 1 cup natural peanut butter
- 1 & ¼ cups finely grated coconut
- ¼ cup raw honey
- 1 tsp vanilla pure
- ½ cup chocolate chips mini

Instructions
- Preheat the oven to 300°F.
- Toast the oats on a baking pan for 15 min.
- Leave to cool after removing from the oven.
- Mix all of the ingredients along with your hands.
- Make 20 1" balls out of the dough.
- Add some water, if necessary, till crunchies stay together when formed into balls.
- On a dish or parchment paper, sprinkle with more coconut.
- Roll your dough in 20 balls and roll each one in coconut.
- Refrigerate the wrapped balls for 1 hr or until they are firm.

Nutrition Information
Calories: 163 kcal, Carbohydrates: 15 g, Protein: 5 g, Fat: 10 g

133. 5-Ingredient Peanut Butter Chocolate Chip Cookies
Prep Time: 10 Mins, Cook Time: 25 Mins, Servings: 6
Ingredients
- 1 cup natural peanut butter
- ½ cup palm sugar coconut
- 1 large, beaten egg
- 1 tsp extract vanilla
- 2/3 cup of chocolate chips

Instructions
- Preheat the oven to 350°F.
- Add peanut butter, beaten egg, coconut sugar, & vanilla extract. Add the chocolate chips and mix well.
- Roll the cookie dough in 1" balls, making 16 balls. Place on the cookie sheet coated with parchment paper.
- To make typical peanut cookie crosshatch markings & flatten your balls, wet the fork & dip it into coconut sugar. Press balls in one way & afterward in the other.
- Bake your cookies for 6 mins in the center oven rack before rotating the baking sheet & bake for another 5-6 mins. Leave to cool for approximately 25-30 mins on a baking sheet before lifting with the spatula. Enjoy!

Nutrition Information
Calories: 171 kcal, Carbohydrates: 16 g, Protein: 4 g, Fat: 11 g

134. Chocolate Strawberry Cups
Prep Time: 10 mins, Cook Time: 40 Mins, Servings: 5
Ingredients
- ½ cup hulled strawberries
- 1 tbsp honey
- 1 tsp lemon juice
- ½ cup canned coconut milk
- 1/3 cup fat-free, softened cream cheese
- 5 oz coarsely chopped milk chocolate

Garnish
- 7 quartered strawberries
- fresh mint leaves

Instructions
- Combine the strawberries, honey, and lemon juice in a blender and puree until smooth.
- Whisk both coconut milk and cream cheese together in a small mixing bowl unless smooth. Chill for around 2 hrs after adding it to a strawberry purée.
- Microwave the chocolate inside a medium microwave-safe dish for 10 seconds at the moment, stirring after each until melted. Be cautious not to burn the food.
- Fill a tiny muffin tray using paper liners & spoon the melted chocolate into each one. Allow to solidify and take off paper liners after rotating to cover both sides.
- Fill your chocolate cups halfway with strawberry cream & the remaining strawberries & mint leaves.

Nutrition Information
Calories: 100 kcal, Carbohydrates: 10 g, Protein: 2 g, Fat: 6 g

135. Chocolate, Fruit, & Nut Clusters
Prep Time: 10 Mins, Cook Time: 55 Mins, Servings: 4
Ingredients
- ¾ cup chips dark chocolate
- ¼ cup chips white chocolate
- 2 tbsp divided coconut oil
- ¼ cup lightly chopped dried fruit
- ¼ cup slivers almond

Instructions
- On a baking sheet that can fit inside the freezer, place a layer of parchment paper.
- In a large saucepan on low heat, melt the dark chocolate. Melt your white chocolate in a second small saucepan. Half of the coconut oil goes into the white chocolate & the other half goes into the dark chocolate. Make a thorough mixture.
- Allow the chocolates to chill somewhat before serving but keep them apart.
- Combine the dried fruit, dark chocolate, & almonds. Drop a spoonful of the batter onto the baking sheet. Melt your white chocolate and drizzle it over each drop. Cover loosely using plastic wrap & freeze for 1 hr or until firm.
- Enjoy!

Nutrition Information
Calories: 159 kcal, Carbohydrates: 16 g, Protein: 2 g, Fat: 11 g

136. Strawberry Yogurt Muffins
Prep Time: 15 mins, Cook Time: 25 mins, Servings: 8
Ingredients
- 1 & ¼ cups of white flour whole-wheat
- 1/3 cup oats old-fashioned
- ½ tsp cinnamon

- ½ tsp soda baking
- 1 tsp powder baking
- ½ tsp salt sea
- 2/3 cup sugar coconut
- ¾ cup of Greek yogurt
- 2 lightly beaten egg large
- 1/3 cup of coconut oil
- 1 cup diced strawberries

Instructions
- Preheat the oven to 375°F. Fill muffin pan with muffin papers.
- Whisk together dry ingredients in a blender or food processor dish.
- Whisk the egg, yogurt, & oil in a separate mixing dish, then fold in strawberries. Pour the wet ingredients into the dry ingredients & whisk just until everything is incorporated.
- Bake for around 25 mins, or till brown and wooden skewer in the center comes out clear. Allow time for the muffins to chill completely before serving. Enjoy!

Nutrition Information
Calories: 177 kcal, Carbohydrates: 24 g, Protein: 4 g, Fat: 8 g

137. Olive Oil Honey Banana Bread
Prep Time: 15 mins, Cook Time: 50 mins, Servings: 4

Ingredients
Wet
- 3 overripe, peeled & mashed brown bananas
- 1/3 cup olive oil extra virgin
- ¾ cup of honey
- 1 large, beaten egg
- 1 tsp vanilla extract real

Dry
- 1 & ½ cups white flour whole-wheat
- 1 tsp soda baking
- 1/8 tsp sea salt or kosher
- ½ tsp cinnamon ground

Instructions
- Preheat the oven to 350°F.
- Using cooking spray, coat the loaf pan.
- In a small mixing bowl, whisk together wet ingredients till smooth.
- Sift all dry ingredients in a second large mixing bowl.
- Combine the wet & dry ingredients in a mixing bowl and whisk with a spoon till barely mixed. But don't over the ingredients.
- If using, toss in walnuts & chocolate chips.
- Fill loaf pan halfway with batter, then bake for around 50-60 mins, or till knife tip comes out clear.
- Leave to cool completely in the loaf pan over a wire rack before cutting.
- Enjoy!

Nutrition Information
Calories: 202 kcal, Carbohydrates: 35 g, Protein: 3 g, Fat: 7 g

138. Clean Eating Chocolate Bundt Cake
Prep Time: 15 mins, Cook Time: 40 mins, Servings: 3

Ingredients
Dry
- 2 cups of flour
- ½ cup powder cocoa
- ½ tsp sea salt or kosher
- 1 tsp soda baking
- ½ tsp powder baking
- 1 & ½ cups palm sugar coconut
- ½ cup chips chocolate

Wet
- ½ cup plain Greek yogurt
- 2 large eggs
- 1 & ½ tsp vanilla
- 1 cup melted coconut oil

- Sauce Chocolate
- ½ cup chocolate chips semisweet
- ¼ cup lite canned coconut milk
- 1 tbsp palm sugar coconut
- ½ tsp vanilla

Instructions
Cake
- Preheat the oven to 350°F.
- A 10-12 cupcake pan should be oiled and floured.
- Set aside all dry ingredients after whisking them together. In a bowl, add the wet ingredients & beat using a mixer until thoroughly blended. Combine the dry & wet ingredients in a mixing bowl and whisk just unless mixed.
- Pour the batter into the pan that has been prepared. Shake the pan to spread the batter evenly. Cook for around 40 mins, till the cake tester inserted in the center, comes out clear. Allow for around 15 mins of cooling within the pan before inverting onto the cooling rack.

Sauce
- In a medium saucepan over medium heat, combine all ingredients & whisk regularly till the chocolate has dissolved & ingredients are combined. Remove from the heat and set aside to cool.
- Place your cake on a cake stand & pour a sauce on it.

Nutrition Information
Calories: 310 kcal, Carbohydrates: 37 g, Protein: 4 g, Fat: 18 g

139. Yogurt & Blueberry Jam Popsicles
Prep Time: 20 mins, Cook Time: 6 hrs 20 mins, Servings: 5

Ingredients
Crunchy Granola
- ½ cup oats old-fashioned
- 1 tbsp oil coconut
- 1 tbsp of honey

Yogurt & Blueberry Mixture
- 2 cups non-fat, plain Greek yogurt
- 1/3 cup almond milk vanilla
- 2 tbsp raw honey
- ½ tsp vanilla extract pure
- 1/3 cup spread blueberry fruit

Instructions
Granola
- Add the oats to a small pan over moderate heat. Toast the oats for 3-4 mins, stirring regularly, until golden. Toss in the oil & honey to coat the grains. Leave to cool after removing from the heat.

Yogurt and Blueberry Mix
- Combine milk, honey, yogurt, & vanilla in a mixing bowl & whisk until smooth. With the butter knife, stir in the blueberry fruit spreading.
- Fill popsicle molds evenly with the yogurt mixture. 1 tbsp granola should be added to the popsicle mixture. Before eating, place within the freezer for 6 hrs.
- To unmold, run the popsicle mold under hot water from the tap for some seconds, taking care not to allow any water inside the mold or leave it on the counter for some time to thaw around the edges.

Nutrition Information
Calories: 161 kcal, Carbohydrates: 25 g, Protein: 25 g, Fat: 3 g

140. Best Ever Applesauce-Spice Muffins
Prep Time: 15 mins, Cook Time: 20 mins, Servings: 8

Ingredients
- 2 & ½ cups of white flour whole-wheat
- 1 & 2/3 cups palm sugar coconut
- 1 & ½ tsp soda baking
- 1 tsp salt sea
- ¼ tsp powder baking
- ¼ tsp allspice
- 1 cup diced walnut pieces

- 2 tsp cinnamon
- ¼ tsp cloves
- 1 cored, peeled, & diced apple
- 2 beaten eggs
- ½ cup of Greek yogurt
- 1 & ½ cups no sugar applesauce
- 1 tsp vanilla pure
- 1/3 cup oil coconut

Instructions
- Preheat your oven to around 350°F.
- In muffin pans, place paper. Combine all the dry ingredients in a mixing bowl.
- Toss in the walnuts with the dry ingredients.
- In a separate medium mixing bowl, whisk the rest of the ingredients until well incorporated. Pour the wet ingredients into the dry ingredients & whisk just until everything is incorporated.
- Fill Eighteen muffin cups two-thirds full of batter and bake for 20 mins.
- Allow time for the muffins to get normal completely before serving. On the second day, those muffins are still fantastic!

Nutrition Information
Calories: 218 kcal, Carbohydrates: 39 g, Protein: 4 g, Fat: 6 g

141. Avocado & Chicken Wrap
Prep Time: 10 Mins, Cook Time: 30 Mins, Servings: 1
Ingredients
- 2 chicken breasts bone-in
- 2 tsp olive oil extra virgin
- ½ tsp sea salt or kosher
- ½ tsp pepper black
- ½ tsp powder chili
- 1 peeled, pitted, & chopped avocado ripe
- 1 tbsp freshly squeezed lime juice
- 1 cup quartered cherry tomatoes
- 4 sliced scallions
- 2 cups chopped bibb lettuce
- 15 oz beans refried
- ½ cup no sugar salsa
- 8 tortillas whole-grain

Instructions
- Preheat the oven to 350°F.
- Clean the chicken breasts by rinsing them and drying them using a paper towel.

Drizzle olive oil over the chicken and season with salt, pepper, & chili powder. Bake for 60 mins, or till juices flow clear when probed using a fork in the oven-safe pan.
- Remove your chicken from the oven & set it aside until it is cold enough to handle. Remove the skin and throw it away.
- Remove your chicken off the bone & shred it into strips with your hands.
- While the chicken cools, mash the diced avocado, remaining pepper, and salt, & lime juice together using a fork. Place stewed beans in your saucepan & heat at medium-low heat till heated.
- Warm tortillas into a dry pan on medium heat for 1 min each side, or till warm. Equal portions of tomatoes, salsa, lettuce, refried beans, shredded chicken, & scallions should be spread on heated tortillas. Each one should be topped with the mashed avocado mix. To serve, tuck its end under & roll every wrap.

Nutrition Information
Calories: 238 kcal, Carbohydrates: 23 g, Protein: 14 g, Fat: 11 g

142. Coconut Halva Balls
Prep Time: 20 Mins, Cook Time: 30 Mins, Servings: 10
Ingredients
- ½ cup diced walnut pieces
- 1 & ½ cups gluten-free oats old-fashioned
- ¼ tsp sea salt or kosher
- 1 cup of tahini
- 1 cup no sugar finely grated coconut
- ¼ cup raw honey
- ½ tsp vanilla pure

Instructions
- Preheat the oven to 325°F.
- Toast the oats & walnuts on a baking sheet for around 12 mins. Leave to cool after removing from the oven.
- In a mixing bowl, add all of the ingredients & whisk to blend.
- On a dish or parchment paper, sprinkle with more coconut. Roll your dough in 18 balls and roll them within the coconut.
- Refrigerate wrapped balls for 1 hr or until firm.

Nutrition Information
Calories: 109 kcal, Carbohydrates: 11 g, Protein: 2 g, Fat: 7 g

143. Grandma's Southern Peach Cobbler
Prep Time: 30 Mins, Cook Time: 40 Mins, Servings: 4
Ingredients
Peach
- 8 peeled, pitted, & sliced peaches
- 1/3 cup sugar coconut
- 1 tbsp cornstarch
- ½ tsp ground cinnamon
- ¼ tsp sea salt or kosher
- 1 tsp freshly squeezed lemon juice
- 2 tbsp water
- 1 tsp vanilla pure

Biscuit Topping
- 1 cup of flour
- 1 tsp powder baking
- ¼ tsp soda baking
- ½ tsp sea salt or kosher
- 2 tbsp sugar coconut
- 4 tbsp butter cold
- ½ cup low-fat buttermilk
- 1 tsp melted butter

Instructions
- Preheat the oven to 375°F.
- Combine the cornstarch, cinnamon, coconut sugar, & salt in a mixing bowl.
- Toss in the peaches, water, lemon juice, & vanilla extract.
- Fill a casserole dish halfway with the ingredients and lay it on the baking sheet.
- While making the biscuit topping, bake the peach mix for 15 mins.
- Meanwhile, combine flour, salt, soda, baking powder, and coconut sugar in a mixing bowl. Cut butter in flour mixture with a pastry cutter till fine crumbs form.
- In the middle of the flour, form a well & gently pour there in buttermilk.
- Stir just long enough to moisten the dry ingredients.
- Drop Ten spoons of dough onto the heated peach filling. Brush the tops of the biscuits with melted butter and coconut sugar. When the dough is baked, it will spread a little.
- Place the cobbler over a baking sheet & bake for 35-40 mins, or until the biscuits are brown and the mixture is bubbling. Leave to cool for a few mins before serving.

Nutrition Information
Calories: 185 kcal, Carbohydrates: 23 g, Protein: 3 g, Fat: 6 g

144. Slow Cooker Apple Crisp
Prep Time: 15 mins, Cook Time: 4 hrs, Servings: 3
Ingredients
- 6 cups diced apples
- 2 tbsp juice lemon
- 1 cup palm sugar coconut
- ¾ cup flour whole-wheat

- ½ cup oats rolled
- 2 tsp cinnamon
- 1 tsp nutmeg
- ½ tsp allspice
- sea salt or kosher
- 4 tbsp coconut oil or butter

Instructions
- In the slow cooker, arrange the apples in a single layer. Toss in lemon juice & mix well. Then, add sucanat & cinnamon, then mix until the apples are coated with the sweetener.
- Flour, oats, & the rest of the sucanat, along with the other spices and salt, should be combined in a different bowl. Add the butter using a pastry blender when the mixture matches coarse crumbs.
- The apples should be fully coated in this crumb mixture.
- Allow your apple crisp to simmer for four hrs on low in your slow cooker.

Nutrition Information
Calories: 218 kcal, Carbohydrates: 42.2 g, Protein: 1.7 g, Fat: 5.1 g

145. Clean Eating Thumbprint Cookies
Prep Time: 20 mins, Cook Time: 10 mins, Servings: 12
Ingredients
- ¼ cup sugar coconut
- ½ cup butter pure
- 1 large, separated egg
- ½ tsp vanilla extract pure
- 1 cup of flour
- ¼ tsp sea salt or kosher
- 1 cup crushed walnuts
- 2/3 cup fruit-sweetened jam

Instructions
- Preheat the oven to 350°F.
- Combine the butter, coconut sugar, & egg yolk in a small bowl & beat at moderate speed until well blended. Mix in the vanilla extract until it is well incorporated.
- Combine flour & salt in a medium mixing bowl. Stir in the flour & salt until everything is well combined. Form the dough into 1" balls & roll them in gently whisked egg whites. Place an individual ball on a baking sheet & roll in smashed walnuts.
- Make a huge indentation in the middle of every ball with your thumb to allow for the addition of jam. Fill cookie centers with fruit spread. Bake for 8-10 mins, or until brown. Remove the cookies from the oven and set them aside to cool until eating.

Nutrition Information
Calories: 223 kcal, Carbohydrates: 23 g, Protein: 4 g, Fat: 14 g

146. Sangria Fruitsicles
Prep Time: 10 Mins, Cook Time: 45 Mins, Servings: 10
Ingredients
- 2 cups wine red
- ¼ cup sec triple
- 2 cups soda club
- ¼ cup juice orange
- ¼ cup of honey
- 1 cup berries frozen mixed
- 1 peeled & sliced kiwi
- 1 small slice of nectarine

Instructions
- Combine the wine, orange juice, club soda, triple sec, & honey in a mixing glass. Fill Eight popsicle molds with appropriate fruit, then pour in the wine mixture.
- Place the sticks in the fridge or freezer, or till completely frozen.

Nutrition Information
Calories: 118 kcal, Carbohydrates: 21 g, Protein: 1 g, Fat: 6 g

147. Strawberry & Rhubarb Galette
Prep Time: 25 Mins, Cook Time: 55 Mins, Servings: 10
Ingredients
Crust
- 1 & ¼ cups of white flour whole-wheat
- 1 tbsp palm sugar coconut
- ¼ tsp sea salt or kosher
- ½ cup of virgin solid coconut oil
- 2-3 tbsp ice-cold water

Filling
- 2 cups halved, hulled strawberries
- 1 cup diced rhubarb
- 2 tbsp sugar coconut
- 2 tbsp water

Instructions
- In a food processor equipped with the s-blade, combine flour, coconut sugar, & salt. To combine the ingredients, pulse them together. Pulse in some coconut oil until the mixture resembles pea-sized fragments.
- If you don't have access to the food processor, you may do it manually by whisking that flour mix first and using your fingers to combine coconut oil till crumbs form.
- Pulse in your processor as you pour an ice water.
- The dough mustn't be too moist to join together after being chilled.
- Make a ball out of the dough. Refrigerate for around 30 mins after wrapping it securely in plastic wrap & pushing to take the ball altogether.
- Meanwhile, in your saucepan over medium heat, combine all filling ingredients. Cook, stirring regularly, for approximately 15 mins, or unless the rhubarb has wilted. The fruit filling may be used right away or kept refrigerated until needed.
- Form your dough into a disc and lay between 2 wax papers, pressing flat using a rolling pin to approximately ½-inch thickness. To make a ring for the galette, place an upturned salad plate over the top of this dough & draw around this using a knife.
- Preheat the oven to around 350°F. On the baking sheet, place your dough. Fill your dough with fruit filling, allowing 2" around all sides. To make a crust, fold the galette's edges over. The leftover coconut sugar should be sprinkled on top.
- Bake for around 20-25 mins, or till golden brown & filling is steaming.

Nutrition Information
Calories: 218 kcal, Carbohydrates: 23 g, Protein: 3 g, Fat: 14 g

148. Corn Bread Cake with Fresh Nectarines
Prep Time: 10 Mins, Cook Time: 35 Mins, Servings: 5
Ingredients
Dry
- 1 & ½ cup of cornmeal
- ½ cup of flour
- ½ tsp sea salt or kosher
- 2 tsp powder baking
- ½ tsp soda baking

Wet
- 1/3 cup sugar coconut
- ¼ cup oil coconut
- 1 & ¾ cup of milk
- 1 beaten egg
- 1 tsp vanilla extract pure

Topping
- 2 thinly sliced nectarines
- 2 tsp oil coconut

Instructions
- Preheat the oven to 400°F.
- A 10" cast-iron skillet should be lightly oiled.
- In a small mixing basin, combine wet ingredients. In a mixing bowl, combine dry ingredients.
- Combine wet & dry ingredients in a mixing bowl and whisk until incorporated.

- In a pan over moderate heat, melt 2 tbsp coconut oil & add nectarines. To soften, sauté for approximately 5 mins.
- Pour the corncake batter into the pan that has been prepared. Nectarines should be arranged in series on the cornmeal mixture.
- Preheat the oven to 350°F and bake for around 25 mins, till a wooden skewer in the middle comes out clear.

Nutrition Information
Calories: 223 kcal, Carbohydrates: 34 g, Protein: 3 g, Fat: 9 g

149. Peach and Blueberry Crumble
Prep Time: 20 Mins, Cook Time: 40 Mins, Servings: 4
Ingredients
Crumble
- 1 cup old-fashioned oats
- ½ cup white flour whole-wheat
- ½ cup sugar coconut
- 1/3 cup melted or solid coconut oil
- sea salt or kosher

Filling
- 1 cup fresh blueberries
- 6 peaches of ripe, peeled, cored still firm
- ¼ cup sugar coconut
- 3 tbsp flour
- ½ tsp cinnamon
- 1/8 tsp salt
- 1 zest & juice lemon

Instructions
- Preheat the oven to 350°F.
- In a medium mixing bowl, crumble ingredients & mix well using a fork. The mixture should resemble a crumbly mixture. Remove from the equation.
- Toss peaches, blueberries, & dry ingredients in a second dish to coat. Stir in the lemon juice and zest until everything is well combined. Fill 8 ramekins halfway with the crumble ingredients and distribute evenly.
- Place the filled ramekins over a prepared baking sheet in the oven. Bake for around 45 mins, or unless the filling is boiling & the tips are brown.

Nutrition Information
Calories: 259 kcal, Carbohydrates: 44 g, Protein: 5 g, Fat: 9 g

150. Mint Chocolate Chip Banana Popsicles
Prep Time: 20 mins, Cook Time: 6 hrs 20 mins, Servings: 7
Ingredients
- 1 tsp extract mint
- 2 large bananas
- 2 & ½ cups almond milk vanilla
- 2 tbsp honey
- 1 cup of mini semisweet dark chocolate chips

Instructions
- Blend bananas, milk, mint extract, & honey in a high-powered blender till a creamy texture is achieved. Toss in the chocolate chips in a mixing dish. Insert the popsicle sticks in popsicle molds or tiny paper cups. Chill for a minimum of 6 hrs.

Nutrition Information
Calories: 184 kcal, Carbohydrates: 27 g, Protein: 3 g, Fat: 7 g

151. Coconut Banana Paleo Cookies
Prep Time: 10 Mins, Cook Time: 45 Mins, Servings: 12
Ingredients
- 3 cups flour almond
- 1 tsp soda baking
- ½ tsp sea salt or kosher
- 1 tsp cinnamon
- ¼ cup butter unsalted
- ¾ cup sugar coconut
- 1 large, beaten egg
- 1 large egg white
- 1 tsp vanilla pure
- 1 ripe, mashed banana
- 1 cup shredded, unsweetened coconut
- 1 cup pieces walnut

Instructions
- In a large mixing bowl, combine baking soda, almond flour, salt, & cinnamon. Stir the walnuts & coconut into the flour mixture.
- Cream the butter & coconut sugar together in a large mixing bowl using an electric mixer. Mix the egg white, egg, & vanilla extract until everything is well blended. Stir in the crushed banana until everything is well mixed.
- Stir till the flour mixture is mixed into the wet ingredients. Cover and chill for 45 mins.
- Preheat the oven to 350°F.
- Drop dough 2" apart on a wide cookie sheet with a scoop. Bake for 8 mins, rotating the cookie sheet halfway through. Bake for another 8 mins, or till brown and firm. Allow your cookies to set for 5 mins over the cookie sheet. Allow cookies to set fully on a cooling rack. Continue to bake cookies till all the dough has been utilized.
- Store for up to 2 days in a sealed jar. When adding those walnuts, add Paleo-friendly white chocolate if preferred.

Nutrition Information
Calories: 194 kcal, Carbohydrates: 13 g, Protein: 5 g, Fat: 15 g

152. Chocolate-Dipped Banana Cream Pops
Prep Time: 15 Mins, Cook Time: 20 Mins, Servings: 6
Ingredients
Pops of Banana Cream
- 2 large, ripe bananas
- 2 cups milk coconut
- 1 tsp extract vanilla
- 2 tbsp raw honey

Chocolate Coating
- ½ cup chocolate chips dark
- 1 tbsp oil coconut

Nuts & Coconut
- ¾ cup unsweetened, shredded coconut
- ¾ cup of nuts finely chopped peanuts, walnuts

Instructions
- Combine bananas, vanilla, coconut milk, & honey in a blender. Pulse until everything is properly blended. Fill Six popsicle molds with the mixture and put them in.
- Freeze for almost 3 hrs, or till frozen solid.
- On one dish, spread coconut, & on another, the nuts. After dipping, line the baking sheet using wax paper to arrange the popsicles.
- Remove your popsicles from the freezer & let them over the counter to defrost for 3-5 mins or wash the molds under extremely hot water for a few seconds to release them.
- In a heavy-bottomed saucepan, melt chocolate & coconut oil over low flame over the stovetop, constantly whisking, till melted, approximately 2-3 mins.
- To cover a popsicle, drizzle chocolate over it & gently pushes it into the almonds & coconut.
- Continue with remaining popsicles & set on the lined using parchment paper. Freeze for almost an hr, uncovered, to solidify the covering. Enjoy!

Nutrition Information
Calories: 344 kcal, Carbohydrates: 34 g, Protein: 6 g, Fat: 26 g

153. Poppy Breakfast Muffins
Prep Time: 30 mins, Cook Time: 25 mins, Servings: 10
Ingredients
Wet
- 1 cup uncooked quinoa
- ¾ cup of milk
- 2/3 cup of honey
- ¼ cup oil olive
- 1 large egg
- 1 & ½ tsp extract almond

Dry
- 2 cups white flour whole-wheat 100%
- 1 & ½ tsp powder baking
- ¼ tsp sea salt or kosher
- ½ tsp soda baking
- 1/3 cup of seeds poppy

Instructions
- Preheat the oven to 350°F. Prepare a muffin tray by lining it using paper liners or lightly spraying it with the cooking spray.
- In a cup of water, put quinoa to a boil. Reduce the heat to low flame, cover, & cook for around 20 mins, or until all the water is absorbed. Using a fork, fluff the mixture.
- Combine all dry ingredients in a mixing bowl.
- Whisk all wet ingredients in a second bowl before adding to dry ingredients.
- Fold the wet and dry ingredients together until just incorporated.
- Fill each muffin tray halfway with batter & bake for around 25 mins, till a wooden skewer in the middle comes out clear.

Nutrition Information
Calories: 254 kcal, Carbohydrates: 41 g, Protein: 6 g, Fat: 8 g

154. 2-Min Chocolate Almond Mug Cake
Prep Time: 10 Mins, Cook Time: 45 Mins, Servings: 4
Ingredients
Dry
- ¼ cup of flour
- 2 tbsp unsweetened cocoa powder
- 2 tbsp chocolate chips dark
- ¼ tsp powder baking

Wet
- 2 tbsp of honey
- ¼ cup of milk or almond milk unsweetened
- 2 tbsp melt coconut oil
- pinch of sea salt kosher
- ¼ cup almond slices slivered

Filling
- ¼ cup natural almond butter
- 1 tsp sugar coconut

Instructions
- Except for the filling ingredients & almonds, whisk together all dry ingredients. Next, combine wet ingredients in a mixing bowl. Combine the dry & wet ingredients in a mixing bowl. Combine almond butter & coconut sugar in a mixing bowl.
- The half chocolate mixture should be divided amongst the cups, followed by the almond filling & the leftover chocolate mixture. Slivered almonds should be sprinkled
on top of the chocolate.
- Microwave for 1 min on medium, covered with a paper towel. Check to see whether everything is finished. If you need extra time, heat for another 10-20 seconds. Allow for another few mins of cooling before serving.

Nutrition Information
Calories: 202 kcal, Carbohydrates: 21 g, Protein: 4 g, Fat: 14 g

155. Coconut Lemon Macaroons
Prep Time: 20 Mins, Cook Time: 35 Mins, Servings: 3
Ingredients
Macaroons
- 13-15 oz whole fat coconut milk
- ¼ cup of honey
- 3 cups flaked; unsweetened coconut shredded
- 1 tsp vanilla extract real
- 1/8 tsp sea salt or kosher

Lemon Curd
- 1/3 cup freshly squeezed lemon juice
- 1/3 cup of honey
- 1 tsp zest lemon
- 2 eggs whole
- 1 yolk egg
- 1 tbsp cornstarch

Instructions
Honey With Coconut Milk
- In a medium saucepan, heat the coconut milk on high heat. Honey should be added at this point.
- Reduce the heat to moderate and cook, stirring periodically, for 45 mins, or until the sauce has thickened & dropped by half. Bubbles will appear in the liquid.

Lemon curd
- In a medium saucepan over moderate heat, combine the zest, lemon juice, & honey to
make the lemon curd.
- In a mixing bowl, whisk the eggs while your lemon-honey sauce warms.
- Pour your lemon-honey sauce into an egg bowl together in the gentle stream when it has just heated up, constantly beating. 2 mins of beating
- Separately, make the slurry with cornstarch and water, stir till dissolved. Add to the lemon curd & cook, constantly stirring, for 3-4 mins on medium-high heat, till it boils and thickens. Remove from heat & let aside in an uncovered dish for around 20 mins.

Macaroons

- Preheat the oven to 300°F. Use the baking spray and coconut oil to coat the baking sheet. Alternatively, use an uncoated silicone baking mat to line your baking sheet. Combine the condensed coconut-honey milk, shredded coconut, vanilla, & salt. Allow chilling in the refrigerator for 5 mins, uncovered in the small bowl.
- Drop mixture in heaping tbsp onto the baking sheet with some space between each, shaped using hand to produce a macaron shape. Repeat for a total of 15 cookies or three rows of five.
- When dealing with macaron mix, wet your hands to prevent it from sticking to your fingertips. Make a small depression in the middle of each cookie with your thumb & push the edges together to form small nests; cookies would be a bit flattened.
- Place in the oven for around 20 mins, or till golden & crisp. If you want a lighter, slightly toasted macaron, bake for just 15 mins. Remove from the oven & cool for around 10 mins over a sheet pan before gently placing each macaron on a dish.
- Before serving, spread lemon curd over baked cookies & keep in the fridge, covered, for almost five days, or eat right away!

Nutrition Information
Calories: 164 kcal, Carbohydrates: 15 g, Protein: 2 g, Fat: 12 g

156. 3-Ingredient Pineapple Skewers
Prep Time: 15 mins, Cook Time: 10 mins, Servings: 6
Ingredients
- 2 tbsp of honey
- 3 tsp of vanilla
- 1 ripe pineapple

Instructions
- Honey & vanilla should be combined in a mixing bowl.
- Remove the core from the pineapple after peeling it and cutting it in half.
- Each half should be cut into six wedges.
- Using skewers, thread the mixture onto the skewers.
- Using the honey-vanilla sauce as a basting agent.
- Grill grates should be lightly oiled, and a skillet should be sprayed using cooking spray.
- Grill over a moderate flame or set a skillet on the moderate flame on the stovetop.
- Cook the pineapple skewers for around 5-6 mins on 1 side once the grill is hot.
- Repeat until pineapple skewers become golden brown & tender, basting with any remaining sauce during cooking.

Nutrition Information
Calories: 51 kcal, Carbohydrates: 13 g, Protein: 15 g, Fat: 2 g

157. Zucchini Blondies
Prep Time: 15 mins, Cook Time: 20 mins, Servings: 2
Ingredients
- ¼ cup melted coconut oil
- 1 tbsp extract vanilla
- 1 tbsp applesauce
- 2 large eggs
- 1 cup sugar coconut
- 1 cup of white flour whole-wheat
- 1 tsp powder baking
- ½ tsp soda baking
- ½ tsp salt
- ½ tsp cinnamon
- 1/8 tsp nutmeg ground
- 1 small, shredded zucchini

Instructions
- Preheat the oven to 350°F.
- Combine the vanilla, applesauce, coconut oil, & egg. Mix thoroughly. Whisk together the sugar, cinnamon, flour, baking soda, baking powder, & salt in a separate basin. Mix in the wet ingredients well. Toss in the zucchini and mix well.
- Line a baking pan using parchment paper. Cook for around 20-25 mins, or until a wooden skewer in the middle comes out clear. Allow for thorough cooling before slicing into squares.

Nutrition Information
Calories: 215 kcal, Carbohydrates: 36 g, Protein: 3 g, Fat: 8 g

158. Quinoa Almond Joy Bars
Prep Time: 10 Mins, Cook Time: 30 Mins, Servings: 2
Ingredients
- 1/3 cup dry quinoa
- 2/3 cup of water
- 12 no whole sugar dates
- ½ cup almonds whole
- ½ cup finely grated coconut
- 2-3 tsp water
- ¼ cup chocolate chips semi-sweet

Instructions
- In a medium saucepan, combine the quinoa & water, cover, then bring to your boil. Reduce to low heat & cook for 15 mins. Allow it cool to ambient temperature before refrigerating for almost 2 hrs. If you already have cooked quinoa, you may use it.
- In your food processor, mix the dates, coconut, almonds, & cooked quinoa, then pulse until thoroughly incorporated & ball forms. Return the ingredients to a mixing bowl and gradually add water until the mix holds together. Make 14 minibars out of the dough.
- Melt chocolate chips in a shallow dish over a low flame. Drizzle every bar with heated chocolate. Leave the chocolate to the firm in the refrigerator. The bars may be kept for a few days in a sealed container.

Nutrition Information
Calories: 94 kcal, Carbohydrates: 10 g, Protein: 2 g, Fat: 6 g

159. Buckwheat Crepes with Fruit Filling and Yogurt
Prep Time: 15 Mins, Cook Time: 20 Mins, Servings: 8
Ingredients
- 3 peeled & diced kiwis
- 1 peeled, pitted & diced mango
- 1 peeled & chopped banana
- 1 cup low-fat, plain Greek yogurt
- 1 tbsp honey
- 1 tsp vanilla
- 5 tbsp melted coconut oil
- 2/3 cup flour buckwheat
- 1/3 cup white flour whole-wheat 100%
- 3 large eggs

Instructions
- Chop the fruit, then combine it with the yogurt, honey, & vanilla extract. In a food processor, mix both flours, coconut oil, & the eggs until well blended.
- In a nonstick pan, melt coconut oil on medium heat. Pour batter into the ladle & swirl to make a flat crepe using the spoon. Cook for around 2 mins, then loosen all edges using a spatula & cook for around 30 seconds more, or until well done. Cover & continue with the remaining mix.
- Warm crepes with fruit & a dab of yogurt are served.

Nutrition Information
Calories: 246 kcal, Carbohydrates: 28 g, Protein: 8 g, Fat: 13 g

160. Sweet Plantains
Prep Time: 10 mins, Cook Time: 10 mins, Servings: 3

Ingredients
- 2 tbsp refined coconut oil
- 2 peeled plantains brown
- ¼ tsp sea salt or kosher

Instructions
- In a medium-sized pan, heat the oil. Plantain pieces should be added at this point. Cook, stirring periodically, for approximately 10 mins, or till soft & golden. Before serving, season with salt.

Nutrition Information

Calories: 168 kcal, Carbohydrates: 29 g, Protein: 1 g, Fat: 7 g

161. Chocolate Coconut Almond Balls
Prep Time: 20 mins, Cook Time: 20 mins, Servings: 11
Ingredients
- ¼ cup rolled oats old-fashioned
- 3 tbsp powder cocoa
- 1/16 tsp sea salt or kosher
- ¾ cup pitted Medjool dates
- 1 & ½ tbsp warm water
- ½ cup unsweetened shredded coconut
- ½ cup coarsely chopped almonds

Instructions
- Combine the cocoa powder, oats, & salt in a mixing bowl. To make a paste, combine dates & water inside your blender. Combine the oats & chocolate powder in a mixing dish. Mix well, if required, with your hands, and roll into balls.
- On a platter, spread the almonds & coconut. Roll the balls, pushing the almonds in them as needed. Makes 12 balls with a diameter of one inch.
- Balls may be kept within the fridge for almost 1 week or frozen for up to two weeks in a sealed jar.

Nutrition Information
Calories: 92 kcal, Carbohydrates: 14 g, Protein: 2 g, Fat: 5 g

162. Chocolate Peanut Butter Energy Bites
Prep Time: 5 Mins, Cook Time: 55 Mins, Servings: 5
Ingredients
- 1 & ½ cups of old fashioned divided rolled oats
- ¼ cup of flax seeds
- ¼ cup powder unsweetened cocoa
- 1/8 tsp sea salt or kosher
- 3 tbsp seeds chia
- 1/3 cup of honey regular or raw
- ½ cup natural & creamy peanut butter
- 1 tsp vanilla extract real

Instructions
- In a food processor, grind oats and flax seeds till they create a powder.
- In a big mixing bowl, combine ground oats & flax seeds. Combine the remaining rolled oats, salt, cocoa powder, & chia seeds in a large mixing bowl. To blend, stir everything together.
- Stir the peanut butter, honey, & vanilla essence in a separate bowl until well blended. Stir thoroughly to incorporate in the big mixing bowl with the dry ingredients. Because the mixture is thick, you may mix it with your hands. Make one-inch balls out of the dough. Approximately 20 balls must be produced. When making the balls, soaking hands, and coating them in canola oil may help prevent the mix from adhering to your hands.
- Refrigerate for almost 2 weeks or freezer for almost 4 days.

Nutrition Information
Calories: 94 kcal, Carbohydrates: 12 g, Protein: 3 g, Fat: 5 g

163. Homemade Date Chocolate Truffles
Prep Time: 20 mins, Cook Time: 1 hr 20 mins, Servings: 6
Ingredients
- 2 cups pitted Medjool dates
- 4 tbsp raw, divided cocoa powder
- 1 tbsp virgin coconut oil
- 1 tsp vanilla extract real
- ¼ cup unsweetened shredded coconut
- 2-3 tbsp water warm
- ¼ tsp sea salt or kosher

Instructions
- In a food processor, purée the dates, cocoa powder, vanilla, coconut oil, & salt. Add a little water at the moment, scraping its sides as needed, and puree till a paste form. If needed, a little additional water might be added to make a paste.
- Roll your paste in balls using wet palms or maybe coconut oil. Approximately 14 balls must be created. On one dish, sprinkle the remainder cocoa powder, & on another, sprinkle some shredded coconut. Half balls should be cocoa-coated, and the other half should be coconut-coated. Refrigerate for 1-2 hrs, wrapped, to set.

Nutrition Information
Calories: 112 kcal, Carbohydrates: 25 g, Protein: 2 g, Fat: 2 g

164. Chocolate Rice Pudding
Prep Time: 5 mins, Cook Time: 30 mins, Servings: 5
Ingredients
- 2/3 cup rice brown
- 3 cups canned coconut milk
- ½ cup palm sugar coconut
- 1/8 tsp kosher salt or sea
- ½ tsp cinnamon
- ½ cup chocolate chips dark
- 1 tsp vanilla extract real

Instructions
- Over high temperature, bring water & rice to your boil. Reduce the heat to a low setting & cover.
- Cook the rice for approximately 15 mins, or till all the water has been absorbed.
- Meanwhile, bring cinnamon, coconut sugar, coconut milk, & salt to your simmer in a different saucepan. Toss in the cooked rice. Reduce heat & simmer, occasionally stirring, for approximately 15 minutes, or until your pudding is fully thickened.
- Remove from the heat and mix in the chocolate chunks and vanilla extract. Serve warm, or chill for one hr before serving cold. If preferred, top with clear eating whipped frosting & a sprinkling of cinnamon.

Nutrition Information
Calories: 325 kcal, Carbohydrates: 34 g, Protein: 3 g, Fat: 22 g

165. Chocolate Peanut Cake Pops
Prep Time: 10 Mins, Cook Time: 30 Mins, Servings: 4
Ingredients
For Cake Pops
- 3 cups of crumbled muffins or cupcakes
- ¼ cup of honey
- ¼ cup of peanut butter
- ¼ cup chocolate chips semi-sweet
- 1 tsp oil coconut

For Coating
- 1 cup chocolate chips semi-sweet
- 1 tbsp oil coconut
- ½ cup chopped nuts

Instructions
For Cake Pops
- Wax paper should be used to line a baking pan.
- In your saucepan, melt peanut butter & honey on moderate flame, stirring constantly. Leave to cool after removing from the heat.
- Half of these nut butter & honey mixture should be poured over cake crumbles & mixed with your hands. Add the leftover honey & nut butter mixture in small increments until these cake crumbs are combined to make a ball. Make 16-18 cake balls out of the mixture.
- Melt chocolate & coconut oil in a medium saucepot, stirring constantly.
- Dip a lollipop stick in the chocolate after it has melted. Make sure that the chocolate-dipped tip of this stick is upright before pressing it into the cake ball. Freeze for 1 hr after repeating with the leftover cake balls.

For Coating
- In your saucepan on low heat, melt the chocolate & coconut oil, stirring frequently.
- Once your chocolate has melted, take cake pops out of the fridge & dip them into it, covering the whole ball and approximately ¼" of that stick. Your cake ball would remain on a stick as a result of this.

- Before chocolate sets, place it over wax paper & top with some chopped peanuts. Repeat with leftover pops & chill till the chocolate is fully solidified, uncovered. Refrigerate the mixture in a sealed jar.

Nutrition Information
Calories: 271 kcal, Carbohydrates: 25 g, Protein: 2 g, Fat: 11 g

166. Best Ever Fudge Brownies
Prep Time: 20 mins, Cook Time: 25 mins, Servings: 10

Ingredients
- ½ cup butter pure
- 1 cup sugar coconut
- ½ cup powder cocoa
- 1 ½ tsp vanilla extract pure
- 2 lightly whipped eggs large
- ½ cup of white flour whole-wheat
- ¼ tsp sea salt or kosher
- 1 cup chips chocolate
- ½ cup of walnut

Instructions
- Preheat the oven to 350°F.
- A baking pan should be lightly oiled on the edges & bottom.
- Melt butter in a wide saucepan over medium heat. Stir in the coconut sugar unless it is completely dissolved. Remove from the heat and quickly mix in the cocoa powder. Add the vanilla & eggs once, stirring well after each addition.
- Stir in the chocolate chips, flour, salt, & walnuts, being cautious not to overcrowd. It is ready to pour into the pan after the flour isn't visible. In a baking pan, evenly spread. Before cooking, if desired, add a few extra walnut pieces over the top. Preheat oven to 350°F and bake for around 25 mins. Remove from the oven and set aside to cool for almost one hr before serving.

Nutrition Information
Calories: 265 kcal, Carbohydrates: 35 g, Protein: 3 g, Fat: 13 g

167. Oatmeal Cranberry-Walnut Cookies
Prep Time: 10 Mins, Cook Time: 20 Mins, Servings: 6

Ingredients
- 2 cups of flour
- 1 tsp soda baking
- ½ tsp sea salt or kosher
- 1 tsp of cinnamon
- 1/8 tsp nutmeg
- 2 cups rolled oats old-fashioned
- 1 cup of unrefined melted coconut oil
- 1 cup palm sugar coconut
- 2 tsp vanilla
- 2 large eggs
- 1 & ½ cups cranberries dried
- ½ cup diced walnuts

Instructions
- Preheat the oven to 325°F.
- When estimating flour, scoop into measurement cup & level off, taking care not to overfill. It's crucial not to scrape flour from the bag since this would compact the flour and result in a thicker cookie.
- Combine flour, salt, cinnamon, baking soda, & nutmeg in a mixing bowl. Stir in the oats until they are evenly distributed.
- In a big mixing bowl, whisk coconut oil & coconut sugar using your electric mixer until well combined, approximately 4 mins. Mix in the vanilla & eggs at a lower speed unless well mixed. Add a bit of the oat mix at the moment, mixing well after each addition. Combine the cranberries & walnuts in a mixing bowl.
- Roll dough into tiny balls & put approximately 2" apart on a cookie sheet. You should have a total of 40 balls. Place cookies over rack gently pressed down. Bake for 7 mins, then flip pan & bake for another 7 mins, or till set. Because the cookies would continue to bake after being taken from the oven, they might be somewhat soft from the middle. Allow 2 mins for the cookies to set before moving to the cooling rack.
- Cool thoroughly before storing in a sealed jar for almost 3 days.

Nutrition Information
Calories: 135 kcal, Carbohydrates: 15 g, Protein: 2 g, Fat: 7 g

168. Clean Eating Pumpkin Pie
Prep Time: 15 Mins, Cook Time: 55 Mins, Servings: 8

Ingredients
Filling
- 15 oz unsweetened pumpkin puree 100%
- 15 oz can coconut milk
- 2 tsp spice pumpkin pie
- 1 tsp extract vanilla
- ½ tsp salt sea
- 2/3 cup palm sugar coconut
- 2 large eggs

Crust
- 1 & ½ cups of white flour whole-wheat
- ¼ tsp sea salt or kosher
- ½ cup refined, solid coconut oil
- 8 tbsp water ice

Instructions
- To make coconut oil firm, put it in the refrigerator almost an hr ahead of time.

For Filling
- Combine all filling ingredients in a large mixing bowl and whisk until smooth.

For Crust
- In your food processor, combine the flour & salt. Blend the oil into the food processor. The flour combination should have the texture of a coarse meal. Next, pulse in a little amount of ice water. Simply pour in enough water to make a dough.
- With the dough, make one flat disc. Freeze for almost one hr & up to 3 days after wrapping it in plastic wrap.
- Preheat the oven to 375°F.
- On a floured surface, roll out the dough flat. To carve a circle all around the pie plate, flip it upside down & cut the circle. Place the dough within the pie pan & push it down. Fold over the edges or use a fork to push around. Prick the bottom & sides of the pastry using a fork. Place a sheet of parchment paper on top of the dough and fill with pie weights before baking for around 15 mins. Leave to cook for another 5 mins after removing the paper & weights/beans.
- Remove the crust & fill your pie with the contents. Place your pie dish on the baking sheet with the full pie inside. Bake for around 30 mins, till a knife poked into the center, comes out clear.

Nutrition Information
Calories: 322 kcal, Carbohydrates: 31 g, Protein: 5 g, Fat: 22 g

169. Pumpkin Chocolate Chip Cookies
Prep Time: 15 mins, Cook Time: 15 mins, Servings: 25

Ingredients
Dry
- 2 & ½ cups white flour whole-wheat 100%
- ¾ tsp soda baking
- ½ tsp powder baking
- ¼ tsp salt
- 1 & ½ tsp spice pumpkin pie
- ½ tsp cinnamon

Wet
- ½ cup olive oil or coconut
- 1 cup of honey or maple syrup real
- 1 cup pumpkin puree pure 100% canned
- 2 large eggs
- 2 tsp extract vanilla
- 2/3 cup chocolate dark

Instructions

- Preheat the oven to 370°F & line the baking sheet using parchment paper.
- Combine all dry ingredients in a mixing bowl.
- Combine all wet ingredients in a mixing bowl. Place some chocolate chips on top.
- Combine the wet & dry ingredients in a mixing bowl and stir until completely combined.
- Scoop the cookie dough into two tbsp & scrape it over the prepared baking sheet. Place cookies on the baking sheet approximately 2" apart. It's worth noting that the mixture is thinner than other cookie doughs, resulting in a soft cookie.
- Bake for approximately 15 mins, or unless the bottoms are brown & firm. Place the cookies on a wire rack to cool. Continue with the rest of the mix.

Nutrition Information
Calories: 106 kcal, Carbohydrates: 16 g, Protein: 2 g, Fat: 4 g

170. Chocolate Cupcakes with Peanut Butter Frosting
Prep Time: 15 mins, Cook Time: 20 mins, Servings: 20
Ingredients
Dry
- 1 & ½ cups of white flour whole-wheat
- ¼ cup unsweetened cocoa powder
- 1 tsp soda baking
- ½ tsp sea salt or kosher

Wet
- 1 cup maple syrup real
- 1 cup café americano or coffee
- 1 tbsp vinegar white
- 2 tsp extract vanilla
- ¼ cup olive oil

Peanut Butter Frosting
- 2/3 cup natural peanut butter
- ¼ cup syrup maple
- 1 tbsp milk

Instructions
- Preheat the oven to 350°F.
- Cupcake liners should be used to cover a muffin tray. In a mixing bowl, combine all dry ingredients.
- Whisk all wet ingredients in a separate bowl. Combine the wet & dry ingredients in a mixing bowl and stir till just incorporated. There is going to be a certain lump.
- Fill every cupcake holder with batter. Cook for around 20 mins until a toothpick inserted within the middle comes out clear.
- In a mixing bowl, combine all frosting ingredients. Spread frosting over cupcakes using the butter knife, elevating your knife to add texture. Enjoy!

Nutrition Information
Calories: 289 kcal, Carbohydrates: 37 g, Protein: 6 g, Fat: 15 g

171. Peanut Butter & Dark Chocolate Squares Recipe
Prep Time: 10 Mins, Cook Time: 35 mins, Servings: 30
Ingredients
Wet
- ½ cup smooth, natural peanut butter
- ½ cup virgin coconut oil
- ¾ cup maple syrup or honey
- ½ tsp extract vanilla

Dry
- 2 cups of rolled oats old-fashioned
- ¼ tsp sea salt or kosher
- ¾ tsp cinnamon

Topping Chocolate
- 10 oz dark semisweet chocolate chips
- 2 tbsp unrefined, virgin coconut oil

Instructions
- Preheat the oven to 350°F.
- Combine all wet ingredients in a mixing bowl. Blend the oats at a fast speed till they are crushed into flour. Combine the salt, oat flour, & cinnamon in a mixing bowl.
- Combine the dry & wet ingredients in a mixing bowl until well mixed, then pour into a baking dish.
- Melt the chocolate with the coconut oil on a medium heat setting. As quickly as the chocolate has melted, remove it from the fire and spread equally on the peanut butter coating. Leave to cool over the stovetop for around 18 mins after baking.
- Refrigerate for almost 2 hrs to allow flavors to meld. The bars must be kept in the refrigerator. Allow for 15 mins at room temp before slicing if kept inside the freezer.

Nutrition Information
Calories: 348 kcal, Carbohydrates: 42 g, Protein: 6 g, Fat: 20 g

172. Caramel Pumpkin Spice Popcorn
Prep Time: 15 mins, Cook Time: 1 hr, Servings: 4
Ingredients
- 12 cups of popcorn
- ½ cup oil coconut
- 1 cup sugar coconut
- ½ cup maple syrup pure
- ½ tsp sea salt or kosher
- 1 tsp spice pumpkin pie
- ½ tsp soda baking
- 1 tsp vanilla pure

Instructions
- Preheat the oven to 225°F.
- Fill a mixing dish halfway with popped corn.
- Combine maple syrup, coconut sugar, coconut oil, & salt in a small saucepan. Stir constantly over low flame until all of the coconut sugar has dissolved. Remove the pan from the heat and add the baking soda, pumpkin spice, & vanilla extract. Toss the cooked popcorn in the sauce to coat it.
- Place buttered popcorn over the baking sheet. Preheat oven to 350°F and bake for

around 1 hr, stirring after 15 mins. Remove from the oven and set aside to cool before serving.

Nutrition Information
Calories: 218 kcal, Carbohydrates: 30 g, Protein: 1 g, Fat: 11 g

173. 3-Ingredient Peanut Butter Cups
Prep Time: 15 mins, Cook Time: 2 hrs 15 mins, Servings: 16
Ingredients
- ½ cup of peanut butter no salt natural
- 1 mashed banana ripe
- 2 tbsp unrefined, melted coconut oil

Instructions
- In a large dish, combine all of the ingredients. Fill paper cups with 1 spoonful of the mixture. Place all cups over the freezer-safe dish and freeze for about 2 hours or until firm.

Nutrition Information
Calories: 110 kcal, Carbohydrates: 5 g, Protein: 3 g, Fat: 9 g

174. Clean Eating Zucchini Bread
Prep Time: 10 Min, Cook Time: 35 Mins, Servings: 14
Ingredients
- ½ cup pieces walnut
- 1 & ½ cups grated zucchini
- 1 & ½ cups of white flour whole-wheat
- 1 tsp powder baking
- ½ tsp sea salt or kosher
- ½ tsp soda baking
- ½ tsp cinnamon
- ¼ cup non-fat buttermilk
- 1 large egg
- 1 large egg yolk
- 1 cup sugar coconut
- 2/3 cup coconut oil melted
- 1 tsp freshly grated ginger
- ½ tsp vanilla pure

Instructions
- Preheat the oven to 350°F. Set aside one loaf pan that has been lightly greased and floured.

- Roast the nuts for around 10 mins over the baking sheet. Allow time for cooling while you prepare the batter.
- Combine flour, baking soda, salt, baking powder, & cinnamon in a medium mixing dish.
- Buttermilk, sugar, ginger, eggs, oil, & vanilla are whisked together in a mixing dish. Assemble the ingredients and make sure they're thoroughly mixed. Add the dry ingredients to the batter and whisk just until blended. Combine the shredded zucchini & nuts in a mixing bowl.
- Bake for around 55-60 mins, till a fork poked into the middle of the loaf, falls out clear.
- Allow it to cool for around 15 mins within the pan before flipping onto the wire rack and delicately running the butter knife over the sides. Before serving, let it cool fully.

Nutrition Information
Calories: 244 kcal, Carbohydrates: 29 g, Protein: 3 g, Fat: 14 g

175. No-Bake Oatmeal Chocolate Chip Energy Bites
Prep Time: 15 Mins, Cook Time: 25 Mins, Servings: 35
Ingredients
- ½ cup chocolate chips dark
- 1 cup smooth almond butter
- 2 & ¼ cups of oats
- 1 ripe, pureed banana medium
- 1 tsp vanilla extract real
- 1/8 tsp of salt
- 3 tbsp seeds chia
- 1/3 cup raw honey
- 1 tbsp powder cocoa
- ¼ cup shredded, unsweetened coconut

Instructions
- A piece of paper wax should be used to line a sealable container.
- In your blender, grind oats until they have a flour-like appearance. In a mixing bowl, pour the oat flour. Combine the ground oats, chia seeds, leftover oats, salt, chocolate powder, & coconut.
- In your blender, puree sliced banana. Toss the oat mix with the chocolate chips, nut butter, vanilla, raw honey, & banana puree, then mix well.
- Make 20 balls with your hands, then set them over wax paper. Once you've completed 1 covering of bites, put another wax paper, then more on the next sheet, & so on.
- Refrigerate for almost 2 hrs before serving. Bites may be frozen in thin layers inside freezer bags for almost 3 months after being refrigerated.

Nutrition Information
Calories: 203 kcal, Carbohydrates: 24 g, Protein: 6 g, Fat: 11 g

176. Apple Pie Flautas
Prep Time: 10 Mins, Cook Time: 40 Mins, Servings: 10
Ingredients
- 4 golden large, seeded delicious apples
- 3 tbsp sugar coconut
- ½ tsp cinnamon
- 1 tbsp cornstarch or flour
- dash sea salt kosher
- 2 tsp butter pure
- 14 flour tortillas whole-wheat

Instructions
- Combine apple chunks, coconut sugar, salt, flour/cornstarch, cinnamon, & butter. If using a slow cooker, combine the ingredients and simmer on low for 2 hrs, or till apples are soft.
- Preheat the oven to 350°F. Preheat oven to 350°F. Line one baking sheet using parchment paper.
- Put 1 heaping spoonful of apple filling inside the middle of every tortilla, roll tightly as possible, and set. Brush every flauta with some coconut oil or spritz it using cooking spray.
- Bake for around 20-25 mins, unless the exterior is gently brown & crisp. Leave to solidify at room temperature unless the filling has reached the temperature it may be eaten.

Nutrition Information
Calories: 196 kcal, Carbohydrates: 36 g, Protein: 4 g, Fat: 4 g

177. Oatmeal Chocolate Breakfast Muffins
Prep Time: 20 mins, Cook Time: 20 mins, Servings: 12
Ingredients
Dry
- 2 cups oats rolled
- ¼ cup unsweetened cocoa powder
- 1/3 cup palm sugar coconut
- 1 ½ tsp powder baking
- ½ tsp soda baking
- ½ tsp cinnamon
- ½ tsp sea salt or kosher
- ½ cup chocolate chips dark

Wet
- 1 cup yogurt Greek
- 2 ripe, large bananas
- 2 large eggs
- ¼ cup raw honey
- 1 ½ tsp vanilla extract pure
- ¼ cup unrefined coconut oil

Instructions
- Preheat the oven to 425°F.
- In a high-powered blender, grind the oats until they resemble flour. Combine the cinnamon, cocoa powder, baking soda, baking powder, coconut sugar, & salt in a mixing dish.
- Blend the honey, yogurt, bananas, coconut oil, eggs, & vanilla in a high-powered blender.
- Pour all wet ingredients within dry ingredients & stir well. Combine the chocolate chips and fold them in. Muffin papers may be used to line the muffin tray. Fill every cup with the mixture. Preheat oven to 350°F and bake for around 20 mins.
- Leave muffins to set on the cake rack when cool enough to manage.

Nutrition Information
Calories: 226 kcal, Carbohydrates: 32 g, Protein: 5 g, Fat: 10 g

178. Peanut Butter Yogurt Honey Dip
Prep Time: 5 mins, Cook Time: 5 mins, Servings: 2
Ingredients
- 1 cup fat-free Greek yogurt
- ½ cup natural peanut butter
- 1 tbsp honey

Instructions
- Combine all the ingredients in a mixing bowl. Serve with fruit or vegetables of your choice.

Nutrition Information
Calories: 89 kcal, Carbohydrates: 4 g, Protein: 4 g, Fat: 7 g

179. Froyo Berry Bites
Prep Time: 15 mins, Cook Time: 6 hrs 15 mins, Servings: 16
Ingredients
- ¼ cup almonds crushed
- 2 tbsp sugar coconut
- 2 tbsp melted coconut oil
- ¾ cup low-fat, plain Greek yogurt
- 2 tbsp honey
- 1 & ½ cups of strawberries

Instructions
- Use silicone to line a muffin tray or bake directly into a nonstick muffin pan.
- Crushed coconut sugar, almonds, & coconut oil are combined in a mixing bowl. A tiny quantity should be spooned into the muffin cup.
- Combine yogurt & honey in a small mixing basin. Cover your crust with 2 tsp of the mixture in every muffin cup.

- Freshly sliced berries may be sprinkled on top. Freeze for 6 hrs or till firm. Remove from the silicone wrapping and leave aside at room temperature for around 8-10 minutes before serving.

Nutrition Information
Calories: 128 kcal, Carbohydrates: 14 g, Protein: 4 g, Fat: 7 g

180. Strawberry Banana Cheesecake Bites
Prep Time: 15 Mins, Cook Time: 25 Mins, Servings: 24

Ingredients
- 24 large strawberries
- ½ ripe banana
- 8 oz low-fat, softened cream cheese
- 2 tbsp honey
- 1 tsp freshly squeezed lemon juice
- 1 tsp vanilla
- liquid stevia
- 1 tbsp crushed almonds
- 1 tbsp sugar coconut
- ¼ tsp cinnamon
- for garnish mint leaves

Instructions
- Remove the green tips from strawberries and set them aside. To make every strawberry stand straight, cut a little bit off the bottom. Dry the tops of every fresh-sliced strawberry using a paper towel. Strawberries should be placed on a serving plate.
- Combine banana, lemon juice, honey, cream cheese, & vanilla in the mixer, then beat the light and frothy. Mix in some stevia till the mixture reaches your desired sweetness level.
- Either pour the banana mix into the icing bag equipped with a big star tip or use an icing bag having a big star tip. Pipe into the tip of each prepped strawberry or pour the banana mix into every strawberry using the gallon size zipper bag & snipping off approximately ½-inch from the bottom corners.
- Coconut sugar, Crushed almonds, & cinnamon are combined in a mixing bowl. Toss with a pinch of salt and pepper on top of the strawberries.
- Serve right away or keep refrigerated till ready to use. Serve between 3-4 hrs after preparation for optimal results.

Nutrition Information
Calories: 100 kcal, Carbohydrates: 9 g, Protein: 2 g, Fat: 7 g

181. No-Bake Almond Joy Cookies
Prep Time: 20 mins, Cook Time: 2 hrs 20 mins, Servings: 25

Ingredients
- 10 big dates
- 2/3 cup of almond meal
- ½ cup grated coconut
- ¼ cup minced almonds
- ¼ cup chocolate chips dark
- 1/8 cup of water

Instructions
- Add fresh dates to your food processor and pulse till they make a ball. Pulse in some almond meal & coconut until thoroughly blended.
- Add both crushed almonds & chocolate chips to the mix in a bowl. Gradually add the water till the mix holds together and resembles cookie dough. It's possible that you won't need all the water. Place in the container covered using parchment paper & cut in 8 cookies. Refrigerate for almost 2 hrs before serving.
- If desired, top with more chocolate chips & chopped almonds.

Nutrition Information
Calories: 197 kcal, Carbohydrates: 29 g, Protein: 4 g, Fat: 9 g

182. Skinny Watermelon Sorbet
Prep Time: 10 mins, Cook Time: 10 mins, Servings: 18

Ingredients
- ½ seedless watermelon
- freshly squeezed lemon juice

Instructions
- Watermelon chunks should be frozen overnight. In your blender, combine frozen pieces & lemon juice. Blend till the texture is smooth, adding extra lemon juice if required. Serve & have fun!

Nutrition Information
Calories: 86 kcal, Carbohydrates: 22 g, Protein: 3 g, Fat: 0 g

183. Chocolate Covered Peanut Butter & Banana Pops
Prep Time: 20 Mins, Cook Time: 25 Mins, Servings: 8

Ingredients
- 2 big bananas, ripe
- 1/3 cup all-natural peanut butter
- 1 ½ cups chocolate chips dark
- 1 tbsp oil coconut

Instructions
- Bananas should be peeled and sliced to a thickness of approximately 1 inch. Half sliced bananas should be spread with peanut butter, then the next piece of banana should be placed over peanut butter to form a "sandwich." If you're using skewers, gently place them in the center of your bananas.
- Place sliced bananas over parchment paper-lined baking sheet and freeze for around 30-60 mins.
- Meanwhile, melt both chocolate chips & coconut oil together in a saucepan on low flame.
- Place some chocolate in a dish and immediately dip the bananas in it. Place the bananas within the freezer for the next 30-60 Mins.

Nutrition Information
Calories: 141 kcal, Carbohydrates: 16 g, Protein: 2 g, Fat: 9 g

184. Mango Shake
Prep Time: 5 mins, Cook Time: 5 mins, Servings: 6

Ingredients
- 1 pitted & peeled mango ripe
- ¼ cup coconut milk lite
- ¼ cup of ice

Instructions
- In your blender, combine the milk, mango, and ice & mix till smooth.
- Serve right away.

Nutrition Information
Calories: 258 kcal, Carbohydrates: 33 g, Protein: 3 g, Fat: 15 g

185. Skillet Peach Cobbler
Prep Time: 15 mins, Cook Time: 15 mins, Servings: 12

Ingredients
For Cobbler
- 8 fresh peeled & sliced peaches
- 4 tbsp melted coconut oil
- 3 tbsp white flour whole-wheat
- 1 & ½ cups grape juice white
- 1/3 cup of pure honey maple syrup
- 1 tsp cinnamon
- 1 tbsp vanilla

For Streusel Topping
- ¼ cup of white flour whole-wheat
- ¼ cup flour coconut
- ¼ cup flour almond
- 1 tsp vanilla
- 2 tbsp milk almond
- 2 tbsp melted coconut oil
- 3 tbsp sugar coconut
- 1 tbsp vanilla

Instructions
- Combine all cobbler ingredients & pour into the cast-iron pan. Combine all streusel topping ingredients in a large mixing bowl. Over peach mix, sprinkle the streusel. Cover skillet and cook over moderate heat for around 15-25 mins, or till peaches are soft & streusel topping fully hardened.
- Serve with a dollop of coconut ice cream & a dusting of blueberries on top.

Nutrition Information
Calories: 260 kcal, Carbohydrates: 31 g, Protein: 3 g, Fat: 14 g

186. Fruit Salad with Poppy Seed Dressing
Prep Time: 15 mins, Cook Time: 15 mins, Servings: 6
Ingredients
- 1 cup peeled & diced kiwi
- 1 cup hulled & diced strawberries
- 1 cup berries mixed
- 1 cup peeled & diced mangoes
- 1 sliced orange
- 1 cup low-fat Greek yogurt
- 4 tbsp honey
- 2 tbsp seeds poppy
- 2 tbsp fresh lime juice
- 1 tbsp oil almond
- fresh mint

Instructions
- Inside a serving dish, toss together all of the fruits & chill as you make the dressing.
- Combine the lime juice, yogurt, poppy seeds, honey, & oil in a shallow dish to prepare the seed dressing. If desired, adjust its sweetness.
- Before serving, toss the fruits with some poppy dressing & top with fresh mint leaves.

Nutrition Information
Calories: 244 kcal, Carbohydrates: 44 g, Protein: 6 g, Fat: 7 g

187. Blueberry Chia Seed Pudding
Prep Time: 5 mins, Cook Time: 3 hrs 5 mins, Servings: 8
Ingredients
- 1 & ½ cups milk almond
- ½ cup seeds chia
- 2 tbsp honey
- ½ tsp extract vanilla
- 1 cup of blueberries
- ¼ cup of granola

Instructions
- In your blender, purée the honey, vanilla, milk, & blueberries till smooth. In a separate bowl, whisk together chia seeds. Fill single ramekins cups, mason jars halfway with the mixture. Cover and chill for almost 3-5 hrs, or till you get a thick consistency.

Nutrition Information
Calories: 206 kcal, Carbohydrates: 29 g, Protein: 5 g, Fat: 9 g

188. No-Bake Strawberry Mug Cakes
Prep Time: 15 mins, Cook Time: 15 mins, Servings: 4
Ingredients
- 1 cup non-fat Greek yogurt
- 1 cup low-fat cream cheese
- 2 cups hulled & quartered strawberries
- 4 tbsp no sugar strawberry preserves
- 2 zested lemons
- 2 tbsp juice lemon
- 2 tbsp sugar coconut
- 6 tbsp crushed almonds
- ¼ cup for garnish blueberries
- 4 fresh mints for garnish leaves

Instructions
- Combine the juice, cream cheese, yogurt, lemon zest, & sugar in a small mixing bowl, then chill while you finish the rest of the recipe.
- Combine the strawberries & preserves in a large mixing dish.
- Prepare 4 separate cups with the yogurt mixture & divide equally. Strawberries and crumbled almonds go on top of the yogurt mixture.
- Serve with blueberries & mint as a garnish. Allow cooling before serving.

Nutrition Information
Calories: 318 kcal, Carbohydrates: 35 g, Protein: 12 g, Fat: 18 g

189. Apricot and Mascarpone Cake
Prep time: 20 Mins, Cook Time: 35 Mins, Servings: 12
Ingredients
- 4 large eggs
- 2/3 cup sugar coconut
- 1/8 tsp of salt
- 1 & 1/8 cups of mascarpone
- 2 & ¼ cups of white flour sifted whole-wheat
- 1 tbsp powder baking
- ½ tsp extract vanilla
- 1 & ¾ lb of apricots or fresh, divided nectarines
- 3 tbsp apricot spread all-fruit
- 1 tbsp cinnamon ground
- 8 fresh mint leaves

Instructions
- Preheat oven to 375°F.
- In a mixing bowl, whisk the sugar, eggs, & salt till the mixture is light & fluffy.
- In a separate dish, soften the mascarpone cheese by stirring it. To keep it a little less dense, throw in one egg and sugar combination. Next, combine the leftover egg and sugar combination in the same dish. Gently combine the ingredients.
- Toss the mascarpone with the baking powder, sifted flour, and vanilla extract. To blend, carefully mix everything.
- Add your apricots, diced (or nectarine). Gently combine the ingredients.
- Transfer the batter to an 11" cake pan, which has been floured and oiled with cooking spray.
- Preheat your oven to 350°F and bake for around 1 hr. If the cake's exterior darkens too much while cooking, wrap it with Al foil & continue cooking.
- Put a toothpick into the middle of the cake to see whether it is done. It's already cooked if it falls out clear. If not, return the cake to the oven for some more mins.
- Allow time for it to cool. Remove it from the pan after it has set.
- Over, arrange some sliced apricots.
- Warm your apricot jam in a saucepan over lower heat for approximately 2 mins.
- Apply some jam over the cut apricots with care.
- Sprinkle cinnamon over the top once you've coated all apricots. Garnish with a few mint leaves.

Nutrition Information
Calories: 280 kcal, Carbohydrates: 41 g, Protein: 7 g, Fat: 11 g

190. Mini Apple Strudel
Prep Time: 20 mins, Cook Time: 30 mins, Servings: 4
Ingredients
- 16 oz whole-grain rectangular puff pastries
- 5 big apples
- ¼ cup of raisins
- 1/8 cup of pine nuts
- 1 tbsp coconut sugar raw
- 1 zest lemon organic
- ½ tsp powder cinnamon
- 1 whisked egg
- sugar icing

Instructions
- Preheat your oven to 350°F.
- Puff pastry should be laid flat over the work surface and divided into four equal sections. Carry on with the next one in the same manner.
- Combine the sugar, apples, lemon zest, pine nuts, raisins, & cinnamon in a mixing bowl.
- Spoon little apple mix into the middle of each little puff pastry, then seal both ends & both edges to form a tight, compact log. Carry on with the rest of the ingredients in a similar manner.
- Place every strudel over a parchment-lined baking sheet.

- On top of every strudel, sprinkle with some egg wash.
- Preheat oven to 350°F and bake for around 30 mins, or till golden brown.
- Drizzle icing sugar over the top and serve with ice cream if preferred.

Nutrition Information
Calories: 85 kcal, Carbohydrates: 17 g, Protein: 1 g, Fat: 2 g

191. Almond Milk Rice Pudding with Cranberries
Prep Time: 10 Mins, Cook Time: 40 Mins, Servings: 3

Ingredients
- 2 tsp extract vanilla
- 1 cup of short-grained uncooked brown rice
- 2 & ½ cups unsweetened almond milk
- 1 tbsp palm sugar coconut
- 2 tbsp of almonds
- ¼ cup cranberries dried
- ½ tsp powder cinnamon

Instructions
- Using a knife, scrape the seeds out of a vanilla pod by slicing them in half along its whole length.
- Pour in the sweetener, almond milk, rice, and vanilla extract into a small saucepan & bring to a boil over high temperature. Lower the heat to a simmer when the water reaches a rolling boil.
- Rice should be stirred constantly to prevent burning or adhering to the pan. Cook the rice for 35 to 45 mins, or until it's done. You may add extra almond milk if you see that the rice is beginning to get dry. The texture should be creamy.
- Over medium heat in a dry saucepan, roast almonds till they become golden brown and aromatic, approximately 3-5 mins. Serve as a side dish or appetizer.
- Dried cranberries blended with more sugar can be soaked in water for approximately 10 mins to remove the extra sweetness. Drain, press out the water, then chop. Set away for later.
- Turn off the heat and remove the vanilla bean from the rice after it's done cooking.
- Top with cranberries & almonds after sprinkling with cinnamon.

Nutrition Information
Calories: 213 kcal, Carbohydrates: 37 g, Protein: 7 g, Fat: 4 g

192. Almond Blueberry Pancakes with Chocolate Ganache
Prep Time: 30 Mins, Cook time: 25 Mins, Servings: 4

Ingredients
- ½ cup of white flour whole-wheat
- ½ cup flour almond
- 1 tsp powder baking
- ¾ cup milk almond
- 1 tbsp sugar honey coconut
- ¼ tsp salt
- 1 large egg
- 1 tsp butter or coconut oil

Instructions
- The egg & sweetener should be mixed with the other ingredients. Mix until a homogeneous mixture is achieved. Refrigerate it for 30 mins.
- If you're making ganache out of chocolate: Melt your chocolate with water in a water bath. Add some liqueur once the chocolate has melted. Switch off the heat and allow 3 mins for your alcohol to evaporate. Set away for later.
- A medium skillet should be warmed up. Use butter to help prevent the pancakes from sticking together. Drop a few blueberries on top of the pancake as soon as the batter hits the skillet. Cook the other side once the pancake begins to move freely in the skillet. Continue this process until the mixture has reached its final consistency.
- Cookie cutters with a 3" diameter can create round shapes. Four smaller pancakes can be made from one large pancake.

Nutrition Information
Calories: 369 kcal, Carbohydrates: 59 g, Protein: 7 g, Fat: 12 g

193. Apple Puffs
Prep Time: 15 Mins, Cook Time: 20 Mins, Servings: 5

Ingredients
- 3 apples medium golden delicious
- 2 tbsp raisins
- 1 tbsp coconut oil
- 3 tbsp syrup maple
- ½ tsp cinnamon ground
- 1 tbsp whole-wheat plain breadcrumbs
- 1 tbsp nuts pine
- 1 tbsp crushed walnuts
- 1 big whole-wheat store-bought puff pastry
- flour
- 1 lightly whisked egg

Instructions
- The oven should be preheated at 375°F.
- The apples should be peeled, cored, and diced.
- Apples & raisins are combined with maple syrup & cinnamon in a big skillet and cooked over moderate flame for approximately 10 mins. Set away for later.
- Combine the pine nuts, breadcrumbs, & walnuts with the maple syrup you have left. Set away for later.
- Lay your puff pastry out on a floured surface, such as a dough board. To prevent them from sticking together, dust the dough with flour. A 3" cookie cutter is ideal for this task.
- For each cut piece of dough, spread the nut and breadcrumb mix in the middle and then spoon some apple filling on top.
- Afterward, squeeze the bag shut by bringing all the corners together and securing them.
- Take a little portion of the dough left over after cutting out the circles and spread it out thinly on a platter. Each bag may be topped with this.
- Your apple puffs should be baked on the baking mat.
- The apple puffs should be egg washed.
- Make sure to bake for around 20 to 25 mins or unless the puffs of apple are golden brown.
- Before serving, allow them to cool for almost 20 mins.

Nutrition Information
Calories: 110 kcal, Carbohydrates: 18 g, Protein: 2 g, Fat: 4 g

194. Cherry Chocolate Trifle
Prep Time: 15 Mins, Cook Time: 25 Mins, Servings: 4

Ingredients
- 4 shots espresso
- 1 tbsp brandy
- 3 tbsp coconut sugar
- 1 cup low-fat, plain Greek yogurt
- 1 cup ricotta cheese part-skim
- 3 tbsp syrup tart cherries
- 3-4 tbsp cherry syrup
- 3 tbsp chocolate chips mini semisweet
- 4 oz ladyfingers

Instructions
- To begin, prepare the whipped topping for a healthy diet.
- The sugar & espresso should be mixed in a mixing bowl. Set away for later.
- Beat the ricotta cheese, yogurt, & pie syrup together in a small bowl. Alternatively, if you don't have the beater, you can mix the ricotta cheese, yogurt, & syrup in your blender & then add it to the bowl before mixing. Add the cherries & chocolate chips to the mixture. Gently fold in whipped topping till it's all mixed in.
- The individual bowls should be prepared. Please take a few ladyfingers and dip them briefly within the espresso

- mix so that they soak up the liquid but don't get soggy. In the bowls, place them just at the base of each one.
- A spoonful of the creamy yogurt mixture is all that is needed to cover the ladyfingers. It's time to do it again! The yogurt mixture should be the final layer.
- The leftover cherries & chocolate chips may be added as a garnish.
- Refrigerate for two hrs before serving, wrapped in plastic.

Nutrition Information
Calories: 244 kcal, Carbohydrates: 24 g, Protein: 8 g, Fat: 13 g

195. Skinny Mint Cookies
Prep Time: 20 Mins, Cook Time: 35 Mins, Servings: 10
Ingredients
For Cookies
- 1 cup of white flour whole-wheat
- ¼ cup powder cocoa
- 5 tbsp melted coconut oil
- 5 tbsp honey maple syrup
- 1 tsp vanilla
- ¾ tsp extract peppermint
- sea salt pinch
- 3-8 drops of water

For Chocolate
- 8 oz chocolate dark
- 2 tbsp oil coconut
- ¼ tsp extract peppermint

Instructions
- Preheat your oven to around 400 deg F.

For Cookies
- Stir together all ingredients in a mixing bowl until you have a creamy dough that is easy to work with. Then chill the dough for at least an hr before using. Keep your dough from crumbling by adding some water if necessary.
- Spread a layer of parchment paper on top of the dough. A quarter of the way through the rollout, "thick and clumsy. Slash in half. "Cut out circles & set them on a baking pan.
- Make sure they're done baking after 7 to 9 mins. Remove and allow to cool to room temperature. When the cookies have cooled, melt the chocolate.

For Chocolate
- You may build a double boiler yourself by putting a small pan on top of a larger water pan, which ought not be contacting the top pan. Add the chocolate chips and stir until they are melted and smooth. Using a spatula, stir the water until it thickens, then remove from the heat. Stir in some coconut oil & peppermint essence after the mixture has cooled. If you need to reheat the coconut oil before adding this to the chocolate, do so first.
- The chocolate chips may also be melted in the microwave by placing them in a microwave-safe glass dish and heating for 15 seconds, stirring, and repeating if required. Add both coconut oil & peppermint essence and mix until well combined.
- You may also melt chocolate and coat the cookies. Return dipped cookies over the baking sheet and bake as directed. Refrigerate the chocolate-covered cookies for at least an hr after they've been dipped.
- Before serving, store cookies in the refrigerator for maximum performance.

Nutrition Information
Calories: 74 kcal, Carbohydrates: 10 g, Protein: 1 g, Fat: 6 g

196. Skinny Strawberry-Banana Bread
Prep Time: 20 Mins, Cook Time: 30 Mins, Servings: 3
Ingredients
- 1 cup over-ripe, mashed bananas
- 2/3 cup milk coconut
- 3 tbsp syrup maple
- 2 & ½ tbsp seeds chia
- 2 tbsp melted coconut oil
- 1 tbsp vanilla
- 1 & ¼ cup flour blend gluten-free
- 2 & ½ tsp powder baking
- 1 tbsp cinnamon
- 2 cup finely chopped strawberries fresh

Instructions
- Preheat the oven to 350°F
- Mix all of the ingredients except the chia seeds & oil in a big bowl until well-combined. Allow thickening for around 5 mins before serving.
- Flour, some baking powder & cinnamon should be mixed and added to wet ingredients before they are mixed in. Mix until it's all incorporated. Add the strawberries and combine well.
- Apply olive oil spray to a 24-count tiny loaf pan. Spread out the batter in a baking pan. Bake for around 8-12 mins, or till muffin pops back once gently pressed. Remove from heat and let it cool for a few mins.
- Cooked loaves may be topped with coconut cream and chia seeds if desired. It's time to eat!

Nutrition Information
Calories: 87 kcal, Carbohydrates: 15 g, Protein: 1 g, Fat: 3 g

197. Ricotta with Honey & Pistachios
Prep Time: 5 mins, Cook Time: 5 mins, Servings: 5
Ingredients
- 16 oz low-fat ricotta cheese
- 4 tbsp buckwheat honey
- 4 tbsp ground pistachios

Instructions
- It's time to serve the ricotta upside down! If you're serving each person individually, measure out into a cup & then pour it out over a plate.
- The honey should be poured on top.
- Spritz the pistachios on top of the cake.
- This may be served on a piece of fruit for an extra dose of sweetness.

Nutrition Information
Calories: 277 kcal, Carbohydrates: 26 g, Protein: 16 g, Fat: 13 g

198. Mango Rice Pudding with Chocolate Shavings
Prep Time: 25 Mins, Cook Time: 30 Mins, Servings: 4
Ingredients
- 2 ripe mangoes
- 1 cup of rice Arborio
- 2 cups of water
- 2 cups of milk coconut
- 2 tbsp palm sugar coconut
- ¼ cup shaved dark chocolate

Instructions
- Using a mandolin, cut mangoes in half and remove all the pulp. Remove the third pulp, dice it, and store it. This will be used as a garnish in the future.
- In your blender, combine the remainder of the mangoes & process until they are finely ground. Set away for later.
- Cook the rice & water in a medium-sized pot on high heat. Add water and bring to your boil.
- Boil it, reduce the heat, and partly cover it till nearly all water has also been absorbed; however, the mixture is still creamy, about an hr.
- In your saucepan, combine the sugar, coconut milk, and salt, then bring to a boil. For approximately 5 mins, cover & cook.
- The mangoes should be added and mixed well. Cover.
- The drink should be absorbed within 8-10 mins. Add extra coconut milk and boiling water if your rice pudding is drying up & rice is firm.
- Let it cool down for around 15 mins once it's done cooking. It is best served at room temperature rather than heated.
- Meanwhile, use a peeler to remove chocolate flakes off a block.

- Individual servings are best. Mango dice & chocolate shavings may be used as garnishes.

Nutrition Information
Calories: 388 kcal, Carbohydrates: 51 g, Protein: 5 g, Fat: 20 g

199. 3-Ingredient Chocolate Chip Macaroons
Prep Time: 15 mins, Cook Time: 20 mins, Servings: 20
Ingredients
- 2 very ripe bananas medium
- 2 cups coconut finely shredded
- 2/3 cup chocolate chips mini

Instructions
- The oven should be preheated to 350°F.
- Mix the bananas & coconut in a medium-sized bowl. Add the chocolate chips and mix well. A cookie sheet should be used to form 16 biscuits or drops. Keep the cookies apart from one other. Bake for about 20-25 mins, or until the cookies are firm and the coconut is brown. While on your baking pan, let it chill to room temp. Keep it in a sealed jar for future use.

Nutrition Information
Calories: 174 kcal, Carbohydrates: 20 g, Protein: 2 g, Fat: 11 g

200. No-Bake Mini Apple Cheesecakes
Prep Time: 15 mins, Cook Time: 35 mins, Servings: 4
Ingredients
- 2 peeled, cored, & diced apples large
- ¼ tsp cinnamon
- 3 tbsp coconut sugar blonde
- sea salt pinch
- 2/3 cup of fat-free softened cream cheese
- 1/3 of cup fat-free plain Greek yogurt
- 4 no sugar dates
- ½ cup halved walnut

Instructions
- Cover a large saucepan with a lid, bring the apples to your boil, lower the heat, and simmer for about 10 minutes. Allow it to simmer for around 30 mins until the meat is fork tender. Applesauce is a slippery slope. Before pouring to dessert plates, let to cool at room temp.
- While the apples are simmering, combine the yogurt, melted cream cheese, and coconut sugar in a wide mixing bowl. For approximately 2 mins, use the electric mixer to whip the mixture unless it's smooth & the sugar has dissolved. Let it sit in the fridge until you're ready to utilize it.
- Process the dates in your food processor unless they're very small dice. Add walnuts, then pulse until the mixture resembles coarse crumbs and dates are mixed in.
- Layer cream cheese, walnut mixture, & finally cooked apples on each dessert plate. Any leftover walnuts may be sprinkled on the top.
- Keeping it in the fridge until you're ready to eat it is recommended.

Nutrition Information
Calories: 165 kcal, Carbohydrates: 26 g, Protein: 5 g, Fat: 6 g

201. Holiday Ginger Spice Cookies
Prep Time: 15 Mins, Cook Time: 45 Mins, Servings: 10
Ingredients
- 2 cups of white flour whole-wheat
- 2 tsp soda baking
- ½ tsp salt sea
- 1 tsp ginger ground
- 1 tsp cinnamon ground
- ½ tsp allspice ground
- ½ cup softened coconut oil
- 1 cup palm sugar coconut
- 1 large egg
- ¼ cup sorghum or molasses
- 1 tsp of water

Instructions
- The oven should be preheated to 350°F. You may use a cookie sheet to prevent the cookies from sticking to the pan.
- Set aside a large bowl & sift the salt, flour, & spices.
- Beat the coconut oil & sugar together in a medium bowl with the electric mixer till they form a creamy & well-combined mixture. Beat in the molasses, egg, & water until they're all incorporated into the batter. With a big spoon, stir all dry ingredients into the mixture. Shape the dough after it has rested for 10 mins at room temp.
- Using your hands or the base of the glass, flatten the 1" balls of dough using your hands or the base of the glass on a piece of parchment paper. Separate the cookies by approximately a half-inch.
- Use Turbinado sugar with bigger crystals to make your cookies extra festive.
- Baking time ranges from 10 to 12 mins, depending on how soft or crunchy you want your cookies. Remove from cookie sheet & let cool entirely on the wire rack for approximately four more mins. Keep it in a sealed jar for future use. Do not freeze your food for the greatest benefits.

Nutrition Information
Calories: 78 kcal, Carbohydrates: 12 g, Protein: 1 g, Fat: 5 g

202. Clean Eating Crème Brulé
Prep Time: 20 mins, Cook Time: 30 mins, Servings: 5
Ingredients
- 5 large egg yolks
- 1 large egg
- 6 stevia drops
- ¼ cup syrup maple
- 1 coconut milk full fat
- 1 scraped vanilla bean
- ¼ cup turbinado sugar or sucanat

Instructions
- A 325°F oven is ideal for baking.
- Mix all ingredients in the blender, including vanilla seeds & egg yolks. Fill six ramekins with the mixture and set them in the refrigerator. A big baking dish should be used to hold the ramekins & water should be poured around the muffin tins. Avoid getting water into the ramekins when cooking.
- Place 27-33 mins in a preheated oven, till the borders are set & the middle is jiggly such as jello. Remove from heat and let it cool for a few mins. Sprinkle a spoonful of sugar over the top and broil for 30 secs; utilize a kitchen flame to caramelize the sugar right before you serve it. It's time to eat!

Nutrition Information
Calories: 288 kcal, Carbohydrates: 20 g, Protein: 8 g, Fat: 20 g

203. No-Bake Skinny Chocolate Cheesecakes
Prep Time: 25 mins, Cook Time: 35 Mins, Servings: 10
Ingredients
Crust
- ½ cup finely ground walnuts
- 1 tbsp oil coconut
- 1 tsp honey

Cheesecake
- 16 oz cream cheese low-fat
- 1 cup vanilla Greek yogurt
- ¼ cup of honey
- 3 tbsp powder cocoa
- 1 tbsp extract vanilla
- ¼ tsp salt sea

Instructions
- A baking dish should be used to press all crust ingredients together.
- In your food processor, combine all cheesecake ingredients & pulse until creamy. At least three hrs before serving spread the mix into a baking dish.
- Serve by slicing into squares.

Nutrition Information
Calories: 119 kcal, Carbohydrates: 9 g, Protein: 4 g, Fat: 8 g

204. No-Bake Peanut Butter Cheesecake
Prep Time: 15 Mins, Cook Time: 30 Mins, Servings: 12

Ingredients
Crust
- 1 cup of almonds
- 1 cup oats old-fashioned
- 3 tbsp melted coconut oil
- 2 oz melted bittersweet chocolate
- 1/8 tsp salt

Filling
- 8 oz low-fat, softened cream cheese
- 15 oz milk coconut
- 1 cup natural peanut butter
- ½ cup sugar coconut
- 1 tbsp melted coconut oil
- 1 tsp vanilla extract pure

Instructions
- The oven should be preheated to 350°F. The crust is baked, but not cheesecake.

Crust
- When melting chocolate, use a boiler. Process the almonds, oats, & salt in a food processor unless they are the consistency of coarse crumbs, about 10 pulses. Mix melted chocolate, almond mixture, & coconut oil in a mixing bowl. One tbsp of the crumbs should be saved for subsequent use.
- To make a pie dish, add the crumbs. The bottom & sides should be equally coated with crumbs. If you don't have a springform pan, you may just push crumbs into the bottom & up the edges of your pan. Remove from the oven and let cool fully before serving.
- Using plastic wrap, push the crumbs into position with one hand.

Filling
- Before opening coconut milk, keep it in the refrigerator for almost 24 hrs. Open this can from the base by flipping it over & using the can opener. Remove all of the liquid from the container. Retain the juice from the coconut for milkshakes or other dishes. To thicken the coconut milk, place it in a large mixing bowl & beat it on a moderate speed with the electric mixer for 5-6 mins. When sugar dissolves, add the cream cheese & continue beating for another 2 mins.
- Beat in the coconut oil, peanut butter, & vanilla. Cool crust before filling. After 5-6 hrs of refrigerating, sprinkle your filling using the remaining crumbs.

Nutrition Information
Calories: 323 kcal, Carbohydrates: 17 g, Protein: 9 g, Fat: 26 g

205. Slow Cooker Molten Lava Cake
Prep Time: 20 Mins, Cook Time: 35 Mins, Servings: 6

Ingredients
For Cake
- 5 large eggs
- 1 cup powder cocoa
- 2/3 cup maple syrup pure
- 2/3 cup finely chopped dark chocolate

For Ice Cream
- 4 ripe, frozen bananas
- ¼ cup nibs' cacao

Instructions
- Cocoa powder, eggs, & maple syrup are whisked in a big basin. Pour into your slow cooker. Chop up some chocolate and sprinkle it on top.
- Cover & cook for around 1-2 hrs on high. Start monitoring your cake after 1 & ½ hrs in the crockpot. When the center is set & pops back to the touch, you know it's done.
- When your cake is ready, unplug your crockpot & keep your cake wrapped until it is time to eat.

Prepare Topping
- A high-speed blender may be used to combine frozen bananas & cacao to create the cream topping.

Nutrition Information
Calories: 240 kcal, Carbohydrates: 37 g, Protein: 7 g, Fat: 10 g

206. Slow Cooker Honey Baked Apples with Granola
Prep Time: 15 mins, Cook Time: 2 hrs, Servings: 16

Ingredients
- 6 medium, cored apples
- 3 tbsp honey
- 2 tsp cinnamon powdered
- ¼ cup dried cranberries or raisins
- 1 cup granola stovetop
- 1/3 cup juice orange

Instructions
- Combine cinnamon, raisins, honey, & granola in a small bowl. Set away for later.
- Scoop out about three-quarters of the apple's internal meat, leaving a bit at the bottom. Fill the apples halfway with the granola mix, and then serve.
- In your slow cooker, mix orange juice & honey. In your slow cooker, place your granola stuffed apples. Cook for 4-5 hrs on low.
- Pour some syrupy liquid from your slow cooker over each apple. Ensure that the food is at room temperature before serving.

Nutrition Information
Calories: 195 kcal, Carbohydrates: 40 g, Protein: 3 g, Fat: 4 g

207. Nutella Fudge Brownies
Prep Time: 10 mins, Cook Time: 15 mins, Servings: 12

Ingredients
- 1 cup of Nutella
- 2 large eggs
- ¾ cup pastry flour whole-wheat
- 1 tbsp powder cocoa
- 1/16 tsp of salt

Instructions
- Preheat the oven to 350°F
- Eggs are added to the Nutella spread & mixed until smooth.
- Add the cocoa powder, flour, & salt to the mixture and mix well. Spread the mixture in an 8" square baking pan that has been lightly oiled. When a toothpick put into the middle comes out clear, it's done baking for 15 mins. Slice into squares when they've cooled to room temperature.

Nutrition Information
Calories: 125 kcal, Carbohydrates: 15 g, Protein: 3 g, Fat: 7 g

208. No-Bake Peanut Butter Bars
Prep Time: 15 mins, Cook Time: 1 hr 15 mins, Servings: 4

Ingredients
Crust
- ¾ cup finely ground peanuts
- 1 tbsp pastry flour whole-wheat
- 1 tbsp of honey
- 1 tbsp melted coconut oil
- ¼ tsp salt sea

Filling
- 1 cup of creamy natural peanut butter
- ¼ cup milk coconut
- ¼ cup of honey
- 2 tbsp melted coconut oil

Instructions
- Using parchment paper, cover a baking pan.
- Gather all crust ingredients & spread them out evenly in a 9-inch by 13-inch baking dish.
- In your food processor, combine filling ingredients & process till smooth & creamy. The mixture should be poured over the crust. Refrigerate for a few hrs till it's solid.
- Cut the dough into squares and bake. Keep in the fridge.

Nutrition Information
Calories: 235 kcal, Carbohydrates: 14 g, Protein: 9 g, Fat: 17 g

209. Slow Cooker Pumpkin Spice Latte Cake
Prep Time: 20 mins Cook Time: 2 hrs, Servings: 4
Ingredients
- 28 oz puree pumpkin
- 2 cups pastry flour whole-wheat
- 3 large eggs
- 1 & 2/3 cups palm sugar coconut
- 2/3 cup of milk almond
- ¼ cup oil canola
- 2 tbsp spice pumpkin pie
- 2 tsp powder baking
- 2 tsp maple extract or vanilla
- 2 tbsp powder espresso
- ½ cup of honey
- nonstick cooking spray olive oil

Instructions
- This recipe calls for a big bowl to be filled with a mixture of half the can of pureed pumpkin, coconut sugar, eggs, almond milk, and pumpkin spice. Combine all ingredients in a large bowl using your electric mixer on low speed until thoroughly blended.
- Combine the leftover pumpkin, egg, pumpkin spice, & honey and mix well.
- Apply cooking spray to a slow cooker's bottom. In the base of your crockpot, spread some cake batter. Spread this pumpkin mixture over the top. Make a cake top using the rest of the batter. Cook on low for two to three hrs, covered.
- Before lifting the cover, let your cake cool down a little.

Nutrition Information
Calories: 248 kcal, Carbohydrates: 47 g, Protein: 4 g, Fat: 6 g

210. Feta, Apple, and Arugula Quesadillas
Prep Time: 20 mins, Cook Time: 20 mins, Servings: 14
Ingredients
- 1 tbsp mustard Dijon
- 2 tsp cider apple
- 4 tortillas flour
- 6 oz low-fat feta cheese
- 1 large apple
- 3 cups of arugula
- ¾ tsp freshly ground black pepper

Instructions
- Mix mustard & cider in a mixing bowl.
- Over medium-high heat, place a large skillet.
- Spread roughly 1 & ½ tbsp of the mustard mix on every tortilla.
- Place a mustard-side up the tortilla in the pan.
- ½ of a tortilla should be covered with cheese slices. Cook the tortilla for one minute unless the cheese starts to melt.
- One-quarter of sliced apples and arugula should be placed on the cheese. Sprinkle with black pepper.
- Press a spatula into the folded tortilla.
- When golden brown, remove from the heat and serve.
- Pull out of the pan.
- Repeat the technique with apple pieces, tortillas, cheese, arugula, & pepper.

Nutrition Information
Calories: 246 kcal, Carbohydrates: 26 g, Protein: 10 g, Fat: 12 g

211. Easy Mint Yogurt with Strawberries
Prep Time: 10 Mins, Cook Time: 20 Mins, Servings: 5
Ingredients
- 3 & ½ cups of low-fat Greek yogurt
- 1/3 cup fresh, packed mint leaves
- ½ cup honey or maple syrup
- ½ cup of water
- 3 & ½ cups fresh, hulled & chopped strawberries

Instructions
- Toss the mint leaves & maple syrup together in a medium saucepan over medium heat. Cook for 2-3 mins after bringing to your boil. Pour the syrup into a large mixing bowl via a mesh sieve. Refrigerate for at least an hr.
- Yogurt and mint syrup may be mixed in a blender. Pour ¼ cup of the syrup into a separate big dish and stir in some strawberries. Strawberries should be placed on top of six separate bowls of blended yogurt.
- Serve right away.
- The excess mint syrup may make other treats, such as cookies.

Nutrition Information
Calories: 167 kcal, Carbohydrates: 31 g, Protein: 7 g, Fat: 2 g

212. Fresh Summer Fruit Salad with Basil Syrup
Prep Time: 10 Mins, Cook Time: 40 Mins, Servings: 4
Ingredients
- ¼ cup fresh basil leaves
- ¼ cup of coconut blonde palm sugar
- ½ cup of water
- 2 cups hulled & quartered strawberries
- 4 peeled & sliced kiwi fruits
- 4 peeled & sliced oranges
- ½ cup goji berries dried
- mint leaves or basil fresh

Instructions
- A little saucepan with sugar, water, & basil is all that's needed to make a syrup. To get the syrupy texture, lower the flame to medium-low once it hits a boil & simmer for around 10-15 mins.
- To preserve the syrup, discard all basil & put it in a shallow dish or jar. Please wait for it to cool down. If you're not going to use it right away, put it in the fridge.
- Goji berries, basil syrup, & water should be mixed in a shallow dish to soften them.
- Serve the fruits & soft goji berries in 4 different dishes.
- Use basil syrup to sweeten.
- Garnish with fresh mint or basil.

Nutrition Information
Calories: 128 kcal, Carbohydrates: 32 g, Protein: 2 g, Fat: 1g

213. Grilled Pineapple with Rum Syrup and Frozen Yogurt
Prep Time: 25 Mins, Cook Time: 45 Mins, Servings: 5
Ingredients
- 6 slices pineapple
- ½ cup of rum
- ¼ cup of water
- ¼ cup of brown sugar unrefined
- 6 yogurt scoops frozen

Instructions
- Pour the water, rum, & sugar into a medium saucepan & bring to a boil over moderate flame. Then decrease the heat & simmer for a few mins till it thickens. Wait for it to cool down. This syrup may be made the next day & stored in the freezer for some days.
- Grill chopped pineapple for approximately 40 secs on all sides over high temperature.
- Frozen yogurt should be placed on top of the pineapple before serving. Pour syrup over the top.
- Serve right away.

Nutrition Information
Calories: 298 kcal, Carbohydrates: 67 g, Protein: 3 g, Fat: 1g

214. Coconut Granita Drizzled with Mango Sauce
Prep Time: 30 Mins, Cook Time: 25 Mins, Servings: 4
Ingredients
- 1 cup of lite canned coconut milk
- 1 cup of water
- 3 tbsp palm sugar coconut
- 1 ripe, peeled & sliced mango
- ½ zest lime
- 1 tsp juice lime

Instructions
- Bring water and sugar to a boil on a moderate flame in your saucepan.

- That coconut milk should be added after the sugar completely melts. When somewhat thickened, remove from heat and let it cool.
- Then let coconut mixture cool down to room temp before putting it in a jar that could be closed with a lid.
- Until it's frozen, put the jar in the fridge. After every hr, use a spoon to stir the granita. Make sure to break up any chunks that have formed and place them within blender shortly before serving if your granita is too difficult to shift around.
- Put mango pulp, lime juice, sugar, & lime zest into the blender, then process until the mixture is smooth. Refrigerate.
- Pour some sauce over the granita before serving.

Nutrition Information
Calories: 181 kcal, Carbohydrates: 20 g, Protein: 2 g, Fat: 12 g

215. 90. Pan-Seared Peaches and Cinnamon
Prep Time: 30 Mins, Cook Time: 40 Mins, Servings: 4

Ingredients
- 4 peeled, cored & halved peaches ripe
- 4 tsp sugar coconut
- 1 tsp cinnamon
- 3 cups yogurt Greek
- fresh mint leaves

Instructions
- In a medium saucepan, bring the sugar to a boil over moderate flame.
- Cook all sides of the peaches unless sugar has dissolved completely.
- Add a dash of cinnamon on top.
- Refrigerate your peaches when they have cooled down.
- They should be served in separate glasses.

Nutrition Information
Calories: 122 kcal, Carbohydrates: 19 g, Protein: 7 g, Fat: 3 g

216. Quinoa Peanut Butter Fudgesicles
Prep Time: 25 Mins, Cook Time: 15 Mins, Servings: 3

Ingredients
- 1 cup cooked & chilled quinoa
- 6 tbsp unsweetened cocoa powder
- sea salt or kosher
- 6 tbsp natural & crunchy peanut butter
- 6 tbsp honey
- 13 & ½ oz milk can lite coconut
- 1 tsp vanilla pure

Instructions
- Add cocoa powder, cooked quinoa, & salt to a blender. Process in batches in a food processor until everything is fully blended. Add the rest of the ingredients and continue to pulse till smooth. Make popsicles by pouring the mixture into ice cube trays and freezing until solid. Run boiled water on the molds for seconds to soften them up for around 10 minutes out from the freezer.

Nutrition Information
Calories: 253 kcal, Carbohydrates: 24 g, Protein: 6 g, Fat: 17 g

217. Healthy Frozen Yogurt with Fresh Fruit Salad and Mint
Prep Time: 5 mins, Cook Time: 5 mins, Servings: 4

Ingredients
- ¼ cup peeled & chopped kiwi
- ¼ cup hulled & quartered strawberries
- 1/8 cup rinsed blackberries
- ¼ cup rinsed blueberries
- 1/8 cup diced pineapple
- 4 fresh mint leaves
- 1 cup low-fat frozen yogurt

Instructions
- Serve fresh fruit in separate dishes. Mint leaves should be minced, and mint should be added to fresh fruit & mixed well. Scoop the yogurt on top of fresh fruit. The leftover mint may be used as a garnish.

Nutrition Information
Calories: 191 kcal, Carbohydrates: 38 g, Protein: 4 g, Fat: 4 g

218. Pan-Roasted Candied Pecans
Prep Time: 15 mins, Cook Time: 15 mins, Servings: 4

Ingredients
- 2 cups halves pecan
- sea salt or kosher
- ¼ cup of honey
- ½ tsp extract vanilla

Instructions
- Pecan halves should be roasted for approximately two mins in a big pot over moderate heat. While roasting nuts in a skillet, rotate them numerous times. Toss the nuts in honey and toss again to coat. For about five mins, keep the mixture constantly whisked.
- Remove from the heat and stir in the vanilla. Leave to cool at room temp before serving. A sealed container is the best way to keep pecans fresh until you're ready to utilize them.

Nutrition Information
Calories: 211 kcal, Carbohydrates: 14 g, Protein: 2 g, Fat: 18 g

219. No-Cook, 5 Min Chocolate Pudding
Prep Time: 5 mins, Cook Time: 5 mins, Servings: 8

Ingredients
- 1 medium avocado
- ¼ cup raw honey
- 1 & ½ tbsp oil coconut
- ¼ tsp vanilla pure
- ¼ tsp vinegar balsamic
- ¼ cup unsweetened cocoa powder
- sea salt or kosher

Instructions
- Mix avocado, vanilla, coconut oil, honey, & vinegar. Pulse till smooth. Using a spatula, scrape the sides of the blender, then add some cocoa powder & salt; pulse till the mixture is smooth and creamy. Serve right away.

Nutrition Information
Calories: 220 kcal, Carbohydrates: 29 g, Protein: 2 g, Fat: 14 g

220. Coconut-Banana Cream Pudding
Prep Time: 30 mins, Cook Time: 30 mins, Servings: 5

Ingredients
- ¼ cup arrowroot or cornstarch
- ¼ tsp of salt
- ¼ cup honey pure
- 1 & ½ cups coconut milk lite
- 2 slightly beaten egg yolks
- 1 tsp extract vanilla
- ½ cup unsweetened coconut flakes
- 2 sliced bananas

Instructions
- Cornstarch and salt should be mixed in a heavy-bottomed pot. Add honey & egg yolks into dry ingredients. Stir in the ingredients, then gradually add the milk until it's all incorporated into a smooth paste. Ensure that the food doesn't cling to the bottom of the pan by constantly stirring it. 8-10 mins of cooking time should be sufficient to get the appropriate thickness.
- Then remove from the stove and toss in the coconut & vanilla extract. Serve individual desserts with a layer of the pudding & a layer of sliced bananas that has cooled for approximately 15 mins. Serve the pudding at room temperature.

Nutrition Information
Calories: 264 kcal, Carbohydrates: 34 g, Protein: 3 g, Fat: 14 g

221. Cantaloupe Granita
Prep Time: 30 Mins, Cook Time: 20 Mins, Servings: 7

Ingredients
- 1 lb chopped cantaloupe pulp
- 2 cups of water
- 3 & ½ oz sweetener natural
- 2 tbsp fresh lemon juice

Instructions

- Take a medium saucepan and bring water & sweetener to your boil, then lower the heat & simmer for around 15 mins.
- Blend your cantaloupe till smooth inside a blender.
- Mix both syrup & the melon in a big bowl. Lemon juice should be added. A variety of flavors are available to suit your palate. Make the cantaloupe combination a little spicier since it would lose some flavors as it freezes.
- Ice cream machine instructions will tell you how to create cantaloupe ice cream after it's cooled down.
- If you don't have an ice cream maker, transfer the mix to the container with a lid and put it within the freezer. Bring it out every 30 mins and stir till it reaches the proper granita consistency.
- If your granita becomes too hard, split it into large pieces & put it in a blender to break it up.

Nutrition Information
Calories: 54 kcal, Carbohydrates: 14 g, Protein: 1 g, Fat: 0 g

222. Protein Fudgesicles
Prep Time: 10 mins, Cook Time: 2 hrs 10 mins, Servings: 16
Ingredients
- 6 tbsp unsweetened cocoa
- sea salt or kosher
- 1 large avocado
- 13 & ½ oz coconut milk lite
- 15 oz drained & rinsed black beans
- 6 tbsp honey
- 1 tsp vanilla pure

Instructions
- Set aside a mixture of cocoa powder and salt. A food processor may mix cocoa powder with salt, beans, honey, coconut milk, avocado, and vanilla.
- Put the fudge mix in popsicle molds. Set in the freezer for a few hrs or till solid. To release the mold, spray it with hot water.

Nutrition Information
Calories: 242 kcal, Carbohydrates: 28 g, Protein: 6 g, Fat: 15 g

223. Grain-Free Lemon Blueberry Lavender Muffins
Prep Time: 15 mins, Cook Time: 15 mins, Servings: 6
Ingredients
- ½ cup sifted coconut flour
- ½ tsp soda baking
- ½ tsp salt
- ¼ tsp nutmeg
- ½ tsp cinnamon
- 2 tbsp lavender dried
- 6 large eggs
- 1/3 cup of honey
- ¼ cup melted coconut oil
- 1 tbsp extract vanilla
- 1 cup fresh blueberries
- 1 zested lemon

Instructions
- Add coconut flour, cinnamon, nutmeg, baking soda, & lavender to a medium bowl, then mix well.
- Eggs, oil, honey, & vanilla are mixed in a big bowl. With a whisk, mix well.
- Whisk the wet and dry ingredients together.
- Using a spatula, incorporate the blueberries & lemon zest.
- The muffin tray should be filled to the brim with batter.
- Bake for around 15-20 mins at 350 F. When the toothpick pushed into the center of a muffin falls out clear, it's done baking.
- Serve when it's cooled down!

Nutrition Information
Calories: 156 kcal, Carbohydrates: 20 g, Protein: 4 g, Fat: 8 g

224. Apple Cinnamon Streusel Cake
Prep Time: 25 Mins, Cook Time: 30 Mins, Servings: 10
Ingredients
- 1 & ¼ cups of white flour whole-wheat
- 1 tsp powder baking
- ½ tsp soda baking
- 1 tsp cinnamon
- ½ tsp salt
- 3 cups thinly diced apple pieces
- ½ cup oil canola
- ½ cup of honey
- 1 slightly beaten egg
- 1 tsp of vanilla
- ½ diced pecans

Streusel
- 2 tbsp white flour whole-wheat
- ¼ cup oats old-fashioned
- ¼ cup finely diced pecans
- 1 tsp cinnamon
- 1 tbsp honey

Instructions
- A 325°F oven is ideal for baking.
- Add flour, sugar, and salt to a small dish and mix well.
- Small mixing basin with ingredients whisked together. Add the honey, egg, canola oil, & vanilla to a mixing bowl, then beat on moderate speed for approximately 2 mins.
- Stir in the apples with a wooden spoon after adding them to the dry ingredients. Mix the wet ingredients with the dry ingredients in a large bowl, including the apples.
- Prepare a cake pan with a little oil. Sprinkle streusel equally on the cake batter after pouring it into the pan. After 30 mins of baking, gently cover the streusel with foil to prevent browning. If the sides of the cake start to brown & peel away from the pan, it's ready to come out of the oven.
- Ensure that the food is at room temperature before serving.

Nutrition Information
Calories: 267 kcal, Carbohydrates: 31 g, Protein: 3 g, Fat: 16 g

225. Quinoa Crisp and Berry Parfait
Prep Time: 20 Mins, Cook Time: 40 Mins, Servings: 6
Ingredients
- 1 cup fat-free Greek yogurt
- 1 tbsp freshly squeezed lemon juice
- 2 tbsp of honey
- 2 cups fresh seasonal berries
- ½ cup crisp quinoa

Quinoa Crisp
- ½ cup pre-rinsed red quinoa
- 1 cup of water
- 2 tsp honey

Instructions
- A tiny mixing bowl is all that is needed for this recipe.
- Cover and store in the refrigerator until needed.
- Quinoa & water should be added to a saucepan and brought to your boil over medium heat before being lowered to simmer. When the quinoa has absorbed all the water, it is done cooking. Stir in the honey. The oven should be preheated to 325°F while Quinoa cools.
- Spread quinoa on a parchment-lined baking sheet. After 15 mins, mix the quinoa & continue cooking for another 10 mins on the center oven rack. Let quinoa crisp come to room temp before serving.
- Add yogurt & quinoa crisp to smoothie dessert plates with berries.
- Eat it as a snack, on top of yogurt, granola, or cereal.

Nutrition Information
Calories: 214 kcal, Carbohydrates: 40 g, Protein: 8 g, Fat: 3 g

226. Vanilla Soft Serve Ice Cream
Prep Time: 10 mins, Cook Time: 10 mins, Servings: 4
Ingredients
- 1 & ½ cups sliced, frozen bananas
- 1 tbsp nonfat Greek yogurt
- 1 tsp vanilla extract pure

Instructions

- To make it smooth, use your food processor. It will take a few stops of the processor before you can use a spoon to push stuff around. After some repetitions, it will become almost undetectable.
- If desired, garnish with fresh fruit.

Nutrition Information
Calories: 110 kcal, Carbohydrates: 26 g, Protein: 2 g, Fat: 0 Fat

227. Piña Colada Pops
Prep Time: 15 Mins, Cook Time: 35 Mins, Servings: 14
Ingredients
- 15 oz chunks pineapple
- 1 ripe banana
- 1 cup milk coconut

Instructions
- Blend all ingredients till smooth & creamy in a food processor. The mixture should be poured into popsicle molds and frozen.

Nutrition Information
Calories: 88 kcal, Carbohydrates: 12 g, Protein: 1 g, Fat: 5 g

228. Clean Eating Almond Butter Fudge
Prep Time: 25 Mins, Cook Time: 40 Mins, Servings: 24
Ingredients
- 1 cup natural, creamy almond butter
- ¼ cup melted coconut oil
- ¼ tsp extract vanilla
- pinch sea salt

Instructions
- In a small bowl, combine all of the ingredients. Stir until the mixture is completely emulsified. Preheat an oven to 350 degrees. Put the mixture in a medium pan & freeze it. Spend several hrs in the freezer. Cut into squares after removing from the pan. Wrap each piece in a sealed container and store it in the refrigerator. Keep in the fridge or freezer.

Nutrition Information
Calories: 129 kcal, Carbohydrates: 3 g, Protein: 3 g, Fat: 12 g

229. Chocolate Banana Wonderland Smoothie
Prep Time: 5 mins, Cook Time: 5 mins, Servings: 4
Ingredients
- 1 cup unsweetened almond milk
- 1 banana unfrozen or frozen
- 2 tbsp raw organic cacao powder
- 1 tsp organic cinnamon
- 2 tbsp natural peanut butter
- 1 tbsp organic virgin coconut oil
- 10 cubes ice

Instructions
- In your blender, combine all ingredients and process until your smoothie is creamy and frothy. Ice cubes can be added to your drink at the beginning of the finish, depending on your preference. If you're using a blender with a blade that can't handle ice, you may want to add it towards the end. Enjoy!

Nutrition Information
Calories: 297 kcal, Carbohydrates: 29 g, Protein: 9 g, Fat: 18 g

230. Three Seed Berry Parfait
Prep Time: 5 mins, Cook Time: 5 mins, Servings: 4
Ingredients
- 2 cups fat-free Greek yogurt
- 2 tbsp honey
- 2 tsp freshly squeezed lemon juice
- 1 cup fresh raspberries
- 1 cup fresh blueberries
- 1 cup fresh, sliced strawberries
- 1 tbsp flax seeds ground
- 1 tbsp seeds chia
- 1 tbsp seeds hemp

Instructions
- In your small dish, mix yogurt, honey, & lemon juice.
- After layering the yogurt with berries & seeds, top your parfait with a sprinkle of seeds. Serve right away.

Nutrition Information
Calories: 128 kcal, Carbohydrates: 21 g, Protein: 6 g, Fat: 3 g

231. Superfood Banana Pops
Prep Time: 10 Mins, Cook Time: 35 Mins, Servings: 6
Ingredients
- 3 large bananas
- 2-3 tbsp raw cacao powder
- 2 drops liquid stevia
- 3 oz water
- ¼ cup raw cacao nibs
- ¼ cup raw goji berries

Instructions
- Freeze two of the bananas by inserting a stick into each one.
- Make a chocolate syrup-like consistency by blending the second banana, stevia, cacao powder, & water in a blender unless smooth.
- Top cacao nibs or goji berries after dipping a frozen banana in chocolate sauce.

Nutrition Information
Calories: 241 kcal, Carbohydrates: 58 g, Protein: 3 g, Fat: 1 g

232. No-Bake Chocolate Coconut Macaroons
Prep Time: 15 mins, Cook Time: 35 mins, Servings: 20
Ingredients
- ¾ cup of honey
- ¼ cup oil coconut
- 1 tbsp vanilla extract pure
- 4 cups finely shredded coconut unsweetened
- 2/3 cup unsweetened cocoa powder

Instructions
- Melt the coconut oil & honey together in a small saucepan over low heat. Using low heat, melt the chocolate.
- Add the vanilla, coconut, & cocoa powder, then mix thoroughly.
- Use parchment paper to cover a baking pan. The dough should be scooped onto the baking sheet using the cookie scoop. Store within an airtight jar in the freezer for approximately 20 mins.

Nutrition Information
Calories: 159 kcal, Carbohydrates: 18 g, Protein: 2 g, Fat: 11 g

233. Chocolate Chia Seed Pudding
Prep Time: 10 mins, Cook Time: 3 hrs 10 mins, Servings: 0.5 cup
Ingredients
- 2 cups milk almond
- ½ cup seeds chia
- ¼ cup butter creamy almond
- ¼ cup unsweetened cocoa powder
- 4 large, pitted & finely chopped dates
- 1 tsp vanilla extract pure

Instructions
- Mix the ingredients in a bowl. Refrigerate for at least 3-4 hrs, or overnight, if possible.
- Blend in blender. Use more milk to soften the pudding if required, puree until smooth & creamy. Add extra fruit, nuts, chia seeds, any other toppings you choose to the chia bowl.

Nutrition Information
Calories: 219 kcal, Carbohydrates: 18 g, Protein: 12 g, Fat: 16 g

234. No-Bake Lemon Berry Cups
Prep Time: 20 mins, Cook Time: 20 mins, Servings: 5
Ingredients
- 1 cup fat-free Greek yogurt
- ½ cup of cream cheese softened low-fat
- 1 juiced & zested lemon
- 2 tbsp sugar coconut
- ¼ cup chopped pecans
- 2 pitted dates
- 1 cup fresh mixed berries

Instructions

- Make a creamy & fluffy mixture by combining the yogurt with lemon juice, cream cheese, & zest.
- Make a crumb-like pecan-date mixture by pulsing in a food processor.
- In tiny dessert cups, combine yogurt, almonds, & fresh berries. The dish could be garnished with more nuts & lemon zest.

Nutrition Information
Calories: 118 kcal, Carbohydrates: 10 g, Protein: 4 g, Fat: 7 g

235. Spiced Chocolate and Avocado Pudding
Prep Time: 10 mins, Cook Time: 10 mins, Servings: 3
Ingredients
- 2 ripe avocados
- 2 tbsp oil coconut
- ¼ cup of honey
- 3 pitted dates
- ½ cup powder cocoa
- ½ tsp powder mild curry
- 1 cup milk coconut

Instructions
- The food processor is all that is needed to make this dish. Add fresh coconut milk gradually until it reaches the desired consistency. Refrigerate for at least an hr to thicken.
- Fruit, seeds, chopped nuts, shredded coconut may be served as a garnish.

Nutrition Information
Calories: 238 kcal, Carbohydrates: 25 g, Protein: 4 g, Fat: 16 g

236. Skinny Mini Blueberry Cheesecakes
Prep Time: 10, Cook Time: 25, Servings: 5
Ingredients
- ½ cup fat-free cream cheese
- 2 tbsp sugar coconut
- ½ cup low-fat Greek yogurt
- 2 tsp freshly squeezed lemon juice
- ¼ cup of blueberry no sugar fruit spread
- 1 cup fresh, whole blueberries

For Crumb Layer
- 1/3 cup whole almonds
- 4 no sugar dates

Instructions
- A mixer should be used to beat together the sugar, cream cheese, yogurt & lemon juice in a medium-sized bowl for approximately 3 mins, till the sugar dissolves and the mixture becomes smooth. Let it sit in the fridge until you're ready to use it.
- Combine blueberries & preserves in a mixing bowl.
- Add almonds in your food processor & pulse until you get a crumb-like texture, but don't overdo it. Pulse the dates into the mixture until they're evenly dispersed. Spread half the almond & date mixture on each dessert plate if you choose to serve it as a dessert.
- Add half of the cheesecake and yogurt batter to every serving container, followed by half of the blueberry mixture, and then the other half. 2 to 3 hrs before serving, chill in the fridge.
- If preferred, Mint may also be added to the dish as a topping.
- When you just can't get enough sugar, these sweets are the ideal solution. A freezer-safe plate may be used to store this dessert for later usage.

Nutrition Information
Calories: 138 kcal, Carbohydrates: 27 g, Protein: 4 g, Fat: 2g

237. Clean Eating Raspberry Oat Bars
Prep Time: 15 mins, Cook Time: 35 mins, Servings: 10
Ingredients
- 1 cup of white flour whole-wheat
- 1 cup oats rolled
- ½ cup palm sugar coconut
- ½ tsp powder baking
- ¼ tsp salt sea
- ½ cup melted coconut oil
- 2/3 cup fruit-sweetened raspberry jam

Instructions
- Preheat the oven to 350°F
- In a mixing bowl, combine all dry ingredients and mix well. Spread oat mixture onto the baking dish that has been gently greased. Using your hands, press the mix down firmly.
- Spread some jam over the top & sprinkle the rest of the oat mix on top. Incorporate the oat mix into a jam with a gentle touch.
- After 35 mins, the top should be golden brown. Before slicing into squares & serving, let the dessert cool down.

Nutrition Information
Calories: 212 kcal, Carbohydrates: 20 g, Protein: 2 g, Fat: 14 g

238. Frothy Chocolate Shake
Prep Time: 5 mins, Cook Time: 5 mins, Servings: 4
Ingredients
- 2 frozen, peeled, & pre-sliced bananas
- ½ cup non-fat Greek Yogurt
- 1 cup unsweetened or almond milk
- ¼ cup syrup chocolate
- ½ tsp vanilla extract pure

Instructions
- Pulse all ingredients together in your blender till they form a homogeneous paste.
- Top with the whipped topping & dark chocolate flakes for an additional special treat.

Nutrition Information
Calories: 269 kcal, Carbohydrates: 47 g, Protein: 25 g, Fat: 3 g

239. Easy Clean-Eating Chocolate Syrup
Prep Time: 20 mins, Cook Time: 20 mins, Servings: 3
Ingredients
- 1 & ½ cups palm sugar coconut
- ¾ cup unsweetened cocoa powder
- 1 tbsp cornstarch
- sea salt or kosher
- 1 cup of lite canned coconut milk
- 2 tsp vanilla extract pure

Instructions
- Whisk corn starch, sugar, cocoa, & salt in a small saucepan. Then add the coconut milk slowly & bring it to your boil on moderate flame. Then lower the heat to your simmer & cook for about 10 mins, stirring occasionally. Remove from the stove and mix in the vanilla extract.
- Remove from heat and store in an airtight container in the refrigerator.

Nutrition Information
Calories: 76 kcal, Carbohydrates: 15 g, Protein: 1 g, Fat: 2 g

240. Clean Eating Chocolate Coconut Muffins
Prep Time: 10 mins, Cook Time: 18 mins, Servings: 16
Ingredients
- 1 & ¾ cup oats rolled
- 3 tbsp unrefined coconut oil
- ½ cup unsweetened applesauce
- ½ cup unsweetened cocoa powder
- ½ cup palm sugar coconut
- 1 tbsp vanilla extract pure
- ½ cup yogurt plain Greek
- ½ tsp tartar cream
- 1 & ½ tsp powder baking
- 1 ½ tsp soda baking
- ½ tsp salt
- 2 cups water hot
- ½ cup chips chocolate
- ¼ cup unsweetened coconut flakes

Instructions
- The oven should be preheated to 350°F. Line the muffin tin with cupcake liners & bake.
- A food processor is all that is needed to combine the other ingredients. Blend till oats are crushed and the

mixture is well-combined. By hand, add the chocolate chips.
- Pour your batter into cupcake liners in an equal layer. Coconut flakes may be sprinkled on top. When a toothpick put into the middle comes out clean, the cake is baking.

Nutrition Information
Calories: 199 kcal, Carbohydrates: 26 g, Protein: 6 g, Fat: 10 g

241. Berries with Homemade Pomegranate Syrup
Prep Time: 5 mins, Cook Time: 45 mins, Servings: 5
Ingredients
- 2 cups fresh blueberries
- 6 tbsp cranberries dried
- 2 cups unsweetened pomegranate juice
- ¼ cup palm sugar coconut
- 2 tsp juice lemon
- 8 fresh mint leaves

Instructions
- Pomegranate juice, sugar, four cut mint leaves, & lemon juice should all be combined in a small saucepan. Bring to your boil on moderate flame, then lower the heat to your simmer & cook for about 45 mins, or until the mixture reaches a syrup-like consistency. Before putting it in a container, let it cool down. Refrigerate until you're ready to serve.
- Combine the cranberries, blueberries, & pomegranate syrup. Please put them in separate serving glasses and serve them at once. The leftover mint leaves may be sprinkled on top of each glass. Keeping it in the fridge until you're ready to eat it is recommended.

Nutrition Information
Calories: 88 kcal, Carbohydrates: 22 g, Protein: 1 g, Fat: 1g

242. Clean Eating Apple Pie
Prep Time: 10 Mins, Cook Time: 25 Mins, Servings: 8
Ingredients
Crust
- 1 & ½ cups pastry flour whole wheat
- ½ cup flour oat
- 1 tbsp coconut or turbinado sugar
- ½ tsp salt
- 2/3 cup cold coconut oil
- water ice cold

Filling
- 3 lb delicious apples golden
- ½ cup palm sugar coconut
- 2 tbsp white flour whole wheat
- 1 juiced lemon
- 1 tsp cinnamon
- ½ tsp cardamom ground
- ½ tsp ginger ground
- ground nutmeg pinch
- sea salt or kosher
- 2 tsp vanilla extract pure
- 1 lightly beaten egg

Instructions
- Combine the sugar, oat flour, wheat flour, & salt. Then, form the crust by kneading the mixture together. Using your hands, incorporate the butter into the flour mixture until it's crumbly.
- To make a dough, gradually add some ice water until you get a firm texture. After approximately a half-hr in the fridge, form your dough, cover it in plastic, & transfer it to a bowl.
- To prepare the filling, combine apples and all other ingredients in a food processor or blender, excluding the egg. Allow the mixture to settle for at least 15 mins before serving. Stir once more.
- Roll out one-half of the pie crust after dividing it in half & lightly flouring your work area. Place the dough within the pie pan with care. The apples will cook down, so fill the crust to the brim with the pieces.
- Lay the rest of the crust on top of the pie. Alternatively, the crust may be crisscrossed on pie filling by cutting it into 1-inch strips. When you're done squeezing & pinching the edges, either with your fingertips or fork, you're done. Use a knife to cut slits in the crust of the pie. Brush your dough with beaten egg.
- For 45-60 mins, bake your pie over a baking sheet in an oven, monitoring the crust frequently to ensure it doesn't burn. If the crust starts browning too rapidly, cover the top with a thin layer of Al foil and bake for the rest of the time.
- Filling and crust are done when they are golden brown & bubbling. Let it sit for a few mins before serving.

Nutrition Information
Calories: 414 kcal, Carbohydrates: 58 g, Protein: 5 g, Fat: 20 g

243. Cinnamon Spiced Coffee
Prep Time: 15 mins, Cook Time: 15 mins, Servings: 8
Ingredients
- 1 water quart
- ¼ cup rapadura or sucanat
- 1 stick cinnamon
- 2 anise pods star
- orange
- ½ cup of dark coarsely ground roasted coffee

Instructions
- Pour in the cinnamon, water, orange peel, anise & sweetener into a small saucepan, then bring it to a boil on medium heat. Take it from the fire after 2 mins of boiling. Stir well. Allow at least five mins of standing time before removing the cover. Serve after straining through a metal mesh filter.

Nutrition Information
Calories: 15 kcal, Carbohydrates: 4 g, Protein: 5 g, Fat: 0 g

244. Sweetly Spiced Granola
Prep Time: 15 mins, Cook Time: 30 mins, Servings: 4
Ingredients
- 3 cups rolled oats old-fashioned
- 1 cup of amaranth
- 1 cup pieces walnut
- ¼ cup oil canola
- ½ cup of honey
- ¼ tsp salt
- 1 tsp anise ground
- ½ tsp cinnamon
- ¼ tsp cardamom ground
- ½ tsp extract vanilla
- 1 cup cranberries dried
- 1 cup chopped dark chocolate

Instructions
- The oven should be preheated to 325°F.
- Line the baking sheet using cooking spray.
- Combine the honey, oil, & vanilla extract in a medium bowl & whisk until well combined.
- Combine the anise, cinnamon, pecans, salt, oats, amaranth, and cardamom in a mixing bowl. Stir in some honey mixture until it is evenly distributed. Make sure to spread your granola out evenly on a baking sheet with a rim around it. Bake for about 30 mins, or until brown on the bottom and top. To avoid overbrowning, stir the granola every ten mins.
- The granola should be fully cooled before adding into cranberries & dark chocolate.
- Use lids to seal granola after it has cooled in containers for gifting. Otherwise, be sure to keep it in a sealed jar. Granola may be kept in the pantry for up to two months.

Nutrition Information
Calories: 199 kcal, Carbohydrates: 29 g, Protein: 5 g, Fat: 8 g

245. Slow Cooker Cranberry Poached Pears
Prep Time: 10 mins, Cook Time: 4 hrs, Servings: 6
Ingredients
- 6 bosc pears

- 6 cups juice cranberry
- ¼ cup syrup maple
- 1 cup of raisins
- 1 peeled orange
- 3 sticks cinnamon
- 1-inch root ginger
- 2 stars anise pods
- 3 tsp starch arrowroot
- 8-10 mint leaves

Instructions
- Crockpot: Add the cinnamon sticks, orange peel, cranberry juice, & ginger. Put the pears inside the crockpot with the skins on. During cooking, pear slices may be

flipped over to ensure even cooking. In a slow cooker, cook for 3-4 hrs.
- Mix the cornstarch and poaching liquid in a dish. Make sure to remove all of the spices by squeezing them out of the saucepan. Save the raisins that have swelled up for dessert.
- Pour the cornstarch slurry into the boiling liquid. For a dense thickness, bring to your boil, then decrease the heat & simmer for around 5 mins.
- Allow cooling completely. Poach your pears within cranberry syrup, then add the raisins & a scoop of whipped cream. If desired, garnish with fresh mint leaves.

Nutrition Information
Calories: 224 kcal, Carbohydrates: 58 g, Protein: 1 g, Fat: 0 g

246. Creamy Holiday Eggnog
Prep Time: 20 Mins, Cook Time: 15 Mins, Servings: 6

Ingredients
- 1 yolk egg
- 2 separated whole eggs
- 2 cups skim milk
- 2 zested oranges
- 1/3 cup syrup maple
- 1 tsp cinnamon ground
- 1/8 tsp freshly grated nutmeg
- ½ tsp vanilla extract pure
- 2 rum shots white

Instructions
- Set aside the egg yolks in a basin and whisk them until they are lightened in color.
- Whip the egg whites with the electric mixer until they form firm peaks in a second dish, then put them aside.
- Pour the milk, sweetener, cinnamon, orange zest, & nutmeg into a small saucepan and bring to your simmer over low heat for around 5-8 mins. While constantly whisking, slowly add egg yolks in spiced milk & heat for 3-4 mins.
- Remove from the heat and stir in vanilla & rum. Pour into glasses, top with extra nutmeg, and enjoy!
- Allow the Eggnog to settle & refrigerate for around 24 hrs if you want it cold.

Nutrition Information
Calories: 202 kcal, Carbohydrates: 19 g, Protein: 2 g, Fat: 7 g

247. Creamy Vanilla Frozen Yogurt
Prep Time: 15 Mins, Cook Time: 25 Mins, Servings: 4

Ingredients
- 3 cups of Greek-style plain yogurt
- 2 tsp extract vanilla
- ¼ tsp salt
- ½ cup syrup maple

Instructions
- In a large bowl, combine all ingredients. To create soft-serve ice cream, follow the manufacturer's instructions.
- Put the yogurt in a sealed jar and put it in the fridge to harden. To avoid ice crystals accumulating on the top, wrap the surface using wax paper & then place the lid on the container for more than a day.
- As an alternative to using an ice cream machine to produce vanilla frozen yogurt, pour the mixture into a large shallow container & freeze it, scraping & stirring every half hr for 1 hr and 30 mins. Cover and refrigerate after it has been thoroughly frozen.

Nutrition Information
Calories: 196 kcal, Carbohydrates: 32 g, Protein: 10 g, Fat: 3g

248. Skinny Chai Cookies
Prep Time: 20 Mins, Cook Time: 35 Mins, Servings: 12

Ingredients
- ¼ cup softened unsalted butter
- ¼ cup solid-state coconut oil
- 1 cup of sucanat
- 1 large egg
- ¼ tsp vanilla
- 1 & ½ tsp cinnamon
- ½ tsp cardamom
- ½ tsp ginger
- ¼ tsp allspice
- 1/8 tsp pepper black
- 2 tsp powder baking
- 1 & ¾ cup flour whole-wheat

Instructions
- Coconut oil, Butter, & sucanat should be mixed in a big dish to prevent the ingredients from separating. Use a hand mixer to blend the ingredients until they are completely combined and creamy.
- Mix in the egg & vanilla extract until completely combined.
- Then, add the black pepper, ginger, allspice, cinnamon, cardamom, and baking powder to the mixture. Stir to combine and stir until everything is well incorporated. When you've finished mixing, add the remaining flour, and continue mixing until all of it is combined.
- Refrigerate for around 30 mins after covering with the plastic wrap.
- Line two baking pans using parchment paper & heat the oven to 350°F. Roll cooled dough into balls after removing it from the fridge.
- Flatten the dough balls with a fork once they've been placed over the baking pan. If desired, top with extra sucanat.
- It takes ten mins to bake cookies. Serve cookies when they've had a chance to cool completely.

Nutrition Information
Calories: 185 kcal, Carbohydrates: 24.1 g, Protein: 2.4 g, Fat: 8.9 g

249. Clean Eating Pumpkin Streusel Bars
Prep Time: 30 Mins, Cook Time: 25 Mins, Servings: 6

Ingredients
- 2 cups of white flour whole-wheat
- 2 tsp powder baking
- 1 tsp soda baking
- 1 tsp cinnamon ground
- ¼ tsp ginger ground
- ½ tsp salt kosher
- 1 & ½ cups palm sugar coconut
- 4 large eggs
- 1 cup oil canola
- 15 oz puree pumpkin
- 1 tsp vanilla extract pure

Streusel
- ¾ cup of flour
- ½ cup palm sugar coconut
- 1 tsp of cinnamon
- ¼ cup melted coconut oil

Instructions
- Set the oven's temperature to 350°F and prepare the oven for baking.
- Combine the first six ingredients in a small bowl and put them aside. In a mixing bowl, combine oil, pumpkin, sugar, eggs, & vanilla extract; use a mixer on moderate speed to beat till light and fluffy. Dry

ingredients should be added to the pumpkin mix & stir just long enough to blend everything.

Streusel
- In a mixing bowl, combine all the ingredients & stir thoroughly with a fork.
- Serve in a baking dish or a 9x13-inch baking pan that has been sprayed with nonstick cooking spray. Using a fork, evenly distribute the streusel topping over the batter. If the cake tester falls out clear after 30 minutes, the cake is baking.
- The bars should be cooled down to room temp before slicing into 20 pieces.

Nutrition Information
Calories: 261 kcal, Carbohydrates: 28 g, Protein: 3 g, Fat: 16 g

250. Apple-Berry Crisp
Prep Time: 10 Mins, Cook Time: 25 Mins, Servings: 8

Ingredients

Topping
- 2 & ½ cups oats rolled
- 1/3 cup of honey
- 2 tbsp oil canola
- ¼ cup chopped walnuts
- cooking spray canola oil or olive oil

Filling
- 2 cups chopped, peeled apples
- 2 cups berries fresh
- 1 zested lemon
- 1 tbsp juice lemon
- ¼ cup of honey
- 1 tsp cinnamon ground
- ¼ tsp nutmeg ground
- 2 tbsp flour or cornstarch

Instructions
- 375° Fahrenheit is the recommended temperature for preheating the oven.
- Crush some oats till flour consistency in a blender. Combine your oat flour with the remaining oats in a small bowl. If using, stir in the chopped walnuts. Mix in the oil & honey until it becomes a crumbly texture.
- Olive should be used on each ramekin. Combine lemon juice, chopped apples, lemon zest, berries, & honey in a medium-sized bowl and mix well. Toss together the spices & cornstarch inside a mixing bowl before adding to the apple-berry combination. Make individual ramekins out of the apple-berry mixture. Add the oat mixture on top. When the top is brown and bubbly, it's done baking.
- Dish out into individual ramekins onto plates and turn out of ramekin on a plate after cutting around the sides with a knife to release.

Nutrition Information
Calories: 280 kcal, Carbohydrates: 38 g, Protein: 5 g, Fat: 8 g

251. Slow Cooker Pumpkin Spice Bread Pudding
Prep Time: 15 mins, Cook Time: 6 hrs, Servings: 10

Ingredients
- 1 & ¼ cups almond milk unsweetened
- ¾ cups no sugar pumpkin puree
- ½ cup of honey or palm sugar coconut
- 1 egg whole
- 4 large egg whites
- ½ tsp ground cinnamon
- ¼ tsp ginger
- 1/8 tsp allspice ground
- ground cloves pinch
- 5 cups bread cubed whole grain

Instructions
- Whisk together all ingredients, excluding the bread, inside a large bowl. Pour your pumpkin mixture over the bread within the slow cooker.

Nutrition Information
Calories: 155 kcal, Carbohydrates: 30 g, Protein: 6 g, Fat: 2g

252. Pumpkin Spice Bread
Prep Time: 15 mins, Cook Time: 55 mins, Servings: 12

Ingredients
- 3 tbsp flaxseed ground
- ½ cup of water
- 1 & ½ cups sugar turbinado
- ½ cup of applesauce
- ½ cup oil coconut
- 2 cups pumpkin puree fresh
- 3 cups flour whole-wheat
- 1 tsp cinnamon
- 1 tsp nutmeg fresh
- 1 tsp ginger ground
- 1 tsp soda baking
- ½ tsp powder baking
- ¾ tsp salt
- 2 cups of chopped walnuts
- oats sprinkles

Instructions
- Set the oven temperature to 350°F.
- Flaxseed & water should be mixed until they form a gel-like consistency. The flax mixture should be incorporated into a mixing bowl with the applesauce, oil, sugar, & pumpkin, then mixed well. Add baking powder, flour, & salt to a medium-sized basin and mix well to include the baking soda, spices, powder, & salt. Add dry ingredients to wet ingredients and mix well. Incorporate the walnuts. Loaf pans should be lightly oiled.
- Either divide the batter between two 8" loaf pans. Sprinkle fresh oats or maybe turbinado sugar on top for decoration. Bake the big loaves for around 55 mins & the smaller pieces of bread for around 40 mins. Remove from pans and let cool for around 20 mins before serving.

Nutrition Information
Calories: 177 kcal, Carbohydrates: 23.8 g, Protein: 3.4 g, Fat: 8.1 g

253. Grilled Peaches with Cinnamon, Vanilla, and Honey
Prep Time: 5 mins, Cook Time: 20 mins, Servings: 6

Ingredients
- 4 quartered & pitted peaches ripe
- 1 tsp extract vanilla
- ¼ cup of honey
- 1 tsp cinnamon ground

Instructions
- Preheat the oven to 400°F.
- Apply cooking olive oil spray to a cookie sheet.
- Gather your ingredients in a medium-sized bowl, including honey, vanilla, & cinnamon, then combine well. In a large bowl, combine peach slices, marinade, and salt and pepper to taste. Roast your peaches for around 20 mins, or unless they are soft & golden brown.

Nutrition Information
Calories: 150 kcal, Carbohydrates: 30 g, Protein: 1 g, Fat: 4 g

Conclusion

About 75 percent of the stomach's volume is reduced with a gastrectomy. There is a banana-shaped stomach on the inner curve & the pyloric valve just at the bottom controls the evacuation of your stomach into your small intestine by dividing the stomach vertical from the top towards the bottom. This suggests that, although being smaller, the stomach's function has not been changed. When you consume tiny meals, you'll lose weight, particularly if you stick to a low-fat, low-sugar diet like the Atkins diet. The sense of fullness would last longer, allowing you to consume just 3 meals per day. Your digestive system remains unchanged, so you won't have to deal with any of the adverse symptoms of gastric bypass patients.

To ensure the long-term effectiveness of the sleeve gastrectomy procedure, read this book and adhere to the dietary guidelines it provides you.

Once the new dietary habits have been formed, you must stick to a healthy diet to sustain your weight reduction. Your reduced stomach will reduce the quantity of food you can consume, but weight gain may still happen if you consume a lot of high-calorie items.

As a result of the reduced amount of food consumption, bowel habits are likely to alter. This, of course, is not a bad thing. In the beginning, you may notice that your bowels are opening less regularly, maybe every 2 - 3 days. However, the following meals may help you get your bowel motions back on track.

Before & after the gastric sleeve procedure, you must adhere to your doctor's prescribed diet. The things you're permitted to consume are meant to aid your body's recovery while also setting you up for a long-term good eating habit. In addition, physical activity is essential.

INDEX

Acorn Squash, 14, 79
Almond, 28, 30, 31, 34, 37, 39, 43, 45, 70, 98, 123, 167, 176, 185, 186, 187, 193, 199, 200, 201, 205, 207, 214
Apple, 16, 21, 29, 33, 37, 38, 39, 40, 81, 87, 97, 106, 107, 112, 131, 133, 134, 146, 159, 160, 164, 166, 169, 171, 180, 182, 183, 189, 193, 196, 204, 206, 207, 209, 211, 213, 216, 218
Arugula, 65, 84, 138, 211
asparagus, 12
Asparagus, 12, 52, 64, 69, 125, 138, 140, 145, 154, 164
Avocado, 28, 35, 38, 51, 65, 82, 83, 85, 121, 123, 126, 128, 139, 149, 160, 161, 164, 165, 167, 176, 186, 196, 215
Bacon, 14, 32, 43, 46, 56, 58, 73, 74, 79, 88, 111, 122, 125, 149, 153
Banana, 21, 25, 28, 30, 33, 37, 38, 39, 40, 42, 99, 114, 132, 139, 140, 166, 168, 170, 174, 186, 187, 194, 195, 198, 199, 205, 208, 212, 214
Bark, 189, 191
Bars, 30, 37, 45, 63, 89, 90, 97, 116, 173, 174, 179, 180, 184, 186, 188, 200, 210, 215, 217
Beef, 26, 45, 67, 84, 117, 130, 131, 159, 163
Black Beans, 20
Blackberry, 129, 173, 183
Blueberry, 22, 24, 30, 34, 38, 39, 45, 59, 74, 75, 106, 108, 164, 173, 174, 185, 195, 198, 206, 207, 213, 215
Bread, 21, 28, 29, 44, 47, 49, 50, 100, 110, 114, 119, 142, 148, 150, 168, 171, 172, 189, 195, 197, 203, 208, 218
Broccoli, 15, 34, 35, 62, 69, 70, 79, 102, 109, 127, 130, 135, 137, 144, 152, 154
brown rice, 18, 21, 26, 35, 37, 66, 69, 71, 79, 82, 83, 130, 149, 207
Brown Rice, 21
Brownies, 167, 182, 185, 186, 190, 202, 210
Brussels Sprout, 61, 66, 71
Brussels Sprouts, 71, 78, 89, 138, 144
Butternut Squash, 23, 74, 85
Cabbage, 88, 131, 142, 151
Cake, 21, 30, 36, 42, 144, 166, 167, 169, 171, 173, 176, 177, 179, 180, 181, 183, 189, 192, 195, 197, 199, 201, 206, 210, 211, 213
Carrot, 21, 30, 38, 42, 72, 73, 79, 178, 179, 188, *See*
Cauliflower, 15, 45, 47, 49, 53, 60, 84, 87, 89, 94, 102, 105, 106, 108, 112, 123, 127, 143, 144, 150, 153, 155, 158, 159, 163
Cheeseburger, 46, 63, 88
Cheesecake, 89, 93, 104, 110, 170, 174, 180, 181, 188, 189, 190, 192, 205, 209, 210
chicken, 10, 12, 13, 14, 16, 17, 18, 19, 20, 26, 27, 28, 32, 33, 34, 35, 36, 44, 46, 47, 48, 49, 50, 51, 52, 53, 54, 55, 56, 59, 61, 62, 63, 64, 65, 66, 71, 72, 76, 78, 79, 80, 81, 82, 84, 85, 87, 88, 90, 91, 92, 93, 94, 96, 101, 102, 103, 104, 107, 108, 109, 110, 111, 112, 113, 114, 115, 116, 117, 118, 119, 120, 121, 122, 125, 127, 128, 129, 130, 131, 132, 133, 134, 135, 136, 137, 138, 140, 141, 142, 143, 144, 146, 148, 149, 150, 151, 152, 153, 155, 156, 157, 158, 159, 160, 161, 162, 163, 164, 196
Chicken, 12, 13, 14, 16, 17, 18, 19, 26, 27, 32, 33, 34, 35, 46, 47, 48, 49, 50, 51, 52, 53, 54, 55, 56, 59, 61, 62, 64, 65, 66, 71, 72, 73, 78, 79, 80, 81, 87, 88, 90, 92, 96, 102, 104, 107, 109, 111, 114, 115, 116, 117, 118, 119, 120, 121, 122, 124, 125, 127, 128, 129, 131, 132, 133, 134, 135, 136, 137, 140, 141, 142, 144, 146, 148, 149, 150, 151, 152, 153, 155, 157, 158, 159, 160, 161, 162, 163, 164, 196
chicken broth, 12
Chickpea, 35, 47, 125, 137, 139
Chocolate, 25, 29, 39, 50, 55, 63, 70, 75, 85, 99, 105, 107, 125, 126, 129, 144, 159, 167, 168, 170, 171, 172, 173, 174, 175, 176, 177, 178, 179, 186, 187, 188, 189, 190, 191, 194, 195, 198, 199, 201, 202, 203, 204, 205, 207, 208, 209, 212, 214, 215
Cinnamon, 21, 28, 29, 37, 40, 41, 81, 93, 97, 98, 100, 103, 107, 110, 113, 134,

153, 182, 190, 191, 193, 212, 213, 216, 218
Cobbler, 173, 182, 196, 205
Coconut, 38, 59, 63, 66, 70, 85, 114, 125, 127, 136, 139, 144, 152, 168, 172, 173, 175, 176, 182, 183, 184, 186, 191, 192, 194, 196, 198, 199, 201, 205, 211, 212, 214, 215, 216, 217
Coffee, 36, 37, 43, 63, 69, 122, 139, 180, 216
Cookie, 37, 87, 99, 114, 166, 174, 175, 177, 184, 188, 207
Cookies, 30, 31, 42, 45, 70, 75, 76, 85, 87, 93, 98, 102, 125, 139, 156, 167, 168, 174, 176, 177, 178, 179, 182, 189, 190, 191, 194, 197, 198, 202, 205, 208, 209, 217
Cranberry, 45, 50, 94, 116, 160, 169, 177, 189, 202, 216
Cupcakes, 172, 175, 178, 187, 203
egg, 13, 14, 15, 21, 22, 23, 24, 25, 27, 30, 36, 40, 41, 42, 43, 44, 46, 47, 49, 51, 55, 56, 57, 59, 60, 61, 62, 64, 65, 70, 71, 73, 74, 75, 76, 77, 79, 80, 81, 82, 83, 84, 85, 86, 87, 88, 89, 90, 91, 93, 94, 95, 97, 98, 99, 100, 101, 102, 103, 104, 107, 110, 112, 113, 114, 117, 119, 120, 121, 122, 123, 125, 126, 127, 132, 135, 141, 143, 144, 146, 148, 149, 151, 152, 154, 156, 158, 161, 164, 165, 166, 167, 170, 173, 174, 175, 176, 177, 178, 179, 180, 181, 182, 183, 184, 185, 186, 187, 188, 189, 191, 192, 194, 195, 197, 198, 199, 200, 203, 206, 207, 209, 211, 212, 213, 216, 217, 218
Egg, 13
Eggplant, 80, 104, 108, 145, 160
Energy Balls, 70, 176
Fish, 97, 118, 119, 131, 141
French Toast, 49, 57, 74, 154
Fudge, 157, 167, 168, 170, 176, 179, 182, 190, 192, 202, 210, 214
Ginger, 13, 62, 68, 87, 129, 145, 160, 163, 209
Goat Cheese, 14, 91, 105, 106
Granola, 25, 30, 37, 45, 72, 186, 195, 210, 216
Greek Yogurt, 28, 37, 44, 101, 108, 146, 176, 215
Grits, 82, 91

Ham, 12, 25, 74, 75, 101, 133
Honey Mustard, 16, 121
Jalapeno, 84, 118, 127, 140
Kale, 12, 24, 32, 35, 61, 64, 68, 74, 132
Lemon, 22, 31, 41, 48, 57, 60, 62, 64, 69, 70, 73, 84, 90, 115, 127, 138, 145, 153, 169, 173, 184, 186, 188, 199, 213, 214
lentil, 15
Lentil, 12, 15, 17, 47, 67, 139
lentils, 17
Mango, 19, 38, 172, 205, 208, 209, 211
Millet, 40
Mint, 50, 65, 105, 187, 198, 208, 211, 212, 215
Muffin, 44, 75, 185, 193, 204
Mushrooms, 19, 45, 72, 75, 115, 120, 143, 152, 154, 158, 187
Oatmeal, 23, 24, 25, 28, 29, 34, 37, 39, 41, 45, 63, 75, 97, 98, 99, 113, 166, 173, 174, 175, 177, 178, 202, 204
Oats, 23, 24, 29, 31, 32, 34, 141, 179
Onion, 45, 46, 102, 165
Onions, 56, 67, 82, 84, 120, 148
Orange, 38, 77, 78, 83, 89, 124, 130, 143, 145, 167, 176, 191
Pancakes, 25, 28, 44, 59, 65, 79, 135, 137, 191, 207
Parmesan Cheese, 69
Pasta, 10, 17, 19, 36, 45, 82, 85, 118
Pea, 12
Peach, 38, 85, 98, 163, 173, 196, 198, 205
Peanut, 28, 29, 30, 37, 38, 63, 75, 91, 93, 99, 108, 109, 139, 140, 150, 156, 170, 173, 177, 179, 187, 190, 194, 201, 203, 204, 205, 210, 212
Peanut Butter, 28, 29, 30, 37, 38, 63, 75, 93, 99, 139, 140, 150, 156, 170, 173, 177, 179, 187, 190, 194, 201, 203, 204, 205, 210, 212
Pear, 39, 183, 191
Pecans, 70, 73, 136, 146, 175, 177, 212
Peppers, 13, 18, 24, 52, 56, 61, 82, 120, 136, 137, 145, 159
Pie, 29, 39, 75, 79, 94, 108, 111, 168, 172, 179, 180, 182, 186, 192, 193, 202, 204, 216
Pizza, 14, 45, 66, 101, 102, 107, 125, 136, 145, 149
Pomegranate, 115, 132, 191, 216

Popcorn, 75, 126, 177, 178, 203
Pork, 18, 81, 87, 89, 92, 103, 119, 122, 129, 133, 139, 157, 158
Portobello, 34, 71, 120
Portobello Mushroom, 34, 71
Pudding, 99, 105, 125, 132, 166, 171, 174, 183, 189, 193, 201, 206, 207, 208, 212, 214, 215, 218
Pumpkin, 15, 29, 39, 41, 49, 78, 79, 85, 89, 98, 100, 110, 168, 172, 178, 181, 182, 192, 193, 202, 203, 211, 217, 218
quinoa, 15, 18, 25, 31, 35, 36, 61, 62, 63, 66, 67, 68, 80, 85, 94, 99, 107, 113, 119, 120, 127, 136, 137, 148, 156, 160, 163, 177, 199, 200, 212, 213
Quinoa, 18
Rice, 26, 35, 47, 49, 53, 98, 102, 112, 114, 201, 207, 208
Salad, 14, 16, 19, 21, 27, 32, 35, 46, 51, 52, 53, 61, 62, 64, 65, 67, 68, 71, 73, 74, 82, 83, 84, 85, 87, 91, 96, 101, 106, 111, 115, 123, 124, 126, 128, 130, 137, 139, 145, 146, 149, 150, 154, 162, 163, 164, 187, 206, 211, 212
salmon, 13, 16, 29, 48, 54, 64, 65, 66, 73, 90, 130, 131, 138, 140, 142, 144, 145, 153, 154, 156, 160
Salmon, 13, 16, 29, 48, 54, 64, 65, 66, 130, 138, 140, 142, 144, 153, 154, 156, 160
Sausage, 28, 44, 45, 47, 50, 55, 56, 58, 81, 82, 85, 92, 96, 99, 100, 132
Shake, 38, 96, 97, 99, 100, 111, 114, 117, 126, 136, 170, 195, 205, 215
Shrimp, 16, 69, 82, 83, 85, 91, 103, 106, 109, 112, 113, 129, 141, 147, 152, 163

Sour Cream, 48, 62, 124
Spaghetti, 26, 27, 47, 80, 91, 103
Spinach, 13, 23, 28, 32, 34, 36, 38, 39, 41, 60, 61, 75, 77, 153, 156, 160, 161, 163, 164
Steak, 26, 86, 98
Strawberry, 24, 25, 33, 39, 48, 96, 97, 104, 167, 169, 172, 178, 184, 194, 197, 205, 206, 208
Sweet Potato, 42, 63, 74, 76, 78, 80, 84, 95, 134, 135, 143, 157, 161, 167, 179, 185
Sweet Potatoes, 72, 76, 156
Taco, 85, 101, 109, 111, 112, 116, 137, 141
Tenderloin, 18, 59, 157, 158
Tofu, 29, 64, 68, 69
Tomato, 13, 52, 67, 69, 72, 75, 82, 84, 85, 92, 117, 118, 121, 138, 142, 145, 148
Tuna, 21, 52, 64, 101, 123, 130
turkey, 13, 14, 16, 23, 24, 43, 44, 49, 58, 59, 61, 62, 68, 71, 74, 76, 77, 78, 79, 80, 81, 82, 83, 84, 88, 94, 95, 97, 98, 99, 100, 102, 105, 111, 115, 116, 121, 122, 125, 126, 127, 129, 132, 133, 134, 136, 137, 138, 140, 141, 142, 149, 151, 153, 154, 158, 165
Turkey Sausage, 23, 68, 81, 82, 126
Vanilla, 29, 30, 68, 169, 175, 177, 193, 213, 217, 218
Waffles, 28, 50
Walnut, 16, 105, 115, 185, 202
Yam, 70, 175
Zucchini, 36, 44, 62, 63, 64, 67, 73, 74, 77, 115, 124, 135, 140, 146, 149, 152, 154, 162, 179, 200, 203

Printed in Great Britain
by Amazon